Building Sustainable Futures for Adult Learners

A volume in
Adult Learning in Professional, Organizational, and Community Settings
Carrie J. Boden-McGill, *Series Editor*

Building Sustainable Futures for Adult Learners

edited by

Jennifer K. Holtz
University of Arkansas at Little Rock

Stephen B. Springer
Texas State University

Carrie J. Boden-McGill
Texas State University

Associate Editors
Nora Cavazos and Melisa Kakas
Texas State University

Assistant Editors
Iris Fulton and Portia Gottschall
Texas State University

INFORMATION AGE PUBLISHING, INC.
Charlotte, NC • www.infoagepub.com

Library of Congress Cataloging-in-Publication Data

A CIP record for this book is available from the Library of Congress
http://www.loc.gov

ISBN: 978-1-62396-871-7 (Paperback)
       978-1-62396-872-4 (Hardcover)
       978-1-62396-873-1 (ebook)

Printed in the United States of America

*It is with profound gratitude and great affection that I dedicate this book
to Lynne Bernabei, Eliza Dermody, and Rima Kapitan, whose professional
and personal concern enabled me to be where I am, doing
what I was meant to do. Thank you.*
—Jennifer K. Holtz

*I would like to dedicate this book to my wife Janice who has supported me through
this and many projects for 40 years. Her competence, comments, and daily
encouragement have made it possible for me to hold multiple roles and take many
journeys through the years. Janice, thank you and I love you.*
—Stephen B. Springer

*I would like to dedicate this book to my family—close and extended—
who, in their own ways, contributed to the project.*
—Carrie J. Boden-McGill

CONTENTS

Stephen B. Springer, Carrie J. Boden-McGill, and Jennifer K. Holtz

PART I

SUPPORTING NEEDS OF ADULT LEARNERS: SUSTAINING ADULT LEARNERS IN HIGHER EDUCATION

viii ▪ Contents

SUPPORTING ADULT STUDENT PARENTS

BUILDING FUTURES THROUGH CURRICULUM REVISION

INTEGRATING ADULT LEARNING EXPERIENCES IN THE "REAL WORLD"

ADVANCING ADULT LEARNING IN THE HEALTH PROFESSIONS

PART II

SUPPORTING ADULT LEARNING IN ORGANIZATIONS, INSTITUTIONS, AND COMMUNITIES: LEADING CHANGE TOWARD A SUSTAINABLE FUTURE FOR ADULT LEARNING

IMPLEMENTING FORWARD-LOOKING, COMPENTENCY-BASED MEASURES OF ADULT LEARNING

SUPPORTING PROFESSIONAL DEVELOPMENT FOR ADULT EDUCATORS

EXPLORING LOCAL AND GLOBAL PARTNERSHIPS TO SUSTAIN ADULT LEARNING

PREFACE

Dear Reader,

Once again, it is with pride in our AHEA organization, its members, affiliates, and friends that I introduce you to our newest contribution to the field: *Building Sustainable Futures for Adult Learners* in the Adult Learning in Professional, Organizational, and Community Settings series. In an age of initiatives, rapid change, global mobility and migration, and many other forms of being in a state of flux, the concept of sustaining, i.e., this process of maintaining, nourishing, and carrying on, is essential to the emotional, intellectual, and spiritual development of communities, across boundaries and barriers, be these situated locally or globally. As such, adult and higher education practitioners have quite the responsibility to sustain themselves as much as others in terms of mutual support, professional currency, and validation of our advocacy efforts, and we need to fill our toolboxes with a great and current variety of instruments to serve our craft well.

Building Sustainable Futures for Adult Learners is a multi-faceted book that speaks to settings, content, contexts, populations, and practices as diverse as our world community. Yet, within these differences we also find similarities of needs and commonalities of corresponding solutions. This book you are about to read is more than a collection of voices and perspectives: it is a slice of the reality of a diverse group of stakeholders. You will be invited into these different realities via the narratives provided. Not only will you glimpse problems and solutions; you may also find validation and fodder for deep reflection on your practices as you consider your colleagues' chapters. Moreover, *Building Sustainable Futures for Adult Learners* speaks not only to innovative programming, empathy, and instructional methods to

Building Sustainable Futures for Adult Learners, pages xiii–xiv
Copyright © 2015 by Information Age Publishing
All rights of reproduction in any form reserved.

sustain learners; it also nudges you to join our network of colleagues for your sustenance.

Our volume editors, Drs. Holtz, Springer, and Boden-McGill along with the generous assistance of Nora Cavazos, Melisa Kakas, Iris Fulton, and Portia Gottschall have, once again, completed a book with care, enthusiasm, and professionalism. They have my deep appreciation, and I commend everyone on the team for their passion for our profession that has had them work in the spirit of collegiality and for the benefit of everyone in our field of Adult Education. Each author who contributed took time to fine tune their original presentations at the joint 2013 AHEA/AAACE Conference to create the chapter you will here read. Beyond the personal gain of adding a publication "notch" to their resumes, our contributing authors to *Building Sustainable Futures for Adult Learners* generously shared their knowledge, skills, and passion with the rest of us toiling in the field of Adult Education. For that, I thank them gratefully. As we continue our advocacy for Adult Education, let us continue to be mindful of the reality that each one of us is both teacher and learner and that together we "make the road by walking," working toward a sustainable, peaceful, and equitable future for all.

—Gabriele Strohschen
President, The Adult Higher Education Alliance

ACKNOWLEDGEMENTS

Any project of this size requires the support of many people, and we have worked with an outstanding group.

The AHEA Board is an integral partner in this series, and we deeply appreciate the opportunity to support the AHEA mission. Special thanks go to Fred Prashun, who has handled the business matters associated with the book so adeptly.

We also appreciate the diligent work and expertise of the Editorial Board members, Theresa Carter, Joellen Coryell, Thomas Cox, Steven Dietz, Matthew Eichler, Bonnie Flynn, Carrie Johnson, Yvonne Hunter-Johnson, Yu-Chun Kuo, Marilyn Lockhart, Omar Lopez, Joan S. Olson, Kathleen Peno, Anne Rapp, Todd Sherron, W. Franklin Spikes III, Gabriele Strohschen, and Jonathan E. Taylor. Thank you for your service to the field of adult education and to AHEA.

Associate Editors Nora Cavazos and Melisa Kakas and Assistant Editors Iris Fulton and Portia Gottschall have excelled in keeping both the project and the editors organized, on task, and on schedule. We are grateful for your abilities and your willingness to help in a myriad of ways.

Special thanks and much gratefulness to the chapter authors, who graciously agreed not only to share their work, but also to live with many months of recommendations, suggestions, and directives. We deeply appreciate each of you.

—Jennifer K. Holtz
Stephen B. Springer
Carrie J. Boden-McGill

INTRODUCTION

Stephen B. Springer and Carrie J. Boden-McGill
Texas State University

Jennifer K. Holtz
University of Arkansas at Little Rock

The editors of this book are pleased to present this publication that provides some unique perspectives in support of adult learners. Coinciding with the goals of the Adult Higher Education Alliance (AHEA) and the American Association of Adult and Continuing Education (AAACE), this volume expands on the joint conference theme, *Building Sustainable Futures for Adult Learners.* The chapters address various aspects of this theme from national and international perspectives.

Supporting the learning of adults for a sustainable future is a formidable endeavor. The U.S. Department of Labor (2012) estimates that most workers will have 10–14 jobs between the ages of 18 and 46. Currently, many of the top in-demand jobs did not exist a decade ago (Casserly, 2012). In many instances, as educators, "We are currently preparing students for jobs that don't yet exist, using technologies that haven't been invented, in order to solve problems we don't even know are problems yet" (Rose, Fisch, & McLeod, 2012). Likewise, the amount of technical information human civilization produces doubles approximately every two years; this means that as much as 50% of what students learn in college will be outdated by the

Building Sustainable Futures for Adult Learners, pages xvii–xxi
Copyright © 2015 by Information Age Publishing
All rights of reproduction in any form reserved.

time they graduate (Peterson, 2009, para. 8). Because of this rapid change, it is very important to address the needs of adult learners by creating what Weimer (2013) calls a learner-centered environment where the product is not learning, which could be static in time, but rather learners, who can learn throughout the lifespan.

Sustaining an environment that produces learners means that the activities of higher education need to be "ecologically sound, socially just and economically viable," so that "they will continue to be so for future generations" (Association of University Leaders for a Sustainable Future, 2008, para. 4). Elements of sustainable practices in education include creating a university environment that increases awareness of environmentally sustainable development, creates an institutional culture of sustainability, educates for environmentally responsible citizenship, fosters environmental literacy for all, practices institutional ecology, involves all stakeholders, collaborates for interdisciplinary approaches, enhances the capacity of primary and secondary schools, broadens service and outreach nationally and internationally, and maintains the movement (Association of University Leaders for a Sustainable Future, 2008).

The chapters in this volume address many of the above-mentioned aspects of sustainability. Others propose theories, methods, or techniques that could be used to build sustainable futures for adult learners. The book is divided into two central sections including Part I, "Supporting Needs for Adult Learners" and Part II, "Supporting Adult Learning in Organizations, Institutions, and Communities." The first subsection begins with the concept of sustaining adult learners in higher education. This dynamic section provides testimony regarding experiences of displaced workers in education by Voelkel. This leads into factors impacting student persistence in education. Bergman, Rose and Shuck provide the reader concrete information regarding persistence while the section is concluded by Collins, Coddington, and Williams, who look at whether formal goals really affected graduation rates.

The second subsection provides key discussion regarding supporting adult student parents. Lovell and Barnes lead with an article regarding college enrollment choices predicted by such areas as social capital and academic encouragement. Convincing arguments are made that indeed numerous factors may impact college enrollment and more life transition research needs to take place. Wu provides a compelling chapter addressing the needs of women in doctoral education. The overall complexity of the lives of women seeking higher education is aptly illustrated.

Leading the third subsection regarding curriculum re-vision, Capozzi provides evidence that creative experiences can improve learning and that the interdisciplinary approach is strong in curriculum matters. Also supporting differences as healthy, Dick concludes the subsection by providing the notion that non-traditional education may be neo-traditional education. Dick impels the reader to consider, or perhaps reconsider, general education requirements for adult learners.

The fourth subsection regarding hybrid and on line learning is heavily supported by Kuo's lead chapter championing the valuable nature of on-line learning. Lockhart and Jackson demonstrate classroom configuration and engagement as being important in the learning environment. Concluding the section Peterson and McGuire provide a documented example of hybrid teaching and learning giving additional support for implementation of hybrid instruction.

Real world application is the center of the discussion in the fifth subsection. Saal provides the reader justification for using authentic texts and promoting comprehension. Hentz urges adult educators not to get in the way of change or allow their own views to cloud the picture. Providing cornerstone and capstone learning options, Springer, Lopez, Eichler, Lasker-Scott, and Boden-McGill indicate specific information on coursework and new changes that promote student understanding and personal application. Harner concludes the section by noting formal learning compared to incidental learning.

The health professions related to adult learning is the focus of the sixth section. Hall leads the section in closely examining a model for self-directed learning. Readiness and different instructor roles are important in the discussion. McDonald, Straker, and Lyons provide a concrete example of a course being blended as well as conclusions and recommendations for practice. They argue that in essence, change must be holistic. Feedback and open ended questions are two issues mentioned in the discussion of training medical faculty to use adult learning in a chapter by Peno, Mangiante, and Kenahan. Concluding this section, Carter and Gogia provide a serious discussion regarding adult education practitioners encountering education in the health field. Siding with previous writers, the authors propose that more adult education methods are needed including active methods and more learner engagement.

Part II of the book, Supporting Adult Learning in Organizations, Institutions, and Communities, provides additional tools and real world examples in support of Part I and beyond. The first section provides chapters clustered around leading change toward a sustainable future for adult learning. In this section, Rice outlines collaborative leadership while Nanton addresses the development of women leaders pointing out that strength cannot be denied regarding women's leadership, it is just facing up to that fact and taking action that is important. Hultquist continues the call for change pointing out that innovation is essential due to the global economy and technological advances.

The second section provides a foundation for competency based measures of adult learning. Leading the section, Merill provides an informative discussion of Prior Learning Assessment (PLA), Massive Online Open Courses (MOOCs), and PLA trends. Prasuhn and Frasard challenge the reader regarding how much learning takes place in the semester hour model. The challenge also includes better defining the learning.

Section 3 leads the reader through "professional identity development for adult educators" and begins with a practical discussion of learning objectives by Fedeli, Felisatti, and Giampaolo. The authors criticize vague objectives and provide recommendations on how to use learning contracts. The next chapter by some of the same scholars, Felisatti, Manzzuco, Fedeli, and Giampaolo, provides an outline regarding personal and professional experiences to develop learning in Teacher's professional qualifications. Technology again is linked to adult education in a chapter by Fabrikant, York, and Morris, who point out that technology is challenging and changing the role of adult education. Concluding this dynamic section, Kirwn and Roumell review successful on line instructor dispositions and also provide comments on self-assessment.

The last section provides relevant discussion regarding creating local and global partnerships to sustain adult learning. Cummings and Franck provide best practices in working to build community coalitions. Reminding the reader of diverse populations Tan, Nabb, and Sammons provide a difficult yet encouraging discussion regarding Appalachian learning that transitions to other cultures. Concluding the section and acknowledging globalization, Rell and Gonzalez demonstrate respect for cultures and provide solid comments regarding partnerships.

In conclusion, this publication promises to lead the reader through the compelling current issues in adult education, provide relevant evidence for directions that need to be taken in the field, and share personal perspectives to augment the book's evidence. We commend the book to you as you take the adventure with the writers. As Zig Ziglar (2000) would say, we will "see you at the top."

REFERENCES

Association of University Leaders for a Sustainable Future. (2008). *About ULSF.* Retrieved from: http://www.ulsf.org/about.html

Casserly, M. (2012). 10 jobs that didn't exist 10 years ago. *Forbes.* Retrieved from: http://www.forbes.com/sites/meghancasserly/2012/05/11/10-jobs-that-didnt-exist-10-years-ago/

Peterson, G. P. (2009). *It's a changing world: Will higher education be prepared?* Retrieved from http://www.president.gatech.edu/publications-presentations/speeches-presentations/its-changing-world-will-higher-education-be

Rose, D., Fisch, K., & McLeod, S. (2012). *Did you know?* Retrieved from: http://www.youtube.com/watch?v=XVQ1ULfQawk

U.S. Department of Labor Bureau of Labor Statistics. (2012). Number of jobs held, labor market activity, and earnings growth among the youngest baby boomers: Results from a longitudinal study. Retrieved from http://www.bls.gov/news.release/pdf/nlsoy.pdf

Weimer, M. (2013). *Learner-centered teaching: Five key changes to practice*. San Francisco, CA: John Wiley & Sons.

Ziglar, Z. (2000). *See you at the top: Twenty-fifty anniversary edition*. Gretna, LA: Pelican Publishing Company.

PART I

SUPPORTING NEEDS OF ADULT LEARNERS:

Sustaining Adult Learners in Higher Education

CHAPTER 1

REBUILDING LIVES

Narratives of the Educational Experiences of Displaced Workers

Margaret A. Voelkel
University of Arkansas–Fort Smith

In the past decade, the United States has lost hundreds of manufacturing jobs as businesses move production lines overseas. As a result, workers are out of work and without the job skills necessary to find new employment. In smaller cities that rely on a manufacturing economic base, the shock waves created by a large pool of displaced workers can be profound.

Partnerships between higher education and Federal and State programs can help displaced workers transition into new fields. Trade Adjustment Assistance (TAA) is a federal program that assists workers who enroll in degree and certificate programs by providing living stipends, tuition assistance, and other assistance (U.S. Department of Labor, n.d.). While such partnerships extend a lifeline to displaced workers, the long term outcomes for displaced workers are not promising. Jacobs (2013) described a "Great Recession hangover" in which the long term jobless have taken part-time work or left the workforce permanently (p. 1). While the American unemployment rate in January 2013 was 7.9%, Jacobs estimated that 14.4% of the workforce was unemployed when those who dropped out and those who worked part time were included. At the same time, 3.5% of unemployed workers had been looking for work six months or more, while an additional 2.3% had been unemployed for at least a year (Jacobs, 2013).

Jacobson, LaLonde, and Sullivan (2005a) found that any job loss had a long term effect on earnings. Displaced workers suffered not only temporary earning losses while unemployed, but long term earning losses associated with the job loss; in other words, many displaced workers ended up in entry level positions earning lower wages than they once earned pre-job displacement (Farber, 2005; Jacobson, LaLonde, & Sullivan, 2005a, 2005b, 2005c; Park, 2012). Farber (2005) estimated that workers who lost a full time job and then found new full time employment received wages that were 13% less than those they earned in the previous job; additionally, those who lost full time jobs earned 17% less on average in their new jobs than they would have earned had they stayed in their previous jobs. Earning losses increased when job displacement was due to a mass layoff. Couch and Placzek (2010) found that the earning deficit was between 7% and 9% six years after a worker lost a job; for those who lost jobs due to a mass layoff, the six year earning deficit was between 13 and 15%. Hironimus-Wendt and Spannaus (2007) further identified social costs associated with job displacement including lower household incomes, bankruptcy, anger, anxiety, depression, and other emotional or psychological issues. Jacobs (2013) pointed to other social costs of job displacement including stress-related health problems such as heart attack or stroke, higher mortality rates, and increased divorce rates. Jacobs also found that job loss affected the children of displaced workers resulting in poorer grade retention and poorer student performance.

The long term unemployed, TAA workers in particular, may be fundamentally different from other unemployed workers. Jacobs (2013) pointed out that the long-term unemployed may not have the job skills and qualifications needed for the job vacancies in today's economy:

> For instance a long-tenure manufacturing worker who lost his job as a line-worker during the recession may be ill-suited for re-employment in a manufacturing sector that is increasingly moving away from basic assembly line work and toward a high-tech, high-skill model of advanced manufacturing. (p. 6)

Reynolds and Palatucci (2012) noted that participants in the TAA program were older and less-educated than other displaced workers. They were also less mobile and therefore less likely to be willing or able to relocate to find work. The TAA workers were also less likely to have the job qualifications that would allow them to easily find re-employment.

The TAA program has three goals: to encourage the rapid re-employment of participants, to provide training and income support to participants, and to assist participants to obtain long-term re-employment at a comparable wage to their prior job; despite these goals, there is little evidence to suggest that the TAA program actually helps participants (Reynolds & Palatucci, 2012). Jacobson, LaLonde, and Sullivan (2011, 2005a, 2005b, 2005c) found that TAA participants who participated in educational programs—particularly academic and vocational programs that were quantitatively oriented—fared better, received higher wages in new employment, and experienced significant benefits from the educational experience. Reynolds and Palatucci (2012) also stated that those TAA participants who take advantage of TAA funded training and educational opportunities were more likely to find new jobs and at higher wages than those TAA participants who did not participate in educational programs.

This study focused on TAA participants in Western Arkansas who were displaced when Whirlpool Corporation closed its manufacturing plant in Fort Smith, AR. Fort Smith is a city of 86,200 located on the Arkansas-Oklahoma border. Fort Smith serves as the economic center of six counties in Arkansas and Oklahoma. Located along the Arkansas River, Fort Smith has long depended upon a manufacturing-based economy. In 2006, Whirlpool Corporation was the area's largest employer with a staff of 4,600; when the company closed the Fort Smith site in June, 2012, there were 826 employees left (Garrett, 2012).

Partnerships between the federal TAA program, the Arkansas Department of Workforce Services, and several institutions of higher education have provided the displaced Whirlpool workers with the opportunity to complete a two-year degree program while earning a living stipend. The University of Arkansas-Fort Smith is a regional university that also retains a two-year mission through its College of Applied Science and Technology. Gordon (2012) analyzed Department of Labor wage figures for Western Arkansas TAA participants who began training programs between July 1, 2006 and June 30, 2008 and completed training no later than June 30, 2010. Gordon found that TAA participants in Western Arkansas earned significantly lower wages upon re-employment than they did during their tenure with Whirlpool; additionally, there was no significant difference in re-employment wages between those TAA participants who completed training programs and those who did not. If TAA participation in education programs did not significantly affect wages, what were the benefits of enrollment in higher education programs?

This qualitative narrative study focuses on how five displaced Whirlpool workers in the TAA program made meaning of their educational experiences after job displacement. The research question was: How do displaced workers use narrative to ascribe meaning to their experiences in higher education? Additional questions guiding the study included:

1. How has the experience of completing a degree program affected displaced workers' assumptions or frames of reference?
2. What role, if any, did generativity (McAdams, 1996) play in motivating the displaced worker to enroll in and complete an associate degree?

PERSONAL IDENTITY AND TRANSFORMATIVE LEARNING

The theoretical framework of the study is based on Mezirow's (1990, 1991, 2000, 2009) transformative learning theory and on McAdams's (1988, 1996, 2006) life story model of identity. Many of the former Whirlpool employees worked in their jobs for decades. This study focused on how educational programs help provide displaced workers with a new way of looking at their lives after the loss of job identity. Specifically, how did educational experiences help students reframe personal identity to encompass new roles such as student, associate degree graduate, college graduate, or employee of some business other than Whirpool? While not all participant educational experiences would necessarily result in transformative learning, transformative learning was one particular tool which might allow the workers to begin to reframe personal identity stories.

Transformative Learning Theory

Mezirow (1990, 1991, 2000, 2009) developed a theory of transformative learning in which the adult uses reflection to make meaning of experience. Mezirow (1991) wrote: "Reflective learning involves assessment or reassessment of assumptions. Reflective learning becomes transformative whenever assumptions or premises are found to be distorting, inauthentic, or otherwise invalid" (p.6). Transformative learning is the process of reflecting on assumptions and transforming them into a more useful or accurate assumption to guide future action. Mezirow and Associates (2000) described transformative learning as a process in which an adult reassesses previously held assumptions to see the world in a different way.

Adult learners come to learning opportunities with a lifetime of previous experience. Mezirow (Mezirow and Associates, 1990) conducted a 1975 nationwide study of women re-entering community colleges. The primary finding of the study was *perspective transformation.* By learning to become critical of their role in society, the women changed the assumptions or frames of reference through which they saw the world.

There are ten phases or steps in the transformative learning process (Mezirow & Associates, 2000, 2009): (1) a disorienting dilemma; (2) self-examination; (3) critical reflection on assumptions; (4) connection of personal discontent to the process of transformation; (5) exploration of potential new role, relationships, or action; (6) a plan of action; (7) acquisition of new knowledge and skills; (8) experimentation with new roles; (9) building competence in new roles; and (10) reintegration of new perspectives into regular life.

In reviewing empirical studies of transformative learning, Taylor (2009) identified six core elements of fostering transformation in students. These included individual experience, critical reflection, dialogue, holistic orientation, context, and authentic practice (p. 4). Methods in use for fostering transformation include arts-based, theatrical approaches (Butterwick & Lawrence, 2009), leadership development (Donaldson, 2009), mentoring (Mandell & Herman, 2009), and storytelling (Tyler, 2009).

Life Story Model of Identity

McAdams (1988, 1993, 1996) formulated the life story model of identity to describe how adults' narratives of their lives form adult identity. McAdams described how the "storied self" creates identity. He also recognized how themes of agency and communion combine to create a uniquely American identity he termed the redemptive self.

The life story model of identity posited by McAdams is based on Erik Erikson's model of adult development. According to Erikson (1980), generativity is the hallmark of the seventh stage of development in which the adult seeks to make a positive contribution to future generations through parenting, mentoring, or leadership. Erikson characterized the middle years as a conflict between generativity and stagnation. McAdams (1988, 1996, 2006a) incorporated the concept of generativity into his life story model of identity. McAdams maintained that the life story was the vehicle through which modern persons create their personal identities and make meaning of their life experiences. According to McAdams (1996) the life story of an adult may be understood in terms of narrative tone, imagery, theme, ideological setting, nuclear episodes, imagoes (alter egos), and the generativity script. Imagoes are alternate selves which represent the various roles that a person plays in life. For example, a person may play concrete roles like spouse, parent, student, worker, or manager. Imagoes may also represent a way of looking at the self in less concrete roles such as victim, protector, or problem solver.

McAdams (2008) identified six principles about life stories. First the self is "storied"—identity is built through the stories persons tell about their lives. Next, stories serve to integrate lives in both synchronic and diachronic patterns. Synchronic patterns bring together the diverse aspects of personality into a cohesive whole of the individual personality; diachronic patterns show how this cohesive person changes through time. Third, stories are told in social relationships. In other words, stories are actually told to others; there is a relationship between the listener and the teller of the story. Fourth, stories change over time. Although a story is about true events, the details and telling of the story subtly morph with each telling. Fifth, stories are cultural texts that reflect the overall environment and culture of the society in which they are set. Finally, some stories are better than others; personality researchers can evaluate stories in terms of good and bad both on their story elements and on the aspects of psychological health that they reveal about the teller.

This study explores the ways that the personal narrative of each participant revealed or did not reveal perspective transformation and transformative learning, as well as the ways in which each participant's telling of the experience revealed changes in identity. A goal of the study was to understand the intangible benefits (those benefits other than wages and earning potential) the TAA program participants gained by completing an associate or bachelor's degree.

METHODS

This qualitative narrative study focused on displaced workers from the closing of a Whirpool plant in Fort Smith, Arkansas. By using a qualitative approach, the researcher was able to ask the participants directly about the meaning that educational participation had for them and to gain a clearer understanding of the benefits of TAA-funded educational programs from the perspective of the participant.

Rationale for Qualitative Research Design

Qualitative research falls within the social constructivist paradigm or worldview. Also called interpretivism, the social constructivist paradigm assumes that reality is subjective and multiple (Creswell, 2007). Individuals socially construct the meaning of their experiences. Research, in this tradition, relies on multiple points of view and attention to the context of lived experiences (Creswell, 2007; Creswell, 2009; Merriam, 2009; Patton, 2002). According to Patton (2002), "qualitative inquiry can be used to discover, capture, present, and preserve the stories of organizations, programs, communities, and families" (p. 196). In this study, a qualitative approach to research is used to "discover, capture, present, and preserve" the stories of TAA participants.

Rationale for the Narrative Approach

According to Patton (2002), stories are memorable and provide better understanding and learning than research that is non-narrative; the language of stories is more accessible to non-researchers. Merriam (2009) maintained that stories are "how we make sense of our experiences, how we communicate with others, and through which we understand the world around us" (p. 32). Maynes, Pierce, and Laslett (2008) framed narrative as distinct in its focus on the whole person. The narrative approach is most useful in its capacity to reveal nuances that may be neglected in other forms of inquiry.

The procedures of the narrative approach require determining a research problem that involves learning the detailed life experiences of an individual or small group. The researcher spends extensive time in the field gathering stories through multiple types of data. The researcher collects information about the context of each story then analyzes, creates, and arranges the story to create a narrative. Finally, the researcher actively involves the participants in the research through collaboration (Clandinin & Connelly, 2000; Creswell, 2007).

Site and Participants

The participants in this study completed either an associate's or bachelor's degree program at the University of Arkansas-Fort Smith while participating in the TAA program. University of Arkansas-Fort Smith is a regional university that also retains a two-year mission, offering associate's degrees and technical certificates through its College of Applied Science and Technology. The study was conducted according to IRB guidelines at the University of Arkansas-Fort Smith. Each study participant was recruited by contact with instructors who recommended former students for participation. Participants were recruited via telephone or email contact according to IRB-approved protocols.

Ultimately, five participants ranging in age from 39 to 51 years of age were recruited (see Table 1.1).

Each displaced worker completed a semi-structured interview that focused on the "story" of their educational experiences. Each interview was audiotaped and transcribed. Each participant had the opportunity to review the typed transcript of the interview. Each participant was assigned an alias to be used throughout the study.

TABLE 1.1 Participant Characteristics

Participant	Age	Race/Ethnicity	Highest Level of Education Completed before Entry into Program	Degree Completed during TAA Participation	Additional Education after TAA Participation
Chad	41	Caucasian	High School Diploma	A.A.S. in Electronics	B.A.S. Electronics
Jimmy	51	Caucasian	High School Diploma	A.A.S. in Workforce Leadership	None
Katie	51	Caucasian	Associate of Arts	B. S. in Organizational Leadership	None
Stella	39	Caucasian	G.E.D.	A.A.S. in Administrative Professional- Human Resources	None
Tom	49	Caucasian	Some College	A.A.S. in Workforce Leadership	None

Positioning the Researcher in the Study

The researcher was a faculty member who had daily contact with TAA students in a University of Arkansas-Fort Smith associate degree program. Two of the study participants were graduates of the researcher's program. Two additional participants were students in one class that the researcher taught several years earlier. Therefore, four of the five participants were acquainted with the researcher before the study began. The fifth participant was the only graduate the investigator had not previously met. The investigator entered the study looking for positive experiences and benefits of the program. In order to counteract this bias, students were asked about low points and disappointments during their educational experiences.

DATA COLLECTION AND ANALYSIS

In qualitative research, the researcher is the key instrument (Clandinin & Connelly, 2000; Creswell, 2007; Creswell 2009; Maynes, Pierce, & Laslett, 2008; Merriam, 2009; Patton, 2002). As Creswell (2007) wrote:

The qualitative researchers collect data themselves through examining documents, observing behavior, and interviewing participants. They may use a protocol—an instrument for collecting data—but the researchers are the ones who actually gather the information. They do not tend to use or rely on questionnaires or instruments developed by other researchers. (p. 38)

In this study the collected data consisted of interview transcripts with the participants, field notes written after each interview, and follow-up email communications with each participant. The investigator met with each participant for a semi-structured interview. The interview protocol included both demographic and open ended questions. Demographic questions included gender, age, ethnicity, level of education before entry into TAA program, graduation date, and degree earned. There were nine open-ended questions:

1. Tell me the story of how you enrolled in college through the TAA program.
2. Please share with me how you chose your program of study.
3. What was the hardest thing about your educational experience?
4. Tell me about a time when you were tempted to give up. What motivated you to keep going?
5. Tell me about an experience when you felt successful in your educational program.
6. What and/or who motivated you to continue your education?
7. Now that you have graduated, tell me about how your life has changed.
8. When you tell your life story, what would the chapter about your participation in TAA say?
9. If you could say something to your earlier self—the person you were before you enrolled in school and completed your program—what would you say?

During each of the interviews, formal structured questions were supplemented with follow-up questions that arose from context of the interview. These included asking for additional detail, asking about personal feelings or reactions to events, or responding with simple prompts such as "What happened then?" Semi-structured interviews lasted on average 45 minutes. The shortest interview was 36 minutes long, while the longest was 70 minutes.

After each interview, the investigator wrote field notes about how the interview progressed and described personal thoughts about the participant's experience. Each interview was audiotaped. Verbatim transcripts of the interviews were used to code the data. Each participant had the opportunity to review the transcripts of the interview for accuracy. In one case, the researcher asked for clarification on a point of fact in an interview that resulted in an exchange of three emails between the researcher and the participant. All transcripts, emails, and field notes were included in the analysis of the data.

Data analysis followed Creswell's (2007) Data Analysis Spiral. The method as described by Creswell is an iterative process that begins with organizing collected data and then moving through memoing, reflecting, classifying, comparing, representing, and ultimately creating a formal matrix of coding (p. 151). The researcher read each interview transcript and identified initial categories. Creswell (2007) describes this process as an attempt to "hear" what the interviewee said (p. 151The investigator used *in vivo* coding in which the exact words used by participants were used to identify categories of information (Creswell, 2007; Merriam, 2009). Initial coding categories were determined based on reading of the data, but additional categories were included that were based on the theoretical frameworks of transformative learning and the life story model of identity. Data analysis was managed by creating tabs in a Microsoft OneNote notebook for each code. Relevant data for each code was copied and pasted onto each notebook tab. After analyzing the coded data, the researcher built a narrative story for each participant based on the interviews and communications. Finally, the investigator re-analyzed the written stories and identified four themes that occurred across the five narratives.

RESULTS

The Stories

Chad's Story

Chad Wilson, age 41, had always been a factory worker. Chad had six years of service with Whirlpool when he elected to take an early layoff and go back to school. As the son of an electrician, Chad's decision to pursue electronics was a "no brainer." Chad excelled in electronics classes, but credits most of his true learning to the opportunity to become a student assistant for the electronics program:

> Mr. M. was looking for a student assistant, and he offered me the job. I took it. Through that I learned more through the electronics program working for him as a student assistant than I did as a student. Because I got to do a lot of reinforcement. (C. Wilson, personal communication, October 30, 2013)

When Chad graduated in 2009, the job market in Fort Smith was in crisis. Carefully weighing his options, Chad applied for Pell grants which were now available to him because of his reduced income. He still had unemployment insurance available, so he chose to enroll in a Bachelor of Applied Science completer program. In December 2011, Chad was a college graduate. While finishing his bachelor's program, Chad applied to work in communications for a local natural gas company. He did not get the job. A year later he applied to the same company as a general laborer. He said:

> Now the construction job—that's a shovel. You don't have the backhoe. You're not a welder. You're sitting there in the cold holding a shovel. And this was like I went for a communications job. There's no way I'm going to put myself in a ditch. (C. Wilson, personal communication, October 30, 2013)

Persuaded by his wife, Chad did take the job. While still in his 90 day probation period, Chad decided to apply for an open position in a more desirable department. Chad's seniority was so low that he had 15 candidates ahead of him for the job. He would only be able to test for the job if each of the 15 candidates failed. To Chad's astonishment, all the candidates failed, and he found himself after 93 days in a more desirable, higher paying department. Within 18 months Chad had been promoted to management thanks in part to his bachelor's degree. At the time of the interview, he had just completed his first year in that position. Chad summed up his experience:

> So going from second and third shift all the time, making decent money, to finishing my degree. Coming out here and starting at the bottom with a shovel and working my way into management. It's made a big difference in my life. (C. Wilson, personal communication, October 30, 2013)

Tom's Story

Originally in the Navy, Tom Carver, age 49, had spent 10 years at Whirlpool at the time of his layoff. A methodical man, Tom committed himself to his studies but struggled consistently with math. He said:

> Things got tough. My math classes were tough. But you can't quit. It's one of things where you just have to push on with. If you are struggling seek help. I took advantage of everything that was here to offer. I stayed after. I did studies. I got study partners. And sometimes it was very humbling because I didn't know some of the things that my math classes were teaching me. I didn't understand it. Whereas my partner, they understood it clearly and they were a bit younger than me. So yeah. It was a real awkward situation. I had to keep it in my mind that I'm here for a purpose. I'm here to learn and it's the only way I can learn. (T. Carver, personal communication, August 27, 2013)

Upon graduation, Tom prepared for a long job search. He was completing an application to work in a temporary job for a delivery company when he accidentally dialed a wrong number. The man who answered that wrong number ran a fastener company that manufactured various screws and other fasteners. He asked to see Tom's resume. After several conversations with Tom, the manager created a quality manager position for Tom. He said:

> During my process of the quality manager I've introduced a lot of the things that I've learned here at school. And some of the things I've learned in the Navy and at Whirlpool. Like lean manufacturing. . . . And I introduced these concepts to our facility now. And we've gotten [rid of] a lot of waste and become more streamlined which in turn saves money because we've become more efficient. So it's nice to finally take some of the applied principles see them in motion. See them working . . . I like to use the tools that I've learned. (T. Carver, personal communication, August 27, 2013)

Jimmy's Story

Jimmy Lensing, at age 51, had a different attitude than the other participants in the study. With job tenure at Whirlpool of only 10 months, Jimmy had the shortest time in with the company and less of an emotional connection to his work there. Jimmy also seems the most pragmatic. He said:

> I knew early on when I was a kid to put stuff back. Put stuff back. Put stuff back. They [other displaced workers] just didn't take care to plan ahead to take care of all that if something did happen. I've had. I've had . . . this is the third company that's actually closed and left since I left [a previous job]. So I already know that it's not guaranteed. You can go to work today and the place could be closed down tomorrow. (J. Lensing, personal communication, October 29, 2013)

Due to his pragmatism, Jimmy did not experience some of the same financial lows as others in the study. Jimmy had the most menial current job-stocking at local discount store. This particular job he saw as consistent with his past warehouse experience. It's not the job he wanted, but he saw it as a way to support himself while he looked for something better.

Katie's Story

Katie Bolton at 51 was the most academically successful student of the participants. Katie completed an associate degree immediately after high school. She spent more than 26 years working for Whirlpool. Her job at Whirlpool was an engineering job although she lacked the engineering credentials. She used the opportunity of TAA to finish her bachelor's degree. She loved the experience and made excellent grades. She said: "I'm proud of myself . . . That I did it. Did the work. Got the grades. It wasn't easy" (K. Bolton, personal communication, September 16, 2013).

Success academically did not translate to success in the work world. Although Katie continued to fill out job applications, she currently works billing insurance companies for nursing home services—a job that any high school graduate can do. Of the five participants, she seemed the most disappointed in how her experience has turned out:

> I'm doing a job that requires a high school education. And the problem is availability of jobs. I'm not going to leave. My kids still need me. You know I'm not going to go somewhere else and find a job. I'm billing insurance companies. And my closest coworker is my best friend's daughter who has a high school diploma. That's all it takes. So I'm not actually using my degree which bothers me.... I took my job out of necessity. I needed to pay the bills. I would rather have a job that I choose because I love it. (K. Bolton, personal communication, September 16, 2013)

Stella's Story

Stella Hewlett at 39 participated in TAA twice. She participated first to go through cosmetology school. While participating in that program, she actually returned to Whirlpool only to take a later layoff. She went on to complete an associate's degree in administrative support with a special focus on human resources. Today she runs her own successful photography studio.

Stella dropped out of high school eventually completing a GED. She described herself as having a "rough life" as a young person. During her layoff and entrance into the TAA program, Stella encountered a number of family problems including a separation from her husband, problems with her teen children, and the deaths of her beloved grandparents. In addition to family challenges, Stella suffered from Attention Deficit Disorder (ADD). Despite these challenges, Stella was determined to complete her associate's degree:

> I had a pretty rough life when I was younger and my grandparents always thought highly of me so as I was going to college my grandparents went into a nursing home and I was hoping that they would make it long enough to see me graduate. Because that's one of the things that my granddad—he, he started crying when he found out I was going to college. And I was not going to quit... (S. Hewlett, September 18, 2013)

Today Stella's business is steady and she enjoys the creativity and freedom of running her own business:

> In most factories you can't horseplay. In my job I get to horseplay. I get to be outside. I get to play with kids. I get to be involved with people. I love people. I love socializing. I love talking... I can walk up to anybody and talk to them and I guess that's what helps me with this.... So I think this degree was a very good thing for me. (S. Hewlett, personal communication, September 18, 2013)

Most important to Stella was a new image of herself: "I feel like a grown up. I don't feel like a child. I don't know, college I guess made me feel like I was smart" (S. Hewlett, personal communication, September 18, 2013).

Themes

Four themes emerged from analysis of the participants' stories and interviews:

Theme 1—Humbling Experiences
In each of the participants' stories, a humbling or humiliating episode was a significant part of the narrative. For some participants, the humbling experience came during the educational experience; for others the humbling experience occurred in trying to re-enter the workplace.

Bureaucracy
Several of the participants mentioned feeling humbled or humiliated in participating in the bureaucratic aspects of the program. Chad said:

> It just felt like they owned you. It was—they made it almost feel like a handout. Instead of us losing our job and them trying to help us it felt like it was more like a handout, like I was going down there to get my food stamps or whatever it was. (C. Wilson, personal communication, October 30, 2013)

Stella had a similar experience:

> Well a lot of times they would lose your paperwork and you would have to go back and forth, back and forth, back and forth and it just seemed like it was, it was more of a hassle to do that than to even go to college. I mean it was very frustrating. The college part, once you were in the door, it was fine. (S. Hewlett, personal communication, September 18, 2013)

Struggles with Math
Another common theme was the struggle to regain lost mathematical skills. Tom's struggle to deal with college level math featured prominently in his story. Stella had a similar experience with college algebra:

> It was two classes at the same time but the class that I took was more advanced where I should have already known College Algebra and it was really tough on me. So I had to drop College Algebra and pick it back up after that because it was really confusing me. Because I should have already known the College Algebra course before I took the other course. (T. Carver, personal communication, August 27, 2013)

Working in a Low Status Job

Another humbling experience was that of working in a low status job after completing the degree program. Katie put it succinctly: "I'm doing a job that requires a high school education" (K. Bolton, personal communication, September 16, 2013). Chad also had this experience:

> I came out here and did my interview. And the construction guys—the director of engineering and or the VP of engineering and the director of construction—they interviewed me. And he says you know you are overqualified for this. He says your resume looks awesome but you understand that you'll be holding a shovel. And I said I understand that we're in an economy now. I've got three kids. I've got to feed them. (C. Wilson, personal communication, October 30, 2013)

Jimmy also worked in a low status job but seemed less troubled by it than the other participants:

> I mean the job's really more physical which I haven't done in years. And uh the job's not bad. It's just that you've got too many people wanting to be the boss and they're trying to tell you what to do and you only got one boss. (J. Lensing, personal communication, October 29, 2013)

Humiliating experiences were a common point of similarity between all five study participants. The source of humiliating experiences was varied. For some participants the stigma against government assistance made the process of turning in weekly paperwork a weekly experience in which they described feeling judged. For others the process of new academic challenges was humiliating; they had moved from seeing themselves as competent workers to a new image of themselves as incompetent in academics. Finally, the reality of taking lower status (and lower paying) work caused feelings of embarrassment and humiliation.

Theme 2—Symbols of Success

For each of the participants, common symbols of academic success were meaningful motivators and personal milestones. Katie said:

> The thing that kind of chokes me up is actually putting on the cap and gown and that would have to be. I mean that was the ultimate goal and something that I had wished that I had done, you know, 30 years earlier. (K. Bolton, personal communication, September 16, 2013)

Tom had a similar experience:

But the best moment I'd say honestly, when you walk across that stage. And, and you just...Wow! And honestly I don't really know if it hits you until afterwards and you're off the stage and say wow it's done. I'm over. I can move forward now. (T. Carver, personal communication, August 27, 2013)

Chad found that the diploma on his wall was a meaningful symbol: "Down in my office they come in and they see my diploma. That was a very expensive piece of paper and yeah I like showing it off" (C. Wilson, personal communication, October 30, 2013). For both Stella and Jimmy grades were important symbols. Jimmy said: "Any time I made an A in a class I knew that I was reaching a goal where I needed to be...Just to know at my age I can still make an A in a college level" (J. Lensing, personal communication, October 29, 2013).

For each of the participants, common academic symbols of achievement such as semester grades or graduate's cap and gown, were meaningful as milestones of accomplishment. In the absence of their Whirlpool jobs, the everyday academic symbols seemed to take on an enhanced power for each of the participants.

Theme 3—Instructor as Mentor

Another theme that emerged was that of instructors stepping out of their instructional roles to serve as mentors. Chad said:

Mr. M. was not just a professor to me he was a mentor. A good solid, you know, no holds barred. If you did something wrong he let you know; if you did something right he let you know. . . . And then they brought in a new teacher, Mr. J. Awesome guy. I never even had him as a teacher. I worked with him because of you know the student assistant and he's . . . Both them men are Godly men. And they are—you can tell by the way they lift people up. (C. Wilson, personal communication, October 30, 2013)

Jimmy also had a mentor:

You know one particular teacher that I had, he had a lot of manufacturing experience and that's why I clicked with him because we knew what was out there and we knew what was expected. . . . The teachers didn't let you down. . . . They knew you were struggling, they tried to help you out. . . . You knew they were there for you. Not the other way around. (J. Lensing, personal communication, October 29, 2013)

Each of the participants mentioned the important role that their instructors took in helping them accomplish both academic and work-related goals. For these adults, entering higher education after a devastating job loss, the importance of personal attention from authority figures emerged again and again in the interviews. The importance of being treated as a fellow adult worthy of their time and attention appeared to be a source of motivation for participants.

Theme 4—Generational Impact.

The final theme that emerged from the interviews was the generational impact that education had on the families of participants. Katie was attending university at the same time as both of her sons:

> They were going through high school they would, you know, be on the dean's list and we would put it on the refrigerator. And we got into college and they just both got stupid all of a sudden and quit making the dean's list. And mom was on the—I was going on the refrigerator and they weren't. So I was trying to be an example and say look your mother is outdoing you and I know y'all are a smarter than I am. I'm working harder than you do. (K. Bolton, personal communication, September 16, 2013)

Chad also saw the impact of his experience on his teen son:

> And the whole time I was in school my boy was going through high school. He didn't know if he wanted to go to college. Well this is his first semester at [local college]. So he knows. He knows that education does work. (C. Wilson, personal communication, October 30, 2013)

Other participants saw their work in college as an opportunity to be a role model for their children. Tom said: "Because I'm dad. And parents need to set a good role [model]" (T. Carver, personal communication, August 27, 2013).

For each of the participants, the impact of the experience of completing a degree was felt throughout the entire family. In each of their stories, the educational experience—to the participants—made a difference to the children of each family allowing the participant to serve as a positive role model.

Discussion

How do displaced workers use narrative to ascribe meaning to their experiences in higher education? How has the experience of completing a degree program affected displaced workers' assumptions or frames of reference? What role, if any, did generativity (McAdams, 1996) play in motivating the displaced worker to enroll in and complete an associate degree? To answer these questions the investigator examined each of the four themes that emerged from the interview data, then looked at each participant story holistically.

Discussion—Humbling Experiences

For the participants who were most successfully employed—Chad, Tom, and Stella—the role of the humbling experience in their narratives appeared to be a narrative technique to help them contrast their current state with the past. McAdams (2006) recognized low points or humbling experiences as part of a uniquely American narrative he calls the "redemptive self." In other words, the low point or humbling experience is told so that the teller of the story can go on to overcome the negative circumstances and emerge changed. Each of these successfully re-employed participants cheerfully shared the humiliating aspects of their experiences and took pains to contrast those experiences with their present state of achievement. In other words, the imago (alter ego or role) they took on was that of the hero—a person who overcomes adversity to reach success.

The less successfully re-employed participants, Jimmy and Katie, shared a slightly different narrative. Despite academic success, both Jimmy and Katie are now working in jobs with lower status and lower wages than their previous employment. Jimmy and Katie took pride in their academic achievements and have incorporated the imago of "good student" into their identity; however, Jimmy and Katie each struggled with the fact that academic success has not translated into success at work. Despite frustration, Jimmy and Katie told stories in which they were still taking action and working toward a goal of financial status comparable to that they enjoyed at Whirlpool. Possibly Jimmy and Katie have incorporated the hero imago into their identities, only in their cases the hero has not yet finished the journey.

The issue of whether transformative learning has taken place is more ambiguous. While each participant seemed to have "transformed" in important ways, only Stella appeared to have experienced transformative learning. Mezirow and Associates (2000, 2009) described transformative learning as beginning with a disorienting dilemma. Surely for each of the participants, the job loss and entry into higher education is a disorienting dilemma. For Chad, Tom, and Stella the telling of the humbling experience is the stage Mezirow and Associates (2009) called "Recognition of a connection between one's discontent and the process of transformation" (p. 19). In other words, the humbling experience was a spur to make a transformation to a new way of looking at the world. But a key component to transformation is the reassessment of assumptions about the world. Stella appears to have changed her assumptions about the world. For instance, Stella says that she now realizes that she does not have to depend on a man for emotional and financial support. She also speaks about the assumption that she hated school and now finds that she loves school and loves learning. Stella appears to have made a transformation from old ways of seeing the world to new paradigms. For the other participants, however, despite impressive achievements and improvements in their lives, there is little evidence that transformative learning as described by Merizow has occurred.

Discussion—Symbols of Academic Success

For each of the participants, the symbolism of academic success—grades, diplomas, commencement ceremonies, academic regalia—were powerful symbols of accomplishment. The participants share instances of "choking up" or feeling pride in these symbols. These symbols seem to help the participants understand the height of their accomplishment, and take on the weight of convincing the participants themselves of their success academically.

McAdams (2008) said that stories are cultural texts that reflect the overall environment and culture of the society in which they are set. In the narrative told by each participant, symbols of academic success figure prominently. The focus on outward symbols of academia seems to indicate that academic success has been incorporated into the personal identity of each participant. In other words, each participant has taken on a new alter ego or imago—that of the "Good Student."

Discussion—Instructor as Mentor

For each of the study participants, instructors who stepped out of typical academic roles and into a mentoring role were important figures. For each of the participants, instructors who took on the mentor role were mentioned in the context of motivation. In answer to a question, "What or who kept you going?" each participant shared stories of instructors who served as mentors. In these narratives, the mentor figures emerged as important characters in the story. Another identity theme that emerged from the stories of mentors was the importance of being seen as an individual by the mentor. This suggests that the mentor is an important figure in reinforcing self-esteem and personal status. If the mentor figure takes the time for a personal relationship with the story teller, then the narrator still retains some of the status associated with previous employment. A mentor figure is an important character in terms of helping the participants try on new roles and relationships, and in formulating action plans to move forward (Mezirow & Associates, 2009). The mentor figure is also important to the McAdams model of identity (1988, 1996, 2006). The mentor who guides the participant through new experience plays the important role in reinforcing self-identity as a person worthy of respect and attention.

Discussion—Generational Impact

McAdams (1988, 1996, 2006) focused on how generativity—a person's need to care for and prepare future generations (Erikson, 1980), helps shape personal identity. For each of the participants, the impact of education on their own children was a motivating factor. Tom felt the need to be a role model for his junior high aged daughter. Chad was pleased that his educational success led his academically unmotivated son to try college. Katie even felt a sense of healthy competition with her academically gifted sons. In each of these cases, concern for children was a strong motivating factor for pursuing the degrees and for persisting in programs of study despite struggles and setbacks. By successfully completing a college degree—either an associate's or bachelor's degree—each participant has the opportunity to make a positive change not just in their own individual life and identity but in the future of the family by affecting the lives and attitudes of their children.

Transformative Learning or a New Identity?

Each of the participants explicitly stated that they benefited from the educational experience of completing a degree through the TAA program. While it may be said that each participant accomplished transformation, or at least improvements in their lives, the participants did not necessarily accomplish transformative learning. Of all the participants, only Stella appeared to question former assumption about the world and adopt new paradigms.

For Jimmy and Katie, the experience was not quite as life changing as for other participants. Because re-entry into employment put both these participants in low status jobs, each of them seems to see their story as incomplete. Jimmy sees his warehouse position as a stepping stone to something better, while Katie continues to look for other employment that will allow her to use her degree. When asked "How is your life different?", each answered that their lives were not different. For the other participants—Chad, Tom, and Stella—the experience seems to have been beneficial on many levels.

While transformative learning is a potential benefit of participation, only one participant appears to have truly experienced transformative learning. The more crucial benefit appears to be the way in which the educational experience has affected identity. For each participant, the educational experience seems to have served the important purpose of forging a new self-identity which is separate from that of "Whirlpool Employee."

IMPLICATIONS AND FUTURE RESEARCH

The experience of completing an associate's or bachelor's degree through participation in the TAA program was generally positive for each of the participants in this study. While the partnership between the federal TAA program, the state Department of Workforce Services, and the university created many administrative and bureaucratic tasks that the participants found frustrating, the successful completion of their programs was an important accomplishment for each participant. While two of the five participants are still struggling to find employment in which to use their new degrees, the other three participants have experienced successful re-employment.

The findings of this study suggest some areas for future research:

- How can educators use symbols of academic success as a motivator for adult students?
- How can educational programs and state and federal programs reduce the burden of paperwork to help TAA participants?
- How can educators use the generative impulses of adult students to help them persist in their academic programs?
- How do the narratives of students who are currently enrolled in TAA programs compare to the narratives of graduates?

So, what is the benefit to participation in higher education through the TAA program? Pragmatic Tom indulged in a metaphor describing his experience:

> I would also summarize it as almost like skydiving for the first time if you've ever done that...I can only imagine jumping out of a plane depending on that parachute to catch you. To catch the wind. To ease the cushion of your fall if that makes any sense at all.... Because when I got into the program I wasn't sure that that chute was there and I wasn't sure that it would open. And I was falling but I was beginning to enjoy the free-fall of it all if I can use that metaphor. When I opened the chute, I knew I was going to make it. (T. Carver, personal communication, August 27, 2013)

REFERENCES

Butterwick, S., & Lawrence, R. L. (2009). Creating alternate realities: Arts-based approaches to transformative learning. In J. Mezirow & E. Taylor (Eds.), *Transformative learning in practice: Insights from community, workplace and higher education* (pp. 35–45). San Francisco, CA: Jossey-Bass.

Clandinin, D. J., & Connelly, F. M. (2000). *Narrative inquiry: Experience and story in qualitative research.* San Francisco, CA: Jossey-Bass.

Couch, K. A., & Placzek, D. W. (2010). Earning losses of displaced workers revisited. *The American Economic Review, 100*(1), 572–589.

Creswell, J. W. (2007). *Qualitative inquiry and research design* (2nd ed.). Thousand Oaks, CA: Sage Publications.

Creswell, J. W. (2009). *Research design: Qualitative, quantitative, and mixed methods approaches* (3rd ed.). Thousand Oaks, CA: Sage Publications.

Donaldson, J. F. (2009). Fostering transformative learning in leadership development. In J. Mezirow & E. Taylor (Eds.), *Transformative learning in practice: Insights from community, workplace and higher education* (pp. 67–76). San Francisco, CA: Jossey-Bass.

Erikson, E. H. (1980). *Identity and the life cycle.* New York, NY: W.W. Norton and Company, Inc.

Farber, H. S. (2005). What do we know about job loss in the United States? Evidence from the displaced workers survey, 1984–2004. *Economic Perspectives, 29*(2), 13–28.

Garrett, R. (2012, June 29). Local Whirlpool production shuts down today. *Southwest Times Record.* Retrieved from http://nl.newsbank.com/nl search/we/ Archives?p_action=list&p_topdoc=21.

Gordon, K. (2012). Pre- and post- wage differences of trade adjustment assistance participants in Arkansas. (Unpublished doctoral dissertation). University of Arkansas, Fayetteville, AR.

Hironimus-Wendt, R. J., & Spannaus, F. (2007). The social costs of worker displacement. *Social Policy, 37*(3/4), 83–89.

Jacobs, E. (2013). *Creating a virtuous circle: Workforce development policy as a tool for improving the prospects of America's unemployed workers.* Governance Studies Discussion Paper. Washington, DC: The Brookings Institution. Retrieved from http://www. brookings.edu/research/papers/2013/02/1-workforce-development-jacobs.

Jacobson, L. S., LaLonde, R., & Sullivan, D. (2005a). Estimating the returns to community college schooling for displaced workers. *Journal of Econometrics, 125,* 271–304.

Jacobson, L. S., LaLonde, R., & Sullivan, D. (2005b). Is retraining displaced workers a good investment? *Economic Perspectives, 29*(2), 47–66.

Jacobson, L. S., LaLonde, R., & Sullivan, D. (2005c). The impact of community college retraining on older displaced workers: Should we teach old dogs new tricks? *Industrial and Labor Relations Review, 58*(3), 398–415.

Jacobson, L. S., LaLonde, R., & Sullivan, D. (2011). Policies to reduce high-tenured displaced workers' earning losses through retraining. Hamilton Project Discussion Paper. Washington, DC: The Brookings Institution. Retrieved from http:/www.hamiltonproject.org/files/downloads_and_links//11_displaced_ JLS_paper.pdf.

Mandell, A., & Herman, L. (2009). Mentoring: When learners make the learning. In J. Mezirow & E. Taylor (Eds.) *Transformative learning in practice: Insights from community, workplace and higher education* (pp. 78–87). San Francisco, CA: Jossey-Bass.

Maynes, M. J., Pierce, J. L., & Laslett, B. (2008). Telling *stories: The use of personal narratives in the social sciences and history.* Ithaca, NY: Cornell University Press.

McAdams, D. P. (1988). *Power, intimacy, and the life story: Personological inquiries into identity.* New York, NY: The Guilford Press.

McAdams, D. P. (1993). *The stories we live by: Personal myths and the making of the self.* New York, NY: The Guilford Press.

McAdams, D. P. (1996). Personality, modernity, and the storied self: A contemporary framework for studying persons. *Psychological Inquiry, 7*(4), 295–321.

McAdams, D. P. (2006). The redemptive self: Generativity and the stories Americans live by. *Research in Human Development, 3*(2&3), 81–100.

McAdams, D. P. (2008). Personal narratives and the life story. In O. John, R. Robins, & L. Pervin (Eds.), *Handbook of personality: Theory and research* (3rd ed.), (pp. 242–263). NY: Guildford Press.

Merriam, S. B. (2009). *Qualitative research: A guide to design and implementation,* (3rd ed.). San Francisco: Jossey-Bass.

Mezirow, J., & Associates (1990). *Fostering critical reflection in adulthood: A guide to transformative and emancipator learning.* San Francisco, CA: Jossey-Bass.

Mezirow, J., & Associates (2000). *Learning as transformation: Critical perspectives on a theory in progress.* San Francisco, CA: Jossey-Bass.

Mezirow, J., & Taylor, E. W. (2009). *Transformative learning in practice: Insights from community, workplace and higher education.* San Francisco, CA: Jossey-Bass.

Mezirow, J. (1991). Transformative *dimensions of adult learning.* San Francisco, CA: Jossey-Bass.

Park, J. (2012). Does occupational training by the trade adjustment assistance program really help reemployment? Success measured as occupation matching. *Review of International Economics, 20*(5), 999–1016.

Patton, M. Q. (2002). *Qualitative research and evaluation methods,* (3rd ed.). Thousand Oaks: CA: Sage Publications, Inc.

Reynolds, K. M., & Palatucci, J. S. (2012). Does trade adjustment assistance make a difference? *Contemporary Economics Policy, 30*(1), 43–59.

Taylor, E. W. (2009). Fostering transformative learning. In J. Mezirow & E. Taylor (Eds.), *Transformative learning in practice: Insights from community, workplace and higher education* (pp. 3–17). San Francisco, CA: Jossey-Bass.

Tyler, J. A. (2009). Charting the course: How storytelling can foster communicative learning in the workplace. In J. Mezirow & E. Taylor (Eds.), *Transformative learning in practice: Insights from community, workplace and higher education* (pp. 136–147). San Francisco, CA: Jossey-Bass.

United States Department of Labor. (n.d.). *Trade Adjustment Assistance State Profile: Arkansas.* Retrieved from: http://www.doleta.gov/tradeact/pdf/AR.pdf.

CHAPTER 2

ADULT DEGREE PROGRAMS

Factors Impacting Student Persistence

Mathew J. Bergman, Kevin J. Rose, and M. Brad Shuck
University of Louisville

As a result of increasing demands for a more educated population, adult degree completion programs are becoming increasingly relevant within the higher education community and are growing at a rapid pace across the United States (Carnevale, Smith, & Stroh, 2010; Taylor, 2000). According to the North Central Association's Higher Learning Commission Task Force on Adult Degree-Completion Programs (2000), an adult degree completion program is one designed specifically to meet the needs of the working adult who, having acquired 60 or more college credit hours during previous enrollments, is returning to school after an extended period of absence to obtain a baccalaureate degree. The institution's promise that the student will be able to complete the program in fewer than two years of continuous study is realized through provisions such as establishing alternative class schedules, truncating the traditional semester/quarter time frame, organizing student cohorts, and awarding credit for prior learning experiences equivalent to approximately 25% of the bachelor's degree credit total (Task

Building Sustainable Futures for Adult Learners, pages 27–50
Copyright © 2015 by Information Age Publishing

27

Force, 2000). Adult degree programs share common characteristics including, but not limited to, distance (online) options, evening course options, weekend course options, test-out (CLEP and DSST) options, and college credit for prior learning in the workplace.

Among the most pressing concerns for colleges and universities across the United States is student retention (Tinto, 2012). While most research on the topic has focused on traditional students, labor statistics indicate that adult degree programs, which typically have low retention rates, are an essential part of the stability and growth of the nation's economy. There are more than 162.3 million people in the United States workforce (Bureau of Labor Statistics, 2012), and 38 million of those are working-age adults (ages 25 and older) who have some college but no degree (Adult Learning in Focus CAEL, 2008). The U.S. labor market now requires postsecondary education for most entry-level positions and virtually all mid-level occupations, and by 2018, 63% of jobs will require some form of postsecondary training (Carnevale et al., 2010). The U.S. economy will have jobs for 22 million workers with college degrees, but a shortage of nearly three million college graduates (Carnevale et al., 2010). These statistics show a growing need for the nation's workforce to acquire more postsecondary credentials. Consequently, colleges and universities must work to better understand why so many adults fail to reach graduation.

Past generations have been able to secure any number of jobs in the public and private sectors with a high school diploma; in today's marketplace, however, possession of a high school diploma alone will not provide the qualifications for entry-level jobs and limits the possibilities of acquiring highly skilled jobs (Klein-Collins, Sherman, & Soares, 2010). In the nation's changing economy, baccalaureate-level education is a necessity for a number of jobs that have never before required it (Bragg, Townsend, & Rudd, 2009). According to Cabrera, Burkum, and LaNasa (2005) "a bachelor's degree is no longer considered a potential stepping-stone to a better life and is fully acknowledged as the gatekeeper to a myriad of social and individual benefits" (p. 2). Even though there are some skeptics of this assertion, a recent Pew Research Study (2014) found an increasing disparity in earnings between those with and without a college degree. Statistics show that college graduates earn roughly $1 million more over their lifetimes, earning on average $48,800 annually compared to $30,800 for workers without a degree (Kazis, Vargas, & Hoffman, 2007; Pew Research, 2014). College graduate unemployment rates are also 30% lower than that of high school graduates with an unemployment rate of 5.5% in 2009, compared with all other persons at 9.3% (Turner & Krumenauer, 2010). They also provide at least $300,000 more over a lifetime in federal taxes (Adult Learning in Focus CAEL, 2008). This significant number of adults with some college and no degree and the demands of the current workforce have facilitated growth in adult degree completion programs, and this reality is directly impacting both traditional and nontraditional colleges and universities. As such, institutions cannot afford to let adult degree completion programs operate on the periphery of their traditional curricula. These changes in demographics are forcing colleges and universities to consider more adult-friendly practices in order to adapt to this underserved population. Between 1970 and 1991, adult participation in higher education rose at a rate of 171.4%. Adult students now comprise more than 50% of all part-time higher education enrollments, and over 33% of total higher education enrollment in the United States (NCES, 2013). As institutions of all sorts cater to larger adult student enrollment, it is imperative for academe to examine both positive and negative factors impacting adult student retention.

ADULT STUDENTS AND RETENTION

Despite research on adult and nontraditional attrition, more depth and breadth is merited by this subpopulation. No single group is more important to the viability of higher education, and the reasons for adult student attrition stem from complex and diverse intervening variables (Tweedell, 2000). Moreover, Tinto (1993, 2012) posited that much of what we think we know about student retention is wrong, or at least misleading, and a good deal of literature is filled with stereotypical portraits of student dropouts. Institutions of higher education are still unable to make sense of student departure because so much remains unknown about its longitudinal character and the complex interplay of forces that lead students to drop out (Tinto, 1993). As the number of "traditional" students continues to decrease, the need for a better understanding of adult students has deepened.

Many factors have been shown to affect students' progress to graduation (see Figure 2.1). Adult students pose a unique challenge to researchers because they do not persist to graduation in the same manner or at the same rates as traditional-aged students (Justice & Dornan, 2001; Soares, 2013). Adult students come to higher education with a variety of academic backgrounds. Some return to college after a gap of several years well prepared for any academic challenge they face. Others require remedial or developmental education to increase academic preparedness. Bergman's (2012) Model of Adult Learner Persistence in Degree Completion Programs provides a comprehensive examination of the salient variables associated with student entry characteristics, external environmental variables, internal/academic campus related variables in relation to the outcome variable of persistence. In the following sections, those factors included in the (Bergman, 2012) model will be overviewed in brief.

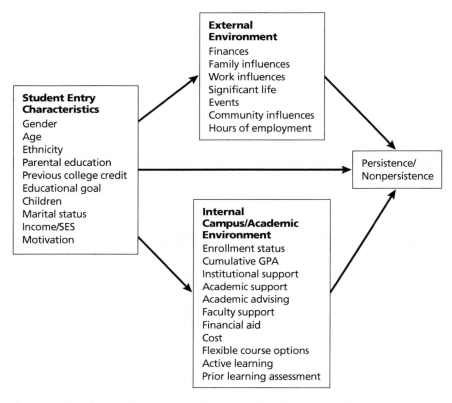

Figure 2.1   (Bergman, 2012) Model of adult learner persistence in degree completion programs.

Student Entry Characteristics

Background or entry characteristics are those that come with adult students returning to the academic setting. These variables include both static and dynamic traits, and colleges and universities can do little to influence them. Entry characteristics relevant to adult learners include socioeconomic status, race/ethnicity, age, gender, marital status including number of children, total previous college credit earned, and goal commitment (Braxton, Hirschy, & McClendon, 2004). Other entry characteristics include high school class rank, standardized test scores, college prep curriculum, and high school friends attending college, but they are often excluded when considering what impacts adult student persistence because of the typical large gap of years between enrollments that exists for most adult learners.

Gender

The strength of association between gender and completion varies, but gender is a factor in most published studies that have adequate sample size and statistical techniques (Choy, 2002; Farabaugh-Dorkins, 1991; Horn, 1998; McCormick, Geis, Vergun, & Carroll, 1995). An analysis of data from the Integrated Postsecondary Education Data System reported that 62% of female adult students graduate from two-year institutions and 57.2% of female adult students graduate from four-year institutions, and men graduate at rates of 38% and 42.8% respectively (Knapp, Kelly-Reid, & Ginder, 2012). Thus, women graduated at higher rates than men did at both the two and four-year levels. On the contrary, Metzner and Bean (1987) did not find a significant association between persistence and gender. Horn and Berger (2005) also did not find a significant difference in the gap in the graduation rates between women and men. Shields (1994) found no effect from gender, although total sample size may have had an influence on this conclusion (N = 97). Woosley (2004) also found no significant differences related to gender. Therefore, it is posited that no gender differences are likely to exist in a degree-completion program composed of adults ages 25 and older.

Age

Scholars do not agree on whether age positively or negatively affects persistence, or if it has any influence at all (DesJardins, Ahlburg, & McCall, 1999; Singell & Stater, 2006). It is true that as the age of the student increases, it is less likely that the parents attained a college degree and older students may have more non-academic responsibilities that influence the dropout decision (Hammer, Grigsy, & Woods, 1998). Simply being older does not mean an individual will have less time to participate in higher education, but it could correlate to competing responsibilities depending on one's career trajectory. Adult learners often make a pledge to balancing other life commitments and have great success in their degree pursuits (Bergman, 2012). In a seminal study, Bean and Metzner (1985) highlighted age as one indirect effect on nontraditional student persistence. However, in and of itself, age has not been shown as a predictor of retention. Thus, it is not age but the associated responsibilities that tend to accompany age that influence a student's persistence (Hammer et al., 1998).

Ethnicity

This variable appears as a factor affecting student persistence in many education studies (Aud, Fox, & Kewal-Ramani, 2010; Aud, et al., 2013). However, the studies that have considered the impact of ethnic origin among adult students have produced mixed results. Many studies, including St. John, Paulson, and Carter (2005), Byrd (1990), and Webb (1989) found ethnicity to be a statistically significant factor in persistence.

Conversely, Bean and Metzner (1985) predicted ethnic origin to be a factor in nontraditional persistence but their 1987 empirical study did not find this variable statistically significant after controlling for other factors. Overall, African Americans and Latinos are less likely to persist than their white peers are, but significant differences in completion rates depend on types of institutions being considered and how persistence is defined (DesJardins, et al, 1999).

Parent's Educational Attainment

Students with parents and other close family members or friends who have graduated from postsecondary institutions are more likely to desire to attain similar educational goals and persist to graduation at a higher rate (Choy, 2002; Tinto, 1993). Those whose parents or family members have not achieved such educational credentials are less likely to be interested or aware of the opportunities that are afforded to those with postsecondary degrees (Horn, 1998). Older students are more likely than traditional age students to be "first generation" students who are less conscious of all of the nuances related to entry and assimilation into colleges and universities (Bergman, 2012). Consequently, these students, both adult and traditional, are more likely to leave before completing their studies (Arbona & Nora, 2007; Choy, 2002; Horn, 1998).

Previous College Credit

Students who have more prior college credits are more likely to persist to graduation (Christensen, 1991; CAEL, 2010; Hanniford & Sagaria, 1994; Harrington, 1993; Martin 1990; Simmons, 1995). St. John and Starkey (1995) also found an association between number of credits completed and persistence except at the senior class level. Wlodkowski, Mauldin, and Gahn (2001) noted that adult students benefit from having significant prior college experience before enrolling in four-year colleges, whether in accelerated or in conventional programs. In other words, those with more college credit often have less remaining course work to reach their goal of a baccalaureate degree, thus increasing the likelihood of program completion. Persistence for nontraditional transfer students can be enhanced when states encourage four-year colleges to form articulation agreements with community colleges to accept transfer credits and guarantee admission to qualified students (Calcagno, Jenkins, Bailey, & Crosta, 2006). Institutions that aim to improve adult learner persistence by offering multiple learning options, such as off-campus learning centers, distance-learning technologies, online material, and flexible course offerings at nontraditional times (like evenings and weekends) can increase the likelihood of adult student retention (CAEL, 2010; Simmons, 1995).

Educational Goal

Kasworm (2005) posited that many adult students have a wavering self-image and limited self-confidence. The collegiate environment tests their sense of self and their external world presents challenges to their participation in college. Often negative messages, as well as self-doubt, lead to limited energies and productivity in college. Further, initial goals and motives may be weak or unrealistic and may be quickly challenged by participation in a competitive collegiate environment (Bergman, 2012). Some adults "self-destruct" when faced with challenges and do not follow through on their initial enrollment application, or stop out from further college enrollment when difficulties are presented. However, those adults who have a higher level of commitment to educational attainment often persist at much higher rate than others with lower educational attainment goals (Bergman, 2012; Cabrera, Nora, & Castaneda, 1993).

Marital Status and Children

Marital status and number of children can be factors in persistence, but their effect may be mediated through a student's age and gender. The number of parents seeking a bachelor's degree peaked in 1989 and declined in 1992 (NCES, 2000). However, the reality that the workforce has a prerequisite of a bachelor's education for most job criteria is driving working adults with children back to American colleges and universities (Cabrera et al., 2005; Lumina, 2011). Unfortunately, much of the literature has found that the presence of children is negatively associated with persistence (Horn, 1998; McCaffrey, 1989; McGivney, 1996; Mercer, 1993; Shields, 1994), and marital status was positively associated with persistence (Mercer, 1993). An early study by Weidman (1985) found that students who report less trouble with children were more likely to persist. Conversely, Byrd (1990) found that students with three or more children experienced more barriers to completion. Another study (Mercer, 1993); however, found no difference in persistence based on marital status or the presence of children when controlling for other factors. It must be noted that the age of the children and the parent attending school are an essential consideration. Older adults with children that have moved away from home and are gainfully employed are less likely to have intervening issues with enrollment (Bergman, 2012).

Income/Socioeconomic Status

Income and socioeconomic status (SES) also play a complex role in the persistence of adult students. One National Center for Education Statistics (2000) study defines SES as a composite variable combining parents' education and occupation, dependent student's family income, and the existence of material possessions in respondent's home. Horn (1998) included all beginning U.S. higher education students from a national database, and

SES was not found to be statistically significant when other variables were controlled. However, this study finding did not isolate adult students. Scott, Burns, and Cooney (1996) found that SES, as measured by spousal and parental income, was a significant factor in the persistence of female adult students. Adults have more financial commitments, and SES/income has been shown to have a direct effect on persistence among adult students (Ashar & Skenes, 1993). Increased financial assistance made available to adult learners increases access to higher rates of degree completion (Hunt & Tierney, 2006). Therefore, a student with fewer concerns regarding their basic living expenses experiences less stress that could lead to departure decisions.

Motivation

There are two roots of voluntary departure: intention and commitment. Individual intentions can change and are not always clear even to the individual. Commitment takes two forms: goal commitment (usually occupational in nature) and institutional commitment. Tinto (1993) found the existence of occupational goals proportionate to the likelihood of completing a degree, and that goal commitment "becomes a motivating force" (p. 38) even for students who were marginally academically prepared. In fact, Tinto found that students with high academic preparation, but weak goal commitment and motivation, were less likely to persist than students with weak academic ability, and strong goal commitment. Additional research has supported this assertion that motivation and commitment is a strong predictor of college students' ability to persist (Braxton, Milem, & Sullivan, 2000; Cabrera, Nora, & Castaneda, 1993; Sadler, Cohen, & Kockesen, 1997). The intent and/or motivation to leave or stay are often the best predictors of actual student departure (Bean, 1980). One cause of early withdrawal is a gap between learner expectations and reality. Returning students are motivated enough to enroll in degree-seeking programs, and many clearly value education, but negative past experiences of school may be too strong (Quigley & Uhland, 2000).

Internal Campus/Academic Environment

Internal environment variables include, but are not limited to the following: financial aid, grade point average, part-time enrollment status, counseling, evening and weekend scheduling, instructor/advisor support, and prior learning assessment. Several factors are not discussed in the current context because they pertain more to traditional-age students, such as housing policies, membership in student organizations, dining services, and student government involvement. Adult education researchers have also investigated the problematic relationship between the adult student and the university environment, noting lack of sufficient policies, procedures, and services to adequately support the success of adult undergraduates (Kasworm, Sandmann, & Sissel, 2000).

Enrollment Status

Part-time status has become much more common, but its effect on persistence is generally negative. Adult students who are able to enroll on a full-time basis persist at much higher levels than do part-time students. However, this often means that adults are committing to full-time enrollment in lieu of full-time employment. The model proposed by Bean and Metzner (1985) included enrollment status as a factor in persistence which was supported by substantial evidence. In sum, the more hours the student takes per term, the more likely they are to persist (Metzner & Bean, 1987; Cuccaro-Alamin, 1997; Horn & Carroll, 1997; McCormick et al., 1995; Mc-Givney, 1996; Mercer, 1993; St. John & Starkey, 1995; Taniguchi & Kaufman, 2005). Conversely, by allowing students to attend part-time, institutions meet a variety of needs and extend educational opportunity to students who otherwise might be dissuaded from participation, or shut out of the system entirely (McCormick et al., 1995).

Cumulative GPA

A growing body of literature supports the notion that the cumulative grade point average (GPA) of students is positively correlated with persistence (Bean & Metzner, 1985; Farabaugh-Dorkins, 1991; Horn, 1998; Kasworm, 1990; McCaffrey, 1989; Mercer, 1993; St. John & Starkey, 1995). Cuccaro-Alamin, Horn, and Carroll (1997) found that a high GPA was positively associated with persistence among nontraditional learners. Conversely, Shields (1994) found no effect from GPA on persistence among adult students. Since adults have been shown throughout the literature to have a stronger commitment to learning, it was hypothesized that higher GPAs would not likely be a significant predictor of adult student persistence. In other words, cumulative GPA was important to measure but not likely substantial among the variables measured.

Institutional Support, Academic Advising, and Faculty Support

Traditional American colleges and universities are not known for their extensive adult learner friendliness. However, Kuh (2008) found academic advising and faculty interaction to be an integral part of any retention, persistence, and student-success initiative. Both help students navigate the resources available to them in and around the campus and classroom. Wlodkowski, Mauldin, & Campbell (2002) found adult learners desired better advising services. Adults view advising and faculty support as customer service that needs to be prompt and efficient in the dissemination of quality information that assists them to efficiently take required courses toward a desired baccalaureate degree program. Effective academic advisors, instructors, counselors, and adult support services all influence adult-student persistence (Bergman, 2012). Beal and Noel (1980) posited that inadequate academic and faculty advising was one of the largest impediments to student retention; however, Habley and Morales (1998) found that only 29% of postsecondary institutions have some form of advisor effectiveness evaluation.

Financial Aid and Cost

Cuts to tuition assistance and revision of policies on state and federally funded loans and grants may weigh heavily in adults' intent to persist. The variety of responsibilities and competing demands for money from adult students' budgets is often cited as a reason for leaving college (Aslanian, 2001; Kasworm, 1990; McCormick et al., 1995). Unfortunately, adult, part-time, and independent students are less likely to receive grants, and what funding they do receive is smaller than traditional students (Lumina Foundation, 2011).

Aslanian (2001) found that most adult undergraduates rely on personal funds to cover college costs. Only 20% use loans, 19% receive grants or scholarships, and 18% receive tuition reimbursement (NCES, 2010). However, when tuition reimbursement is available, 70% of adults use this benefit (NCES, 2010). Financial sources including federal aid, foundation support, and tuition discounts provide avenues to assist adult students, whether they are in accelerated learning programs or in conventional learning formats. Unfortunately, adult students receive much less financial aid than their traditional counterparts (Lumina Foundation, 2011).

Astin's (1993) work suggested that, for traditional students, state and federal need-based financial aid displays "no discernible impact on traditional student development" (p. 368). This study overturned the earlier finding (Astin, 1975) that grants and scholarships were positive and loans were negative. Astin and Oseguera's (2002) later work concludes that merit-based awards have a positive effect for nontraditional students. The role of financial aid for adult students is also complex. Receiving financial aid is generally positive for persistence among adult students (Cuccaro-Alamin, 1997; Kasworm, 1990; McCormick et al., 1995). For full-time adult students, financial aid is consistently positive (McCormick et al., 1995), but for part-time adult students, the type of aid is crucial (grants were positive, loans more negative). As mentioned previously, adult students do not receive aid as often as traditional students, in spite of broad eligibility (St. John & Starkey, 1995). For part-time students, the primary form of aid is employer tuition reimbursement (McCormick et al., 1995). To counter the effects of rising tuition costs and offer equal opportunities to adult students, especially those of low socioeconomic status, student aid needs to be increased to that group (Lumina Foundation, 2011).

Flexible Course Options

Adult learners are engaging in work and education, particularly distance education, at an unparalleled rate, and higher education professionals need to understand the unique challenges nontraditional students face in order to facilitate a positive learning environment. It has been suggested that the flexibility of distance education courses and programs may be particularly helpful in encouraging Americans with family and work obligations to pursue and complete post-secondary credentials (Kolowich, 2010). The flexibility of the online environment has become increasingly more appealing to adult learners who are trying to balance work, family, and education.

Adult learners' increased utilization of online learning is further supported by Ashby's (2002) Government Accounting Office (GAO) report on adult learners and distance education. In an analysis of the National 2002 Postsecondary Student Aid Study (NPSAS), Ashby reported the average age for distance learning students was 30, and students were more likely to be married, working full-time and studying part-time, with women comprising 65% of the online undergraduate population. Ashburn (2010) noted that simply offering more online courses is not sufficient to attract and retain the growing adult student population. Adult learners with numerous life and familial commitments also prefer evening and weekend courses alongside online course and program options.

Active Learning

Ahson, Gentemann, & Phelps (1998) provided further evidence that many students leave college voluntarily, rather than because of involuntary reasons such as academic performance. In a sample composed of both traditional and nontraditional students, Horn and Carroll (1997) found that academic integration and active learning were positively associated with persistence. To measure active learning and skills development, they used student responses to questions about how often they participated in the following activities: "attend career-related lectures, participate in study groups with other students, talk over academic matters with faculty, and meet with their advisor concerning academic plans" (p. 52). In summary, students who were isolated both from the resources of the college and from other students are less likely to persist. Adult students, in particular, exhibit a more problem-centered or skills development focus in the formal academic environment. This population seeks out more active learning because they are self-directed, experiential, problem-centered, and internally motivated (Knowles, Swanson, & Holton, 2011).

Research findings from other studies confirm that positive involvement with peers and faculty encourages adult students to persist (New England Adult Research Network, 1999; Tinto, 1998). The study of persistence among traditional age students has stressed the importance of social integration in persistence (Tinto, 1993). Traditional age students who become involved on campus and make friends, join clubs, and participate in activities are far more likely to persist. It is important to re-work this concept to address the persistence of adult students.

Prior Learning Assessment

Prior Learning Assessment (PLA) is a process that colleges use to evaluate college-level knowledge, skills, and abilities gained outside the confines of the classroom for academic credit (CAEL, 2010). There are two primary forms of prior learning assessment (PLA): course-specific PLA and the broader portfolio form. In course-specific PLA, adult learners can test-out of courses via challenge exams or take CLEP or DSST tests that are universally accepted as the equivalent of various core courses. If students are able to demonstrate mastery of any of a number of content areas, they are exempted from those courses and awarded college credit for that requisite knowledge. The Council on Adult and Experiential Learning (CAEL, 2010) collected data from 62,475 students at 48 postsecondary institutions and found PLA students had better academic outcomes, particularly in terms of graduation rates and persistence, than other non-PLA students. More than 56% of PLA students earned a postsecondary degree, while only 21% of non-PLA students did so (CAEL 2010). The CAEL study also revealed that many PLA students also graduate sooner than other non-PLA students. Another study by the College Board Advocacy (2009) found that 1500 adults rated "credit for prior learning policy" as more important than "small class size" or "availability of financial aid." Smith and McCormick (1992) suggest that learning from experience can often be equivalent, if not superior, to college classroom learning.

External Environment Variables

Some of the major environmental factors include finances, family support, employer support (tuition, flextime, work hours), and significant life events. Environmental factors, including family problems, lack of childcare, and job demands are often cited as factors for withdrawal or stop-out behaviors of adult students. The balancing act of managing family, work, community, and academic responsibilities can pose great challenges for adult students.

Adults have to cope with a variety of work, life, and academic roles. In addition, negative experiences from the past may affect adults' confidence. Kasworm (2001) stated that

> being an adult student is fraught with time and resource issues related to actively pursuing homework assignments and final projects, getting to and from

courses and the library, typing papers, collaborating with study groups, and engaging in other activities to support academic success. (p. 33)

Many adult learners need more time to dedicate to their academic life than they have available. In these circumstances, the academic responsibilities shift to the bottom of the priority list, and the guilt and frustration related to this balancing act often leads to departure decisions. The competing demands of life make it very challenging for adult learners to strike a balance that helps them reach their academic goal of completing a baccalaureate degree. These learners experience a wide variety of life circumstances, such as work, family, financial pressures, and community responsibilities that weigh heavily on their intentions to return and persist in degree programs (Kasworm, 2003b; Kazis et al., 2007). The ability to juggle multiple roles and responsibilities can often lead to a level of stress that produces higher rates of attrition than that of traditional-aged learners.

Finances

Bean and Metzner (1985) suggested in their model that finances would be a significant factor in departure decisions only to find that it was not statistically significant in their subsequent 1987 study. However, many studies have suggested that finances or low income were a significant factor in persistence to graduation (Christensen, 1991; Hall, 1997; Horn & Caroll, 1997; Losty & Kreilick, 1982; McCaffrey, 1989; Mercer, 1993; Zajkowski, 1997; Titus, 2006). In exit surveys, adult students who leave college often say they cannot afford it any longer. The cost of enrollment, tuition, books, and child-care can prevent adults from completing a degree. Some employers have tuition assistance, however there may be caps on the amount available based upon federal government regulation. Others must shoulder the entire financial burden, viewing it as too monumental to overcome on their own.

It is possible that departing students fail to mention other obstacles that might be contributing to the dropout decision. For these students, the challenges add to the overall financial and emotional cost of the program and thus decide to abandon their educational pursuits. A related set of studies also support the idea that adult students persisted at higher rates if they reported higher income (Choy & Premo, 1995; Losty & Kreilick, 1982; Stinebrickner & Stinebrickner, 2003; Titus, 2006), more financial security (Cabrera et al. 1992), or that finances were not much of a problem (Mercer, 1993). However, men generally express fewer financial problems than women, but they do not persist as often as women (Ryder, Bowman, & Newman, 1994). Money certainly has an impact on adult students. However, the influence of money may be overstated in persistence studies unless money crises (such as the loss of a job) occur after studies have been initiated. The student's expression of financial difficulty can be financial difficulty, but it can also be an expression of declining commitment to education attainment.

Family and Community Influences

For their adult learner study, Hammer, Grigsy, and Woods (1998) examined the following three sets of variables: work and family, enrollment status, and gender and age. The dependent variable was the degree of conflict between work, family, and school. They found a statistically significant correlation between the dependent and independent variables including credit hours, hours of employment, perceived effectiveness of support services, and satisfaction with the academic environment. Kimmel and McNeese (2006) reported family care and financing issues as primary deterrents for nontraditional students. Wldokowski (2001) noted that lack of time was the dominant theme for leaving college. He found that adult students repeatedly and emphatically cite competing priorities and not having enough time to meet the demands of family, community, work, and school as a deterrent to completion of their academic degree program. Wldokowski (2001) found that among adults in the school with an accelerated program, the top two reasons for leaving college indicated were conflict between job and studies (60%), and home and community responsibilities were too great (59%).

Work Influences and Hours of Employment

Employment, like age, has been found to have both motivational and detrimental influence on adult student participation (Kasworm, 2003a). Bradburn (2002) reported that nontraditional students were "less likely than traditional students to cite academic problems or the need to work as the reason for leaving" (p. 55). Many adults have a stronger tie to career culture than to academic culture. Adult learners often re-enter an academic setting to achieve advanced positions and higher wages. However, the same factor that has driven many adults back to the classroom is often the greatest barrier to their completion of the degree. Wlodkowski et al. (2002) found that lack of time was the dominant theme among all adult learners leaving college. The various competing priorities, including job responsibilities, often generate a feeling of being overwhelmed to the point of not being effective as a student.

As Berker, Horn, and Carroll (2003) reported, 76% of adult students who work full-time are enrolled in school part-time. Only 19% of the students were working full-time and taking classes full-time. In general, adult students are less likely to persist than their traditionally aged, non-working counterparts (NCES, 2002). Kirby, Biever, Martinez, and Gomez (2004) examined the influence of school responsibilities on family, work, and social interactions for students in a nontraditional weekend college program. In this study, students who indicated they had support from work reported significantly lower stress levels. However, even with work and family support, full-time employment was a significant predictor of school-related stress. Berker, et al. (2003) also examined the relationship between work and school, finding that adult students who classified themselves as employees who were attending school, were less likely to persist than those who classified themselves as students who chose to work. In other words, if a person identifies as an employee or a student, that identity becomes the priority and receives more attention. However, Pascarella, Terenzini, and Wolfle (1991) controlled for 15 student background characteristics and college experiences and considered both on- and off-campus employment; they found only modest and inconsistent evidence to suggest that either form of work seriously inhibits students' learning or cognitive development. There was, however, some evidence in the third year of the study to suggest that reasonable amounts of part-time on- or off-campus work actually facilitated learning.

Significant Life Events

Some significant life events include health issues, family health issues, death in the family, divorce, marriage, birth of a child, military deployment, and employment changes including job loss, promotion, or relocation because of job. Sometimes a significant life change will trigger a return to college, propelling a student to return to college and finish a long-delayed goal (Aslanian, 1989). Unfortunately, these events can have multiple results. While these occasions weigh heavily on adult learners' intentions to return, these scenarios often lead to greater levels of stress that produce higher rates of attrition (Mercer, 1993; Kazis, et al., 2007). It is typical for adults to accrue more responsibilities with advanced years in the workforce. Therefore, competing responsibilities and challenging life events are a natural occurrence in most adults' lives. It is essential for adults returning to the academic environment to mitigate the chances of these events occurring when possible.

RECOMMENDATIONS FOR POLICY AND PRACTICE

The confluence of factors that affect adult learners in an academic environment is daunting to say the least. Although the field of student retention has been studied for close to eighty years (Braxton & Hirschy, 2005), additional empirical research is merited for this growing subpopulation of students. Many of these individual variables are positively correlated with persistence of adults in degree completion programs, but have never been measured collectively (Bergman, 2012). Further study of the variables from the model could provide insight into the validity of the proposed Theory of Adult

Learner Persistence in Degree Completion Programs (Bergman, 2012). This model provides support for utilizing each of the variables examined for the development of specific action-oriented interventions to aid in adult student persistence. Development of policy at the institutional, local, state, and national level could result from the data analysis of age, ethnicity, educational goal, PLA credits, financial aid, active learning, institutional support, and external influences of adult learners in degree completion programs.

Further, a multivariate analysis of a broad range of adult friendly institutions could provide a glimpse into the experiences of adult learners at varied types of colleges and universities. This research could also provide avenues toward innovative student tracking via an early alert system to provide intervention for adult learners. Thus, colleges and universities could improve their adult retention and graduation rates in comparison to those for traditional-aged students. Producing more accountability for each program would also promote a culture of discipline encouraging students to become more accountable for their learning and educational attainment.

This review and conceptual model introduction illuminates the need for additional convenience options including weekend and online course offerings while maintaining the rigor of the academic curriculum. The value students place on flexible course options and prior learning assessment mirrors that of previous research and advances the case for creating adult-friendly practice nationwide. The ability to integrate credit for prior learning through experiential credit evaluation helps relieve some of the fears and anxiety of returning adults and empowers them through the reflection on the depth and breadth of learning they already have accumulated.

This review of variables associated with adult student retention also debunks many misconceptions about the requirements of undergraduate study. Because many adults in degree completion programs have failed in previous attempts as traditional-aged students, they often feel nervous about their ability to complete formal academic work at a high level. Although the reintegration into a formal academic setting is challenging, many adult learners indicate that it is no more overwhelming than their current workload in their current job (Hammer, Grigsy, & Woods, 1998). Orientation and PLA courses provide an avenue for adults to assimilate into a world in which they often were not previously successful.

Another recommendation concerns the need to address affordability and accessibility. Although progress has been made on finding additional scholarships, grants, and loans specifically for adults, the amount of funding in comparison to that of traditional high school seniors is miniscule (Lumina, 2011). As significant numbers of adult learners are coming back to complete degrees, it is necessary for institutions and legislature to designate additional resources for this growing population. The federal government has made strides in its reform of the G.I. Bill; however, adults outside of the military and lower socioeconomic groups find it difficult to secure scholarships or financial aid. This is a growing and complex challenge.

This chapter has displayed the value placed on faculty and staff to aid in the students' continued enrollment and eventual graduation. Adults have little to no time to integrate in co-curricular activities on campus, so having a single point of contact or familiar office can build a relationship that helps foster success. Even though the advisor or faculty member might not remain the key contact once a student is enrolled, adults often maintain their relationships with faculty and staff throughout their college experience, continuing to seek assistance and support from these individuals until they graduate. Students have indicated that having someone available to listen to them and try to answer their questions is often enough to help them stay enrolled. Therefore, an essential component of any degree completion program is a single or small group of academic or faculty advisors available for timely and knowledgeable feedback.

Finally, we note that adults are focused on real-world relevance and expect a level of service that they receive in the business environment. Unfortunately, the innovative student support and learning strategies described above are rarely found in traditional university programs (Ross-Gordon, 2011). It is essential that more adult friendly practices (PLA, convenient course options, and evening and online student support) become fully integrated into the fabric of traditional four-year colleges and universities. If programs are able to manage the demands of students that identify as worker, spouse or partner, parent, caregiver, and community member with timely and informed feedback and guidance, higher levels of student persistence is likely to follow.

CONCLUSION

Few issues in higher education have received as much attention as persistence and retention (Bean 1980; Braxton, Hirschy, & McClendon 2004; Cope & Hannah, 1974; Iffert, 1957; Lang & Ford 1988; McNeely, 1937 Pantages & Creedon, 1978; Raimst 1981; Spady 1970, 1971; Summerskill, 1962; Tinto, 1975, 1993, 2012). Prior research has shown that adults persist at lower rates than that of their traditional counterparts. In addition, little is known about factors that increase rates of persistence among an increasingly broad base of flexible and convenient degree-completion programs at four-year colleges. With the advent of PLA and offerings that include evening, online, and weekend options, one would assume that nontraditional students might persist to graduation at much higher rates. Accurate modeling of nontraditional student attrition behavior, however, is difficult due to the heterogeneity of the population (Metzner & Bean, 1987).

More students in the United States attain degrees of higher education than anywhere else in the world (Lumina Foundation, 2011). However, degree-attainment levels are increasing in every industrialized or post-industrial country in the world except the United States (Lumina Foundation, 2011). Simply waiting for youth to fill the workforce needs, however, will not meet the demands of this rapidly changing economic landscape (Merriam, Caffarella, & Baumgartner, 2007).

Thus, it is important to understand the obstacles faced by adult students who return to the academic setting to pursue bachelor's degrees. Various work, family, financial, and community responsibilities have been shown to impact attrition and persistence behavior of adult learners. Researchers must continue to examine these factors and how they interact to increase or decrease likelihood of persistence to graduation among adult learners in a single institution's four-year degree completion program.

REFERENCES

Adult Learning in Focus (2008). *National and state-by-state data CAEL and NCHEMS published report.* Retrieved from http://www.cael.org/pdf/ALIF_highlights_%20PRINT.pdf

Ahson, N. L., Gentemann, K. M., & Phelps, L. (1998). *Do stop outs return? A longitudinal study of re-enrollment, attrition, and graduation.* Paper presented at the 38th Annual Forum of the Association for Institutional Research. (ERIC Document Reproduction Service No. ED424800).

Arbona, C., & Nora, A. (2007). The influence of academic and environmental factors on Hispanic college degree attainment. *Review of Higher Education, 30*(3), 247.

Ashar, H., & Skenes, R. (1993). Can Tinto's student departure model be applied to nontraditional students? *Adult Education Quarterly, 43*(2), 90–100.

Ashburn, E. (2010). City U. of New York plans "a grand experiment": A new college. *The Chronicle of Higher Education.* Retrieved April 25, 2010 from http://chronicle.com/section/Home/5

Ashby, C. (2002). *Report on adult learners and distance education.* Washington DC: Government Accountability Office. Retrieved September 27, 2010, from http://www.gao.gov/new.items/d03905.pdf

Aslanian, C. B. (1989). What triggers adult participation in higher education. *Equity and Excellence, 24*(3), 5–8.

Aslanian, C. B. (2001). *Adult students today.* New York, NY: The College Board.

Astin, A. (1975). *Preventing students from dropping out.* San Francisco, CA: Jossey-Bass.

Astin, A. (1993). *What matters in college? Four critical years revisited.* San Francisco, CA: Jossey-Bass.

Astin, A. W., & Oseguera, L. (2002). *Degree attainment rates at American colleges and universities.* Los Angeles: Higher Education Research Institute, UCLA.

Aud, S., Fox, M., & Kewal-Ramani, A. (2010). *Status and trends in the education of racial and ethnic Groups* (NCES 2010-015). U.S. Department of Education, National

Center for Education Statistics. Washington, DC: U.S. Government Printing Office.

Aud, S., Wilkinson-Flicker, S., Kristapovich, P., Rathbun, A., Wang, X., & Zhang, J. (2013). *The condition of education 2013* (NCES 2013-037). U.S. Department of Education, National Center for Education Statistics. Washington, DC. Retrieved from http://nces.ed.gov/pubsearch.

Beal, P. E., & Noel, L. (1980). *What works in student retention.* Iowa City, IA: American College Testing Program.

Bean, J. P. (1980). Dropouts and turnover: The synthesis and test of a causal model of student attrition. *Research in Higher Education, 12*(2), 155–187.

Bean, J. P., & Metzner, B. S. (1985). A conceptual model of nontraditional student attrition. *Review of Educational Research, 55*(4), 485–540.

Bergman, M. (2012). *An examination of factors that impact persistence among adult students in a degree completion program at a four-year university.* Doctoral dissertation, University of Louisville, Louisville, KY. Retrieved April 1, 2012, from author.

Berker, A., Horn, L., & Carroll, C. (2003). Work first, study second: Adult undergraduates who combine employment and postsecondary enrollment. Postsecondary Educational Descriptive Analysis Reports. Retrieved from EBSCO*host* http://nces.ed.gov/pubs2003/2003167.pdf

Bradburn, E. M. (2002). *Short-term enrollment in postsecondary education: Student background and institutional differences in reasons for early departure, 1996–1998.* (NCES 2003-153). Washington, DC: U.S. Department of Education.

Bragg, D. D., Townsend, B. K., & Ruud, C. M. (2009). *The adult learner and the applied baccalaureate: Emerging lessons for state and local implementation.* Office of Community College Research and Leadership (2009, January).

Braxton, J. M., & Hirschy, A. S. (2005). Theoretical developments in the study of college student departure. In Seidman,, A. *College student retention* (pp. 61–88) Westport, CT: Praeger Publishers.

Braxton, J. M., Hirschy, A. S., & McClendon, S. A. (2004). Understanding and reducing college student departure. *ASHE-ERIC Higher Education Report, 30*(3).

Braxton, J. M., Milem, J. F., & Sullivan A. S. (2000). The influence of active learning on the college student departure process. *The Journal of Higher Education, 71*(5), 569–590.

Bureau of Labor Statistics (2012). United States Department of Labor census data. Retrieved from http://www.bls.gov/

Byrd, S. (1990). *Perceptions of barriers to undergraduate education by nontraditional students at selected non-public, liberal arts institutions in the mid-south.* Paper presented at the annual conference of the Mid-South Educational Research Association, New Orleans, LA.

Cabrera, A., Nora, A., & Castaneda, M. B. (1993). College persistence: Structural equations modeling test of an integrated model of student retention. *Journal of Higher Education, 64*(2), 123–139.

Cabrera, A. F., Burkum, K. R., & LaNasa, S. M. (2005). Pathways to a four-year degree: Determinants of transfer and degree completion. In A. Seidman (Ed.), *Student retention: Formula for student success* (pp. 155–214). New York, NY: Rowman & Littlefield.

Cabrera, A. F., Nora, A., & Castaneda, M. B. (1992). *The role of finances in the persistence process: A structural model.* Paper presented at the annual meeting of the American Educational Research Association, San Francisco, CA.

Calcagno, J., Crosta, P., Bailey, T., & Jenkins, D. (2006). Stepping stones to a degree: The impact of enrollment pathways and milestones on community college student outcomes. *Research in Higher Education, 48*(7), 775–801.

Carnevale, A. P., Smith, N., & Strohl, J. (2010). *Help wanted: Projections of jobs and education requirements through 2018.* Georgetown University Center on Education and the Workforce, 45–46.

Choy, S. (2002). *Nontraditional students. The condition of education 2002* (NCES 2002–2012). National Center for Education Statistics. Washington, DC: U.S. Department of Education.

Choy, S., & Premo, M. (1995). *Profile of older undergraduates: 1989–90.* (NCES 95-167). U.S. Department of Education, National Center for Education Statistics. Washington, DC. Retrieved from http://nces.ed.gov/pubs95/web/95167.asp

Christensen, P. (1991). Comparison of adult baccalaureate graduates and nonpersisters. Paper presented at the Midwest Research-to-Practice Conference., St. Paul, MN. (ERIC Document Reproduction Service No. ED 378 307)

College Board Advocacy (2009). *How colleges organize themselves to increase student persistence: Four-year institutions.* Retrieved September 24, 2010 from http://pas.indiana.edu/cb.index.cfm

Cope, R. G., & Hannah, W. (1974). *Revolving college doors.* New York, NY: John Wiley & Sons.

Council for Adult and Experiential Learning (CAEL). (2010). Fueling the race to postsecondary success: A 48-institution survey of prior learning assessment and adult student outcomes. [Online]. Available from http:// www.cael.org/pdf/PLA_Fueling-the-Race.pdf

Cuccaro-Alamin, S. (1997). *Postsecondary persistence and attainment.* (NCES 97- 984). Washington, DC: U. S. Department of Education. Office of Educational Research and Improvement. National Center for Education Statistics.

DesJardins, S. L., Ahlburg, D. A., & McCall, B. P. (1999). An event history model of student departure. *Economics of Education Review, 18*(3), 375–390.

Farabaugh-Dorkins, C. (1991). *Beginning to understand why older students drop out of college: A path analytic test of the Bean/Metzner model of nontraditional student attrition.* Tallahassee, FL: The Association for Institutional Research. (ERIC Document Reproduction Service No. ED332598)

Habley, W., & Morales, R. (1998). *Current practices in academic advising: Final report on ACT's Fifth National Survey of Academic Advising.* National Academic Advising Association & Act Inc. Monograph Series No. 6.

Hall, N. (1997). Variables that enhance the persistence of older female graduate students. *Dissertation Abstracts International, 53,* 1610.

Hammer, L. B., Grigsby, T. D., & Woods, S. (1998). The conflicting demands of work, family, and school among students at an urban university. *The Journal of Psychology, 132*(2), 220–226.

Hanniford, B., & Sagaria, M. (1994). *The impact of work and family roles on associate and baccalaureate degree completion among students in early adulthood.* Paper presented at the annual meeting of the American Educational Research

Association (New Orleans, LA). (ERIC Document Reproduction Service No. ED 370 520).

Harrington, J. (1993). Why they stay: A study on the persistence of re-entry women. *Initiatives, 55*(4), 17–24.

Horn, L. (1998). *Stopouts or stayouts? Undergraduates who leave college in their first year* (NCES 1999-087). Washington, DC: U.S. Department of Education.

Horn, L., & Carroll, C.D. (1997). *Nontraditional students: Trends in Enrollment from 1986 to 1992 and persistence and attainment among 1989–90 beginning postsecondary students* (NCES 97-578). Washington, DC: U.S. Department of Education.

Horn, L., & Berger, R. (2005). *College persistence on the rise?: Changes in 5-year degree completion and postsecondary persistence rates between 1994 and 2000* (NCES 2005-156). Washington, DC: U.S. Department of Education.

Hunt J. B., & Tierney, T. J. (2006). *American higher education: How does it measure up for the 21st century?* San Jose, CA: The National Center for Public Policy and Higher Education.

Iffert, R. E. (1957). *Retention and withdrawal of college students.* U.S. Office of Education, Bulletin 1957, no. 1. Washington, DC: U.S. Government Printing Office.

Justice, E. M., & Dornan, T. M. (2001). Metacognitive differences between traditional age and non-traditional age college students. *Adult Education Quarterly 51*(3), 236–249.

Kasworm, C. (1990). Adult undergraduates in higher education: A review of past research perspectives. *Review of Educational Research, 60,* 345–372.

Kasworm, C. (2001). A case study of adult learner experiences of an accelerated degree program. Paper presented at the American Educational Research Association Conference, Seattle, WA, April 2001.

Kasworm, C. (2003a). Adult meaning making in the undergraduate classroom. *Adult Education Quarterly, 53,* 81–98.

Kasworm, C. (2003b). Setting the stage: Adults in higher education. *New Directions for Student Services, 102,* 3–10.

Kasworm, C. (2005). Adult student identity in an intergenerational community college classroom. *Adult Education Quarterly, 56,* 3–20.

Kasworm, C., Sandmann, L. R., & Sissel, P. A. (2000). Adult learners in higher education. In A. L. Wilson & E. R. Hayes (Eds.), *Handbook of adult and continuing education,* (pp. 449–463). San Francisco, CA: Jossey-Bass.

Kazis, R., Vargas, J., & Hoffman, N. (2007). *Double the numbers: Increasing postsecondary credentials for underrepresented youth.* Boston, MA: Harvard Education Press.

Kimmel, S. B., & McNeese, M. N. (2006). Barriers to business education: Motivating adult learners. *Journal of Behavioral and Applied Management, 7*(3), 292–303.

Kirby, P. G., Biever, J. L., Martinez, I. G., & Gomez, J. P. (2004). Adults returning to school: The impact on family and work. *The Journal of Psychology, 138*(1), 65–76.

Klein-Collins, R., Sherman, A., & Soares, L. (2010). Degree completion beyond institutional boarders: Responding to the new reality of mobile and nontraditional learners. Center for American Progress: The Council for Adult and Experiential Learning. Retrieved from http://www.cael.org/Forum_and_News/IndexNov2010_files/CAPandCAELExecSummary.pdf

Knapp, L. G., Kelly-Reid, J. E., & Ginder, S. A. (2012). *2011–12 Integrated Postsecondary Education Data System (IPEDS) Methodology Report* (NCES 2012-293). U.S. Department of Education. Washington, DC: National Center for Education Statistics. Retrieved from http://nces.ed.gov/pubsearch

Knowles, M. S., Swanson, R. A., & Holton, E. F. (2011). *The adult learner: The definitive classic in adult education and human resource development.* Burlington, MA: Butterworth-Heinemann.

Kolowich, S. (2010). Buying local, online. *Inside Higher Ed.* Retrieved September 6, 2011. Retrieved from http://www. insidehighered.com/news/2010/07/23/online

Kuh, G. (2008). Diagnosing why some students don't succeed. *Chronicle of Higher Education, 55*(16), A72.

Lang, M., & Ford, C. A. (1988). *Black student retention in higher education.* Springfield, IL: Charles C. Thomas.

Losty, B., & Kreilick, D. (1982). Who succeeds? Perceptions of graduates and inactive students of a nontraditional bachelor of arts degree program. *Alternative Higher Education: The Journal of Nontraditional Studies, 6,* 258–267.

Lumina Foundation (2011). *Goal 2025: Increasing Postsecondary Attainment.* Retrieved from http://www.luminafoundation.org/goal_2025/goal3.html

Martin, L. (1990). Dropout, persistence, and completion in adult secondary and prevocational programs. *Adult Literacy and Basic Education, 14,* 159–174.

McCaffrey, S. (1989). *A key to survival: The retention of adult students in an external degree program.* Paper presented at the annual meeting of the Association for the Study of Higher Education, Atlanta, Georgia. (ERIC Document Reproduction Service No. ED 313 974)

McCormick, A., Geis, S., Vergun, R., & Carroll, D. (1995). *Profile of part-time undergraduates in postsecondary education: 1989–90.* (NCES 95-173). Washington, DC: U.S. Department of Education. Office of Educational Research and Improvement. National Center for Education Statistics.

McGivney, V. (1996). *Staying or leaving the course: Non-completion and retention of mature students in further and higher education.* Leicester, England: National Institute of Adult Continuing Education.

McNeely, J. H. (1937). *College student mortality.* U.S. Office of Education, Bulletin 1937, no. 11. Washington, DC: U.S. Govt. Print.

Mercer, D. (1993). Older coeds: Predicting who will stay this time. *Journal of Research and Development in Education, 26,* 153–163.

Merriam, S. B., Caffarella, R. S., & Baumgartner, L. (2007). *Learning in adulthood: A comprehensive guide.* San Francisco, CA: John Wiley & Sons.

Metzner, B., & Bean, J. (1987). The estimation of a conceptual model of nontraditional undergraduate student attrition. *Research in Higher Education, 27*(1), 15–38.

National Center for Public Policy in Higher Education. (2006). *Measuring up 2006.* San Jose, CA: Carnegie Corporation.

New England Adult Research Network. (1999). *Factors influencing adult student persistence in undergraduate degree programs.* Amherst, MA: Victoria Dowling, University of Massachusetts.

Pantages, T. J., & Creedon, C. F. (1978). Studies of college attrition: 1950–1975. *Review of Educational Research, 48*(1), 49–101.

Pascarella, E. T., Terenzini, P. T., & Wolfle, L. M. (1991). Orientation to college and freshman year persistence/withdrawal decisions. *The Journal of Higher Education, 57*, 155–175.

Pew Research Center. (February, 2014). *The rising cost of not going to college*. Retrieved from http://www.pewsocialtrends.org/2014/02/11/the-rising-cost-of-not-going-to-college/

Quigley, B. A., & Uhland, R. L. (2000). Retaining adult learners in the first three critical weeks: A quasi-experimental model for use in ABE programs. *Adult Basic Education, 10*(2), 55. Retrieved August 1, 2011, from Career and Technical Education.

Ross-Gordon, J. M. (2011). Research on adult learners: Supporting the needs of a student population that is no longer nontraditional. *Association of American Colleges and Universities, 13*, 1–6.

Ryder, R., Bowman, R., & Newman, P. (1994). Nontraditional students: Perceived barriers to degree completion. *College Student Affairs Journal, 13*(2), 5–13.

Sadler, W., Cohen, F., & Kockesen, L. (1997). *Factors affecting retention behavior: A model to predict at-risk students*. AIR Annual Forum Paper. (ERIC Document Reproduction Service No. ED 410 885).

St. John, E., & Starkey, J. (1995). The influence of prices on the persistence of adult undergraduates. *Journal of Student Financial Aid, 25*(2), 7–17.

Scott, C., Burns, A., & Cooney, G. (1996). Reasons for discontinuing study: The case of mature age female students with children. *Higher Education, 31*, 233–253.

Shields, N. (1994). Retention, academic success, and progress among adult, returning students: A comparison of the effects of institutional and external factors. *NACADA Journal, 14*, 13–24.

Simmons, D. (1995). Retraining dislocated workers in the community college: Identifying factors for persistence. *Community College Review, 23*(2), 47–58.

Singell, L. D., & Stater, M. (2006). Going, going, gone: The effects of aid policies on graduation at three large public institutions. *Policy Sciences, 39*(4), 379–403.

Soares, L. (2013). "Post-traditional learners and the transformation of postsecondary education: A manifesto for college leaders". *American Council on Education*. Retrieved from http://www.acenet.edu/news-room/Documents/Soares-Post-Traditional-v5-011813.pdf

Spady, W. (1970). Dropouts from higher education: An interdisciplinary review and synthesis. *Interchange, 1*, 64–85.

Spady, W. (1971). Dropouts from higher education: Toward an empirical model. *Interchange, 2*, 38–62.

Stinebrickner, R., & Stinebrickner, T. R. (2003). Understanding educational outcomes of students from low-income families: Evidence from a liberal arts college with a full-tuition subsidy. *The Journal of Human Resources, 38*(3), 591–617.

Summerskill, J. (1962). Dropouts from college. In N. Sanford (Ed.), *The American college* (pp. 627–657). New York, NY: John Wiley & Sons.

Taniguchi, H. and Kaufman, G. (2005), Degree Completion Among Nontraditional College Students. *Social Science Quarterly, 86*, 912–927. doi: 10.1111/j.0038-4941.2005.00363.x

Task Force on Adult Degree Completion Programs. (2000, June). *Adult degree completion programs.* Retrieved from http://www.ncacihe.org/resources/ adctf/ ADCPRept.pdf

Taylor, J. A. (2000). *Adult degree completion programs: A report to the board of trustees from the Task Force on Adult Degree Completion Programs and the award of credit for prior learning at the baccalaureate level.* North Central Association of Colleges and Schools, Chicago, IL. Commission on Institutions of Higher Education.

Tinto, V. (1975). Dropout from higher education: A theoretical synthesis of recent research. *Review of Educational Research, 45,* 89–125.

Tinto, V. (1993). *Leaving college: Rethinking the causes and cures of student attrition* (2nd ed.). Chicago, IL: University of Chicago Press.

Tinto, V. (1998).Colleges as communities: Taking research on student persistence seriously. *The Review of Higher Education, 21,* 167–177.

Tinto, V. (2012). *Completing college: Rethinking institutional action.* Chicago, IL: The University of Chicago Press.

Titus, M. A. (2006). Understanding college degree completion of students with low socioeconomic status. *Research in Higher Education, 47*(4), 371–398.

Turner, B., & Krumenauer, G. (2010). *The value of a bachelor's degree.* WorkSource Quality Information, Oregon Employment Department. Retrieved August 19, 2011 from http://www.qualityinfo.org/olmisj/ArticleReader?itemid = 00001862

Tweedell, C. B. (2000, October). *A theory of adult learning and implications for practice.* Paper presented at the meeting of the Midwest Educational Research Association Annual Meeting. Chicago, IL.

Webb, M. (1989). A theoretical model of community college student degree persistence. *Community College Review, 16*(4), 42–49.

Weidman, J. (1985). Retention of nontraditional students in postsecondary education. Paper presented at the Annual Meeting of the American Educational Research Association, Chicago, IL. (ERIC Document Reproduction Service No. ED 261 195)

Wlodkowski, R. J., Mauldin, J. E., & Campbell, S. (2002). *Early exit: Understanding adult attrition in accelerated and traditional postsecondary programs. Synopsis: Higher education research highlights.* Indianapolis, IN: Lumina Foundation for Education, July, 2002.

Wlodkowski, R. J., Mauldin, J. E., & Gahn, S. W. (2001). *Learning in the fast lane: Adult learners' persistence and success in accelerated college programs.* Indianapolis, IN: Lumina Foundation for Education.

Woosley, S. (2004). Stop-out or drop-out? An examination of college withdrawals and re-enrollments. *Journal of College Student Retention, 5,* 293–303.

Zajkowski, M. (1997). Price and persistence in distance learning. *Open Learning, 12,* 12–23.

CHAPTER 3

DO GRADUATE STUDENTS WHO SET FORMAL GOALS REALLY GRADUATE AT HIGHER RATES?

Robert Collins and Jill Coddington
College for Professional Studies

Dorothy Williams
Regis University

There is a long-standing historical context for the relationship between goal setting and persistence and reaching desired outcomes, including the development of successful degree programs within the field of higher education. A growing concern for one university's college for professional studies, and possibly other institutions offering graduate programs for adult learners, is the rate at which students complete their degrees and the reasons they do or do not finish. Not only is there a concern about whether such programs are achieving expected outcomes, but also about the efficiency of admitting large numbers of new students while at the same time losing existing students at a high rate. Many universities believe that retaining more students in their

Building Sustainable Futures for Adult Learners, pages 51–64
Copyright © 2015 by Information Age Publishing
All rights of reproduction in any form reserved.

programs until they graduate is a more efficient use of resources than is admitting more students who may drop out at higher rates. The question of efficiency and maintaining a stronger revenue stream for the university forms the basis for research described in this chapter.

Related literature indicates that other researchers are strongly interested in goal setting (Bandura, 1986, 1997; Dweck, 1986; Grant and Dweck, 2003; Eppler and Harju; 1997; Klein and Lee, 2006; Locke and Latham 2002). However, much of this literature applies to students in elementary/secondary schools and traditional age college students while little research is available that applies to adult nontraditional learners in graduate degree programs. More research that applies directly to programs that offer accelerated, intensive and online learning formats is clearly needed.

Locke and Latham (2002) reviewed literature and research conducted over a 35 year period, the outcome of which was a proposed theory of goal setting and task motivation. Their work forms a likely theoretical foundation for further research that may link goal setting to task motivation. While much of their work was conducted in the workplace, it was done with adults. Therefore, this theory base was an appropriate place to begin. Their work in this review is based on Ryan's (1970) premise that conscious goals affect action. Locke and Latham (2002) concluded that two variables, goal specificity and goal difficulty, are at the core of goal setting theory. Further, they concluded that Moderators or variables that impact goal setting include Goal Commitment, Goal Importance, Self-Efficacy, Feedback, and Task Complexity. Mechanisms or related variables that impact performance are Choice/direction, Effort, Persistence, and Strategies. All of these variables are believed to affect performance or actions of individuals.

Bandura (1986) proposed a social cognitive theory that established the foundation of the study of self-efficacy and motivation. Bandura's research provides a useful theoretical framework for the analysis of the relationship between goal setting and self-efficacy. Schunk (1990) examined goal setting and self-efficacy using Bandura's theory. This research supported the belief that goal setting and self-efficacy are important self-regulated learning processes. Dweck (1986) and Schunk (1990) examined goal orientations and academic performance. They found support for the notion that people "...who believe they are capable select tasks at which they can succeed, persist longer, and expend effort..." p. 82).

Other researchers (Fleming, 2002; Glynn, Aultman, and Owens, 2005; and Ironsmith, et.al. 2003) also examined motivation and academic performance. Results of these studies support a positive relationship between motivation, goal setting, and academic performance. Yet, other researchers (Metzner, Lauer, & Rajeciki 2003; Taniguchi & Kaufman, 2005) focused their research on factors related to persistence. Metzner, Lauer, and Rajeciki (2003) found moderate support for factors that implied a dimension of commitment to future goals. Taniguchi and Kaufman (2005) found that part-time enrollment deters college completion while high cognitive ability and a high status occupational background seem to increase the chance of completion. McGivney (2004) summarized recent data in an effort to understand persistence patterns of adult learners, reporting eight factors that contribute to persistence of adult learners, the first of which was motivation. Adult learners were generally acknowledged as being more motivated than their younger traditional student counterparts. More specific reasons for motivation level of adults were reported including: a strong desire to pursue an educational program, a desire to prove themselves capable of learning, and obtaining qualifications for employment. While the specific practice of setting goals was not mentioned, logic dictates that these reasons are a likely foundation for goals that adult learners may establish as they enter and pursue continued education.

In a qualitative study, Cox (2008) interviewed 15 adult students who were graduates of the University of Memphis Master of Arts in Liberal Studies degree, the purpose of which was to describe factors that contributed to persistence toward completion of their degree. Five findings were reported including motivation to get a better job, desire for efficacy, family support and support from others, student/teacher relationships, and faith and religion. Cox concluded that the factors described were consistent with personal experience and were also consistent with the work of Houle (1988) who described goal oriented learners, activity oriented learners, and learning oriented learners in the book *The Inquiring Mind.*

A practical application of using goals to motivate learners is described by Meyer (2006) in a book titled *Attitude is Everything.* Meyer has long been accepted by many in the field of motivating adults to succeed as the founder of S.M.A.R.T. Goal setting. Each letter in the title represents a descriptor for defining effective goals. Meyer posits that effective goals should be specific (S), measurable (M), attainable (A), realistic (R), and tangible (T). While motivational presenters, including the late Stephen Covey (2004), have adopted or adapted this concept into their programs, there is little scholarly research evidence that confirms their effectiveness. However, many adult learners have been exposed to motivational programs either because they were drawn to them for personal reasons or because of on the job training and development programs. Practical application of goal setting process is beyond the scope of this study thus further scholarly investigation is needed. While this review was not exhaustive, literature related to the focus of this study were examined. Much of the research reviewed was conducted using participants other than those on which the current study was focused: non-traditional adult graduate students.

Given that much of the research relevant to goal setting has been done with audiences other than the non-traditional adult learner, the authors undertook research that does involve this audience. The authors' interest was to determine whether formal goal setting requirements increases the rates at which adult learners complete their graduate degrees, and to look for trends in data that may help our university increase graduation rates over all.

The authors' study was focused on four graduate degree programs and was designed to investigate a possible connection between formal goal setting as a program requirement and completion of degrees. The study was conducted in 2013 examining longitudinal data reaching back to 2007. The Master of Arts (MA), developed in 2005, was designed to provide an individualized graduate learning program for students based on their learning and professional goals. The program is interdisciplinary by nature as almost all of its students choose to study across more than one academic discipline. Nearly all MA students enter the program with professional goals in mind. An integral part of the program is a formal goal setting process. Students and faculty advisors work closely together to develop and document formal goals for the degree. The program allows students to monitor and adjust their learning goals and their degree program(s) as they complete courses. In addition, students are required to include an interdisciplinary core course to be completed at the mid-point of the degree plan. This course includes a review of formal learning goals, and the students' progress toward achievement of those goals. Thus, the MA program contains a formal goal setting and monitoring process not found in the other degrees in the study. The formal goal setting design of the MA program was thought to be necessary to provide a clear focus for students who need a unique, individualized graduate learning program. Because the MA program design is uniquely focused on formal goal setting, the researchers theorized that students would be more motivated to complete their degrees at higher rates than other comparable graduate programs.

CENTRAL RESEARCH QUESTIONS

This project was designed to examine the relationship between formal goal setting requirements in a MA degree program and persistence of graduate students to complete their graduate degrees. More specifically, the researchers analyzed whether formal goal setting improves the likelihood that students will complete their degrees. In this study, persistence of students enrolled in a MA degree program that requires formal goal setting was compared to students enrolled in other comparable degree programs. In addition, a secondary goal was to anaylze trends in all programs to attempt to determine recommendations that could improve persistence across all programs included in the study.

METHOD

This research was quantitative in nature for several reasons. First, quantitative studies can be reproduced in order to do future comparative analyses based on facts. Second, they can statistically support the hypothesis. Third, if the hypothesis is supported, it can be used to generalize about the target population.

The method for this research was to compare the persistence (degree completion) of MA degree students to their counterparts in other comparable graduate degree programs. The purpose of the project was to determine whether formal goal setting and monitoring features required in the MA program affect the persistence of students to complete the degree. The reseachers hypothesized that since students in the MA program set formal goals as part of their degree planning requirements, and further that they had formal review of goal status later in their program, they would graduate at higher rates than students in other comparable degree programs that did not incorporate goal setting and monitoring activities. In addition, a secondary goal was to determine trends within each program based on credit hours and time in program for both graduates and dropouts. While the authors recognized that other variables may exist and may influence the outcome, the focus of this study remained on formal goal setting. Control of additional variables was considered beyond the scope of this study. The size of the population was thought to offset some of these other variables as well.

Existing student data were collected for students in the MA degree and for students in four comparable Masters degree programs. Data were compared to determine whether graduation rates for programs that do not incorporate formal goal setting and monitoring activities are different from those of the MA degree that does include formal goal setting and monitoring activities. Quantitative analytical methods, including calculations of mean P-value tests, were used to analyze the group data. The p-values were calculated in Minitab for the difference between 2 population proportions with independent samples. The confidence interval was .05. For purposes of this project, persistence was defined as completion of the degree as originally intended by the learner. In an attempt to hold structural variables constant, comparable programs that were selected to be included in this study were those that require the same number of total credit hours, include a specialization, and include core course requirements. The primary variable examined in this project was whether or not degree programs incorporate formal goal setting and monitoring activities. Other variables also included in this study that may be related to persistence were: total credits required, number of credits transferred from other institutions, grade point average (GPA), active duty military service, and gender. Therefore, it was the researchers' intent to gather data relative to each of these variables as well as for the primary variable for the secondary purpose of trend analysis. Individual students were not identified in the data collection process. This was intentional for two reasons. First, the Institutional Review Board (IRB) approved this as a blind study. Second, with the size of the data set, it would be too difficult to contact individual students. While this limited the amount of data on each student, the researchers believe this was mitigated by the number of students in the study.

While persistence is defined as degree completion, the researchers acknowledge that CPS students are adults who have competing priorities, one of which is their education. Therefore, they will, from time to time, step out of classes for a term or two, then return to complete their degree. A pattern often recommended to students by faculty advisors is to remain enrolled one course per 8 week term, or two courses per semester. Doing so would allow students to graduate in six semesters or two academic years. However, the researchers found that average of three years or nine semesters is the average for students who were reasonably persistent in working toward graduation.

The target population of this study consisted of degree seeking graduate students from the following graduate programs: Master of Arts (MA), Master of Nonprofit Management (MNM), Master of Science in Accounting (MSA), Master of Science in Database Management (MSDM), Master of Science in Information Assurance (MSIA), Master of Science in Information Technology Management (MSITM), Master of Science in Software Engineering (MSSE), and Master of Science in Systems Engineering (MSCS).

When the data were collected and analyzed, the number of records in the five technology degrees did not warrant a statistical analysis of each of those degrees independently. Therefore, the researchers grouped all of these degrees together as one unit of analysis. This unit was named the Master of Science in Computer Science (MSCS) and were referenced in this way in the data analysis and findings sections below. Thus, there were four data sets to be included in the analysis of data. One for each of the following: MA (Master of Arts), MNM (Master of Nonprofit Management), MSA (Master of Science in Accounting) and MSCS (Master of Science in Computer Science).

Data were collected from records of students who began their programs from September, 2007 through August, 2013. A total of 1,767 student records including all programs were examined. Records included for each of the four programs examined were: 400 from MA, 417 from MNM, 289 from MSA, and 661 from MSCS. The beginning date was chosen to coincide with the term in which the four schools were originally founded. August, 2013 was the end of the summer semester and included the latest data available for this study. The data acquired included: (1) term of first course; (2) term of last course; (3) number of credits completed by August, 2013; (4) term of graduation; (5) GPA; (6) active duty military service; and (7) gender.

There were two categories of students who had not graduated. The first was dropouts. These were defined as students who had not completed at least one course prior to the last term included in this study. The second group was the current students, defined as those who had completed at least one course prior to the last term included in this study and they were considered current students. There is little research focused on persistence or retention for graduate level programs; however, in one study (Voigt & Hundrieser, 2008) the importance of credit hours completed was clear. Thus credit hours completed was included as a consideration in this research.

DATA ANALYSIS

A statistical analysis of the data was conducted including calculations of the percentages for graduates, current students, dropouts, and P-value tests between each of the four data sets. In addition, the mean was calculated for the number of years in each of the programs and the number of credit hours. The data collected included a number of other fields such as gender and veteran status that may improve granularity. However, there were not sufficient numbers in each sub-category to support generalizations aside from gender, which was not analyzed in detail for this project. Thus, the four populations as a whole were analyzed. Overall, the MNM program had the highest overall graduation rate (62.8%), and was significantly better than the graduation rate for the MA (50.5%) and the MSCS (36.5%) program. The MSA program graduation rate (60.9%) was significantly better than the graduation rate for MA and the MSCS program. Moreover, the MA program graduation rate was significantly better than the graduation rate for MSCS. Note that the hypothesis of this study was that the MA program that included goal setting and monitoring would have graduation rates significantly better that the other degree programs.

FINDINGS

The purpose of this research was designed to examine the relationship between formal goal setting requirements in a graduate degree program and persistence of graduate students to complete their degree, as compared to other degree programs at this university that do not require a formal goal setting plan. The subjects in this study were all degree seeking graduate students from the following programs: Master of Arts (MA), Master of Nonprofit Management (MNM), Master of Science in Accounting (MSA), and Master of Science in Computer Science (MSCS). Data were accessed from those students who started their programs from September 2007 through

August 2013. This research set out to investigate the hypothesis that students who had a formal goal setting plan would graduate at a higher rate than those who did not have a formal goal setting plan. The outcome would be success or failure to graduate.

The findings did not support the hypothesis that a formal goal setting plan does correlate to a higher graduation rate. Using a .05 confidence interval, the difference between the graduation rates of all four programs was statistically significant. This means that the ranking in graduation rates is appropriate. These values are shown in Table 3.1.

According to the data presented in Figure 3.1, the MA students did graduate at a higher rate (50.5%) than those in the MSCS program (36.5%), but did not graduate at a higher rate than the MNM (62.8%) or MSA students (60.9%). The same holds true for analyzing the overall graduation rates not including current students across the four programs.

Figure 3.2 displays how the MA students did graduate at a higher rate (58.6%) than those in the MSCS program (44%), but did not graduate at

TABLE 3.1   P-value Comparisons

Degree 1	Degree 2	P-value
MSA	MNM	.02579
MSA	MA	.01215
MSA	MSCS	$7.3215 * 10^{-3}$
MNM	MA	.01046
MNM	MSCS	$51212*10^{-5}$
MA	MSCS	$4.325*10^{-2}$

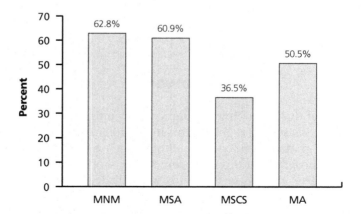

Figure 3.1   Calculated percentage graduation rates. *Note:* Graduation rates are per program. Students currently taking classes are included.

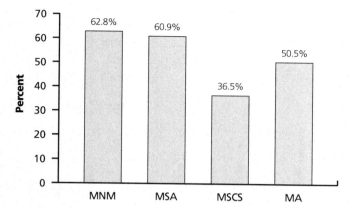

Figure 3.2 Calculated percentage graduation rates. *Note:* Graduation rates per program where students all students who have not graduated are included.

a higher rate than the MNM (70.6%) or MSA students (69.3%). What is notable is that the MNM students graduated more students than all other programs in both categories (overall graduation rate and graduation rate not including current students).

Figure 3.3 shows the average number of years to graduate from the shortest amount of time to the longest amount of time. The students in the MSA program took an average of 2.32 years to complete the program followed by the students in the MNM taking an average of 2.78 years. The MA students took an average of 2.92 years to graduate while the students

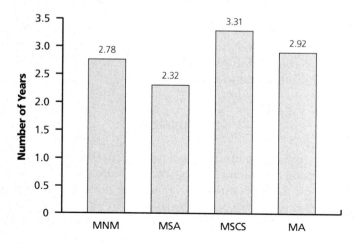

Figure 3.3 Calculated number of years to graduate. *Note:* Average number of years to graduate per program.

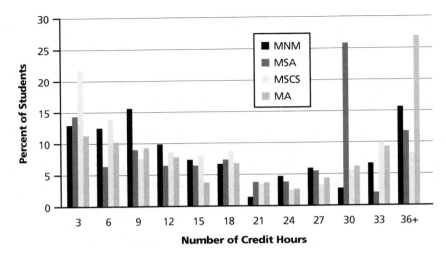

Figure 3.4 Calculated percentage of students who did not graduate. *Note:* Credit hours earned are included in Figure 3.4 for all students in the study who had not yet graduated.

in the MSCS program took an average of 3.31 years to graduate. Whereas the MNM students had a higher overall graduation rate as well as a higher graduation rate not including current students, the MSA students graduated in a shorter amount of time on average. This would indicate that the university might need to reevaluate the effectiveness of a formal goal setting plan as an indicator of student success in graduation.

According to the data presented in Figure 3.4, students in the MSA program and the MA program showed a significant completion of hours yet did not graduate. It is worth further investigation to determine the reasons for the spike of completion of 30 or more credit hours of graduate work and without continuing on to graduation.

DISCUSSION

This research project began with a purpose of investigating the impact of formal goal setting and monitoring activities of adult non-traditional graduate students on their persistence to complete their degree. The second purpose of this researh project was to analyze trends across all programs. The data analysis and findings indicate that the hypothesis that goal setting would increase degree completion was not supported.

The researchers also acknoweldge that there are several limitations of this study. The first of which is that the target population for this study was from one university and may or may not adequately represent all adult graduate students in non-traditional master's degree programs. Other limitations include the possibility that other uncontrolled variables such as those identified by Collins (2011) may have a more significant impact on persistence to graduate than the single variable that was tested in this study. Because data were collected from September 2007 through August 2013, a total of six academic years, the overall number of records analyzed is statistically significant and provides a wide range of data. The researchers suggest that continued research is necessary to identify and test other relevant variables, including those identified by Locke and Latham (2002), who suggest that goals that are specific and challenging are more likely to produce the desired outcome.

The results of this study are significant for colleges and universities throughout the country that have accelerated graduate degree programs for adult students, specifically for those adult students who have gone back to school to help them achieve either professional or personal learning goals. Most notable in this research was the spike in the number of non-graduates who dropped out of the program and did not continue taking classes in year four of their programs. This was consistent with all programs—Master of Science Accounting, Master of Arts, Master of Science Computer Science, and Master of Nonprofit Management. In addition, it is to be noted that there is a large number of non-graduating students in all programs who were close to completing their degree, but did not. It is the recommendation of these researchers to further analyze these two issues to look for answers to two questions. They are: (1) What are the variables that cause students who are well into their programs to drop out? (2) Do final thesis or capstone requirments create a hurdle that cannot be overcome?

FURTHER RESEARCH

Based on the data analysis and end results of this study, follow up research is needed to determine how and why students are motivated to complete graduate degrees. The researchers believe the following recommendations will help to guide the design of further research.

1. Consider a replication of this study adding populations from other comparable universities.
2. Consider designing a study to examine learning format as a variable. Would a student who takes his/her classes only in an online environment have a different graduation success rate as compared to only a ground-based enrollment, or would a combination of online and ground-based enrollment have such an effect?

3. Explore the differences and similarities of learning goals among genders and whether certain graduate degrees with and without goal setting plans predict success.
4. Explore whether age group differences predict success in completion of graduate degrees with and without goal setting requirements.
5. Explore whether active, retired, or reserve military service predicts success in completion of graduate degrees with and without goal setting requirements.
6. Explore additional variables Collins (2011) identified in the planning of further research.

Collins (2011) identified and interviewed 30 graduate students associated with accelerated degree programs designed for adult learners at three Jesuit Universities. Three groups of students were selected from programs at each university, including current students, drop-outs, and graduates. The purpose of this qualitative study was to look for connections between goal setting and degree completion. While the study was exploratory, a number of variables that may be associated with learner goal setting and motivation to complete degrees were identified. Table 3.2 contains the variables and sub-variables.

Consideration of these variables in further research seems appropriate to the researchers given that goal setting as a single varible in the current study did not appear to increase degree completion. Goal setting may involve a number of variables and sub-variables that may increase the motivation of adult graduate students to complete their degree. Future research and analysis should include consideration of these variables and will need to be designed to measure and evaluate the effect of such variables on degree completion.

TABLE 3.2 Variables and Sub-variables

Variables	Sub-variables
Vision	Perceived personal happiness, workplace success, career enhancement, ambition
Goal setting purpose	Personal development, work/performance, career development, hope, optimism, social support
Goal setting process	Specific, documented goals, measurable goals, challenging goals, goal assessment
Learning program selection	Goal/program congruence
Learning program initiation	Perceived urgency, timeline of goals, learner needs
Learning program continuation	Intrinsic motivation, extrinsic motivation, goal validity, self-efficacy, academic success, feedback, goal changes, value of goals, value of life-long learning
Goal Achievement	Perceived closure, impact on vision, setting new goals

RECOMMENDATIONS

The authors believe that several recommendations are appropriate, given the results of this study. Recommendations are intended to be useful for universities that offer non-traditional graduate degree programs for adult learners. The recommendations are as follows:

1. Based on the analysis of the trends from this research, it would be beneficial for the university to create intervention programs at certain points in students' graduate programs to assist the students towards graduation.
2. Intervention may be needed after completion of the first course, after students have completed three years in the program, and at a point when students have completed all 30 credits and have not enrolled in thesis or capstone credits.
3. In conjunction with various departments (i.e., advisors, faculty and staff) at the university, it would be important to develop methods to monitor students' progress throughout their degree programs, and to put into place additional interventions designed to raise the graduation rate per program.
4. Further analysis should be undertaken by the university to determine why some students take one class then drop out.
5. A notable issue that arose from this research was the percentage of students who dropped out in year four, having completed over 30 credit hours of a 36- hour program. The data support the point that the university might need to evaluate the thesis and capstone requirements to determine if they are a roadblock to graduation and determine if changes are needed.

In conclusion, the researchers hope this study will provide interest for future studies that will continue to examine the processes of students' success in completing their graduate degrees. This research was driven by the authors' professional desires as graduate faculty to suggest that colleges and universities reevaluate their degree programs and processes designed to offer the guidance and tools necessary to help students achieve their academic and personal goals.

Indeed, as this research suggests, there may be certain times in a student's graduate work in which added support and encouragement is needed in order to help ensure student success. It is important to understand that adult students are highly motivated and mature abstract thinkers. It is the responsibility of higher education professionals and institutions to ensure that students have the assistance needed to be able to be successful.

REFERENCES

Bandura, A. (1986). Social *foundations of thought and action: A social cognitive theory.* Englewood Cliffs, NJ: Prentice-Hall.

Bandura, A. (1997). Self-*efficacy: The exercise of control.* New York, NY: Freeman.

Collins, R. D. (2011). *Goal setting behaviors and persistence.* Unpublished research manuscript, Regis University, Denver, CO.

Covey, S. R. (2004). *The seven habits of highly effective people.* New York, NY: Free Press.

Cox, T. D. (2008). Students who persist in a MALS Program. *Confluence: Journal of the Association of Graduate Liberal Studies, 8*(2), 136–143.

Dweck, C. S. (1986). Motivational processes affecting learning. *American Psychologist, 41,* 1040–1048.

Eppler, M. A., & Harju, B. L. (1997). Achievement motivation goals in relation to academic performance in traditional and nontraditional college students. *Research in Higher Education, 38*(5), 557–573.

Fleming, V. M. (2002). Improving students' exam performance by introducing study strategies and goal setting. *Teaching of Psychology, 29*(2), 115–119.

Glynn, S. M., Altman, L., & Owens, A. M. (2005). Motivation to learn in general education programs. *Journal of General Education, 54*(2), 150–170.

Grant, H., & Dweck, C. S. (2003). Clarifying achievement goals and their impact. *Journal of Personality and Social Psychology. 85*(3), 541–553.

Houle, C. O. (1988). *The inquiring Mind* (2nd ed). University of Wisconsin Press.

Ironsmith, M., Mara, J., Harju, B., & Pepper, M. (2003). Motivation and performance in college students enrolled in self-paced versus lecture-format remedial mathematics courses. *Journal of Instructional Psychology, 30*(4), 276–284.

Klein, H. J., & Lee, S. (2006). The effects of personality on learning: the mediating role of goal setting. *Human Performance, 19*(1) 43–66.

Locke, E. A., & Latham, G. P. (2002). Building a practically useful theory of goal setting and task motivation. *American Psychologist, 57*(9), 705–717.

McGivney, V. (2004). Understanding persistence in adult learning. *Open Learning 19*(1), 33–46.

Metzger, B. S. Lauer, J. B., & Rijeka, D. W. (2003). Predicting persistence among psychology majors at an urban university. *North American Journal of Psychology, 5*(1), 55–60.

Meyer, P. J. (2006). *Attitude is everything.* Leading Edge Publishing Company.

Ryan, T. A. (1970). *Intentional behavior.* New York, NY: Ronald Press.

Schunk, D. H. (1990). Goal setting and self-efficacy during self-regulated learning. *Educational Psychologist, 25*(1), 71–86.

Taniguchi, H., & Kaufman, G. (2005). Degree completion among nontraditional college students. *Social Science Quarterly,* 86(4), 912–927.

Voigt, L., & Hundrieser, J. (2008). Noel-Levitz retention codifications student success, retention, and graduation: Definitions, theories, practices, patterns, and trends. Retrieved from http://www.stetson.edu/law/conferences/highered/archive/media/Student%20Success,%20Retention,%20and%20Graduation%20Definitions,%20Theories,%20Practices,%20Patterns,%20and%20Trends.pdf

PART I

SUPPORTING NEEDS OF ADULT LEARNERS:

Supporting Adult Student Parents

CHAPTER 4

COLLEGE ENROLLMENT CHOICES PREDICTED BY SOCIAL CAPITAL, ACADEMIC ENCOURAGEMENT, ENVIRONMENT, AND STUDENT-PARENT DIFFERENCES

Elyse D'nn Lovell
Highlands College University of Montana

Dustin Barnes
University of Montana

The purpose of this study was to understand predictors among college students' enrollment choices by considering students' academic encouragement and learning environments as minors and adults. As instructors and administrators have greater understanding of the diversity among non-traditional students, they are more equipped to strengthen services corre-

Building Sustainable Futures for Adult Learners, pages 67–86
Copyright © 2015 by Information Age Publishing
All rights of reproduction in any form reserved.

sponding to this diverse group, thereby enhancing services for students' enrollment and academic persistence. Delayed college enrollment beyond the recent completion of a high school diploma describes non-traditional students in the broadest sense, yet non-traditional students are extremely diverse when considering their roles and responsibilities as adults in combination with their student status (National Center for Education Statistics, 2013). Social capital and parental status (student-parent or non-parent) are two prime examples suggesting some of the significant variance among non-traditional students beyond traditional measures of age. This study explored the social capital role of student-parent for further understanding.

Today, instructors, program directors, and administrators note increased enrollments among adult students reflecting a changed student culture. Recent economic conditions and a greater legislative emphasis has encouraged adult enrollment in higher education (Capps, 2012; Goodman & Simms, 2005). Nearly 125 million adults age 25 years and older do not have a college degree (Applegate, 2010). According to the U.S. Department of Education, National Center for Education Statistics (2009), the percentage of college enrollments of non-traditional-aged students is expected to increase more significantly than traditional-aged students over the next ten years. According to the National Post-Secondary Student Aid Study (2008), non-traditional students can be categorized by their independent status (i.e., those independent of their parents for support).

The Lumina Foundation recently titled non-traditional students as "non-traditional no more" which is a reflection of the increased number of non-traditional students projected in future enrollments. Also, there is anticipation that non-traditional students will be recognized more often as the new majority as they increase in enrollment (Lumina & WICHE, 2010). The increasing numbers of newly identified non-traditional students leads to a dynamic environment as adult students and their needs are being identified (Maehl, 2004). Literature suggests unique barriers occur for non-traditional students in enrollment, retention, motivation, and persistence including academic, financial, social, cultural, and personal issues (Dougherty & Woodland, 2009; Fusch, 2010; Spellman, 2007).

Non-traditional aged students are a growing student-population with differing needs when compared to traditional aged students. It is the purpose of this study to understand differences among traditional and non-traditional students in the pursuit of their academics when considering their academic environments as minors and adults. Variables used to assess predictors for delayed enrollment included: age, parental status, socioeconomic status, and social capital. Indices were developed to assess academic encouragement as a minor, academic environment as a minor, and academic environment as an adult. Three research questions were utilized to explore findings: Can academic encouragement as a minor to enroll in college be an indicator of college student status: age, parental status, socio-economic status as a minor, and social capital? Can academic environment as a minor be an indicator of college student status: age, parental status, socioeconomic status as a minor and social capital? Can academic environment as an adult be an indicator of college student status: age, parental status, socioeconomic status as a minor, and social capital?

LITERATURE REVIEW

The related literature describing the vast expanse of non-traditional students is explored. A section follows on the specific category of students who are parents. Last, literature in the areas of social capital and socioeconomic status is investigated.

Non-Traditional Students

Historically, a non-traditional student would have been defined by age, socioeconomic status, and race (Ogren, 2013).The most common definition today is for students that are of the age 25+, but the true definition has shown significantly more indicators (Compton, Cox, & Laanan, 2006). According to the U.S. Department of Education National Center for Education Statistics (2013), the traditional students attend college full-time immediately after high school graduation attending full-time, while the non-traditional students are anyone who does not follow this time frame.

The non-traditional student is defined by age (25+), and this is a cohort often used for comparison to the traditional student age (18–24), thereby identifying differing needs. Non-traditional students are in several studies characterized as adult students (Compton, Cox, & Laanan, 2006). Many adult students are still familiar with college as they may experience stop-out enrollment meaning a re-enrollment (Horn, 1996).

According to Jacobs and King and King (2002), 82.28% of women newly enrolled in college were enrolled previously. Their backgrounds and needs are still different than their younger counterparts. The majority has been in the workforce for a number of years and view themselves as workers rather than students (Compton, Cox, & Laanan, 2006). Some lacked academic skills to pursue higher education after high school, and most likely weak academic skills continue once enrolled in college (U.S. Department of Education, National Center for Education Statistics, 2002). Non-traditional students are more likely to have already moved into adult life transitions such as parenthood (Roksa & Velez, 2012).

Student-Parent

A limited number of studies have compared delaying college enrollment and being a parent (Bozick & De Luca, 2005; Roksa & Velez, 2012). According to Teachman and Polonko (1988), being a parent is directly related to delayed enrollment. Another study showed delayed enrolling parents were 67.6% compared to 26.9%, who were not delayed enrollment parents (U.S. Department of Education, National Center for Education Statistics, 2002). The longer the delay in entering college, the probability will heighten for becoming a parent (Rindfuss, Swicegood, & Rosenfeld, 1987). Parents who have children before enrollment beginning college have an average of delayed enrollment of 40.98 months compared to 6.68 months when having a child while enrolled (Bozick & DeLuca, 2005).

Delaying enrollment in higher education is especially true for the younger parent (Teachman & Polanko, 1988). According to Evans, Wallace, and Schwab (1992), teenage pregnancy correlates with dropping out of high school and low socioeconomic status. Limited resources and attention focused on raising newborns results in reduced time to pursue and complete academics (Bozick & DeLuca, 2005). It then becomes more difficult for these parents, who are mostly female, to go back to school since they were more likely to be single and unemployed (Solem, Christophersen, & Martinussencm, 2011). As a group, female single parents tend to be less educated, more stressed, and have with less of a social network than their peers; they are also more likely to have children with behavioral problems (Solem, Christophersen, & Martinussencm, 2011). However, the probability of college enrollment has been shown to become higher after the first couple years of parenthood (Teachman & Polanko, 1988).

The effects of parenthood and other life transitions in adulthood on delayed college enrollment have not been fully studied (Roksa & Velez, 2012). Having children could give parents avenues to be involved in new activities to have more social capital; for example, parents gain valued social capital through other parents and their children's teachers, yet this may not enhance enrollment or academic success within college (Perna & Titus, 2005). According to Corrigan (2003), once enrolled in college, 47% of these student-parents are more likely to stop-out compared to 31% of low income dependents after three years of enrollment (p.29).

Social Capital

Social capital has been described as having an effect on delayed enrollment (Lareau, 1987; Perna & Titus, 2005), and has been studied quantitatively (Rowan-Kenyon, 2007). There has been more than one perception of how to measure the variable of social capital. Coleman's definition of social capital has been referenced for delayed enrollment in numerous studies (Coleman, 1988; Perna, 2000; Rowan-Kenyon, 2007). Coleman (1988) explained social capital as the amount and quality of knowledge, resources, and social ties in an individual's surroundings, and can come in the form of parental involvement for their children to enroll into college. Coleman's findings suggest the relationship between social capital in academic surroundings as a minor and adult are an indicator for college students' enrollment.

Immediate relationships, other than family, are forms of social capital (Coleman, 1988). According to Hofferth, Boisjoly, and Duncan (1998), children within higher socioeconomic brackets have greater access to educational benefits from their families' economic resources and social capital within academic settings when compared to those in lower socioeconomic brackets. Higher socioeconomic peers are more likely to enroll into college without delay, further compounding positive academic success (Corrigan, 2003; Perna & Titus, 2005). Teachers and counselors give them more valued attention to better situated students, which heightens the amount of academic knowledge conveyed (Bradley & Corwyn, 2002; McLoyd, 1998; Stanton-Salazar, 1997). Hence, these students are more likely to be properly academically prepared to pursue higher education. Adolescents and children are reliant on their parents and immediate surroundings for economic, social, and emotional support for their education (Pallas, 1993), but in adulthood individuals have more autonomy and control for their own support.

Socioeconomic Status

The evidence is overwhelming that a minor from a lower socioeconomic background is more likely to delay enrollment into college after high school compared to students from a higher socioeconomic background (Bozick & DeLuca, 2005; Cabrera & LaNasa, 2001; Hearn, 1992; Niu & Tienda, 2013; Perna, 2000; Rowan-Kenyon, 2007). This is not surprising since an insurmountable number of stressors are more common in lower socioeconomic environments that hinder educational growth. These include lack of basic necessities such as clothes, shelter, food, unstable residence, stimulating experiences, child maltreatment, insecure neighborhoods, low quality of schools, and less of a stable social network. There is also more reported exposure to dangerous toxins through unstable housing, child maltreatment described by social services, and reduced stimulating academic experiences within social settings (Brooks-Gunn & Duncan, 1997). These environments disable parents' ability to be able to fulfill all of their children's academic needs.

Parents are likely to be more academically involved in their children's education with a higher socioeconomic status; they are more likely to pass their knowledge on to their children, thereby minimizing impediments to academic success (Bradley& Corwyn, 2002; Perna & Titus, 2005). Parental involvement is described as more frequent among higher socioeconomic students when compared to lower socioeconomic peers, and increased parental support shows a correlation to increased academic opportunities (Coleman, 1988). According to Lareau (1987), most parents stated that they want their children to obtain college degrees, but higher socioeconomic parents are more likely to provide the resources, college insight, and parental involvement to bring fourth this goal.

METHOD

The purpose of this quantitative comparative analysis study was to determine the factors that contribute to differences in delayed college enrollment among 158 undergraduate college students by considering their academic choices and surroundings as a minor and adult. The study explores the entire sample with indices (dependent variables): academic encouragement as a minor, academic surroundings as a minor, academic surroundings as an adult, and predictors (independent variables) traditional and non-traditional age, parental status, socioeconomic status as a minor, and social capital-academic standing of those closest to you as an adult.

Participants

Participants in this study were undergraduates within two rural Rocky Mountain communities with populations of 30,000 to 35,000 within each community, located within 60 mile proximity. The students in this study were all enrolled in Introduction to Psychology. The sample included all students who filled out the entire survey ($n = 158$). Students provided their consent to participate following institutional review board guidelines, and researchers were not present during the distribution and collection of all surveys.

The history of the colleges included several name and branding changes. The name changes have in part responded to the cultural shift of the increased number of adult students. It is the intent of these Rocky Mountain institutions to increase vocational training, and more specifically, two-year degrees. The Board of Regents has heavily promoted two-year credentialing over recent years. The increased promotion of two-year credentialing has recognized the cultural shifts as non-traditional aged students' enrollments are increasing.

Assessment Instrument

The survey was a self-report measure with comparative, associational, and descriptive approaches. The survey items were a combination of close-ended, unordered items, and close-ended questions with ordered choices. Convergent and discriminate evidence was enhanced by using research questions from an existing study about predictors of delayed enrollment and the impact of socioeconomic status (Rowan-Kenyon, 2007). After using the guidelines and similar format of the Rowan-Kenyon survey, some adjustments were made by adding National Center for Education Statistics (NCES) variables to more specifically narrow the scope of parental status and non-traditional student variables. The survey was distributed in the fourth week of classes. Since previous literature for the population of student-parents is particularly limited, and no studies were found which specifically measured this cohort, some adjustments were made for measurement. Cronbach's alpha was run for each index to assure relationships among each group of questions (factors) for measurement reliability.

Assessment Measurement

Descriptive and Quantitative and quantitative analyses were used including six tables. Table 4.1 reviewed the descriptive analyses by the entire sample and by two subgroups: Subgroup (1) parents (2) non-parents with mean, standard deviation, and frequency (percentage) distribution. Table 4.2 reviewed the questions for each index with Cronbach's alpha scores. Table 4.3 reviewed results with t-tests to further explore differences between sub-populations (parents and non-parents).

RESULTS

Descriptive data (see Table 4.1) for dependent and independent variables included means and standard deviations. Dependent variables include academic encouragement as a minor, academic environment as a minor, and academic environment as an adult. Independent variables included age, parental status, and socioeconomic status as a minor, and academic status of those closest to the adult student. The entire sample shows a majority of participants are 18–24 years old, non-parents, middle income or above, and those closest to them did not have a college degree.

Considering parent and non-parent differences in means for dependent variables, student-parents identified less encouragement toward their academic encouragement to enroll in college as a minor, weaker academic

TABLE 4.1 Frequency Distribution of Dependent and Independent Variables

Variable	Entire Sample (N = 158)		Parent (n = 45)		Non-Parent (n = 113)	
	(M)	(S)	(M)	(S)	(M)	(S)
Dependent Variables						
Acad Encor Minor	2.72	.935	2.07	.907	2.98	.813
Acad Env Minor	2.84	.745	2.52	.747	2.96	.709
Acad Env Adult	3.27	.505	3.19	.521	3.29	.499
Independent Variables						
Age			*Scale:*			
18–24 (Trad)	(107) 68%		Age			
25 + (Non-Trad)	(51) 32%		0 = Trad			
			1 = Non-Trad			
Parental Status			Parent Status			
Non-parent	(113) 72%		0 = Parent			
Parent	(45) 28%		1 = Non-Parent			
Income as Minor			Income Minor			
Poverty	(48) 30%		0 = Poverty			
Middle Income +	(110) 70%		1 = Middle +			
Academic Standing			Closest Adult/Acad			
Closest to Adult			0 = degree			
College Degree	(63) 40%		1 = no degree			
No College Degree	(95) 60%					

environments as minors, and the differences between parents and non-parents appeared to be less significant as they became adults.

A Cronbach's alpha was used to test internal consistency reliability of questions grouped by indices: Academic Environment Minor (.87) with six questions, academic environment as a minor (.86) with eight questions, and academic environment as an adult (.71) with seven questions (see Table 4.2). Since the questions and indices for this survey came from one survey with some modifications (Rowan-Kenyon, 2007), no further tests were run for the reliability of questions grouped by indices. The coding and responses used for the questions in each index were Likert scale which included four levels: 1 = strongly disagree, 2 = disagree, 3 = strongly agree, 4 = strongly agree.

Levene's test for equality of variances was used for reporting significant differences between traditional and non-traditional status (Age 18–24/25+), parental status (student-parents/non-parents), socioeconomic status as a minor (poverty/middle income and above), and academic social capital

TABLE 4.2 Three Indices with Questions in Each Index

Indices	Questions
Acad Encor Minor (.87)	1. While I was under 18, I read information about financial aid for college. 2. While I was under 18, I talked with a school rep. about fin. aid for college. 3. While I was under 18, a teacher encouraged me to attend college. 4. While I was under 18, a friend encouraged me to attend college. 5. While I was under 18, a family member encourage me to enroll in college. 6. While I was under 18, an employer or co-worker encouraged enroll college.
Acad Env Minor (.86)	1. I believe that others saw me as an academic success in K–12th grade. 2. The school or schools I attended in K–12th grade were above average. 3. My parents or guardians participated in school activities and/or volunteered at school/etc. 4. In my home, there were academic materials to read. 5. In my home, parents or guardians helped me with homework. 6. I had good relationships and support with and from my teachers. 7. I participated in art, music, sports, or extracurricular activities that were outside of my K–12. 8. My friends thought it was important to do well in school (grades, attendance, etc.).
Acad Env Adult (.71)	1. I believe that today, others see me as an academic success in my pursuit of a college degree. 2. The people I'm living with encourage the pursuit of my college degree. 3. In my home, there were academic materials to read. 4. In my home, the people I'm living with encourage me to do homework. 5. I participate in social activities like art, music, sports, or extracurricular activities in my community. 6. My spouse/partner/and or friends think it is important to succeed in college. 7. My employer and or co-workers think it is important that I succeed in college.

(closest adults who hold a college degree/do not have a college degree). The variance in response was described with the three indices: enrollment as a minor, surroundings as a minor, and surroundings as an adult.

For academic encouragement as a minor, results showed significant differences between traditional and non-traditional aged students, parents and non-parents, socioeconomic status, and closest adult to the student who has a college degree. Weaker academic encouragement was found for non-traditional aged students (25+), parents, those who lived in poverty, and those closest to the adult-student did not have a college degree.

For academic environment as a minor, there were significant differences between traditional and non-traditional aged students, parents and non-parents, socioeconomic status, and closest adult /college degree. Weaker academic environments as a minor were found for non-traditional aged students, student-parents, and those who lived in poverty; in addition, those closest to the adult-student did not have a college degree.

Results showed no significant differences for academic environments as an adult when comparing parents and non-parents, but there were significant differences between traditional and non-traditional aged students, socioeconomic status, and closest adult/college degree. Weaker academic environments as a minor were found for non-traditional aged students, those who lived in poverty, and those defined by the student as closest to them that did not have a college degree.

A Pearson's chi-squared test was used to investigate student-parents or non-parents for further understanding in regard to differences by their parental status. Pearson's chi-squared tests were run to determine if there was a statistically significant relationship between independent variables (dichotomous). The relationship of student parental status was statistically significant showing significance for each relationship analyzed between parents and non-parents with each variable (age, income as a minor, and those closest to the adult-student today did not have a college degree) $p < .05$. The results were as follows: Age ($\chi^2 = 29.78$, $df = 1$, $N = 158$, $p < .001$), Income as a minor ($\chi^2 = 5.86$, $df = 1$, $N = 158$, $p < .05$), Academic standing of those closest ($\chi^2 = 6.25$, $df = 1$, $N = 158$, $p < .05$). This indicated greater certainty that student parents and non-parents were statistically significant in their relationship by their parental status to age, income as a minor, and academic standing of those closest. Age among all students ($\chi^2 = 29.78$, $df = 1$, $N = 158$, $p < .001$) showed a majority by traditional age students and non-parents, yet non-traditional age students were a majority of parents; understanding these differences, there was a significant relationship with variables. Income as a minor for all students ($\chi^2 = 5.86$, $df = 1$, $N = 158$, $p < .05$) showed a majority by middle income and above and non-parents, and middle income and above were a majority of parents; recognizing these differences there was a significant relationship with variables. For the academic standing of those closest to the adult student, ($\chi^2 = 6.25$, $df = 1$, $N = 158$, $p < .001$). The majority of students were non-parents with those closest to them without a college degree. Among the parents, those closest to them did not have a college degree; acknowledging this difference, a significant relationship exists with variables.

Phi was used to determine the strength of the association between two variables (Effect Sizes) between parent status and all other variables. Academic encouragement minor, phi (.519) large effect; academic environment minor, phi (.438) large effect; academic environment adult, phi (.302) medium effect; age, phi (−.434) large effect; income as a minor, phi (.198) small effect; those closest to you academic standing, phi (−.199) small effect. A synopsis of effect sizes showed that enrollment as a minor, surroundings as a minor, and present age as the largest effect sizes.

In Table 4.3, simple linear regression analyses were utilized to explore how academic encouragement as a minor, academic environment as a minor, and academic environment as an adult can be predicted by parental status and then multiple regressions were used controlling for combined variables.

TABLE 4.3 Regressions: Academic Encouragement Minor, Acad Env Minor, Acad Env Parent

Variable/Model	B	β	t	p	Adjust R²
Set 1, Model 1					
(*Acad Encor Minor DV¹ = Parent/Non-Parent*)	.92	.44	6.19	.000***	.192
Set 1, Model 2					
(*Acad Encor Minor DV¹ = Parent/Non-Parent, Age, Inc Minor, Social Cap*)				.000***	.341
Parent/non-parent	.48	.23	3.16	.002*	
Age	−.82	−.41	−5.64	.000***	
Income as a minor	.14	.07	1.01	.315	
Social capital – those closest/college degree	−.20	−.11	−1.56	.120	
Set 2, Model 1					
(*Acad Env Minor DV¹ = Parent/Non-Parent*)	.44	.27	3.48	.001**	.066
Set 2, Model 2					
(*Acad Env Minor DV¹ = Parent/Non-Parent, Age, Inc Minor, Social Cap*)				.000***	.296
Parent/non-parent	.06	.04	.489	.626	
Age	−.48	−.30	−4.07	.000***	
Income as a minor	.36	.22	3.16	.002***	
Social capital – those closest/college degree	−.43	−.28	−4.01	.000***	
Set 3, Model 1					
(*Acad Env Adult DV¹ = Parent/Non-Parent*)	.10	.09	1.13	.259	.002
Set 3, Model 2					
(*Acad Env Adult DV¹ = Parent/Non-Parent, Age, Inc Minor, Social Cap*)				.001***	.087
Parent/non-parent	−.04	−.04	−.428	.669	
Age	−.13	−.12	−1.46	.147	
Income as a minor	.16	.14	1.79	.075	
Social capital – those closest/college degree	−.24	−.23	−2.87	.005*	

Research Question One (Regression Set 1)

Can academic encouragement given as a minor (variable: enroll minor) be an indicator of college student status: age, parental status, socioeconomic status as a minor and social capital?

The regression analysis in Set 1, Model 1 (acad encor minor DV^1 = parent/non-parent) revealed academic encouragement as a minor was significantly predicted by parental status, $F(1,156) = 38.29$ observed F value, $p = .000$, significance level ($p < .05$), adjusted $R^2 = .19$. As shown by the adjusted R^2 predicting19% of the variance of academic encouragement as a minor could be predicted by parental status. According to Cohen (1988), this would be a typical effect size. The positive direction showed parents experienced significantly lower academic encouragement to enroll in college as minors when compared to non-parents.

When the other variables were added, Set 1, Model 2 (acad encor minor DV^1 = age, parental status, income as a minor, and social capital – those closest/college degree status) they significantly improved the prediction, $F(4,153) = 21.32$ observed F value, $p = .000$, significance level ($p < .05$), adjusted $R^2 = .341$. The entire group of variables significantly predicted 34% of the variance for the academic encouragement given as a minor. This is a larger than typical effect size according to Cohen (1988). When considering each variable separately, non-traditional aged students (.000) and parents (.002) were significantly less likely to be given academic encouragement as minors to enroll in college.

Research Question Two (Regression Set 2)

Can academic environment as a minor be an indicator of college student status: age, parental status, socioeconomic status as a minor, and social capital?

The regression analysis in Set 2, Model 1 (acad env as a minor DV^2 = parent/non-parent) revealed academic environment was significantly predicted, $F(1,156) = 12.10$ observed F value, $p = .001$ significance level ($p < .05$), adjusted $R^2 = .07$. As shown by the adjusted R^2 predicting 7% of the variance of academic environment as a minor could be predicted by parental status. According to Cohen (1988), this is a smaller than typical effect size. The positive direction suggests parents experienced significantly less positive academic environments as minors when compared to non-parents.

When the other variables were added, Set 2, Model 2 (acad env as a minor DV^2 = age, parental status, income as a minor, and social capital – those closest/college degree status) this significantly improved the prediction, $F(4,153) = 17.52$ observed F value, $p = .000$significance level ($p < .05$), adjusted $R^2 = .30$. The entire group of variables significantly predicted 30% of the variance for the academic environment as a minor. This is a typical effect size according to Cohen (1988). When considering each variable separately, non-traditional aged students were significantly less likely to be living in a positive academic environment as a minor ($p = .000$). Participants who were raised in middle income or above had significantly higher indicators for being raised in a positive academic environment ($p = .002$). Students stating those closest to them in their adult lives are without a college degree are significantly more likely to have lived in a less positive academic environments when they were children ($p = .000$).

Research Question Three (Regression Set 3)

Can academic environment as an adult be an indicator of college student status: age, parental status, socioeconomic status as a minor, and social capital?

The regression analysis in Set 3, Model 1 (acad envadult DV[3] = parent/non-parent) revealed academic environment as an adult was not significantly predicted, $F(1, 156) = 1.28$ observed F value, significance level ($p < .05$). R^2 was .002. As shown by the R^2 predicting less than 1% of the variance of academic environment as an adult (surroundings as an adult) could be predicted by parental status.

When the other variables were added, Set 3, Model 2 (acad env adult DV[3] = age, parental status, income as a minor, and social capital − those closest/college degree status) they significantly improved the prediction, $F(4, 153) = 4.72$ observed F value = .001 significance level ($p < .05$). The entire group of variables significantly predicted 9% of the variance for the academic environment as an adult. This is a smaller than typical effect size according to Cohen (1988). When considering each variable separately, the academic environment as an adult showed that students stating those closest to them are without a college degree are significantly more likely to be living in a less positive academic environment today ($p = .000$).

DISCUSSION

The purpose of this study was to understand differences among college students' parental status, their ages, socioeconomic status as a minor, and social capital in adulthood as potential predictors for academic and enrollment choices. Further investigation measured academic encouragement received as a minor to enroll in college, academic encouragement within learning environments as a minor, and the academic learning environments as an adult.

The amount of academic encouragement that a minor receives to enroll in college and their academic learning environment were prominent indicators for enrollment choices. Academic learning environments as adults revealed limited indicators for enrollment choices. These findings coincide with the literature that factors for academic encouragement to enroll in college and learning environments among minors indicates college enrollment choices (Rowan-Kenyon, 2007). Notably, the amount of literature about enrollment choices based on adult's academic learning environments (non-traditional aged students) is more limited, yet there is recognition for the importance to achieve greater understanding of adult's enrollment choices because this population is growing (Roksa & Velez, 2012). Minors' academic encouragement and enrollment choices have been studied by the influence and dependence of family (Pallas, 1993). In adulthood, the scope of academic encouragement and the decision to enroll in college becomes more complex to measure as individuals have more autonomy to blend with a broader base of social groups thereby making their influences more complex to measure. Non-traditional students are defined as adults age 25+ (Horn, 1996).

Many non-traditional aged students have been enrolled in college over longer periods of time for their degree completion, and some experience stop-outs thereby increasing their number of enrollments and drop outs (Jacobs & King, 2002). The non-traditional aged students showed less academic social capital in the form of those closest to them having a college degree, which correlates positively with weaker academic outcomes among non-traditional students in literature (Rowan-Kenyon, 2007). Non-traditional aged students were more likely to be from a lower socioeconomic status as a minor similarly corresponding to weaker academic outcomes (Rowan-Kenyon, 2007). Although non-traditional students are most commonly defined by age 25+, parents are also non-traditional students. Reasonably, most student-parents are older which may lengthen the delay of their enrollment, thereby increasing the chances that non-traditional aged students have children (Rindfuss, Swicegood, & Rosenfeld, 1987). A positive correlation was shown between non-traditional aged students and student-parents, and it was the intent of this study to further clarify non-traditional student sub-groups; the needs of parents as a non-traditional group appears limited. Research clarifies differences for the enrollment and persistence needs of student-parents (Roksa & Velez, 2012).

Student-parents identified themselves as having lower levels of encouragement to enroll in college and weaker academic environments when they were minors and the differences were significant when compared to non-parents who identified higher levels of academic encouragement and to enroll in college. Literature and national data describes student-parents as a majority female, head of household, and living in poverty. Parents appear to be an at risk group when considering reduced academic and enrollment encouragements as minors, parental and student responsibilities being balanced, and challenged economic status as minors and adults. The combination of these stressors suggests more academic encouragement is needed when considering the significant differences between parents and non-parents in this study and literature. Student-parents may be encouraged to take care of their children rather than encouraged to enroll or persist in college as the needs of their children place demands on their schedules, thereby reducing time for academic responsibilities (Bozick & DeLuca, 2005). If student-parents were recognized as a group with specific services accommodating their differing needs, given more encouragement to enroll and support to stay in college particularly after stop-outs, retention outcomes may be enhanced. According to Bozick and DeLuca, (2005), parents who have already had previous college credit delay enrollment for a substantially less amount of time than those without college credit. A short delay to enroll or stop-out can happen after having a newborn, and specific student-parent support services may assist further success.

Social capital is clarified as students identify the people closest to them that have a college degree, and this was a significant predictor of academic surroundings as a minor and adult. The status of non-traditional aged students was a predictor for reduced encouragement to enroll in college and also showed weaker academic learning environments as minors. The parents of today's college students may have promoted and known that higher education was important for their children, but those parents lacked the resources and knowledge to provide an academic learning environment or effective support to successfully assist their children to enroll in college (Lareau, 1987).

Students with lower socioeconomic status as minors corresponded to reduced academic learning environments as minors. Reduced socioeconomic status as a minor showed a correlation with people closest to you not having a college degree. Yet, when considering academic surroundings as an adult, the income as a minor was not a significant predictor, but adults with weaker academic surroundings were significantly predicted by most of the people around them who do not have a college degree. This suggests that people with a college degree immediately surrounding the college student could possibly offset the effects of lower socioeconomic status within the adults' academic surroundings.

Limitations

There were limitations to this study. The study was measured by self-report method, and non-traditional students have had a long length of time between being a minor and enrolling in college, and this could have affected the validity of their answers. What precise age an individual became a parent and how they were encouraged before and after to pursue their academics may have helped to determine when and why they were receiving lower amounts of encouragement compared to non-parents. Closest people to you with a college degree was an extremely broad variable, and it may have helped to narrow more specifically who was considered to be closest to the student. Further clarification of who students consider their closest people to be would help to understand specific relationships of influence. Similarly, further understanding of adult life transitions, like marriage, may have provided insight influencing students' academic choices.

CONCLUSIONS AND FUTURE PROSPECTS

These findings had several implications to generate recommendations. First, adults are a diverse group, and specific factors of individuals' surroundings may have an unobservable effect on the model for delayed enrollment within a quantitative analysis. A qualitative study is recommended to better understand the nuances of life transitions, those closest to the student, and the circumference of their social capital. Social capital is broadly defined in previous research as an indicator for delayed enrollment and academic success (Bozick, & DeLuca, 2005; Capps, 2012; Coleman, 1988).

Second, college students' academic experiences as minors and adults showed that when the people closest to them had a college degree, this was a predictor for increased social capital creating more positive academic environments for students' learning. This suggests academic support which extends beyond the classroom for students could benefit enrollment choices and academic persistence. Students who are not surrounded by college graduates at home may benefit from outreach academic support to their home environment. These students are at a disadvantage with the lacking comradely academic support at home, thereby generating weaker academic environments. Curriculum could be designed within the classroom to include family members and friends in an effort to promote and manufacture academic learning home environments with take home group assignments.

Lastly, the status of student-parent shows weaker encouragement to enroll in college and academic learning environments when students were minors; these students were disadvantaged academically as children, and today they are trying to excel in academics while simultaneously raising their own children. Shown below, Diagram 1 reflects the grinding of student-parents academic gears, and they are coping with a heightened disadvantage as they have not been academically encouraged as minors with necessary oil for the high functioning gears of learning within higher education. Their academics are further compromised as they simultaneously assume responsibility for their children's learning. The student-parent who comes from an academically underprepared environment is navigating an academic terrain often without having the proper academic tools for success. This results in

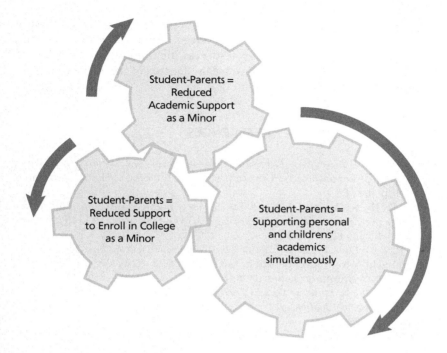

Figure 4.1 The challenged gears of academic and enrollment success for student-parents.

the suggested need for faculty and administrators within higher education to consider providing tools which are individual responding to the differing needs of student-parents.

   In conclusion, as educators and administrators consider further exploration of the vast differences among non-traditional students, it is probable that qualitative research would enhance quantitative results. Given the diversity among adults when considering their academic and enrollment support as minors and adults, qualitative research may assist with the nuances of differences thereby enhancing understanding. Non-traditional students' home environments suggested reduced academic support when compared to traditional aged students. Non-traditional students' home environments may be enhanced by faculty and administration's development of familial support reaching out to home environments. Administration could consider campus functions encouraging family attendance. Educators may distribute homework which necessitates family participation thereby providing academic enrichment and encouragement to the students' home environment. A further reverberation may occur as the student-parents could include their children in homework assignments. The inclusion of student-parents' children with homework assignments may simultaneously secure future generations' interests in college. Administration and faculty could incorporate familial plans for success including parents and their children which could help to achieve balance securing greater potential for academic success among future generations.

REFERENCES

Applegate, J. (2010, August). *Lumina Foundation it's not ALL about the kids.* Paper session presented at The Governor's Forum Building a Skilled Workforce, Kalispell, MT.

Bradley, R. H., & Corwyn, R. F. (2002). Socioeconomic status and child development. *Annual Review of Psychology, I,* 371–399. doi: 10.1146/annurev.psych.53.100901.135233

Bozick, R., & DeLuca, S. (2005). Better late than never? Delayed enrollment in the high school to college transition. *Social Forces, 84*(1), 531–554. Retrieved from http://www.jstor.org/stable/3598316

Brooks-Gunn, J., & Duncan G. J. (1997). The effects of poverty on children. *The Future of Children, 7*(2), 55–71. Retrieved from http://www.jstor.org/stable/1602387

Capps, R. (2012). Supporting adult-student persistence in community colleges. *Change: The Magazine of Higher Learning, 44*(2), 38–44.

Cabrera, A. F., & La Nasa S. M. (2001). On the path to college: Three critical tasks facing America's disadvantaged. *Research in Higher Education, 42*(2), 119–149. Retrieved from http://www.jstor.org/stable/40196425

Cohen, J. (1988). *Statistical power and analysis for the behavioral sciences* (2nd ed.). Hillsdale, NJ: Lawrence Erlbaum Associates.

Coleman, J. S. (1988). Supplement: organizations and institutions: sociological and economic approaches to the analysis of social structure. *American Journal of Sociology, 94,* S95–S120. Retrieved from http://www.jstor.org/stable/2780243

Compton, J. I., Cox, E., & Laanan, F. S. (2006). Adult learners in transition. *New Directions for Student Services, 114,* 73–80. doi: 10.1002/ss.208

Corrigan, M. E. (2003). Beyond access: Persistence challenges and the diversity of low-income students. *New Directions for Higher Education, 121,* 25–34. doi: 10.1002/he.99/pdf

Dougherty, C. B., & Woodland, R. (2009). Understanding sources of financial support for adult learners. *The Journal of Continuing Higher Education, 57*(3), 181–186. doi: 10.1080/07377360903250445.

Evans, E. N., Wallace, O. E., & Schwab, R. M. (1992). Measuring peer group effects: a study of teenage behavior. *Journal of Political Economy, 100*(5), 966–991. Retrieved from http://www.jstor.org/stable/2138631

Fusch, D. (2010). Re-enrolling stop-outs: Overcoming the barriers. Higher Ed Impact Weekly Analysis for Academic Impressions, 1–4.

Goodman, P., & Simms, S. (2005). Student success through policy and practice. *Community College Journal, 76*(1), 42–43.

Hearn, J. C. (1992). Emerging variations in postsecondary attendance patterns: An investigation of part-time, delayed, and non-degree enrollment. *Research in Higher Education, 33*(6), 657–687. Retrieved from http://www.jstor.org/stable/40196146

Hofferth, S. L., Boisjoly, J., & Duncan, G. J. (1998). Parents' extrafamilial resources and children's school attainment. *Sociology of Education, 71*(3), 246–268. Retrieved from http://www.jstor.org/stable/2673204

Horn, L. (1996). *Nontraditional undergraduates, trends in enrollment from 1986 to 1992 and persistence and attainment among 1989–90 beginning postsecondary students* (NCES 97–578) Washington, DC: U.S. Government Printing Office.

Jacobs, J. A., & King, R. B. (2002). Age and college completion: A life-history analysis of women aged 15–44. *Sociology of Education, 75*(3), 211–230. Retrieved from http://www.jstor.org/stable/3090266

Lareau, A. (1987). Social class differences in family-school relationships: The importance of cultural capital. *Sociology of Education, 60*(2), 73–85. Retrieved from http://www.jstor.org/stable/2112583

Lumina Foundation & Western Interstate Commission for Higher Education (WICHE). (2010, November). Task force policy solutions for adult learners. Bringing adults back to college: Designing and implementing a statewide concierge model. Boulder, CO: Author.

Maehl, W. H. (2004). Adult degrees and the learning society. *New Directions for Adult and Continuing Education, Developing and Delivering Adult Programs, 103*, 5–16.

McLoyd, V. C. (1998). Socioeconomic and child development. *American Psychological Association, 53*(2), 185–204. doi: 10.1037/0003-066X.53.2.185

National Center for Education Statistics, (2002). *Non-Traditional Undergraduates* (NCES 2002–012) Retrieved from http://nces.ed.gov/pubs2002/2002012.pdf

National Center for Education Statistics. (2009). National student data base. [data file]. Retrieved from http://www.nces.ed.gov/

National Center for Education Statistics. (2013). National student data base. [data file]. Retrieved from http://www.nces.ed.gov/

National Center for Education Statistics, (2013). *Nontraditional Undergraduates: Trends in Enrollment from 1986 to 1992 and Persistence and Attainment Among 1989–90 Beginning Postsecondary Students, Who is Non-Traditional?* (NCES 97-578) Retrieved from http://nces.ed.gov/pubs/web/97578e.asp

National Post Secondary Student Aid Study. (2008). National Student Data Base. [data file]. Retrieved from http://nces.ed.gov/surveys/npsas/

Niu, S., & Tienda, M. (2013). Delayed enrollment and college plans: Is there a postponement penalty? *The Journal of Higher Education, 84*(1), 1–27. Retrieved from http://www.jstor.org/stable/23324212

Ogren, C. A. (2013). Rethinking the "nontraditional" student from a historical perspective: State normal schools in the late nineteenth and early twentieth centuries. *The Journal of Higher Education, 74*(6), 640–664. Retrieved from: http://www.jstor.org/stable/3648233

Pallas, A. M. (1993). Schooling in the course of human lives: The social context of education and the transition to adulthood in industrial society. *Review of Educational Research, 63*(4), 409–447. Retrieved from http: //www.jstor.org/stable/1170495

Perna, L. (2000). Differences in the decision to attend college among African Americans, Hispanics, and whites. *Journal of Higher Education, 71*(2), 117–141. Retrieved from http://www.jstor.org/stable/2649245

Perna, L. A., & Titus, M. A. (2005). The relationship between parental involvement as social capital and college enrollment: An examination of racial/ethnic group differences. *Journal of Higher Education, 76*(5), 485–518. Retrieved from: http://www.jstor.org/stable/3838837

Rindfuss, R. R., Swicegood, G. C., & Rosenfeld, R. A. (1987). Disorder in the life course: How common and does it matter? *American Sociological Review, 52*(6), 775–801. Retrieved from http://www.jstor.org/stable/2095835

Roksa, J., & Velez, M. (2012). A late start: delayed entry, life course transitions and bachelor's degree completion. *Social Forces, 90*(3), 769–794. Retrieved from http://www.jstor.org/stable/41682677

Rowan-Kenyon, H. T. (2007). Predictors of delayed college enrollment and the impact socioeconomic status. *The Journal of Higher Education, 78*(2), 188–214. Retrieved from http://www.jstor.org/stable/4501202

Solem, M., Christophersen, K., & Martinussencm, M. (2011). Predicting parenting stress: Children's behavioral problems and parents' coping. *Infant & Child Development, 20*(2), 162–180.

Spellman, N. (2007). Enrollment and retention barriers adult students encounter. *Community College Enterprise, 13*(1), 63–79.

Stanton-Salazar, R. D. (1997). A social capital framework for understanding the socialization of racial minority children and youth. *Harvard Educational Review, 67,* 1–40. doi:10.1177/0044118X10382877

Teachman, J. D., & Polonko, K. A. (1988). Marriage, parenthood, and the college enrollment of men and women. *Social Forces, 67*(2), 512–523. Retrieved from http://www.jstor.org/stable/2579193

CHAPTER 5

TORN BETWEEN THREE WORLDS

Examining the Graduate School Experience of Women Balancing Doctoral Education, Motherhood, and Work

Aimee Tiu Wu
Teachers College, Columbia University

The theme of this volume, "Building Sustainable Futures for Adult Learners," highlights the changing landscape of adult education in the twenty-first century. The current chapter considers the theme by maintaining that the journey towards this sustainability entails a shift in perspective about what it means to be an adult learner today and how learners, adult educators, and organizations make meaning in light of on-going personal and social responsibilities within families and communities (Denham, 2007).

Adult learners, in particular women balancing multiple roles, are a growing population in higher education today. Recent statistics illustrate that women earned 52.2% of all doctoral degrees in 2012, an enormous 49.4% increase since 1961 (Council of Graduate Schools, 2013; Department of

Building Sustainable Futures for Adult Learners, pages 87–113
Copyright © 2015 by Information Age Publishing

Professional Employees, 2010). Moreover, women comprised more than 47% of the total U.S. labor force and are projected to increase in size in the next ten years (U.S. Department of Labor, 2011). This reality is a testament to the dramatic surge of the number of women in the workforce in recent years due to the massive feminist movement in the 1960s (Berkeley, 1999).

Despite the number of women who combine the daunting challenge of graduate school and motherhood, contemporary society still holds women responsible for the majority of work associated with child-rearing and home management (England, 1996; Hochschild & Machung, 2003; Palladino Schultheiss, 2009). As far as expectations and commitments to graduate education go, Murphy and Cloutier-Fisher (2002) contended that "female doctoral students with a dual commitment to parenting and academic life often find themselves facing pressures equivalent to holding down two full-time jobs" (pp. 37–38). With competing responsibilities and commitments in both private (home) and public (academia and work) spheres, doctoral student mothers, like other women with multiple roles, face the postpartum dilemma of transitioning back to work as they try to manage a "double workday" (Hochschild, 1997). Inherent in the process is the transition between multiple life roles and responsibilities as well as the transition from being a student to that of a working professional (Golde, 1998; Weidman, Twale, & Stein, 2001). As a result, women often experience sleep deprivation, loss of leisure time, and struggle with feelings of guilt, overload, and stress (Presser, 1995; Hochschild, 1997). Moreover, they are "more directly affected by family planning issues, a forced choice between caregiver and professional, and discrimination in the work setting" (Wall, 2008, p. 226).

This research was conducted to reveal some of the complexities of the lived experience of academic mothers. It is important because it provided a venue for the voices of doctoral student mothers to be heard. Insight and knowledge obtained from this research has contributed to the general understanding of the support systems and engagement needed to enhance the learning of mothers who are pursuing academic studies, family lives, and professional careers. Furthermore, institutions of higher education may benefit from this study by gaining an improved understanding of the needs of this growing population of non-traditional students.

This chapter includes the results of a study of 20 doctoral student mothers who are pursuing doctoral degrees while mothering young children and working at the same time. In the literature, there are three areas that influence a doctoral student mother's journey of navigating doctoral studies, motherhood, and work. Finally, the chapter concludes with recommendations to build a sustainable future for doctoral student mothers and offers suggestions for future research around motherhood in academia.

LITERATURE REVIEW

In examining how doctoral student mothers navigate their roles as doctoral students, mothers, and professionals, the literature review begins with an introduction into the three worlds that they occupy to present the competing responsibilities surrounding their three salient roles. Second is a general overview of women and graduate school to illustrate the trend in graduate attrition, retention, and persistence. Third is an examination of the challenges experienced by women in academia to provide a backdrop of the realities facing women pursuing doctoral education.

Torn Between Three "Greedy" Worlds

Academic women have long decried the academic community for being oblivious to their struggle in combining academic studies, work, and motherhood (Evans & Grant, 2009). Doctoral student mothers are expected to conform to the unspoken norms and expectations of the three institutions they concurrently serve—academia, family, and the workplace. This notion of total commitment and voluntary compliance among its members is what Coser (1974) referred to as "greedy institutions with omnivorous demands for exclusive and undivided loyalty" (p. 33). In academia, higher education is a "greedy institution" because it requires devotion and commitment from its students to fulfill its academic requirements. Doctoral students are expected to balance their own coursework and conduct their own research while teaching or working. For the doctoral student mother, she is simultaneously expected to perform her roles as a partner, mother, and primary caregiver to conform to the demands of another "greedy institution"—her family. Additionally, when she has to work outside the home, she is expected to give the same amount of commitment and devotion to the job as obligated by the third "greedy institution"—her employer. Clearly, the roles and expectations of these "greedy institutions" continue to intersect at a colossal speed, but they persist and continue to create significant conflict and imbalance, often leaving the woman physically exhausted and emotionally drained (Grant, Kennelly, & Ward, 2000).

WOMEN AND GRADUATE SCHOOL

Socialization is a theoretical construct commonly associated with research in doctoral attrition (Gardner, 2010). This concept is grounded in Tinto's (1993) notion of academic and social integration in academic communities. In a study of the socialization experience of 60 doctoral students across six disciplines, Gardner (2010) cited four core themes that drive their socialization experience: (1) support from family, peers, and faculty members; (2) self-direction in the progression of the program; (3) ambiguity associated with institutional guidelines and requirements; and (4) transition between roles and expectations. These findings are in line with Mallinckrodt and Leong's (1992) survey of 440 graduate students at a large university in the middle eastern section of the United States, where they found that the two main sources of social support for graduate students are family/peers and faculty in the academic program. With a strong mentoring relationship in place, this social support becomes even more crucial (Gardner, 2010). In relation to Gardner's theme of transition, Mallinckrodt and Leong's (1992) study also concluded that women graduate students reported more anxiety and depression related to life event changes and higher likelihood of role strain as they balance multiple life roles, demands, and concerns, particularly in terms of living conditions, financial resources, and child-rearing.

Doctoral Student Attrition and Completion

While the term attrition is loosely understood as departure from an academic institution or even "dropout," Tinto (1975) defined student attrition as:

> a longitudinal process of interactions between the individual and the academic and social systems of the college during which a person's experiences in those systems... continually modify [her] goals and institutional commitments in ways which lead to persistence and/or to varying forms of dropout/ (p. 94)

In general, women have higher estimated attrition rates from graduate school than men across all fields of study, which may be a result of their disproportionate enrollment in fields that have higher attrition rates (Herzig, 2004). In line with the concern over women's attrition in doctoral education, studies have examined factors that impact time between entry into graduate study and completion of the doctoral degree (Allan & Dory, 2001; Nerad, 1991). Not surprisingly, findings from such studies suggested that having dependents lengthens the time for completion of the doctorate for women more than for men (Allan & Dory, 2001; National Science Foundation, 1994; Nerad, 1991).

Berelson (1960) in his seminal work, *Graduate Education in the United States*, cited six reasons for attrition at the doctoral level, which are still very much relevant today: lack of financial resources, lack of intellectual ability to do the work, lack of proper motivation, lack of necessary physical and emotional stamina, found degree was not necessary for what they wanted to do, and disappointment in graduate study resulting in quitting. Similarly,

Allan and Dory (2001) determined five factors that influence attrition as (1) psychological (e.g., procrastination, lack of motivation); (2) structural (particularly in the dissertation process); (3) external (funding, work and family obligations); (4) institutional (lack of faculty support, lack of research training to complete requirements); and (5) capability (personal shortcomings). More recently, research like Golde's (2005) suggested that for both female and male students, attrition—at least in the sciences—is to a large extent due to the perceived imbalance between academic, family, and work responsibilities.

There is also some disparity between men and women in terms of completion rate. While data from the National Center for Education Statistics (2010a) reported that students pursuing doctoral degrees have increased from 12.4% in 1995–1996 to 15.1% in 2007–2008, with the most prominent increase evident among female students, women still take longer to complete their doctorates than men. Recent results from the PhD Completion Project, which examined doctoral study and completion of PhD programs in the U.S. and Canada, revealed that 57% of doctoral students complete their degrees within 10 years (Council of Graduate Schools, 2008). Men are ahead with 58%, while women trail behind by three points at 55% (Council of Graduate Schools, 2008). However, there is some disparity in completion rates across fields of study, with men leading in the fields of engineering (65%), life sciences (64%), math and physical sciences (59%), and women leading in social sciences (57%) and humanities (52%) (Council of Graduate Schools, 2008).

Clearly, the consequences of doctoral student departure are immensely costly not only for the faculty, university, and society in general, but the greatest disadvantage falls on the individual who leaves graduate school without a degree (Lovitts, 2001). The costs of departure for the individual do not only affect personal finances and time but also the resources provided by the institution during the duration of their stay in the program (Lovitts, 2001). Adult educators, in particular graduate school faculty, dissertation advisors, and mentors, play a crucial role in promoting retention, persistence, and ultimately successful program completion among doctoral students (Fischer, Gokalp, Gupton, Pena, & West, 2011).

CHALLENGES OF ACADEMIC MOTHERHOOD

Despite changes in women's participation in academia and the labor force, the experience of motherhood remains a central event for most women. While a substantial amount of research on motherhood in academia has been published, very little has been documented about the experience of motherhood of doctoral students and how it contributes to their learning, growth, and development. Previous studies like Ward and Wolf-Wendel (2004), Wolf-Wendel and Ward (2006), and Tiu Wu (2013) demonstrated how certain factors associated with work-life balance influence women's meaning making while highlighting outcomes related to work–family conflict. While a great amount of research has been done on women's persistence in the STEM fields (Cuny & Aspray, 2000; Goulden, Frasch, & Mason, 2009; Greenhouse, 2011; Herzig, 2004; Mason, 2008b) and minority women's experience and persistence in doctoral programs (Bailey-Iddrisu, 2010; Herzig, 2002, 2004), research on the experience of motherhood while in graduate school has been slowly gaining traction as well. A recent study by CohenMiller (2013) introduced a model called Phenomenon of Motherhood in Academia Online (PMAO), which illustrated the complexity of an academic women's personal experience/story, biology (physical experience of pregnancy and childbearing), and experience of academic pressures leading to advise and empower other women and offer specific suggestions on how to improve practices within institutions of higher education.

Unequal Career Trajectories Between Male and Female Doctoral Students

Feminist researchers like Mason (2008a, 2008b, 2009) continued to point out the stark differences of combining academic life and parenthood between men and women. In an in-depth study utilizing the Survey of Doctorate Recipients (SDR), a comprehensive employment database following more than 160,000 PhD recipients across all disciplines in the United States, Mason and Goulden (2004b) found some astonishing facts about women in academia: (1) men with "early babies" (having a child within five years of receiving their PhD's) are 38% more with likely than women with "early babies" to achieve tenure; (2) women who have babies early on in their career leave academia before obtaining their first tenure track job; (3) single mothers are more successful than married mothers; (4) women with late babies do as well as women without children; (5) women who have tenure are more than twice as likely to be single twelve years after earning their PhDs; (6) in terms of work hierarchy, a high percentage of women with babies opt to become part-time instructors, adjuncts, and lecturers; and (7) academic women are more likely to experience divorce or separation than their male counterparts. The cumulative disadvantage of losing talented female scholars has been referred to as the *leaky pipeline* (Mason, Goulden, & Frasch, 2011). Similarly, other researchers pointed out barriers that hinder academic women's advancement in graduate school, which include: overt and subtle gender discrimination experienced in the workplace (Monroe, Ozyurt, Wrigley & Alexander, 2008), lack of female leadership and role models in the field (Berg & Ferber, 1983), lack of social support (Mallinckrodt & Leong, 1992), and power relationships between students and male/female advisors (Thibodeaux, 2003).

Role Strain

As they face resource constraints and manage multiple competing demands, doctoral student mothers continue to experience increased levels of stress due to their perceived inability to meet the expectations set forth by the multiple roles they play (Mallinckrodt & Leong, 1992; Tiu Wu, 2013). With increasing complexity in life roles and expectations, an individual experiences role strain as two or more life domains come in conflict (Bomar, 2004; McBride, 1990). This is particularly evident in women with "superwoman syndrome," or those who desire to perform all their roles exceptionally well (Gray, 1983; Nicolson, 2002). This is the case of academic mothers, who are "expected to accommodate the new role of student or working spouse without a significant lessening of their responsibilities as wife, homemaker and...mother" (Mallinckrodt & Leong, 1992, p. 716).

As academic women continue to experience the complexity of managing their private and professional lives, social support such as family, peers, and faculty becomes more significant (Tiu Wu, 2013). The development of strategies to help women manage multiple demands is also warranted. For example, identifying sustaining factors (belief in traditional values that motherhood work is meaningful, ability to utilize their inborn sense of structure, support of an emotionally and financially supportive spouse) and hindering factors (belief in gendered expectations as a result of traditional values, personal and professional sacrifices, unsupportive spouses, changing marital dynamics as a result of parenthood) may help women understand the complexity of their expanding social roles (Vejar, Madison-Colmore & Ter Maat, 2006). Some other coping strategies include organization, empathy, delegation, and stalling (O'Keefe, 1991), spacing the birth of children (Bird, 1984), compartmentalization, delegation, lowered housekeeping standards, and engagement in physical, intellectual, or artistic pursuits (Villadsen & Tack, 1981).

Childcare Challenges

Large increases over the last 20 years in the number of women in doctoral programs and in the workforce have significant implications for childcare. Data from the National Center for Education Statistics (2010b) indicate that 76.7% men and 71.7% women who applied for federal financial aid in

2007–2008 received an average amount of $23,800. Among individuals pursuing a PhD (except in education), 18.8% were married with dependents and 4.8% were unmarried with dependents. Among those in doctoral programs in education, 43.3% were married with dependents and 11.5% were unmarried with dependents. Moreover, 41.9% of graduate student parents have a dependent child less than five years of age (National Postsecondary Student Aid Study, 2013). In fact, Gerencher (2002) confirmed the trend that graduate students with dependents are more likely to be women, married, and caring for young children. This reality has clear implications for many doctoral mothers with young children who have a need for childcare services (Cole & Zuckerman, 1987; Gasser & Gasser, 2008). While house chores can be delegated or even outsourced by some, in their survey of 20,000 employees, Emlen and Koren's (1984) found that women in general still carry the burden of worrying about childcare and work and life balance, with 47% of women as compared to 28% of men reporting childcare-related stress. Not much has changed in the last thirty years, as recent studies continue to demonstrate the trend that women still assume greater childcare-related responsibilities in the United States leading to increased stress and risk of poverty (Smith, Appio & Cho, 2012).

RESEARCH DESIGN AND METHODOLOGY

The purpose of the study was to examine the experiences of doctoral student mothers pursuing doctoral education, motherhood, and professional work. Using an exploratory field study approach, this research explored how women made meaning as they navigate these three roles. Since the researcher's goal was to gather in-depth data that capture the participant's experience navigating motherhood and work during their journey through doctoral studies, a qualitative research method was deemed most suitable to probe more deeply into the problem and to gain a detailed understanding of the phenomenon (Creswell, 2007). Such an investigation required inquiry into the nature of the participants' experience, particularly the way in which they are constructing the meaning of that experience.

Research Question

Undergirding this study was the question, *how do women doctoral students learn to navigate and balance the conflicts and intersections that arise from their roles as student, mother, and professional?* The sub-question emerging from the main research question was: *How has motherhood changed/influenced/impacted their graduate school experience?*

Participant Demographics

Doctoral student mothers who had completed at least one year of their academic program in any discipline were invited to participate in the study. There were three main criteria in the selection of participants. First, completion of at least one year in the program of study was specified in order to recruit participants with some experience with doctoral study. Second, participants must be a primary caregiver of a child/ren (age 0–13) since birth because literature (e.g., Home, 1997; Mikolaj & Boggs, 1991) indicated that female students with dependents under the age of 13 reported higher incidence of role strain. Given that the needs of children from this age group are greater, it was assumed that the experience of balancing roles would be more intense given the competing demands of each role. Third, participants were required to be engaged in full- or part-time employment because as Home (1992) pointed out that working women experienced more role strain and were more likely to drop out from school than those without multiple roles to manage.

In an effort to make the study inclusive and representative of the population of professional women in doctoral programs, efforts were made to recruit female doctoral students: (a) in a committed same-sex relationships with a child/ren; (b) not in a committed relationship but with a child/ren; (c) pregnant for the second time; (d) with adopted child/ren; and (e) with more than one child. Of these additional criteria, only two were represented in the study—women expecting a second child and women with multiple children within the ages of 0–13 years old. There were no participant volunteers representing criteria (a), (b), or (d). In the end, a total of 20 women, married and ranging in age from mid-20s to late-30s, met the criteria and agreed to participate in the study. Participants were predominantly White and/or came from professional or middle class family backgrounds. Ethnically, 14 were White, 3 were Asian, 2 were Hispanic/Latina, and 1 was African American. The majority (70%) had one child, three participants (15%) had two children, two (10%) had three children, and one (5%) had four.

Procedure

Utilizing demographic surveys, critical incidents, interviews, and focus group discussion, the responses obtained were analyzed for emergent themes and patterns related to the specific learning involved in the experience of balancing doctoral studies, motherhood, and professional work. In order to pay close attention to validity threats and biases, I followed Maxwell's (2005) suggestion of writing personal memos or "researcher identity memo" after each interview to keep track of my reflections and bracket my assumptions and experiential knowledge.

The sequence of data collection was important for ensuring richness of content and controlling for researcher bias in this exploratory field study. The first step was to construct a brief demographic survey and an interview protocol, which was pilot tested with a small sample of women who shared similar backgrounds as the participants of the study. Feedback from the pilot study contributed to the finalization of the demographic survey and the interview protocol, which was developed and guided by literature review and consisted of four sections: warm up, navigating roles, looking ahead, and concluding thoughts. For the actual study, 20 research participants were identified through purposeful sampling (Maxwell, 2005).

After collecting demographic data, participants were invited to do one round of a semi-structured interview lasting approximately 60–90 minutes. Next, perceptual data on how doctoral student mothers navigate the intersections of their roles as student, mother, and professional, and how motherhood changed/influenced/impacted their graduate school experience were gathered from the critical incidents, interviews, and focus group discussion. Prior to the interview, participants were sent a critical incident questionnaire to complete via email. Participants were then asked to relate two narratives about their experience navigating school, motherhood, and work: one in which they successfully navigated all three roles, and the other they perceived as a moment of challenge or failure in managing the roles. After the interview, a transcript, along with a brief introduction of the participant, was sent to each woman for review. The final step was the focus group discussion, where participants came together to discuss their shared experience of navigating their roles as well as recommendation for institutions of higher education. This method enabled me to obtain multiple views and perspectives as well as provided the women a safe venue to reveal their thoughts, insights, and emotions in a social setting with other women who share a similar journey.

Data Analysis

Data analysis began after all interview recordings were transcribed and organized. I utilized Atlas.ti to manage, explore, code, compare, and integrate the 282 pages of data into meaningful results. The initial coding scheme was developed based on the literature review, data from the pilot interviews, and by combining organizational, substantive, and theoretical codes (Maxwell, 2005). In the process of open coding, the researcher started to notice a pattern of similar or recurring codes, which were eventually merged into one cohesive code. As categories and themes emerged, the researcher began the process of interpreting the data or what Patton (2002) referred to as "attaching significance to what was found, making sense of the findings, offering explanations, drawing conclusions, extrapolating lessons, making inferences, considering meanings and otherwise imposing order" (p. 480). Once all data had been coded, I reviewed the data and the codes focusing on themes that did not fit the emerging patterns, and I looked for other plausible explanations as to why they did not fit the patterns established (Creswell, 2007). Finally, when no additional data were found or a saturation point had been reached (Strauss & Corbin, 1997), the researcher summarized the vast amount of codes, categories, and patterns into a meaningful written report, taking the reader to the specific instances of the phenomenon (Marshall & Rossman, 2006).

FINDINGS AND DISCUSSION

Significance of the Relationship with Faculty Advisor

Similar to the experience of Grenier and Burke (2008), participants in this study benefited from a supportive relationship with faculty advisors, particularly in light of their responsibilities as mothers. Given the multiple roles doctoral student mothers play and the load associated with these roles, support from faculty was crucial to their continued academic and personal success. Based on the data, it was evident that the faculty advisor's role was critical in providing emotional support and academic guidance in the patriarchal environment of higher education. Moreover, findings indicated that relationship with their faculty advisor was a lifeline in completing their doctorate. In general, all but one out of the 20 women expressed overall satisfaction with their relationship with their faculty advisors. Participants who were highly satisfied with their advisors described them as trusted mentors and professional/collegial friends. For example, one woman shared a time when she seriously considered quitting her program, but her advisor encouraged and motivated her throughout. She recalled the experience, saying:

> I have the world's greatest sponsor.... [A]s far as our social identities go, we're very different. (Laughs)....And I have an affectionate name for him. I call him my coach. Because when I'm having a tough time, I go to my coach and say I don't know what to do about this...(Laughs). [So he'll say] ...Stick with it! Don't let it break you!...But also with him being a scholar, he...say[s], "Well, think about what it means if you drop out of the program....what does it mean as far as your area's scholarship, who won't be helped if you don't get your work out there? (personal communication, September 17, 2011)

This type of emotional support and academic encouragement not only demonstrated the faculty advisor's commitment to the education and training of the student, but also as future member of the academic community.

Altered Career Plans

Although a great majority of the women felt that their advisors were their allies in their academic journey, the realities of motherhood altered their career plans. This was particularly true for participants working in academia. More than half (65%) of participants noted how their career plans had changed as a result of their multiple roles, particularly in light of motherhood. For instance, motherhood prompted one participant to take on a job on the West Coast to be closer to family. Others noted how they became disillusioned with the politics in academia and started to entertain job options outside teaching. For instance, a few participants alluded to the hostile remarks made by their department chairs and faculty upon knowing about their pregnancies. Others shared how motherhood changed the way they viewed their potential work schedule and how they used to have strong aspirations to work in research universities.

These sentiments were supported in the literature on academic motherhood, which seemed to suggest that a balance between an academic career and family might be unattainable (Armenti, 2004; Gardner, 2008; Mason, 2009; Mason & Goulden, 2002, 2004a, 2004b). While not completely conclusive, findings in this study lent some support to this body of literature, since 65% of the participants noted shifts in their career plans as a result of motherhood. While a good majority aspired for a faculty position, others desired to work as researchers or administrators in higher education. While inconclusive, it was striking to note the participants' vocal disinclination for working in research universities, their non-desire and reluctance to become "famous" scholars in their fields due to perceived "motherhood penalty." Correll, Benard, and Paik (2007) described motherhood penalty as women being "penalized on a host of measures, including perceived competence and recommended starting salary" (para. 1).

To counter possible challenges, which abound in academic careers, participants in this study, as in Golde and Dore's (2001) observation, opted for non-tenure-track positions or work at less research-intensive institutions. Similarly, Ward and Wolf-Wendel (2004) found that academic women deliberately make career decisions based on institutional priorities and culture, as well as their ability to balance family and career in academia. These sentiments were spurred in part by the "publish or perish" mentality in higher education and the notion of "Mommy Track," which is a "socio-economic phenomenon that working women who get pregnant and have children experience lower expectations at work, lower opportunity, and lower pay than those who not have children" (Cater-Steel, 2010, p. 32).

Diminished Level of Effort and Output Toward Academic Work

There was a general thread in the data where participants talked about how much to give in terms of time, energy, and resources to academic activities like reading, studying, writing their dissertation, going to conferences, etc. Effort and output referred to the physical, mental, and even financial exertion needed to fulfill one's academic role. Given the magnitude of work involved in doctoral study, the women were often confronted with limitations of time and energy when it came to fulfilling academic-related obligations. There was a general theme around the idea of a "good and dedicated student" delicately intertwined with the role of being a doctoral student found in the data. As one woman observed, "it's probably the Type A personalities who go into doctoral programs." Type A personalities are often characterized as high achievers, highly ambitious, organized, persistent, and able to multi-task (Schulz-Aellen, 1997). For example, one self-confessed Type A student admitted to "satisficing" her academic work, or doing a subpar work to pass the course due to lack of time and sheer exhaustion. Aside from the physical, mental, and psychological effort and output required to meet academic requirements, attitudes toward their field of specialty have also changed as a result of motherhood. One woman candidly shared her view toward school in comparison to her childless peers:

> I've always noticed in comparison to my other cohort members, I just don't have the time to worry about academic things in the way that they do. I produce the paper, it's my best paper I can produce and I can't worry about finding more sources....My other cohort members...they're in love with the discipline and the field in a way that I can't. I can't muster the time or the space in my own life to do that kind of work. And I worry that I'm not as good as they are....I can't go into the library for ten hours a day and go in all the meetings....I just can't let it bleed into my everyday life and I try not to let what's happening at home bleed into my work. (personal communication, September 23, 2011)

This woman's sentiments aptly captured the feelings of all women in this study. Feelings of self-doubt and comparison to others would set in particularly in times of stress and pressure to meet deadlines.

Interestingly, research by Carney-Crompton and Tan (2002) found that nontraditional students, like the women in this study, perform at a higher academic level than traditional students, even though they experience more stress brought about by other roles they need to fulfill. However, when demands of the two other more salient roles (i.e., being a mother or a professional) become more pressing, the student role is usually the first to be compromised (Home, 1992). Like participants in Sears's (2001) study, some women in this study were able to reframe their definition of a good student and create an alternate definition outside the dominant ideology (be it intensive mothering or that of a good student or ideal worker). While some were better than others in living out their alternate definitions of a good student, these women had learned to reconcile their ideology with their reality. Meanwhile, others felt compelled to live up to the dominant ideology of a good student (complete focus and dedication to her studies).

Continued Funding Became a Determinant for Persistence

Managing multiple roles also brought forth the reality of funding as a strong determinant for continued persistence in graduate school. This study showed that women, particularly those from public institutions, demonstrated financial uncertainty towards persisting in their education. Maher, Ford and Thompson's (2004) observation that "lack of stable and/or relevant funding [often] plagued" women doctoral students could not be more true in this case (p. 399). For instance, financial aid and scholarship in the forms of teaching assistantship were important factors for the women to stay in school. Similar to the findings of Lynch (2008), the most important source of funding for women in this study was financial aid in the form of scholarships, Teaching Assistantship, Graduate Assistantship, and Research Associate. Data indicated that 45% of the participants were funded through some form of academic fellowships like teaching assistantships and research assistantships, 25% through employee benefits (tuition remission), and 30% through a combination of personal resources and outside funding. While graduate school funding was a challenge for doctoral students in general, the ability for women from public institutions to secure funding seemed even more insecure (Berg & Ferber, 1983).

Lack of Flexibility in Schedule

While consensus was centered around the need for flexibility in schedule to help them find a balance between academics and their personal and professional lives, all women highlighted their lack of flexibility compared to their childless peers in graduate school. Among the women in this study, one participant experienced the most abrupt transition from being a doctoral student/stay-at-home mom to a full-time working professional and breadwinner when her husband got into a serious motor vehicle accident and fell into coma for three months.

Lack of flexibility in schedule also impacted the choice of classes doctoral mothers could take because they needed to coordinate childcare arrangements prior to signing up for classes. Since required courses were designed with traditional students in mind, they were usually in conflict with non-traditional students' schedules (Veney, O'Green, & Kowalik, 2012). For some women in this study, the juggling act proved extremely challenging from a scheduling standpoint because doctoral classes were few and far between and were set up in specified time slots that were not congruent with their schedule. Meanwhile, another participant decided to take a semester off when her second child was born. Prior to the arrival of their second child, she and her husband, who was also a doctoral student, had a working arrangement that allowed them to alternate between going to classes and taking care of their eldest. Now with two young children, she knew it was not possible to fit in classes while taking care of the kids.

Changed Perspective and Relationship with Higher Education

Data also suggested that the women experienced feelings of being marginalized and disempowered as a result of balancing motherhood with doctoral studies. This perception contributed to their changed relationship with "greedy" (Coser, 1974) institutions of higher education. Consistent with the study of Gardner (2008) on the socialization experience of doctoral students who did not "fit the mold" of traditional graduate education (in particular women, students of color, older students, students with children, and part-time students), several women in this study alluded to negative interactions with higher education institutions. Gardner, (2008) referred to these as "structural impediments to success" and "general feelings of 'differentness'." For example, a few women (25%) reported receiving offhand comments from their departments about combining motherhood with doctoral study. Likewise, others noted a general lack of departmental support for student mothers and unfounded questioning of their commitment to their doctoral studies.

Influence of Family on Decision and Choice of Graduate School

The doctoral journey begins with the decision to enter a doctoral program, a decision that has tremendous implications for one's family life, finances, and time. Consistent with Wall's (2008) study of doctoral women at a Canadian university, three participants in this study explicitly articulated that their decision to begin a doctoral program was heavily influenced by family and/or motherhood. Given the magnitude of the decision to undertake a doctorate, it is important to note that for women in this study, the choice of institution and programs was based on reasons closely tied to the family. Although participants reported a general sense of satisfaction with their choice of institution or program, their decision did not come without professional and personal compromises. For a small number of participants (15%), the decision to pursue a doctorate was driven by circumstances surrounding their families or significant others.

For instance, in order to help care for and support her mother-in-law, who was diagnosed with pancreatic cancer, one participant and her husband decided to move back to their old town and buy the family house from his parents. She recalled the decision to apply for doctoral study and said "[it] is the only school around town ... so I applied and luckily I got in." Another woman, on the other hand, met her then-boyfriend-now-husband in graduate school and made a decision to pursue her doctorate by staying in the same city, where her husband had already established career. For her, the decision to pursue doctoral study meant limiting her choices in terms of location, institutional type, and potential return of investment.

CONCLUSIONS

In general, all women acknowledged some sort of diminished experience compared to their childless peers in graduate school as a result of managing multiple roles but remained driven to succeed and make the most out of their doctoral experience. Understanding that their life circumstances greatly differed from those of their childless counterparts, these women vocally shared stories of marginalization, disempowerment, and disappointment as a doctoral student mother, while at the same time highlighting successes, achievements, and joy brought about by the experience of being in school. The findings of this study support previous research on perceived load and power and the added challenge of doctoral studies and motherhood (Grenier & Burke, 2008; Home & Hinds, 2000; Maher et al., 2004). Moreover, this study found that the women were constantly finding that delicate balance among their roles as doctoral students, mothers, and professionals. This was in line with Garey's (1999) findings in her study of female hospital workers with children who "negotiated her own way through the structural complexities of combining (academics), employment and motherhood" (p. 194). Through their balancing act, they learned to embrace the complexity of their roles and the responsibilities that came with them.

The learning curve in reaching this "new synthesis," while not a seamless process, allowed them to become self-directed and learn from their experience to reconfigure their roles to balance the demands of graduate school, motherhood, and professional life (O'Donnell, 1985). In other words, they learned to find a way to manage the complexities of their roles by "recognizing that it is possible to have different priorities at different times" (O'Donnell, 1985, p. 156).

Similar to the research by Ward and Wolf-Wendel (2004), this study also found that multiple roles involving school, family, and professional work can be both possible and fulfilling for academic women. In fact these roles "are not impossible to reconcile, and there are many successful examples of women who do both well" (Ward & Wolf-Wendel, 2007, p. 1). While the majority of the women in this study were able to navigate the challenges of combining motherhood with their academic and professional pursuits, "the effort required personal commitment and endurance" (Wolf-Wendel & Ward, 2006, p. 501). Moreover, this balancing act required work efficiency, realistic expectations of their productivity, and reliance on their own strength and ability (Wolf-Wendel & Ward, 2006). This finding could be due to design of the self-selection process, whereby more self-directed and motivated women are more likely to pursue a doctorate. The decision to assume additional roles, such as that of a mother and a professional, was made with thorough planning, greater awareness, and commitment to adapt to the demands of these roles. Further, these women felt competent in themselves and knew that taking on additional roles would not severely compromise their other roles and responsibilities (Carney-Crompton & Tan, 2002).

The Path Forward: Key Factors for Building a Sustainable Future for Doctoral Student Mothers

The journey toward sustainability necessitates a fundamental shift in how we view adult learners managing multiple roles in life. Advancement in this direction is critically determined by adult educators, educational leaders, policy makers, and most importantly, by us- doctoral student mothers who feel marginalized and as though we do not belong to the existing graduate school "mold." While the idea of a sustainable future is highly complex, findings from this study and the emergent themes across the literature provide headway for adult educators to forge forward. The path recommended henceforth highlights individual, relational, and structural components and is a beginning of a dialogue, not a conclusion. It is an earnest attempt to stimulate discussion and initiate research to build a truly sustainable future for all adult learners managing multiple and highly complex life roles.

Individual Components

Forming a Strong Support Network

Numerous studies have shown the importance of having an adequate personal support system for learners to persist and succeed in their educational goals (Council of Graduate Schools, 2009; Gardner, 2010; Link, 2006; Maher, Ford & Thompson, 2004). Personal support system is comprised of families, relatives, friends, colleagues, community, and support groups. This system is further classified by Comings and Cuban (2002) as personal (one's family and relatives), official (educators, librarians, counselors), and intermediate or those who fall in between (pastors, counselors, tutors, mentors). Hence, the saying *it takes a village to raise a child* holds true in the case of adult learners.

Developing Self-Efficacy

While self-efficacy is beyond the scope of this study, data indicated that it accounted for the participant's ability to manage the responsibilities in their lives. Moreover, various studies on adult learner retention, persistence, and achievement point to the concept of self-efficacy in the form of self-esteem, capacity, persistence, and commitment (Allan & Dory, 2001), making the system work for them (Maher, Ford & Thompson, 2004), and not engaging in self-sabotaging or self-handicapping behaviors (over-commitment, procrastination, perfectionism) (Kearns, Gardiner & Marshall, 2008). Bandura (1986) defined self-efficacy as an individual's "judgment of [his/her] capabilities to organize and execute courses of action required to attain designated types of performances" (p. 391). In other words, self-efficacy is "a global feeling of being able to accomplish most tasks" (Link, 2006, p. 2). Cultivating self-efficacy can be achieved through sufficient training on how to conduct research or write a dissertation (Allan & Dory, 2001); participation in meaningful research (Maher, Ford & Thompson, 2004); strong commitment to finish in a timely manner, as prolonging the program may have financial ramifications (Maher, Ford & Thompson, 2004); and recognition of self-destructive thought patterns and self-management of time and resources (Kearns, Gardiner & Marshall, 2008).

Relational Components

Belongingness

Gardner (2008) contended that attrition is high among students who feel that they do not "fit the mold" of a graduate student. These are often under-represented students, or those who differ with regard to gender, race, age, enrolment (part-time), and familial status from the traditional graduate student. Strayhorn (2012) argued that socialization is crucial for graduate students across academic disciplines, and student's sense of belongingness is shown to impact persistence, grade point average (GPA), and overall academic satisfaction. Social class, in particular one's financial situation, has also been shown to influence sense of belongingness (Ostrove, Steward, & Curtin, 2011). Socialization can be enhanced, and sense of belongingness can be fostered formally through introduction to a department's customs and mentoring, and informally through various social events (orientation, symposiums) (Strayhorn, 2012).

Positive Working Relationship with Faculty

The role of faculty, advisors, and mentors could not be underestimated since faculty-student interactions are critical for student persistence, retention, and development as scholars (Allan & Dory, 2001; Heinrich, 1995; Maher, Ford & Thompson, 2004). Recall that a great majority of the women in this study were generally satisfied with their advisors, and this relationship is pivotal in the participant's doctoral journey. Department chairs and deans should consider offering training for faculty and staff to increase awareness of nontraditional students' needs. Through awareness training, faculty members may be better able to identify and acknowledge the presence of female students, as well as to anticipate and understand their needs as they become mothers or manage multiple roles and suggest better ways to cope with personal and academic demands (Medved & Heider, 2002). Most importantly, advisors' flexibility and understanding have been shown to enhance students' satisfaction and degree progress, since other life demands may reduce the time student-parents dedicate to campus visits, thereby reducing interactions with faculty members (Thibodeaux, 2003).

Structural Components

Increased Institutional Support

From an organizational standpoint, increased support in three areas is crucial. First is provision of consistent and stable educational funding for adult learners (Allan & Dory, 2001; Council of Graduate Schools, 2009; Maher, Ford & Thompson, 2004). Second is improved programs in general, modified schedules, access to childcare, increased financial aid, subsidized housing, and support systems will greatly benefit student mothers (Chater & Hatch, 1991). And third, in response to the grave need for childcare, Chater and Hatch (1991) actively called for institutions of higher education to be cognizant of the growing number of non-traditional students like student mothers and to consider "programs and policies enabling them to combine and cope with the demands of academics, home, and work" (p. 33). In the same vein, Boswell (2003) argued that the significant increase in the number of women faculty and student parents in American colleges calls for institutions of higher education to provide campus childcare.

Increased Research and Dialogue in Academia and Beyond

This study contributes to the adult learning literature on how women balance multiple roles through personal and the systemic perspective. Preparing women to navigate higher education addresses the symptom of a system that is deeply patriarchal and inequitable (LaMonica, 2010). Additional studies should be done on the systems level to create institutions that are more equitable, with the goal of providing different types of scaffolding and support to adult learners with multiple life roles. Moreover, the complexity of the experience of "motherhood may be an especially socially-needy time in which the mother needs just as much support as the child from a community" because recent shifts in maternal and social practices have made "motherhood more conflicted than ever" (Narvaez, 2012, p. 198). Social support through dialogue within and outside academia is greatly needed if we want to promote and enhance an environment where women's public and private spheres are more permeable and where work, home, and other life roles are more integrated into a sustainable future for adult learners.

Recommendations for Future Research

This study contributes to the adult learning literature on how women balance their roles as students, mothers, and professionals. While this study was limited to the experiences of 20 doctoral student mothers, replication of this research utilizing a larger sample size may further reinforce the themes and subthemes of this study. Expansion of sample size to include more women in the STEM fields may yield some interesting data. Additionally, future studies may also consider the inclusion of deviancy discourse, which includes single, lesbian, and older mothers, to look at the similarities and/or differences in their experiences that occur as a result of not "fitting the mold" of higher education. Moreover, since gender no longer defines motherhood, future studies on how fathers and lesbian mothers navigate the dominant ideology of heterosexual motherhood should be explored.

The use of mixed methods to identify significant relationships among variables should also be considered in future studies. For example, previous studies on female doctoral students and academic women have focused on their socialization experience (Gardner, 2008), degree progress (Maher et al., 2004), health behavior (Vancour, 2009), Canadian Ph.D. students (Wall, 2008), ideology of a "good mother" and a "good student" (Sears, 2001), academic life and motherhood based on institutional type (Wolf-Wendel & Ward, 2006), and stress levels (Arric, Young, Harris & Farrow, 2011).

Last, for researchers interested in student retention, another area to examine is the women who did not persist in their doctoral endeavors. It is important to understand the learning that transpired from their experience and how they translate their own experiences in order to assist other women to keep them in the academic pipeline.

FINAL THOUGHTS

This study found that mothering had important implications for doctoral student mothers. Like Brown and Watson (2010), I found that the experience of motherhood has a profound effect on women pursuing their doctorate as they navigate their academic responsibilities, domestic demands and professional pursuits. While research on this particular demographic is slowly gaining traction (Brown & Watson, 2010; CohenMiller, 2013; Eisenbach, 2013), additional studies need to be undertaken to further understand and reveal the complexity that exist for mothers within doctoral programs. The implications that arose from these findings highlight the role of institutions of higher education, educators, and mentors of graduate students. Female graduate students, in particular women pursuing a terminal degree, are an important resource in academia and beyond. Support of these women can be made possible through implementation of work-family programs and changes and enhanced academic and personal leave policies. It is hoped that this study will bring attention to the experiences of women in graduate school and initiate dialogues about how to help support their learning and development amidst a background of complexity in life roles.

REFERENCES

Allan, P., & Dory, J. (2001). Understanding doctoral program attrition: An empirical study. *Faculty Working Papers.* Retrieved July 25, 2011, from http://digitalcommons.pace.edu/lubinfaculty_workingpapers/17

Armenti, C. (2004). May babies and post tenure babies: Maternal decisions of women professors. *Review of Higher Education, 27*(2), 211–231.

Arric, L., Young, K., Harris, S., & Farrow, V. (2011). An analysis of stress levels of female graduate students in an online program. *Advancing Women in Leadership, 31,* 144–152.

Bailey-Iddrisu, V. L. (2010). Women of African descent: Persistence in completing a doctorate. *FIU Electronic Theses and Dissertations.* Paper 327. Retrieved March 10, 2011, from http://digitalcommons.fiu.edu/etd/327.

Bandura, A. (1986). *Social foundations of thought and action: A social cognitive theory.* Englewood Cliffs, NJ: Prentice-Hall.

Berelson, B. (1960). *Graduate education in the United States.* New York, NY: McGraw Hill.

Berg, H. M., & Ferber, M. A. (1983). Men and women graduate students: Who succeeds and why? *Journal of Higher Education, 54*(6), 629–648.

Berkeley, K. (1999). *The women's liberation movement in America.* Westport, CT: Greenwood Press.

Bird, G. W. (1984). Family and career characteristics of women and men college and university administrators. *Journal of National Association of Women Deans, Administrators, and Counselors, 44*(4), 21–28.

Bomar, P. J. (2004). *Promoting health in families: Applying family research and theory to nursing* (3rd ed.). Philadelphia: WB Saunders.

Boswell, T. (2003). Campus childcare centers. Retrieved August 14, 2011, from *ERIC Digest* at http://www.ericdigests.org/2005-2/child-care.html.

Brown, L., & Watson, P. (2010). Understanding the experiences of female doctoral students. *Journal of Further and Higher Education, 34*(3), 385–404.

Carney-Crompton, S., & Tan, J. (2002). Support systems, psychological functioning, and academic performance of nontraditional female students. *Adult Education Quarterly, 52*(2), 140–154.

Cater-Steel, A. (2010). *Women in engineering, science and technology: Education and career challenges.* Hershey, PA: IGI Global.

Chater, S. S., & Hatch, A. A. (1991). Student, worker, mom: On campus, in need. *Educational Record, 72*(1), 32. Retrieved December 23, 2011, from http://eric.ed.gov/?id=EJ421591

CohenMiller, A. (2013). Motherhood in academia: A grounded theory pilot study of online texts. *The Researcher, 25*(1), 47–66.

Cole, J. R., & Zuckerman, H. (1987). Marriage, motherhood, and research performance in science. *Scientific American, 255,* 119–125.

Comings, J., & Cuban, S. (2002). *Sponsors and sponsorship: Initial findings from the second phase of the NCSALL Persistence Study.* Retrieved December 2, 2013, http://www.ncsall.net/index.html@id=221.html.

Coser, L. (1974). *Greedy institutions.* New York, NY: Free Press.

Council of Graduate Schools. (2008). *PhD completion rates.* Retrieved May 23, 2011, from http://www.cgsnet.org/portals/0/pdf/N_pr_PhDC_bookII.pdf.

Council of Graduate Schools. (2009). *Ph.D. completion and attrition: Findings from exit surveys of Ph.D. completers.* Retrieved May 29, 2011, from http://www.phd completion.org/information/Executive_Summary_Exit_Surveys_Book_III.pdf.

Council of Graduate Schools. (2013). *Graduate enrollment and degrees.* Retrieved June 9, 2014, from http://cgsnet.org/ckfinder/userfiles/files/GEDReport_2012.pdf.

Correll, S. J., Benard, S., & Paik, I. (2007). Getting a job: Is there a motherhood penalty? *American Journal of Sociology, 112*(5). Retrieved January 3, 2014, from http://www.jstor.org/stable/10.1086/511799

Creswell, J. W. (2007). *Research design: Qualitative inquiry and research design: Choosing among five approaches* (2nd ed.). Thousand Oaks, CA: Sage.

Cuny, J., & Aspray, W. (2000). Computing research association. *CRA Home | Computing Research Association.* Retrieved January 12, 2011, from http://www.cra.org/uploads/documents/resources/...history.../rrwomen.pdf.

Denham, G. (2007). Adult students in postsecondary education. Retrieved September 8, 2013, from http://www4.aacrao.org/semsource/sem/index2cc6.html?fa=view&id=3569

Eisenbach, B. (2013). Finding a balance: A narrative inquiry into motherhood and the doctoral process. *The Qualitative Report, 18*(34), 1–13.

Emlen, A. C., & Koren, P. E. (1984). *Hard to find and difficult to manage: The effects of child care on the workplace.* Portland, OR: Regional Institute for Human Services.

England, K. (1996). Mothers, wives, workers: The everyday lives of working mothers. In K. England (Ed.), *Who will mind the baby? Geographies of child care and working mothers* (pp. 109–122). New York, NY: Routledge.

Evans, E., & Grant, C. (2009). *Mama PhD: Women write about motherhood and academic life.* New Brunswick, NJ: Rutgers University Press.

Fischer, L., Gokalp, G., Gupton, J., Pena, E. V., & West, I. J. Y. (2011). Exploring effective support practices for doctoral students' degree completion. *College Student Journal, 45*(2), 310–323.

Gardner, S. K. (2008). Fitting the mold of graduate school. *Innovative Higher Education, 33*, 125–138.

Gardner, S. K. (2010). Contrasting the socialization experiences of doctoral students in high- and low-completing departments: A qualitative analysis of disciplinary contexts at one institution. *Journal of Higher Education, 81*(1), 62–68.

Garey, A. I. (1999). *Weaving work and motherhood.* Temple University Press, Philadelphia: USA.

Gasser, H. S., & Gasser, R. F. (2008). Facing the baby blues? Serving student parents on campus college. Retrieved May 10, 2011, from http://nccp.nsuok.edu/LinkClick. aspx?\fileticket=zrDuYc4lopQ%3D&tabid=77

Gerencher, K. (2002). *More women invest in grad school: Females drawn to teaching, health care; lag in business.* Retrieved March 22, 2011, from http://www.marketwatch.com/story/more-women-attend-grad-school-even-with-family-duties?pagenumber=2

Golde, C. M. (1998). Beginning graduate school: Explaining first year doctoral attrition. *New Directions for Higher Education, 101*, 55–64.

Golde, C. M. (2005). The role of the department and discipline in doctoral student attrition: Lessons from four departments. *Journal of Higher Education, 76*(6), 669–700.

Golde, C. M., & Dore, T. M. (2001). *At cross purposes: What the experiences of doctoral students reveal about doctoral education.* Philadelphia, PA: Report prepared for the Pew Charitable Trusts. Retrieved from on June 18, 2012 from http://www.phd-survey.org.

Goulden, M., Frasch, K., & Mason, M. A. (2009). *Staying competitive: Patching America's leaky pipeline in the sciences.* Center for American Progress. Retrieved December 8, 2010, from http://www.americanprogress.org/issues/2009/11/women_and_sciences.html

Grant, L., Kennelly, I., & Ward, K. B. (2000). Revisiting the gender, marriage, and parenthood puzzle in scientific careers. *Women's Studies Quarterly, 28*, 62–85.

Gray, J. D. (1983). The married professional woman: An examination of her role conflicts and coping strategies. *Psychology of Women Quarterly, 7*, 235–243.

Greenhouse, S. (2011). Keeping women in science on a tenure track. —NYTimes. com. The economy and the economics of everyday life—Economix Blog— *NYTimes.com*. Retrieved May 11, 2011, from http://economix.blogs.nytimes. com/ 2011/01/05/keeping-women-in-science-on-a-tenure-track/

Grenier, R. S., & Burke, M. (2008). No margin for error: A study of two women balancing motherhood and Ph.D. studies. *Qualitative Report, 13*(4), 581–604.

Heinrich, K. (1995). Doctoral advisement relationships between women: On friendship and betrayal. *Journal of Higher Education, 6*(4), 447–469.

Herzig, A. (2002). Where have all the students gone? Participation of doctoral students in authentic mathematical activity as a necessary condition for persistence toward the Ph.D. *Educational Studies in Mathematics, 50*(2), 177–212.

Herzig, A. (2004). Becoming mathematicians: Women and students of color choosing and leaving doctoral mathematics. *Review of Educational Research, 74*(2), 171–214.

Hochschild, A. (1997). *The time bind: When work becomes home and home becomes work.* New York, NY: Metropolitan Books.

Hochschild, A., & Machung, A. (2003). *The second shift.* New York, NY: Penguin Books.

Home, A. (1992). Women facing the multiple role challenge. Adult women studying social work and adult education in Canada: A study of their multiple role experiences and of supports available to them. Ottawa, Canada: Social Sciences and Humanities Research Council of Canada, Ottawa (Ontario). Retrieved January 14, 2012 from http://www.eric.ed.gov/ERICDocs/data/ericdocs2sql/content_storage_01/0000019 b/80/15/8d/e7.pdf

Home, A. (1997). Learning the hard way: Role strain, stress, role demands, and support in multiple role women students. *Journal of Social Work Education, 33*, 335–347.

Home, A., & Hinds, C. (2000). *Life situations and institutional supports of women university students with family and job responsibilities.* Unpublished manuscript, Department of Educational Studies, University of British Columbia, Vancouver, Canada. Retrieved from http://www.edst.educ.ubc.ca/aerc/2000/ homea&hindsc- final.pdf

Kearns, H., Gardiner, M., & Marshall, K. (2008). Innovation in PhD completion: The hardy shall succeed (and be happy!). *Higher Education Research and Development, 27*(1), 77–89.

LaMonica, L. T. (2010). *Becoming a worker-mother: Understanding the transition.* Ed.D. dissertation, North Carolina State University, United States -North Carolina. Retrieved February 29, 2011, from Dissertations & Theses: Full Text.

Link, T. (2006). Adult student persistence: What factors make the difference? Retrieved December 6, 2012, from www.portal.state.pa.us/portal/server.pt/ document/fn06retention_pdf⊠

Lovitts, B. E. (2001). *Leaving the ivory tower: The causes and consequences of departure from doctoral study.* Lanham, MD: Rowman & Littlefield.

Lynch, K. (2008). Gender roles and the American academe: A case study of graduate student mothers. *Gender & Education, 20*(6), 585–605. doi: 10.1080/09540250802213099

Maher, H., Ford, M., & Thompson, C. (2004). Degree progress of doctoral students: Factors that constrain, facilitate and differentiate. *Review of Higher Education, 27*(3), 385–408.

Mallinckrodt, B., & Leong, F. T. (1992). Social support in academic programs and faculty environments: Sex differences and role conflicts for doctoral students. *Journal of Counseling and Development, 70,* 716–723.

Marshall, C., & Rossman, G. B. (2006). *Designing qualitative research* (4th ed.). Thousand Oaks, CA: Sage.

Mason, M. A. (2008a). Balancing act: Frozen egg. *Chronicle of Higher Education.* Retrieved February 12, 2011, from http://ucfamilyedge.berkeley.edu/ Frozen%20Eggs%20Article.pdf.

Mason, M. A. (2008b). Do babies matter in science? Advice. *Chronicle of Higher Education.* Retrieved March 11, 2011, from http://chronicle.com/jobs/news/2008/10/2008101701c.htm

Mason, M. A. (2009). Why so few doctoral-student parents? *Chronicle of Higher Education.*

Mason, M. A., & Goulden, M. (2002). Do babies matter? *Academe, 88*(6), 21–27.

Mason, M. A., & Goulden, M. (2004a). Do babies matter (Part II)? *Academe, 90*(6), 3–7.

Mason, M. A., & Goulden, M. (2004b). Marriage and baby blues: Redefining gender equity in the academy. *Annals of the American Academy of Political and Social Science, 596,* 86–103.

Mason, M. A., Goulden, M., & Frasch, K. (2011). Keeping women in the science pipeline. *Annals of the American Academy of Political and Social Science, 638*(1), 141–162.

Maxwell, J. A. (2005). *Qualitative research design: An interactive approach* (2nd ed.). Thousand Oaks, CA: Sage.

McBride, A. B. (1990). Mental health effects of women's multiple roles. *American Psychologist, 45,* 381–384.

Medved, C. E., & Heisler, J. (2002). A negotiated order exploration of critical student-faculty interactions: Student-parents manage multiple roles. *Communication Education, 51*(2), 105–120. doi:10.1080/03634520216510

Mikolaj, E. L., & Boggs, D. L. (1991). Intrapersonal role conflicts of adult women undergraduate students. *Journal of Continuing Higher Education, 39*(2), 13–19.

Monroe, K., Ozyurt, S., Wrigley, T., & Alexander, A. (2008). Gender equality in academia: Bad news from the trenches, and some possible solutions. Retrieved June 2, 2014, from http://www.apsanet.org/imgtest/PerspectivesJun08MonroeEtal.pdf

Murphy, B. L., & Cloutier-Fisher, D. (2002). Balancing act: Graduate school and motherhood. *Great Lakes Geographer, 9*(1), 37–47.

Narvaez, D. (2012). Mothers, dialogues, and support: Commentary on Garvey & Fogel and on Duarte & Gonçalves. In M. C. Bertau, M. M. Gonçalves, & P. T.F. Raggat (Eds.), *Dialogic formations: Investigations into the origins and development of the dialogical self.* Charlotte, N.C.: Information Age Publishers.

National Center for Education Statistics. (2010a). *Profiles of graduate and first professional students: Trends from selected years 1995–1996 to 2007–2008.* Retrieved June 12, 2011, from http://nces.ed.gov/pubs2011/2011219.pdf.

National Center for Education Statistics. (2010b). *Trends in student financing in graduate and first-professional education: Selected years 1995–1996 to 2007–2008.* Retrieved June 12, 2011, from http://nces.ed.gov/pubs2011/2011217.pdf.

National Postsecondary Student Aid Study. (2013). *Full-scale methodology report.* Retrieved February 12, 2014, from http://nces.ed.gov/pubs2014/2014041_1.pdf

National Science Foundation, Division of Resources Studies. (1994). *Women, minorities, and persons with disabilities in science and engineering.* Retrieved June 12, 2011, from http://www.nsf.gov/statistics/wmpdse94/chap7/sidebar3.htm.

Nerad, M. (1991). *Doctoral education at the University of California and factors affecting time-to-degree.* Oakland: Office of the President, University of California.

Nicolson, P. (2002). Having it all: Choices for today's superwoman. Hoboken, NJ: John Wiley & Sons.

O'Donnell, L. N. (1985). *The unheralded majority: Contemporary women as mothers.* City, Canada: D.C. Heath.

O'Keefe, D. (1991). Women and leadership in American Universities. *McGill Journal of Education, 26*(3), 303–322.

Ostrove, J. M., Stewart, A. J., & Curtin, N. L. (2011). Social class and belong: Implications for graduate students' career aspirations. *The Journal of Higher Education, 82*(6), 748–774.

Patton, M. Q. (2002). *Qualitative research and evaluation methods* (3rd ed.). Thousand Oaks, CA: Sage.

Palladino Schultheiss, D. E. (2009). To mother or matter: Can women do both? *Journal of Career Development, 36,* 25–48.

Presser, H. B. (1995). Are the interests of women inherently at odds with the interests of children or the family? A viewpoint. In K. O. Mason & A. Jensen (Eds.), *Gender and family change in industrialized countries.* New York, NY: Oxford University Press.

Schulz-Aellen, M. F. (1997). *Aging and human longevity.* York: PA: Maple Vail Press.

Sears, A. L. (2001). Of diapers and dissertations: The experiences of doctoral student mothers living at the intersection of motherhood and studenthood. Digital Dissertations.

Smith, L., Appio, L. M., & Cho, R. J. (2012). The feminization of poverty: Implications for mental health practice. In P. K. Lundberg-Love, K. L. Nadal, & M. A. Paludi (Eds.), *Women and mental disorders: Understanding women's unique life experiences.* Santa Barbara, CA: Praeger.

Strauss, A., & Corbin, J. (1997). *Grounded theory in practice.* Thousand Oaks, CA: Sage.

Strayhorn, T. (2012). *College students' sense of belonging: A key to educational success for all students.* New York, NY: Routledge.

Thibodeaux, A. M. (2003). *A critical analysis of female doctoral students advisement: Implications for program satisfaction.* Digital Dissertations.

Tinto, V. (1975) Dropout from higher education: A theoretical synthesis of recent research. *Review of Educational Research, 45,* 89–125.

Tinto, V. (1993). *Leaving college: Rethinking the causes and cures of student attrition* (2nd ed.). Chicago, IL: University of Chicago Press.

Tiu Wu, A. (2013). *Learning to balance: Exploring how women doctoral students navigate school, motherhood and employment* (Doctoral dissertation). Retrieved from Pro-Quest UMI Dissertations Publishing. (3556422)

U.S. Department of Labor, Bureau of Labor Statistics, *Employment and Earnings,* January 2011, Annual Averages. Retrieved March 15, 2012, from http://www.bls.gov/opub/ee/empearn201101.pdf

Vancour, M. L. (2009). Motherhood, balance and health behaviors of academic woman. *Journal of the Association for Research on Mothering, 11*(1), 151–166.

Vejar, C. M., Madison-Colmore, O. D., & Ter Maat, M. B. (2006). Understanding the transition from career to fulltime motherhood: A qualitative study. *The American Journal of Family Therapy, 34,* 17–31.

Villadsen, A. W., & Tack, M. W. (1981). Combining home and career responsibilities: The methods used by women executives in higher education. *Journal of National Association of Women Deans, Administrators and Counselors, 45*(1), 170–175.

Veney, C., O'Green, V., & Kowalik, T. F. (2012). Role strain and its impact on nontraditional students' success. Retrieved January 19, 2011, from http://www4.aacrao.org/semsource/sem/index0790.html?fa=view&id=5292.

Wall, S. (2008). Of heads and hearts: Women in doctoral education at a Canadian University. *Women's Studies International Forum, 31,* 219–228.

Ward, K., & Wolf-Wendel, L. (2004). Academic motherhood: Managing complex roles in research universities. *Review of Higher Education, 27,* 233–257.

Ward, K., & Wolf-Wendel, L. (2007). The chair's role in helping faculty negotiate work and family issues. *The Department Chair, 18*(1), 1–3.

Weidman, J. C., Twale, D. J., & Stein, E. L. (2001). *Socialization of graduate and professional students in higher education: A perilous passage?* San Francisco, CA: Jossey-Bass.

Wolf-Wendel, L., & Ward, K. (2006). Academic life and motherhood: Variations by institutional type. *Higher Education, 52*(3), 487–521.

PART I

SUPPORTING NEEDS OF ADULT LEARNERS:

Building Futures through Curriculum Revision

CHAPTER 6

ENHANCING MEANING IN ADULT HIGHER EDUCATION THROUGH ARTS BASED LEARNING

Lisabeth Eames Capozzi
Penn State University

If adult educators want to make higher education sustainable, they must be open to re-examining how we approach teaching and learning in light of today's increasingly interconnected world. People make sense of their world in multiple ways (Erikson, 2007; Gardner, 2006; Lindeman, 1926) tapping into not only the cognitive domain, but also engaging the emotional, spiritual, kinesthetic, and experiential ways of knowing. One method of making meaning that can engage the affective, kinesthetic, experimental, spiritual, and social constructivist domains of knowing is the use of arts-based learning processes that involve artistic or creative forms of expression (Dirkx, 2001; Green, 1995; Kasworm, Rose, & Ross-Gordon, 2010; Kowalski, 1988; Lawrence, 2005; Orr, 2005; Tisdell, 2003; Wodlowski, 2008).

This chapter is a discussion of the effective use of artistic modes of expression as creative tools to enhance adult learning within academia. First

Building Sustainable Futures for Adult Learners, pages 117–131
Copyright © 2015 by Information Age Publishing
All rights of reproduction in any form reserved.

is a discussion of the importance of arts-based learning as a complement to higher education classes such as education, social sciences, and business. Next is a discussion of the different types of arts-based teaching methods, some of which will be explored in more detail within the chapter. This will be followed by an in-depth literature review of the successful use of arts-based creative teaching and learning methods within higher education settings. The chapter will conclude with implications and suggestions for practice and curriculum design, as well as potential areas for future research.

IMPORTANCE OF ARTS-BASED WAYS OF LEARNING

Following a long tradition of positivistic approaches to education, higher education has been characterized by an emphasis upon the rational and provable within the social sciences as well as engineering and the physical sciences. However, there have been notable dissenters to this approach along the way such as Lindeman (1926, 1961), Greene (1995), and Dirkx (2001), who have advocated for more creative, meaningful, and diverse approaches to the learning experience, those meant to engage all the senses, feelings, and spirit beyond just the mind. One powerful way to deepen the meaning of learned material for many adult learners is through arts-based teaching methods.

Greene speaks of the power of the imagination, in the book *Releasing the Imagination* (Greene, 1995). Greene takes the reader on a compelling and richly woven journey showing how powerfully the imagination and its related forms of art and literature can shape learning throughout the lifespan. Greene weaves in numerous examples from her own life and the lives of others of the power of the imagination; she then shows how the imagination can play a role in providing superior education and in driving social change.

Lindeman spoke of the power of the arts to more fully engage adult learners in making sense of their worlds. "Light comes from learning—just as creation comes everywhere—through integrations, syntheses, not through exclusions" (Lindeman, 1923, published 1961, p. xiv). Professors in higher education cannot simply limit our teaching practices to the cognitive domain. As Lindeman points out, "if adult education is to save itself from degenerating into another type of intellectualism, it will teach people how to make their thinking glow with the warmth of honest feeling" (Lindeman, 1923, p. 105). Lindeman suggests that the aesthetics of the arts is a powerful way to engage the warmth of these feelings. Lindeman also suggests the most potent use of arts-based education involves active participation in the arts through doing, creating, and discussing, rather than passively observing. This emphasis on the kinesthetic component of arts-based learning is described below.

We get a more intense feeling of beauty and more valid meanings when the "sense of beauty" is an accompaniment of some activity... The highest aesthetic values are probably not those which somehow get themselves registered in books, paintings, statues, but rather those which are realized in motion. (Lindeman, 1926, p. 107)

Building arts-based learning methods into the teaching curriculum also engages other forms of knowing beyond the cognitive, extending into more holistic learning methods favored by non-western societies (Merriam, Caffarella & Baumgartner, 2007). Art can engage these alternative ways of knowing, including "the spirit, mind, body, and emotional components of learning," (Merriam, Caffarella & Baumgartner, 2007, p. 238). Indeed, the constructivist approach to learning, whereby learners actively create or co-create meaning, can use the arts as vehicles to enhance critical dialogue during the learning process (Merriam, Caffarella, & Baumgartner, 2007). Constructive developmental theory stresses that the most profound way in which adults develop is in how we know ourselves and our environment, and how we construct these understandings (Kasworm, Rose, & Ross-Gordon, 2010). "Artistic knowing can" also "be transpersonal, creating an opening to transcend the small individual self," (Kasworm, Rose, & Ross-Gordon, 2010, p. 38).

An arts-based approach has been found to be helpful in educating adults within the workplace (Manning, Verenikina, & Brown, 2010), management and leadership development (Edwards, 2013; Gaia Wicks & Rippin, 2010; Hansen & Bathhurst, 2011; Kerr & Lloyd, 2008), the healthcare setting (Cueva, 2010; de la Croix, Rose, Wildig, & Willson, 2011), and within secondary education (Davis, 2012; Lewis & Rainer, 2012). Interestingly, little has been written of the use of arts-based learning within the academic classroom, or its effectiveness as a method of increasing meaning and enhancing learning.

VARIETIES OF ARTS-BASED LEARNING METHODS

Those wishing to build arts-based learning into their academic curriculum have a rich variety of options from which to choose. Auto-ethnography is a powerful tool to help individuals, especially those who have been historically marginalized, to tell their personal stories in their own words (Davis, 2012), and this art form can be linked to the subject matter being studied in a number of ways. Photography, in a process known as photovoice, has likewise been used as a method by which adults can tell their personal stories (Morton, 2012).

Poetry is a powerful way to ground a subject matter (Lorde, 1984; Pendergast & Leggo, 2007), and can be a powerful punctuation at the beginning or conclusion of an academic class session. Poetry can also be created collectively with socially constructed meaning, which will be discussed below. Aside from poetry, the power of the written word, through either original composition, collective creation, or through reading works of literature, has the power to forge bonds with the existing psychological schemas of meaning held within the human brain. Music can be used to create mood, to portray meaning through both the melody as well as the lyrics, or to involve students more viscerally in the learning process. Examples of the use of music and song within learning communities will be discussed in the next section.

Artistic images engage the visual and the affective capacities of learners and can take many forms. Learners can create visual art either singly or collectively within the classroom or as part of the class requirements. Original art creations enable the learner to bring whatever skill level they possess into creating images that are most meaningful to themselves. Visual art in the form of paintings, drawings, or sculpture can be shown either directly or through computer images or books, and these can be powerful symbolic representations of the issue at hand that is being studied. The potential forms of visual arts are almost limitless and can even take such forms as quilts, needlework, or finger paints.

Film is an art form that is seen more often in today's academic classrooms and combines the visual with the dramatic to help students see the meaning of areas of study in ways that mere reading or hearing cannot. Likewise, drama can be used as a powerful tool outside of conventional sources of film. Live drama, where learners either watch or participate, can mirror life in such a way as to drive home the importance of an area of study. With ready access to computers and the Internet, today's classrooms are beginning to employ the use of digital stories as ways in which students can creatively convey their thoughts, studies, or stories and share them with others. The next sections discuss the ways in which arts-based learning has been employed within higher education, as well as in other forms of adult learning. The limited literature on the effectiveness of arts-based learning methods is also discussed (Armstrong, 2005; Carroll, 2008; Conti, Amabile, & Pollak, 1995; Karsten, 2004).

Literature on the Successful Use of Arts-Based Learning within Academia

Although the literature providing examples of arts-based learning actually within the academic classroom is sparse, there are a few examples available. From these supports can be gathered that arts-based learning heightens the depth of meaning within higher education and may lead to better memory of the subject matter. There is also some research that suggests that arts-based learning may lead to better academic performance and higher self confidence in some students (Carroll, 2008).

Types of Learning Enhanced through Arts-Based Teaching Methods

Arts-Based Learning Heightens Depth of Meaning

The use of creative expression within the context of teaching classes in higher education is clearly linked to a deepening of meaning for the learners. Armstrong (2005) used a combination of autobiography, storytelling, and photography in a process called auto-photography where adults recorded important life images over a 12-year period. This method was later used with non-traditional college students. The students used critical reflection methods in considering the images they selected and found this a powerful method for increasing meaning within the learning environment. This approach, reflecting Freire's liberatory educational philosophy (Merriam, Caffarella, & Baumgartner, 2007), was used as a means to help marginalized individuals re-construct an identity founded upon choice rather than societal imposed stereotypes (Armstrong, 2005). This study, along with other qualitative research on the use of photography to increase meaning within a learning environment (Morton, 2012), demonstrate that the use of creative expression can deepen meaning, and thus learning, and lead to increased social justice within higher education. The arts provide a medium by which individuals can more personally relate to the material being learned and apply personal meaning to the subject matter.

Improved Memory for Learned Material

Adults learn and process information in many different ways, including cognitive, aesthetic, spiritual, kinesthetic, affective, and somatic learning (Erikson, 2007; Gardner, 2006; Kasworm, Rose, & Ross-Gordon, 2010; Wlodkowski, 2008). Creative expression is naturally linked to affective and aesthetic learning, but there is some evidence that the use of creativity can actually increase memory of learned material. In a two by three factorial design, Conti, Amabile, and Pollak (1995) demonstrated that students who engaged in a creative pre-task showed increased memory for material they read five days afterward, compared to students who engaged in a non-creative pre-task. They also varied the motivational framework of the participants by giving instructions that either emphasized the importance of the material for passing a test (extrinsic motivation), focused solely on the task itself (intrinsic motivation), or emphasized both testing as well as importance of the task (both). They found that the creative pre-task improved long-term retention, but only in the intrinsic motivation condition.

They conclude that creativity can improve learning but only in the absence of evaluation expectation. This would suggest that the use of arts-based instructional techniques can improve learning if the emphasis at the time of learning is not strongly associated with testing and evaluation.

This assertion is further supported by the cognitive processing research on how long term memory is coded into thematic groups, or schemas, within the brain (Swartz, 2011; Taylor & Lamoreaux, 2008). During the past twenty years, neuroscience has made advances that suggest that there are great individual differences in how people learn (Glass, Meyer, & Rose, 2013). Because artistic ways of knowing transverse multiple learning domains, the use of arts-based teaching techniques can more readily engage a diverse group of learners. This suggests that, "providing multiple, accessible, and flexible pathways to learning may be a promising strategy to address" the complexity of the learning environment (Glass, Meyer, & Rose, 2013, p. 99). In another study with artistically gifted students in a leading post-secondary art college, Carroll (2008) demonstrated that by engaging multiple ways of learning, teachers could link learning to students' specific strengths and both increase academic learning as well as build confidence. By providing multiple ways in which content is presented, discussed, and reflected upon, the instructor can engage diverse groups of learners across a variety of the affective, recognition, and strategic neural networks.

Enhanced Learning of Subject Matter

In another study based within higher education, Karsten (2004) demonstrated enhance learning in a college computer applications course through using holistic, arts-based teaching methods. "Participants who previously felt a lack of expertise with computer technology were transformed by discoveries that enhanced creativity and confidence" (Karsten, 2004, p. 1). The students were able to construct knowledge of computer applications through the use of drama and storytelling, perhaps because "storytelling, creative drama, multimedia, presentation skills, facility with the World Wide Web are all forms of creative problem-solving" (Karsten, 2004, p. 13). By using a holistic, arts-based approach, the instructor was able to help students successfully construct technical knowledge in the computer related subject of the course.

Music has been successfully used across a number of higher education curricula to teach various concepts (Levy & Byrd, 2011). Issues of culture, diversity, and black history have all been taught using either music or musical lyrics to illustrate key concepts. In college courses in the helping professions, music has been taught as a means to facilitate forms of therapy, to increase the helper's own empathy, and to understand differences among people (Levy & Byrd, 2011). Music has also been shown to help illustrate key sociology concepts and to promote discussions in sociology courses.

All of these studies within the higher education arena lend support to the contention that arts-based learning enhances adult learning and memory. Although the research on the effectiveness of arts-based learning methods within higher education are limited, there are a number of studies within other learning venues that provide further evidence of the link between artistic ways of knowing and learning. For example, adults who engaged in an arts-based professional development training program found the arts-based approach to be a refreshing change from traditional lecture-style training and to be a powerful form of learning (Manning, Verenikina, & Brown, 2010) They also appreciated the hands-on, interactive nature of the arts-based learning approaches used.

In another study, medical students enjoyed using creative writing, theater, and movement sessions as part of their medical school curriculum and felt that "learning the techniques that are helpful to actors in overcoming anxiety and presenting themselves confidently" would help them to overcome performance anxiety and "to present themselves more confidently as doctors" (de la Croix et al., 2011, p. 1094). This increase in confidence through employing the arts in learning was also found by Carroll (2008). In a grounded theory study, Sutherland (2012) studied the descriptive essays of executive MBA students in a leadership development program who participated in a class on choral conducting (Sutherland, 2012). Thematic analysis of the students' essays revealed that this arts-based learning format allowed them to engage in aesthetic reflexivity that created memories that could inform their future leadership practices. Sutherland developed a three-stage model grounded in experiential learning theory of the experiential processes involved in arts-based learning methods, which suggests that artistic experiences create aesthetic workspaces that then place people in the frame of mind to reflect which, in turn, creates powerful memories that embed learning and can drive future action (Sutherland, 2012). Participants related how the choral class created a separate aesthetic workspace where the music "relaxed us and put us into a completely different situation than we normally were in at school" (participant Calvin from Sutherland, 2012, p. 30). Sutherland points out that the mere presence of art or music does not "transform environments into aesthetic workspace" but "as an emergent property of art and music, aesthetic workspaces...arise through interactions between individuals, groups and artistic products and events" (Sutherland, 2012, p. 31). It is through this interactive discourse that arts-based learning can create meaning and imbed subject matter more thoroughly. In arts-based learning, the art object or activity is made meaningful through the human interaction with it. It is "a dynamic part of a more pervasive system *with* which we make experience *through* emerging associations of the arts-based experience" (Sutherland, 2012, p. 35, emphasis in original).

The creative arts were employed to teach literacy to adults in post-conflict Northern Ireland by enabling instructors to engage learners in text-free methods which helped level the playing field and promote social justice and equality (Mark, 2008). Non-text methods used included the visual arts, drama, storytelling, image theater, and music. Using a participative approach, learners helped shape the literacy project as well as engage in the learning process. By actively engaging in the art making process, from storytelling to collage creation, learners were able to represent their own unique points of view and gain legitimacy within the learning process rather than coming from a place of less than (Mark, 2008).

The process of making art has been used within the academic workplace itself, resulting in informal learning and deepened relationships among participants (Upitis, Smithrim, Garbati & Ogden, 2008). Faculty at Queen's University in Nigeria participated in an art-making group in conjunction with a seven-year project studying the effectiveness of an art education program called Learning Through the Arts. This group spent roughly two hours per week making art together over almost six years and found that working together in the creative process of art making led to better group cohesiveness and interpersonal understanding, where members gained better insight into one another. The co-construction of art was also found to be personally fulfilling and brought "colour, and imagination, and real possibility" into the work world (Upitis, Smithrim, Garbati, & Ogden, 2008, p. 16).

The literature is also richly populated with examples of theoretical articles as well as expository pieces proposing the use of more arts-based education or arts-based learning approaches within schools or organizations. For example, Nissley (2010) suggests that, "economic adversity can inspire extraordinary innovation" within U.S. businesses "if we choose to engage the arts as enablers of business creativity" (Nissley, 2010, p. 9). In advocating for the use of drama in secondary education in order to propagate authentic learning, Lewis and Rainer (2012) suggest that drama can "promote learning across a wide range of curriculum areas" beyond simply the humanities and other forms of the arts to include "English and literacy, Science and Personal Social and Health Education" (Lewis & Rainer, 2012, p. 1). The use of the dramatic arts can engage learning that is authentic in that it is "rooted in real-world issues, dilemmas and narratives" (Lewis & Rainer, 2012, p. 1).

Greene is a strong advocate for the use of arts within elementary and secondary education, and many of her arguments easily apply to higher education as well (Greene, 1995). Greene suggests the need to integrate imagination through the arts into education in order to energize students and drive change. "We must make the arts central in school curricula because encounters with the arts have a unique power to release the imagination" (Greene, 1995, p. 27). Student engagement occurs through the process of creating linkages between the subject matter being taught and the storied lives of the students themselves. "Through proffering experiences of the arts and storytelling, teachers can keep seeking connection points among their personal histories and the histories of those they teach" (Greene, 1995, p. 42).

Dirkx (2001) speaks of a "vision for integrating emotion within alternative ways of knowing in adult and higher education," that includes "the role of the arts in adult learning," (Dirkx, 2001, p. 16). In discussing the role of transformative learning within adult education, Dirkx suggests that effective adult learning must include a "more integrated and holistic understanding of subjectivity . . . that reflects the intellectual, emotional, moral, and spiritual dimensions of our being in the world" (Dirkx, Mezirow, & Cranton, 2006, p. 125). Dirkx expresses the desire to know more of the "inner world" of people, that subjective arena that "reveals its presence through art, poetry, music, theater, and film," and that is ". . . refracted through the lens of image and metaphor and story" (Dirkx, Mezirow, & Cranton, 2006, p. 127). Beyond helping us to understand this inner world, the arts can impact "the deep meaning-making processes that are at the core of learning" (Dirkx, Mezirow, & Cranton, 2006, p. 130). Arts-based learning methods can drive the meaning-making process within higher education. The next section discusses suggestions for adopting arts-based learning methods in academic curriculum.

Implications for Practice and Curriculum Design

The ways in which the arts can be built into academic curriculum design are limitless. Educators bring their own life experiences, subject matter knowledge, and comfort levels to their teaching endeavors. Likewise, each class of students can greatly vary in their learning preferences, personal experiences, and comfort levels. However, it may be helpful for educators to have examples of ways in which the arts can be integrated into their lesson plans so that they can have the flexibility to select what might work best in each given situation.

Story-Based Methods of Artistic Learning

There are many examples in the literature of different art forms used to tell a story; either an autobiographical story or another story related to the subject being learned. For example, GED students who had previously dropped out of high school where given an assignment called autoethnography (Davis, 2012), which involved writing their own stories about what led to their leaving high school. Once they had completed the written version of their story, they each gave a verbal reading in front of others in their academic community. These auto-ethnographies offered both read-ers and listeners alternative ways of understanding why people drop out of high school and had the potential to dislodge previously held stereo-types on this topic. These first-person accounts told of the students' very human struggles and their subsequent quest to complete their education. The auto-ethnographies could also be shared in other classrooms by having different people play individual parts as they retold the stories. In this way, the actors reading the stories found themselves part of the story and were likewise powerfully impacted. This is an example of how arts-based learning can be used to illuminate the experiences of marginalized groups.

Photography is another story-based approach that can be used to give voice to marginalized groups. Armstrong (2005) used a combination of au-tobiography, storytelling, and photography in a process called auto-photog-raphy to enhance meaning among adults over a 12-year period, and later with non-traditional college students. Students photographed images that were meaningful to them in their lives. The images could be "actual or metaphoric examples of his or her life world" (Armstrong, 2005, p. 34), and students were instructed to critically reflect on the meaning of the images and then share these reflections in groups. Armstrong states that "autobiography and photography are remarkably powerful media because others often recognize some part of their own life experiences in what they see and read" (Armstrong, 2005, p. 33). This Freirean approach was used "to influence the identity of participants, allowing them to move away from imposed identity toward an emergent identity of choice" (Armstrong, 2005, p. 38), where auto-photography could be used as "a forum for the lesser known voices of society to be heard" (Armstrong, 2005, p. 41). Armstrong found that this process drew students closer together and led to broader perspectives and an expanded sense of social justice (which is often a goal of many higher education classes, particularly in the social sciences). Stu-dents realized that "everybody has some part of his or her life that 'delivers an interesting message'" (p. 41).

Digital story telling has become a widespread arts-based method used in academia. Students use computer software to create a story that may include still photographs, video, voice narration, and music to tell such stories as the history of a movement or scientific discovery, biographical histories, career aspirations, or creative development processes. Extending the art of storytelling to the digital arena, digital story telling can engage learners that are more comfortable with computer-based technologies than with traditional written discourse (Karsten, 2004).

Written Forms of Artistic Learning

While term papers continue to flourish within academia, there are other arts-based forms of writing that can anchor learning when added into a varied learning curriculum. Poetry can act as a poignant source of grounding in a subject matter (Lee & Taylor, 2011; Lorde, 1984; Prendergast& Leggo, 2007; Stuckey, 2009). A class of chemical engineers who are studying chemical spills may benefit from anchoring the beginning of class with a poem about the community effects of such an occurrence. A political science class studying war may find learning enhanced by closing class with a powerful poem about war.

Poetry can be written individually or collectively. There are many methods of launching a collective poetry endeavor, such as having students individually write descriptive words about the topic of learning and then blend these together. Another approach is to have one person write a line of poetry on what a certain experience meant to them, and then pass it to the next person who adds their own (see Trentin, 1999). Before passing it to the third person, the top line is covered by folding the paper. In this way, each person who adds a line can only see the line before theirs. A student or the professor reads the entire finished poem, which blends in the various individual thoughts into a form that can be quite lovely.

Creative writing can also be used to embed learning as students create and portray their own metaphors and thoughts pertaining to the area of study. Students can also record thoughts pertaining to the subject being studied through formats such as student journals, but these tend to be less arts-based and treated more as a requirement by students, since they are usually evaluated for content, leading to less creativity and more emphasis upon meeting the required objectives. Literature, both classical and current, can be used to introduce variety and meaning to academic studies in areas that are not based on English or literature. For example, a professor teaching students to speak Arabic may include works of literature that involve the Arabic culture as a means of engaging students and piquing interest in mastering the language.

Music Based Methods of Learning

Music in all of its various forms can be used within the classroom to create mood, engage emotion, and enhance meaning (Sussman & Kossak, 2011; Tisdell, 2006). Music is one of the easiest ways to introduce an alternative way of knowing into the classroom. What is also powerful, but less common, and arguably more challenging to blend into academic curriculum, is the art form of dance. Yet dance engages multiple ways of knowing, including the kinesthetic domain involved with movement (Minton, 2008). Just the process of watching a dance performance can engage the parts of the brain linked to movement as the watcher's mind "mirrors" the movements of the dancers (Cheville, 2005).

Drama Based Ways of Learning

Drama is a form of storytelling that can take many forms. Students can either view or participate in the various forms of drama within the classroom. In *Drama at the Heart of Secondary School: Projects to Promote Authentic Learning,* Lewis and Rainer (2012) provide a wealth of teaching techniques utilizing drama that can be used while teaching a wide variety of topics. These techniques could easily transfer to the academic classroom environment. Next, the paper will discuss some possible areas for research to focus on going forward.

POTENTIAL AREAS OF FUTURE RESEARCH

The most glaring gap in the literature is the lack of research studies demonstrating the impact that arts-based forms of instruction have on adult learning in the academic classroom. Studies that employ a qualitative or mixed methods design can help better inform practitioners on how students experience classrooms that include arts-based learning activities and how these experiences differ from the traditional approach to academic instruction. A related area of research to explore is how arts-based approaches can mediate cultural differences in the classroom, perhaps providing more universal approaches to learning. Finally, there are a number of examples in the literature of arts-based learning that has been successfully used in adult learning venues other than the academic classroom. Some of these studies could be replicated within the academic setting.

CONCLUSIONS

Both college administrators as well as researchers in adult education need to focus more closely on how creative expression can enhance the learning experience across the spectrum of university classes. As Armstrong (2005) suggests, the arts can be transforming to students. For example, "when stories of people's lives are delivered as art, they are more powerful (life changing) for the presenter as much as for the listeners" (Armstrong, 2005, p. 42). University administrators can help foster creativity and alternative ways of learning through fostering an interdisciplinary approach to learning across the university's different colleges (Kandiko, 2012). Such an approach not only leads to better learning connections on important issues, but also can help open professors and students alike to the possibility of blended forms of learning within each discipline.

In *Releasing the imagination: Essays on education, the arts, and social change,* Greene (1995) offers a compelling argument for the importance of the arts in primary and secondary education to develop citizens engaged and committed to social change. Her arguments apply equally well to higher education. Greene argues that the human condition is integral to education and suggests a multi-disciplinary approach to help us to build an increasing awareness of the social complexity around us. Green contends, "we must make the arts central in school curricula because encounters with the arts have a unique power to release the imagination" (p. 27). Greene advocates the arts, including literature, as a critical educational vehicle to help us imagine things as they could be.

REFERENCES

Armstrong, K. B. (2005). Autophotography in adult education: Building creative communities for social justice and democratic education. *New Directions for Adult and Continuing Education,* (107), 33–44. Retrieved from http://search.proquest.com/docview/62018585?accountid=13158

Carroll, K. L. (2008). In their own voices: Helping artistically gifted and talented students succeed academically. *Gifted Child Today, 31*(4), 36–43. Retrieved from http://search.proquest.com/docview/61939178?accountid=13158

Cheville, J. (2005). Confronting the problem of embodiment. *International Journal of Qualitative Studies in Education, 18*(1), 85–107.

Conti, R, Amabile T. M., & Pollak, S. (1995). The positive impact of creative activity: Effects of creative task engagement and motivational focus on college students' learning. *Personality and Social Psychology Bulletin, 21,* 1107–1116.

Cueva, M. (2010). Readers' theatre as cancer education: An organic inquiry in Alaska awakening possibilities in a living spiral of understanding. *Journal of Cancer Education, 25*(1), 3–8. doi:http://dx.doi.org/10.1007/s13187-009-0002-4

Davis, A. (2012). Performing hidden voices: The path from high school to GED. *Live session at the American Association of Adult and Continuing Education Conference,* Las Vegas, NV.

de la Croix, A., Rose, C., Wildig, E., & Willson, S. (2011). Arts-based learning in medical education: The students' perspective. *Medical Education, 45,* 1090–1100.

Dirkx, J. M. (2001). The power of feelings: Emotion, imagination, and the construction of meaning in adult learning. *New Directions for Adult and Continuing Education, 89,* 63–72. Retrieved from http://search.proquest.com/docview/62362314?accountid=13158

Dirkx, J. M., Mezirow, J., & Cranton, P. (2006). Musings and reflections on the meaning, context, and process of transformative learning: A dialogue between John M. Dirkx and Jack Mezirow. *Journal of Transformative Education, 4*(2), 123–139. doi: 10.1177/1541344606287503

Edwards, G. (2013). Critical and alternative approaches to leadership learning and development. *Management Learning, 44*(1), 3–10.

Erikson, H. L. (2007). Philosophy of holism. *Nursing Clinics of North America, 42*(2), 139–164.

Gardner, H. (2006). *Multiple intelligences: New horizons in theory and practice.* New York, NY: Basic Books.

Glass, D., Meyer, A., & Rose, D. H. (2013). Universal design for learning and the arts. *Harvard Educational Review, 83*(1), 98–119,266,270,272. Retrieved from http://search.proquest.com/docview/1326778711?accountid=13158

Greene, M. (1995). *Releasing the imagination: Essays on education, the arts, and social change.* San Francisco: Jossey-Bass.

Hansen, H., & Bathhurst, R. (2011). Aesthetics and leadership: In A. Bryman, D. Collinson, & K. Grint et al. (Eds.), *The SAGE handbook of leadership.* SAGE: London, 255–266.

Kandiko, C. B. (2012). Leadership and creativity in higher education: The role of interdisciplinarity. *London Review of Education, 10,* 191–200.

Karsten, S. (2004). WebStars: Holistic, arts-based college curriculum in a computer applications course. *College Quarterly, 7*(1), 1–16. Retrieved from http://search.proquest.com/docview/61839260?accountid=13158

Kasworm, C. E., Rose, A. D., & Ross-Gordon, J. M. (Eds.) (2010). *Handbook of adult and continuing education.* San Francisco: Jossey-Bass.

Kerr, C., & Lloyd, C. (2008). Pedagogical learnings for management education: Developing creativity and innovation. *Journal of Management and Organization, 14,* 486–503.

Kowalski, T. J. (1988). *The organization and planning of adult education.* Albany, NY: State University of New York Press.

Lawrence, R. L. (2005). Knowledge construction as contested terrain: Adult learning through artistic expression. In R. Lawrence (Ed.), *Artistic ways of knowing: Expanded opportunities for teaching and learning.* New Directions for Adult and Continuing Education, no. 107 (pp. 3–11). San Francisco: Jossey-Bass.

Lee, N., & Taylor, P. (2011). Insights from an E-dialogue of practitioners on arts in transformative learning. *Journal of Adult and Continuing Education, 17*(2), 80–95. Retrieved from http://search.proquest.com/docview/1018482125?accountid=13158

Levy, D. L., & Byrd, D. C. (2011). Why can't we be friends? Using music to teach social justice. *Journal of the Scholarship of Teaching and Learning, 11*(2), 64–75. Retrieved from http://search.proquest.com/docview/889929628?accountid=13158

Lewis, M., & Rainer, R. (2012). *Drama at the heart of secondary school: Projects to promote authentic learning.* Taylor and Francis. Retrieved from http://www.eblib.com

Lindeman, E. C. (1926). *The meaning of adult education.* Montreal: Harvest House.

Lindeman, E. C. (1961). *The meaning of adult education.* Norman, OK: Oklahoma Research Center for Continuing Professional and Higher Education.

Lorde, A. (1984). Poetry is not a luxury. From *Sister Outsider.* Freedom, CA: Crossing Press.

Manning, C., Verenikina, I., & Brown, I. (2010). Learning with the arts: What opportunities are there for work-related adult learning? *Journal of Vocational Education and Training, 62*(3), 209–224.

Mark, R. (2008). Exploring equality through creative methods of learning in adult literacy: Findings from a peace funded project. *Adult Learner: The Irish Journal of Adult and Community Education,* 77–83. Retrieved from http://search.proquest.com/docview/61801268?accountid=13158

Merriam, S. B., Caffarella, R. S., & Baumgartner, S. M. (2007). *Learning in adulthood: A comprehensive guide* (3rd ed.). San Francisco: Jossey-Bass.

Minton, S. C. (2008). *Using movement to teach academics: The mind and body as one entity.* Rowman & Littlefield Education: Lanham, Md.

Morton, J. L. (2012). *Giving light to voice: Individual stories of photovoice research participation* (Doctoral Dissertation). Available from ProQuest Dissertations and Theses, 346. (1034598622).

Nissley, N. (2010). Arts-based learning at work: Economic downturns, innovation upturns, and the imminent practicality of arts in business. *Journal of Business Strategy, 31*(4), 8–20.

Orr, D. (2005). Minding the soul in education: Conceptualizing and teaching the whole person. In J. Miller, S. Karsten, D. Denton, D. Orr, & I. Kates (Eds.), *Holistic learning and spirituality in education: Breaking new ground* (pp. 87–100). Albany: State University of New York Press.

Prendergast, M., & Leggo, C. (2007). Astonishing wonder: Spirituality and poetry in educational research. *International Handbook of Research in Arts Education* (pp. 1459–1477). The Netherlands: Springer.

Stuckey, H. (2009). Creative expression as a way of knowing in diabetes adult health education. *Adult Education Quarterly, 60,* 46–64.

Sussman, A., & Kossak, M. (2011). The wisdom of the inner life: Meeting oneself through meditation and music. *New Directions for Adult and Continuing Education,* 2011, 55–64. doi: 10.1002/ace.421

Sutherland, I. (2012). Arts-based methods in leadership development: Affording aesthetic workspaces, reflexivity and memories with momentum. *Management Learning, 44*(1), 25–43, doi: 10.1177/1350507612465063.

Swartz, A. (2011). Wisdom, the body, and adult learning: Insights from neuroscience. In E. Tisdell & A. Swartz, *Adult education and the pursuit of wisdom.* San Francisco. Jossey-Bass.

Taylor, K., & Lamoreaux, A. (2008). Teaching with the brain in mind. *New Directions for Adult and Continuing Education, 119,* 49–59. doi: 10.1002/ace/305

Tisdell, E. (2003). *Exploring spirituality and culture in adult and higher education.* San Francisco: Jossey-Bass.

Tisdell, E. (2006). Teaching to the music of my soul: Catching on to the beat of learners' hearts. In W. Ashton & D. Denton (Eds.), *Spirituality, ethnography, & teaching: Stories from within* (pp. 264–277). New York, NY: Peter Lang International Academic Publishers.

Trentin, G. (1999). Telematics, narrative and poetry: The parole in jeans project. *International Journal of Instructional Media, 26*(4), 409. Retrieved from http://search.proquest.com/docview/204260698?accountid=13158

Upitis, R., Smithrim, K., Garbati, J., & Ogden, H. (2008). The impact of art-making in the university workplace. *International Journal of Education & the Arts, 9*(8), 1–25. Retrieved from http://search.proquest.com/docview/61967481?accountid=13158

Wlodkowski, R. J. (2008). *Enhancing adult motivation to learn: A comprehensive guide for teaching all adults.* San Francisco: Jossey-Bass.

CHAPTER 7

RE-VISIONING GENERAL EDUCATION THROUGH THE ADULT BACCALAUREATE LEARNING EXPERIENCE

Diane Dick
Capella University

While questions regarding general education purpose, content, and outcomes have long been of interest in higher education discussions (AACU, 2011; DiConti, 2004; Fong, 2004; Gaff, 2004; Schlossberg, Lynch, & Chickering, 1989; Sheridan, 1998), these questions have not as frequently been considered in light of adult learning needs and the adult-focused baccalaureate experience. Adult-focused baccalaureate programs usually adapt existing general education programs to adult learning needs. Such adaptations acknowledge the adult learning differences, as identified in experience and as captured in adult learning literature. They simultaneously affirm the essentiality to the degree of the general education requirement as designed for post-high school learners (Dick, 2011). Adult-focused baccalaureate programs continue to grow in enrollments and in market share of baccalaureate degree seekers (U.S. Department of Education, 2012).

Building Sustainable Futures for Adult Learners, pages 133–155
Copyright © 2015 by Information Age Publishing
All rights of reproduction in any form reserved.

Given adults' increasing presence as learners in baccalaureate programs, how might the values, interests, goals, and expectations of adult degree seekers offer some perspectives on the purpose(s) for, and content of, the general education component?

As a starting place for exploring this question, a qualitative study completed in 2011 sought to understand how academic decision-makers in traditional colleges navigated the adaptation of their general education curricula for use in adult-focused programs (Dick, 2011). In November 2013, at a joint conference of AHEA and AAACE, a round table discussion examined four premises derived from that study's findings. Two of the premises focused on the role of general education in the baccalaureate program and in the institution: (a) General education is the distinguishing component for the baccalaureate degree; and (b) General education is the expression of the character of the academic institution offering the degree. The other two focused on adult learner characteristics and expectations in relation to their educational pursuits: (c) Adult learners share traits with post-high school college learners, but have distinguishing characteristics that should be accounted for; and (d) Adult learners are interested in educational transformation as well as academic credentialing. The participating adult education professionals applied their expertise during the discussion in order to critique, modify, and enrich understanding of the proposed four premises regarding the intersection between adult learning and general education. Participants engaged with the issues of adult learners' experiences of general education and considered how theories of adult learning interact with ideas of what it means to be broadly and deeply educated beyond professional preparation.

This chapter's discussion of these issues begins with a brief review of the literature considered and the findings resultant from the 2011 study, focusing particularly on general education as adapted for adult-focused liberal arts programs. That review is followed by an exploration of each of the four premises derived from the study, the observations and discussion contributed by participants at the round table, and a discussion of the implications for adult-focused general education, and general education as the expression of the university's character.

The 2011 Study: Adult-focused Revision of Traditional General Education Curricula

The dissertation study completed in 2011 was a multi-case study of three traditional private colleges where adult-focused degree program models were created from existent traditional baccalaureate programs. Participants were decision-makers serving in academic leadership, in faculty, and as directors of general education or adult degree programs. Participants described their institution's curriculum revision decisions and discussed their own perceptions and ideals regarding their institution's approach to general education, the baccalaureate program, and adult learners. The researcher administered two open-ended questionnaires and one intervening interview to gather this information. Published and internal documents provided by the colleges were also examined and analyzed, and data were analyzed using question and concept categories (Yin, 1989) to identify themes, disparities, gaps, and general characteristics of responses regarding general education, adult learners, the adult degree program, and the baccalaureate degree.

Overview of Literature Informing the Study

The question regarding what it means to be college educated is inextricably linked to concepts of general education (Glyer & Weeks, 1998; Lucas, 1998). The American Association of Colleges and Universities (AACU) described a liberal arts education as "a philosophy of education that empowers individuals with broad knowledge and transferable skills, and a strong sense of values, ethics, and civic engagement" (AACU, 2011, Advocacy section, para. 3). As such, the liberal arts core of a baccalaureate degree, expressed in the general education curriculum, would reach beyond the specialized preparation for professional life and promote the inculcation of "broad knowledge and transferable skills" in a common curriculum shared by students across disciplines, "empower[ing]" students for lifelong learning (AACU, 2011).

General Education as the Evolving Expression
of Community Aspirations

From the establishment of the first American university in the seventeenth century through the present, concepts of general education have changed in concert with changes in contemporary concepts of what it means to be college-educated. The earliest colonial universities, such as Harvard, Yale, and William and Mary, were established to prepare young men for vocations in the ministry, with a "single canon" (Awbrey, 2005, p. 2) of required study rooted in the classical languages, philosophy, metaphysics, and science (Geiger, 1999; Glyer & Weeks, 1998; Lucas, 1998). Emerging from the European Reformation, these American universities reflected European influences of Calvinist, Puritan, and Anglican theology. As colonies grew increasingly prosperous, local communities were able to support those institutions and establish new ones, influencing their academic institutions to diversify their offerings and develop educational programs for secular professional programs in law, medicine, and business (Geiger, 1999). This relationship between academic institutions and the communities they serve has persisted, and universities and colleges continue to respond to the needs of a developing culture and economy, adding curricula that support preparation for a widening array of professions.

As economies and industries change, employer and occupational needs also change, requiring a reexamination of knowledge needs, degree requirements, and a reconsideration of the value proposition for the liberal arts core, as well as for the baccalaureate degree itself. Job growth continues to favor the more highly skilled and paid service sectors, including areas such as finance, marketing, management, education, and health care, all relying heavily on the non-technical intellectual competencies found in a liberal arts curriculum (Carnevale & Strohl, 2001). Economist Alan Greenspan explored the interrelationship between economic development and the need for a liberal arts emphasis in education, arguing that, "the ability to think abstractly will be increasingly important across a broad range of professions . . . fostered through exposure to philosophy, literature, music, art, and languages . . . all aspects of human intellectual activity" (Greenspan, 1999, para. 28). As Greenspan predicted, intellectual skills and advanced knowledge, synthesis and application of literary, artistic, and philosophical histories, embodying "all aspects of human intellectual activity," are increasingly requisite for participation in a dynamic and unpredictable marketplace. While adult degree seekers and education providers alike recognize the need for advanced professional preparation and respond to that need through their participation in adult-focused programs, it is the general education component of these programs that offers the greatest opportunity for formal exposure to "all aspects of human intellectual activity."

The Academy's Struggle to Respond to a Changing Learning Community

While the abstract and critical thinking skills pursued through liberal arts study might have the potential to strengthen the ongoing ability of working adults to be resilient participants in a rapidly changing work culture, nevertheless, academic communities, business communities, and degree-seekers tend to avoid any significant re-examination of the liberal arts and the general education curriculum in response to societal changes (Carnevale & Strohl, 2001). Although academic communities are well-equipped to study, understand, and predict educational needs trending in the larger community, they are often not constituted as an organizational culture to respond nimbly to those needs, nor are academic organizations' finances such that the best changes can easily happen. Further, employers and adult learners are not usually in a position to advise academic decision-makers regarding curriculum revision. "[A]dult learners and their employers, while perhaps appreciating the value of questions about the role of the liberal arts and the higher purposes of education, may tend to see these as questions for another day—after they have graduated" (Dick, 2011, p. 70).

There are other impediments to a re-examination of the general education or liberal arts component. A 2001 study examining general education development found that, despite the fact that a majority of institutions surveyed were engaged in ongoing general education review and reform projects, an analysis of responses to the survey also suggested that, for many of these institutions, "shared educational values" were not considered or even articulated in the review and reform process (Ratcliff et al, 2001, p. 18). Gaff (2004) later observed that local academic communities can come to neglect the philosophical foundations that informed their core curriculum, in part due to turnover in faculty over time, as well as a departmental focus on resources and staffing, rather than a focus on philosophies of learning (Gaff, 2004; Trainor, 2004).

This tendency to neglect "shared educational values" and to attend instead to more immediate local departmental and administrative factors is where the local institution departs from the industry-wide dialogue regarding general education reform. Recent literature on general education reform considers the larger issues of the values and philosophies informing general education and focuses on a series of preferences arising from those philosophies: (a) curricular prescription versus curricular choice; (b) an information-orientation versus a skills-orientation ("Are courses built to inculcate ongoing learning skills in various disciplines or are they built to instill knowledge of historically accumulated content of those disciplines?"); and (c) a liberal arts-oriented curriculum versus a professional preparation focus (Dick, 2011; DiConti, 2004; Geiger, 1999; Glyer & Weeks, 1998; Latzer, 2004b; Lewis & Legler, 1998; Lucas, 1998; Sheridan, 1998; Tetreault & Rhodes, 2004).

Discussions of these issues have often focused on questions of content selection, particularly regarding how power holders and cultural ideology influence the selection or marginalization of various perspectives on subjects such as literature, philosophy, the arts, politics, history, and even the sciences (Latzer, 2004b; Sheridan, 1998; Tetreault & Rhodes, 2004). A contrasting concern is that some traditional knowledge foundations may be disappearing as the expectations for a common curriculum diversify until intentionality disappears. In a study of the general education curricula of fifty Ivy League, "Big Ten," and other prominent colleges and universities (Latzer, 2004a), the American Council of Trustees and Alumni articulated seven overarching content categories that college trustees and alumni considered essential to the general education foundation of the baccalaureate curriculum, and evaluated these 50 institutions to see how their "core curriculum" addressed the seven categories. Of the 50 institutions, only one addressed as many as six of the seven categories. Seventy percent of the institutions addressed three or fewer of the seven categories and nearly half (48%) of the academic institutions addressed two, one, or none of the core curriculum categories. None of the institutions addressed all seven categories (Latzer, 2004a).

In a later commentary for the *Chronicle of Higher Education,* Latzer observed that most other institutions around the country followed the lead of the Ivy League institutions in revising their general education curricula, all settling on the Ivy League model of a "distribution system" maximizing student choice within broad subject categories and de-emphasizing a clear articulation of outcomes (Latzer, 2004b). Most distribution system models encourage a proliferation of narrowly defined courses reflecting special interests and designated as fulfilling general subject areas. Students are often motivated to complete their "generals" as painlessly as possible so that they can concentrate on their major coursework.

Latzer found that non-demanding courses in popular and familiar subjects tend to draw the most student registrations. Unfamiliar subjects that require the development of new learning skills tend to wither and die from lack of interest. Latzer noted in his analysis that such "trivialization" of the general education core in practice served as a contradiction to the promotion of the general education core in the stated philosophy, noting as an example, Princeton's description of general education requirements that "transcend the boundaries of specialization and provide all students with a common language and common skills" which, Latzer commented, "simply cannot be taken seriously" (Latzer, 2004b, p. B20). Thus, when general education curriculum developers exclude considerations of their institution's mission, values, and philosophy, disregard emergent scholarly work in curriculum development, and ignore the curricular expectations of alumni and trustees, it is likely that they will also neglect the considerations of the particular needs of adult students.

Overview of Study Findings

The Role of General Education in the Baccalaureate Degree

Study participants were academic leaders, program decision-makers, and full-time faculty who were in some way involved in the adult-focused revision of their college's general education curriculum. The participants described the features of a baccalaureate degree that distinguish it from profession-specific training. The distinguishing features they identified were (a) the general education and liberal arts core; (b) the values, mission and learning philosophy of the college; (c) an advanced analytical framework; and (d) assessment of outcomes. The two most consistently identified features were the general education component or liberal arts core, and the inculcation of institutional values, mission, and learning philosophy. The values, mission, and learning philosophy of the institution was recognized as a core distinguisher of the baccalaureate degree, which academic decision-makers confirmed was established through common foundations courses required for all undergraduate degree-seekers as part of their general education requirements. Another feature of the baccalaureate degree consistently mentioned was an advanced analytical framework. Participants saw this feature established through the program of general education, and, ideally, reiterated and interwoven throughout the courses for the major. Finally, participants emphasized the importance of an institution-wide approach to outcomes assessment that articulated and measured knowledge and skills outcomes for the curriculum, reinforcing the purpose and value of the requirements for the degree (Dick, 2011).

The Purpose and Content of the General Education Curriculum

The consensus among participants regarding the distinguishing role of general education in the baccalaureate degree seemed to inform participants' views of the purposes of the general education curriculum, particularly, to establish an institutionally-based philosophy of learning, to cultivate a framework for advanced analytical thinking, and to build knowledge and skills, measuring them through assessment of learning. The content of a general education curriculum, then, would offer a breadth of knowledge comprised of information outside the content of the major and common to all who complete the degree. The curriculum would cultivate skills that are not particular to the major, but which foster adaptability in life-long learning within and beyond the major. Finally, the curriculum would be rooted in the philosophy of the learning community, reflecting the ethos of the local academic institution, and aligning with a larger culture of knowledge-building and interchange (Dick, 2011).

General education program structure for each of the colleges' traditional baccalaureate degrees tended to be comprised of subject categories that could be satisfied through an undergraduate student's choice among a wide array of courses that qualified to fulfill that requirement (see Figure 7.1). Thus, one student, in attempting to fulfill a cultural diversity requirement could choose a course on gender and global commerce, while another student might choose a course on Japanese baseball, and another might study abroad for a semester in Brazil. Finally, in the required core of this common baccalaureate general education curriculum is the (usually freshman level) introduction to college learning course, which combines the institution's core values and mission to establish the institution's philosophy of learning and to inculcate the ethos of the college. Figure 7.1 captures the supporting structure of the liberal arts requirements on the

Distribution Course Array　　　　　　**Required Core**

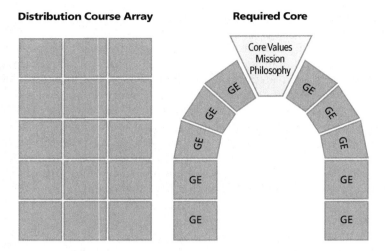

Figure 7.1 Traditional general education structure.

right, with the accumulated array of corresponding general education distribution courses on the left.

Traditional Academics' Perceptions of Adult Learner Differences

Study participants were academics at traditional private colleges that had adult-focused baccalaureate programs. Their responses to questions regarding the differences between adult college learners and traditional post-high school college students mingled to reveal six emerging themes: Adult learners (a) are alert to a sense of calling; (b) have an experiential context for what they learn; (c) value efficient achievement of their goals; (d) bear the weight of past failures and current responsibilities; (e) greet irrelevance and incompetence with impatience; and (f) are in some ways very much like their 18-year-old counterparts (Dick, 2011).

Participants remarked repeatedly regarding the effect of adult learners' sense of calling as they pursued their degree programs, and participants saw this as a significant difference from most post-high school college students. This sense of calling was understood by participants to be not only a motivator for returning to or initiating college study, but more significantly was understood to influence the quality of their academic performance. One participant captured the reason for adults' sense of calling insightfully, remarking on the "vocational maturity" of adult students, while noting that recent high school graduates, while also adult, are in the discovery stage of their professional pursuits, and hold their goals more tenuously.

On the other hand, adult degree seekers were also seen to expect to encounter new experiences since their decision to pursue a degree (unlike the traditional freshman) was an intentional departure from the expected path in mid-career. One participant, a professor of literature, explained that while adult learners expect that their required courses can be shown to be useful for their goals, they also are willing to follow their instructors into new territory. "They are willing to go with you . . . sort of an 'OK, I've never read much literature, but I'll take what you put out there!'" (Dick, 2011, p. 153). The consensus among participants was that adult life experience created a rich context within which new learning could flourish and proliferate meaning and where new skills gained immediate relevance and practical value in solving old or emerging problems.

Alongside the benefits of greater life experience, participants also discussed the "baggage" accumulated in the personal histories of adult learners, representing past academic failures, false starts in vocational direction, and missteps in professional development. Participants noted the insecurity that many adult learners bring to their studies and described the toll of life responsibilities on adults' ability to persist in their academic progress. Struggling to learn amid these challenges inherent in their situations, adult learners were seen to be more intolerant of irrelevant learning, bureaucratic impediments, and academic incompetence in their college learning experience. Participants agreed that adult learners, while generally more serious, more dogged, and more capable in their studies, were in some ways more fragile, and more dependent on well-crafted academic program models that accounted for adult learning needs.

Nevertheless, one assertion of participants was that in some significant ways, traditional post-high-school students were not so different from adult learners. One faculty member who was a co-founder of his college's adult-focused degree programs, explained that thirty years of program development from an adult learning perspective had taught him and his colleagues how to view traditional college students as experienced adults, inculcating the experiential learning perspective in the youngest college freshman:

> What we have learned is that everybody has experience that should be respected, even an 18–24 year old. I think what we learned from making learning experiential, and trying to draw on students' experience, we can draw on the experience of traditional students, too—they know something about distribution, inventory, things that go wrong, as observers rather than as decision-makers, some realistic sense of the complexity of business . . . If we take it seriously, we respect it, we pull it out of them, it's not 'OK you are here to learn from me you don't know anything.' We don't treat the traditional students as a blank slate. (Dick, 2011, pp. 153–154)

The Adaptation of the General Education Curriculum for Adult-Focused Programs

Alongside these participant perceptions regarding the characteristics of adult learners and their descriptions of their institution's general education program, participants also described how general education was revised for the adult-focused degree program at their college. Participants identified the central challenge that they believed shaped the development of the adult programs, which was to maintain the integrity of the general education curriculum while adapting the program to accommodate adult learners. Several questions complicated this effort, including: (a) How can we retain the content, but allow changes in delivery? (b) Might delivery changes offer an opportunity to rethink curricula? (c) Will changes in delivery alter the learning experience in unintended ways? (d) Can (and should) the role of faculty governance be maintained in the adult program? (e) Can the new program be an integral part of the college's mission, or is it merely a revenue supplement for the real work of the college?

Faculty and administrators involved in the development of an adult-focused revision of their general education program agreed—emphatically so—that the content of the general education curriculum would remain the same for adult learners. Scheduling, advising, teaching methods, availability of student services were auxiliary issues that needed to be reconsidered, but the curriculum itself also needed to be adjusted to allow flexibility and ensure that adult students had access to the required learning for their programs. One college president explained that his college's program attempted to demonstrate adaptability without compromising learning outcomes. "I think people have tried to take seriously the importance, both of general education and the different place in life for non-traditional adult learners." He acknowledged that addressing adult learning differences was new territory for his faculty and deans, having developed programs solely for post-high-school students through the years. "We . . . then tried to put it together for people at very different points [in their lives]. There has been an attempt to incorporate learning styles, experience, different life pressures. People have tried to be flexible without selling out" (Dick, 2011, p. 156).

The challenge to ensure that "selling out" did not happen was faced mainly at the program director and faculty level. One faculty member explained how the scheduling changes influenced new strategies for teaching and learning: "We had to figure out how to take a big chunk of time in the weekend lengthy courses and make it work. The courses were really very engaging, using small group work with reporting out and presentations" (Dick, 2011, p. 157). This participant also noted that the weekend schedule was a mixed blessing, explaining that while the extended time off during the work week allowed more time for reflection and assignment development, having the week days off also tended to break continuity and limited learner access to developmental feedback along the way. This program developed other strategies that fostered inter-discipline collaboration and encouraged new approaches to delivering required general education content, designing courses around carefully articulated themes or issues, allowing learners to synthesize the perspectives of different disciplines to "foster a scholarly cross-discipline collegiality in developing integrative approaches to the liberal arts portion of the general education requirements" (Dick, 2011, p. 158). Another faculty member who was a founding director of the college's adult degree program explained the rationale for the interdisciplinary collaborations: "We wanted to create interesting, compelling courses that would give the biggest bang for the buck in terms of pulling together key knowledge from general education…students really loved those courses!" (p. 159).

Such an approach, a history professor in the program observed, was more demanding for both faculty and students:

> It's not just a challenge for the students, but for the faculty. In the first liberal arts course, a six credit course, I could teach them some of the aspects of critical thinking as a historian, but I also had to teach them about understanding literature and dealing with the world through literary imagination, to ask questions like a philosopher. (p. 158)

However, the adult degree program for this college (renamed in the study as "Alexandrine College") was the exception, in that the baccalaureate program was revised in its entirety to account for adult learning characteristics, and this revision was done by full-time faculty who were together responsible for the ongoing development and integration of all academic programs at the college. Participants from the other two colleges (renamed in the study as "Benedictine" and "Clementine") were less satisfied with the delivery-only adaptation, expressing their worry, cynicism, and even alarm regarding their institutions' approach to preserving the general education content in their adult programs. In particular, faculty who were not asked to contribute to the actual formation of their college's adult focused program tended to look at the program with significant distrust. One faculty member described the faculty response when their administration had introduced the plan for the new program:

> While [we] wanted to talk about this, the vice president said that "all we are talking about here is a delivery system—it doesn't have anything to do with curriculum—it's not something that faculty really need to have a say in." And so we didn't say anything about it—we accepted it. We weren't happy about it, but it's a delivery system, which meant the curriculum would be identical— there is no need to alter anything. For a long time, I think that's the way it

was—the distance sites had to take their same curriculum and figure out ways to implement it. (Dick, 2011, p. 160)

A faculty colleague at the same college characterized the effects of evening scheduling of adjunct-taught general education courses this way:

... a pretty thorough lack of intentionality... "OK, we aren't going to be able to staff a full range of general education courses, so we'll just get somebody to teach something and that will be the general education course for that time." Practical realities of those programs have led to not much consideration of adult learners in terms of the curriculum... practical issues have really trumped the more idea-based or more coherent curricular issues. (Dick, 2011, p. 135)

Several administrators and faculty acknowledged this lack of intentionality as a hazard of the effort to accommodate adult learners through alternate delivery methods. One administrator noted the administrative impracticality of offering some general education distribution courses when only a few students needed it and acknowledged that it was often more cost effective to send those few students to a community college to obtain the requirement. Several of the adult programs that were studied regularly scheduled only one course option to fulfill a general education requirement for all learners. This resulted in adult learners at one campus having no flexibility in fulfilling that requirement. For example, one college required a year of language study for the baccalaureate degree. The only adjunct qualified for foreign language instruction taught Russian, so any adult students needing that requirement studied Russian, regardless of their own learning goals.

In these cases, despite the intention of program developers to preserve the academic requirements, and simply change the delivery model, the academic experience for adult degree-seekers was considerably different from that of post-high-school freshman, for whom the general education programs were originally designed. Nowhere was this more evident than in the omission of the first-year requirement that served as an introduction to baccalaureate study and to the ethos of the college. Each college had such a requirement for incoming freshman, and the course could not be satisfied through transfer credit, since it was considered a foundation for study at that particular college. The implication of this non-transfer rule was that the institution-specific course was necessary to inculcation of the mission and values of the college granting the degree. Nonetheless, at Benedictine and Clementine, this foundational course was waived for students in the adult program, as it was seen as not necessary.

The omission of this requirement is significant, considering that an inculcation of institutional values and mission was considered by all participants to be a standard—and even defining—feature of their general education curriculum. The director of one of the programs that eliminated this requirement recognized the problem and indicated that an effort was being made to find other ways to include the adult program's students in the culture of the college and inculcate the college's mission and values. Another academic administrator described the concerns expressed by regional accreditors regarding adult programs developed at private colleges, observing that "other institutions have gotten hit quite hard for their lack of a [unified college] philosophy, and lack of quality control in their off campus programs." Reiterating the common phrase—"cash cows"—used derogatorily by faculty regarding their college's adult degree programs, she commented:

> You can't just milk them for all they're worth. You have to figure out how they relate to the rest of your programs, you have to ensure quality control, put resources into it and assess whether you really are meeting your outcomes in these programs too. (Dick, 2011, p. 164)

Participants who contributed directly to the founding of their adult programs all cited academic assessment as a critical piece in the effort to adapt general education curricula. The director of general education at one college acknowledged the challenges of developing a robust assessment model for the general education requirements (whether in the traditional or the adult program) was challenging, given that so many of the distribution courses that could satisfy specific requirements (nearly 300 courses that qualified to satisfy fourteen requirements) were actually developed as courses for a major. When used for general education, these courses needed to identify the outcomes that answered to the general education requirements and determine how those outcomes would be assessed—an ongoing effort that tended to fall to the bottom of tenured faculty members' priority list. In the adult-focused programs, this became more difficult in the colleges where full time faculty were entirely divorced from the academic oversight of their courses as taught in the adult programs. As one faculty member commented, "So, since we were excluded from any decision-making power, essentially we gave [the adult program] no thought at all" (p. 162). An academic administrator described the unanticipated logistical problems in extending outcomes assessment to the adult programs, as an unaddressed quality control issue: "We haven't really figured out how to outcomes assess things here, when we've got the programs here, and faculty [t]here . . . the whole package will be a lot harder" (p. 164).

When colleges allow course and adjunct availability to dictate adult learners' options for fulfilling general education requirements, eliminate first-year courses introducing the institutional ethos as a framework for study, and neglect a robust assessment of the general education outcomes in both the traditional and adult programs, the result is a general education

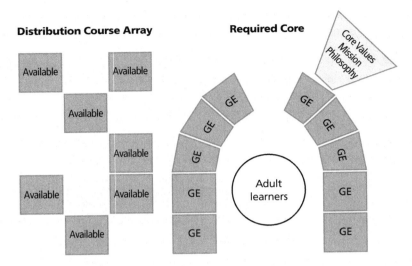

Figure 7.2 General education in adult degree programs: "The Same."

experience for adult learners that differs not only in delivery method, but in academic outcomes. In programs revised for adults (see Figure 7.2), the structure looks very different from the structure originally designed for post-high-school learners (Figure 7.1).

This very different model of "the same" general education experience exposes, not only the lack of intentionality and lack of philosophical orientation for the adult learner experience, but, by implication, also undermines the college's commitment to its educational and learning philosophy and iterates the lack of intentionality in the original general education model (Figure 7.1). While a proliferation of choice among general education distribution courses may arguably be a benefit (as in one college's 300 course choices eligible to satisfy fourteen requirements), it is also a symptom of a school's lack of intentionality regarding the outcomes of those distribution requirements. When that wide range of choices is reduced by administrative convenience to eighteen available courses for fourteen requirements, intentionality is all but eliminated. When a college requires that all incoming students, including transfer students, complete a course inculcating the college's educational philosophy but exempts adult degree-seekers from that requirement, the college' commitment to that philosophy can legitimately be questioned.

Discussion of the Four Premises

The adult-focused model of general education programs and the traditional model from which it was adapted provided a discussion starting place for the round table participants at the AHEA 2013 conference. The participants considered four premises regarding general education and adult learners and critiqued those premises based on their knowledge of theories of adult learning, as well as their expertise derived from working with adult learners and adult-focused programs. Their critiques offered further insights regarding how adult-focused revisions of the general education or liberal arts components of their baccalaureate programs might inform the philosophical framework for general education development. The premises are: (a) General education is the distinguishing component for the baccalaureate degree; (b) General education is the expression of the character of the academic institution offering the degree; (c) Adult learners share traits with post-high school college learners, but have distinguishing characteristics that should be accounted for; and (d) Adult learners are interested in educational transformation as well as academic credentialing. An analysis of these premises and their critiques follows.

General Education is the Distinguishing Component for the Baccalaureate Degree

The features that distinguish the baccalaureate degree from vocational training were identified by study participants as (a) the general education curriculum; (b) an inculcation of the institution's values, mission and learning philosophy; (c) an advanced analytical framework; and (d) a system for assessing learning outcomes. The perspectives of these participants regarding the baccalaureate degree's distinguishing features align with the perspectives of higher education regulators, scholars of higher education, prospective employers, and, indeed, students themselves (AACU, 2011; Carnevale & Strohl, 2001; Hutton, 2006; Latzer, 2004a; 2004b; Ratcliff, Johnson, LaNasa, & Gaff, 2001; Ratcliff, Johnson & Gaff, 2004; Trainor, 2004). It is precisely this differentiation that persuades working adults to pursue the completion of a bachelor's degree despite the cost and the increased demands on their time and energy.

While the general education curriculum is one of those four distinguishing features, it is also a significant delivery system for the other three (an inculcation of the institution's values, mission, and learning philosophy; an advanced analytical framework; a system for assessing learning outcomes). Though it is likely that the values, mission, and learning philosophy of the institution will be implicit in the ongoing baccalaureate experience, those ideas must be established in the freshman year, orienting incoming degree-seekers and enabling ongoing learners to recognize and cultivate those values along the way. Though it is assumed that each course for the major will require an advanced analytical framework, the general education requirements would also require that same higher order thinking across a diverse array of subjects. Further, just as the major program is designed to certify through assessment the achievement of outcomes for the major, ideally, assessment of program outcomes will certify that the student has also gained breadth of knowledge and of transferrable skills, as well as depth of knowledge in a specific discipline.

Participants in the 2013 AHEA discussion roundtable considered the findings of the 2011 study and responded with several observations regarding this premise. An observation that drew consensus was that while adult learners accept the general education requirements of their programs, many regard these requirements critically, challenging the requirements' utility and looking for shortcuts in completing them. This observation in experience is borne out by the literature about adult learning characteristics, where adult learners seek to know the reasons for what is required of them, and analyze those requirements in terms of their educational or professional needs (Knowles, 1984; Merriam, 2001a). As the roundtable participants noted, it is the general education requirements that are going to seem to adult learners to be the most distant from their goals in obtaining the degree, despite the fact that general education is recognized to be a distinguishing feature of the baccalaureate degree.

General Education Expresses the Character of the Academic Institution

Particularly in required freshman foundation courses, baccalaureate students are expected to become acquainted with the philosophical and educational foundations of the institution, its mission and values, and learning philosophy. As the ethos of the college culture, the mission, values and learning philosophy have the best opportunity for introduction and reinforcement within the context of the general education requirements, since these are the requirements common to all the majors.

The comments offered in discussion of this premise in the AHEA roundtable centered on the gap between the ideal and the real. Discussion participants wished that more institutions successfully expressed their educational ethos in their general education requirements, but lamented that this was seldom the case. There was no disagreement about the desirability of laying such a foundation in the beginning of a baccalaureate experience and of reinforcing those values all through the degree program. There was full agreement that inculcation of the college's mission, values, and learning philosophy was incomplete in traditional programs, and sometimes missing altogether in adult degree programs, where more transfer credit supplanted opportunities to integrate such values.

Though adult-friendly programs allow, and usually encourage, the transfer of credits, the courses transferred must conform to the intent and content of the required courses of the receiving institution's program, which will preserve to some degree the requirements of the receiving institution. However, when it comes to those features in the general education program that mark the student's educational experience with the ethos of the degree-granting institution, the adult transfer student is unlikely to reconceive learning from another institution's courses in those subtle ways. Further, it is the "first year" or freshman courses that are most likely to introduce that philosophical framework, and, as was seen in both Benedictine College and Clementine College, these were the general education requirements most readily waived, since they were never designed for "adult" learners. In this passive way, adult learners find themselves cut off from the philosophical foundations of their degree-granting institution, reinforcing the notion that the general education requirements are just "courses to get out of the way" before getting down to the real learning in the major (Awbrey, 2005; Latzer, 2004a; 2004b).

Adult Learner Traits are Distinct From and Shared with Post-High-School Learners

Differences between adult learners and their post-high school counterparts have long been explored resulting in rich insights regarding adult learning characteristics, as well as characteristics of effective and self-directed learning, applicable to all stages of human development. However, the required common core in the general education portion of the baccalaureate program may pose a challenge to the conclusions of andragogy, and the differentiating characteristics of adult learners may present a critique to the assumptions underlying an institution's core curriculum (Brookfield, 1995; Cross & Zusman, 1979; Merriam, 2004; Schlossberg, Lynch, & Chickering, 1989).

Roundtable participants agreed with the conclusions of the 2011 study participants concerning the situational and experiential differences in adult learners compared to post-high-school students. Adult students bring a wealth of life experience, with an experiential context in which to place new learning, but bring with that experience "baggage" in terms of past failures and current responsibilities. They may be attuned to a sense of vocation as they attempt to align their career path with their aspirations, but this sense of calling heightens their impatience with what seems unnecessary or extraneous to those aspirations. The round table participants added that the motivations of adult learners mark the effectiveness of their learning efforts since adults come to their programs out of their own choice, rather than in response to the expectations of their parents. The inference of participants was that such internal motivations would more likely result in more successful learning efforts. Round table participants also noted a difference in how adult learners constructed the hierarchy of roles making up their identity, seeing themselves as employees who are learning, rather than as students who are working.

Adult Learners are Interested in Transformation as well as Credentialing

Though adult degree-seekers are often driven by practical considerations of career advancement, adults as learners may possess other expectations during their pursuit of the degree. Adult learners sort quickly between what they already know (in transfer credit and through life experience), and what they need to know in remaining degree requirements. However, they are alert to the value to be gained in the degree and value life enrichment as well as opportunity for advancement (Brookfield, 1995; Dick, 2011; Kasworm, Sandmann, & Sissel, 2000; Maehl, 2004, Sissel, Hansman, & Kasworm, 2001).

Roundtable participants responded to this premise with some disagreement and some concession. Some commented that while adult students may not describe their experience as *transformation*, such transformation does happen, and they may recognize it when it occurs. Other participants acknowledged that academic administrators and faculty might expect that their programs and courses will have a transforming effect, but that learners may not come with that expectation. One participant observed that getting the credential can, in itself, be transforming. However, all agreed that transformation is a goal as easy to miss as it is to yearn for in the quest to be a college-educated person.

An Adult Focus for General Education: Seeking Coherence and an Educational Ethos

Implicit in these careful critiques of the four premises regarding baccalaureate programs, their general education curricula, and the adult learners who pursue them, was dissatisfaction with what has been exposed in traditional general education under the gaze of the adult degree-seeker: a flabbiness of overabundant options, a dissipated intentionality, a confusion of journey and destination until neither is effectually consummated. Missing in adult-focused programs and, in the traditional baccalaureate programs from which they are derived, is a formal inculcation of the college's educational ethos in the general education or core curriculum. Missing for adult learners and, for their post-high school counterparts, is the opportunity to develop out of their general education experience a personal learning ethos that is deeply influenced by the characteristics of the institution that granted the degree.

Expressing an Institution's Educational Ethos and Cultivating a Personal Learning Ethos

While general education is understood to be a distinguishing feature of baccalaureate education, and a significant means of delivering other distinguishers of the baccalaureate degree, the diminished role of general education in programs adapted for adult degree-seekers exposes the deterioration of this understanding for both degree-granting institutions and the students seeking their degrees. As AHEA round table participants noted, general education programs often exhibit a significant gap between expectations and outcomes, intentions and actions, the ideal and the real. Participants in both the study and the round table agreed that their own institutions' distribution courses ought to satisfy in a well-defined way the general education and baccalaureate program outcomes, and that those program outcomes should reflect the mission, values, and learning philosophy of the institution. However, participants were agnostic as to whether this was actually the case. Concomitantly, adult learners seek a credential that is differentiated from professional training, first, by the degree's required core curriculum of general education and second, by the institution's accreditation, which is earned through documented adherence to mission, values and philosophy of learning. Nonetheless, those same adult learners doubt the practical relevance of both general education and the philosophical foundations of their learning experience. What are the impediments—and the remedies—for bridging these gaps between the ideal and the real in general education as the distinguishing feature of a college's baccalaureate degree and the expression of the institution's character?

One impediment is in the selection of courses that satisfy general education requirements. Adult learners, while accepting the necessity of completing general education requirements, maintain their view of them as a "mere" necessity, rather than as integral to their own educational goals. Academic institutions tend to foster this perspective by offering to adult learners a limited array of general education course offerings chosen for administrative convenience, with little attention paid to substantive coherence or adaptability to the learner's interests and learning goals. Such convenience-driven course scheduling emphasizes the "mere necessity" of fulfilling the requirement, rather than the value of the course itself. The problem runs deeper, however, into the option-rich environment of the college's traditional "day school" where post-high school students wade through dozens of esoteric and special interest course subjects, all qualifying to fulfill one particular general education requirement but many providing only faint indicators of the program outcomes addressed.

A second impediment that reaches deeper than the first is a degree-granting institution's failure to inculcate its mission, values, and learning philosophy throughout degree program requirements and failure to cultivate that educational ethos in its learning environment. The colleges participating in the 2011 study each required first year courses that oriented students to an approach to learning in that college, and the literature for those colleges promoted the inculcation of specific values. However, the individual participants of the 2011 study, including directors of general education, vice presidents of academic affairs and college presidents, consistently expressed doubts about whether any of the many general education distribution courses that fulfilled their core curriculum were developed with institutional values or learning philosophy in mind. Participants in the 2013 AHEA round table discussion, when considering the premise that general education is an expression of the institution's character, responded emphatically that this should be so, but that it was seldom the case. Further, when participating educators in both the 2011 study and the 2013 round table discussion shifted their gaze to the programs revised for adult degree-seekers, they saw that first-year courses introducing the college's learning philosophy were usually removed, and remaining courses offered little that would furnish an organizing principle synthesizing the learning experiences across degree requirements, except the understanding that "these are the courses required if I am to graduate."

Just as the impediments to coherence and an inculcation of mission, values, and learning philosophy are most magnified in the adult-focused degree programs, so might some remedies be found there. First, required first year orientation courses still offer an opportunity for colleges to establish for all incoming students a philosophical foundation for college-level study, acquainting incoming students with the educational ethos of the college, and guiding students in what they should expect to gain from each of the general education requirements ahead. The assumption underlying traditional general education is that eighteen-year-old student life experience is parochial and needs broadening in specified ways that are pertinent to degree completion. Older, more experienced students may find this to be not as much the case—or the gaps may be different and may seem to be unaddressed by the general education curriculum.

For adult learners, the underlying philosophy guiding curricular choices may need to be made all the more explicit, so that they, along with post-high school learners, understand what each of these general education requirements is for. Thus, rather than waiving this first year foundational course for adult learners, the course could be used to show adult learners how their prior learning—both through transfer credit, and life experience—might be reconceived through the lens of the college's educational ethos, bringing coherence to their experiential learning through institution-focused prior learning assessment, and preparing adult learners for ongoing integration of the learning just ahead. As the educational ethos of the institution is introduced in the first course and expressed with intentionality through the general education core curriculum, students may be awakened to their opportunity to cultivate a learning ethos of their own.

Adult Learning and General Education as the Soul of Higher Education Institutions

Left unaddressed during the round table discussion was a subset of outlying findings from the 2011 study in which several academic decision-makers found that some characteristics of adult learners can be observed in post-high-school learners as characteristics-in-development. These decision-makers were seasoned faculty who had led in the formation of their college's adult-focused programs and had created the general education curriculum for the college's baccalaureate programs based on the premise that all college learners should be cultivated and respected as adults who can direct their own educational path with intentionality. This premise led to a collaborative approach by liberal arts faculty in developing general education courses designed to foster in all their students (traditional weekday and non-traditional weekend) a self-assessing purposiveness in learning that transcended situational and experiential differences between the two learning populations. The outlying findings derived from the experience of these faculty members were that all students merit acknowledgement of their life experience, whether as observers (those new to the work force) or as decision-makers (seasoned employees). Youthful, less discerning college learners, as well as mature adults, seek a rationale and a context for what they learn. All students can handle complexity if it is introduced early and built upon through the curriculum (Dick, 2011).

These outlying premises of commonality among learners of varying ages and experience may be best explored and refined in programs where learners share a core curriculum. Consistently over the last few decades, adult degree-seekers and post-high-school degree seekers have shared nearly equal parts of the education market. As a result, traditional colleges are faced with a changing academic and economic landscape that requires a re-examination of cultural and philosophical assumptions regarding what an academic institution does, how it does it, and how what it does contributes to the culture in which it operates. As adult degree programs increasingly transition from being seen as "non-traditional" to being accepted as "neo-traditional," they will move closer to the heart of what colleges expect to do. A dialogue about what a college education should accomplish will necessarily follow. At the heart of that discussion will be general education—the center of the baccalaureate degree, and the defining expression of the institution's soul.

REFERENCES

Association of American Colleges and Universities. (2011). *What is liberal education?* Retrieved April 28, 2011, from http://www.aacu.org/advocacy/What_is_liberal_education.cfm

Awbrey, S. (2005). General education reform as organizational change: Integrating cultural and structural change. *Journal of General Education 54*(1), 1–18.

Brookfield, S. (1995). Adult learning: An overview. International Encyclopedia of Education. A. Tuinjman (Ed.). Oxford: Pergamon Press.

Carnevale, A., & Strohl, J. (2001). The demographic window of opportunity: Liberal education in the new century. *Peer Review 3*(2): Washington D.C.: Association of American Colleges and Universities. Retrieved July 2, 2006, from http://www.aacu.org/peerreview/pr-wi01/pr-wi01feature1.cfm

Cross, K., & Zusman, A. (1979). The needs of nontraditional learners and the response of nontraditional programs. In C. Stafford (Ed.), *An evaluative look at nontraditional postsecondary education*. Washington, D.C.: National Institute of Education.

Dick, D. (2011). *Liberal arts for a 21st century baccalaureate learner: Traditional faculty and administrator perceptions of adult-focused degree programs and general education*. (Doctoral dissertation). Retrieved from UMI Dissertations Publishing, 2011. 3460928.

DiConti, V. (2004). Experiential education in a knowledge-based economy: Is it time to reexamine the liberal arts? *Journal of General Education 53*(3–4), 167–183.

Fong, B. (2004, winter). Looking forward: Liberal education in the 21st century. *Liberal Education, 90*(1), 8–13.

Gaff, J. (2004, fall). What is a generally educated person? *Peer Review, 7*(1), 4–7.

Geiger, R. (1999). The ten generations of American higher education. In P. Altbach, R. Berdahl, & P. Gumport (Eds.), *American higher education in the twenty-first century: Social, political, and economic challenges* (pp. 38–69). Baltimore, MD: Johns Hopkins University Press.

Glyer, D., & Weeks, D. (1998). Liberal education: Initiating the conversation. In D. Glyer & D. Weeks (Eds.), *The liberal arts in higher education: Challenging assumptions, exploring possibilities* (pp. ix–xv). Lanham, MD: University Press of America.

Greenspan, A. (1999, February 16). Remarks made by Chairman Greenspan at the *81st Annual Meeting of the American Council on Education*, Washington DC.

Hutton, T. (2006, fall). The conflation of liberal and professional education. *Liberal Arts*, 54–59.

Kasworm, C., Sandmann, L., & Sissel, P., (2000). Adults in higher education. In A. Wilson, & E. Hayes (Eds.), *Handbook of adult and continuing education* (pp. 449–463). San Francisco, CA: Jossey-Bass.

Knowles, M. (1984). *The adult learner: A neglected species* (3rd Ed.). Houston, TX: Gulf Publishing.

Latzer, B. (2004a, April). *The hollow core: Failure of the general education curriculum.* Washington DC: American Council of Trustees and Alumni.

Latzer, B. (2004b, October). Common knowledge: The purpose of general education. *Chronicle of Higher Education 51*(7), B20.

Lewis, P., & Legler, R. (1998). Integrating liberal arts and professional education. In D. Glyer & D. Weeks (Eds.), *The liberal arts in higher education: Challenging assumptions, exploring possibilities.* (pp. 47–60). Lanham, MD: University Press of America.

Lucas, C. J. (1998). *Crisis in the academy.* New York, NY: St. Martin's Press.

Maehl, W. (2004). Adult degrees and the learning society. *New Directions for Adult and Continuing Education 103*, 5–16.

Merriam, S. (2001, Spring). Andragogy and self-directed learning: Pillars of adult learning theory. *New Directions for Adult and Continuing Education 89*, 3–13.

Merriam, S. (2004). The changing landscape of adult learning theory. In J. Comings, B. Garner, & C. Smith (Eds.), *Review of adult learning and literacy: Connecting research, policy, and practice* (pp. 199–220). Mahwah, NJ: Lawrence Erlbaum Associates.

Ratcliff, J. L., Johnson, D. K., & Gaff, J. G. (2004, spring). Changing general education: Editor's notes. *New Directions for Higher Education 125*, 1–8.

Ratcliff, J. L., Johnson, D. K., La Nasa, S. M., & Gaff, J. G. (2001). *The status of general education in the year 2000: Summary of a national survey.* Washington, DC: Association of American Colleges and Universities.

Schlossberg, N. K., Lynch, A. Q., & Chickering, A. W. (1989). *Improving higher education environments for adults.* San Francisco, CA: Jossey-Bass.

Sheridan, D. (1998). Modern and post-modern challenges to liberal education. In D. Glyer & D. Weeks (Eds.), *The liberal arts in higher education: Challenging assumptions, exploring possibilities* (pp. 25–46). Lanham, MD: University Press of America.

Sissel, P., Hansman, C., & Kasworm, C. (2001, Fall). The politics of neglect. *New Directions for Adult and Continuing Education, 91*, 17–27.

Tetreault, M., & Rhodes, T. (2004). Institutional change as scholarly work: General education reform at Portland State University. *Journal of General Education, 53*(1), 81–106.

Trainor, S. (2004). Designing a signature general education program. *Peer Review, 7*(1), 16–19.

U.S. Department of Education, National Center for Education Statistics. (2012). *Digest of Education Statistics, 2011*(NCES 2012-001), Chapter 3.

Yin, R. (1989). *Case study research: Design and methods.* London, England: Sage.

CHAPTER 8

ONLINE LEARNING AND APPLICATION OF ACTIVE LEARNING STRATEGIES

Adult Learners in Online Settings

Yu-Chun Kuo
Jackson State University

Active learning is an instructional technique that involves students' active participation in the learning process through a variety of activities (Bonwell & Eison, 1991; Escribano, Aguera, & Tovar, 2013; Hativa, 2000). Traditional active learning methods that are usually implemented in traditional classroom environments evolved away from the static lectures to a learning environment where students actively engage in the learning process (Strage, 2008). Due to the rapid development of emerging technologies, online education has become one of the major approaches to learning for adult learners (Allen & Seaman, 2008; Parsad & Lewis, 2008). The percentage of the online student population has been increasing, from 9.6% in 2002 to 32% in 2011 (Allen & Seaman, 2013). Online learning shifts the use of active learning for adult learners from traditional classroom learning to web-

Building Sustainable Futures for Adult Learners, pages 157–182

based learning with the use of various technologies (Muncy & Eastman, 2012; Paetzold & Melby, 2008; Shieh, Chang, & Tang, 2010). A substantial amount of research has shown that there are no significant differences between the effectiveness of online learning and traditional face-to-face learning, and that the active learning strategies applied in a traditional classroom environment may also be applied to online learning (Allen, Bourhis, Burrell, & Mabry, 2002; Brown & Liedholm, 2002; Johnson, Aragon, Shaik, & Palma-Rivas, 2000). It is necessary to explore the application of active learning in accordance with the characteristics of adult learners. In addition, it is important to understand how online learning and active learning strategies can assist adult learners in developing their competencies for sustainable futures and becoming successful lifelong learners in the information explosion era.

EMERGING TECHNOLOGY, ONLINE LEARNING, AND ADULT LEARNERS

Integration of Information and Communication Technology (ICT) into teaching and learning has become the trend in the twenty-first century. Online education allows adults to learn at their own pace and, ultimately, to become life-long learners (Jarvis, 2010; Knowles, Holton, & Swanson, 2012; Merriam, Caffarella, & Baumgartner, 2007). This section describes the influence of technology on adult learning, the current trend of online learning in adult and higher education, and how online learning is aligned with the characteristics and learning needs of adults.

Current Trend of Online Learning in Adult and Higher Education

There has been an increasing enrollment of non-traditional students in the higher education market (Hanover Research, 2012). Increasing degree completion in colleges and universities contributes to the economic growth of the United States (Allen & Seaman, 2013). Adult students attend or return to college to seek the bachelor or advanced degrees for a number of reasons, which may include personal professional development, promotion, and post-training (Hanover Research, 2012). Due to the increase of online enrollment, many institutions have realized the profitable market of adult undergraduates and have initiated distance education programs in accordance with the needs of traditional and non-traditional adult learners (Aslanian Group, 2008; Hanover Research, 2012). Offering online programs with proper design and support may significantly increase enrollment numbers and revenue for an institution. It is necessary to understand the current trends of online learning in adult and higher education.

Over the last ten years, enrollment in online courses at U.S. colleges and universities has grown at a greater rate than overall enrollment in higher education (Hanover Research, 2012). For example, according to surveys conducted by the College Board and the Babson Survey Research Group, the online course enrollment at degree-granting postsecondary institutions increased by 21% from the fall of 2008 to the fall of 2009 (Parker, Lenhart, & Moore, 2011). Over the same one-year period, the total higher education enrollment increased by only 1.2%. Offering online courses has been considered as a critical part of an institution's long-term goals and strategies (Seaman, 2011).

Thirty-two percent of higher education students, about 6.7 million, have taken at least one course online (Allen & Seaman, 2013). According to a report from the Pew Research Center, more than 75% of the U.S. colleges and universities offer some form of online learning (Parker, Lenhart, & Moore, 2011). Among the presidents of 1,055 colleges and universities who participated in the survey, 50% of them agree that online courses prepare students for the working world by providing the same educational value as the courses taken in the classroom. The majority (91%) of two-year institutions offer online courses. Four-year public institutions appear to have been less skeptical about the value of online learning and offered more online courses than four-year private institutions. For example, 89% of the presidents of four-year public colleges and universities reported that their institution offers online classes, while 60% of the presidents of four-year private institutions reported the same. In a study of online learning trends in private institutions, Seaman (2011) indicated that there is a steady but small increase in the proportion of private-sector leaders with positive views of online learning outcomes.

Fourteen percent of public and 11% of private college and university presidents indicated that more than half of their undergraduate students had taken an online course in 2011 (see Figure 8.1). Forty-five of public and 37% of private institution presidents predicted more than half of students taking online courses in 10 years (Parker, Lenhart, & Moore, 2011). Generally, public institutions (66%) are more likely than private institutions (47%) to grant degrees with the courses completed online. Among college graduates who have taken at least one online class, 15% have earned a degree entirely online (Parker, Lenhart, & Moore, 2011).

According to a survey of online learning by the Sloan Consortium (Seaman, 2009), there was about one-third (34.4%) of public institution faculty who had taught courses online, although more than one-half had recommended an online course to students. The majority (80%) of the faculty who taught online have developed an online course. They indicated that

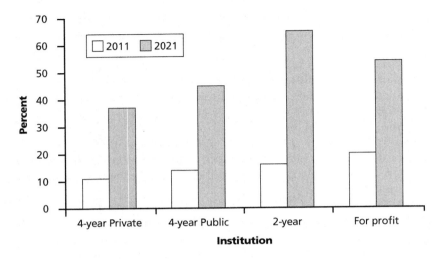

Figure 8.1 Percent of presidents reporting more than half of students had taken and will take an online course. Adapted from Parker, K., Lenhart, A., & Moore, K. (2011). *The Digital Revolution and Higher Education.*

more efforts were needed to teach an online course than a face-to-face course. Student needs (i.e., flexible access and the best approach to reaching particular students) were the primary factor that drives faculty to teach online courses. However, faculty who taught online seem unsatisfied with campus support structures that include support for online course development, course delivery, and students' policies on intellectual property, recognition in tenure and promotion, and incentives for developing and delivering online courses.

A survey from the Chronicle of Higher Education (2010) indicated that 10 academic fields accounted for 81% of all online enrollments, including criminal justice, computer and information technology, health care, business, nursing, public administration, liberal arts, communication, education, and psychology. Among these fields, computer and information sciences, business, general studies, education, and health care were identified by the National Center for Education Statistics as the most popular fields for both online courses and online undergraduate programs (Radford & Weko, 2012). The report from the US News & World Report (2013) also showed similar trends where criminal justice, business degrees, nursing programs, and allied health programs were four of the most popular areas of online degree programs at the Bachelor degree level. Specifically, criminal justice accounts for over one fourth of all online undergraduate degree programs at U.S. institutions.

By 2018, there will be about 63% of jobs in the United States that require some form of postsecondary training. Although approximately 22 million jobs require a college degree, there will be a shortage of 8 million workers to fill these positions (Bryant & Wertheim, 2010). There has been a focus on increasing the percentage of U.S. adults that obtain a Bachelor degree because a skilled workforce that is able to learn and adapt to new challenges and the rapid changes in society is necessary to support and stimulate America's economy. The needs of improving knowledge and skills to succeed in a competitive workforce also lead to an increasing amount of adult population seeking education opportunities for an undergraduate degree. These adults have unique needs that differentiate them from traditional students when returning to undergraduate education or pursuing advance studies.

Aligning the Characteristics and Needs of Adult Learners with Online Learning

Understanding adults' characteristics and learning needs is important, as these factors are critical to the design of online courses. According to Knowles, Holton, and Swanson (2012), the characteristics of adult learners include: (a) self-concept of the learner: Adult learners are self-directed and generally desire to have control over their learning; (b) motivation to learn: Adult learners are motivated to learn due to internal factors, such as personal goals, interests, values, and beliefs; (c) prior experiences of the learner: Adult learners prefer to draw upon past experiences as a resource in their learning efforts; (d) readiness to learn: Learning readiness of adult learners is related to the roles of their job or life; (e) orientation to learn: Adult learners are goal oriented and expect to immediately apply new knowledge in problem solving; and (f) learner's need to know: Adults need to know the reasons of learning and prefer to be respected by others. Online learning allows adults to learn at any time or any place, as long as there is Internet access. The advantages that online courses can offer for the adult learners include convenience, flexibility, individual attention, financial benefits, enhancing self-discipline skills, and promoting life-long learning (Dabbagh, 2007). These features of online learning appear to fit the characteristics of adult learners.

Institutions need to pay attention to adult learners' needs or desires in pursuing an undergraduate degree because they are different from traditional undergraduate students. These needs typically include different kinds of information about their educational options, institutional flexibility in curricular and support services, academic and motivational advising supportive of their life and career goals, and recognition of experience and work-based learning already obtained (Council for Adult and Experiential Learning, 2000).

According to a 2011 study (The 2011 National Adult Learners Satisfaction-Priorities Report) conducted by the Council for Adult and Experiential Learning (Noel-Levits, 2011), of over more than 20 factors identified, the six most important factors that influence adult learners' decision when choosing a college or university include availability of their desired program, convenient time and locations of classes, flexible pacing for completing a program, time required to complete the program, availability of financial assistance, and cost. "Availability of online courses," ranking 10th among these influential factors, reflects the desires of adults towards online learning as well as the importance and potential of offering courses online for an institution to enhance student retention and success.

Based on the adult learner inventory with 47 items (Noel-Levits, 2011), eight scales provided a basis for the principles of effectiveness for serving adult learners, including "outreach, life and career planning, financing, teaching-learning process, technology, transitions, student support systems, and assessment of learning outcomes." As shown in Table 8.1, "outreach" was identified as the most important category by adult learners, while "assessment of learning outcomes" was least important. The largest performance gap between student expectations and satisfaction is found in "life and career planning," followed by "financing" and "outreach," while the smallest performance gap is in "technology" that follows "teaching-learning process."

Based on the characteristics and needs of adult learners, online learning seems to be a good alternative that can overcome the barriers or limitations of traditional classroom learning and help adult learners to fulfill their goals of further education. Innovative technology-mediated learning environments and flexible course delivery schedules are attractive to adult learners (Dabbagh, 2007). In addition, previous studies have shown that adults who have taken a course online have a more positive view toward the values of online learning formats (Parker, Lenhart, & Moore, 2011).

AN OVERVIEW OF ACTIVE LEARNING

This overview will include the history of active learning based on a review of existing literature on active learning. Also introduced are the types of active learning strategies along with the theories that support active learning. Last, learning outcomes that are relevant to active learning are discussed as well as the advantages of utilizing active learning strategies.

TABLE 8.1 Principles of Serving Adult Learners Effectively

Importance Rank[a]	Satisfaction Rank[a]	Principles	Description
1	3	Outreach	Outreach assesses the way the institution conducts its outreach to adult learners by overcoming barriers of time, place, and tradition in order to create lifelong access to educational opportunities.
2	8	Life and Career Planning	Life and career planning assesses how the institution addresses adult learners' life and career goals before or at the onset of enrollment in order to assess and align its capacities to help learners reach their goals.
3	6	Financing	Financing assesses the way the institution promotes choice using an array of payment options for adult learners in order to expand equity and financial flexibility.
4	1	Teaching-Learning Process	Teaching-learning process assesses how the institution's faculty use multiple methods of instruction (including experiential and problem-based methods) for adult learners in order to connect curricular concepts to useful knowledge and skills.
5	2	Technology	Technology assesses the institution's use of information technology to provide relevant and timely information to enhance the learning experience.
6	4	Transitions	Transitions assesses how the institution supports guided pathways leading into and from its programs and services in order to assure that students' learning will apply to successful achievement of their educational and career goals.
7	5	Student Support Systems	Student support system addresses how the institution assists adult learners using comprehensive academic and student support systems in order to enhance students' capabilities to become self-directed, lifelong learners.
8	7	Assessment of Learning Outcomes	Assessment of learning outcomes looks at the way the institution defines and assesses the knowledge, skills, and competencies acquired by adult learners both from the curriculum and from life/work experience in order to assign credit and confer degrees with rigor.

Note: Adapted from "National Adult Learners Satisfaction-Priorities Report," by Noel-Levits, 2011.
[a] Rank refers to the order of importance or satisfaction of 8 principles indicated by the adult learners enrolled in four-year colleges and universities.

An Introduction to Active Learning

Active learning is a student-centered approach to learning that focuses on students' active involvement in the learning process (Deneve & Heppner, 1997; Escribano, Aguera, & Tovar, 2013; Mumoz, Martinez, Cardenas, & Cepeda, 2013). Bonwell and Eison (1991), the leaders of active learning, have contributed much to its development and the acceptance of active learning as a feasible approach to enhancing student learning. Student activity and engagement in the learning process are the two major elements of active learning (Prince, 2004). In active learning, students take responsibility for their own learning. Students learn best through "learning by doing," in which students are required to actively participate in meaningful learning activities and think about what they are doing (Gardner & Belland, 2012). Active learning may fit the needs of adult learners because adults are self-directed learners who intend to control their learning progress and prefer to work on something practical that connects life experiences and learning (Merriam, Caffarella, & Baumgartner, 2007).

Bonwell and Eison (1991) summarized the general characteristics that are associated with the use of active learning strategies, including (a) students are more involved than in passive listening; (b) students are engaged in activities such as reading, discussing, and writing; (c) student motivation is increased; (d) students can receive immediate feedback; and (e) students may be engaged in higher-order thinking, such as analysis, synthesis, and evaluation. Active learning is aligned with the adult learning principles (see Table 8.2). Active learning engages adults in a series of learning processes through which adults know the reasons of learning, regulate the progress, and relate concepts or principles to their social roles in life (Knowles,

TABLE 8.2   Alignment of the Characteristics of Active Learning with the Adult Learning Principles

Characteristics of Active Learning	Addressed Adult Learning Principles
Students are more involved than in passive listening,	Learner's need to know; self-concept of the learner
Students are engaged in activities such as reading, discussing, and writing	Learner's need to know; self-concept of the learner; readiness of learn; orientation to learn
Student motivation is increased	Motivation to learn
Students can receive immediate feedback	Learner's need to know; orientation to learn; motivation to learn
Students may be engaged in higher-order thinking, such as analysis, synthesis, and evaluation	Learner's need to know; prior experience of the learner; readiness to learn; orientation to learn

Holton, & Swanson, 2012). It fulfills the intrinsic motivations of adult learners and enhances their orientation to learn by providing problem-centered contexts involving immediate feedback and application (Wlodkowski, 2008). In active learning contexts, adults develop higher-order thinking skills by engaging themselves in the activities that involve real life problems and connect theories with their previous or current life experiences and tasks (Caffarella & Daffron, 2013).

Active learning strategies encompass various activities (see Table 8.3), such as icebreakers, class discussions, question and answer pairs, short written exercises, cooperative learning, student debates, games, role playing, case study methods, fieldwork, independent study, jigsaw, and computer-aided instruction (Bonwell & Eison, 1991; Escribano, Aguera, & Tovar, 2013; Gardner & Belland, 2012; Mumoz, Martinez, Cardenas, & Cepeda, 2013; Prince, 2004). Selection of appropriate active learning methods depends on the level of students and the content that is being taught. Learner motivation increases when active learning strategies are appropriately adopted in an instruction (Carroll & Leander, 2001).

TABLE 8.3 Activities or Exercises in Active Learning

Activities	Description
Icebreakers	Icebreakers are short "getting to know you" activities or discussions used to help individuals feel comfortable in a group setting. Ice breakers may involve physical or purely mental activities (Jessop, 2010). They allow students to establish trust and communicate with one another (Chlup & Collins, 2010)
Class discussions	Class discussions engage students in the process of communication, including ideas sharing and exchanges (Normore & Blaylock, 2011). This method, which can be conducted with any class size, allows students to think critically and reflect on the content subject matter (Lynch, 2010). Discussions improve students' communication and problem-solving skills (Hamann, Pollock, & Wilson, 2012).
Question/answer pairs	Question/answer pairs allow students to ask and answer questions on a topic by interacting with their instructor or classmates (Schreyer Institute for Teaching Excellence, 2007). The instructor can use this method to review taught content or to prepare students for a quiz. Through this strategy, students can identify their level of understanding through provided questions (Kwong & Yorke-Smith, 2012).
One minute paper	One minute papers engage students by having them review course materials and respond questions in writing at the end of a class session. This method requires students to provide feedback by concisely summarizing what they have learned. It takes about one or two minutes to complete the exercise (Eison, 2010; Stead, 2005).

(continued)

TABLE 8.3   Activities or Exercises in Active Learning (continued)

Activities	Description
Cooperative learning	Cooperative learning refers to any instructional method in which students work together in small groups to complete tasks towards academic goals (Hussain, Khan, & Ramzan, 2013; Ogletree, 2013). Students learn through the processes of sharing their knowledge and exchanging information (Hussain, Khan, & Ramzan, 2013). The instructor may become a vacillator in such cooperative learning settings (Ogletree, 2013).
Student debates	Debates are an active form of oral pedagogy through which students gather information and seek reasons to support their points of view by explaining to others (Healey, 2012). Debates can also be in a written format. Student debates not only engage students in the learning process to become deep thinkers, but also develop students' oral and written skills, as well as the ability to work in teams (Khan, Omar, Babar, & Toh, 2012).
Games	A class game is often considered an enjoyable and effective way to learn, because it not only helps students learn course content by reviewing the provided information or course materials, but also engages students in a series of learning processes that involve exploration, demonstrations, and decision-making (Blanchard & Thacker, 2012). Educational games that provide simulated contexts reflect the actual operations of an event or a task (Silberman, 2006). They increase students' motivation to learn (Olson, 2010).
Role-playing	This method is an experiential learning technique that gives students an opportunity to act out roles in a scenario (Lan, Tseng, & Lai, 2008). The instructor usually provides students with a description of the context, including a topic with goals or objectives, a general description of a situation, a description of assigned roles, and the problem students may confront (Blanchard & Thacker, 2012). Role-playing allows students to practice some skills through the constructive methods of confrontation (Silberman, 2006).
Case study method	A case study provides learners a real or fictitious situation that students may encounter in the future (Silberman, 2006). The students is usually presented with a written history with sufficient details for further analysis, including a description of the situation, key elements, and the potential issues faced by a unit (Blanchard & Thacker, 2012). This method enables students not only to apply learned concepts to a real or fictitious situation but also to identify the solutions and discovering new principles (Blanchard & Thacker, 2012).
Fieldwork	Fieldwork, sometimes referred to as field research, gives students first-hand experience of processes of collecting information and resources outside of a classroom, laboratory, library, or workplace environment (Lai & Lam, 2013; Larkin & Watchorn, 2012). This method has been used in various disciplines. Field work, which

(continued)

TABLE 8.3   Activities or Exercises in Active Learning (continued)

Activities	Description
	brings theory and practice together, involves a range of activities including informal interviews, collective discussion, direct observation, and analysis of historical documents (Grindsted, Madsen, & Nielsen, 2013; Lai & Lam, 2013).
Independent study	Independent study is a form of education that is typically undertaken by an individual with support and guidance but no supervision from the instructor, based on the topic that is agreed upon by both the instructor and the student (Cuthbert, 2001; Thompson & Seward, 2012). Through this method, students take the responsibility for the progress of a project. They acquire knowledge and develop skills for inquiry and problem solving by focusing on lifelike problems (Powers, 2008).
Jigsaw	The jigsaw technique is a method of organizing classroom activities that make students dependent on each other to learn a coherent body of knowledge or skills (Silberman, 2006). The method splits classes into mixed groups to work on small problems that the group collates into a final outcome. Each participant in the group is assigned with one segment of a topic or a piece of an assignment to complete that does not overlap with that of other group members (Doymus, 2007). Student learns from each other while combing materials.
Computer-aided instruction	This refers to the instructional strategy that involves the use of computers to enhance student learning experiences (Kaplan, Ozturk, & Ertor, 2013). This method helps instructors not only to teach academic knowledge on a subject, but also to promote interactions and the development of a deep understanding of the major concepts for students (Kaplan, Ozturk, & Ertor, 2013). Computer-based exercises and tutors are examples of computer-aided instruction (Martin & Pear, 2011).

Active learning strategies have been developed as effective methods to complement traditional classroom learning that is primarily static lecture-based (Paetzold & Melby, 2008). Applying active learning instruction will help increase student interaction and knowledge retention in the traditional classroom learning environment (Paetzold & Melby, 2008). Passive learning, as opposed to active learning, does not require students to actively participate in learning activities. Instead, passive learners are instilled knowledge from the instructor through lecture-based instruction or receive information by reading course materials on their own (Phillips, 2005; Prince, 2004; Wilson, Pollock, & Hamann, 2007). Fewer higher-order cognitive learning skills, such as analysis and critical thinking, are developed through passive learning, and lower-level learning, including rote memory and reciting, often becomes the outcome. Dale's (1969) cone of learning, a visual metaphor for learning modalities, indicates the differences between active learning and passive learning in terms of the degree or levels of learning that takes place with different learning modalities involved. The progression of learning is displayed from the bottom of the cone that involves the most concrete experiences (e.g., presentations, discussions, hands-on activities) to the top of the cone that includes the most abstract experiences (e.g., lectures, graphs, demonstrations, field trips) (Lord, 2007; Wagner, 1970). The activities through speaking and doing in the bottom of the cone exemplify active learning, while those through reading, hearing, and seeing at the top of the cone illustrate passive learning (Dale, 1969; Lord 2007). The percentage of knowledge retention is higher through active learning than through passive learning, from 90% for doing and 70% for speaking to 50% for hearing and seeing, 30% seeing, 20% hearing, and 10% reading (Dale, 1969; Dwyer, 2010).

When examining a variety of active learning strategies, it became clear that active learning strategies address the adult learning principles to a large degree (see Table 8.4). For example, among the active learning strategies indicated in this article, the activity of icebreakers enhances only two of the adult learning principles (i.e., prior experience of the learner and

TABLE 8.4   Active Learning Activities and Adult Learning Principles

Active Learning Activities	Adult Learning Principles					
	Learner's need to know	Self-concept of the learner	Prior experience of the learner	Readiness to learn	Orientation to learning	Motivation to learn
Ice breakers	–	–	v	–	–	v
One minute paper	v	–	v	–	–	v
Question/answer pairs	v	–	v	v	v	v
Class discussions	v	v	v	v	v	v
Student debates	v	v	v	v	v	v
Role playing	v	v	v	v	v	v
Games	v	v	v	v	v	v
Cooperative learning	v	v	v	v	v	v
Jigsaw	v	v	v	v	v	v
Case study method	v	v	v	v	v	v
Fieldwork	v	v	v	v	v	v
Independent study	v	v	v	v	v	v
Computer-aided instruction	v	v	v	v	v	v

Note: The sign "v" refers to the activity that represents the principle, and "–" indicates that the activity does not well represent the principle.

motivation to learn). "One-minute paper" follows by addressing another adult learning principle (i.e., learner's need to know) beyond what is covered in the icebreaker activity. The rest of the active learning strategies, except for questions/answer pairs, appear to address all of the six adult learning principles. This again demonstrates the connection between active learning activities and adult learning.

Underlying Theories of Active Learning

The claim of constructivism that people learn by constructing their own understanding and knowledge of the world based on previous experiences and prior knowledge serves as the foundation of active learning. In the view of constructivist, learning is a process of knowledge construction instead of knowledge recording or absorption (Anthony, 1996; Chalufour, 2014; Füllsack, 2013). The role of learners is shifted from a passive recipient of knowledge to an active constructor of knowledge who builds an internal illustration of knowledge and a personal interpretation of experience. Learners are knowledge-dependent as they build on current knowledge to construct new knowledge. Moreover, active learners are often aware of the processes of cognition and can control or regulate them based on their needs or situations. These assumptions of constructivism are in line with the core elements of active learning.

Cognitive constructivism and social constructivism are relevant theories that promote active learning. Cognitive constructivism, developed based on Piaget's (1968) theory, focuses on the development of abilities through a cognitive approach that stresses mental process (learners' mental models in their heads). Piaget's theory proposes that learners cannot immediately understand and use new information that they are taught or given. Instead, learners construct their understandings based on their existing cognitive structure or intellectual framework. Experiences enable learners to create schemas that can be changed, enlarged, and made more sophisticated through two cognitive processes, assimilation and accommodation (Ewing, 2011). The principle of Piaget's cognitive constructivism–learning is an active process that should be whole, authentic and real–has reflected the concept of active learning.

In social constructivism, one of the major assumptions is that "learning is collaborative with meaning negotiated from multiple perspectives" (Smith & Ragan, 1999, p. 15). According to Vygotsky (1978), meaningful learning occurs in a social context that involves collaborative activities to enhance social interaction of a group. In such contexts, learners construct knowledge when they are given psychological tools (language, diagrams, mathematics) of their culture, and then the opportunity to create artifacts (a common or shared understanding of some phenomenon) through their interaction with others and the environment (Snowman & Biehler, 2000). The emphasis of social and cultural interactions within a group of learners through collaborative activities addresses the concept of collaboration underlying active learning.

Another theory relevant to active learning approaches is experiential learning. Experiential learning, proposed by Kolb (1984), emphasizes the important role of experiences based on the assumption that people learn from relevant experiences that include cognitions, environmental factors, and emotions. Knowledge acquisition occurs through a cyclical process that capitalizes on learners' experiences. Kolb's Experiential Learning Model (ELM) illustrates the four stages of experiential learning, including concrete experience, reflective observation, abstract conceptualization, and active experimentation (Chan, 2012). Gaining experiences and transforming experiences are two dimensions of ELM that include two modes relevant to each other in each dimension. By engaging in these continuous processes, learners construct meaning that is unique to themselves by incorporating the cognitive, emotional, and physical aspects of learning. In addition, through the experiential processes, learners' analytical and problem-solving skills are developed. The focus of knowledge construction through the transformative reflection on learners' experience that leads to the development of higher-order thinking corresponds largely to the characteristics of active learning.

Learning Outcomes as a Result of Active Learning

Active learning has been linked to better learning outcomes, including achievement, attitudes, and behaviors (Michel, Cater, & Varela, 2009; Taraban, Box, Myers, Pollard, & Bowen, 2007). Particularly, research has shown that active learning strategies enhance learners' higher-order thinking, including critical thinking, problem-solving, synthesis, analysis, and evaluation (Bonwell & Eison, 1991; Richmond & Hagan, 2011). Development of higher-level thinking becomes one of the most significant aims for active learning (Pundak, Herscovitz, & Schacham, 2010). In terms of different levels of learning, Bloom's taxonomy categorizes learning outcomes into three domains (Bloom, 1956): the cognitive domain (knowledge construction and the development of intellectual and mental skills), the affective domain (the way learners face things emotionally, including feelings, values, motivations, and attitudes), and the psychomotor domain (physical movement, coordination, and use of motor skills).

Higher-order thinking often refers to application, analysis, evaluation, and creation in the six levels of cognitive learning in Bloom's taxonomy that are measured based on the degrees or levels of difficulty. Knowledge and understanding are lower-level of cognitive learning outcomes. A wide range of evidence supports the importance of active learning in receiving higher-order thinking, and its superior role over traditional learning methods. For example, in a study conducted by Dori and Herscovitz (2005), learners were found to achieve higher conceptual understanding through active learning approaches than those who studied in the same course through traditional learning approaches. Learners constructed new knowledge through problem solving and interpretations in active learning.

The conceptual framework of active learning proposed by Watkins, Carnell, and Lodge (2007), which implicitly depicts the cognitive learning domain of Bloom's taxonomy, provides a basis of the measurement of learning outcomes for active learning. The three distinct dimensions in this framework include behavioral (active employment and development of resources), cognitive (active thought about experiences to make sense and so foster construction of knowledge), and social elements (active interaction with others through a collaborative and resource-driven basis) (Watkins, Carnell, & Lodge, 2007). This framework rests on two relevant constructivist theories, cognitive constructivism and social constructivism.

The Advantages of Applying Active Learning Strategies

Based on the positive learning outcomes from active learning, researchers have discussed the benefits of active learning (Bonwell & Eison, 1991; Phillips, 2005; Watkins et al., 2007). In addition to its academic advantages, active learning has been shown to bring social and psychological benefits (Gavalcova, 2008; Slavin, 1996). These benefits of applying active learning include an increase of learners' motivation to learn, self-confidence, and self-reliance; enhancing the opportunities to retrieve previously learned knowledge; fostering social interdependence and support; improving attitudes towards subject areas and student retention; and enhancing skills to collaborate, communicate, or interact with others (Gavalcova, 2008; Kane, 2004; Phillips, 2005; Watkins et al., 2007). Moreover, active learning is found to be positively related to perceived course quality (Taylor & Ku, 2011).

ACTIVE LEARNING AND ADULT LEARNERS IN ONLINE LEARNING ENVIRONMENTS

Applying active learning strategies in online learning helps decrease the isolated feeling of online learners and increase learner interaction with the instructor and other students. In this section, the readers are expected to gain an understanding of how to apply active learning in an online or technology-supported setting through a proper design by taking adult learners' characteristics or learning styles into account. I indicate the factors that have an impact on the design of online active learning among adult learners from a summary of relevant literature as well as provide suggestions of designing active learning based on instructional design principles. In addition, it is necessary to understand the encountered challenges of incorporating active learning strategies in online settings. Last, I address the problems encountered through the implementation of active learning strategies from the perspectives of faculty and students.

Application of Active Learning among Online Adult Learners

The active learning strategies applied in a traditional classroom may be also applied to an online course with adult learners, as long as the multiple learning styles of adult learners are considered (Paetzold & Melby, 2008). Cost, individual learning styles, instructional skill sets, and technology support are important factors that influence an instructor's decision of selecting active learning strategies (Phillips, 2005). Although there are different types of active learning strategies, not all of them can be properly applied in online settings. For example, Table 8.5 shows a comparison among various active learning activities in terms of contexts, complexity, and communication. Fieldwork and independent study can only be conducted partially online in some situations and may be best for face-to-face settings. Each active learning strategy involves a different level of complex problems or tasks. Adult learners' communication with the instructor or other students cannot be successfully achieved in some types of active learning activities. Instructors need to understand the needs of online adult learners with different learning styles and be prepared to utilize active learning strategies to help each style of adult learners (Paetzold & Melby, 2008; Phillips, 2005; Vincent & Ross, 2001).

Visual adults learn best with presentations that include videos and pictures. They may lose interest and become impatient with a lack of visual instructions. Video clips, taped lectures, and short movies are effective when used in an online course (Austin & Mescia, 2001). The auditory learners gain information and knowledge by listening to directions or hearing step by step instructions. Podcasts are excellent aids to online learners because they can provide an overview of course materials, directions to problems, and review of work. These podcasts can be accessed through personal mobile devices and allow adult learners to take the instructions with them. The action oriented adults learn best from the assignments or tasks that require them to

TABLE 8.5 Comparison of Active Learning Activities in Terms of Contexts, Complexity, and Communication

Description	Contexts	Complexity	Communication
Activities	*Online*	*Levels of complexity*	*With the instructor or among students*
Icebreakers	v	Low	With the instructor; among students
One minute paper	v	Low	None (Individual work)
Question/answer pairs	v	Low	With the instructor or among students
Class discussions	v	Medium	Among students
Student debates	v	Medium	Among students
Role playing	v	Medium	Among students
Games	v	Medium	Among students
Cooperative learning	v	High	Among students
Jigsaw	v	High	Among students
Case study method	v	High	Among students
Fieldwork	v (In certain situations)	High	None (People outside of the classroom context)
Independent study	v (In certain situations)	High	With the instructor
Computer-aided instruction	v	Medium/ High	With the instructor; among students

Note: The sign "v" refers to the activity that can be conducted in the online context.

perform an action, or create something tangible with their efforts. Discussions, group projects, and quizzes are good active learning strategies for such learners in an online course (Paetzold & Melby, 2008; Vincent & Ross, 2001).

Previous research has demonstrated equivalent learning outcomes between traditional courses and online courses (Allen & Seaman, 2008; Parsad & Lewis, 2008). Online courses can be effective as long as the medium used to deliver course content is properly selected based on course design and learning styles of adults. To incorporate active learning techniques into online learning, instructors must know the technology they choose for an online course (e.g., the strengths and weaknesses of technology tools, main features, potentials, quality), and think about whether the selected technology tool can efficiently engage adult learners in active learning activities, and thus, enhance student learning outcomes (Parker, Lenhart, & Moore, 2011; Phillips, 2005). For example, a learning management system (e.g., Blackboard, Moodle) provides tools that instructors can manipulate, based on the characteristics of selected active learning strategies along with course content, to engage learners in interactive and collaborative learning processes through which learners build knowledge and higher-order thinking (Phillips, 2005). Although the selection of proper technology tools is important for an online course with adult learners, the focus should not be the technology, but the development of an online course that incorporates active learning.

Important Factors for the Design of Online Active Learning

A proper design of active learning in online settings is necessary to facilitate student learning processes. Hutchings, Hadfield, Howarth, and Lewarne (2007) indicated seven principles that guide the design and development of active learning in web-based learning environments. Formed based on Kolb's (1984) experiential learning cycle and Laurillard's (2002) conversational framework, these guiding principles of active learning design emphasize the relationships between learning process and the role that teachers play to guide learners by taking both learner-centered and teaching-focused approaches into consideration. These seven design principles include variety (engaging and maintaining learner's attention), action (asking learner to do things), application (encouraging learner to apply their learning in another context), interaction (allowing learners to change or comment on content), feedback (supporting learners in reviewing and reflecting on what they have done or understood), scaffolding (guiding learners with frameworks and connections for learning), and evaluation (enabling learners to contribute to learning design through feedback). These principles also represent the important factors that instructors or instructional designers should consider when developing an online or web-based course with active learning.

Challenges and Difficulties of Implementing Active Learning in Online Settings

Although much evidence has shown the benefits of applying active learning, many faculty members are reluctant to utilize it in the class due to the obstacles they have encountered, especially in online courses. These obstacles include content coverage issues, time consumed, fears of new learning techniques, student reaction, teacher characteristics, technology, and pedagogical issues (Faust & Paulson, 1998; Michael, 2007). When applying active learning in a course to incorporate more student-centered activities, an instructor may not be able to cover as much material as they were in a course without active learning. Weighing content coverage against the amount of active learning activities becomes a task for the faculty. They will need to decide to either teach more course content with students learning less of it, or teach less but students learning more (Faust & Paulson, 1998).

It takes too much time for faculty to prepare for a course incorporating active learning techniques, especially for those who teach a new course or who are using active learning the first time (Michael & Modell, 2003). Faulty may have less control in an active learning class (Michael, 2007). With a wide range of active learning strategies that show different levels of complexity, the faculty may be more inclined to choose the learning techniques that require little preparation time, such as questions and answers, discussions, or one-minute papers (Michael, 2007). A fear of utilizing new innovative learning strategies is another impediment to incorporating active learning. Faculty may feel more comfortable maintaining the same teaching style than making changes to include active learning strategies. Inclusion of active learning may possibly result in negative reactions or poor evaluations from the students when the strategies are not properly applied in accordance with the design of a course.

Interaction is an important component to determine student satisfaction in online learning (Kuo, Walker, Belland, & Schroder, 2013). Although active learning can enhance the interaction among students, requirements of too many online activities among students reduce student satisfaction toward an online course (Kuo, Walker, Schroder, & Belland, 2014). It may not be easy for an instructor to identify the amount of active learning strategies that should be conducted in online settings. In addition, lack of teacher maturity and perceptions of colleagues may influence the adoption of active learning.

In addition to the problems that the teachers encounter, students may also experience some barriers in an active learning class (Michael, 2007). First, students may not know what to do in the class with active learning, as they are expected to learn course content through participating in different activities. Second, lack of preparation before coming to class is another issue that leads to low effectiveness of applying active learning. Students may also not possess the maturity needed for active learning. Third, students' expectations towards learning and heterogeneity are barriers to active learning. Students have different learning styles, and it is difficult to apply an active learning strategy that makes each student satisfied. Moreover, students may be unwilling to engage in active learning, but are forced to do so.

CONCLUSION

This chapter included a review of the major trend of online learning in adult learning, the concept of active learning, and the application of active learning in online learning environments. Public and private institutions have been offering more online courses or degrees than before. Online learning provides extended opportunities for adults in the workforce to earn a college or an advanced degree, which helps resolve the shortage of future positions in the United States. Adults return to school for many reasons, and facing the changes in life and career plans appears to rank the top of the list for adults to continue their education. Online learning benefits adults in several ways (convenience, life transitions, professional development, and increased chances for future promotions). It is important to design effective online learning by considering the characteristics and learning needs of adults. Active learning is an instructional method that can facilitate adults' learning in online settings. It has the potential to increase adult learners' levels of engagement in the learning processes and, thus, enhance the effectiveness of online learning.

Through a review of literature on active learning, I found that (a) active learning is aligned with the principles of adult learning to a large degree; (b) active learning promotes higher-order thinking and problem-solving skills; (c) constructivism and experiential learning are two major theories in support of active learning; (d) factors affecting the design of active learning in online learning; and (e) the academic, social and psychological benefits of applying active learning and challenges of implementing active learning strategies. These findings suggest instructors and practitioners (instructional designers, curriculum developers, and program leaders) consider course subjects as well as adults' learning styles and available resources (technology tools and institutional support) before incorporating active learning strategies into online learning. Selection of active learning strategies should be based on the course objectives, subject areas, and teachers' readiness of adopting active learning. Institutions can offer a series of training to help the faculty apply active learning strategies in online settings and gather suggestions or comments from faculty members in different disciplines. Evaluation, including quantitative or qualitative methods, is necessary to determine the effectiveness of applying active learning in online learning.

Although active learning is popular in K–12 and higher education, there is limited research of active learning in the adult education literature. Few researchers have addressed the role of active learning in continuing education from the perspectives of adult learning. The majority of active learning research was completed through case studies. On one hand, there is a lack of online active learning studies at program or institutional levels. It is necessary to include the viewpoints of the faculty, program directors, or institutional leaders for active learning. On the other hand, researchers should investigate non-traditional adult learners' perspectives of attending online courses involving active learning strategies. In addition, this study did not draw on the literature in training. Future studies should extend the application of active learning to both formal (courses offered towards a degree program) and informal (training) learning settings, and compare the use of such instructional methods in two different settings.

REFERENCES

Allen, M., Bourhis, J., Burrell, N., & Mabry, E. (2002). Comparing student satisfaction with distance education to traditional classrooms in higher education: a meta-analysis. *The American Journal of Distance Education, 16*(2), 83–97. doi:10.1207/S15389286AJDE1602_3

Allen, I. E., & Seaman, J. (2008). *Staying the course: Online education in the United States, 2008.* Retrieved from http://www.sloan-c.org/publications/survey/pdf/staying_the_course.pdf

Allen, E., & Seaman, J. (2013). *Changing course: Ten years of tracking online education in the United States.* Retrieved from http://www.onlinelearningsurvey.com/reports/changingcourse.pdf

Anthony, G. (1996). Active learning in a constructivist framework. *Educational Studies in Mathematics, 31*(4), 349–369. doi:10.1007/BF00369153

Aslanian Group. (2008). *Undergraduate adult student and graduate student market analysis.* Retrieved from www.sdstate.edu/accreditation/upload/University-Center-Aslanian-Studyt.pdf

Austin, D., & Mescia, M. D. (2001). *Strategies to incorporate active learning into online teaching.* Retrieved from http://www.icte.org/T01_Library/T01_245.pdf

Blanchard, P. N., & Thacker, J. (2012). *Effective training.* Upper Saddle River, NJ: Prentice Hall

Bloom, B. S. (1956). *Taxonomy of educational objectives, Handbook I: The cognitive domain.* New York, NY: David McKay Co.

Bonwell, C., & Eison, J. (1991). *Active learning: Creating excitement in the classroom* (ASHE-ERIC Higher Education Report No. 1). Washington, DC: The George Washington University, School of Education and Higher Education.

Brown, B. W., & Liedholm, C. E. (2002). *Can web courses replace the classroom in principles of microeconomics?* Retrieved from https://www.msu.edu/~brownb/brown-liedholm%20aea%202002.pdf

Bryant, J., & Wertheim, J. (2010, November). *ALFI assessments: Tools to identify institutional priorities to help adult learners.* Paper presented at the Annual Meeting of the Council for Adult and Experiential Learning (CAEL), San Diego, CA.

Caffarella, R. R., & Daffron, S. R. (2013). *Planning programs for adult learners.* San Francisco, CA: Jossey-Bass.

Carroll, L., & Leander, S. (2001). *Improving student motivation through the use of active learning strategies.* Unpublished thesis, Saint Xavier University, Chicago, ERIC Document No. ED455961.

Chalufour, I. (2014). Constructivism across the curriculum in early childhood classrooms: Big ideas as inspiration. *Science & Children, 51*(6), 28–29.

Chan, Y. K. (2012). Exploring an experiential learning project through Kolb's Learning Theory using a qualitative research method. *European Journal of Engineering Education, 37*(4), 405–415.

Chlup, D. T., & Collins, T. E. (2010). Breaking the ice: Using ice-breakers and re-energizers with adult learners. *Adult Learning, 21*(3/4), 34–39. doi:10.1177/104515951002100305

Chronicle of Higher Education. (2010). *Online learning: By the numbers.* Retrieved from http://chronicle.com/article/Online-Learning-Enrollment/125202/

Council for Adult and Experiential Learning. (2000). *Serving adult learners in higher education: Principles of effectiveness.* Retrieved from http://www.carrollcc.edu/assets/forms/PTA/Summary%20of%20Alfi%20Principles%20of%20Effectiveness.pdf

Cuthbert, K. (2001). Independent study and project work: Continuities or discontinuities. *Teaching in Higher Education, 6*(1), 69–84. doi: 10.1080/1356 2510020029617

Dabbagh, N. (2007). The online learner: Characteristics and pedagogical implications. *Contemporary Issues in Technology and Teacher Education, 7*(3), 217–226.

Dale, E. (1969). *Audiovisual methods in teaching.* New York, NY: The Dryden Press.

Deneve, K. M., & Heppner, M. J. (1997). Role play simulations: The assessment of an active learning technique and comparisons with traditional lectures. *Innovative Higher Education, 21*(3), 231–246.

Dori, Y. J., & Herscovitz, O. (2005). Case-based long-term professional development of science teachers. *International Journal of Science Education, 27*(12), 1413–1446.

Doymus, K. (2007). The effect of a cooperative learning strategy in the teaching of phase and one-component phase diagrams. *Journal of Chemical Education, 84*(11), 1857–1860. doi:10.1021/ed084p1857

Dwyer, F. (2010). Edgar Dale's cone of experience: A quasi-experimental analysis. International. *Journal of Instructional Media, 37*(4), 431–437.

Eison, J. (2010). Using Active learning instructional strategies to create excitement and enhance learning. Retrieved from http://www.cte.cornell.edu/documents/presentations/Active%20Learning%20-%20Creating%20Excitement%20in%20the%20Classroom%20-%20Handout.pdf

Escribano, B. M., Aguera, E. I., & Tovar, P. (2013). Television format or research project? Team work and the opportunity of choosing classroom-led activities reinforce active learning. *Advances in Physiology Education, 37*, 207–209. doi:10.1152/advan.00108.2012

Ewing, J. C., Foster, D. D., & Whittington, M. S. (2011). Explaining student cognition during class sessions in the context Piaget's theory of cognitive development. *NACTA Journal, 55*(1), 68–75.

Faust, J. L., & Paulson, D. R. (1998). Active learning in the college classroom. *Journal on Excellence in College Teaching, 9*(2), 3–24.

Füllsack, M. (2013). Author's response: Constructivism as possibility? *Constructivist Foundations, 9*(1), 23–25.

Gardner, J., & Belland, B. R. (2012). A conceptual framework for organizing active learning experiences in biology instruction. *Journal of Science Education and Technology, 12*(4), 465–475. doi:10.1007/s10956-011-9338-8

Gavalcova, T. (2008). On strategies contributing to active learning. *Teaching Mathematics and its Applications, 27*(3), 116–122.

Grindsted, T. S., Madsen, L. M., & Nielsen, T. T. (2013). One just better understands.....when standing out there: Fieldwork as a learning methodology in university education of Danish geographers. *Review of International Geographical Education Online, 3*(1), 9–25.

Hamann, H., Pollock, P. H., & Wilson, B. M. (2012). Assessing student perceptions of the benefits of discussions in small-group, large-class, and online learning contexts. *College Teaching, 60,* 65–75. doi: 10.1080/87567555.2011.633407

Hanover Research. (2012). *Trends in online and adult education.* Retrieved from http://www.hanoverresearch.com/wp-content/uploads/2012/10/Trends-in-Online-and-Adult-Education.pdf

Hativa, N. (2000). *Teaching for effective learning in higher education.* Dordrecht: Kluwer.

Healey, R. L. (2012). The power of debate: Reflections on the potential of debates for engaging students in critical thinking about controversial geographical topics. *Journal of Geography in Higher Education, 36*(2), 239–257. doi:10.1080/03098265.2011.619522

Hussain, I., Khan, H. M., & Ramzan, S. (2013). Integrating cooperative learning activities to instruction at tertiary education level: A qualitative portrayal of the experience. *Journal of Educational Research, 16*(1), 33–50.

Hutchings, M., Hadfield, M., Howarth, G., & Lewarne, S. (2007). Meeting the challenges of active learning in Web-based case studies for sustainable development. *Innovations in Education and Teaching International, 44*(3), 331–343.

Jarvis, P. (2010). *Adult education and lifelong learning: Theory and practice.* New York, NY: Routledge.

Jessop, A. (2010). Bayes ice-breaker. *An International Journal for Teachers, 32*(1), 13–16.

Johnson, S. D., Aragon, S. R., Shaik, N., & Palma-Rivas, N. (2000). Comparative analysis of learner satisfaction and learning outcomes in online and face-to-face learning environments. *Journal of Interactive Learning Research, 11*(1), 29–49.

Kane, L. (2004). Educators, learners and active learning methodologies. *International Journal of Lifelong Learning, 23*(3), 275–286.

Kaplan, A., Ozturk, M., & Ertor, E. (2013). The efficiency of computer-aided instruction and creative drama on academic achievement in teaching of integers to seventh grade students. *International Journal of Academic Research, 5*(2), 49–56. doi: 10.7813/2075-4124.2013/5-2/B.7

Khan, S. A., Omar, H., Babar, M. G., & Toh, C. G. (2012). Utilization of debate as an educational tool to learn health economics for dental students in Malaysia. *Journal of Dental Education, 76*(12), 1675–1683.

Knowles, M. S., Holton, E. F., & Swanson, R. A. (2012). *The adult learner.* New York, NY: Routledge.

Kolb, D. A. (1984). *Experiential learning.* London, England: Prentice Hall.

Kuo, Y. C., Walker, A., Belland, B. R., & Schroder, K. E. E. (2013). A predictive study of student satisfaction in online education programs. *The International Review of Research in Open and Distance Learning, 14*(1), 16–39.

Kuo, Y. C., Walker, A., Schroder, K. E. E., & Belland, B. R. (2014). Interaction, Internet self-efficacy, and self-regulated learning as predictors of student satisfaction in online education courses. *The Internet and Higher Education, 20,* 35–50. doi:10.1016/j.iheduc.2013.10.001

Lai, K. C., & Lam, C. C. (2013). School–based assessment of fieldwork in Hong Kong: Dilemmas and challenges. *Geography, 98*(1), 33–40.

Lan, C. H., Tseng, C. C., & Lai, K. R. (2008, July). *Developing a negotiation-based intelligent tutoring system to support problem solving: A case study in role-play learning.* Paper presented at the Eighth IEEE International Conference on Advanced Learning Technologies. Cantabria, France.

Larkin, H., & Watchorn, V. (2012). Changes and challenges in higher education: What is the impact on fieldwork education? *Australian Occupational Therapy Journal, 59,* 463–466. doi: 10.1111/1440-1630.12002

Laurillard, D. (2002). *Rethinking university teaching: A framework for the effective use of educational technologies* (2nd ed). London, England: Routledge.

Lord, T. (2007). Society for college science teachers: Revisiting the cone of learning. *Journal of College Science Teaching, 37*(2), 14–17.

Lynch, J. (2010). Fostering incisive, topic-building class discussions. *The LLI Review, 5,* 38–44.

Martin, G., & Pear, J. (2011). *Behavior modification: What it is and how to do it.* (9th ed.). Upper Saddle River, NJ: Pearson Prentice Hall.

Merriam, S. B., Caffarella, R. S., & Baumgartner, L. M. (2007). *Learning in adulthood: A comprehensive guide.* San Francisco, CA: Jossey-Bass.

Michael, J. (2007). Faculty perceptions about barriers to active learning. *College teaching, 55*(2), 42–47.

Michael, J. A., & Modell, H. I. (2003). *Active learning in secondary and college science classrooms: A working model of helping the learner to learn.* Mahwah, NJ: Lawrence Erlbaum.

Michel, N., Carter, J. J., & Varela, O. (2009). Active versus passive teaching styles: An empirical study of student learning outcomes. *Human Resource Development Quarterly, 20*(4), 397–418.

Muncy, J. A., & Eastman, J. K. (2012). Using classroom response technology to create an active learning environment in marketing classes. *American Journal of Business Education, 5*(2), 213–218.

Mumoz, M., Martinez, C., Cardenas, C., & Cepeda, M. (2013). Active learning in first-year engineering courses at Universidad Católica de la Santísima Concepción, Chile. *Australasian Journal of Engineering Education, 19*(1), 27–38. doi:10.7158/D12-017.2013.19.1

Noel-Levitz, LLC, & CAEL. (2011). *National adult learners satisfaction-priorities report.* Retrieved from https://www.noellevitz.com/documents/shared/Papers_and_Research/2011/ALI_report%202011.pdf

Normore, L. F., & Blaylock, B. N. (2011). Effects of communication medium on class participation: Comparing face-to-face and discussion board communication rates. *Journal of Education for Library and Information Science, 52*(3), 198–211.

Ogletree, G. L. (2013). Eight practices for successful cooperative learning groups. *New Teacher Advocate, 21*(2), 4–5.

Olson, C. (2010). Children's motivations for video game play in the context of normal development. *Review of General Psychology, 14*(2), 180–187. doi: 10.1037/a0018984

Paetzold, S. P., & Melby, N. J. (2008). Active learning strategies for computer information systems education in online courses. *The Journal of Global Business Issues*, 13–17.

Parker, K., Lenhart, A., & Moore, K. (2011). *The digital revolution and higher education*. Retrieved from http://www.pewsocialtrends.org/2011/08/28/the-digital-revolution-and-higher-education/2/

Parsad, B., & Lewis, L. (2008). *Distance education at degree-granting postsecondary institutions: 2006–07*. Retrieved from http://nces.ed.gov/pubs2009/2009044.pdf

Piaget, J. (1968). *Six psychological studies*. New York, NY: Vintage Books.

Phillips, J. M. (2005). Strategies for active learning in online continuing education. *Strategies for Active Learning Online, 36*(2), 77–83.

Powers, E. A. (2008). The use of independent study. *Gifted child today, 31*(3), 57–65. doi: 10.4219/gct-2008-786

Prince, M. (2004). Does active learning work? A review of the research. *Journal of Engineering Education, 93*(3), 223–231.

Pundak, D., Herscovitz, O., & Schacham, M. (2010). Attitudes of face-to-face and e-learning instructors toward active learning. *European Journal of Open, Distance and E-Learning, 2*, 1–12.

Radford, A. W., & Weko, T. (2012). *Learning at a distance: Undergraduate enrollments in distance education courses*. Retrieved from http://nces.ed.gov/pubs2012/2012154.pdf

Richmond, A. S., & Hagan, L. K. (2011). Promoting higher level thinking in psychology: Is active learning the answer? *Teaching of Psychology, 38*(2), 102–105. doi: 10.1177/0098628311401581

Seaman, J. (2009). *Online learning as a strategic asset*. Retrieved from http://sloan-consortium.org/publications/survey/APLU_Reports

Seaman, J. (2011). *Online learning trends in private-sector colleges and universities*. Retrieved from http://www.babson.edu/Academics/Documents/babson-survey-research-group/online-learning-trends-private-sector.pdf

Schreyer Institute for Teaching Excellence. (2007). *Question and answer pairs*. Retrieved from https://www.schreyerinstitute.psu.edu/pdf/alex/questionanswerpair.pdf

Shieh, R. S., Chang, W., & Tang, J. (2010). The impact of implementing technology-enabled active learning (TEAL) in university Physics in Taiwan. *The Asia-Pacific Education Researcher, 19*(3), 401–415.

Silberman, M. (2006). *Active training: A handbook of techniques, designs, case examples, and tips*. San Francisco, CA: Pfeiffer.

Slavin, R. W. (1996). Research on cooperative learning and achievement: What we know, what we need to know. *Contemporary Educational Psychology, 21*, 43–69.

Smith, P. L., & Ragan, T. J. (1999). *Instructional design* (2nd ed.). Upper Saddle River, NJ: Prentice-Hall, Inc.

Snowman, J., & Biehler, R. (2000). *Psychology applied to teaching* (9th ed.). Boston, MA: Houghton Mifflin Company.

Strage, A. (2008). Traditional and non-traditional college students' descriptions of the ideal professor and the ideal course and perceived strengths and limitations. *College Student Journal, 42*(1), 225–231.

Stead, D. R. (2005). A review of the one-minute paper. *Active Learning in Higher Education, 6*(2), 118–131. doi:10.1177/1469787405054237

Taraban, R., Box, C., Myers, R., Pollard, R., & Bowen, C. W. (2007). Effects of active-learning experiences on achievement, attitudes, and behaviors in high school biology. *Journal of Research in Science Teaching, 44*(7), 960–979.

Taylor, J. E., & Ku, H. Y. (2011). Measuring active learning to predict course quality. *Performance Improvement Quarterly, 24*(1), 31–48.

Thompson, S. B., & Seward, B. (2012). Learn to do something new: Collaboration on McNair Middle school's independent study offers fresh skills for gifted students. *Knowledge Quest, 40*(4), 68–72.

US News & World Report. (2013). *Top online bachelor's programs.* Retrieved from http://www.usnews.com/education/online-education

Vincent, A., & Ross, D. (2001). Personalize training: Determine learning styles, personality types and multiple intelligences online. *The Learning Organization, 8*(1), 36–43.

Vygotsky, L. (1978). *Mind in society.* London, England: Harvard University Press.

Wagner, R. W. (1970). Edgar Dale: Professional. *Theory into Practice, 9*(2), 89–95.

Watkins, C., Carnell, E., & Lodge, C. (2007). *Effective learning in classrooms.* London, England: Sage.

Wilson, B. M., Pollock, P. H., & Humann, K. (2007). Does active learning enhance learner outcomes? Evidence from discussion participation in online classes. *Journal of Political Science Education, 3*, 131–142. doi:10.1080/15512160701338304

Wlodkowski, R. J. (2008). *Enhancing adult motivation to learn.* San Francisco, CA: Jossey-Bass.

CHAPTER 9

COLLABORATIONS AND PARTNERSHIPS

The Foundation of Technology Enhanced Active Learning

Marilyn Lockhart and Lindsey R. Jackson
Montana State University

Collaborations and partnerships yield superior results in the workplace (Burke, 2011; Davidson, 2012) and in the classroom (Brookfield, 2005; Millis, 2010). Collaborators share knowledge, resources, and perspectives through communication and interaction with one another (Mattessich, Murray-Close, & Monsey, 2001). In partnerships, individuals participate in collaborative relationships with common goals (Bailey & Dolan, 2011). Strong collaborations and partnerships involve people who are equally engaged and committed to working together (Nelson & Quick, 2005).

In the workplace, businesses have moved towards emphasizing building connections and networks to enable creativity and improvements (Davidson, 2012; Eisner, 2010). People collaborating together can share experiences, learn from one another, and, as a result, create innovation that can

Building Sustainable Futures for Adult Learners, pages 183–209

be used to make business changes and improvements (Kanter, 1996; Senge, 1990). Cross-functional teams, consisting of individuals with a variety of job responsibilities and experiences, can be particularly valuable (Kanter, 1996). There is a growing body of literature that views groups as learning entities themselves (Kasl, Marsick, & Dechant, 1997; Yorks & Marsick, 2000). However, in higher education, where the culture is for individuals to work more autonomously, collaborative relationships are not widespread (Kezar & Lester, 2009).

Adult learning theorists have written about the importance of experience in learning. The importance of sharing experiences, a critical step of collaboration and partnerships (Burke, 2011), has been described by several adult learning theorists. Fenwick (2003) wrote that the outcome of individuals with a variety of experiences working together is that the group can create new practices, refine existing practices, or discontinue existing practices. In Fenwick's description, (2003) collaboration with others provides a rich opportunity for learning. Knowles' (1980) work on adult learning states that the experience of adults is a valuable resource for learning. Transformative learning, a fundamental change in the way an individual views the world and considered by some adult learning theorists as the most significant learning in adulthood (Mezirow, 2000, Taylor, 2000), has also been connected to individuals working together. Team opportunities in the workplace that include action and reflection can result in individual and group transformation (Lamb, 2003; Yorks & Marsick, 2000). This transformation can lead to the organization more effectively achieving its goals (Yorks & Marsick, 2000) as well.

Developing self-directed learners and life-long learners should be a goal of educational programs (Schrader-Naef, 2000). Knowles (1980) first described self-directed learning in his theory of adult learning. One of his primary assumptions of adult learning is that "as a person matures, his or her self-concept moves from that of a dependent personality toward one of a self-directing human being" (p. 44). Fink (2013) writes that active learning experiences, such as group discussions and group in-depth reflection, deeply engage the student with content. Such experiences result in individuals who become self-directed learners and then have the skills to learn throughout their lifetime. Hammond and Collins (1991) see self-directed learning as the ultimate goal of instruction, and teachers should empower individuals "to use their learning to improve the conditions under which they and those around them live and work" (p. 14).

The Millennial Generation, born between 1980 and 2000 (ages 34 to 14) and numbering 80 million people, is found in the college classrooms and the workplaces of today (Green, Coke, & Ballard, 2013). A Pew Research Center study (2014) of the Millennial Generation reported that because of the time period they have lived, this generation is networked with friends and colleagues. Additionally, they have grown up with digital technology rather than having to adapt to it and are comfortable using technology in their lives (Pew Research, 2014). According to Knowles, Holten, & Swanson (2011), active and engaging learning is more important to this generation than any other. Since this generation has grown up working in groups and teams, collaboration and activities that engage the learner with content as compared to passively listening to lectures is important (Green, Coke, & Ballard, 2013). Green, Coke, and Ballard (2013) write that millennial learning preferences need to be considered when designing classes, and since this generation is comfortable with technology, incorporating technology into the classroom is desirable. Additionally, designing instruction for the Millennial Generation that is based on adult learning principles is more important than previous generations (Knowles, Holten, & Swanson, 2011).

The characteristics of the Millennial Generation described in the above paragraph coincide well with well-known principles of college student learning. These principles state that learning is grounded in making connections, established in a social context, and affected by the educational climate that includes settings and surroundings (Bowen, 2012; Millis, 2010). Learner-centered environments in which individuals are engaged, active, and collaborative, as compared to teacher-centered, lecture-based classrooms, result in greater student success (Brookfield, 1987; Davis & Arend, 2013; Doyle, 2011; Fink, 2013). Bowen (2012) considers college students as developing adults and, therefore, Perry's model of college student intellectual development is important. Perry (1999) believed that college students can and should transition from dualistic thinkers (only one answer is correct) to relativism (one more than one answer may be correct and there are grey areas) and that adult educators have a responsibility to create an environment that enables this transformation. Bowen states that group work exposes learners to diverse perspectives, experiences, and opinions and helps them make this transition (2012). However, the application of active and engaging teaching approaches remains difficult for instructors to implement for numerous reasons, including resistance, lack of skills, and the amount of time required to make changes (Bowen, 2012; Millis, 2010).

BACKGROUND OF THE STUDY

In the past few years, increasing importance has been given to the physical design of college classrooms to increase student success and create a learner-centered environment that is active and engaging (Brooks, 2012; Gardner, 2013; Hunley & Schaller, 2009). While traditional classrooms look much as they did in nineteenth century images, with rows of chairs and desks, students facing the backs of other students, and the instructor at the front of the room, innovative classrooms have movable chairs, students facing each other at round tables, and no front of the room. Long lectures are discouraged by this physical design, and instructors circulate throughout the room facilitating group discussion of content and interacting with the students. Whiteboards are located around the room for students to record their work, questions, and comments. Technology is a key tool for in-class group work with computer connections for each team at the table. Teams can display their computer work to the rest of the table or to the entire class on an adjacent monitor (Graetz & Goliber, 2002). Leaders in the development of innovative classroom spaces are North Carolina State University, the University of Minnesota, and Massachusetts Institute of Technology (Brooks, 2012). Terminology for the rooms varies from institution to institution, however, the designs are similar. North Carolina State University refers to its rooms as Student-Centered Activities for Large Enrollment Undergraduate Programs (SCALE-UP; Beichner, et al., 2007), Massachusetts Institute of Technology classrooms are labeled Technology Enabled Active Learning (TEAL) classrooms (Dori & Belcher, 2005), and the University of Minnesota's rooms are called Active Learning Classrooms (ALC; Brooks, 2012).

While research on the outcomes of these classrooms is sparse (Brooks, 2012), initial results from assessments are positive. Researchers at North Carolina State reported that SCALE-UP classrooms promoted active and collaborative learning, student engagement, and more interaction between instructors and students (Beichner, et al., 2007). Students taking an electromagnetism course in a TEAL classroom at the Massachusetts Institute of Technology and using an activity based curriculum were more successful, as measured by passing rates, than students in a traditional teacher-centered lecture designed classroom (Dori & Belcher, 2005). At the University of Minnesota using a quasi-experimental design, students taking an introductory biology class taught in an ALC classroom were compared to those taking the same course in a traditional classroom (Brooks, 2012). The researcher at the University of Minnesota found that ALC rooms had a significantly positive effect on student learning as measured by grades. Brooks' research (2012) also revealed that instructors in ALCs moved throughout the room interacting with students, and traditional room instructors were more often located at the podium in the front of the class and distanced from the students.

CONTEXT AND PURPOSE OF THE STUDY

Montana State University (MSU) is located in the Rocky Mountain West, has an enrollment of 15,000 students, 900 faculty, and a Carnegie classification of "very high research intensive." A primary goal of the strategic plan is to increase student graduation rates. In working towards this goal, senior administrators identified courses with low passing grades, targeted introductory algebra and statistics classes for improvement, and asked the Director of the Center for Faculty Excellence, one of this chapter's authors, and the Academic Technology Specialist to become partners in planning an approach for improvement. The benefits of active and collaborative learning to increase student success and the use of technology quickly became topics of dialogue. In accordance with the writings from individuals such as Brookfield (2005), Knowles (1980) and Merriam, Caffarella, and Baumgartner (2007), we wanted the faculty of these classes to offer learner-centered classes that were active and engaging as well as classes that encouraged individuals to work together and learn from one another. In addition to individuals in the Center for Faculty Excellence offering workshops for faculty to enhance their teaching practices, the administrators decided to renovate two classrooms following the models of those at North Carolina State, Massachusetts Institute of Technology, and the University of Minnesota. The administrators, the Director for the Center of Faculty Excellence, and the Academic Technology Specialist wanted the physical design of the classes to be one that encouraged changes in instructor behavior.

Our initial planning group knew that in order to have a successful outcome of the project, we needed a substantial amount of assistance and support. Based upon our readings of the value of collaboration and partnership (Burke, 2011; Davidson, 2012), we believed that creating these types of relationships with constituencies that are not commonly seen working together in higher education, as described by Kezar & Lester (2009) and at our institution, was critical to accomplishing our goals. Yorks & Marsick (2000) advance in their writing on organizational learning and transformation that teams can enable an organization to more effectively reach its goals, and we hoped that the partnerships we established would lead to our university achieving its goal of increasing student success.

The purpose of this chapter is to present the internal and external partnerships established, challenges experienced, student outcomes, and the lessons learned through the design and implementation of what we labeled Technology Enhanced Active Learning (TEAL) classrooms. Our project asked:

1. What were the outcomes, as they related to collaborations and partnerships, of a cross-functional planning team of administrators, faculty, and staff that was formed to design and renovate two traditional classrooms into a TEAL room?
2. What was the student and faculty assessment of all classes taught in TEAL as measured by student and faculty surveys?
3. What was the student success rate, as measured by grades at C and above, of algebra and statistics classes conducted in TEAL classrooms.

DESIGN OF THE ROOMS

Knowles proposed that the physical environment of the classroom should be one of "adultness" (1980, p. 47) that creates a "spirit of mutuality between teachers and students as joint inquirers" (1980, p. 47). Weinstein (1981) argues that "learning is optimized only when the physical environment is treated with the same care as curricular materials and teacher preparation (p. 14). According to Silberman (1995) the physical design of a room can "make or break active learning" (p. 5). He states that there is no one best way to lay out a room; however, active learning requires a design where the participants can easily interact with one another (Silberman, 1995). Research on the influence of the physical design of learning spaces is sparse, and low levels of knowledge on how space impacts learning has kept public consideration of the topic very low (Chism, 2002).

The goal of our cross-functional team was to create a room that increased opportunities of student-student interaction and teacher-student interaction as compared to standard classrooms. We scaled the design to fit into the square footage area available for renovation. Each room consisted of five round tables that were seven feet in diameter and that could accommodate three teams of three students each for a total of nine students at a table. The maximum class size would be 45. Three computer connections at each table would provide a computer hook-up for each group. A flat screen display panel for each table, for a total of five in the room, would enable one group's work to be displayed to the entire table or to the whole room. The instructor would use a work station located in the middle of the room to control the display of content from student computers to the monitor close to an individual table or to all displays in the room. The instructor work station would also have a computer, document camera, and room light adjustment. A large screen at one end of the room would allow for a large display of content from the Internet or from instructor prepared material. Student groups could record their work on white boards located around the room. No instructor podium would be placed in the room.

The round tables, students facing one-another, movable chairs, white boards, and instructor station in the middle of the room created the active learning design for the classroom. This plan encourages student interaction, group work, instructor to student interaction, and student to content contact. The hook-ups for three computers at each table, display monitors, and document camera were the technology portion of the classroom. Figure 9.1 shows the design of the room.

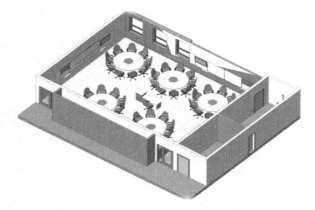

Figure 9.1 Conceptual diagram of MSU TEAL classroom.

METHODS

This section presents the four steps that transpired in our TEAL classroom start-up:

1. Planning and renovating,
2. Scheduling,
3. Preparing faculty, and
4. Assessment of outcomes.

These four steps are adapted from Caffarella and Daffron's (2013) Interactive Model of Program Planning that emphasizes the overarching importance of relationship building, adult learning, and technology in planning and implementing programs. Caffarella and Daffron's Model is composed of eleven components:

1. Context,
2. Support,
3. Needs assessment,
4. Goals and objectives,
5. Instruction,
6. Learning transfer,
7. Evaluating,
8. Scheduling,
9. Budgets,
10. Marketing, and
11. Details (Caffarella and Daffron, p. 29).

Their model is a non-linear model rather than a step-by-step process, and Caffarella and Daffron (2013) write that individuals planning programs may "find all of the components applicable or they may use the relevant parts of the model in any order and combination based upon the planning situation" (p. 30). Each of Caffarella and Daffron's components is nestled within the four steps of our project and are described in varying amounts of detail, and the reader of this chapter will see them incorporated in the narrative of the four steps. Descriptions of internal and external partners and collaborators, the overall process they followed, and the value of these relationships are given for each step.

Planning and Renovating

The process followed during TEAL classroom planning and renovation differed from that of traditional classrooms by the individuals who participated. The members of the cross-functional team during the planning and renovation steps included the Associate Provost, individuals from the Facilities Management Department, the Director for the Center for Faculty Excellence (CFE), the Academic Technology Specialist (who reports within the CFE and is also chair of the Classroom Committee), faculty at the institution, an external architect, an individual from the Information Technology Center, an individual from the Registrar's Office, and learning space leaders at the University of Minnesota and North Carolina State University. The Associate Provost asked all of the individuals at the university to participate in the project. The Director of the CFE and the Academic Technology Specialist had met individuals from the two universities at technology and teaching conferences and asked them if they would be willing to consult with us on the project. Additionally, the Director of the CFE consulted with the faculty scheduled to teach in TEAL rooms once they had been identified. The faculty provided additional input to details of the room, such as configuration of the technology control mechanism. The partners and collaborators in this stage differed from the usual collaborations that occur in renovating a classroom at our institution in that the Associate Provost, the Director for CFE, faculty, and individuals at other universities were included in the planning process.

The new partners made unique and critical contributions. For example, The Director of the CFE and the Academic Technology Specialist learned, after consulting with individuals at North Carolina State University, that seven foot tables are the recommended size for this type of room. Smaller tables do not allow sufficient room for groups of three, the optimum size, and larger tables result in groups too large for equal participation. Individuals at the University of Minnesota provided the architect, facilities planning, and information technology staff the design of their active learning rooms and the technology connections. The Director of the CFE, a long-time faculty member, offered an additional faculty perspective of teaching in a classroom and teaching methodology considerations. As an experienced member of the university's classroom planning committee, the Academic Technology Specialist gave a view of faculty reactions to previous new and redesigned spaces. The Associate Provost kept the group on track, demanded a fast-track schedule, and moved this phase forward at a faster rate than earlier standard classroom renovations.

Scheduling

The procedure for scheduling classes into TEAL followed an unusual path. The collaborators and partners during this phase consisted of the Director of the CFE, an individual in the Registrar's Office, the chair of the math department, and faculty—all new contributors to the standard process. The new participants served as significant players in identifying and scheduling classes into the TEAL rooms. Since senior administrators targeted algebra and statistics for increased student success rates, the chair of the math department entered into the development of course schedules and had first priority in identifying the math sections for the TEAL classroom. The department head selected three sections of entry level algebra and four sections of entry level statistics courses into the classroom the first semester. The department chair placed instructors who had indicated an interest in pioneering the new approach into the room. The Center for Faculty Excellence offered an information session about the innovative classroom for all faculty at the university while the room was in the design phase. At the end of this session and for the next several weeks, faculty in other disciplines signed up to teach in the room. Instead of the Registrar's office scheduling classes, as in the past, the Director of the CFE planned the timetable for classes. This was done for two reasons (a) to ensure that all the math classes had a time period, with the remainder of classes scheduled around them, and (b) to have a list of TEAL instructors for teaching and technology training. The Director gave the schedule to the Registrar's Office. This was the first time in the history of the university that classes were not scheduled directly through the Registrar's Office.

Preparing Faculty

We viewed the preparation of faculty for new teaching methods in the room as vital to the success of TEAL and devoted a considerable amount of time and effort to this aspect. Three meetings occurred with faculty before they began teaching in TEAL spring semester and three sessions occurred after they began teaching. The partners and collaborators during this step consisted of the two individuals in the Center for Faculty Excellence, the Associate Provost, and individuals working at the University of Minnesota. The addition of the Associate Provost and individuals from other universities were distinctive in this step.

For session one, the two individuals in the Center for Faculty Excellence and the Associate Provost conducted a "Welcome to TEAL" workshop the semester prior to the room opening. In order for faculty to learn information about the teaching methodology intended for these rooms before we met, we provided a link to University of Minnesota Center for Teaching Learning (2013) web site titled "Considerations for Teaching in Active Learning Communities," that provided an excellent overview. By using this approach, faculty would be more knowledgeable about teaching practices before attending so that a more analytical and deep dialog could occur during the session. Hence, we modeled "flipping the classroom," a key strategy of teaching in an active learning classroom. In a "flipped classroom" content is first delivered outside of class thereby enabling a more comprehensive examination of the subject when the face-to-face session occurs (Bowen, 2012). The Associate Provost, Director of the CFE, and the Academic Technology Specialist, facilitated a discussion with eleven instructors about teaching in the room. Topics included what they were excited about, how teaching methods would differ, and any concerns and questions they had about teaching in TEAL. Our conversations focused on student collaboration and faculty-small group interaction. Individuals learned from each other by sharing experiences of active teaching in their current traditionally designed classrooms as well as their ideas for new approaches. The facilitators made a list of questions and concerns that had not been answered by the end of the session and gave these to the Director of the Center of Teaching and Learning at the University of Minnesota.

For the second session, the Director of the Center of Teaching and Learning at the University of Minnesota gathered three individuals who had been teaching in their University's Active Learning Classrooms, gave them our questions and concerns, and conducted a live Skype Internet discussion session. During the meeting, their experts addressed each question and concern as well as answered additional questions posed to them during the consultation. Our new instructors found this session reassuring, and it also provided them with strategies they had not considered.

Meeting three occurred one week before classes began. The Director of the Center for Teaching and Learning at the University of Minnesota traveled to our University and conducted a group session for all the new TEAL instructors. The group session contained specific methods for teaching in that type of classroom. Additionally, he consulted one-on-one with TEAL faculty if they had questions regarding the content of their specific course.

We believed that ongoing support immediately before and after classes began was important. Therefore, the Academic Technology Specialist met with TEAL faculty immediately before the classes started to provide training in using the technology in the room. After the semester began, the Director of the CFE and the Academic Technology Specialist provided ongoing support by conducting three brown bag lunches to answer questions. During these gatherings, faculty collaborated with one another to share experiences, challenges, and how they tackled difficulties. Strategies for designing and managing group activities were the predominant topic of conversation.

Assessment of Outcomes

Two faculty members from the Department of Education with expertise in assessment, the Director of the CFE, and a graduate student from the Department of Education joined to form an assessment team. The first question of the project asked "What were the outcomes, as they related to collaborations and partnerships, of a cross-functional planning team of administrators, faculty, and staff that was formed to design and renovate two traditional classrooms into a TEAL room?" To answer this question, the assessment team gathered information by interviewing the Associate Provost, an individual from the Facilities Management Department, the Academic Technology Specialist, an individual from the Information Technology Center, and an individual from the Registrar's Office throughout the project and at the end. We asked them questions about the collaborations and partnerships that occurred during the planning process, specific events that transpired as a result of the individuals working together, challenges that occurred, and the unique contributions of individuals. The Director of CFE kept detailed notes as the project progressed as well as provided her experiences and perceptions. The assessment team conducted an analysis of all the data by examining it in detail and looking for descriptions of events as they related to the interactions among the group members. Our analysis followed Gay, Mills, and Airasian's (2012) method of starting with a "large set of data representing many things and seeking to narrow them progressively into small and important groups of data" (p. 466). Additionally, we looked for unique interactions among the group members that illustrated the concepts described in the collaboration and partnership literature, such as sharing experiences, innovation, creativity, new practices, and improvements. To establish validity, the assessment team members used peer debriefing (Gay, Mills, & Airasian, 2012) by consulting with each other to reflect on the data gathered and the analysis. Assessment team members believed that the answers to the second and third questions of our project provided important information about the outcomes of the cross-functional planning team as well.

The second question of our project asked "What was the student and faculty assessment of all classes conducted in TEAL, as measured by student and faculty surveys?" The team chose the University of Minnesota's assessment instrument, contacted them for permission to use their survey, and distributed the survey at the end of the semester. The team created two survey instruments: one for students and one for faculty. Questions for both surveys asked for the same information, with the faculty questions reworded slightly to query their perceptions of students learning and experiences as well as their evaluations of the room. The survey contained twenty questions on a four-point Likert scale of 1 = strongly disagree, 2 = disagree, 3 = agree, and 4 = strongly agree. The four point Likert scale is what Losby and Wetmore (2014) label a forced choice survey instrument because there is no middle category. According to Losby and Wetmore (2014), a forced choice survey forces people to make an evaluation and people may be more discriminating and thoughtful with their responses. An additional benefit is that it avoids possible misinterpretation of a middle point (Losby & Wetmore, 2014). Following the format of the University of Minnesota instrument, the survey queried student and faculty assessment of the learning outcomes and the room design, and the questions were divided into the categories of (a) course specific; (b) development of skills beyond the classroom; and (c) room design/use of technology. The team administered the surveys online using Survey Monkey. The questions on the student survey are shown in Table 9.1 and are grouped by category.

The questions on the faculty survey are shown in Table 9.2 and are grouped by category.

The third question of our project asked "What was the student success rate, as measured by grades at C and above, of algebra and statistics classes conducted in TEAL classrooms?" To answer this question, the assessment team calculated student success rate (grades at C and above) for algebra and statistics classes taught in TEAL at the end of each of the two semesters.

RESULTS

Montana State University's first TEAL classroom opened spring semester of 2013 and a second room became ready for classes fall semester of the same year. During spring 2013, 380 undergraduate students with majors in seven colleges enrolled in 14 classes. These classes included four sections of introductory statistics, three sections of introductory algebra, two education classes, and one section each of horticulture, engineering, political

TABLE 9.1   Student Feedback Survey Item

Category	Survey Item Stem: As compared to the layout and design of other classrooms, I believe the design of this Classroom...
Category 1: Content	Increases my excitement to learn. Facilitates multiples types of learning activities. Promotes discussion. Encourages my active participation. Makes me want to attend class regularly. Helps me develop connections with my classmates. Engages me in the learning process. Is an appropriate space to hold this class. Enhances in-class exercises. Helps me be more successful.
Category 2: Development of skills beyond the classroom	Helps me develop professional skills that can be transferred to the real world. Helps me develop confidence in working in small groups. Helps me define issues or challenges and identify possible solutions. Assists me in understanding someone else's views by imagining how an issue looks from another perspective. Improves my confidence that I can speak clearly and effectively. Encourages me to create of generate new ideas, products, or ways of understanding.
Category 3: Room design/ use of technology	The technology helps me learn the content of this course. The writing boards on the wall helped me learn the material. The instructor was effective in using the technology in the classroom. The instructor was effective in using the classroom for instructional purposes.

TABLE 9.2   Faculty Feedback Survey Item

Category	Survey Item Stem: As compared to the layout and design of other classrooms, I believe the design of this classroom...
Category 1: Content Specific	Increases my students' excitement to learn. Facilitates multiples types of learning activities. Promotes discussion among students. Encourages my student's active participation. Makes my students want to attend class regularly. Helps my students develop connections with classmates. Engages my students in the learning process. Is an appropriate space in which to hold this particular course. Enhances in-class exercises.

(continued)

TABLE 9.2   Faculty Feedback Survey Item (continued)

Category	Survey Item Stem: As compared to the layout and design of other classrooms, I believe the design of this classroom...
Category 2: Development of skills beyond the classroom	Helps my students develop professional skills that can be transferred to the real world.
	Helps my students develop confidence in working in small groups.
	Helps my students define issues or challenges and identify possible solutions.
	Assists my students in understanding someone else's views by imagining how an issue looks from another perspective.
	Improves my student's confidence so that they can speak clearly and effectively.
	Encourages my students to create of generate new ideas, products, or ways of understanding.
Category 3: Room design/ use of technology	I was able effectively to use the technology available in the classroom for instructional purposes.
	I felt physically comfortable in this room.
	I was able effectively to use the classroom for instructional purposes.
	The in-class exercises for this course are enhanced by the features of this classroom.

science, chemistry, and geography. These classes were taught by 11 instructors. For fall 2013, 930 undergraduates enrolled in 24 classes in six sections of introductory algebra, seven sections of introductory statistics, two sections of algebra II, six sections of business courses, and one section each of engineering, education, and geography. Seventeen instructors taught in the TEAL class rooms during fall 2013.

Cross-Functional Planning Team

According to everyone interviewed, the internal and external partnerships were important, effective, and beneficial in the design and building of the TEAL classrooms. According to the individuals interviewed, the new participants included in each step contributed varied viewpoints and outlooks, and the collaborations among all individuals created results and a synergy that would not have occurred otherwise. Individual and group learning occurred.

Doz (1996) reports that, without purpose, over 50% of collaborations fail. All internal members of our group shared the common goal of wanting to build an innovative classroom that would be successful and increase student learning. The task directed objective of the partnerships and the reliance on each other to accomplish this goal provided a strong impetus for the individuals at the University to work together. For example, the willingness of the Registrar's Office to direct faculty who would be teaching in TEAL to the Director of the CFE enabled identification of who to contact for training and support. The foundation of the relationships helped when the team learned that the first TEAL classroom would not be ready at the beginning of the semester. With the late arrival of technology equipment from the outside vender on the horizon, early notification by our Facilities partner to the Registrar's Office partner permitted timely rescheduling of classes into alternate classrooms for the first two weeks of the semester and notification to students.

An important outcome of collaboration can be innovation that would not have transpired without the coalition (Paulus & Nijstad, 2003; Senge, 1990), and this benefit occurred in the project. The involvement of faculty in classroom design and equipment outfitting added aspects that had not been considered. Faculty input resulted in document cameras for each student table so that groups could project written work (hence the name "document") on table monitors as compared to the ability to post only computer work. However, the desire to create a nationally innovative classroom led to some difficulties. The latest design of *frosted* glass white boards by classroom furniture designers resulted in boards for our first TEAL room that were attractive and innovative but somewhat difficult to read at a distance. Feedback from faculty about this challenge resulted in a different style of white board ordered for the second TEAL room.

Because external collaborations are viewed as key to mergers and financial success, the business literature has devoted attention to the importance of outside alliances (Saxton, 1997). External collaborators in higher education typically consist of accrediting agencies, professional organizations, K–12 schools, and researchers in the same or similar disciplines or areas of interest (Kezar & Lester, 2009). Reaching out to make connections with other universities that had experience with TEAL type classrooms developed networks that supplied the team with information and support. Individuals at North Carolina State University shared their research on improved student learning outcomes in the sciences and the most effective room design. Individuals at the University of Minnesota furnished best practices in teaching in this type of room and how to address the challenges that can be experienced.

Research on teamwork reveals that having individuals with different areas of expertise expands perspectives and can lead to powerful outcomes (Eisenstat & Cohan, 1990; Neumann & Wright, 1999), and individuals involved in the project described this effect. The Associate Provost added an overall institutional outlook, which included attention to the University's strategic plan and goals. Additionally, this individual provided energy and momentum to the project. For example, if another partner expressed concern about the project's time schedule, he intervened to remove doubts and eliminate institutional barriers. The Director of the CFE added the perspective of faculty who would be teaching in the rooms and brought up unique considerations during the design and renovation steps. Members of the team stated that they learned about the responsibilities of others in the group and expected this knowledge would transfer to other projects and be beneficial.

Student Assessment of TEAL Classrooms

At the end of spring semester 2013, 243 students completed the end-of-semester surveys that assessed their perceptions of learning outcomes and room design in TEAL as compared to other classrooms for a response rate of 63%. Of these respondents, 32% were freshmen, 34% sophomores, 21% juniors, 12% seniors and 1% master's students. Fifty percent of the respondents were males and 50% females. Sixty-nine percent of the students were in the 18–21 age range, 24% in the 22–30 age range, and 7% in the 30+ range.

At the end of fall semester 2013, 307 students returned the end-of-semester surveys for a response rate of 33%. Of these respondents, 42% were freshman, 28% sophomores, 20% juniors, 7% seniors, and 3% 5+ years. Forty-six percent of the respondents were males and 54% females. Seventy-three percent of the students were in the 18 to 21 age range, 21% in the 22–30 age range, and 6% in the 30+ age range.

The assessment team calculated the mean and standard deviation of the student survey responses for each of the categories and the results are shown in Table 9.3 for spring and fall 2013 semesters. Calculating the mean and standard deviation by category makes the report of survey results more meaningful and also improves the reliability of the scores (Gay, Mills, & Airasian, 2012). Table 9.3 shows a positive mean (3 = agree on the 4 point Likert scale) for all categories in spring 2013 and a positive mean for all categories with the exception of the Development of Skills category in fall 2013. The fall 2013 mean for the category of Development of Skills, 2.83, was only .18 below a positive mean. For both semesters, students gave

TABLE 9.3   Student Responses: Average and Standard Deviation By Category

Category	Spring 2013		Fall 2013	
	Mean	SD	Mean	SD
Course Specific	3.22	0.76	3.10	0.70
Development of Skills	3.06	0.76	2.83	0.72
Room design/use of Tech	3.27	0.82	3.06	0.75

Note: N = 243 Spring, N = 307 Fall. 4 = strongly agree, 1 = strongly disagree.

positive responses, on average, to the TEAL rooms as compared to other classrooms for the majority of categories. While the standard deviations were less than 1, by using a 4 point Likert scale, the authors considered the responses as reflecting some variance of positive and negative responses.

Calculating the percentages of positive and negative responses for individual questions is an additional method of analyzing the results of a Likert scale survey and can provide further insight to the results (Losby & Wetmore, 2014). According to Losby & Wetmore (2014), a calculation of positive and negative responses can be particularly informative in a forced choice Likert scale survey with no middle response. For our four-point Likert-scale of 1 = strongly disagree, 2 = disagree, 3 = agree, and 4 = strongly agree, positive responses were 3 and 4 level responses and negative responses were 1 and 2 responses. Accordingly, the authors calculated these figures and these percentages are shown in Table 9.4 in a descending order of positive comments for spring 2013.

When asked to compare the TEAL room to other classrooms, the majority of students gave positive responses to all twenty questions in all categories for both semesters. At the end of spring semester 2013, items in the Content Category that received the highest percentage of positive responses were 94% to promoting discussion, 93% to facilitating multiple types of learning activities, and 91% to encouraging active participation. Highest positive percentage items in the Development of Skills Beyond the Classroom Category were positive responses of 85% to helping develop confidence working in small groups, 80% to improving confidence to speak clearly and effectively, and 79% to assists in understanding others' views, helping to define issues and identify solutions, and encouraging the creation of new ideas, products or ways of understanding.

For fall 2013, students also indicated very positive responses to the TEAL room in a similar order as spring, with 93% positive to facilitating multiple types of learning activities, 92% positive to promoting discussion, and 91% to engaging in the learning process.

Faculty Assessment of TEAL Classrooms

Seven of the 11 instructors teaching in spring 2013 and 17 of 17 teaching in fall 2013 returned the end-of-semester survey that asked about their perceptions of student learning and room design. The assessment team calculated the mean and standard deviation of the faculty survey responses for each of the categories and the results are shown in Table 9.5 for the two semesters. Table 9.5 reports positive mean scores (3 = agree on the 4 point Likert scale) for all categories in spring and fall 2013 semesters. The standard deviation of faculty responses was smaller than those of student responses.

TABLE 9.4   Student Responses: Percentage of Positive and Negative Responses

Questions	Spring 2013		Fall 2013	
	Positive	Negative	Positive	Negative
Category 1: Content				
Promotes discussion.	94%	6%	92%	8%
Facilitates multiple types of learning activities.	93%	7%	93%	7%
Encourages my active participation.	91%	9%	84%	16%
Helps me develop connections with my classmates.	90%	10%	90%	10%
Is an appropriate space to hold this class.	87%	13%	89%	11%
Engages me in the learning process.	87%	13%	91%	9%
Enhances in-class exercises.	87%	13%	91%	9%
Increases my excitement to learn.	81%	19%	82%	18%
Helps me be more successful.	77%	23%	74%	26%
Makes me want to attend class regularly.	70%	30%	62%	38%
Category 2: Development of Skills Beyond the Classroom				
Helps me develop confidence in working in small groups.	85%	15%	90%	10%
Improves my confidence that I can speak clearly and effectively.	80%	20%	69%	31%
Assists me in understanding someone else's views by imagining how an issue looks from another perspective.	79%	21%	67%	33%
Helps me define issues or challenges and identify possible solutions.	79%	21%	70%	30%
Encourages me to create or generate new ideas, products, or ways of understanding.	79%	21%	71%	29%
Helps me develop professional skills that can be transformed to the real world.	78%	22%	69%	31%
Category 3: Room Design/Use of Technology				
The instructor was effective in using the technology in the classroom.	86%	14%	83%	17%
The instructor was effective in using the classroom for instructional purposes.	86%	14%	87%	13%
The technology helps me learn the content of this course.	81%	19%	75%	25%
The writing boards on the wall helped me learn the material.	78%	22%	78%	22%

Note: N = 243 Spring, N = 307 fall. Positive = 3 & 4 on 4 point Likert scale, negative = 1 & 2. Percentages rounded to equal 100%.

TABLE 9.5   Faculty Responses: Average and Standard Deviation by Category

Category	Spring 2013		Fall 2013	
	Mean	SD	Mean	SD
Course Specific	3.63	0.59	3.36	0.48
Development of Skills	3.32	0.63	3.16	0.52
Room design/use of Tech	3.41	0.76	3.17	0.65

Note: N = 7 Spring, N = 17 Fall. 4 = strongly agree, 1 = strongly disagree.

The assessment team calculated positive and negative percentages of faculty responses as well, and these numbers are shown in Table 9.6 in a descending order of positive responses for spring 2013.

Faculty had high positive responses to the questions with the majority of faculty giving positive responses to all the questions in all categories for both semesters. For spring 2013, 100% of responding faculty stated that the room, as compared to other classrooms, increases students' excitement to learn, facilitates multiple types of learning activities, promotes discussion, encourages students' active participation, helps students develop connections with classmates, engages students in the learning process, enhances in-class exercises, and will increase student retention. In the Development of Skills Beyond the Classroom category, 100% of responding faculty also strongly agreed or agreed that the room design helps students develop professional skills that can be transferred to the real world, develop confidence in working in small groups, define issues and identify possible solutions, and understand someone else's views.

Faculty had similar responses in fall 2013. One hundred percent of responding faculty indicated the room increases students' excitement to learn, facilitates multiple types of learning activities, promotes discussion, and engages students in the learning process. In the Development of Skills beyond the Classroom Category, 100% of responding faculty also strongly agreed or agreed that the room design helps students develop confidence working in small groups. The majority of the faculty gave positive responses to the room design. At the end of the semester, one of the instructors related informally to one of the researchers that they preferred to lecture hence some negative responses were not surprising.

Student Success Rates of Algebra and Statistics

Student success rates, as measured by grades of C and above, of individuals enrolled in the algebra and statistics TEAL classrooms were calculated. For comparison, non-Teal classrooms were calculated for both semesters

TABLE 9.6   Faculty Responses: Percentage of Positive and Negative Responses

	Spring 2013		Fall 2013	
Questions	Positive	Negative	Positive	Negative
Category 1: Content				
Increases my student's excitement to learn.	100%	0%	100%	0%
Facilitates multiple types of learning activities.	100%	0%	100%	0%
Promotes discussion.	100%	0%	100%	0%
Encourages my students' active participation.	100%	0%	85%	15%
Helps my students develop connections with classmates.	100%	0%	93%	8%
Engages my students in the learning process.	100%	0%	100%	0%
Is an appropriate space to hold this class.	100%	0%	100%	0%
Enhances in-class exercises.	100%	0%	92%	8%
I think this class will increase student retention.	100%	0%	83%	16%
Makes my students want to attend class regularly.	71%	29%	84%	15%
Category 2: Development of Skills beyond the Classroom				
Helps my students develop professional skills that can be transferred to the real world.	100%	0%	85%	15%
Helps my students develop confidence in working in small groups.	100%	0%	100%	0%
Helps my students define issues or challenges and identify possible solutions.	100%	0%	91%	8%
Helps my students in understanding someone else's views by imagining how an issue looks from another perspective.	100%	0%	85%	15%
Encourages my students to create of generate new ideas, products, or ways of understanding.	85%	15%	85%	15%
Improves my student's confidence that they can speak clearly and effectively.	71%	14%	82%	16%
Category 3: Room Design/Use of Technology				
I felt physically comfortable in this room.	100%	0%	92%	8%
I was able effectively to use the classroom for instructional purposes.	100%	0%	92%	8%
I was able effectively to use the technology available in the classroom for instructional purposes.	85%	15%	92%	8%
The in-class exercises for this course are enhanced by the features of this classroom.	85%	15%	53%	47%

Note: N = 7 Spring, N = 11 Fall. Positive = 3 & 4 on 4 point Likert scale, negative = 1 & 2. Percentages rounded to equal 100%.

TABLE 9.7   Student Success Rates (Grades at C and above)

Class	Spring 2010– Fall 2012 (6 semesters prior to TEAL) Pre-TEAL	Spring 2013		Fall 2013	
		TEAL	Non-TEAL	TEAL	Non-TEAL
Algebra	54%	81%	63%	78%	71%
	(N = 2,817)	(N = 94)	(N = 298)	(N = 252)	(N = 361)
Statistics	56%	86%	65%	80%	69%
	(N = 4,089)	(N = 139)	(N = 464)	(N = 268)	(N = 487)

and success rates of students enrolled in algebra and statistics for the previous six semesters, spring 2010—fall 2012, before the TEAL classrooms were built are shown as well. These results are shown in Table 9.7 and it reveals that before TEAL classrooms were built, student success percentages of algebra classes averaged 54% and statistics classes 56%. For spring semester 2013, student success rates in introductory algebra classes taught in TEAL increased to 81% and introductory statistics to 86%. For fall 2013, student success rates classes taught in TEAL for introductory algebra were 78% and success rates for introductory statistics were 84%. An interesting comparison is classes taught in non-TEAL classrooms for the two semesters. While the non-TEAL success rates for both semesters were lower than the TEAL classes, the rates were higher than the previous six semesters. The non-TEAL success rates increased from spring 2012 to fall 2013. All pre-TEAL and non-TEAL classes were of similar enrollment size as those of the TEAL rooms.

DISCUSSION AND RECOMMENDATIONS FOR PRACTICE

The results revealed positive outcomes of the collaborations and partnerships of the cross-functional planning team that was formed to design and renovate two traditional classrooms into a TEAL room. The relationships provided the foundation for building and opening the classroom. The common goal of everyone helped to create the camaraderie among individuals. Sharing knowledge and experiences resulted in learning that benefited the individuals, the group, and the university. One person stated, "now that I have worked so closely with someone in the Registrar's Office, I understand better the challenges of their work and this will be helpful in other situations when we work on a project or in anyway." The university, as an organization, benefited from the collaboration as shown by the positive responses from students and faculty as well as the increases in student success in algebra and statistics classes. One drawback is that with operational classrooms, the interaction among all these individuals is no longer focused on the task, causing some difficulty in addressing remaining minor issues. For example, one of the rooms is lacking a clock to help the instructor and students monitor group discussion time. A significant positive consequence is that the rapport formed among individuals in the partnerships is ongoing for other long and short-term projects.

The positive student and faulty survey responses aligned with results obtained on the University of Minnesota's survey (Brooks, 2012). The salient feature of the new design, according to faculty and students, was the increase in student engagement and interaction with the course content and each other. Working in teams established connections with each other and with the content of the course. Key concepts described in the adult learning literature, such as sharing knowledge and experience (Knowles, 1980) and group reflection and action (Lamb, 2003) occur while individuals are learning together. Group work in TEAL provides many rich opportunities for students to hear a variety of perspectives and opinions. However, the literature reports that some learners are resistant to group work and prefer to sit passively in a classroom (Millis, 2010). Hence, the authors of this chapter would not expect all students to evaluate the room positively.

The dramatic rise in student success rates in the introductory algebra and statistics classes is equal to that found in studies of physics classes (Beichner et al., 2007) but exceeds the increase of the limited research in other disciplines (Brooks, 2012). An increase in student success rates in a class can mean less repeating of a failed class, which can be a savings of resources to the university in terms of needed classroom space and faculty salary. Additionally, the impact of student engagement extends beyond that of individual classes; those who are engaged in the classroom are more likely to persist in their academic career (Millis, 2010; Wasley, 2006). A learner-centered classroom creates an environment of caring for the student and the positive impact of engagement in the classroom is particularly true for students who are underserved minority populations and students entering college with lower levels of achievement (Braxton, Jones, Hirschy, & Hartley, 2008; Wasley, 2006).

Of interest to the authors was the rise of success rates in non-TEAL classes. After the results of this study were calculated, a conversation with the chair of the math department and two of the TEAL instructors by the Director of the CFE yielded some insight into the results. The chair and instructors stated that the chair had encouraged instructors in the non-TEAL classes to use some of the team-work approach used in TEAL, and this had occurred. While the technology of TEAL was not available to them, they believed that the increase in the use of team-work in non-TEAL classes accounted for the increase from previous semesters.

The majority of learners in this study were Millennnials and, therefore, it is not surprising that the majority were comfortable working in teams and using technology. McCraw and Martindale (2012) state that good teaching appears to be universal across generations—independent of age. Based upon principles of adult learning, we believe that individuals of all ages could find TEAL classrooms of benefit. While earlier generations may have less experience with technology, the simplicity of the technology of TEAL can easily be learned and the increased engagement with content and each other will benefit all ages.

The following recommendations that are presented can be used for a project similar to ours or can be extended to others as well.

1. Create classrooms designed for student engagement as this is critical to improving success and developing skills that can be used after graduation. Students and faculty alike cited student engagement and collaboration an important outcome of the new design.
2. Consider carefully individuals who may serve as key alliances for projects and think outside the box when deciding who to include in the project. Involving a diverse group and people who have not been included in previous projects can lead to unique and vital perspectives that will improve outcomes.
3. Expect things to not go as planned or anticipated. However, we found that the foundations in relationships that were built gave us new ways of dealing with these challenges.
4. Maintain positive relationships with partners throughout the process, as these can be useful for other projects and can reach beyond the boundaries of the project into the future.
5. Assess outcomes by gathering data regarding goals of the project. Outcomes give feedback to those involved and those providing resources so that they can make revisions, if needed, or proceed with expanding or reducing projects.

In conclusion, the collaborations and partnerships established during our project served as the foundation for the success of building our TEAL classrooms. These occurred among administrators, faculty, and staff within the institution, with individuals external to the institution, and between students. The learner-centered environment and innovative design of the room brought about increased engagement, success, and the development of skills that can be used by students beyond their individual classes. At the conclusion of Dori and Belcher's research study (2005), with positive outcomes from their TEAL room, they stated that "we view the TEAL project as a step towards preparing tomorrow's citizens, leaders, and experts for future roles by engaging them in a technology enhanced environment that supports peer discussion and collaboration" (p. 275). We agree and believe that this innovative learning environment builds a sustainable future for learners. Hopefully, readers of this chapter will find this description of value in providing guidance and motivation to those considering building a TEAL room or considering renovating any classroom. Individuals should consider the culture of their own institution and other relationships that might be of importance in forming their own partnerships and collaborations. The participants of this project are optimistic that taking classes in a TEAL or a similarly designed room can help students towards building successful and prosperous lives in new ways. We believe that other institutions using classrooms that incorporate the fundamentals of our TEAL rooms will find comparable results.

REFERENCES

Bailey, F., & Dolan, A. (2011). The meaning of partnership in development: Lessons in developmental education. *Policy & practice: A developmental education review, 13*, 30–48. Retrieved from http: //www. Developmentededucationreview.com/issue13-focus2

Beichner, R., Saul, J., Abbott, D., Morse, J., Deardorff, D., & Allain, R. (2007). Student centered activities for large enrollment undergraduate programs (SCALE-UP) project. In E. Redish & P. Cooney (Eds.), *Research-based reform of university physics* (pp. 1–42). College Park, MD: American Association of Physics Teachers.

Bowen, J. A. (2012). *Teaching naked: How moving technology out of your college classroom will improve student learning.* San Francisco, CA: Jossey-Bass.

Braxton, J. M., Jones, W. A., Hirschy, A. S., & Hartley, H. V., III. (2008). The role of active learning in college persistence. In J. M. Braxton (Ed.), *New directions for teaching and learning: The role of the classroom in college student persistence, 115* (pp. 71–83). San Francisco, CA: Jossey-Bass.

Brookfield, S. (1987). *Developing critical thinkers: Challenging adults to explore alternative ways of thinking and acting.* San Francisco, CA: Jossey Bass.

Brookfield, S. (2005). *The skillful teacher: On technique, trust, and responsiveness in the classroom.* San Francisco, CA: Jossey-Bass.

Brooks, C. D. (2012). Space and consequences: The impact of different formal learning spaces on instructor and student behavior. *Journal of Learning Spaces, 1*(2). Retrieved from http://libjournal.uncg.edu/index.php/jls/article/view/285/275

Burke, W. (2011). *Organization change theory and practice.* San Francisco, CA: Jossey-Bass.

Caffarella R., & Daffron, S. (2013). *Planning programs for adult learners: A practical guide* (3rd ed.) San Francisco, CA: Jossey-Bass.

Chism, N. V. (2002). A tale of two classrooms. In N. V. Chism, & D. J. Brickford (Eds.), *New Directions for Teaching and Learning, 92*(4), pp. 5–12.

Davidson, J. (2012). *Framing decisions: Decision making that accounts for irrationality, people, and constraints.* San Francisco, CA: Jossey-Bass.

Davis, J. R., & Arend, B. D. (2013). *Facilitating seven ways of learning.* Sterling, VA: Stylus.

Dori, J., & Belcher, J. (2005). How does technology enabled active learning affect undergraduate students' understanding of electromagnetism concepts? *The Journal of Learning Spaces, 14(2),* 243 –279.

Doyle, T. (2011). *Learner-centered teaching: Putting the research on learning into practice.* Sterling, VA: Stylus.

Doz, Y. L. (1996). The evolution of cooperation in strategic alliances: Initial conditions of learning processes. *Strategic Management Journal, 17,* 55–83.

Eisner, M. (2010). *Working together: Why great partnerships succeed.* New York, NY: NY: Harper Collins Books.

Eisenstat, R. A., & Cohen, S. G. (1990). Summary: Top management group. In J. R. Hackman (Ed.), *Groups that work (and those that don't): Creating conditions for effective teamwork.* San Francisco, CA: Jossey-Bass.

Fenwick, T. (2003). *Learning through experience: Troubling orthodoxies and intersecting questions.* Malabar, FL: Krieger.

Fink, L. D. (2013). *Creating significant learning experiences.* San Francisco: CA, Jossey-Bass.

Gardner, L. (2013, October 4). Colleges adapt (slowly) to classrooms 2.0. *The Chronicle of Higher Education,* B22–B24.

Gay, L. R., Mills, G. E., & Airasian, P. (2012). *Educational research: Competencies for analysis and application* (10th ed.). Upper Saddle River, NJ: Pearson.

Graetz, K. G., & Goliber, M. J. (2002). Designing collaborative learning places: Psychological Foundations and new frontiers. In N. V. Chism, & D. J. Brickford (Eds.), *New directions for teaching and learning, 92*(4), pp.13–22. San Francisco: CA: Jossey-Bass.

Green, G., Coke, K. L., & Ballard, M. (2013). The new nontraditional student in higher education: Best practices to sustain the Millennial Generation. In C. J. Boden-McGill & K. P. King (Eds.), *Developing and sustaining adult learners* (pp. 83–99). Charlotte, NC: Information Age Publishing.

Hammond, M., & Collins, R. (1991). *Self-directed learning: Critical practice.* London, UK: Nichols/GP Publishing.

Hunley, S., & Schaller, M. (2009). Assessment: The key to creating spaces that promote learning, *Educause Review, 44*(2), 26–35.

Kanter, R. (1996). Collaborative advantage: The art of alliances. *Harvard Business Review,* 96–108.

Kasl, E., Marsick, V. J., & Dechant, K. (1997). Teams as learners: A research-based model of team learning. *Journal of Applied Behavioral Science, 33,* 227–246.

Kezar, A., & Lester, J. (2009). *Organizing higher education for collaboration.* San Francisco, CA: Jossey-Bass.

Knowles, M. S. (1980). *The modern practice of adult education: From pedagogy to andragogy* (2nd ed.). New York, NY: Cambridge Books.

Knowles, M. S., Holten, E. F., & Swanson, R. A. (2011). *The adult learner: The definitive classic in adult education and human resource development.* Oxford, UK: Elsevier.

Lamb, S. (2003). Best practices on fostering transformative learning in the workplace. In C.A. Weissner, S. R. Merys, N. L. Pfhal, & P. G Neaman (Eds.), *Proceedings of the 5th International Conference on Transformative Learning* (pp. 263–268). New York, NY: Teachers College, Columbia University.

Losby, J., & Wetmore. (2014). *Using Likert scales in evaluation research*. Retrieved from http://www.cdc.gov/dhdsp/pubs/docs/CB_February_14_2012.pdf

McCraw, M. A., & Martindale, T. (2012). *Instructing multigenerational students*. Retrieved from http://www.memphis.edu/icl/idt/clrc/clrc2012-mccraw-martindale.pdf

Mattessich, P., Murray-Close, M., & Monsey, B. (2001). *Collaboration: What makes it work: a review of research literature on factors influencing successful collaborations* (2nd ed.). Saint Paul, MN: Amherst H. Wilder Foundation.

Merriam, S. B., Caffarella, R. S., & Baumgartner, L. M., (2007). Learning in adulthood: A comprehensive guide (3rd ed.). San Francisco: CA: Jossey-Bass.

Mezirow, J. (2000). Learning to think like an adult: Core concepts of transformation theory. In Mezirow, & Associates (Eds.), *Learning as transformation: Critical perspectives on a theory in progress* (pp. 3–33). San Francisco, CA: Jossey-Bass.

Millis, B.J. (2010). Why faculty should adopt cooperative learning approaches. In B. J. Mills (Ed.), *Cooperative learning in higher education*: Across the disciplines, across the academy (pp. 1–9). Sterling: VA, Stylus Publishing.

Nelson, D. L., & Quick, J. C. (2005). *Understanding organizational behavior* (2nd ed.). Mason, OH: Thompson/South-Western.

Neumann, G. A., & Wright, J. (1999). Team effectiveness: Beyond the skills and cognitive ability. *Journal of Applied Psychology, 84,* 376–389.

Paulus, P. B., & Nijstad, B. A. (2003). *Group creativity: Innovation through collaboration.* New York, NY: Oxford University Press.

Perry, W. (1999). *Forms of intellectual and ethical development in the college years.* San Francisco: CA, Jossey-Bass.

Pew Research Center (2014). *Millennials in Adulthood.* Retrieved from http://www.pewsocialtrends.org/2014/03/07/millennials-in-adulthood/

Saxton, T. (1997). The effects of partner and relationship characteristics on alliance outcomes. *Academy of Management Journal, 40,* 443–461.

Schrader-Naef, R. (2000). Foundations of self-directed lifelong learning. In G.A. Straka (Ed.), *Conceptions of self-directed learning* (pp. 143–169). New York, NY: Waxmann.

Senge, P. (1990). *The fifth discipline: The art and practice of the learning organization.* New York, NY: Doubleday.

Silberman, M. (1995). *101 ways to make to make training active.* San Francisco: CA: Jossey-Bass.

Taylor, K. (2000). Teaching with Developmental Intention. In Mezirow, & Associates (Eds.), *Learning as transformation: Critical perspectives on a theory in progress* (pp. 151–167). San Francisco, CA: Jossey-Bass.

Wasley, P. (2006, November 17). Underprepared students benefit most from "engagement." *Chronicle of Higher Education,* A39–A40.

Yorks, L., & Marsick, V. (2000). Organizational Learning and Transformation. In Mezirow, J. and Associates (Eds.), *Learning as Transformation: Critical perspectives on a theory in progress (pp. 253–281).* San Francisco, CA: Jossey-Bass.

University of Minnesota Center for Teaching Learning. (2013). Considerations for teaching in active learning classrooms. Retrieved from: http://www1.umn.edu/ohr/teachlearn/alc/considerations/

Weinstein, C. S. (1981). Classroom design as external condition for learning. *Educational Technology, 21,* 12–19.

CHAPTER 10

ADOPTING AND IMPLEMENTING ADULT LEARNER-FOCUSED HYBRID TEACHING AND LEARNING

One Institution's Journey

Lori A. Peterson and Daniel M. McGuire
Augsburg College

Building sustainable education programming for adult learners requires attention to many varied parameters: appropriate use of learning technology, flexible scheduling, marketable program offerings, and adult-focused services. This chapter describes the work underway to transform teaching and learning in adult learner programs at a private Midwestern liberal arts college. It begins by presenting the college's carefully researched approach to determine a path forward for adult learner programs, describes the path chosen (blended/hybrid teaching and learning), and assesses the work the college has done to implement this approach.

Building Sustainable Futures for Adult Learners, pages 211–229
Copyright © 2015 by Information Age Publishing
All rights of reproduction in any form reserved.

THE CHOICE OF HYBRID TEACHING AND LEARNING

Vaughan (2012) has noted that over 80% of higher education institutions in the United States offer courses in a blended format (Arabasz, Boggs & Baker, 2003), and the projection is that in the near future over 80% of all courses in higher education will be blended. In the words of Gladwell (2000), we have gone over the tipping point; blended learning has become an educational epidemic. The three societal forces (the perfect wave) that have converged to drive this epidemic are technology, financial constraints, and quality concerns. In addition to the three forces named by Vaughan, the college described in this chapter (hereafter referred to as "the college") had a desire to better serve its adult learner population and grow its adult learner programs.

At the college, a task force of faculty and staff was assigned to research options for moving forward. In a recommendation forwarded to an administrative and faculty team on academic program structure, the taskforce cited the U.S. Department of Education's (2010) meta-analysis of research on online and hybrid learning. Of particular importance to the taskforce was the conclusion that hybrid instruction was a viable instructional model that produced results not only similar to, but often even better than, face-to-face only instruction (Means, Toyama, Murphy, Bakia, & Jones, 2010). The carefully researched recommendation of the task force (and attending documents with recommendations for implementation considerations) found favor with faculty, administration, and staff at the college. In 2012, the decision was made to move forward in development of hybrid teaching and learning across all adult learner programs. Since the task force research on options was conducted, several authors (Dziuban, Hartman, Cavanagh & Moskal, 2011; Moskal, Dziuban, & Hartman, 2012; Vaughan, Cleveland-Innes, & Garrison, 2013) have affirmed blended learning's efficacy for improving student success, satisfaction, and retention. Moskal, Dziuban, & Hartman (2012) cite a recent market research study predicting a significant drop in the number of students enrolled in face-to-face courses and an increase in the number enrolled in blended and hybrid courses.

What follows in this chapter is an examination of how the college's experiences align with what the literature reports is needed for a successful hybrid implementation: infrastructure, leadership at the highest levels of the institution, faculty professional development, technical support capacity, and a shared purpose. The blended learning adoption and implementation framework developed by Graham, Woodfield, and Harrison (2013) will be used to describe the college's process as it unfolded and continues to unfold, and to assess the college's alignment with the framework. The pedagogical design considerations at the heart of the hybrid teaching and learning practices will be examined using Garrison and Vaughan's (2008) blended learning framework (also referenced in Vaughan, Cleveland-Innes, and Garrison, 2013). The authors will illustrate how this framework provided inspiration for the development of tools that moved the college and its faculty forward in the work. Finally, the authors will share faculty responses to teaching in the hybrid/blended modality and note the work that remains to be done to assess the overall efficacy of the use of blended learning in the college's adult learner programs. It is hoped that this writing contributes to the growing knowledge base on hybrid/blended learning in the higher education, instructional technology, and adult learning fields, and that it serves to share the authors' learning so that other institutions contemplating such an implementation may build upon it.

THEORETICAL FRAMEWORKS

Graham, Woodfield, and Harrison (2013) utilized case study methodology to explore issues surrounding the adoption and implementation of blended learning (BL) practices and policies in higher education institutions. They brought together research in innovation and change (Casanovas, 2010; Rogers, 2003), as well as research directly related to blended learning strategy (institutional direction, mission, policy); structure (technology, ownership, definitions/seat time, incentives, evaluation); and support (technological, pedagogical) to craft a framework for analysis. Then, they analyzed the degree to which institutions with varying levels of blended learning practice implementation had adopted and implemented such practices and policies. The findings from their research were mapped into the framework shown in Table 10.1.

TABLE 10.1   Matrix of BL Adoption Stages and Key Markers

Category	Stage 1—Awareness/ Exploration	Stage 2— Adoption/Early Implementation	Stage 3—Mature Implementation/ Growth
Strategy			
Purpose	Individual faculty/ administrators informally identify specific BL benefits	Administrators identify purposes to motivate institutional adoption of BL	Administrative refinement of purposes for continued promotion and funding of BL
Advocacy	Individual faculty and administrators informally advocate	BL formally approved and advocated by university administrators	Formal BL advocacy by university administrators and departments/ colleges

(continued)

TABLE 10.1   Matrix of BL Adoption Stages and Key Markers (cont.)

Category	Stage 1—Awareness/ Exploration	Stage 2— Adoption/Early Implementation	Stage 3—Mature Implementation/ Growth
Implementation	Individual faculty members implementing BL	Administrators target implementation in high impact areas and among willing faculty	Departments/colleges strategically facilitate wide-spread faculty implementation
Definition	No uniform definition of BL proposed	Initial definition of BL formally proposed	Refined definition of BL formally adopted
Policy	No uniform BL policy in place	Tentative policies adopted and communicated to stakeholders, policies revised as needed	Robust policies in place with little need for revision, high level of community awareness
Structure			
Governance	No official approval or implementation system	Emerging structures primarily to regulate and approve BL courses	Robust structures involving academic unit leaders for strategic decision making
Models	No institutional models established	Identifying and exploring BL Models	General BL models encouraged not enforced
Scheduling	No designation of BL courses as such in course registration/ catalog system	Efforts to designate BL courses in registration/catalog system	BL designations or modality metadata available in registration/catalog system
Evaluation	No formal evaluations in place addressing BL learning outcomes	Limited institutional evaluations addressing BL learning outcomes	Evaluation data addressing BL learning outcomes systematically reviewed
Support			
Technical	Primary focus on traditional classroom technological support	Increased focus on BL/online technological support for faculty and students	Well established technological support to address BL/online needs of all stakeholders
Pedagogical	No course development process in place	Experimentation and building of a formal course development process	Robust course development process established and systematically promoted

(continued)

TABLE 10.1   Matrix of BL Adoption Stages and Key Markers (cont.)

Category	Stage 1—Awareness/ Exploration	Stage 2— Adoption/Early Implementation	Stage 3—Mature Implementation/ Growth
Incentives	No identified faculty incentive structure for implementation	Exploration of faculty incentive structure for faculty training and course development	Well-established faculty incentive structure for systematic training and implementation

Note: Adapted From "A framework for institutional adoption and implementation of blended learning in higher education," by Graham, D.R., Woodfield, W., & Harrison, J.B., 2013, *Internet and Higher Education, 18*(3), 4–14. doi:10.1016/j.iheduc.2012.09.003

Innovation in the pedagogical techniques used when teaching in a blended learning modality was examined by Garrison and Vaughan (2008). These authors advocate for an approach based upon a community of inquiry (CoI) framework. This collaborative constructivist approach is particularly appropriate for the education of adults, who approach education for distinctive purposes that are primarily job-related and life transition-motivated (Merriam, Caffarella, & Baumgartner, 2007), and for whom learning is at its best a social, collaborative process (Knowles, 1973, 1977). Garrison and Vaughan's (2008) CoI-based approach "recognizes the social nature of education" (interaction, collaboration, and discourse) in a community of learners "whose purpose is to critically analyze, construct, and confirm worthwhile knowledge" (p. 9). To achieve this purpose, a CoI integrates social presence, teaching presence, and cognitive presence and "provides a means to design deep and meaningful educational experiences" (p. 9). Bringing together these two frameworks, the first related to institutional adoption and implementation of blended learning, and the second related to blended learning best practices, offers a way forward for institutions who see blended learning as the means to best grow and sustain adult learner programs.

APPLICATION OF ADOPTION/IMPLEMENTATION FRAMEWORK

Earlier researchers suggest that a successful deployment of blended learning initiatives requires a combination of institutional elements such as infrastructure, leadership at the highest levels of the institution, faculty professional development, technical support capacity, etc. (Garrison & Kanuka, 2004; Niemiec & Otte, 2009; Piper, 2010; Wallace & Young, 2010). Graham, Woodfield and Harrison's (2013) summary of these elements (see

Table 10.1) provides a useful framework for our analysis of a private Mid-western liberal arts college's deployment of its blended learning program for adult learners. An analysis of each of the major categories of the adoption and implementation framework (strategy, structure, support) in relationship to the college's work follows.

Strategy: Purpose, Advocacy, Implementation, Definition, and Policy

Garrison and Kanuka (2004) noted that a clear institutional direction is critical to successfully adopting a blended learning initiative. Graham, Woodfield, and Harrison (2013) carried forward this discussion by including a category of strategic elements important to consider when adopting and implementing blended learning. These elements include

- alignment of the purpose for adopting this approach with institutional priorities;
- top level and wide-spread support for the initiative and leadership involvement in its implementation;
- a clear definition of the institution's approach to blended learning; and
- creation, adoption, and implementation of policies for blended learning.

(key for blending)

As in all of the three categories (strategy, structure, and support), institutional adoption and implementation in the strategy category may vary along a continuum from Stage 1 (Awareness/Exploration) to Stage 3 (Mature implementation/Growth).

The college is now between Stage 2—adoption/early implementation, and Stage 3—mature implementation/growth, in the strategy category. The college's strategic decision to move all of its adult learner program offerings (undergraduate and graduate) to a blended/hybrid model of teaching and learning, finalized in 2012, was the result of many years of study and dialogue. Prior to this decision, the use of blended and online learning was highly inconsistent and thereby difficult to manage by curriculum committees and others. In 2011, the college engaged a higher education market research firm to assist in clarifying where it stood in its use of technology for teaching and learning, how best to move forward, and how to claim a consistent identity in this arena. The research demonstrated that the college would do best by using the strength of its name regionally; further expanding its reach by capitalizing on that name bolstered by the use of technology, and in doing so, offer more flexibility for existing students. It became clear that the best modality to do so was via deployment of hybrid/blended (online and face-to-face) teaching and learning. This strategy could bring together the college's reputation for high quality, intensive, face-to-face connections with students with consistently high quality, interactive on-line teaching and learning techniques. In 2012, the faculty approved a proposal to formally establish hybrid teaching and learning as its approach to adult education—and perhaps more importantly, to become consistent in its approach to teaching and learning for adult learners.

Garrison and Kanuka (2004) explain that asynchronous Internet communication technology has

> the ability to facilitate a simultaneously independent and collaborative learning experience. That is, learners can be independent of space and time—yet together. A concomitant property of learning with Internet communication technology is the significant educational implication resulting from an emphasis on written communication. Under certain circumstances, writing can be a highly effective form of communication that encourages reflection and precision of expression. When thoughtfully integrated with the rich dynamic of fast-paced, spontaneous verbal communication in a face-to-face learning environment, the educational possibilities are multiplied. (p. 97)

The full realization of the potential described by Garrison and Kanuka does not occur automatically just by creating a new class meeting schedule coupled with online sessions on a learning management system, even with a clearly expressed policy that requires the courses to employ hybrid teaching and learning. The transformation process is different for individual faculty, and it requires technical support and pedagogical support in order to be brought to fruition.

In order to gain deep and wide support for the hybrid strategy, extensive deliberation over just what was meant by the term hybrid was required. Initially, the college had utilized the term hybrid to refer only to the scheduling behind the model of blended instruction adopted (that classes would meet face-to-face and online), while the term blended was used in reference to the pedagogical considerations. However, as the college worked to become clearer in its use of definitions and to more fully communicate the intent of the design, the decision was made to use the term hybrid to refer to the entire program structure. It was felt that this term signified the importance placed on instructor presence in the online sessions as well as in the face-to-face classroom; both are necessary not only to satisfy credit hour requirements, but also to maintain the continuity between face-to-face and online. Therefore, the college uses the term hybrid to convey the idea of a new way of teaching and learning, not just a combination of two more traditional ways of teaching and learning.

The college has also begun to capitalize on the natural synergy between writing and online work by collaborating with the Writing Across the Curriculum initiative that has been an ongoing general education focus. The learning management system's assessment and feedback tools–marking guides, rubrics, forum ratings, the workshop activity module, and system text templates, comprise the basic framework for responding to student writing. It is anticipated that this synergy will be more fully realized as the implementation moves into its second year.

Structure: Governance, Models, Scheduling, Evaluation

Graham, Woodfield, and Harrison's (2013) framework uses the category structure to refer to the "issues relating to the technological, pedagogical, and administrative framework facilitating the blended learning environment, including governance, models, scheduling structures, and evaluation" (p. 7). The college has a robust structure in place to facilitate the institutionalization of hybrid teaching and learning on its campuses. In this area, the college is near to or at Stage 3—implementation moving to maturity.

Development of a shared understanding of and commitment to a quality standard for hybrid teaching and learning was key to the development of the governance and models now deployed. Department chairs, program directors, curriculum committees of the faculty, and the Hybrid Teaching and Learning Team (experts in online/blended learning with Sloan certification) at the college worked together to ensure that quality standards for teaching and learning in the hybrid model were defined up front in order to ensure pedagogical consistency, student satisfaction, and faculty proficiency. These standards are best seen in the document known as the Hybrid Course Design and Implementation Checklist (see Table 10.2).

This document serves as both a statement of policy and a tool for practice. Faculty are asked to utilize the document as a resource and a guide as they prepare courses for hybrid delivery. In addition, the Checklist organically and naturally shapes the professional community of inquiry as it serves individual faculty members, departments, and the institution as a whole in its drive toward quality and consistency in approach.

Governance of hybrid teaching and learning is integrated with the traditional academic governance structures at the college, via the work of its Academic Affairs Committees (AAC–undergraduate curriculum review committee, and GAAC–graduate curriculum review committee). For a hybrid course to be approved by either of these committees, faculty submit an Addendum for Courses with Regularly Scheduled Online Components (see Table 10.3), a form that is added to the course descriptions the committees use to officially approve course offerings. The document's construction

---

TABLE 10.2   Hybrid Course Design and Implementation Checklist

Department: _____ Course Number: _____ Instructor: _____

Center for Teaching & Learning Consultant: _____ Date Reviewed: ___/___/___

Recommend (y/n): _____

The following provides feedback regarding the course identified above.

C = completed, P = placeholder present, N = not present.

Section 1 (oversight by department and dean's office)

☐ Instructor has adequate preparation in online pedagogy to design and facilitate an effective course.

☐ Instructor possesses the technical skill to complete the majority of the course design and manage the class within the online environment.

☐ All required synchronous class meetings are published in the course schedule.

Section 2: Course Design Components (verification by AAC/GAAC during approval or revision process)

☐ First content section welcomes students to the class and provides clear "getting started" directions.

☐ Syllabus is posted in the first content section prior to the first day of class, according to the policy of the program in which the course is offered.

☐ Course procedures are clearly outlined in the syllabus or in a separate document.

☐ A course calendar with due dates for key activities and assignments as well as any synchronous meetings is included.

☐ Instructor's preferred contact information and expected response time is made clear in the syllabus or first content section. Instructors should use their Augsburg e-mail account.

☐ A section containing information about the instructional technology used in the course is included and available to students at least one week before the course begin. These tools will be designed in cooperation with the academic LFC's and available for instructors to load into their Moodle site as needed.

☐ An introduction forum is included.

☐ Instructor has an articulated plan for evaluating and sharing feedback on student work. Use of the Moodle gradebook for this purpose is recommended.

☐ Learning objectives/goals are described for each topic or lesson.(One sample session as minimum for AAC/GAAC verification)

☐ Learning activities include student-to-student and student-instructor interaction each week. (One sample session as minimum for AAC/GAAC verification)

Section 3: Facilitation expectations (oversight by department and dean's office)

☐ Regular instructor presence is maintained in the course.

☐ External links are checked regularly to verify they are working.

---

reflects the institution's purpose, definition, policy, implementation, advocacy, governance, model, schedule, and supports for hybrid implementation. In practice, this form also serves as a mechanism for faculty/departments to notify the Hybrid Teaching and Learning Team that a course has

TABLE 10.3 Addendum for Courses with Regularly Scheduled Online Components

Courses listed as "Hybrid" in course schedule.

Course # _____

Instructor Name _____

Course Coordinator (if other than Chair) _____

1. What will be the ratio of online to face-to-face instruction used in this course?

    ☐ standard 4 credit undergraduate   ____ F2F and ____ online sessions

    ☐ standard 3 credit undergraduate/graduate ____ ____ F2F and ____ online sessions

    ☐ standard 3 credit MBA   ____ F2F and ____ online sessions

    ☐ other (please explain)   ____ F2F and ____ online sessions

2. What is the rationale for using online sessions for this particular course? (please explain)

3. Please describe the training in effective online teaching and learning the instructor(s) for this course has completed. Indicate if this training occurred at Augsburg College or elsewhere. If the instructor has not yet participated in training but plans to do so, please indicate this as well.

4. Has the syllabus and course been designed using the Augsburg Online and Hybrid Course Design and Implementation Checklist and/or the Quality Matters rubric?

    ☐ Yes   ☐ No (please explain): _____

    Note: The Augsburg Online and Hybrid Course Design and Implementation Checklist and the Quality Matters rubric are available on the Faculty Senate moodle site in the AAC section.

5. Have you or others in your department worked with an LFC in the development of this course in an e-learning format? (delete the line below that does not apply)

    ☐ Yes, we have worked with: _____

    ☐ No, (please explain): _____

6. When the Moodle site for this course is ready for review, rename and save this document as 'Full Course # Hybrid Addendum' and attach this document to an email to HTLT.Team@augsburg.edu with 'Full Course # Hybrid Addendum' in the subject of the email.

    (The Moodle site is ready for review when all course design elements outlined in Section 2 of the Augsburg Online and Hybrid Course Design and Implementation Checklist are present. In addition to the introductory materials (in Section 0), a minimum of one online session must be completed to serve as a sample for how the instructor plans to design the rest of the sessions.

been readied for hybrid instruction. The Hybrid Teaching and Learning Team then reviews the tools and techniques proposed (using the Hybrid Course Design and Implementation Checklist, noted above), and offers recommendations to the proposing faculty and to the curriculum committees regarding whether the proposed course meets the quality standard set by them. Once approved by the appropriate curriculum committee, the quality of teaching is monitored on an ongoing basis by department chairs, program directors, and the Academic Affairs office at the college.

In the last year, the Addendum itself has evolved from a paper document with a long distribution list and routing process to a Google document submitted simultaneously to the Hybrid Teaching and Learning Team and the Dean's office, where the curriculum committees' agendas and meeting materials are prepared and distributed. Future practice will likely involve even more streamlining of the process with fewer redundant steps and even more efficiency. While seemingly mundane, the evolution of official document handling is representative of the cooperation, collaboration, and communication that the administration, departments, faculty, and support staff each need to exercise in order to achieve oversight for and successful implementation of hybrid teaching and learning.

The college has developed designations in the registration system that clearly demonstrate to students the format of a given course. Online and printed materials also designate the format of degree programs and courses. The college chose asynchronous instruction via its learning management system as the primary mode of instruction for online sessions and created a policy that at least some faculty-led instruction occurs in each online session. The schedule of classes in most of the hybrid program offerings is one four hour face-to-face session every other week with one online session between each of the face-to-face sessions over a sixteen week semester. Some of the graduate programs utilize intensive face-to-face sessions mixed with online learning. One example is the Master of Arts in Leadership program, which offers courses that meet for three four-hour face-to-face sessions with the remainder of the courses online. Regardless of the pattern of face-to-face and online meetings, the online instruction component of any hybrid course is required to be interactive; either instructor to student, or student to student with the instructor monitoring, assessing, and commenting on the student to student interaction. The Forum module in the learning management system is designed for this purpose and allows for a wide variety of types of interaction, including both informal communication that is similar to common social media as well as more formal academic discourse relying primarily on the written word (although other types of media are also becoming increasingly common in formal academic discourse).

Collection and analysis of evaluative data on hybrid teaching and learning is in the beginning stages, given that the college is in its first full year of the implementation of its hybrid strategy. At present, course teaching evaluations provide opportunity for students to report on the format of the course, and thus, some evaluative data can be linked to the hybrid courses. Some of the graduate programs using this teaching and learning format for the second or third year have gathered informal feedback from students beyond the teaching evaluation data. Anecdotal data from faculty indicate satisfaction with the support they have received, with the hybrid teaching and learning format, and with the learning they perceive students are realizing. Further work in the assessment and evaluation of student satisfaction, student learning, faculty satisfaction, and overall outcomes is needed. The learning management system deployed by the college will provide some of this data, as it has a built-in analytics capacity that was not previously available in higher education. This review is expected to generate refinements and/or modifications. It is also expected to reveal: (a) the potential for program revision for those programs not yet included in the project; (b) the potential for expansion and development of some programs (international programs are one likely possibility); and (c) the opportunity for more collaboration between departments.

Support: Technical, Pedagogical, Incentives

Graham, Woodfield, and Harrison's (2013) framework uses the category support to refer to the "issues relating to the manner in which an institution facilitates the implementation and maintenance of its blended learning design, incorporating technical support, pedagogical support, and faculty incentives" (p. 7). In this area, the college demonstrates maturity (Stage 3) in providing a variety of integrated technical and pedagogical supports for the hybrid teaching and learning initiative. The technology infrastructure is robust, and instructional technology experts (known as Liaisons for Computing) are assigned to specific departments. They assist faculty and staff with everything from e-mail to working on online instruction, and have become trusted partners of the faculty due to their relational, consultative approach. Just as these Computing Liaisons are assigned by department, so too are library resource staff professionals. These staff members specialize in select academic areas, attend most departmentally focused hybrid teaching and learning workshops, and oftentimes co-present information on accessibility and use of embedded videos and links to source materials. Both of these professional groups and their extended staff counterparts are also deployed to support students from a distance and at flexible times.

As mentioned earlier in this chapter, the Hybrid Teaching and Learning Team includes a team leader well versed in the implementation of learning management systems, with special emphasis in achieving quality in hybrid learning environments. This team is made up of the team lead and 5–6 others—the Director of the Center for Teaching and Learning (CTL), the Lead of the Computing Liaisons, and 3–4 faculty (known as CTL Consultants). The Hybrid Teaching and Learning Team reviews course sites, conducts workshops, and often works one on one with faculty in course development activities. The CTL Consultants of the Hybrid Teaching and

Learning Team are faculty who are already well versed in and excited about hybrid/online pedagogy. They model the academic expertise necessary for successful hybrid teaching and foster in other faculty the courage to try innovative practices. Their expertise and support bolster faculty who might have doubts about this new way of doing things. The richness of the communication between the CTL Consultants, computing and library liaisons, individual faculty, department chairs, and the college administration is living evidence of all of the components of the adoption and implementation framework (strategy, structure, and support).

As part of the implementation of hybrid teaching and learning, the Hybrid Teaching and Learning Team developed a comprehensive plan for faculty professional development from start-up to implementation and beyond. For example, in start-up, all stakeholders engaged in conversations about teaching considerations within disciplines. These conversations led to the identification and resolution of needs particular to the disciplines and the professional development required to meet these needs. For the first semester of the hybrid implementation, a standard learning management system course layout was used. In the second semester, faculty were encouraged to use a collapsed topics format to reduce the page scroll on the front page of their courses. This evolution is an example of changes in professional development required as faculty engage in and expand their competency and confidence in teaching hybrid courses. To date, there have been a variety of professional development activities, including

- weekly general learning management system labs and departmental/program-focused workshops, on average once each week and including library liaisons;
- a course design support site, with a resource list (and links)
- postings of recorded content from the learning management system labs and focused workshops;
- learning management system Huddles (20 minute, repeated segments of learning topics) in the summers, repeated over a series of days/times;
- video/audio feed of workshops/labs to remote locations.

Department chairs have expressed a need for a formal process to identify the needs of individual faculty in their development as hybrid program teachers. Traditional self-reporting and evaluation techniques along with the learning diagnostics and analytics available with the learning management system will inform future professional development.

The college has recognized that implementing its hybrid teaching and learning strategy has required extra commitment by the faculty and sought ways to demonstrate this recognition. Where multiple sections of a course are taught, many departments and programs have utilized a course lead approach to developing the on-line learning portions of their courses. Course leads have received small stipends for developing the initial course site and for training any adjunct faculty about the layout of the site. The CTL consultants group are compensated with annual stipends. Part-time adjunct faculty also receive small stipends for attending professional development offerings. The college is aware that compensation for and recognition of the time and energy required for this work is crucial going forward.

USE OF A PEDAGOGICAL/ANDRAGOGICAL FRAMEWORK

Graham, Woodfield, and Harrison's (2013) adoption and implementation framework provides a useful construct for assessment of an institution's stage of adoption and implementation of a blended/hybrid learning initiative. What we believe is missing from the model is the efficacy that a combined and intentionally overlapping system for technical/pedagogical support can provide, once the basic technological infrastructure is in place. Building learning environments for adult learners that are collaborative constructivist in nature requires attention not only to pedagogical/andragogical theory, but also to the tools to ensure that the practice fulfills the theoretical aspirations.

As noted earlier in this chapter, the college has utilized Garrison and Vaughan's (2008) community of inquiry-based pedagogical framework so as to create a collaborative constructivist learning environment in its hybrid teaching and learning program. This type of environment is one where discourse is encouraged, content is carefully selected, and attention is paid to setting a climate of collaboration. To achieve this, Garrison and Vaughan note that faculty must integrate social presence, teaching presence, and cognitive presence (see Figure 10.1).

Social presence establishes and fuels open communication, group cohesion, and affective/personal interaction. "Cognitive presence maps the cyclical inquiry pattern of learning from experience through reflection and conceptualization to action and on to further experience" (p. 21). It often progresses from a triggering event through to resolution. Teaching presence is "essential to bring all of the elements together and ensure that the community of interest is productive" (p. 24). Teaching presence, therefore, must be embedded in the design and organization of the course, the facilitation of discourse, and in the direct instruction activities.

In the on-line environment, forums provide a means for direct instruction and the integration of the three presences. In the start-up phase, the college paid specific attention to this integration by encouraging faculty to use a forum module. The forum allows students to connect online activity

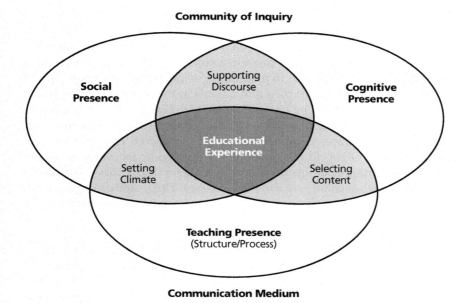

Figure 10.1 Community of inquiry framework. *Source:* Garrison, D. R. & Vaughan, N. D. (2008). *Blended learning in higher education: Framework, principles, and guidelines.* San Francisco, CA: Jossey-Bass.

to work in the face-to-face classroom. Further, it expands student learning via: (a) discussion of a topic from a previous class session or as a result of assigned reading; (b) exploration of new concepts in dialogue with their faculty member and each other; and/or (c) feedback on analysis or synthesis of ideas. At full implementation, faculty have expanded upon their use of forums by including other on-line interactive learning activities that enhance the community of inquiry.

DISCUSSION

Evidence exists that the college is effectively demonstrating the use of Garrison and Vaughan's (2008) CoI model. Beyond this, the college's work is aligned with Vaughan, Cleveland-Innes, and Garrison's (2013) expanded application of the CoI Framework. In order to achieve an assurance that the various elements of presence called for by Garrison and Vaughan are expressed in its adult learner courses, the college has created and deployed the use of a hybrid course template. The template is added to the shell of each course that is listed as Hybrid in the Registrar's course listing. An initial learning management system workshop, the Lab for Hybrid Design, uses the template as an organizer for coaching faculty who are new to the learning management system and/or hybrid teaching and learning. The purpose of the template is to provide a consistent visual and navigational experience for students and to provide a teaching and learning design format that is consistent for faculty and attends to the three presences (Garrison & Vaughan, 2008). The consistent course design also has the advantage of making professional development more consistent for the support staff leading it. The template includes elements considered best practice components for most hybrid courses—such as a welcome banner and a Latest News and Announcements posting which allows instructors a convenient way to develop social presence in their courses. The introductory section of the template, or Week Zero section, includes six pages of information useful in any course. The six pages are

1. A Getting Started in [x Course] page: including basic information for the course and links to other support pages. Each of the pages includes text generic to all courses and those items that need to be edited for each individual. The rationale is to make it as easy as possible for faculty to create a workable hybrid course that is also easy for students to navigate because it is similar in look and feel to other hybrid courses at the College.
2. The Course Procedures page: lists technology items necessary for participation in a hybrid course, a narrative description of how the course is organized, contact information for the instructor, and other pertinent course information.
3. A Course Syllabus: The learning management system front page serves as a syllabus, however, it is also useful to have a traditional syllabus available.
4. A Course Schedule: Commonly found in a traditional syllabus, it has been useful for students to have an easy way to access the schedule, especially if students are new to a hybrid format.
5. A Technology Support and Accessibility page: Including institutional support facilities and online resources available to all students.
6. The Technology Guide page: provides links and information regarding technologies specific to a course (Voice Thread, Adobe Connect, Google Apps suite, etc.).

A Question and Answer Forum was added to the introductory section of the template. This general use forum is used as a method for answering generic questions that might be common to all students. It creates an archive for students' future reference and has proven to be a time saver for faculty as they find they answer fewer emails and phone calls than they otherwise might have. Also, a general use forum entitled The Introduction Forum has been placed in the introductory section of the Moodle course. The introduction forum is a standard best practice in online or hybrid courses, and it's where both students and faculty often first notice the power of the hybrid format to enhance and increase the possibilities for social presence in a course.

As Fink (2013) and others have noted, the key to good course design, in any delivery mode, is determining the particular activities students should do to best achieve the desired learning. The hybrid template format provides the opportunity and the responsibility to decide what works best in the face-to-face on-campus sessions and what will work best in the online sessions to establish a community of inquiry. Faculty are encouraged to use the template design but are free to modify the design to fit their teaching objectives. Many faculty have reported that having the components of the template already laid out for them made the transition to the hybrid format easier to envision. This left the faculty with more time to focus on their re-visioning of the design of the course, which was one of the major new skills required of first time hybrid instructors. Having the ability to make choices about what types of activities to use for students to better understand content is requiring faculty to take a more thoughtful approach to how course material is presented.

CONCLUSION

Using Graham, Woodfield, and Harrison's (2013) adoption and implementation framework has provided a means to assess the stage of one college's hybrid teaching and learning implementation, within each of the three categories of strategy, structure, and support. Mature implementations, and those that are best suited to adult learners, we suggest, will not only have ample technological and pedagogical support, but attend to the marrying of the two. This college's use of Garrison and Vaughan's (2008) CoI framework, embedded computing liaisons and library resources, the presence of a Hybrid Teaching and Learning Team, and the development of appropriate tools in the learning management system, demonstrate not only the desirability of such a practice, but point out how they jointly pave the way toward teaching and learning efficacy. At the same time, it is clear that further work in the areas of assessment and evaluation of student satisfaction, student learning, faculty proficiency and satisfaction, and overall outcomes is needed. Learning management systems will provide some of this data as they have built in analytics capacity that was not previously available in higher education. Higher education institutions will need to determine which data to analyze—institutionally, by department or program, at the course level, and at the classroom level. Additionally, the larger institutional assessment of the use of the hybrid program format for adult learning will be important. A sustainable future for adult learning using hybrid teaching and learning models will likely require repeated renewal of commitment and courageous collaboration among all components of a higher education institution; and leadership at all levels of the technical, academic, and support systems of these institutions.

REFERENCES

Arabasz, P., Boggs, R., & Baker, M. B. (2003). Highlights of e-learning support practices. *ECAR Research Bulletin.* Retrieved from http://www.educause.edu/ecar

Casanovas, I. (2010). Exploring the current theoretical background about adoption until institutionalization of online education in universities: Needs for further research. *Electronic Journal of e-Learning, 8*(2), 73–84. Retrieved from www.ejel.org.

Dziuban, C., Hartman, J., Cavanagh, T., & Moskal, P. (2011). Blended courses as drivers of institutional change. In A. Kitchenham (Ed.), *Blended learning across disciplines: Models for implementation* (pp. 17–37). Hershey, PA: IGI Global.

Fink, L. D. (2013). *Creating significant learning experiences: An integrated approach to designing college courses, revised and updated.* San Francisco, CA: Jossey-Bass.

Garrison, D. R., & Kanuka, H. (2004). Blended learning: Uncovering its transformative potential in higher education. *The Internet and Higher Education, 7*(2), 95–105. Retrieved from http://dx.doi.org/10.1016/j.iheduc.2004.02.001

Garrison, D. R., & Vaughan, N.D. (2008). *Blended learning in higher education: Framework, principles, and guidelines.* San Francisco, CA: Jossey-Bass.

Gladwell, M. (2000). *The tipping point: How little things can make a big difference.* San Francisco: Back Bay Books.

Graham, D. R., Woodfield, W., & Harrison, J. B. (2013). *A framework for institutional adoption and implementation of blended learning in higher education.* Internet and Higher Education, *18*(2013), 4–14.

Knowles, M. S. (1973). *The adult learner: A neglected species.* Houston, TX: Gulf.

Knowles, M. S. (1977). *The adult education movement in the United States.* New York, NY: Krieger Publishing Co.

Means, B., Toyama, Y., Murphy, R., Bakia, M., & Jones, K. (2010). *Evaluation of evidence-based practices in online learning: A meta-analysis and review of online learning.* Center for Technology in Learning, U.S. Department of Education. Retrieved from http://www.ed.gov/about/offices/list/opepd/ppss/reports.html

Merriam, S. B., Caffarella, R. S., & Baumgartner, L. M. (2007). *Learning in adulthood: A comprehensive guide* (3rd ed.). San Francisco, CA: Jossey-Bass.

Moskal, P., Dziuban, C., & Hartman, J. (2012). Blended learning: A dangerous idea? *Internet and Higher Education, 18,* 15–23.

Niemiec, M., & Otte, G. (2009). An administrator's guide to the whys and hows of blended learning. *Journal of Asynchronous Learning Networks, 13*(1), 19–30.

Retrieved from http://www.eric.ed.gov/ERICWebPortal/contentdelivery/servlet/ERICServlet?accno=EJ837541)

Piper, T. (2010). *What policy changes do experts recommend K–12 instructional leaders enact to support the implementation of online instruction and learning?* (Doctoral Dissertation). Available from ProQuest Dissertations and Theses database. (UMI No. 343–711).

Rogers, E. (2003). *Diffusion of innovations* (5th ed.). New York, NY: Free Press.

Vaughan, N. D. (2012). Designing an Inquiry-Based Approach to Blended Learning. Presentation at Sloan-C Blended Learning Conference and Workshop: Milwaukee, WI.

Vaughan, N. D., Cleveland-Innes, M., & Garrison, D.R. (2013). *Teaching in blended learning environments: Creating and sustaining communities of inquiry.* Edmonton, AB: AU Press.

Wallace, L., & Young, J. (2010). Implementing blended learning: Policy implications for universities. *Online Journal of Distance Learning Administration, 13*(4), 7.

PART I

SUPPORTING NEEDS OF ADULT LEARNERS:

Integrating Adult Learning Experiences
in the "Real World"

CHAPTER 11

GIVE ME A REAL WORLD EXAMPLE

Teaching Adults Critical Comprehension Using Authentic Complex Texts

Leah Katherine Saal
Arkansas State University

In February 2011, Bauerlein published "Too dumb for complex texts?" in *Education Week*. In the article, the author questions the readiness of potential postsecondary students to critically confront complex texts and writing. Recent studies by the National Center for Educational Statistics (2009) support this hypothesis, reporting 50.4% of beginning college students take remedial courses. Of those students, 19.4% enroll in three or more remedial courses. Additionally, on the National Assessment of Educational Progress in 2009, only 38% of twelfth-graders in the U.S. performed at or above the *proficient* level in reading.

Many students in both junior and four-year colleges lack the level of reading comprehension skill needed to succeed in the university curriculum (Bettinger & Long, 2005). The ACT (2006) report found the difference

Building Sustainable Futures for Adult Learners, pages 233–252
Copyright © 2015 by Information Age Publishing
All rights of reproduction in any form reserved.

between those college students who were and were not prepared for college or career was an understanding of and ability to independently learn from complex (expository) texts. Critical reading skills affect a student's ability to analyze material to connect ideas to their own life as well as across the disciplines (Gruenbaum, 2012).

Freshman level postsecondary textbooks offer more dense content (hoping to give the novice an overview of the entire discipline) than higher-level courses' texts, which are usually more content/idea specific (Flippo & Schrum, 2009). Unlike in the K–12 system, postsecondary textbooks are not controlled for readability or text complexity and can easily reach postgraduate levels (Flippo & Schrum, 2009). As a result, one of the foundations of the National Governors Association's Common Core State Standards (2010) for the K–12 system is an integration of increasingly complex levels of text into the curriculum. Standards and corresponding assessments are being adopted across the K–12 system for reading instruction focused on preparation for postsecondary reading tasks. However, what is being done for those students who are already experiencing higher education or adult education curriculum without the requisite skill? This innovative practice case study addresses the need for contextualized/authentic critical literacy skill development within higher education.

LITERATURE REVIEW

Active engagement by learners, opportunities to collaborate in groups, frequent interactions and multiple occasions for feedback, and connections to real world/authentic contexts have long been established as characteristics of effective adult learning practices, particularly when considering technological integration within adult learning settings (Knowles, 1990). Opportunities for practicing and applying concepts while learning versus passively receiving new information in lecture style format are linked to adults' increased ability to apply new knowledge when solving novel problems (Bransford, Franks, Vye, & Sherwood, 1989). One of the most important advancements in teaching adults contextualized literacy skill has been the incorporation of the "social practices" approach from the field of New Literacies (Barton, Hamilton, & Ivanic, 2000; Gee, 2001, Street, 1993). This approach acknowledges the diverse ways that people use literacy and numeracy in their day-to-day lives and signifies the primacy of learner-centered goals in language instruction at all levels of instruction (St. Clair & Belzer, 2010). When focusing on literacy development with adults, the importance of explicitly teaching critical comprehension skills using authentic texts will be outlined below.

Critical (Advanced) Literacy & Comprehension

Dagostino and Carifio (1994) describe four spheres a learner progresses through with age and exposure to print. The spheres begin with the most basic, *functional* sphere, and move through *specialized*, multi-*cultural*, and end with *critical* literacy. Critical literacy is achieved when the reader not only understands what they are reading but can use the information to transform his or her life (Freire, 1970). An analogous term used to define the level of literacy required of postsecondary students is advanced literacy. Advanced literacy is the reading and writing done in tertiary schooling, which requires the reader to deeply comprehend and critically question both text content and author's purpose (Dean & Dagostino, 2007).

The RAND Reading Study Group (2002) defined reading comprehension as "simultaneously extracting and constructing meaning" (p. 1). Reading comprehension becomes an interactive process between the text's information and the background knowledge of the reader (RAND, 2002). When readers effectively process text, new information affects the reader's existing knowledge and improves their schema, or existing knowledge base (Anderson & Pearson, 1984). To achieve the goal of critical (advanced) comprehension, students in postsecondary must become strategic readers (Palincsar & Brown, 1984; Pressley, 2000). According to Alvarez and Risko (2009), strategic readers can "self-regulate and monitor their comprehension by knowing *what to do* (e.g., selection of appropriate study strategy) and *when* to employ appropriate strategies in order to increase their understanding of content and increase their intrinsic motivation for learning" (p. 201).

Flavell (1979) first acknowledged metacognition in reading comprehension as "one's knowledge concerning one's own cognitive processes and products or anything related to them" (p. 906). The two components of metacognition are knowledge about one's thinking and the ability to regulate one's thinking (Alexander, 2005; Baker & Brown, 1984; Martinez, 2006; Pintrich, 2002; Sperling, Howard, Staley, & Dubois, 2004). Knowledge about one's cognition is both stable where the reader understands his/her own cognitive load capacity (Baker & Brown, 1984) and stable in that the reader can explain his or her cognitive processes to others (Holschuh & Aultman, 2009). Self-awareness of comprehension is domain specific and varies greatly depending on the complexity and kind of text the person is interacting with (Alexander, 2005; Pintrich, 2002).

Self-regulation, on the other hand, includes the planning and monitoring of strategies used to comprehend text as well as understanding how to monitor one's own thinking to apply a different strategy when comprehension breaks down (Pintrich, 2002). Specifically, it includes the ability to "detect errors or contradictions in text, knowledge of different strategies to use with different kinds of texts, and the ability to separate important from unimportant information" (Holschuh & Aultman, 2009, p. 122). In environments where independent reading processes are central to success, such as postsecondary studies or authentic/real world complex texts (like health care insurance forms, and tax forms), those lacking metacognitive awareness will be more likely to experience problems (Baker & Brown, 1984).

Teaching Strategy within Authentic Tasks for Improved Comprehension

Many adult readers begin to struggle with the idea of having to read informational text before they even begin. History has proven to them that reading is hard, especially in the critical reading required to learn or form an opinion, and provides little or no enjoyment (Pitcher, Martinez, Dicembre, Fewster, & McCormick, 2010). As adult students read these types of text, they may struggle from either the linguistic (text based) or non-linguistic (metacognitive) components of comprehension (Lei, Rhinehart, Howard, & Cho, 2010). Students may lack vocabulary, prior knowledge, or may spend so much effort trying to decipher complex text structures, that meaning is lost. Sorting through what information is important, contradictory, and extraneous becomes an arduous task unless students are offered frequent practice opportunities across numerous contexts.

Explicitly Teaching Comprehension Strategy

To address student concerns, as well as increased comprehension skills required by students to address the rise in text complexity within higher education, teachers can employ instruction of advanced reading strategies. Instructors who teach reading strategies using purposeful and systematic instruction are more likely to have students who achieve in reading comprehension (Ross & Frey, 2009). Teaching reading strategies arms students (from elementary to adult) with the metacognitive awareness to help them succeed in the comprehension of complex reading materials (Baker & Brown, 1984). In the Self Regulated Strategy Development Model (SRSD), teaching involves instruction on how to choose and employ strategies for comprehension within context where the teacher: (a) develops background knowledge; (b) discusses the steps of the strategy; (c) models the strategy; (d) helps students memorize the strategy; (e) guides the students in attempting the strategy; and (f) gives opportunities for independent practice of the strategy within course content (Schumaker, Denton, & Deshler, 1984). This process allows teachers to observe students in skill practice as well as reinforce and clarify strategy use where necessary.

Contextualizing Strategies Using Authentic Tasks

While skills and strategy instruction are vitally important for teaching students how to navigate the comprehension process, providing students with numerous real world/authentic experiences that allow them to see *why* their comprehension strategy skills are important and *how* those skills apply to their "real lives" is key (Parsons & Ward, 2011). Because authentic tasks imitate the literacy undertakings in which adults engage daily, authentic tasks serve to contextualize a student's strategy learning and have the effect of increasing student motivation for strategy use while also increasing the likelihood of transfer and retention of knowledge (Blumenfeld, Soloway, & Marx, 1991; Bransford & Schwartz, 1999; Duke, Purcell-Gates, Hall, & Tower, 2006; Freire, 1970). "Real World" activities that incorporate student-led evaluation and questioning can also serve to increase students' academic vocabularies (Parsons & Ward, 2011). Teachers should not be teaching literacy skills to adults to merely "*do school,* teachers should be teaching them how to *do life*" (Pearson, Raphael, Benson, & Madda, 2007, p. 36) by structuring their curriculum in ways that prepare them for the twenty-first century literacy skills they will face in their daily lives (Organization for Economic Co-operation and Development [OECD], 2013)

CASE STUDY: CRITICAL LITERACY WITH AUTHENTIC/REAL WORLD TEXTS

This case study curricular model explores the use of explicit comprehension strategy instruction along with authentic textual practice opportunities to positively affect adult students' metacognition and comprehension of complex texts. To provide authentic practice of comprehension strategy, an innovative formative assessment, My Environmental Text Analysis (META) was designed. The META utilizes the students' real world/authentic complex texts to evaluate their changing metacognitive awareness and reading comprehension strategy use. The strategic instructional model for comprehension as well as formative and summative assessment design will be discussed as an exemplar innovative case for implementing a data-driven, authentic exemplar of adult critical literacy development in higher education settings. Implications for practitioners as well as challenges of using a real world/authentic application model for critical comprehension will also be discussed.

Purpose and Research Question

Case study method (CSM) has various definitions; however, all definitions pinpoint CSM's use in examining critical question(s) using several data points within a specific system and time (Creswell, 2007, 2009; Merriam, 1998; Stake, 1995; Yin, 2003, 2009). This instrumental case study's purpose was to examine the effect of an explicit paraphrasing strategy with real world/authentic complex texts on students' metacognition and comprehension as measured by pre-post assessments in a reading and study skills course at a four-year research-intensive university in the southeastern United States.

Research Questions

1. Is there a significant difference in students' comprehension in pre-post conditions as measured by average values of MAZE probe and a test of silent sustained reading?
2. Is there a significant difference in students' metacognition in pre-post conditions as measured by average values of a survey of meta-cognitive awareness of reading strategies?

Context and Demands of Setting

The course is set within a full-time, four-year, U.S. News & World Report designated top-tier university in the southeastern region of the United States. The admissions standards are increasing, with an average ACT of 26 and a GPA of 3.4. The faculty-student ratio is officially 1:21; however, general education classes are frequently in excess of 1:150 or more due to financial constraints. Students must maintain a 2.0 GPA for retention within the institution, and admission into senior colleges requires 30 hours of credit at the institution and a 3.0 GPA minimum. The institution maintains a tracking and placement system on all students based on GPA and persistence through capstone classes within their respective degree programs. If a student twice fails to make adequate progress, the institution will remove the student from his or her chosen field and place him or her in a major or course of study, which provided the fastest opportunity for graduation. Although the case study was conducted within a voluntary elective course, the class is recommended for freshman, transfers, students who have been specially admitted into the institution, first generation college students, students registered with the Office of Disability Services, students in the University College for Advising and Counseling (UCAC), or students who are not making adequate progress toward their degree as designated by the tracking system.

Participants

Forty-eight participants were recruited from an elective college study skills course at a large university in the southeastern region of the United States granting bachelors through doctoral degrees. The researcher solicited a convenience sample of participants by making an announcement in class sections, at which time four potential participants chose not to participate. Although listed as a freshman level class, the majority of participants were in their sophomore year. Of the participants, 46.2% were male and 53.8% were female. Participants represented nine college classifications. Two of the college classifications were special designations within the college. University College for the Freshman Year (UCFY) was for undecided freshman or those who have not met the requirements of their senior college and have earned less than 30 hours of credit. UCAC enrolled students who have earned 30-plus hours of college credit and who have not yet met the admission requirements for one of the University's degree-granting senior colleges. In the case study, 40.2% of the participants were members of either UCAC or UCFY.

Procedure

In this case study, the reading strategy of RAP (Read-Ask-Paraphrase) (Hagaman, Luschen, & Reid, 2010; Karbalaei & Azimi Amoli, 2011; Lei, Rhinehart, Howard, & Cho, 2010; Schumaker, Denton, & Deshler, 1984) was modified to PIE (Point-Importance-Real World Example). In past practice with adults, the instructor found the RAP strategy to lack an explicit cognitive model for paraphrasing with real world/authentic complex print or multimedia texts. Therefore, the strategy was amended to provide more specific cognitive directives for adult higher education students. See Table 11.1 for an explanation of the SRSD stages in PIE strategy teaching.

The PIE strategy was applied broadly over the course of the curriculum to assess/paraphrase print and multimedia complex texts. To provide practice paraphrasing using PIE strategy, an innovative formative assessment structure, My Environmental Text Analysis (META), was developed to utilize a student's real world/authentic texts to evaluate student's developing metacognitive awareness and reading comprehension.

Formative assessment—My Environmental Text Analysis (META)

My Environmental Text Analysis (META) is a face-to-face or electronic curricular probe (or short recurring assessment), which gives students five minutes to paraphrase (using PIE strategy) a print or multimedia text. The instructor's choices for META texts came from the students' lives, including journal paragraphs from students' declared fields of study, insurance information, financial disclosures, health documents, legal documents, and even video/multimedia advertisements and articles. This assessment was repeated 10–15 times (using different texts) throughout the semester and

TABLE 11.1 SRSD Stages in PIE Strategy

SRSD Stage	PIE Activity
1. Develop Background Knowledge	• Teach students what the "point" of a text might be. Ex: Show a video with "the caption below a news story" or "the title of a YouTube clip." • Discuss what the "big idea" of various real world texts might be -safety instruction manuals, a job application, or a prescription for medication.

2. Discuss the Strategy	• Explain to students how schemata works—i.e., new knowledge is stored by connecting it to things already in our memories. Learning comprehension strategies, especially paraphrasing, helps train our brain to make more matches and store information for retrieval later.
	• Describe all of the steps of PIE:
	• In 3 sentences or less:
	  1. What is the **P**oint of the text in 12 (or less) of your own words?
	  2. Why is this text **I**mportant, What are the key details?
	  3. What is a "real world" **E**xample?
	• Sell the strategy and build investment/commitment for its use.

3. Model the Strategy	• The teacher models the 3 steps of PIE in an example using "think aloud." Teacher talks through the "hows" and "whys" of each step making his/her thinking explicit to students as he/she completes strategy within a text.
4. Memorize the Strategy	• Student memorizes the PIE steps fluently with automaticity. This allows student's attention to focus on text.
5. Guide Students in Strategy Use	• Teacher scaffolds the student(s) in first attempt(s) at the PIE strategy using an exemplar text. • Strategy procedure is gradually released to students.
6. Independent Practice	• Student(s) practice using PIE strategy independently. • Teacher monitors performance

was completed immediately upon entering the classroom or as an electronic, timed assignment linked into the online course platform (Blackboard).

METAs teach students, through the use of a rubric, to continuously analyze their use of the PIE strategy to efficiently self-monitor (metacognate) their own comprehension in novel real world/authentic complex applications from their studies and life. Following student's independent adoption of PIE strategy, the teacher uses the rubric to teach students to evaluate their strategy use. The SRSD steps (Table 11.1, left column) are repeated when teaching students to utilize the META rubric to analyze the effectiveness of their PIE strategy use. After students have acquired an independent level of evaluation skill using the rubric, they can monitor their own PIE strategy use over time and different examples, compare their perceived

TABLE 11.2   My Environmental Text Analysis (META) Rubric

Points	Description
5 Excellent Paraphrase	• Paraphrase contains 3 sentences or less. • Main idea is clearly stated in the first sentence. • All key details are included. • Uses own wording. Avoids copying phases and sentences from the text. • Has detailed sentences with examples that link to main idea in logical order. • No spelling or grammar errors.
4 Satisfactory Paraphrase	• Paraphrase contains 3 sentences or less. • Main idea is stated in the first sentence. • Most important details are included. • Uses mostly original wording. Avoids copying phases and sentences from the text. • Details and examples are logically linked to the main idea. • Few (2–3) mechanical errors.
3 Below Average Paraphrase	• Paraphrase contains 3 sentences or less. • Main idea is present but hard to locate. • Some important details are missing. • Copies some phrases and sentences. • Detail of sentences and examples lack logical connection to main idea. • Some (4–5) mechanical errors.
2 Ineffective Paraphrase	• Paraphrase contains more than 3 sentences. • Main idea is vague and hard to locate. • Some important details are missing. • Many copied phrases and sentences. • Disorganized details, randomly presented within sentences. • Lacking examples. • Many (6+) mechanical errors
1 Incomplete Paraphrase	• Paraphrase contains more than three sentences. • The main idea is absent. • Details are missing or vague. • Disorganized details, randomly presented in sentences. • Many copied phrases and sentences. • Lacking examples. • Many (6+) mechanical errors.

paraphrasing effectiveness to that of the teacher, as well as provide timely and accurate peer review for classmates. Consequently, evaluation of strategy becomes the sixth step of the SRSD model. Find the META Rubric (Table 11.2) for further detail on evaluation components.

Data Collection

To assess the effectiveness of the strategy instruction and evaluation, assessments were performed with participants ($N = 48$) in the case study. All measurements were administered pre-post during two class periods (the first and last of the semester) for approximately 25 minutes. Assessments included a maze probe of comprehension, a survey of metacognitive awareness of reading strategy and a silent sustained reading comprehensions test. One (1) participant did not complete the MAZE pre assessment and one (1) did not complete the MAZE post assessment.

Instruments

Expository MAZE probe.   One of the hindrances in measuring comprehension is imitating the students' actual academic or authentic/real world tasks. A MAZE probe provides an opportunity to accurately and quickly assess students' abilities to comprehend *within* their curricular or real world/ authentic materials (Mollach, 1972; Williams, Ari, & Santamaria, 2011). A set of MAZE probes measuring comprehension were constructed for this case study using an introductory sociology text written at a 14.8 (postsecondary) reading level, as indicated by Microsoft's Flesch-Kincaid Readability Scale.

To create a MAZE comprehension probe assessment from *any* complex text (Parker, Hasbrouck, & Tindal, 1992):

1. Choose a passage 200 to 400 words in length. For longer texts, select a passage located near the middle of the text.
2. Assess the reading level using Microsoft's Flesch-Kincaid Readability Scale (found as an option inside of the Review Tab, Spelling and Grammar Check) for appropriateness.
3. Start with the second sentence of the passage, delete every seventh word, and replace it with three answer choices (one that correctly completes the sentence and two distractors).
4. Leave the last sentence of the passage intact.

Although the pre-post assessment for the case study was created using an academic text, the MAZE assessment can also be created using an authentic/ real world expository text if more appropriate to the context and demands placed the students by their setting.

In scoring the MAZE assessment, 90% accuracy and above indicates *independent* comprehension level within that text, which means that students can independently read and comprehend the text at that level. Accuracy from 75% to 90 % indicates *instructional* comprehension level within the text, which means that students can comprehend the text with assistance and scaffolding from the teacher. Below 75% accuracy indicates a *frustrational* comprehension level within the text, which means that the material is currently beyond a student's comprehension level even with assistance (See

Appendix A for exemplar from the case study using expository academic text and Appendix B for exemplar using real-world complex text).

Mokhtari & Reichard's (2002) Metacognitive Awareness of Reading Strategies. The instrument was used gauge the students' abilities to metacognate through complex expository (informational) text. Overall scores as well as three subscale scores were calculated for each participant's pretest and posttest (Mokhtari & Reichard, 2002). The three subscales of Mokhtari & Reichard's assessment give an indication of participants' awareness of both *bottom up processing*, or text to meaning strategies in text comprehension, and *top down processing*, or meaning to text strategies in comprehension (Linden, 2007). The first subscale, *Global Reading Strategies*, consists of 13 items for assessing global, or "top down," reading comprehension strategy use by participants. The second subscale, *Problem Solving Strategies*, consists of eight items assessing participants' awareness for solving problems when text becomes too difficult to read. The third subscale, *Support Reading Strategies*, consists of nine items centered on participants' willingness to use outside references, note taking, and other practical strategies to support comprehension when encountering problems while reading.

Expository Silent Sustained Reading Passage. A 300-word expository silent sustained reading comprehension (SSR) passage from a communication studies text was read independently by the students. The assessment then asked students to answer 10 multiple choice comprehension questions related to the passage.

Data Analysis

To investigate the potential effect of explicit strategy instruction (PIE) using META probes for assessment, descriptive statistics were explored. A paired sample t-test was performed to determine whether there was a significant difference between the average values of each of the three instruments' measurements made under the pre-post conditions with the matched samples from participants. This case study assumed the null hypothesis that the differences in the mean values are zero. H0: $d = \mu1 - \mu2 = 0$; where d is mean value difference and $\alpha = .05$.

In checking for out of range values using frequencies, two miscoded cases were found and corrected. In an initial check for outliers using box plots, two more miscoded variables were found. After calculating Z scores and studentized residuals, a number of values greater than or less than 2.5 were found. The outliers were investigated and determined valid. Normality, homogeneity of variance, and linearity were investigated and found tenable.

DATA RESULTS

Descriptive statistics were first computed. In all three pre-post measures, the posttests had significantly higher mean and median scores. Table 11.3 summarizes the descriptive statistics for the pre-post assessments related exclusively to comprehension scores for participants on the MAZE probe and the SSR test.

Although the mean on the MAZE pretest placed the mean of the participants at the *independent* comprehension level within their course materials, the posttest documented improvement. Interestingly, on the silent sustained reading test, the average between the pre-post condition rose by over 12 points. On the MAZE assessments, 45 of the 46 students pre-post tested improved, and, on the SSR test 47 of the 48 students improved across the pre-post condition.

Scores greater than or equal to 3.5 out of 4.0 on the instrument indicate relative strength within any scale of the instrument. On subscale measures of metacognition, all four scales saw marked improvement. Interestingly indicative of the effectiveness of the PIE and META strategy instruction, the *Global* and *Support* subscales scores for metacognition showed the greatest improvement. Similar to the Nash-Ditzel (2010) case study, which tracked student improvement in self-regulation through think aloud procedures following strategy training, students were more aware of the need for

TABLE 11.3 Pre/Post Data from Comprehension Assessments

Sample	MAZE Assessment			Silent Sustained Reading		
	M	Median	SD	M	Median	SD
Pretest	93.29	94.28	7.76	70.00	70.00	17.26
Posttest	97.74	100.00	4.17	82.34	80.00	12.72

Note: M = Mean; SD = Standard deviation.

TABLE 11.4 Pre/Post Data from Metacognition Assessment

Subscale	Pretest			Posttest		
	M	Median	SD	M	Median	SD
Global	3.31	3.38	.55	3.71	3.62	.61
Problem	3.62	3.69	.58	3.98	3.88	.56
Support	2.79	2.78	.56	3.18	3.22	.63
Overall	3.23	3.26	.49	3.62	3.53	.53

Note: M = Mean; SD = Standard deviation.

TABLE 11.5   Paired Samples *t*-tests Between Pre–Post Conditions

Pair	Mean Diff	t	df	Sig. (2-tailed)
Pair 1 MAZE–MAZE Post	4.16	4.651	45	.000
Pair 2 Global–Global Post	0.389	4.75	47	.000
Pair 3 Problem–Problem Post	0.358	4.782	47	.000
Pair 4 Support–Support Post	0.374	4.536	47	.000
Pair 5 Overall–Overall Post	0.38	5.74	47	.000
Pair 6 SSR–SSR Post	12.34	5.67	47	.000

understanding the "big idea" in a passage/text as well as ways they could fix up their understanding when it was perceived to have broken down.

In the paired sample t-tests, each pre-post assessment pair (MAZE, all four subscales of the metacognition instrument, and the silent sustained reading test) was found to indicate a significant difference between the average values of the three instruments' measurements made under the pre-post conditions with the matched samples from participants. Paired samples *t* tests revealed a statistically reliable differences indicating $p = .000$, $\alpha = .05$ (See Table 11.5).

Results are indicative that the strategic comprehension instruction of PIE along with the META formative assessment had a statistically significant effect on the case study participants' comprehension and metacognition scores as measured by selected instruments.

DISCUSSION

The limitations of this study include the convenience sample, small sample size, as well as the singular placement of the students within a higher education institution. Replication is necessary with different populations and placements for more definitive data on the applicability of results to other populations and contexts. Further, informal written evaluations from the students indicated that the students did not "like" the repeated use of the PIE strategy or META probes. Many reported "running out of time," disliking the repetition, and "having a difficult time understanding the METAs." The challenging texts and time constraint caused them small levels of anxiety. However, following the course, most participants also anecdotally expressed that they were better at understanding how to paraphrase, cite appropriately, and understand what they read more quickly.

At the beginning of the course, scores on the METAs were very low as judged by the instructor and very high as judged by the students. However, over time the students' and instructor's scores using the rubric became more analogous with practice. In practice, learning to paraphrase complex texts, apply them to real life, and evaluate them appropriately takes a great deal of time, modeling, and rehearsal across contexts. While, it may not be a "likable" experience, the practice does equate to better comprehension and metacognition—both of which are vital for students to advance in higher education and life skills. The largest advantage of the strategy, assessment, and curriculum was that, in its authenticity, it was immediately applicable to the students' lives.

With this adaptable strategy, the content could be amended, as needed, based on the level and academic/life goals of the student. For example, for those in working in developmental education at the higher education level, the METAs could consist of a greater number and variety of the students' expository texts. For those working in Adult Secondary Education (ASE), the METAs could be amended to include increasing levels of complex text across the curriculum as outlined by the Common Core State Standards Appendix A. Instructors or tutors in Adult Basic Education (ABE) settings could use METAs to model comprehension of real world/authentic texts like health care insurance application forms, immigration paperwork, driver's license manuals, safety manuals, nutrition information, or childcare text topics.

Challenges for Practitioners Using a "Real World" Critical Literacy Curriculum

In many ways, the largest advantage of the strategy is also the largest challenge. While linking context to the students' lives honors their background, scaffolds prior knowledge, fosters understanding for relevancy and cross-disciplinary applications of comprehension skill, and can build student motivation and academic vocabulary, authentic/real world critical literacy curriculum is also challenging for the practitioner. Instead of using stock curriculums and materials, designing each lesson to meet the interests, backgrounds, and needs of students in the current classroom is intellectually demanding and time consuming. First, planning requires a conscious effort to acquire and organize background information from students at the onset of each semester. One way to accommodate would be to provide students with a limited background history questionnaire on the first day, which can be used to gain information about their past experiences in education as well as their current major, interests, and courses. Second, teaching with a "real world" curriculum requires teachers to have access to a wide variety of materials and the ability to ascertain the appropriateness of those materials for each class.

Designing an assessment like a META requires planning before each designated class to create an authentic probe that is both relevant and incrementally challenging. Third, authentic/real world curriculum requires the teacher to be knowledgeable about METAs and be able to provide explicit and systematic instruction on the procedures to follow during the strategy implementation and the assessment. Last, this type of instruction and assessment requires time. Time in class is needed to teach and model the procedure and assessment. Real world/authentic curriculum also requires quite a bit of ongoing planning out of class, since the curriculum is not set at the beginning of the semester and static, but constantly changing with student development. However, the challenges are more than worth the gains in students' understandings and abilities to "do life." To address Bauerlein's concerns, adult students are not too dumb for complex texts; adult students need to be systematically taught using complex texts and given frequent opportunities to practice their skills in understanding.

APPENDIX A
MAZE Assessment Using Expository Academic Text

Read the following passage. **Circle one word** in each set of **bold words** that best completes the passage.

Ex: Tom may be strong, (**but**, and, since) he does not work out much.

Dependency theory is a model of economic and social development that explains global inequality in terms of the historical exploitation of poor nations by rich ones. This analysis, which follows the social-conflict (**singularity, approach, geography**), puts primary responsibility for global poverty (**off, on, of**) rich nations, which for centuries have (**systematically, haphazardly, inadvertently**) impoverished low-income countries and made (**targets, friends, them**) dependent on the rich ones. This (**collective, destructive, advantageous**) process continues today.

Everyone agrees that (**while, before, around**) the Industrial Revolution, there was little (**affluence, poverty, animosity**) in the world. However, dependency theory (**asserts, affronts, admonishes**) that people living in poor countries (**was, were, are**) actually better off economically in the (**future, past, present**) than their descendants are now. A. G. Frank, (**a, on, was**) noted supporter of this theory, argues (**which, that, what**) colonial processes that helped develop deeply (**rugged, rich, caring**) nations also underdeveloped poor societies. Dependency (**analysis, theory, motive**) is based on the idea that (**a, an, the**) economic positions of the rich and (**famous, poor, powerful**) nations of the world are linked (**but, and, which**) cannot be understood apart from one (**nation, process, another**). Poor nations are not simply lagging (**behind, around, between**) the rich ones on the "path of progress," (**so, rather, and**) the prosperity of the most developed (**friendships, pathways, countries**) came largely at the expense of (**more, greatest, less**) developed ones. In short, some nations (**remained, contained, became**) rich only because others became poor. (**Neither, Both, Either**) are the result of the global (**economic, information, movement**) system that began to take shape (**seventy, five, fifteen**) centuries ago.

Late in the fifteenth (**age, century, year**), Europeans began surveying the Americas to (**toward, the, touch**) west, Africa to the south, and (**Africa, America, Asia**) to the east in order to (**dismantle, export, establish**) colonies. They were so successful that (**a, an, the**) century ago, Great Britain controlled about one-fourth (**off, of, on**) the world's land, boasting that "the (**earth, sun, star**) never sets on the British Empire." Formal colonialism has almost disappeared from the world; however, according to dependency theory, political liberation has not translated into economic independence.

Macionis, J. J. (2012). *Society: The basics (12th International Edition)*. New York, NY: Pearson.
Flesch-Kincaid Reading Ease: 14.8 (Postsecondary Reading Level)

APPENDIX B
MAZE Assessment Using Expository "Real World" Text

Read the following passage. **Circle one word** in each set of **bold words** that best completes the passage.

Ex: Tom may be strong, (**but,** and, since) he does not work out much.

*WARNING: Avoid a dangerous environment. To reduce the risk of electrical (**shock, wave, flow**) do not use in rain, in (**dry, damp, bumpy**) or wet locations, or around swimming (rafts, pools, parties), hot tubs, etc. Do not expose (**from, near, to**) snow, rain, or water to avoid (or, an, the) possibility of electrical shock. Use a (**voltage, party, beverage**) supply as shown on unit. Avoid (**advantageous, dangerous, entertaining**) situations. Do not use in the (**presence, nuance, future**) of flammable liquids or gases to (**prepare, prevent, approve**) creating a fire or explosion and/or (**effecting, remaining, causing**) damage to unit. To reduce the (**risk, level, type**) of electrical shock, this equipment has (**the, a, an**) polarized plug (one blade is wider (**through, on, than**) the other) and will require the (**type, correction, use**) of a polarized extension cord. The appliance plug will fit into a polarized extension cord only one way, so, if the plug does not fit fully into the extension cord, reverse the polarized plug or call a certified electrician for modification of wall unit.

* This passage, found in the instructions of a Poulan pruner saw, assessment was amended from its full 300 + word length as an exemplar.

Flesch-Kincaid Reading Ease: 6.3 (Middle School Reading Level)

REFERENCES

ACT. (2006). *Reading between the lines: What the ACT reveals about college readiness in reading.* Iowa City, IA: ACT.

Alexander, P. A. (2005). The path to competence: A lifespan developmental perspective on reading. *Journal of Literacy Research, 37,* 413–436.

Alvarez, M., & Riskco, V. (2009). Motivation and study strategies. In R. Flippo & D. C. Caverly (Eds.), *Handbook of college reading and study strategies* (2nd ed., pp. 199–219). New York, NY: Routledge.

Anderson, R. C., & Pearson, P. D. (1984). A schema-theoretic view of basic processes in reading comprehension. In P. D. Pearson, R. Barr, M. L. Kamil, & P. B. Mosenthal (Eds.), *Handbook of reading research* (pp. 255–291). New York, NY: Longman.

Baker, L., & Brown, A. L. (1984). Metacognitive skills and reading. In P. D. Pearson (Ed.), *Handbook of reading research* (pp. 353–391). New York, NY: Longman.

Barton, D., Hamilton, M., & Ivanic, R. (2000). *Situated literacies: Reading and writing in context.* New York, NY: Routledge.

Bauerlein, M. (2011). Too dumb for complex texts? *Educational Leadership, 68*(5), 28–32.

Bettinger, E. P., & Long, B. (2005). *Addressing the needs of under-prepared students in higher education: Does college remediation work?* Cambridge, MA: National Bureau of Economic Research.

Blumenfeld, P. C., Soloway, E., & Marx, R. W. (1991). Motivating project-based learning: Sustaining the doing, supporting the learning. *Educational Psychologist, 26,* 369–398.

Bransford, J. D., Franks, J. J., Vye, N. J., & Sherwood, R. D. (1989). New approaches to instruction: Because wisdom can't be told. In S. Vosniadou & A. Ortony (Eds.), *Simlarity and analogical reasoning* (pp. 470–497). New York, NY: Cambridge University Press.

Bransford, J. D., & Shwartz, D. L. (1999). Rethinking transfer: A simple proposal with interesting implications. In A. Iran-Nejad & P. D. Pearson (Eds.), *Review of research in education* (Vol. 25, pp. 61–101). Washington, DC: American Educational Research Association.

Creswell, J. (2007). *Research design: Qualitative, quantitative, and mixed methods approaches* (2nd edition). Thousand Oaks, CA: Sage.

Creswell, J. (2009). *Research design: Qualitative, quantitative, and mixed methods approaches* (3rd ed.). Thousand Oaks, CA: Sage.

Dagostino, L., & Carifio, J. (1994). *Evaluative reading: A cognitive view.* Boston, MA: Allyn and Bacon.

Dean, R. J., & Dagostino, L. (2007). Motivational factors affecting advanced literacy learning of community college students. *Community College Journal of Research and Practice, 31,* 149–161.

Duke, N. K., Purcell-Gates, V., Hall, L. A., & Tower, C. (2006). Authentic literacy activities for developing comprehension and writing. *Reading Teacher, 60*(4), 344–355.

Flavell, J. H. (1979). Metacognition and cognitive monitoring: A new area of cognitive developmental inquiry. *American Psychologist, 34,* 906–911.

Flippo, R., & Schumm, J. (2009). Reading tests. In R. Flippo & D. Caverly (Eds.), *Handbook of college reading and study strategies* (2nd ed., pp. 408–432). New York, NY: Routledge.

Freire, P. (1970). *Pedagogy of the oppressed.* New York, NY: Seabury Press.

Gee, J. (2001). Identity as an analytic lens for research in education. In W. Secanda (Ed.), *Review of research in education* (Vol. 25, pp. 99–125). Washington, DC: American Educational Research Association.

Gruenbaum, E. A. (2012). Common literacy struggles with college students: Using the reciprocal teaching technique. *Journal of College Reading and Learning, 42*(2), 110–116.

Hagaman, J. L., Luschen, K., & Reid, R. (2010). The "RAP" on reading comprehension. *Teaching Exceptional Children, 43*(1), 22–29.

Holschuh, J. P., & Aultman, L. P. (2009). Comprehension development. In R., & Caverly Flippo, D. (Ed.), *Handbook of college reading and study strategies* (2nd ed., pp. 121–144), New York, NY: Routledge.

Karbalaei, A., & Azimi Amoli, F. (2011). The effect of paraphrasing strategy training on the reading comprehension of college students at the undergraduate level. *Asian EFL Journal, 13*(3), 229–245.

Knowles, M. (1990). *The adult learner: A neglected species* (4th ed.). Houston, TX: Gulf.

Lei, S. A., Rhinehart, P. J., Howard, H. A., & Cho, J. K. (2010). Strategies for improving reading comprehension among college students. *Reading Improvement, 47*(1), 30–42.

Linden, D. E. (2007). The working memory networks of the human brain. The neuroscientist, 13(3), 257–269.

Macionis, J. J. (2012). *Society: The basics (12th International Edition).* New York, NY: Pearson.

Martinez, M. E. (2006). What is metacognition?. *The Phi Delta Kappan, 87*(9), 696.

Merriam, S. (1998). *Qualitative research and case study applications in education: Revised and expanded from case study research in education (2nd ed.).* San Francisco, CA: Jossey-Bass.

Mokhtari, K., & Reichard, C. (2002). Assessing students' metacognitive awareness of reading strategies. *Journal of Educational Psychology, 94*(2), 249–259.

Mollach, F. (1972). The use of cloze procedure to study the reading capabilities of community college freshmen. *Research in the Teaching of English, 6*(1), 20–35.

Nash-Ditzel, S. (2010). Metacognitive reading strategies can improve self-regulation. *Journal of College Reading and Learning, 40*(2), 45–63.

National Center for Education Statistics. (2009). *Beginning postsecondary students.* Washington, DC: Institute of Education Sciences, U.S. Department of Education.

National Governors Association Center for Best Practices & Council of Chief State School Officers. (2010). *Common Core State Standards for English language arts and literacy in history/social studies, science, and technical subjects.* Washington, DC: Authors.

Organization for Economic Co-operation and Development (2013), *OECD Skills Outlook 2013: First results from the Survey of Adult Skills.* Paris, France: OECD Publishing. Retrieved from http://dx.doi.org/10.1787/9789264204256-en

Palincsar, A. S., & Brown, A. L. (1984). Reciprocal teaching of comprehension-fostering and comprehension-monitoring activities. *Cognition and Instruction, 1*(2), 117–175.

Parker, R., Hasbrouck, J. E., & Tindal, G. (1992). The maze as a classroom-based reading measure: Construction methods, reliability, and validity. *Journal of Special Education, 26*(2), 195–218.

Parsons, S., & Ward, A. (2011). The case for authentic tasks in content literacy. *Reading Teacher, 64*(6), 462–465.

Pearson, P. D., Raphael, T. E., Benson, V. L., & Madda, C. L. (2007). Balance in comprehensive literacy instruction: Then and now. In L. B. Gambrell, L. M. Morrow, & M. Pressley (Eds.), *Best practices in literacy instruction* (2nd ed., pp. 30–54). New York, NY: Guilford.

Pintrich, P. R. (2002). The role of metacognitive knowledge in learning, teaching, and assessing. *Theory into Practice, 41*(4), 219.

Pitcher, S. M., Martinez, G., Dicembre, E. A., Fewster, D., & McCormick, M. K. (2010). The literacy needs of adolescents in their own words. *Journal of Adolescent & Adult Literacy, 53*(8), 636–645.

Pressley, M. (2000). What should comprehension instruction be the instruction of? In M. L. Kamil, P. B. Mosenthal, P. D. Pearson, & R. Barr (Eds.), *Handbook of reading research* (Vol. 3, pp. 545–562). Mahwah, NJ: Erlbaum.

RAND Reading Study Group. (2002). *Reading for understanding: Toward an R&D program in reading comprehension.* Santa Monica, CA: RAND.

Ross, D., & Frey, N. (2009). Learners need purposeful and systematic instruction. *Journal of Adolescent & Adult Literacy, 53*(1), 75–78.

Schumaker, J. B., Denton, P. H., & Deshler, D. D. (1984). The paraphrasing strategy. Lawrence: University of Kansas.

St. Clair, R., & Belzer, A. (2010). Adult basic education. In C. E. Kasworm, A. D. Rose, & J. M Ross-Gordon (Eds.), *Handbook of adult and continuing education* (pp. 189–199). Thousand Oaks, CA: Sage.

Stake, R. (1995). *The art of case study research.* Thousand Oaks, CA: Sage.

Sperling, R. A., Howard, B. C., Staley, R., & DuBois, N. (2004). Metacognition and self-regulated learning constructs. *Educational Research and Evaluation, 10*(2), 117–139.

Street, B. (1993). *Cross-cultural approaches to literacy.* New York, NY: Cambridge University Press.

Williams, R., Ari, O., & Santamaria, C. (2011). Measuring college students' reading comprehension ability using cloze tests. *Journal of Research in Reading, 34*(2), 215–231.

Yin, R. (2003). *Case study research: Design and methods* (3rd ed.). Thousand Oaks, CA: Sage.

Yin, R. (2009). *Case study research: Design and methods* (4th ed.). Thousand Oaks, CA: Sage.

CHAPTER 12

SUSTAINABILITY AND TRANSITIONAL LEARNING

Exploring the Influence of Adult Learners' Mental Models on Adaptive Change

Brian S. Hentz
University of Connecticut

The early twenty-first century presents a range of interconnected phenomena (environmental uncertainties, global neoliberal markets, rapid technological innovations) that leave many adults contending with what Bauman (2007) describes as a "crisis of knowing;" grappling with the "hidden curriculum of life" (Kegan, 1998), adults are increasingly challenged to meet the demands of their daily lives, which can seem "paradoxically certain and uncertain all at the same time" (Stacey & Griffin, 2005, p. 7). In many ways, current methods of resource and energy allocation, as well as articulations of the "good life," are proving insufficient and/or limited, insomuch as they fail to recognize the limits of our external environments and the emerging contexts in which we live. In response to this disconnect, sustainable devel-

Building Sustainable Futures for Adult Learners, pages 253–267
Copyright © 2015 by Information Age Publishing
All rights of reproduction in any form reserved.

opment has gained significant traction of late, with sustainability—for the purposes of this chapter—here defined as "development that meets the needs of the present without compromising the ability of future generations to meet their own needs" (United Nations, 1987).

Learning how to think and act sustainably presents an adaptive challenge, and as early twenty-first century life unfolds, adults who learn to think and act adaptively likely increase their capacity for living—and thriving—amidst complexity (Heifetz, 1994), despite the challenges that sustainability presents. Specifically, meeting these challenges becomes a threshold for transitional learning, in which adults faced with unpredictable changes in the interplay between their lives and their transforming contexts must anticipate, handle, and reorganize these changing aspects of life (Stroobants, Jans, & Wildemeersch, 2001). As transitional learning consists of the skills, behaviors, and psychosocial adjustments adults demonstrate to take on new roles and accommodate changes in their life circumstances (Aslanian, 2001; Rossiter, 2007a), facilitators of adult learning charged with promoting sustainable, adaptive problem-solving among a range of stakeholders require skillful means to make sustainability seem less daunting and more inviting. As the adage suggests, "change is difficult," and sustainability necessarily challenges well-ingrained habits of mind that allow adults to make sense of their lives.

Facilitators of adult learning can develop these skillful means by gaining a fuller appreciation of mental models, the neurological and biological basis for learning that helps explain how adults in transition develop adaptive mindsets conducive to sustainable development. In particular, mental models allow adults to represent knowledge and experiences across various contexts, so they may understand and interpret future situations in order to take action. Johnson-Laird (1983) argues that these models—essentially, cognitive maps—reflect what individuals learn and presume to know; moreover, these models, largely derived from reasoning and encoding, then coalesce to form more complex representations of knowledge (Markman & Gentner, 2001). Transitioning to more sustainable ways of living necessarily requires more complex ways of meaning making, and learning facilitators who appreciate this neurological basis for learning can help adults think and act in qualitatively different ways in the world.

This chapter begins with an overview of transitional learning in order to then situate the adaptive changes that typify sustainable development within this learning domain. It then proceeds to discuss mental model formation as a basis for transitional learning and to discuss the ways in which sustainability educators can leverage analogical reasoning to encourage learners' safe risk taking as they develop more complex ways of meaning making. Finally, the chapter concludes with reflections for facilitators of adult learning charged with helping adults not to simply "meet" the demands of the emerging century for which sustainability offers a provisional road map, but to do so boldly, compassionately, and reflexively.

Sustainability and Transitional Learning

Broadly conceived, transitional learning seeks to explain how adults respond to change, either in their own lives directly or the contexts and environments in which they live out their lives. In part, transitional learning is grounded in lifespan and life stage development theories (Bee & Bjorkland, 2004; Bridges, 1980, Levinson, 1978) with attention paid to the psychosocial and emotional adjustments that adults make as they take perspective and make meaning of the uncertainties that accompany natural and expected transitions across the life course. Other applications of transitional learning have focused on particular life events, including divorce (King & Raspin, 2004), adults returning to college (Aslanian, 2001; Kasworm, Polson, & Fishback, 2002), and career changes (Ibarra, 1999, 2003; Plimmer & Schmidt, 2007; Schlossberg, 1984), among others. Context aside, a central premise of transitional learning is that transitions—anticipated, inevitable, or otherwise—offer possibilities for meaning making, thereby requiring the active participation of adults as they learn to live critically with the conditions in which they conduct their lives (Glastra, Hake, & Schedler, 2004).

A particularly relevant aspect of transitional learning with respect to sustainability is that of potentiality and possibility, inasmuch as ensuring a planet and society for future generations to meet their needs challenges adults to think and act differently in the world. In large part, the paths that adults take to ensure this cross-generational contract "will rest with the reflexivity of human consciousness, our capacity to think critically about why we think what we do [in the future]—and then to think and act differently" (Raskin, 2008, p. 469). Adults' representations of themselves in this future—what Markus and Nurius (1986) call "possible selves"—can provide specificity for and direction to adults' individual aspirations for acting and thinking sustainably, but—importantly—also amplify their fears. In short, adaptive change is demanding, and as Rossiter (2007b) argues, possible selves that reflect transitional learning often result from adults' taking ample opportunities to rehearse attitudes and behaviors as they visualize themselves into their new selves.

Understandably, making the transition from "business as usual," short-term decision-making to more intentional, steady state possibilities is an adaptive challenge—in varying degrees—for all adults. Although developmentally mature adults do interpret themselves and their worlds with more complexity (Hy & Loevinger, 1996), numerous, interrelated institutions preclude more nimble, adaptive responses from adults to the systemic changes that sustainability demands. Specifically, contemporary economic, political, and cultural institutions are woefully inadequate for addressing the destabilizing environmental, security, and social tensions that they have created (Held, McGrew, Goldblatt, & Perraton, 1999). From a public health perspective, living in times of heightened complexity—coupled with this institutional unresponsiveness—comes with a cost: the World Health Organization projects that coronary disease and depression will be the leading global public health concerns by 2020 (Murray & Lopez, 1996), due to chronic stress underpinning adults' resistance to large-scale, systemic change.

In more practical terms, how might this resistance make itself manifest, as we collectively transition to a more sustainable society? Currently, numerous corporations are eager to demonstrate their commitment to sustainability; in turn, new high-level leadership corporate roles (chief sustainability officers) and corporate-wide practices (carbon accounting) are emerging to help corporations show their responsiveness to ecological concerns. In so doing, such corporations are also seeking to position themselves as socially responsible entities. However, from a sustainability perspective, these various initiatives fail to address the unsustainable construct of endless economic growth, rendering their efforts inadequate. As economist Joel Magnuson writes in *Mindful Economics* (2008):

> The crux of the matter is that a sustainable system is a steady-state system, and capitalism cannot operate in a steady-state environment anymore than a polar bear can survive on a vegetarian diet...the issue is not that sustainability is incompatible with business or industry; it is incompatible with capitalism. Capitalism requires exponential growth and no matter how intelligently you design it, it is not sustainable. Continuous economic growth, like cancerous cell growth, will eventually kill its habitat. (pp. 401–402)

As Magnuson aptly points out, a transition that is responsive to limits and future generations' needs is one that necessarily transcends the present capitalist paradigm.

How else might this collective resistance to change make itself manifest, as we seek more sustainable responses to the future? Social gerontologists posit that we are on the precipice of a newly unfolding life course (Carstensen, 2009; Dychtwald, 2000, 2012; Riley Kahn, & Foner, 1994; Riley & Riley, 2000), one in which age no longer serves as the primary determinant of one's anticipated or normative role. This transition—shifting from an age-segregated life course to an age-integrated life course—asks of us to balance simultaneously the spheres of labor, education, and leisure across the entire life course to ensure the most judicious, sustainable use of available resources and time throughout our lives. We are living longer, and as we enter a global, post-capitalist era that calls into question the feasibility of traditional, full-time employment in the market economy for all (Donkin,

2009; Rifkin, 1996), we face a substantive depletion of financial, human, and ecological resources. These collective trends mandate that we think differently about nothing less than the meaning of a well-lived life.

In many ways, the two previous passages point to the complexities inherent in adaptive change. As adults envision possible selves and strive to make necessary transitions that will ensure sustainable livelihoods for future generations, a range of assumptions very likely form the framework upon which adults build their intentions and possibilities for individual change. Central to transitional learning, then, is the recognition that change requires adults to not only tend to their future selves, but also let go and figuratively "die" to their previous ways of knowing. As Rossiter (2007b) points out, this process entails letting go of meaning perspectives that previously offered safety and predictability, so that new developmental growth can occur; such growth can often reflect adults' newfound or more enhanced capacity for relativistic thinking that eschews reductive understandings of the world (Perry, 1981). For a sustainability transition to occur, Raskin (2008) argues that a sharp upswing in public awareness and engagement is required of adults, and developmental growth supports such capacity building.

Adults who develop more complex, nuanced ways of meaning making will likely discover that discarding prior ways of knowing may have initially seemed akin to a breakdown, when—in reality—they experienced a breakthrough for learning through uncertainty. Clearly, this type of learning requires facilitators of adult learning to appreciate the developmental readiness of adults, as they entertain the possibilities of adaptive change that sustainability requires. For many adults, such learning can be—to use Gregory Bateson's terminology—"dangerous," for the problem to which this learning responds is a "solution" that consists of systematic contradictions in experience (Bredo, 1989), thereby resulting in potentially threatening "dilemmas of participation" in learning (Tosey, Mathison, & Michelli, 2005). Because educational relationships function as the context within which adult learners' existing possible selves can be more fully developed (Rossiter, 2007a), facilitators who appreciate their learners' mental models—the neurological basis for learning and change—are well positioned to create educative spaces and holding environments that are safe for risk taking and conducive to "dangerous" learning.

Mental Models and Adaptive Change

Mental models can be thought of as maps that allow individuals to represent both knowledge and experiences across various contexts, so they may understand and interpret situations in order to take action. Johnson-Laird (1983) argues that these cognitive representations reflect what individuals learn and what they presume to know, while Markman and Gentner (2001) add that these models are largely comprised of schemata, or abstractions and generalizations, derived from reasoning and encoding that then coalesce to form more complex representations of knowledge. Further, Gentner (2002) confirms that mental models serve very specific, useful purposes that

> [p]eople use mental models to reason with; they are not merely a convenient way of talking. Second, mental models can facilitate problem solving and reasoning in a domain. Third, mental models can yield incorrect results as well as correct ones". (p. 9685)

Hence, mental models serve as a compass of sorts, directing individuals' attention in ways that allow them to take action, even if those actions may seem limited or insufficiently responsive to emerging contexts. For example, for many adults who may have only a cursory understanding of "sustainability," the term may only encourage adults to think about recycling; certainly, making more mindful and expedient use of recyclables is a part of sustainability, but clearly, just that: one particular activity that can demonstrate more sensitivity to ecological limits. Adults who regularly see recycling bins are more likely to recycle, and—as they see peers and colleagues recycle as well—the activity will not seem unorthodox to them.

Even if mental models may seem insufficiently responsive to emerging contexts, mental models do provide individuals with a sense of stability and permanence (however tenuous), and this cognitive economy encourages individuals to seek "goodness of fit" (Eckert & Bell, 2005) between their current mental models and situations they encounter. In large part, this fit is based upon deeply ingrained assumptions that influence how individuals understand their worlds and how they take action (Senge, 1990). Hence, learning is necessary for changes in mental models to occur. Importantly, mental models largely reflect individuals' tacit knowledge; grounded in lived experiences, this knowledge, more broadly, also reflects individuals' values and beliefs. As inventions of the mind that represent, organize, and restructure domain-specific knowledge (Seel, 2006), mental models are essentially fluid, possessing boundaries open to change, depending upon situations and learners' level of expertise (Park & Gittleman, 1995). To promote more permeable mental models, facilitators of adult learning serve their learning community well by providing adults with new experiences, as well as cultivating safe learning spaces conducive to making tacit knowledge explicit (Sheckley & Bell, 2006), thereby foregrounding the potential for more expansive perspective taking and possibilities for action.

Because our mental models are comprised largely of unconscious reasoning processes that allow us to make causal inferences and "get on" with our daily lives, it's useful to consider the role that these processes play in shaping adults' collective views towards the promise of a more sustainable future, especially inasmuch as they reify the ideological state apparatus (Althusser, 1971) of Western, industrial, neocapitalist societies. Johnson-Laird and Yang (2008) succinctly write of the power of—and concerns over—unconscious reasoning processes:

> Some inferences [we make] are wholly unconscious. They are initiated unconsciously, carried out unconsciously, and *yield unconscious conclusions* (emphasis added). You might wonder how psychologists have detected their occurrence. That answer is that these inferences affect our behavior without our realizing it. (p. 61)

Of course, proceeding with our lives would be impossible without relying on these unconscious reasoning processes. Our brains reserve working memory for information that requires conscious attention, thereby efficiently and economically allowing us to seemingly go on "autopilot" when performing a wide range of rather quotidian tasks (driving, responding to routine emails). However, as Johnson-Laird points out, unconscious reasoning necessarily leads to unconscious conclusions, and systemic, "10,000 foot" challenges that require our collective, conscious attention—so we may necessarily think and act in qualitatively different ways—are steeped in complexity that, for many adult learners, is uninvited and unwelcomed. Specifically, when cognitive dissonance—or what cultural historian Morris Berman (2013) aptly calls "existential strain"—arises and adults' unconscious, unchallenged ways of unknowing fail to help them respond to new challenges, core emotions such as anger and fear can easily short-circuit critical thinking and lead to reactionary, inflammatory, and reductive thinking. As Lehrer (2009) writes,

> A person [can be] so eager to silence the amygdala . . . or suppress some bit of the limbic system that he or she ends up making a bad decision. A brain that's intolerant of uncertainty—that can't stand the argument—often tricks itself into thinking the wrong thing. (p. 203)

From a sustainability perspective, that "wrong thing," unfortunately, is usually more of the same behavior that contributed to unsustainable systems, for "biological evolution is driven by the tendency of all organisms to expand their habitat and exploit the available resources". (Ophuls, 2012, p. 9)

Understandably, in efforts to hold these negative core emotions at bay, individuals may unknowingly slip into the unconscious reasoning process that Johnson-Laird and Yang (2008) call "magical thinking," or erroneous conceptions of cause and effect that simplify complexity and constrain induction. In many ways, magical thinking seems guided by simplistic principles that, while rooted in prior experience, seem more like instrumental, quick-fix propositions to more complex problems. In *One-Dimensional Man*, Marcuse (1964) laments that such one-dimensional thought—thinking that trains individuals to feel a deep need to stay within their existing frameworks of analysis—precludes creative problem-solving and liberation, and, in its extreme, leads to "a massive indoctrination effort intended to stop people questioning what they see around them" (Brookfield, 2004, p. 191). To the point that adults fail to act reflexively, Fromm (1941), in *Escape from Freedom*, argues that adults succumb to automaton conformity, the process of social manipulation that results in adults striving to adjust their thinking to that of the collective. Hence, following Seel (2006), adults' individual mental models and broader, shared conceptual models that help explain phenomena are distinct, yet the power of cognitive economy and "fit" often conflate these ways of knowing.

To take just one example of "magical thinking," our shared, collective understanding of the age-segregated life course in the West—essentially, a social contract—can, in many ways, be construed as a mental model writ large. When Western adults consider the life course, the natural expectation is that one's trajectory through life is separated into distinct phases with primary foci: education serves as the primary sphere of activity in one's formative years, then employment in the market economy serves as the primary focus for the significant portion of one's adult years, with leisure largely structuring one's life activities in later life. In fact, a common question adults often ask upon meeting someone new remains, "What do you do?" When posing this question, adults are often guided by their unconscious reasoning system—that which does not rely on working memory (Johnson-Laird and Yang, 2008)—to assume standard responses that reinforce the cognitive economy of our mental models and ensure "fit" between their queries and others' responses. While adults, of course, understand that the boundaries that delineate work, education, and leisure can be muddled a bit, adults still largely expect that, at certain chronological stages of our lives, one of these spheres of activity will serve as the primary focus of self-identity.

However, a wealth of public policy briefs and research confirm that we are, indeed, becoming an older society, and the very age-segregated life course that Western adults have presumed to be normative and non-negotiable in industrialized times appears ill-suited—and, hence, unsustainable—with respect to the current global aging boom. AARP ("World's 65," 2009) notes that, by 2030, nearly 20% of the US population will be at least 65 years old, and the fastest growing cohort (with respect to %) are adults above the age of 85. Kotlikoff and Burns (2005) point to two key variables that help explain the impending boom: increased life expectancy and birth rate fluctuations. Particularly in developed nations, birthrates have plummeted over the past 50 years, leading to a more even distribution across the ages. This more even age distribution, accordingly, offers up a unique challenge: that of integrating the spheres of education, labor, and leisure more equitably and evenly across the life course. Freedman (2011) welcomes this challenge, arguing that "we need a new map of life. We've been making do with one that was fashioned for an expected longevity of threescore and ten. We shouldn't knock that legacy . . . [b]ut we can't stuff a 21st century life span into a life course designed for the 20th century" (p. 5).

An age-integrated model offers a sustainable response to more equitable age distribution. First, activities are no longer dictated by age (Riley & Riley, 1994). People may move in and out of education, work, and leisure over the course of their lives, and no one sphere of activity ever monopolizes one's identity. When there are no longer rigid age norms that govern people's actions at certain ages, the foundations of age-segregation incur fissures, challenging age barriers and reinforcing Keith's argument that "life stages are culturally situated and socially constructed" (Sokolovsky, 2009, p. 146). Moreover, when individuals are more or less equally attentive to and engaged in the spheres of work, leisure, and education, cross-age interaction is more likely, as people of different ages will interact with one another more frequently. These two aspects of age integration—both the spheres of activity themselves and the interaction across generations—are related because more of either type is likely to be accompanied by the other (Riley & Riley, 1994). An age-integrated approach to the life course, then, seems to offer just the creative, adaptable, and flexible mental model that twenty-first century demands require not just of older adults, but of us all.

Appreciating mental models and, hence, the neurological basis for how adults learn provides a basis for designing transitional learning interventions more likely to resonate with adults feeling overwhelmed by the "hidden curriculum of life" (Kegan, 1998). However, providing safe spaces for risk taking and the consideration of possible selves in a sustainable future is not sufficient for promulgating adaptive change and developmental growth. Rather, interventions that leverage analogical reasoning offer paths for growth and potential selves that respect adult learners' mental models, especially in ways that acknowledge these learners' lived experiences.

Analogical Reasoning: Expanding Mental Models

If mental models serve as the neurological and biological basis for action and change in adults' lives, then analogical reasoning serves as a vital process in helping adult learners revise and adapt these models to meet new demands in their lives. When adults encounter new experiences that fail to fit comfortably into their existing mental models, then neural patterns are triggered that heighten their awareness, signaling to them that these new experiences do not quite fit into their pre-existing, tacit understanding of how and why things work. Hence, the schemas (Markman & Gentner, 2001) that underpin adult learners' mental models fail to accommodate these new experiences, and thus an opportunity for learning and growth surfaces, in which these adults make inferences and abstractions about these new experiences to revise and possibly expand their pre-existing schema (Holyoak, 2005). Analogous to trying to fit the square peg into the proverbial round hole, adults encounter situations in their lives which—while frustrating or disruptive at times—provide opportunities for them to develop more complex neural patterns and complex, even contradictory ways of knowing to accommodate the novelty they have encountered.

Central to analogical reasoning is the relationship between base (source) and target analogs (Gentner & Markman, 1997), and this relationship is especially important in helping adults explore and challenge their current ways of understanding. Comprised of prior experiences, a base analog exists in long-term memory and provides a current pattern for understanding sensory input; in contrast, a target analog offers a new experience that allows individuals to retrieve cues from the new experience that can then be compared, or mapped, to the base analog to look for similar features (Holyoak, 2005). This mapping, both of superficial and structural attributes (Gentner & Markman, 1997), then allows individuals to make inferences about the target analog and make meaning about that new experience in ways that allow for mental models to change accordingly.

Analogical reasoning serves as a useful way to think of building bridges of understanding with adults who may be struggling to adapt to emerging conditions and, understandably, find comfort in clinging to "business as usual" ways of thinking; in helping adults negotiate the demands imposed on them, leaders of transitional learning should appreciate that change efforts must begin with compassion for learners whose mental models preclude entertaining other possibilities, ones that might actually promote more sustainable living alternatives in the face of twenty-first century demands. In helping adults and organizations explore ways for allocating their time and energies in ways that make sense for an emerging age-integrated society, for example, it's helpful to consider ways that learning facilitators might introduce new experiences—the target analogs—to others and, in so doing, make explicit either alignable or non-alignable differences (Gentner & Markman, 1997) so as to help make learners' mental models more permeable and open to new possibilities. For example, as traditional, full-time opportunities in the market economy fail to show a robust rebound since the onset of the 2008 global financial crisis, a bevy of skilled, well-educated adults of all ages find themselves either out of work, underemployed, or constructing creative, piecemeal approaches to a livelihood.

The counter to this trend is that wealth creation in the social economy—through volunteerism, time banks, and a range of other systems of mutuality and collective care—has offered a resilient response to this weakened market economy. To recognize an investment in community as "wealth" is, arguably, a perspective itself that seems foreign to many for, as Daloz (2000) writes, "in a world that ruthlessly offers greater material incentives and a bombardment of encouragement to place one's own welfare before that of the larger community, to care for the larger good seems almost an act of civil disobedience" (p. 121). Nonetheless, facilitators of adult learning across numerous alternative initiatives—ranging from the Transition Towns Movement (Hopkins, 2008) to "free skools" (Shantz, 2010)—can use analogical reasoning to make sustainable responses to emerging contexts even more generative and expansive. The source analog (labor in the market economy) and the target analog (labor in the social economy) share numerous structural similarities: both require an investment of one's time, both allow for skills development, and both allow for networks of mutuality and care to flourish. The "wealth" accrued and invested in the social economy offers social capital that eroded precipitously during the past several decades (Putnam, 2000), and advocates of "slow living" (Andrews, 2006; Honore, 2004) and sustainable, alternative responses to "careerism as secular salvation" are teaching others that "wealth" is a broadly conceived and multifaceted construct, and that emerging demands require more complex ways of meaning making.

Clearly, more reflexive orders of consciousness are required to meet the adaptive challenges to which sustainable development responds, especially as learners encounter the "conceptual emergency" (O'Hara, 2007) when new, emerging contexts simply cannot be understood adequately with their present mental models. While mental models form the basis for adults' action in the world, they importantly reflect an ontological awareness (Jarvis, 2007)—a "learning how to be"—that underscores the inner transformation required to act and think sustainably and transition into new ways of perceiving and being in the world.

CONCLUSION

For adults to meet adaptive challenges that require more sustainable responses, they must be prepared to undertake a certain modicum of "unlearning," and it serves leaders of adult learning well to recognize that unlearning can sometimes be the most perplexing and unnerving, especially for adults who may not be developmentally ready to question the very foundation that supported their lives. For adults to expand their developmental capacity and entertain alternatives that lead to growth and adaptation in their lives, they must be ready to take perspective on their ways of knowing, which—for many—remain tacit; in turn, these ways of knowing—largely unconscious and implicit—must be made explicit, in ways that allow adults to engage in more deliberate reasoning.

In this chapter, I have attempted to highlight how an understanding of mental models and analogical reasoning can help facilitators of adult learning learn from and with adult learners as, together, they address a range of unprecedented challenges that will render "business as usual" obsolete. Helping adults discover new ways to think sustainably necessarily respects a neurological basis for learning, and addressing the complexity of sustainability requires adult learning facilitators who have the skillful means to create safe educative spaces with developmentally-appropriate supports and challenges that will encourage learners' mental models to expand and include wider sets of creative possibilities for living well under different sets of conditions. In particular, these skillful means, when grounded in what we know about how the brain uses lived experiences to create meaning, offer richer possibilities for adaptive change and resilient responses to herculean challenges. In doing so, facilitators of adult learning also do well to heed Kegan's (2000) advice to be careful and not get in their way and become completely captive of their own theories, so that they can recognize their own incompleteness, and allow themselves to stand in relation to paradox and contradictory systems simultaneously.

REFERENCES

Althusser, L. (1971). Ideology and ideological state apparatuses. In L. Althusser (Ed.), *Lenin and philosophy and other essays*. New York, NY: Monthly Review Press.

Andrews, C. (2006). *Slow is beautiful: New visions of community, leisure, and joie de vivre*. Gabriola Island, British Columbia: New Society Publishers.

Aslanian, C. B. (2001). *Adult students today*. New York, NY: College Board.

Bauman, Z. (2007). *Consuming life*. Cambridge, UK: Polity.

Bee, H. L., & Bjorkland, B. R. (2004). *The journey of adulthood* (5th ed.). Englewood Cliffs, NJ: Prentice Hall.

Berman, M. (2013). The existential strain. Retrieved from http://morrisberman. blogspot.com/2013/07/the-existential-strain_20.html

Bredo, E. (1989). Bateson's hierarchical theory of learning and communication. *Educational Theory, 39*(1), 27–38.

Bridges, W. (1980). *Transitions: Making sense of life's changes*. Reading, MA: Addison-Wesley.

Brookfield, S. D. (2004). *The power of critical theory: Liberating adult learning and teaching*. San Francisco, CA: Jossey-Bass.

Carstensen, L. (2009). *A long bright future: An action plan for a lifetime of happiness, health, and financial security*. New York, NY: Random House.

Daloz, L. A. P. (2000). Transformative learning and the common good. In J. Mezirow & Associates (Eds.), *Learning as transformation: Critical perspectives on a theory in progress.* (pp. 103–124). San Francisco: Jossey-Bass.

Donkin, R. (2009). *The future of work.* London, England: Palgrave Macmillan.

Dychtwald, K. (2000). *Age power: How the twenty-first century will be ruled by the new old.* New York, NY: Penguin Putnam.

Dychtwald, K. (2012). A new vision for twenty-first century aging: Seven critical course corrections. Keynote address, American Society on Aging conference. March 27th. Washington, DC.

Eckert, E., & Bell, A. A. (2005). Invisible force: Farmers' mental models and how they influence learning and actions. *Journal of Extension, 43*(3).

Freedman, M. (2011). *The big shift: Navigating the new stage beyond midlife.* New York, NY: Public Affairs Press.

Fromm, E. (1941). *Escape from freedom.* New York, NY: Holt.

Gentner, D. (2002). Psychology of mental models. In N. J. Smelser & P. B. Bates (Eds.), *International encyclopedia of the social and behavioral sciences* (pp. 9683–9687). Amsterdam: Elsevier Science.

Gentner, D., & Markman, A. B. (1997). Structural alignment in analogy and similarity. *American Psychologist, 52*(1), 45–56.

Glastra, F. J., Hake, B. J., & Schedler, P. E. (2004). Lifelong learning as transitional learning. *Adult Education Quarterly, 54*(4), 291–307.

Heifetz, R. A. (1994). *Leadership without easy answers.* Cambridge, MA: Harvard University Press.

Held, H., McGrew, A., Goldblatt, D., & Perraton, J. (1999). *Global transformations: Politics, economics, and culture.* Palo Alto, CA: Stanford University Press.

Holyoak, K. J. (2005). Analogy. In K. J. Holyoak & R. G. Morrison (Eds.), *The Cambridge handbook of thinking and reasoning* (pp. 117–142). Cambridge, UK: Cambridge University Press.

Honore, C. (2004). *In praise of slow: How a worldwide movement is challenging the cult of speed.* New York, NY: HarperCollins.

Hopkins, R. (2008). *The transition handbook: From oil dependency to local resilience.* White River Junction, VT: Chelsea Green Publishing.

Hy, L. X., & Loevinger, J. (1996). *Measuring ego development* (2nd ed.). Mahwah, NJ: Erlbaum.

Ibarra, H. (1999). Provisional selves: Experimenting with image and identity in professional adaptation. *Administrative Science Quarterly, 44*(4), 764–792.

Ibarra, H. (2003). *Working identity: Unconventional strategies for reinventing your career.* Boston, MA: Harvard Business School Press.

Jarvis, P. (2007). *Globalization, lifelong learning, and the learning society: Sociological perspectives.* London, England: Routledge Press.

Johnson-Laird, P. N. (1983). *Mental models: Toward a cognitive science of language, inference, and consciousness.* Cambridge, MA: Harvard University Press.

Johnson-Laird, P. N., & Yang, Y. (2008). Mental logic, mental models, and simulations of human deductive reasoning. In R. Sun (Ed.), *The Cambridge handbook of computational psychology* (pp. 339–358). Cambridge, UK: Cambridge University Press.

Kasworm, C. E., Polson, C. J., & Fishback, S. J. (2002). *Responding to adult learners in higher education.* Malabar, FL: Krieger.

Kegan, R. (1998). *In over our heads: The mental demands of modern life.* Cambridge, MA: Harvard University Press.

Kegan, R. (2000). What "form" transforms?: A constructive-developmental approach to transformative learning. In J. Mezirow & Associates (Eds.), *Learning as transformation: Critical perspectives on a theory in progress* (pp. 35–69). San Francisco, CA: Jossey-Bass.

King, L. A., & Raspin, C. (2004). Lost and found possible selves, subjective well-being, and ego development in divorced women. *Journal of Personality, 72,* 603–632.

Kotlikoff, L. J., & Burns, S. (2005). *The coming generational storm: What you need to know about America's economic future.* Cambridge, MA: MIT Press.

Lehrer, J. (2009). *How we decide.* Boston, MA: Houghton Mifflin Harcourt.

Levinson, D. J. (1978). *The seasons of a man's life.* New York, NY: Balllantine Books.

Magnuson, J. (2008). *Mindful economics.* New York, NY: Seven Stories Press.

Marcuse, H. (1964). *One-dimensional man: Studies in the ideology of advanced industrial society.* New York, NY: Routledge.

Markman, A. B., & Gentner, D. (2001). Thinking. *Annual Review of Psychology, 52,* 223–247.

Markus, H., & Nurius, P. (1986). Possible selves. *American Psychologist, 41,* 954–959.

Murray, C., & Lopez, A. (Eds.) (1996). *The global burden of disease: A comprehensive assessment of mortality and disability from diseases, Injuries, and risk factors in 1990 and projected to 2020.* Cambridge, MA: Harvard University Press.

O'Hara, M. (2007). Strangers in a strange land: Knowing, learning, and education for the global knowledge society. *Futures, 39*(8), 930–941.

Ophuls, W. (2012). *Immoderate greatness: Why civilizations fail.* New York, NY: CreateSpace Independent Publishing Platform.

Park O. C., & Gittelman S. S. (1995). Dynamic characteristics of mental models and dynamic visual displays. *Instructional Science, 23,* 303–320.

Perry, W. G. (1981). Cognitive and ethical growth: The making of meaning. In A. W. Chickering (Ed.), *The modern American college.* San Francisco: Jossey-Bass.

Plimmer, G., & Schmidt, A. (2007). Possible selves and career transition: It's who you want to be, not what you want to do. In M. Rossiter (Ed.), *Possible selves and adult learning: Perspectives and potential.* New Directions for Adult and Continuing Education, no. 114. San Francisco: Jossey-Bass.

Putnam, R. D. (2000). *Bowling alone: The collapse and revival of American community.* New York, NY: Simon and Schuster.

Raskin, P. D. (2008). World lines: A framework for exploring global pathways. *Ecological Economics, 65,* 461–470.

Rifkin, J. (1996). *The end of work: The decline of the global labor force and the dawn of the post-market era.* New York, NY: Tarcher.

Riley, M. W., Kahn, R. L., & Foner A. (Eds.). (1994). *Age and structural lag: Society's failure to provide meaningful opportunities in work, family, and leisure.* New York: John Wiley and Sons.

Riley, M. W., & Riley, J. W. (2000). Age integration: A conceptual and historical background. *The Gerontologist, 40*(3), 266–270.

Rossiter, M. (2007a). Possible selves in adult education. In M. Rossiter (Ed.), *Possible selves and adult learning: Perspectives and potential* (pp. 87–94). San Francisco, CA: Jossey-Bass.

Rossiter, M. (2007b). Possible selves: An adult education perspective. In M. Rossiter (Ed.), *Possible selves and adult learning: Perspectives and potential* (pp. 5–15). San Francisco, CA: Jossey-Bass.

Schlossberg, N. K. (1984). *Counseling adults in transition: Linking practice with theory.* New York, NY: Springer.

Seel, N. M. (2006). Mental models and complex problem solving: instructional effects. In J. Elen & R. E. Clark (Eds.), *Handling complexity in learning environments: Theory and research* (pp. 43–66). Amsterdam: Kluwer.

Senge, P. M. (1990). *The fifth discipline: The art and practice of the learning organization.* New York, NY: Doubleday Business Press.

Shantz, J. (2010). *Constructive anarchy: Building infrastructures of resistance.* Burlington, VT: Ashgate Publishers.

Sheckley, B. G., & Bell, S. (2006). Experience, consciousness, and learning: Implications for instruction. In S. Johnson & K. Taylor (Eds.), *The neuroscience of adult learning: New directions for adult and continuing education, 110,* (pp. 43–52). San Francisco: Jossey-Bass.

Sokolovsky, J. (Ed.) (2009). *The cultural context of aging: Worldwide perspectives* (2nd ed.). Westport, CT: Praeger.

Stacey, R., & Griffin, D. (2005). *A complexity perspective on researching organizations.* London, England: Routledge.

Stroobants, V., Jans, M., & Wildemeersch, D. (2001). Making sense of learning for work: Towards a framework of transitional learning. *International Journal of Lifelong Education, 20,* 114–126.

Tosey, P., Mathison, J., & Michelli, D. (2005) Mapping Transformative Learning: The potential of neuro-linguistic programming. *Journal of Transformative Education, 3*(2), 140–167.

United Nations (1987). Our common future: Report of the world commission on environment and development. Retrieved from http://conspect.nl/pdf/Our_Common_Future_Brundtland_Report_1987.pdf

"World's 65 and over population to triple by 2050." (June 23, 2009). *AARP International.* Retrieved from http://www.aarpinternational.org/news/news_show.htm?doc_id=953328

CHAPTER 13

NEGOTIATING EXPERIENCE AND THEORY

Piloting Cornerstone and Capstone Courses to Build a Sustainable Future for an Interdisciplinary Graduate Degree Program

Stephen B. Springer, Omar S. Lopez, Matthew A. Eichler, Tennille J. Lasker-Scott, and Carrie J. Boden-McGill

Adult-oriented programs in higher education serve an ever-growing and diverse group of learners. Particularly within large state universities, which consider the core-mission of the institution to serve traditionally-aged learners, adult-serving programs are often over-shadowed by traditional programs. To serve the needs of adult students, programs must remain flexible and responsive to the particular needs of students (Coulter & Mandell, 2013); this flexibility must exist at several levels within the structure of adult-serving programs. Adult learners have specific needs which require flexibility and adult-oriented services in advising, financial aid, scheduling,

Building Sustainable Futures for Adult Learners, pages 269–294
Copyright © 2015 by Information Age Publishing
All rights of reproduction in any form reserved.

and delivery format (online, hybrid, etc.) as well as environments that include active and experiential learning.

The Master of Science in Interdisciplinary Studies (MSIS) in the Occupational, Workforce, and Leadership Studies (OWLS) Department at Texas State University has been uniquely situated to serve the needs of working adults in the surrounding metropolitan and rural areas. Previously, the program had existed in several forms, a division of the Department of Technology, an office, and later as a program belonging to a college. Before the MSIS was available, a personalized bachelor's degree existed, based on academic core subjects, assessment of prior learning in the workplace, an internship, and courses chosen to enhance a student's ability to succeed in the workplace. Given the nature of the personalized bachelors, a customized master's degree option fit the existing faculty unit at that time. Initially, it was developed with a few masters courses being taught by the unit and using courses from elsewhere in the university (Sherron, Boden-McGill, & Springer, 2013).

As this unit merged with a small unit within another division of Technology involved in career and technical education, additional graduate courses and faculty became available to serve graduate students. Later, prior to becoming a department, the Occupational Education Program negotiated with the College of Education to completely administer the Master of Education in the Management of Technical Education. The department currently contains three tenured faculty members (which include the Chair of the department and Dean of the college), three tenure-track faculty members, two full-time teaching faculty, and two part-time teaching faculty. Additionally, a number of per-course faculty are hired to teach each term. Of this continuing faculty, eight are qualified to serve as graduate faculty members and have terminal degrees (PhD or EdD). These faculty have offices in one of three areas, the main campus in San Marcos, the Round Rock campus (an upper division campus near Austin), or throughout the San Antonio metropolitan area at an off-campus teaching facility. Courses are offered in face-to-face, blended (hybrid), or online formats. The department is currently working to have all courses available online within the next couple years. Currently a number of the courses are available online, enough that a student can complete the degree program with quite a limited array of course choices in an all-online fashion. As the program has added new faculty and began this transition to an online program, the faculty have begun to examine the degree program carefully in order begin to change and update the program. Additional considerations in updating the program include generating more student course enrollments within the department rather than sending students to other departments to fulfill degree requirements (Sherron, Boden-McGill, & Springer, 2013).

Adults in the MSIS program come from a variety of workplace backgrounds, whether military, governmental, or private sector. Others have not had long-term careers and are looking for a steady career in the future, which brings them to seek a degree. Initially the program sought industrial and military (or past military) students and later expanded its base to serve a variety of workers (Springer, 2010). As Faculty looked to updating the program and building a sustainable model for the future, they had to consider new markets for graduate students, the need to increase enrollments, the role of new faculty who were hired into the department in the last five years, as well as the need to increase student enrollment hours within the department. One major initiative was to strengthen the degree program overall and to improve writing and thinking skills students hone throughout the program. Essentially faculty also saw the opportunity to revise the program as a way to be in contact with students who were otherwise taking courses that were in other departments.

REVIEW OF RELATED LITERATURE

No longer are the hallways of higher education only filled with the traditional student who is a recent high school graduate with limited to no work or life experience. According to the National Center for Educational Statistics learners 25 years old and older comprise more than 50% of part-time and 33% of full-time enrollment in higher education in the United States (Aud, Wilkinson-Flicker, Kristapovich, Rathbun, Wang, & Zhang, 2013) and the majority of those participants in graduate school (Snyder & Dillow, 2012). It is a relatively recent and continuously more prevalent trend that adults are a more significant proportion of the higher education landscape; however, the field of adult education has been flourishing in the United States for quite some time.

Lindeman (1926) first contributed to the literature by supplying what adult learning entailed. Lindeman's assumptions on adult learning are that: adults are motivated to learn as they experience needs and interests that learning will satisfy, the orientation to learning for adults is life-centered, experience is the richest and primary resource of an adult's learning, adult learners seek self-directed learning experiences where the teacher is a facilitator in the learning process, and that the individual differences among people increase with age. Following Lindeman, Malcolm Knowles popularized the theory of adult learning in the United States (1968; 1970). Knowles (1970) also presented the terminology of andragogy as meaning "the art and science of helping adults learn" (p. 43). Knowles (1974) identified the following four principles that portrayed adult learners: they are self-directed and able to take responsibility for their own actions and learning, they have extensive experience (both work and life), they are active learners, ready to immerse themselves into the learning process, and they are motivated. Knowles' (1974) identifications have grown and redeveloped through the years.

Harbour, Daveline, Wells, Schurman, and Hahn (1990) also recognized six characteristics of the adult learner (as cited in Ott, 2011). Those characteristics are the following: adults like to learn from organized materials and structure; adults learners need to connect their new knowledge with their old knowledge and experience; adults bring a significant world experience and education into the classroom; adults are most interested in relevant and practical subjects that are applicable to their life; adults need to feel both a psychologically and physically comfort in their environment; mistakes made by the adult learner sometimes affect their attitude and/or self-esteem. Similar characteristics are also mentioned in Zemke and Zemke's (1984) article, "30 things we know about adult learners."

Unfortunately, another characteristic of adult learners and nontraditional students is a high attrition rate. Studies (Andres & Carpenter, 1997; Bean & Metzner, 1985; Park & Choi, 2009; Sandler, 1999) suggest that it may be due to unsuccessful integrations into the higher education environment, especially eLearning or online programs (Nash, 2005; Tyler-Smith, 2006). Kenner and Weinerman (2011) state that "educators must understand the background of adult students and develop a curriculum that addresses their particular needs." (p. 90). Those needs are met by having an awareness of the adult learners' differing learning styles, framing the curriculum in ways that that adult will find useful, and improve the integration into the higher education environment through competition and repetition (Kenner &Weinerman, 2011). Individualized interdisciplinary programs that effectively utilize reflective practices and experiential learning may be one method that increases persistence of adult learners in graduate programs.

Interdisciplinary programs are ideal for students who have an interest or background in more than one discipline. They are also ideal for adult learners who may come to their studies with various life experiences, professional backgrounds, and interests. The programs allow students to explore and research connections of two or more separate disciplines, emerging them to create a unique learning experience (Newswander & Borrego, 2009). Interdisciplinary education is well-known in the scientific community but has become more popular in academic institutions (Association of American Universities-AAU, 2005; Brint, 2005; Feller, 2002; Morse, Nielsen-Pincus, Force, &Wulfhorst, 2007; Rhoten, 2004). The Association of American Universities (AAU, 2005) asserts this increase is a reflection of the demands for the use of combinations of disciplinary research and knowledge in an effort to solve problems that are both new and complex to the changing environment. Gibbons (1998) and Brainard (2002) attest to the use of interdisciplinary approaches for addressing real-life issues. The interdisciplinary approach has been applied in varying disciplines, such as psychology, sociology, geography, organization studies, sciences, and education (Brint, Turk-Bicakci, Proctor, & Murphy, 2009). Developing curriculum for these programs is no easy achievement. Planning an effective curriculum that is truly interdisciplinary requires the participation of faculty members from different backgrounds, fields, and differing perspectives (Stone, Ballard, & Harbor, 2009).

For graduate students, interdisciplinary education may occur in four dimensions (Manathunga, Lant, & Mellick, 2006). These dimensions include

- The relational, mediated, transformative and situated learning experiences (Lattuca, 2002).
- The intercultural knowledge and skill development that is needed to assist the student to transfer beyond disciplinary to interdisciplinary (Cornwell & Stoddard, 2001).
- The student reaches a higher level of critical thinking skills through the constant deliberation within the differing disciplinary perspectives (Klein, 2001; Ivanitskaya et al., 2002).
- The student's epistemological beliefs about their original discipline and how it contrasts from the other discipline is enhanced (Bradbeer, 1999; Jones et al., 1999; Ivanitskaya et al., 2002).

These dimensions of interdisciplinary education are fluid and can also occur in face-to-face or online course delivery. As Smith (2005) noted, adult learners are increasingly finding online courses to be a notable way to deliver professional development and educational courses.

Adult learners participating in graduate education are also best fit for flexible programs, such as online or hybrid courses, that utilize their educational, cultural, professional, and personal narratives and experiences. As noted by Cornelius, Gordon, and Ackland (2011), an effective collaborative approach occurs when faculty assist the learners in decision making and developing critical thinking, organization, management, and leadership skills. Effective programs also use the existing skills of the learner to connect to the new knowledge to existing frameworks (Weatherley, Bonn, Kerr, & Morrison, 2003). Similarly, this collaboration also calls for the learner to practice reflection.

Reflection or reflective practice is the art of conscientiously and methodically taking one's actions, specifically personal actions, into consideration (Schön, 1987). Reflective practice, through the collaborative approach of the learner, the instructor, and peers, guides the participants into correctly associating the coursework with real-life and professional situations. After the

concept of reflective practice was introduced by Schön (1987), many organizational and academic institutions began to concentrate on the practice.
Concentrations on areas such as experiential learning theory, which significantly includes the practice of reflection, made an impact among adult learners (Compton, Cox, & Laanan, 2006; Klein-Collins, 2011; Roessger, 2012).

According to Kolb (1984), one of the leading theorists of experiential
learning, reflection is one of the major stages in a four-stage learning process
in which experiential learning occurs. In Kolb's model, a learner must witness
and endure concrete experience. The learner must then reflect on the experience in order to draw conclusions from experiences through abstract conceptualization that will eventually develop into active experimentation are then
applied to new concrete experiences. Reflection dictates a significant part of
the learning experience. Reflections are assimilated and distilled in abstract
concepts from which new implications for action can be drawn (Passarelli &
Kolb, 2011). Reflection is an experiential and transformative form of learning
that benefits both the student and the instructor (Boden et al., 2009).

Experiential learning theory argues that learning style is not a psychological trait but a dynamic state resulting from synergistic transactions between the person and the environment; this dynamic state arises from an
individual's preferential resolution of the dual dialectics of experiencing or
conceptualizing and acting or reflecting (Passarelli & Kolb, 2011). Because
adult learners have preferred learning styles and preference for how they
receive and process information, experiential learning preferences such as
personality type, career choice, current job role, educational specialization,
and adaptive competencies (Centenary College New Jersey, 2013) all affect
their personal reflective learning.

Unfortunately, while there is widespread use of experiential learning
models at the undergraduate level, they are not as popular at the graduate
level, especially for hybrid or online courses, perhaps because they have
presented many unique challenges for students, instructors, and clients
(Hagan, 2012). The literature clearly indicates that adult learners have particular needs and learn in ways that are different than their traditionally
aged counterparts. Adult learners are at a disadvantage as many universities
still need to incorporate models that best fit this specific student population. One program, the Master of Science in Interdisciplinary Studies, pulls
together adult learning theory and best-practices in the literature to serve
the unique needs of adult graduate students.

MASTER OF SCIENCE IN INTERDISCIPLINARY STUDIES

The degree program was designed to build on students' already existent
skills in the workplace as well as moving them toward a career trajectory

planned by each individual student in consultation with an advisor. Although the degree itself is not preparation for a specific career, students can plan to customize the degree in ways that support their developmental needs and interests to meet their career goals. The degree plan begins with an entry sequence of nine hours (three regular courses), an academic module of 21 hours (seven regular courses), and an exit sequence of nine hours (three regular courses). The degree is interdisciplinary and must meet a number of rule sets in regard to class choices. First, all courses within the program must be approved by the graduate advisor of the department and further approved by the Graduate College of the university. Second, no more than 15 hours in one discipline (or course designator) may be used for the degree program without approval. Third, three disciplines (represented by departments) must have at least six hours in the program. Fourth, four disciplines must be represented in program from at least three colleges (Department of Occupational, Workforce, and Leadership Studies, 2013). In general, the three courses in the entry module are about communications, ethics, and human relations. The academic module is open to any graduate level courses across the university that addresses the student's needs and goals. Finally, the exit module is a three course research sequence in which the first course is a methods course, and the remaining two courses are independent courses in which the student plans, conducts, and reports on an independent research project.

Changes made to the program include an "Interdisciplinary Studies in OWLS" course, which is taken as part of the entry sequence on the first long semester of a student's time in the program. The second change involves the addition of a practitioner sequence in which the student takes an overview of interdisciplinary research course, plans a practicum experience, executes a professional practicum, and then reflects on the experience in her chosen career area. These changes were supported by three findings by the faculty, one that students were not prepared for the rigors of an exit sequence and had not written about their interdisciplinary program (or thought about it) programmatically. Second, some students were stuck in the exit sequence unable to form and complete independent research projects in a timely fashion. Third, through anecdotal advising encounters, the faculty surmised that the MSIS was also attracting a group of students that desired opportunities to apply their learning in both academic and practical contexts. By giving students an introduction experience in the beginning and creating an additional opportunity for students in a practitioner exit track, we believe the program will be strengthened through better course completion, ongoing advising, and preparation for the culmination of the interdisciplinary program through an exit sequence that ties together the interdisciplinary coursework.

TABLE 13.1

Module	Courses
Entry Module	3 courses in communications, ethics, or human relations to include: OCED 5360E Interdisciplinary Studies in OWLS, and Two other courses related to communications, ethics, or human relations
Academic Module	7 courses chosen around student need and interest. No specification other than needing to meet general rule sets.
Exit Module	3 courses—chose one of two of the following: Research Project Sequence: 　OCED 5300—Interdisciplinary Research Methods 　OCED 5301—Applied Interdisciplinary Research I 　OCED 5302—Applied Interdisciplinary Research II OR Practitioner Sequence: 　CTE 5330—Overview of Interdisciplinary Research 　OCED 5360C—Reflective and Experiential Learning Techniques 　OCED 5360D—Professional Practicum

The degree construction is seen in Table 13.1, and courses are inserted where appropriate.

The program has addressed the ongoing needs of students through two distinctive curriculum revisions, namely the addition of an *introductory* course and an additional *exit sequence* option.

INTERDISCIPLINARY STUDIES IN OWLS

Graduate advisors have faced some of the often overlooked concerns in regard to readiness to learn, degree plan direction, and skill bases to be successful in graduate education. We may assume that the working adult, recently graduated bachelor's level student, and other students have a determined direction, self-confidence, and a strong knowledge and skill bases to do well in graduate college (Ismail, Abiddin, Hassan, 2011; Willson & Gibson, 2011).Unfortunately, graduate students may still struggle balancing life issues and time while working toward the advanced degrees (Lovitts & Nelson, 2000).

Texas State University's Response

Texas State University's OWLS Department has taken an affirmative step to address the issues of students seeking the advanced degrees. The OWLS department has designed a course that introduces graduate students to essential academic skills to include such areas as project planning and communication. In effect, there are nine modules that contain lectures and assignments that are specifically designed to accomplish two goals. First, these skill sets may improve performance in courses in the graduate college, and second, the skills sets may have a positive effect on workplace performance.

The content of the course also includes the opportunity for the student to assess his or her skill sets and to dialog with the Graduate Advisor regarding courses that might remediate any areas as defined as problematic (Applegate, 2012; Bahr, 2008; Gentry, 2012; Kane, Roy, &Medina, 2012). In essence, the exposure to high level skills in the course reminds the student of his or her responsibility to address areas identified as needing "more work." Because of the flexibility of the master's level degrees offered by OWLS, this inventory of the student's skills can be translated into coursework to augment the student's skill bank.

Although there are numerous skills and subject areas that could be infused into the course to meet requirements, those chosen carry the broadest applicability. The following eight subject areas of determining a career direction, preparing a degree plan, tools for researching the literature, decision making processes, improving oral communication skills, project management and life balance, and critical thinking are all important for graduate students. The following sections provide a discussion of what the topics consist of and how they are addressed in the course.

Module I: Determine Career Directions

The first module introduces students to assessment of his or her career direction. Because students come with varying degrees of readiness to learn and goals, it is important to make certain the institution fully understands the direction the student is seeking. According to Bahr (2013), the structure of non-traditional educational programs and institutions may result in a diversity of goals among students. This flexibility sometimes results in the students being overwhelmed and confused. At times understanding the direction the students are seeking may be difficult; therefore, the OWLS course provides assistance within the first module. First, the students are given a career inventory to provide data to consider regarding some of the career options that might be favorable (Bloom, Tripp, Shaffer, 2011). Second, the students are challenged to look at their skills and determine two things. Essentially the students must determine if the skills possessed are sufficient to address the position desired, and if not, how to add those skills through coursework. In addition, once the students have inventoried their skills, a culminating assignment is provided where the students make the career choice and defend that choice. The value of this module is designed to open the course and the students' options as the course begins. It can shake the very bedrock of the students' thinking in a positive manner (Erford & Crockett, 2012).

Module II: Prepare Degree Plan

This module provides the opportunity to translate the planning stage regarding a career direction or promotion within the same career to specific coursework (Tate, Klein-Collins, & Steinberg, 2011). The MSIS, MAIS, and MEd (Management of Technical Education) all have some degree of flexibility to accommodate numerous career directions. However, in the event that there was not a match with the OWLS department, the students would be directed to other plans early in their careers.

This step of translating need to solution is one of the strongest reasons that this module is useful and essential. Dvarishkis (1990) proposed a guide for adult education career exploration that consists of presentations about self-concept, interests, information, and action planning, then resources on resumes writing and discussing the job interview. A search of departments and coursework can help translate the directions the students provided in Module I with "real-life" course options. Although complex, this process can make a major difference in the overall life satisfaction individuals may have with their career direction (Galles & Lenz, 2013).Exploring the courses, careers, and future options with the instructor and the graduate advisor can be extremely valuable.

Module III: Tools for Researching the Literature

Another skill in required of graduate students to be successful is the strong understanding of research tools and the APA writing style (Ondrusek, 2012). This need, often unfilled by the graduate students' backgrounds, becomes extremely important as the students begin enrollment in the specialized curriculum that is chosen from Modules I and II. Basically, it is hoped that as the students begin the coursework, they will gain some degree of understanding of using American Psychological Association (APA) citations, searching databases, and utilizing academic library or other outside resources.

Because of the "real life application" of this OWLS course, there is an activity where students actually correct a sample essay developed by one of our department graduate assistants (Bitchener & Ferris, 2011; Van Beuningen,

De Jong, Kuiken, 2012). This promotes the hands-on work and demonstrates how important it is to have a basic understanding of academic writing. In addition, students must also show their understanding of databases available to them. Although at this stage it may be difficult for students to understand for certain the transferability of these knowledge and skill areas, the students will have a rudimentary exposure to important research and writing concepts.

Module IV: Decision Making

Module four addresses the difficult problem of decision making. How do the students make decisions that are both ethical and useful when they have so many work, school, and personal issues to balance in their daily lives? This module provides another directed discussion of this critical skill. As educators know, many individuals, despite their high level of education, often struggle with decision making. According to Mitchell, Shepherd, and Sharfman (2011), decision-making is central to modern organizations, and it is only effective if consistent. Cognitive experiences and external environment determine the quality of decision-making process, with positive experiences and environment making decisions also more positive. In some instances, decisions may be made without gathering facts or significant evidence that supports the decisions. Therefore, the SWOT analysis is taught as a decision making tool in the course (Addams & Allred, 2013). SWOT is a marketing tool used to identify strengths, weaknesses, opportunities, and threats of an action or an organization in order to gain better understanding of it (Goodrich, 2013). As with the other modules, this discussion is designed to be immediately useful for graduate students. Learning the SWOT can affect the critical decisions made in and out of graduate education (Jonassen, 2012).

Module V: Improve Oral Communication Skills

According to Wilkes (2012), graduate students are often afraid to speak in public which is detrimental for the development of their communication skills. How do graduate students communicate concisely and yet accurately both in their extensive written requirements and their oral presentations in class and at conferences (Conrad & Newberry, 2012; Ondrusek, 2012)? This module is not extensive enough to totally remediate all oral and written skills; rather, it is an awareness module. In essence, the assignments assist students in identification of personal communication issues as well as encouragement for change (Nelson, Range, & Burck-Ross, 2012; Simpson, 2012).

Module VI: Time Management and Life Balance

Both in undergraduate and graduate education, the need for time management is evident (Maher & Mitchell, 2010; Wilson & Gibson, 2011), and this is the topic for Module VI. Late assignments, failure to record events on the work and personal calendars, overbooking and misplaced importance of competing events, are all serious barriers for success in college as well as the workplace. In keeping with the need to present realistic solutions, this module requires the student to report activities and events that took place during a week. This and other assignments are geared again to awareness. Change is recommended and expected; however, it may not always take place.

Module VII: Project Management

This module focuses on project management. Students often work in groups to present at a conference or submit a graduate-level group project to the instructor. However, at times students do not know how to superintend a project from the conception to the delivery. Instead, procrastination, confusion, and concerns block the students' work from being delivered on time or perhaps at all. According to DiMartino and Castaneda (2007), graduates need applied project management skills for success. Students are currently ill-prepared for the demands of the workforce. The project management module is another practical module that provides as much as the student really wants to learn about managing a project of any type. Students should look carefully at the project management concepts and then move from that point to learning how to better manage the projects in their lives.

Module VIII: Critical Thinking for the Present and Future

The final instructional module centers on critical thinking. Within the context of OWLS, critical thinking encompasses the application of knowledge after careful and measured examination of all information and viewpoints to make decisions that are non-egocentric in nature (Flores, Matkin, Burbach, Quinn, & Harding, 2012). Critical thinking among graduate students has been identified as a major deficiency, and the faculty of OWLS has worked to address this issue with the students. However, despite major efforts, students still demonstrate major concerns in the final oral exam regarding critical thinking. Therefore, this module is designed to augment other classes taught by OWLS that promote critical thinking and to open the student's current thinking to this important concept.

In conclusion, this new course combines multiple areas of general concern to the faculty and attempts to address those concerns early and effectively though a mandatory entry course. Students are familiarized with several academic and life skills in the Interdisciplinary Studies in OWLS course. These skills of determining a career direction, preparing a degree plan, conducting library research, making decisions, improving oral and written communication skills, time management and life balance, and critical thinking, are reinforced throughout the graduate plan of study, particularly the Reflective and Experiential Learning Techniques and Professional Practicum courses, and measured in the comprehensive oral and written exit examinations for the program.

REFLECTIVE AND EXPERIENTIAL LEARNING TECHNIQUES

Reflective and Experiential Learning Techniques is the second of an online three-course exit sequence. The first course, Overview of Interdisciplinary Research in OWLS, prepares students to understand basic research concepts and to conduct research in applied settings. The second course, Reflective Experiential Learning Techniques, is designed to assist graduate students with planning and completing a practicum in their chosen profession. In the first 11 weeks of the Reflective and Experiential Learning Techniques course, students learn about tools of inquiry and engage in field-based activities to identify possible locations for their practicum. In the remaining four weeks of the course, they write a proposal to implement the practicum in the second course, Professional Practicum. The course goals for Reflective and Experiential Learning Techniques are to synthesize interdisciplinary coursework and career goals, select a practicum appropriate to learning objectives, identify academic literature related to the proposed practicum experience, learn reflective practices appropriate to professional and career settings, compose a practicum proposal appropriate for goals and coursework, and deliver an online video presentation of highlights from the practicum plan. The following narrative provides a module-by-module description of the topics and learning objectives that define the Reflective and Experiential Learning Techniques course.

Module I: Practicum Course Overview and Planning

At the end of this module, students are required to articulate in a *Practicum Site Plan* the relationship between their prior and current experience and graduate coursework to three potential practicum sites. The site plan contains a student's contact information, biography, and a practicum goal statement. Students develop up to seven learning objectives that define measurable and observable learning objectives from which the student and site supervisor will select three to four during the site-visit interview. These select learning objectives define the student's practicum experience. Students in the final section of the site plan list four to five organizations where they might explore the possibilities of a practicum based on their learning objectives and goals (Hahn, 2010; Scovill & Waite, 2012; Zwozdiak-Myers, 2012).

Module II: Foundations of Reflective Thinking

At the end of this module, students compare theoretical models of reflection (Dewey, 1933; Kolb, 1984; Schön, 1983) as they relate to the workplace. Students achieve this learning objective through the module readings (Ng, 2012; Stevens & Cooper, 2009), and by responding to the online forum prompt: *Describe and explain aspects from theoretical models of reflection you would consider and not consider for use in the practicum.*

During Module II, the students conduct their first site visit to identify a viable location for their practicum experience. To prepare students, the module includes mini-lectures on scheduling, planning, and conducting these interviews, much like a job interview. After the practicum site-visit, students complete a reflection exercise where they rate their initial impressions of the practicum site-visit. These impressions include how well a practicum at that site would allow them to integrate theory and research learned in prior courses with practice.

Module III: Forms of Reflective Writing

At the end of this module, students describe different ways of reflective writing. Students achieve this learning objective through the module readings (Fade, 2006; Hume, 2009; Moon, 2004), and by responding to the following online forum prompt: *Describe and explain aspects from theoretical models of reflection (Dewey, 1933; Kolb, 1984; Schön, 1983) you would consider and not consider for use in the practicum.* During Module III, the students conduct their second site visit to identify a viable location for their practicum experience. After the practicum site-visit, students again complete the reflection exercise outlined earlier in Module II.

Module IV: Experiential Learning

At the end of this module, students distinguish among different types of experiential learning such as service learning, volunteerism, community, internships, field education, and clinical practice. Students achieve this learning objective through the module readings (Purdue University, 2013; Scovill & Waite, 2012), and by responding to the online forum prompt: *Describe and explain how your practicum would differ by type of experiential learning, e.g., service, volunteerism, community, internships, field education, and clinical practice.* During Module IV, the students conduct their third and final site visit to identify a viable location for their practicum experience. After the practicum site-visit, students again complete the reflection exercise outlined earlier in Module II.

Module V: Selecting the Practicum Site

At the end of this module, students engage in a decision-making process that results in the selection of the practicum site that best meets the learning objectives and goal in their *Practicum Site Plan.* To achieve this learning objective, students compare and rank each impression, factor, and comments from the three post-practicum site-visit reflections. Further readings on Kolb (1984) support the students' work for this exercise (Clark, 2011). Upon completion of their analysis, students write a two-page summary of their analysis, describing the tradeoffs among the site possibilities as well as why they selected the proposed practicum site. Students then respond to the following online forum prompt: *State what site you selected and summarize why you made this site selection. Include in your response a description of the interdisciplinary experiential learning (e.g., service, volunteerism, community, internships, field education, or clinical practice) you intend to acquire during your practicum.*

Module VI: Practicum Proposal Draft

At the end of this module, students are required to submit for instructor feedback a *Practicum Proposal* draft. Chapter 1 of the proposal introduces the practicum followed by subsections describing the student's learning objectives, assumptions, and limitations. Chapter 2 of the proposal is the practicum support literature. Chapter 3 of the proposal contains a narrative describing the students' activities with approximate start and completion dates and estimated hours to achieve each learning objective. Students are to complete 120 hours of practicum activities within a 10-week period.

Chapter 4 of the proposal is the practicum evaluation plan. The formative evaluation consists of a timesheet that the site supervisors initial each week of the practicum verifying the hours the students worked on-site. The site supervisors also use a *Practicum Activities Evaluation* form to score the students' weekly activities using a 5-point scoring scale (Unsatisfactory to Excellent). The formative evaluation components combined count for 20%

of the practicum grade. Other formative assessments include weekly reflections through an online blog, which counts for 20% of the practicum grade.

The students' final *Practicum Report* serves as the summative evaluation, which they base on their practicum reflections relevant to the goals and learning objectives articulated in their *Practicum Proposal*. The final report has a weight of 40% of the course grade. Upon completion of the report, the students provide a video presentation for online access and review by other students and the instructor. The students' presentation counts for 10% of the course grade. Students submit a critique of each other's presentations and this assignment counts for the last 10% of the course grade.

Following the references after Chapter 4 comes the most important section of the practicum proposal—the *Practicum Contract*, which formally establishes the practicum as an agreement among the students, site supervisors, and instructor. The contract includes the responsibilities of each party followed by policy guidelines for terminating the practicum, if needed. For students conducting their practicum where employed, there is also a form certifying the practicum is not part of the students' normal work. The timesheet and *Practicum Activities Evaluation* form are the final two components in the proposal. At the end of Module VI, students submit their proposal draft to the instructor for feedback.

Module VII: Final Practicum Proposal

In Module VII, the instructor provides students with feedback by email on the draft of the *Practicum Proposal*. In this manner, the instructor maximizes the likelihood that students have properly prepared the proposal for final submission. In the final proposal, the contract must contain signed and dated signatures of both the student and site supervisor. Upon resubmission, the instructor again reviews the proposals and may return it to the students for further revisions, if needed. If completed properly, however, the instructor signs and dates the contracts. At that moment, the inclusion of all signatures binds the students, site supervisors, and instructor into the practicum agreement. Shortly thereafter, the instructor notifies the students and site supervisors by email that the proposal has final approval for implementation.

Module VIII: Practicum Site Presentations and Review

While waiting for instructor review and approval, students develop a storyboard to produce an online video presentation of highlights from their practicum proposal. Here, they record the presentation using *Camtasia*

Relay video software for upload to the online learning management system. The course resources contain directions for students on how to use the video recording software for posting online for viewing. Students review each other's presentations and follow with a response to the following online forum prompt: *Among the practicum presentations, select 2 and provide a general commentary noting the main features of the proposed practicum projects that would contribute to a successful experience.* This final activity concludes the students' work in Reflective and Experiential Learning Techniques.

PROFESSIONAL PRACTICUM

Professional Practicum is the second of an online two-course sequence that engages graduate students in a field-based, interdisciplinary practicum they designed in Reflective and Experiential Learning Techniques. Students in the first 10 weeks of the course implement their field-based practicum and concurrently use the inquiry tools acquired in Professional Inquiry to collect on-going reflections of their practicum experience. In the remaining five weeks of the course, they write a final report based on these reflections. The course goals for Professional Practicum are to synthesize the practicum experience using weekly reflections, identify new literature relevant to the practicum experience, compose a practicum report that articulates new insights from the practicum synthesis, and deliver an online video presentation of highlights from the practicum experience. The following narrative provides a module-by-module description of the topics and learning objectives that define the Practicum course.

Module I: Practicum Course Overview and Initiation

In this module, students introduce themselves and their practicum within the context of its learning objectives to the instructor and classmates using the online blog feature in the online learning management system. Meanwhile, they begin Module I in their first week of the practicum at the selected site. Activities during this week may include signing HR paperwork, setting up computer access, and becoming familiar with workplace protocols, resources, and facilities (vending machine, restrooms, lunchroom, etc.).

Module II: Practicum

This module consists of the remaining nine weeks of the practicum at the selected site. Each week, students are required to synthesize the practicum experience using weekly reflections and identify new literature relevant to the practicum experience. In so doing, students consider the relationship between their on-going practicum experience and the learning objectives they established for the practicum. To facilitate the reflective process, they use a set of questions organized into four themes: strengths, weaknesses, opportunities, and threats (SWOT) to facilitate and guide them in the reflective process (Hanney, 2012; Wang, 2009).

Students use the strength-related questions to guide their understanding of what they are doing well during the practicum and under what circumstances they are able to learn, develop, and perform best. In comparison, they use the weakness-related questions to guide their understanding of knowledge, skills, and abilities where they may need improvement relevant to the practicum and to overall professional growth and development. The opportunity-related questions keep students alert to resources, people, and activities—including those outside the practicum plan—that may help them succeed during and after the practicum as they pursue their professional career goals. As students progress through the practicum, the threat-related questions ask them to consider how personal and professional ideologies support or limit their professional career plans.

In their weekly blog update, students organize their responses around these questions per theme and introduce new literature appropriate to their practicum. Here, they explain how the new material helped them to benefit from the practicum experience. After completing this activity, students respond to the posted blogs of at least two other students. In this manner, the students become a *community of learners* (Akella, 2012; Chang, 2012; Ehiyazaryan-White, 2012) during their 10-week practicum experience.

Module III: Practicum Report and Storyboard Presentation Drafts

By Module III, students have completed their 120-hour, 10-week practicum and will spend two weeks preparing a Practicum Report draft for instructor feedback. Based on APA-style guidelines, Chapter 1 of the report includes a brief introduction to the practicum that includes the student's learning objectives, assumptions, and limitations. Chapter 2 requires students to narrate a story in first-person based on their practicum experience and may include up to three visuals (photographs, diagrams, artwork, etc.) for illustrative purposes. Chapter 3 is the practicum support literature. Here, students introduce each learning objective followed by the books and peer-reviewed articles identified weekly during the practicum. In their response, they provide a synthesis as to how, where, when, and why the materials helped them in the practicum.

In their weekly reflections, students considered the relationship between their ongoing practicum experience and the learning objectives they established for the practicum. To facilitate the reflective process, students use a set of questions organized into the following four themes: strengths, weaknesses, opportunities, and threats (SWOT) to facilitate and guide them in the reflective process (Hanney, 2012; Wang, 2009). In Chapter 4, students synthesize their weekly practicum reflections into the four themes.

Chapter 5 of the report is the practicum evaluation. In the chapter, students first introduce their activities for each learning objective. Next, they present the results from the timesheet and the *Practicum Activities Evaluation* form that the site supervisor used to evaluate the completed activities on a 5-point Likert scale (Unsatisfactory to Excellent). In the introduction of these evaluation components, the students provide a brief overview of how the supervisor used these instruments to evaluate their practicum performance.

These two evaluation components combined count for 20% of the practicum grade. Other formative assessments include the weekly reflections through an online blog, which also count for 20% of the practicum grade. The students' *Practicum Report* serves as the summative evaluation, which counts for 40% of the course grade. Another 10% of the course grade comes from the students' online video presentations of highlights from the practicum experience. Students submit a critique of each other's presentations, and this final course assignment counts the last 10% of the course grade. Following the references after Chapter 5, students include their site supervisor's signed and dated formative components—timesheet and *Practicum Activities Evaluation* form. Upon completion, students submit the *Practicum Report* to the instructor for scoring toward the course grade.

Module IV: Practicum Presentation

After submitting the report, students develop a storyboard to produce an online video presentation of highlights from their practicum experience. Here, they record the presentation using *Camtasia Relay* video software for upload to the online learning management system. The course resources contain directions for students on how to use the video recording software for posting online for viewing.

Module V: Showcase Practicum Presentation

During Module V, the instructor compiles these student video presentations on the department's YouTube channel. Faculty and other students within the department can access these presentations for viewing and commentary. Students completing the practicum, however, review each other's presentations and follow with a response to the following online forum prompt: *What makes a great practicum experience?* This final activity concludes the students' work in Professional Practicum. The long journey the students have traveled is formally over; however, skills such as presenting, critical thinking, using technology, and other important life skill have improved and augmented through this course pathway.

DISCUSSION AND CONCLUSION

The revised introductory and exit course sequences outlined in this chapter strengthen the experience of the students enrolled in the Master of Interdisciplinary Studies program in the Department of OWLS at Texas State University. In developing these sequences, faculty reviewed the foundational and contemporary literature and used this information to structure a learning experience that builds upon adult learning theory and published best practices. The revised curriculum includes practices that allow students to be increasingly self-directed in their studies, take responsibility for their actions and learning, build on their extensive experience, and study subjects which they are motivated to learn, feel psychologically and physically comfortable in their environment, and learn from practical experiences (Knowles, 1974; Lindeman, 1926; Ott, 2011). For the online components of the program, faculty address the unique needs of adult learners by including "hands-on" approaches and assignments. These high-touch approaches are intended to respond to the national trends of high attrition rates in online courses. The interdisciplinary approaches we advocate and promote in the program, relational, mediated, transformative, and situated learning experiences, intercultural knowledge development and skills, critical thinking development and scaffolded practice, and personal epistemological development through various disciplinary approaches to learning, allow the student to gain discipline-specific knowledge while also developing knowledge and skills that span disciplinary boundaries. Reflection is a key component in the program (Kolb, 1984; Schön, 1987) and is used in ways that are experiential and transformative for both the students and the instructors (Boden et al., 2009). While the revised curriculum is only being piloted and still in the nascent stages, the initial informal feedback indicates success. Data gathered from subsequent semesters will give us more information for future directions and further revisions. Currently, the model presented in this chapter provides a pathway for integrating the work and life experiences of students, academic theory, and real-world applications in practice to create a more holistic approach to personal development.

These elements are key to building a sustainable future for interdisciplinary graduate degree programs.

REFERENCES

Addams, L., & Allred, A. T. (2013). The first step in proactively managing students' careers: Teaching self-SWOT analysis. *Academy of Educational Leadership Journal, 17*(4), 43–51.

Akella, D. (2012). Creating a community of learners online: Connect, engage & learn. *International Journal of Technology in Teaching and Learning, 8*(1), 63–77.

Applegate, J. L. (2012). Graduating the 21st century student: Advising as if their lives (and our future) depended on it. *NACADA Journal, 32*(1), 5–11.

Andres, L., Carpenter, S., & British Colombia Council on Admissions and Transfer. (1997). Today's higher education students: Issues of admission, retention, transfer, and attrition in relation to changing student demographics. Retrieved from http://www.academia.edu/618532/Todays_higher_education_students_Issues_of_admission_retention_transfer_and_attrition_in_relation_to_changing_student_demographics

Association of American Universities. (2005). *Report of the interdisciplinarity task force Washington, DC.* Retrieved from http://www.aau.edu/WorkArea/DownloadAsset.aspx?id=462

Aud, S., Wilkinson-Flicker, S., Kristapovich, P., Rathbun, A., Wang, X., & Zhang, J. (2013). *The condition of education 2013* (NCES 2013-037). U.S. Department of Education, National Center for Education Statistics. Washington, DC. Retrieved from http://nces.ed.gov/pubsearch.

Bahr, P. R. (2008). "Cooling out" in the community college: What is the effect of academic advising on students' chances of success? *Research in Higher Education, 49*(8), 704–732.

Bahr, P. R. (2013). The deconstructive approach to understanding community college students' pathways and outcomes. *Community College Review, 41,* 137–153.

Bean, J. P., & Metzner, B. S. (1985).A conceptual model of nontraditional undergraduate student attrition. *Review of Educational Research, 55*(4), 485–540.

Bitchener, J., & Ferris, D. R. (2011).*Written corrective feedback in second language acquisition and writing.* New York, NY: Routledge.

Bloom, A. J., Tripp P. R., &Shaffer, L. S. (2011). Academic and career advising of scanners. *NACADA Journal, 31*(2), 55–61.

Boden, C. J., Gibson, D., Franklin Guy, S., Lasker-Scott, T., Scudder, R., & Smartt, J.T. (2009). Seven methodologies professors use to promote student epistemological development and self-directedness. *The International Journal of Learning, 15*(11), 11–22.

Bradbeer, J. (1999). Barriers to interdisciplinarity: Disciplinary discourses and student learning. *Journal of Geography in Higher Education, 23*(3), 381–396.

Brainard, J. (2002). US agencies look to interdisciplinary science. *The Chronicle of Higher Education, 48*(40), 20–25.

Brint, S. (2005).Creating the future: 'New directions' in American research universities. *Minerva, 43*(1), 23–50.

Brint, S. G., Turk-Bicakci, L., Proctor, K., & Murphy, S. P. (2009). Expanding the social frame of knowledge: Interdisciplinary, degree-granting fields in American colleges and universities, 1975–2000. *The Review of Higher Education, 32*(2), 155–183.

Chang, H. (2012). The development of a learning community in an e-learning environment. *International Journal of Pedagogies and Learning, 7*(2), 154–161.

Clark, D. (2011). Kolb's learning styles and experiential learning model. Retrieved from http://www.nwlink.com/~donclark/hrd/styles/kolb.html

Conrad, D., & Newberry, R. (2012). Identification and instruction of important business communication skills for graduate business education. *Journal of Education for Business, 87*, 112–120. doi:10.1080/08832323.2011.576280

Cornwell, G. H., & Stoddard, E. W. (2001). Toward an interdisciplinary epistemology: Faculty culture and institutional change. In B. L. Smith & J. McCann (Eds.), *Reinventing ourselves: Interdisciplinary education, collaborative learning, and experimentation in higher education* (pp. 160–178). Bolton, MA: Anker Publishing.

Centenary College New Jersey. (2013). *In Experiential learning at Centenary.* Retrieved from http://www.centenarycollege.edu/cms/sp/accelerated-and-online/degree-completion/experiential-learning/

Compton, J. I., Cox, E., & Laanan, F. S. (2006). Adult learners in transition. In F. S. Laanan (Ed.), *New directions for student services,* No. 114: Understanding Students in Transition (pp. 73–80). San Francisco, Jossey Bass.

Cornelius, S., Gordon, C., & Ackland, A. (2011). Towards flexible learning for adult learners in professional contexts: An activity-focused course design. *Interactive Learning Environments, 19*(4), 381–393.

Coulter, X., & Mandell, A. (2013). Can adult students transform our universities? In C. J. Boden-McGill & K. P. King (Eds.), *Conversations about adult learning in our complex world* (pp. 143–159). Charlotte: Information Age Publishing.

Department of Occupational, Workforce and Leadership Studies. (2013). Master of Science in Interdisciplinary Studies, MSIS. Retrieved from http://www.owls.txstate.edu/graduate-degrees/interdisciplinary-studies.html

Dewey, J. (1933). *How we think: A restatement of the relation of reflective thinking to the educative process.* New York, NY: D.C. Heath & Co.

DiMartino, J., & Castaneda, A. (2007). Assessing applied skills. *Educational Leadership, 64*(7), 38–42.

Dvarishkis, M., & Montana State Dept. of Public Instruction, Helena Division of Adult Education. (1990). *Pathways to Careers: Exploring Career Options.*

Ehiyazaryan-White, E. (2012). The dialogic potential of e-portfolios: Formative feedback and communities of learning within a personal learning environment. *International Journal of ePortfolio, 2*(2), 173–185.

Erford, B. T., & Crockett, S. A. (2012). Practice and research in career counseling and development-2011. *Career Development Quarterly, 60*(4), 290–332.

Fade, S. (2006). *Learning and assessing through reflection: A practical guide.* London, England: London Region Dietitians.

Feller, I. (2002). New organizations, old cultures: Strategy and implementation of interdisciplinary programs. *Research Evaluation, 11*, 109–116.

Flores, K. L., Matkin, G. S., Burbach, M. E., Quinn, C. E., & Harding, H. (2012). Deficient critical thinking skills among college graduates: Implications for leadership. *Educational Philosophy and Theory, 44*(2), 212–230.

Galles, J. A., & Lenz, J. G. (2013) Relationships among career thoughts, vocational identity, and calling: Implication for practice. *The Career Development Quarterly, 61*(3), 240–248.

Gentry, R. (2012). Clinical experience for teacher candidates: Taking preparation beyond four walls. *Research in Higher Education Journal, 15,* 1–13.

Gibbons, M. (1998).*Higher education relevance in the twenty-first century*. Retrieved from http://ec.europa.eu/education/external-relation-programmes/doc/confbalkans/material/21stcentury_en.pdf

Goodrich, R. (2013). SWOT analysis: Examples, templates, & definition. *Business News Daily*. Retrieved from http://www.businessnewsdaily.com/4245-swot-analysis.html

Hagan, L. (2012). Fostering experimental learning and service through client projects in graduate business courses offered online. *American Journal of Business Education, 5*(5), 623–632.

Hahn, J. A. (2010). *Practicum projects of value: A successful strategic partnership between nurse executives and master's level academia*. Retrieved from https://www.nursingeconomics.net/ce/2012/article28143158.pdf

Hanney, R. (2012). Are we any good at it: Using risk as a tool for reflection and critical enquiry: Report of research in progress. *Art, Design & Communication in Higher Education, 10*(1), 103–109.

Harbour, J., Daveline, K., Wells, R., Schurman, D., & Hahn, H. (1990). *Distributed training for the reserve component: Instructor handbook for computer conferencing*. Boise, ID: Idaho National Engineering Laboratory and Boise State University.

Hume, A. (2009). Promoting higher levels of reflective writing in student journals. *Higher Education Research and Development, 28*(3), 247–260.

Ismail, A., Abiddin, N. Z., &Hassan, A. (2011). Improving the development of post graduates' research and supervision. *International Education Studies, 4*(1).

Ivanitskaya, L., Clark, D., Montgomery, G., & Primeau, R. (2002). Interdisciplinary learning: Process and outcomes. *Innovative Higher Education, 27*(2), 95–111.

Jonassen, D. H. (2012). Designing for decision making. *Educational Technology Research and Development, 60*(2), 341–359. doi:10.1007/s11423-011-9230-5

Jones, P. C., Merritt, J. Q., & Palmer, C. (1999). Critical thinking and interdisciplinarity in environmental higher education: The case for epistemological and values awareness. *Journal of Geography in Higher Education, 23*(3), 349–357.

Kane, S.T., Roy, S., & Medina, S. (2012) Identifying college students at risk for learning disabilities: Evidence for use of the learning difficulties assessment in postsecondary settings. *Journal of Postsecondary Education and Disability, 26*(1), 21–33.

Kenner, C., &Weinerman, J. (2011). Adult learning theory: Applications to non-traditional college students. *Journal of College Reading and Learning, 41*(2), 87–96.

Klein, J. T., Grossenbacher-Mansuy, W., Häberli, R., Bill, A., Scholz, R. W., &Welti, M. (2001). *Transdisciplinarity: Joint problem solving among science, technology, and society: An effective way for managing complexity*. Basel, Switzerland: Birkhäuser Basel.

Klein-Collins, R. (2011). Strategies for becoming adult-learning focused institutions. *Peer Review, 13*(1), 4–7.

Knowles, M. S. (1968). Andragogy, not pedagogy. *Adult Leadership, 16*(10), 350–352, & 386.

Knowles, M. S. (1970). *The modern practice of adult education* (Vol. 41). New York, NY: Association Press.

Knowles, M. S. (1974). Human resources development in OD. *Public Administration Review, 34*(2), 115–123.

Kolb, D. A. (1984).*Experiential learning: Experience as the source of learning and development.* Englewood Cliffs, NJ: Prentice-Hall.

Lattuca, L. R. (2002). Learning interdisciplinarity: Sociocultural perspectives on academic work. *The Journal of Higher Education, 73*(6), 711–739.

Lindeman, E.C. (1926). *The meaning of adult education.* New York, NY: New Republic.

Lovitts, B. E., & Nelson, C. (2000). The hidden crises in graduate education: Attrition from Ph.D. programs. *Academe, 86*(6), 44–50.

Maher, J., & Mitchell, J. (2010). I'm not sure what to do! Learning experiences in the humanities and social sciences. *Issues in Educational Research, 20*(2), 137–148.

Manathunga, C., Lant, P., & Mellick, G. (2006).Imagining an interdisciplinary doctoral pedagogy. *Teaching in Higher Education, 11*(3), 365–379. doi:10.1080/13562510600680954

Mitchell, J. R., Shepherd, A., & Sharfman, M. P. (2011). Erratic strategic decisions: When and why managers are inconsistent in strategic decision making. *Strategic Management Journal, 32*(7), 683–704.

Moon, J. A. (2004).*Resources. A Handbook of reflective and experiential learning: Theory and practice* (pp. 183–230). London, England: Routledge-Falmer.

Morse, W. C., Nielsen-Pincus, M., Force, J. E., & Wulfhorst, J. D. (2007). Bridges and barriers to developing and conducting interdisciplinary graduate-student team research. *Ecology and Society, 12*(2), 8.

Nash, R. D. (2005). Course completion rates among distance learners: Identifying possible methods to improve retention. *Online Journal of Distance Learning Administration, 8*(4).

Nelson, J. S., Range, L. M., & Burck Ross, M. (2012).A checklist to guide graduate students' writing. *International Journal of Teaching and Learning in Higher Education, 24*(3), 376–382.

Newswander, L. K., & Borrego, M. (2009).Engagement in two interdisciplinary graduate programs. *Higher Education, 58*(4), 551–562.

Ng, S. L. (2012). Reflection and reflective practice: Creating knowledge through experience. *Seminars in Hearing, 33*(2), 117–134.

Ondrusek, A. L. (2012). What the research reveals about graduate students' writing skills: A literature review. *Journal of Education for Library and Information Science, 53*(3), 176–188.

Ott, K. D. (2011). Technology and adult learning: Understanding e-learning and the lifelong learner. *The International Journal of Technology, Knowledge and Society, 7*(3), 31–36.

Park, J., & Choi, H. J. (2009).Factors influencing adult learners' decision to drop out or persist in online learning. *Educational Technology & Society, 12*(4), 207–217.

Passarelli, A. M., & Kolb, D. A. (2011). The learning way: Learning from experience as the path to lifelong learning and development. *The Oxford Handbook of Lifelong Learning*. doi: 10.1093/oxfordhb/9780195390483.013.0028

Purdue University (2013). *Types of experiential learning*. Retrieved from http://webs. purduecal.edu/exl/types-of-experiential-learning/

Rhoten, D., & Parker, A. (2004).Risks and rewards of an interdisciplinary research path. *Science (New York, N.Y.)*, *306*(5704), 2046.

Roessger, K. M. (2012). Toward an interdisciplinary perspective: A review of adult learning frameworks and theoretical models of motor learning. *Adult Education Quarterly*, *62*(4), 371–392.

Sandler, T. (1999).The past and future of terrorism research. *Revista de Economía Aplicada*, *50*, 5–25.

Schön, D. A. (1983). *The reflective practitioner: How professionals think in action*. New York, NY: Basic Books.

Schön, D. A. (1987). *Educating the reflective practitioner*. San Francisco: Jossey-Bass.

Scovill, S. M., & Waite, M. D. (2012).Linking theory to practice: Experiential learning in an employee wellness practicum. *American Journal of Health Sciences*, *3*(4), 261–268.

Sherron, T., Boden-McGill, C. J., & Springer, S. B. (2013). *Historical review and future directions of prior learning assessment at Texas State University*. Paper presented at the 25th Annual National Institute on the Assessment of Adult Learning. Atlantic City, NJ.

Simpson, S. (2012). The problem of graduate-level writing support: Building a cross-campus graduate writing initiative. *WPA: Writing Program Administration —Journal of the Council of Writing Program Administrators*, *36*(1), 95–118.

Smith, R. O. (2005). Working with difference in online collaborative groups. *Adult Education Quarterly*, *55*(3), 182–199.

Snyder, T. D., & Dillow, S. A. (2012).*Digest of education statistics 2011* (NCES 2012-001). National Center for Education Statistics, Institute of Education Sciences, U.S. Department of Education. Washington, DC. Retrieved from http://nces.ed.gov/pubs2012/2012001.pdf

Springer, S. B. (2010). Assisting new populations: Veterans returning to education. *NCPN Connections*, *(20)*5, 11–12.

Stevens, D. D., & Cooper, J. E. (2009). Reflection and learning from experience. In D. D. Stevens & J. E. Cooper (Eds.), *Journal keeping. How to use reflective writing for learning, teaching, professional insight and positive change*. Sterling, Virginia: Stylus Publishing. Retrieved from http://commons.gc.cuny.edu/wiki/images/Reflection_JournalKeeping_Chapter.pdf

Stone, T., Bollard, K., & Harbor, J. M. (2009).Launching interdisciplinary programs as college signature areas: An example. *Innovative Higher Education*, *34*(5), 321–329.

Tate, P., Klein-Collins, R., & Steinberg, K. (2011). Lifelong learning in the USA: A focus on innovation and efficiency for the 21st century learner. *International Journal of Continuing Education and Lifelong Learning*, *4*(1), 23.

Tyler-Smith, K. (2006). Early attrition among first time eLearners: A review of factors that contribute to drop-out, withdrawal and non-completion rates of adult learners undertaking eLearning programmes. *Journal of Online learning and Teaching, 2*(2), 73–85.

Van Beuningen, C. G., De Jong, N. H., & Kuiken, F. (2012). Evidence on the effectiveness of comprehensive error correction in second language writing. *Language Learning, 62*(1), 41.

Wang, S. (2009).Inquiry-directed organization of e-portfolio artifacts for reflection. *Interdisciplinary Journal of E-Learning and Learning Objects, 5*(1), 419–433.

Weatherley, C., Bonney, B., Kerr, J., & Morrison, J. (2003). *Transforming teaching and learning: Developing 'critical skills' for living and working in the 21st Century.* Stafford, UK: Network Educational Press.

Wilkes, G. L. (2012). The importance of oral communication skills and a graduate course to help improve these skills. *CEE: Chemical Engineering Education. 46*(4), 251–259.

Willson, S., & Gibson, E. (2011). Graduate school learning curves: McNair scholars' postbaccalaureate transitions. *Equity & Excellence in Education, 44*(2), 153–168.

Zemke, R., & Zemke, S. (1984). 30 things we know for sure about adult learning. *Innovation Abstracts, 6*(8), 8.

Zwozdiak-Myers, P. (2012). *The teacher's reflective practice handbook: Becoming an extended professional through capturing evidence-informed practice.* London, England: Routledge.

CHAPTER 14

INCIDENTAL LEARNING AND COMPLEXITY IN THE WORKPLACE

Michael D. Harner
University of Illinois at Chicago

Organizations operate in a complex fast-paced environment where they need to adapt to new factors that arise in the process of providing services or producing products. Strategy is developed and tactics deployed through policies and procedures as organizations attempt to overcome challenges. Leaders and workers interact informally and impact how tactical factors take place. The interaction that occurs among people in the workplace impacts how worker learning happens and also has influence on how an organization evolves.

Traditional human resource development utilizes formal adult education and training methods to assist personnel in learning efforts. Assessment of organizational direction guides leaders to identify the skills that are required to progress toward strategic and visionary goals. Resources are limited and priorities established to determine how to invest in training and development. As development plans are determined, organizations hope for effective results from training endeavors. Organizations expect a positive transfer of training and learning to jobs and duties.

Building Sustainable Futures for Adult Learners, pages 295–321

Learning and development through training efforts are a substantial area for organizational expenditure. In 1985, an estimated $30 billion was spent on employee training (Noe, 1986); in 1997, $58.6 billion (Yamnill & McLean, 2001), and it is estimated in the United States in 2008, $137.7 billion was spent on direct formal training (Kazbour, McGee, Masica, & Brinerhoff, 2013). If informal training costs are included, expenditures increase to $200 billion per year (Yamnill & McLean, 2001). Knowledge acquisition and skills developed through training must transfer to the job or the training will not be valued (Yamnill & McLean, 2001). Estimates indicate that only 40% of training is transferred immediately after training, 25% after six months, and only 15% after one year following the training (Kim & Lee, 2001).

There is a large percentage of adult learning connected to the workplace and a strong linkage involving work life and participation in adult education (Merriam, Caffarella, & Baumgartner, 2007). Organizations, based upon educational investment, indicate a clear relationship between achieving strategic objectives and investing in adult education. The trouble with assuming formal workplace education is effective and complete is that informal and incidental learning commences. Workers perform designated job duties using prescribed systems. System creators are unable to anticipate the spectrum of possibilities and incidental learning fills the formal workplace education void. The disorderliness of Incidental learning persists in spite of formal educational activities and creating policies to preserve the accuracy and efficiency of the workplace.

The purpose of the study in this chapter was to investigate incidental learning activities as a part of formally established systems in a complex healthcare work environment. The research location for this study took place in three University operated primary care family medicine outpatient clinics. The operational organization illustration of the patient-visit cycle (Figure 14.1) represents a model from the research locations used in this study depicting the process and various people a patient interacts when they come for an appointment. It assumes employees fill a variety of defined roles where they interact consistently. Progressing through the cycle necessitates each person to complete tasks as part of their respective job parameters. One of the challenges inherent in accomplishing their tasks is producing solutions to unforeseen dilemmas that surface. Contending with these dilemmas may involve incidental learning that may contribute to changes in the formally created networks. The workplace is an abundant environment for incidental learning to thrive. In the patient visit cycle depicted in Figure 14.1 created from the research location used for the basis of this chapter participants engaged in interaction and communication exemplified by asking questions with an intention to find answers in order to address uncertainties and complete job tasks.

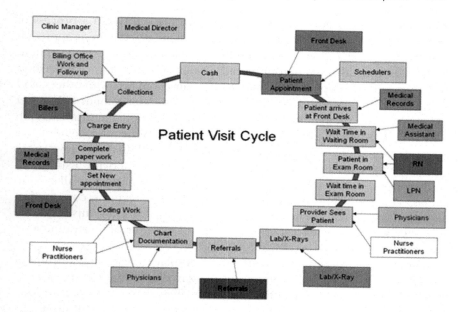

Figure 14.1 Patient visit cycle and position descriptions.

The personnel in the study environments have formally acquired education and knowledge related to medicine, nursing, technology, management, and several other areas of expertise. The formally acquired knowledge to perform their jobs does not prepare them for the result of what they learn through relations with one another. The study locations are complex workplace environments where medical student education takes place at the same time patient healthcare services occur. In completing these tasks, personnel interact with one another as a necessity to task completion resulting in workplace learning. This study seeks to understand what factors are influential as a part of workplace incidental learning.

FRAMEWORK

Traditional management practices embrace a structured and controlled method for organizing people using a Newtonian paradigm method, which is:

> Based on a mechanistic philosophy that states that the enormous diversity of things found in the world can all be reduced completely and perfectly and unconditionally to nothing more than the effects of some definite and limited general framework of laws. (Dooley, Johnson, & Bush, 1995, p. 288)

The Newtonian paradigm applies in the workplace through a process of reductionism conceived by Frederick Taylor. This management approach uses an analytical and logical methodology based in Taylor's management principles summarized into four points: develop a science for each person's job, train and develop the work person, heartily cooperate with others, and divide work and responsibility between labor and management (Dooley et al., 1995). Controlling and anticipating actions and outcomes for each job condensed to basic functional elements. Using scientific management and controls defined by laws, standardized behavior, and analysis allows every operation to be predicted (Dooley et al., 1995). The underlying assumption in this approach is that the system creators are able to anticipate all eventualities. The obstacle with this assumption is that interactions, communication, and incidental learning take place. Prescribed worker duty variances are not anticipated. Figure 14.1 symbolizes an example of illustrating a reductionist scheme of the study environment.

System and process designers in the workplace create and document workflows and write policies and procedures in efforts to generate efficiencies for completing work duties and tasks. The diagram in Figure 14.2, adapted from Stacey (1996), displays a conceptual representation of a legitimate created network. The legitimate network is created by the most powerful and influential members of an organization. The solid lines illustrate the legitimate network and the directional flow of how decision makers have constructed a hypothetical system to work. The intention of

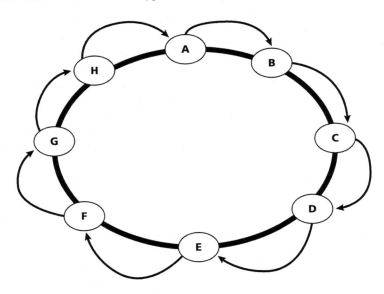

Figure 14.2 Legitimate network.

creating such a system and training people to operate within it is to accomplish certain tasks in a timely and accurate method with as few mistakes as possible. However, the legitimate formalized system does not account for all of the informal interactions, communications, and idiosyncrasies associated with the different personalities of an organization. The formally created systems cannot anticipate incidental interactions among coworkers and how people send and receive verbal or written communication. In addition, elements of power relations among members of the workplace factor into the incidental interactions.

Figure 14.3 represents a combination of legitimate and shadow networks. The dashed lines symbolize the shadow network connections that evolve through the dynamics of communication, power, and interactions that occur every day among coworkers that are the basis of incidental learning. Embodied in the dashed lines of the shadow network are fundamental elements of incidental learning, spontaneous interaction, problem solving, dialogue, debate, and experiencing mistakes. The stress of completing work-related tasks during a particular day at work can be demanding. Contrary to formal training efforts, task completion modifications emerge. Incidental learning perpetuates the new way through interactions among coworkers as they think, do, and communicate in their jobs in shifting conditions resulting in unanticipated process evolution.

Human networks have characteristics of nonlinearity. The interactions and communications of people in organizations pertain to survival and

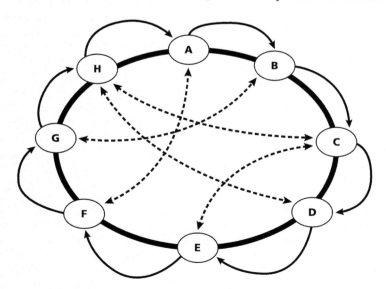

Figure 14.3 Legitimate and shadow networks.

making a living while getting things done on a day-to-day basis (Stacey, 1996). The intertwined legitimate and shadow networks develop over time through feedback where people discover and sense the state of the elements in the organization and the surroundings they are in contact with, choose a response from various tacit and explicit rules, and then act (Stacey, 1996). How agents choose a response is dependent upon factors implicit within the individuals in the organization. How all of the agents interact with one another coupled with how they interact with the environment and how the environment interacts with the agents shapes how process and systems evolve. When coworkers interact there are two fundamental factors, communication and power, that contribute to the outcome of an interaction.

Communication and Power

Within the context of a patient-care environment, employee interaction is pervasive. A crucial ingredient to incidental learning in the workplace is communication. The circular gesture-response communication interaction suggested by Mead (1934) may have a profound influence on how incidental learning occurs. Effective communication is an intricate process. Uncertainty arises after conveying a message until a response follows the receipt of information. Transmission interpretation may not happen as intended or insufficient listening may lead to confusion or misinterpretation.

> Meaning, therefore, does not lie in the gesture alone but in the social act as a whole. In other words, meaning arises in the responsive interaction between actors; gesture and response can never be separated but must be understood as moments in one act. (Stacey, 2011, pp. 331–332)

The dynamic of a communication interchange can be complicated due to workplace velocity and how power factors influence transmissions between co-workers. Elias (1991) suggested that the interdependence of a complex environment puts all employees in need of one another. Yet, even as system participants are inter-reliant, facets of power may play a role in how incidental learning transpires. An intrinsic element of workplace interaction is power. The basis of Power factors is discernible from different perspectives. Gender, race, socioeconomic status, and class as associated with levels of education are areas of power that need to be recognized (Merriam, Caffarella, & Baumgartner, 2007). Complexity science as applied to a workplace environment recognizes power as an element that is part of personnel interactions. The systems and people in a clinical workplace comprise an interdependent environment where cooperating and communicating are required for things to get accomplished. As Stacey (2010) explained:

Interdependence explains how both the good and the bad arise, indeed how particular judgments or ideologies arise. If human individuals are interdependent in this way, it follows that we need each other, and it is this need which explains why power is an aspect of every act of human relating. Since I need others, I cannot do whatever I please; and since they need me, neither can they. We constrain each other at the same time as enabling each other, and it is this paradoxical activity that constitutes power. (Stacey, 2010, p. 181)

Elements of power are ubiquitous and varied throughout a workplace environment. The occurrences of power comprise a dyadic interface between two agents (French & Raven, 1959). The following points assist in framing how power interactions take place among agents. "(A) What determines the behavior of the agent who exerts power? (B) What determines the reactions of the recipient of this behavior?" (p. 150). Answering questions A and B result in the manner of how agents exert and respond to power.

This dyadic relationship is the basis for the power produced by O to influence person P. French and Raven identify five bases of O's power: 1) reward power, based on P's perception that P has the ability to mediate rewards for him; 2) coercive power, based on P's perception that O has the ability to mediate punishment for him; 3) legitimate power, based on the perception by P that O has legitimate right to prescribe behavior for him; 4) referent power, based on P's identification with O; 5) expert power, based on the perception that O has some special knowledge or expertness. (French & Raven, 1959, pp. 155–156)

Throughout the course of activities within the workplace, each of these power relationships may materialize. The power dynamic manifested through workplace interaction influences behavior as communication takes place.

Elias (1991) stressed the use of language as people interacted with each other while forming competitive and cooperative power relations. Elias contended that power is not a thing that someone possesses and is not simply force or violence but, rather, power is a structural characteristic of all human relationships in that it reflects the fact that we depend on each other. Power and communication become indistinguishable in that patterns of power relating are also models of communicating; they both allow and confine participants in a relationship (Stacey, 2004). Patterns of individual belief emerge through themes of repetitive communication that contribute to power relations (Stacey, 2004). Power associations among workplace colleagues contain "a fundamental aspect of social relationships, namely the constraints they impose on members of a group, and therefore, the power differentials they create" (Stacey, 2004, p. 176).

Leaders proactively devise legitimate networks anticipating possible contingencies for producing organizational output. However even as system designers attempt to codify how workers accomplish their tasks and duties in the workplace anticipating all types of scenarios is not possible.

> No system can encompass every eventuality and, therefore, ordinary daily human freedom is exercised to weave actions into an around the system, the known, in order to cope, at the same time, with the daily unknown. This acting, in an ordinary day-by-day way into the known-unknown, requires an explanation that systems thinking on its own cannot provide because this thinking always entails some human chooser standing outside the system and acting upon it. (Stacey et al., 2000, pp. 186–187)

Organizations expect to make progress toward a stated vision or goal employing plans and tactics. Inherent constraints of organizational system development are imperfect information, intrusion of unexpected factors, time pressure and the inability to control human interaction. Yet, "human systems are assumed to change in ways that unfold or reveal what is already there, and their futures are therefore knowable, or formative in nature" (Stacey et al., 2000, p. 184). This way of thinking assumes that there are special forms of humans that have the freedom and power to choose, design, and construct forms in new novel ways that have formally not existed (Stacey et al., 2000). Humans involved in the decisions become part of the interaction of the system they have just designed. The system designers, in constructing a legitimate network, cannot control the interactions of the shadow network. Decisions and learning behavior surface in the shadow network. In spite of how well a system is developed, organizations expect tasks are completed. Humans exercise freedom in their interactions and the organization may evolve into processes that advance in a departure from the formally designed system, undermining the ability of someone stepping outside the system and choosing a future and the design to achieve it (Stacey et al., 2000).

Organizations are comprised of activities of interdependent people that can lead to a particular perspective on learning (Stacey, 2003). Individuals makeup a workplace and create their own unique environment based upon formal rules and informal relations. Interactions of people through communication and activities take the form of persistently iterated meanings and power configurations (Stacey, 2003). Constructivist learning theory emphasizes the role of individual interaction with the socio-cultural environment in the progression of knowledge construction (Fenwick, 2003). Because of the nonlinear unpredictable nature of human beings, there is the potential for transformative shifts in legitimate network stability (Stacey, 2003). System creators presume that they have created orderliness and that interaction through communication is ideal. This presumption discounts or ignores the learning that results from interaction among employees taking place in a workplace. Learning will take place incrementally through communicative interactions and power relations and the emerging shifts in the patterns of human activity. Learning materializes simultaneously through individual behaviors and collective patterns as shifts in meaning take place. Inter-reliant people learn as work related activities transform as a consequence of exchanges and power relating (Stacey, 2003). Individual learning is an emergent process arising through interaction depending upon several factors (Harkema, 2003). Incidental learning and complexity are underlying factors that support this study and require a review of literature.

LITERATURE REVIEW

Incidental Learning

The majority of learning in the workplace is informal and incidental despite the resources invested in formal training projects (Merriam et al., 2007). Incidental learning, a subcategory of informal learning, may occur anywhere, even under formal conditions (Straka, 2009). Incidental learning takes place as a result of interactions with others without the conscious intention of learning or knowledge acquisition (Marsick, Volpe, & Watkins, 1999). Previous incidental learning studies (Le Clus, 2011) include learning characterized through conversation (Van den Tillaart, van den Berg & Warmerdam 1998), observation, repetition, social interaction (Cahoon, 1995), and problem solving (Kerka, 2000). Under-examined compared to informal learning, incidental learning is often less clearly defined and explored (Hunter, 2014). Learning incidentally takes place unintentionally and unplanned resulting from activities while at work, often characterized as tacit (Kerka, 2000). Human experiences, including intentional learning actions, are prospective situations for incidental learning (Watkins, Marsick, & de Álava, 2014). There is an implicit component to incidental learning where people learn after exposure to things through sight or hearing without awareness they were learning (Eraut, 2004). "Incidental learning differs from informal learning in that messages that are being conveyed are often buried in the interaction" (Marsick & Watkins, 1990, p. 14). Learning incidentally can happen in many ways including observation, communication with colleagues about tasks or projects, experiencing mistakes, assumptions, and adapting to new situations (Kerka, 2000). Cyclical, non-sequential and non-routine situations involved in social interactions contribute to incidental learning as transactions take place in the workplace (Wofford, Ellinger, & Watkins, 2013). Learning in the workplace perceived as predictable, controlled, and formal (Cronin, 2014) cannot anticipate events impacting behavior in the workplace where formalized systems are unable to adapt to the pace of events. The social nature of incidental learning plays a role that knowledge and learning are considered to be contextually situated

(White, 2010). Hierarchy and authority can impact worker interactions and may either expand or diminish incidental learning events (Marsick & Watkins, 1990). Interactions take place resulting in specific and general knowledge based upon the relations between workers (Marsick & Watkins, 1990). Learning that is unintentional and unexpected and takes place unconsciously is characterized as incidental and can be depicted as implicit (Cseh, Watkins, & Marsick, 1999, Eraut, 2004). Allied health professionals did not fully realize and appreciate incidental learning in the workplace (Lloyd, Pfeiffer, Dominish, Heading, Schmidt, & McCluskey, 2014). There is a reactive component of incidental learning that occurs in the middle of task completion when there is little time to think compared to formalized learning activities (Eraut, 2004). Interaction among coworkers and the decisions required to perform job requirements are inherent aspects of working. An exchange among coworkers in their day-to-day work routines is the curriculum of the job setting. Tasks and relations among employees happen in a way that "the processes of thinking and acting become indistinguishable from learning" (Billet, 2004, p. 111).

The broad concept of informal learning necessitates reflection to enable learning (Marsick & Watkins, 2001); yet, incidental learning suggests learning can occur without reflection established in the myriad of interactions of co-workers. In a complex workplace, the elements of communication and power may influence the learning as a result of the numerous incidental contacts required by employees as job duties are completed. An inherent feature of incidental workplace learning is interaction between people. The following section of literature examines the elements of complexity science that also contains interaction as a root component.

Complexity Science

The commerce of academic patient care is complex. The health care industry is highly regulated, and health care employees must adhere to policies linked to the regulations. The complexity of providing patient care coupled with the documentation of the patient visit and subsequent insurance transactions requires a group of employees with an array of clerical and health care knowledge to interact at a high performing level. The consequences of these factors are elevated levels of complexity. This section will review literature of complexity science and the connection to incidental learning. "Complexity science is the study of complex adaptive systems, the patterns of relationships within them, how they are sustained, how they self-organize, and how outcomes emerge" (Zimmerman, Lindberg, & Plsek, 2001, p. 5). A primary care patient-visit environment is a complex adaptive system (CAS). "Complex adaptive systems (CAS) are composed of a diversity of agents that interact with each other, mutually affect each other, and in so doing generate novel behavior for the system as a whole" (Lewin & Regine, 2001, p. 6). Nonlinearity is a characteristic of a CAS. Patterns of behavior in a CAS are not necessarily consistent because, as the environment changes, either internally or externally, the behavior of the agents may also change resulting in adaptation (Lewin & Regine, 2001). In this nonlinear dynamic, everything exists in relationship with everything else, and the interactions can lead to complex and unpredictable outcomes (Lewin & Regine, 2001). Complexity theory helps explain how, through agent interaction, an emergence of self-organization can happen without central control. Learning is continuous invention and exploration generated through relations, actions, interactions, and structural dynamics of complex systems (Fenwick, 2003). Even as formalized systems are created, all eventualities cannot be anticipated, and shadow networks develop based upon interactions of the people involved as they cope with the unknown (Stacey, Griffin, & Shaw, 2000).

Within the workplace environment, there are legitimate networks constituting the formal system created for a purpose, and there are also shadow (informal) networks that develop through the interactions of the individual actions of agents that perform independently. The consequence of the interface of the legitimate and shadow networks, as a part of complexity thinking, is the creation of novel unanticipated learning based upon the interaction and subsequent reactions. Complex adaptive systems consist of a number of components, or agents that interact with each other that require them to examine and respond to each other's behavior (Stacey, 1996). Systems with agents that operate in this manner comprise incidental learning situations. Workplaces create formalized systems supported by policies and procedures in hopes of creating efficient predictable outcomes. In contrast, complex systems generate innumerable interactions resulting in behaviors anticipated and unanticipated. Organizations are made up of a collection of interacting objects or agents, where the object's behavior is affected by memory and/or open system, where the system appears to be alive and exhibits emergent phenomena which are generally surprising and may be extreme, where emergent phenomena typically arise in the absence of any sort of central controller, and where the systems show a complicated mix of ordered and disordered behavior (Johnson, 2010).

To refer to complex systems is to submit a form of explanation (Paley & Eva, 2011). Complex systems are nonlinear based generated through interactions components resulting in something qualitatively different from the sum of the parts (Lewin & Regine, 2001). The resulting patterns of behavior emerge based upon the interactions of the component parts in an unpredictable manner, "this has been called distributed control, in contrast to central control" (Lewin & Regine, 2001, p. 27). Unpredictability is another factor because agents in the system change, and changes from the environment outside of the system have an unknowable system effect (Chaffee & McNeil, 2007). Agents, objects, and components in the context of this study all refer to people in a workplace setting who interact in efforts to successfully accomplish their prescribed job duties. A workplace involving a number of people who interact is a complex adaptive system. When the people in a workplace interact, incidental learning transpires resulting in changes to job duty related behavior. Formal education and rule setting cannot capture how the activities will evolve among coworkers as a consequence of incidental learning. Interaction through communication may help educators understand how complexity and incidental learning intersect. In a collective activity, participants each contribute within the dynamic changing others and the atmosphere where they reside. Decisions, actions, and perceptions impact actors where they adapt and learn (Fenwick, 2003).

METHODS AND RESEARCH QUESTIONS

This study examined incidental workplace learning. Incidental learning and complexity science were the literature basis for the study. The purpose of the study was to better understand how incidental learning activities take place as a part of formally established systems in a complex work environment. A qualitative research method was used to answer two research questions: (1) What incidental learning elements do employees use to complete work tasks? (2) What transpires within a formalized system to influence incidental learning?

The study included interviewing front desk/receptionist employees, medical assistants, licensed practical nurses, registered nurses, and employees involved with patient referrals. The employees work within a university based primary care health care system. The clinic environments operate under standardized policies and procedures. The employees are orientated with clinic practices, policies, and workflows. Uniformity and consistency with training exercises are targeted goals. When individual employees begin working at a respective clinic they are immersed in dissimilar cultures. Clinic leadership and other employees interpret and implement policy divergently and with various levels of accuracy.

The IRB of the host institution reviewed and approved the study. A list of interview questions was prepared as a guideline and served as a consistent starting point for the questioning. The interviews evolved independently. The interviews took place in offices and/or conferences rooms in each respective clinic. Twenty-one interviews took place over four months in three separate primary care health care centers. The interviews ranged in time from 30 to 120 minutes. Multiple individuals participated in the interview process from each clinic site. Participants enrolled who had the same and different job functions. Evaluation of responses and experiences allowed follow up questions to subsequent participants on various scenarios that took place from multiple sources to obtain a full range of perspectives. Observations of personnel took place during clinic meetings that assisted in pursuing lines of questions on topics that overlapped participants with different roles. The intent was to fully examine an issue and the participants experience from a variety of perspectives. The three hundred pages of transcribed audio recordings underwent analysis. The participants were unidentifiable on the audio tape. The transcripts and audio tapes went through a verification process. A semi structured interview format offered flexibility in how the interviews progressed. This format allowed participants the freedom to respond their own frame of reference (Bogdan & Biklen, 2007). The tacit nature of incidental learning contributed to selecting a semi structured interview that assists in exploring all possibilities regarding information sought (Merriam & Simpson, 2000). Employees, with the same job classification within and across clinics sites, participated in the study in an effort to provide internal validity to the study. Topics emerged from the semi structured format that allowed the researcher to pursue inquiry from other participants in subsequent interviews.

Researcher Position

In addition to being the researcher and interviewer in this study, I am also an employee of the university that oversees these medical facilities. My position in the organization is the Director of Financial Affairs. My position as the researcher is an insider from the point of view of the entire organization, but an outsider from a purely clinical point of view. Another position consideration is my status as a middle-aged white male. All of the study participants were women with a variety of races, ages, and ethnicities represented. These differences required acknowledgment and consideration while preparing for and conducting the interviews. Even though the people I interviewed or observed do not report to me directly, my profile as the "money person" of the organization comes with perceptions that could affect how people communicate with me. To address this issue, I established the parameters and purposes for speaking with the different participants to ensure not only confidentially, but also to explain the research project would not affect their job, their employment, or lead to appraisals of their job performance. The clinical environments were not completely foreign to me, and the interviewees had familiarity with me. I used my knowledge of processes and roles in the clinic to support the discussion if participants' responsiveness was hesitant. Interviewing more than one person in the same job allowed for follow up questions on common aspects of these jobs to gain perspectives from different participants and added to the depth of the data.

Data Analysis

Analyzing the interview transcripts included exploring the data for phrases in support of developing areas and clusters of categories (Creswell, 2007). Common categories emerged after a concentrated transcript analysis was completed. Significant statements combined into larger groups based upon meaning or categories. Participant experiences from transcript excerpts added to the "textural description." Relevant category excerpts from the interviews were grouped based upon one or more categories that were captured either in the comment of the participant or through the dialogue of the interview. Category grouped data was analyzed to accurately portray the factors involved with incidental learning. Data materialized concerning participants' decision making, communication, and power perceptions. Five categories emerged (incidental experiential learning, collaborative learning, power, learning environment, and complexity) contributing to answering the two research questions.

RESEARCH ENVIRONMENT

The participants who joined in this research project work in one of three University-operated, outpatient family practice healthcare clinics that provide patient services and medical student educational activities. Each of the participants (nurses, medical assistants, receptionists, schedulers, and medical records personnel) came to their jobs with a range of formal education and practical experience. All of the participants were woman. Furthermore, except for male physicians, all other employees of the three clinics were women. Participant recruitment was unencumbered due to the pool of participants. It is not possible to ascertain how male participants may have influenced the consistent experiences expressed by female participants. Some of the participants had worked in a clinical setting before and others had not. Training and orientation for participants was varied. Several participants believed they received adequate instruction; others sensed they had entered a new situation with little or no training. The employees work in a fast paced complex environment where they experience levels of uncertainty and incomplete knowledge.

Figure 14.1, illustrates a model of a typical patient visit cycle in the research study location. This figure exhibits the steps of a standard patient visit surrounded by the variety of employees necessary to successfully conclude a patient visit. This illustration is representational and does not portray the multitude of interactions that take place, nor all of the paperwork, or technology based tasks required. The illustration contributes to visualizing the complexity and interaction elements of the study, and is not a part of policy or training documents. The university that oversees these clinic environments is a very large, multifaceted, and bureaucratic with an extensive set of policies and procedures for employees to have knowledge of and to follow The research sites engaged in this study make use of additional policies (locally created and unique to the study environment) that pertain directly to the clinics where participants work. There are 68 policies under several categories: administration (15), continuum of care (5), environment of care (8), management of human resources (3), infection control (5), management of information (1), patient financial accounts (10), care of patients (19), and patient rights and ethics (2). The policies intend to improve or control the activities of employees in support of patient care, compliance, and financial purposes.

FINDINGS

The categories that surfaced from this study came out of a workplace characterized as a complex adaptive system. In this workplace, incidental learning took place among the workers. The purpose of the study was to better understand the factors involved with the incidental learning that was transpiring. Five categories emerged from the data collection and analysis. Two categories (incidental experiential learning and collaborative learning) related to the first research question: What incidental learning elements do employees use to complete work tasks? Three categories (power, learning environment, and complexity) contributed to understanding the second research question: What transpires within a formalized system to influence incidental learning?

Incidental Experiential Learning

The first category identified how participants experience searching for information related to their specific job tasks. Participants, presented with circumstances of uncertainty and doubt, uniformly asked questions to meet their knowledge needs. All participants admitted they would ask anyone for help in pursuing their efforts to successfully accomplish their prescribed duties. Generally they would begin with immediate peers or coworkers in the same role, but then they would quickly move on to search for answers from other employees who might have completely unrelated roles or different training, and coincidentally might just be randomly walking past a workstation. The following distinct study participant responses from front desk workers, medical assistants, and individuals that answer the phone reflect the incidental nature of how they learned in workplace.

> At first, I didn't think I was really going to get it because there was a lot to learn from my previous job and this was totally out of my realm....Very overwhelmed... relying on coworkers and the boss, mostly coworkers. (Susan, personal communication, June 2013)

> Yeah, kind of just pushed in there and not any training. This is what we do, this is how we do it, and there you go, but they were all very, very helpful. I think the only complaint that I really have as far as not having the training because I do learn being just pushed in there, is that you didn't know you were doing anything wrong until you did it wrong... I would ask anyone that was here, and they again reinstructed me on how to do it... my coworkers at the front desk because they were there. (Maria, personal communication, July 2013)

> No, I did it [training] here. The girls up at the front—it was kind of like a day-by-day scenario. They gave me the basics of what I needed to know, and then every time a situation arose that I wasn't familiar with, I would ask. (Amy, personal communication, June 2013)

> I go to the nurses....Yeah, or I look over their shoulder while they're doing something on the computer and watch what they're doing. (Linda, personal communication, June 2013)

> It was hard at first because, it's like a whole different terminology from what you've had before. It's kind of hard....I just asked anybody who was sitting by me, whoever was there...the medical assistants, the nurses. (Lisa, personal communication, July 2013)

The participants searched for solutions to their needs and also expressed anxiety with the real job facing them without an immediate source to help if they had difficulty. Participants turned to coworkers who have an imperfect range of relevant knowledge. As an incidental interaction takes place, the worker asking the question lacks the immediate ability to verify the correctness of the information provided. Workers grasp for help to solve an instantaneous need to complete a task. Assessing the reliability of the information received is not as imperative as completing the task. Incidental learning of this type can result in assorted information, knowledge, and priorities of behavior for the learner based upon the perception of the significance of the information they are receiving. Yet, in the context of an organization that attempts to train its employees and that utilizes a considerable number of policies and procedures to orient and prepare its employees, this finding amplifies the fact that incidental learning takes place even if policies and procedures are abundant. The learning outcomes may prove to have benefits or create deficiencies, but incidental experiential learning persists. The quotations from participants provide examples of how behavior could change overtime depending upon the coworker the question is directed and the reply. The incidental learning that takes place through these interactions and the incremental changes to work patterns should force supervisors and managers to reflect upon how systems once created evolve through communication and power factors.

Collaborative Learning

The second, but less prevalent, category that emerged was collaboration. Participants alluded to incidental moments of collaboration when a particular issue would gather sufficient awareness among coworkers. The following participant responses represent illustrations of how collaboration incidentally transpires in the workplace.

> Well, for the most part, it's my colleagues and I. We all kind of go, "Well, this isn't working and this is why it's not working. I can't do whatever it is I need to do," so we all kind of have like a little chat session and we go, "Okay, what can we do to get that information into the system or whatever it needs to be to get it done?" We all kind of throw our ideas out there and then we try it. It's kind of a trial and error kind of thing... Rather than think about it for a few days on your own, there are other people out there who are probably having that same issue. If you start talking it out and getting it out in the open, it is more, "Oh, hey, okay, let's try this or let's try that." (Susan, personal communication, June 2013)

> We work well together and communicate. (Emily, personal communication, July 2013)

> I think that's a really good testament to how we all work together... There's been ups and downs here, mostly ups, but we just talk about it, work it out, find another way to do it if that's not working. We're all willing to try something new to make it work... (Emily, personal communication, July 2013)

> Yeah, I think we all kind of brainstorm about it. Like somebody on the unit brings something up... (Emily, personal communication, July 2013)

> Right, as the unit. Then, of course, everybody is going to have their input on it, yeah or nay. (Emily, personal communication, July 2013)

In some cases where incidental learning occurred collaboratively the results of the learning resulted in eventual change to the formal system process.

> Well, then we take it to the nurse manager from there. She will take it to the clinic manager. (Emily, personal communication, July 2013)

Once we do figure it out, of course, then we talk to the office manager....
(Susan, interview by the author, July 2013)

The participants engage in coming together as small groups to figure out a problem or find a solution to something they have encountered. The situations happen incidentally as an event or issue arises, and co-workers learn among themselves in the moment.

Power

Power is the first of three categories contributing to the second research question. Power is widely understood to have influence on adult learning. Power, realized or unspoken, affects learning situations (Hansman & Wilson, 2002). Exercising power, consciously or unconsciously, influences incidental learning. "The exercise of power perpetually creates knowledge and conversely knowledge constantly induces effects of power ... it is not possible for power to be exercised without knowledge, it is impossible for knowledge not to engender power" (Foucault, 1980, p. 52). Power contributes to and determines what accepted knowledge is. "What constitutes and what is accepted as knowledge is determined by power" (Merriam, Caffarella, & Baumgartner, 2007, p. 251). A central component to incidental learning is interaction. Power relations are manifest in all adult education interactions, even those that seem the freest and most unconstrained (Brookfield, 2001). The perception of power impacts how an interaction takes place. Perceptions of power impact the communication cycle resulting in nuances of incidental learning that may be different in absence of a power element. In the clinical environment of this study, there is a clear hierarchy of education (physicians, nurses, other). Deference is given to the person with more education, regardless of the issue being addressed, influencing incidental learning. Expert power was the power factor that contributed to incidental learning in this study. Knowledge or the perception of knowledge attributed to one person over another defines the basis of expert power (French & Raven, 1959). Power can be exercised, knowingly or unknowingly, and can also be an influential function in the incidental learning process as people interact. Research study participants indicated an esteem of other coworkers based upon their formal education.

I was kind of intimidated by them at first because they [physicians] have so much more education than I do.... I've never gotten anybody really grumpy at me, like yelling at me, but they could be upset with like, "I need this chart. Where is at?" I'm like, "Okay, I'll find it. Let me go down and check it out." I think more so my supervisor would hear about it. (Susan, personal communication, June 2013)

> I had never worked with a group of doctors before. Where I come from, there is a certain level of respect that goes with that. They are like, "Call me by my first name," and I still don't feel comfortable doing that. It is very hard for me. I was raised to be very respectful; and if you've earned the title, then that's what you should be called. (Susan, personal communication, June 2013)

Consistently, over the course of participant responses, less formally educated participants conceded to more formally educated coworkers. Changing their behavior based upon the incidental interaction in spite of the systems and policies implemented by their direct supervisors, and in some cases in conflict with their formal education and training.

> When I started, it used to be the doctors would say, "This child needs immunizations." They would either tell us what they needed or we would have to figure out for their age group what they had, what they needed, if it was documented in the computer. It had to be documented so we knew what they needed. There was an instance where I had a director tell me, "This child needs this shot," so knowing—I'm trying to think of the exact situation—but he told me to give a particular shot. I gave it and it ended up being the incorrect shot. . . . It wasn't the wrong medication but the dose. Everybody should have known, and it doesn't matter that it's a director [physician] that told me. It's the fact that you're supposed to know . . . But I was learning. (Michelle, personal communication, July 2013)

This incident illustrates how expert power influenced this particular employee, even though in hindsight they should have known better. In this case the interaction remained in the clinical domain. In other cases, the expert power extends beyond the specific educational expertise into operational areas of the organization where the expert does not have superior knowledge. Deference to the expert transcends specific knowledge into other areas of the workplace. In the following case nurses are instructing a phone scheduler to change to complete a task in spite of how the scheduler's supervisor would have desired.

> We have had things like that where we're told . . . like this nurse told us to schedule this way and somebody [supervisor] will ask us, "Why did you schedule like this?" "Well, we were told to do it that way." (Lisa, personal communication, June 2013)

The change of behavior concedes to the direction of the perceived expert versus the formal organizational structure. Enduring incidental learning perpetuates the new way of completing tasks, based upon the influence of power, through interaction among peers as they search and ask questions to accomplish their work. The marginal changes in task completion persist—creating new unanticipated work patterns. The lesser educated defer to the more educated at points of uncertainty. Workers are predisposed to respect expert power and the assumption of relevant knowledge.

Learning Environment

The second category supporting the second research question is the learning environment. Different learning environments evolve, rooted in leadership styles, communication techniques, and the feedforward and feedback provided to employees. Data analysis indicates disparity of participant perception of the situated learning environment. These two participant replies indicate an environment that is more positive.

> Oh, very, very positively because we have a really great group of people that we work with. It is kind of rare that if you get that many ladies in an office that there is not attitude issues and whatnot, but we all work together really, really well and rely on each other, so that is kind of. (Molly, personal communication, June 2013)

> Very comfortable. There is no trepidation as far as "I feel stupid asking." That is not it. If you need to know it, you need to know it. That goes for all of us. (Lucy, personal communication, June 2013)

Compared with other participants in different buildings how they felt about the environment they were working.

> I didn't feel welcomed . . . I was like infringing on their territory. (Penny, personal communication, July 2013)

> I didn't want to be there. (Amy, personal communication, June 2013)

> I don't know how other people did it, but I was a little stifled there. (Penny, personal communication, July 2013)

Diverse surroundings are creating consequences on incidental learning. Worker uncertainty exists and will prompt questions, yet the extended impact of openness to learning versus an unenthusiastic attitude toward acquiring new knowledge may affect coworker interaction and incidental learning in constructive or unconstructive ways. In this case, the participant felt empowered to offer suggestions and openly offer alternatives to the status quo.

> I just go, "Does it have to be done that way?" "Well, that's the way we've always done it." "Well, what would it hurt if we tried this?" Sometimes they'll say, "Okay, try it and see what happens." Yep, go ahead, do it, so that's what I did.

They liked that. I feel comfortable bringing up suggestions and saying, "Help me think of how we can work it." (Beth, personal communication, June 2013)

Whereas in another clinic the attitude of an individual portrays a much different mind-set about the environment they feel situated.

I'm pretty much the type of person who just, "This is how it's done. Okay, I'm not going to ask questions. Just do it." Right, and I'm not going to complain or try to change. I just kind of like to follow what they say and do it that way. Honestly, I really haven't thought of anything that I could say, "Oh, we could do it different." (Anne, personal communication, July 2013)

These contrasting thoughts contribute to how a workplace environment evolves with respect to a way of thinking and acting. Regardless of the learning environment that exists, incidental learning is tacitly taking place and marginally affecting patterns of how work is completed.

Complexity

Complexity as the final category is an amalgamation of the other themes. This category combines the interactions of the employees through communication and power influencing incidental learning. Complexity theory through incidental learning suggests that regardless of codified knowledge, the progression of learning proceeds. The best made plans and controls cannot account for the variations of communication, power, and incidental learning that occur through the interactions of humans in a workplace. I had the occasion to observe an all-clinic meeting at the Medium sized clinic location. The description of the observation assists in illustrating how complexity confuses the learning interactions.

Regularly scheduled staff meetings disseminate pertinent financial and operational information. The meeting provides a forum to discuss problems or changes happening in the building. Near the completion of the meeting, there is an opportunity for open discussion about anything anyone would like to talk about. Front desk personnel, nurses, and providers discussed a frustrating issue.

This clinic operates a morning walk-in clinic. The purpose of the walk-in clinic is to provide access to patients who have "acute" medical issues. Acute exams do not include annual physicals, chronic health issues, or routine health concerns. The issue concerned how to define an acute visit. This relatively straightforward inquiry by a nurse led to an interesting dialogue among the clinic employees.

A hypothetical case involves a patient coming in and indicating they have a medical issue. Front-desk personnel listen to the patient, and determine the issue is acute. The patient is registered and waits until notified for the exam. The difficulty begins depending upon which provider is working the morning clinic. Providers have different tacit definitions of an "acute" visit. Patients are lead back to an exam room, checked in, and visited by the provider. Staff receive feedback from providers concerning if the visit should be considered acute or not. Communication is given to nurses, or not, and flows to the front desk personnel, where ambiguity ensues. Front desk personnel do not have sufficient medical knowledge to triage a patient's claim of the acute nature of the desired visit. They are unsure how to proceed so now must ask nursing or other medical assistant personnel whether a particular visit is acute or not. The nurses are not always certain either depending upon the provider. Uncertainty is pervasive. Patients receive mixed responses from front-desk or nursing personnel due to staff uncertainty. Patients ascertain they will obtain a visit if they mention more serious medical issues. Adding the patient to the level of complexity adds another factor to the determination of acuteness for personnel.

This set of circumstances helps to illustrate how the categories of this study combine to impact incidental learning in the workplace. The front-desk personnel find themselves in a situation where they do not have the knowledge to help them make adequate decisions. Looking to their front desk peers for learning help is superficial. They can only look to prior experience and the knowledge of the provider who is working to help guide their decision making. The nurses also find themselves in similar states of hesitation regarding how to interpret an acute visit. The advantage the nurses have is medical knowledge, and this provides them with some knowledge over the front-desk personnel. The nurses can feel confident about the acuteness regardless of the provider, but not in every case. There are still situations where nurses get feedback, and yet expert power enters the interaction and the nurse will defer to the provider due to expert knowledge.

The learning environment may also be a contributing factor for the enduring confusion and frustration over this issue. Even though there was an attempt to resolve the uncertainty over the definition of acute, the all-clinic meeting was not successful. During the meeting, I witnessed disjointed communication, where the different people were speaking past one another, rather than listening and trying to come to a decision that could benefit employees and relieve confusion for patients as well. The incidental learning taking place was chaotic and disjointed, and the meeting seemed to create additional confusion and opportunity for additional interaction and incidental learning. Front-desk and nursing personnel (in hopes of finding clarification) came away with increased frustration and confusion. It was evident that there had been segregated attempts at collaboration among employees in similar roles but not collaboration between roles. Ultimately there was a void of leadership to create a consensus among the providers, those with the expert power, to help the other employees in the clinic learn how to function effectively in the situation that arises almost daily (Harner, 2013).

The excerpt portrays the uncertainty that is a consequence from an environment of confusion over a straight forward pragmatic question. Expert power, exercised by providers, is an element that impacts learning and future behavior. Interaction and communication is bewildering, driving supplementary questions about how to do things, and, as a result, engaging in a complex mixture of incidental learning activity. Co-workers interact, asking questions, and collaborating, due to uncertainty, in hopes of constructing ways of completing tasks. Communication and power variances produce unanticipated methods of task completion and establish new patterns and shadow systems. Novel means for completing tasks are different from what the creators of the system had anticipated. New patterns emerge as a result of the incidental learning.

DISCUSSION

Participation in adult education is a result of a desire for learning across life related to economic and work related purposes (Halttunen, Koivisto, & Billet, 2014). Participation in formal adult education demands resources from individuals, government, employers, and educational institutions (Merriam, Caffarella, & Baumgartner, 2007). Formal training and adult education exercises in the workplace determined by people in power roles consume 70% of learning resources (Watkins, et al., 2014). However, learning is omnipresent in the workplace; estimates indicate as much as 80% workplace learning is informal and incidental (Watkins, et al., 2014).

This study examines incidental learning situated in the workplace. Incidental learning involves dynamic interchanges among workers. The range and multitude of interactions are uncontainable resulting in unconscious learning affected by power factors, the learning environment, and elements of communication. Administrators strive to create codified policy and procedure to control education materials directing how employees accomplish their tasks. The perception of the workplace environment (Cronin, 2014) is predictability and control over processes accomplished through formal training and education programs; however, incidental learning sustains its potency in shaping the evolution of workplace activities. Documenting a policy in written format and communicating expected action through formal education efforts may contribute to an administrator's feeling of comfort, but incidental interaction and learning continues, tacitly adjusting how work is completed. Communication utilizing a sender-receiver modality assumes the receivers are listening and consuming a message consistent with the sender's assumptions. Individuals on the receiving end of communication consistently do not have the opportunity to respond leaving to chance the intent of the communication in spite of what the sender assumes. Upon returning to individual workstations, incidental interaction takes place among co-workers based upon disaggregated assumptions where power elements solidify new incidental learning.

This study informs researchers and practitioners about how incidental learning perpetually occurs in the workplace. Interaction among peers affects incidental learning in different fashions depending upon the perceived level of knowledge of the inter-actors. Employees perceived to possess greater levels of knowledge may affect learning through incidental interaction in a different way. Expert power, exerted for employees positioned in the perceived subordinate position, impacts the learning dynamic. Systems, policies, and rules typically cannot suppress the occurrence and the unforeseen directions of incidental learning situations. Adult Education activities in the workplace seek to assist adults in their desire to acquire new knowledge, skill, or ability consistent with the desires of decision makers (Merriam, Caffarella, & Baumgartner, 2007). Learners are attaining new knowledge through courses or training efforts in the present. Incidental learning takes place in the immediate future through interaction leading to unanticipated ways of doing and thinking. Individuals learn as they interrelate and partake in an environment with assumptions, rules, culture, and history utilizing technology and other artifacts in working through the moment's activities (Fenwick, 2000). Adult education can be a link that assists learners to understand that once formally acquired knowledge is applied incidental learning begins. Decision makers and learning researchers can benefit from understanding how incidental learning and the principles of complexity theory affect the evolution of workplace actions and learning.

REFERENCES

Billet, S. (2004). Learning through work: Workplace participatory practices. In H. Rainbird, A. Fuller, & A. Munro (Eds.), *Workplace learning in context* (pp. 109–125). London, England: Routledge.

Brookfield, S. (2001). Unmasking power: Foucault and adult learning. *The Canadian Journal for the Study of Adult Education, 15*(1), 1–23.

Cahoon, B. B. (1995). Computer skill learning in the workplace: A comparative case study. (unpublished doctoral dissertation). University of Georgia. Athens, GA.

Chaffee, M. W., & McNeil, M. M. (2007). A model of nursing as a complex adaptive system. *Nursing Outlook, 55*(5), 232–241.

Creswell, J. W. (2007). *Qualitative inquiry & research design: Choosing among five approaches.* Thousand Oaks, CA: Sage Publications.

Cronin, C. (2014). Workplace learning—a healthcare perspective. *Education and Training*. 56(4), 329–342.

Cseh, M., Watkins, K. E., & Marsick, V. J. (1999). Re-conceptualizing Marsick and Watkins' model of informal and incidental learning in the workplace. In K. P. Kuchinke, (Ed.), *Academy of Human Resource Development Conference Proceedings*, Arlington, VA.

Dooley, K. J., Johnson, T. L., & Bush, D. H. (1995). TQM, chaos and complexity. *Human Systems Management, 14*(4), 287–302.

Elias, N. (1991). *The society of individuals.* Cambridge, MA: Basil Blackwell.

Eraut, M. (2004). Informal learning in the workplace. *Studies in Continuing Education, 26*(2), 247–273.

Fenwick, T. (2000). Expanding conceptions of experiential learning: A review of the five contemporary perspectives on cognition. *Adult Education Quarterly, 50*(4), 243–272.

Fenwick, T. (2003). *Learning through experience: Troubling orthodoxies and intersecting questions.* Malabar, FL: Krieger Publishing Company.

Foucault, M. (1980). *Power/knowledge: Selected interviews & other writings, 1972–1977.* New York, NY: Pantheon Books.

French, R. P., & Raven, B. (1959). The bases of social power. In D. Cartwright (Ed.), *Studies in social power.* Ann Arbor, MI: University of Michigan.

Garrick, J. (1998). Informal learning in corporate workplaces. *Human Resource Development Quarterly, 9*(2), 129–144.

Halttunen, T., Koivisto, M., & Billett, S. (2014). Promoting and recognising lifelong learning: Introduction. In *Promoting, assessing, recognizing and certifying lifelong learning* (pp. 3–18). Springer Netherlands.

Hansman, C. A.,, & Wilson, A. L. (2002, May). Situating cognition: Knowledge and power in context. In *Proceedings of the 43rd Annual Adult Education Research Conference* (pp. 141–146).

Harner, M. D. (2013). *Incidental learning in a complex clinical workplace.* (Unpublished doctoral dissertation). Northern Illinois University, Dekalb, IL.

Harkema, S. (2003). A complex adaptive perspective on learning within innovation projects. *The Learning Organization, 10*(6), 340–346.

Hunter, C. (2014). Perspectives in AE-intentional incidental learning in the workplace: Implications for adult learning. *New Horizons in Adult Education & Human Resource Development, 26*(2), 49–53.

Johnson, N. (2010). *Simply complexity: A clear guide to complexity theory.* Oxford, England: Oneworld Publications.

Kazbour, R. R., McGee, H. M., Masica, T. L., & Brinderhoff, R. O. (2013). Evaluating the impact of a performance-based methodology on transfer of training. *Performance Improvement Quarterly, 26*(1), 5–33.

Kerka, S. (2000). *Incidental learning: Trends and issues alert no. 18.* Columbus, OH: ERIC Clearinghouse on Adult, Career and Vocational Education. Retrieved from www.ericacve.org.fulltext.asp

Kim, J. H., & Lee, C. (2001). Implications of near and far transfer of training on structured on-the-job training. *Advances in Developing Human Resources, 3*(4), 442–451.

Le Clus, M. (2011). Informal learning in the workplace: A review of the literature. *Australian Journal of Adult Learning, 51*(2), 355–373.

Lewin, R., & Regine, B. (2001). *Weaving complexity and business: Engaging the soul at work.* New York, NY: Texere.

Lloyd, B., Pfeiffer, D. Dominish, J., Heading, G., Schmidt, D., & McCluskey, A. (2014). The New South Wales allied health workplace learning study: Barriers and enablers to learning in the workplace. *BMC Health Services Research.* 14, 134–151.

Marsick, V. J., & Watkins, K. E. (1990). *Informal and incidental learning in the workplace.* New York, NY: Routledge.

Marsick, V. J., Volpe, M., & Watkins, K. E. (1999). Theory and practice of informal learning in the knowledge era. *Advances in Developing Human Resources, 1*(3), 80–95.

Marsick, V. J., & Watkins, K. E. (2001). Informal and incidental learning. *New Directions for Adult and Continuing Education, 2001*(89), 25–34.

Mead, G. H. (1934). *Mind, self, and society.* Chicago, IL: University of Chicago Press.

Merriam, S. B., Caffarella, S., & Baumgartner, L. M. (2007). *Learning in adulthood: A comprehensive guide* (3rd ed.). San Francisco, CA: Jossey-Bass.

Merriam, S. B., & Simpson, E. L. (2000). *A guide to research for educators and trainers of adults.* Malabar, FL: Krieger.

Noe, R. A. (1986). Trainees' attributes and attitudes: Neglected influences on training effectiveness. *Academy of Management Review, 11*(4), 736–749.

Paley, J., & Eva, G. (2011). Complexity theory as an approach to explanation in healthcare: A critical discussion. *International Journal of Nursing Studies, 48*(2), 269–279.

Stacey, R. D. (1996). *Complexity and creativity in organizations.* San Francisco, CA: Berrett-Koehler Publishers.

Stacey, R. D. (2003). Learning as an activity of interdependent people. *The Learning Organization, 10*(6), 325–331.

Stacey, R. D. (2004). *Complex responsive processes in organization: Learning and knowledge creation.* New York, NY: Routledge.

Stacey, R. D. (2010). *Complexity and organizational reality: Uncertainty and the need to rethink management after the collapse of investment capitalism.* New York, NY: Routledge.

Stacey, R. D. (2011). *Strategic management and organizational dynamics: The challenge of complexity,* (6th ed.). Harlow, England: Pearson Education.

Stacey, R. D., Griffin, D., & Shaw, P. (2000). *Complexity and management: Fad or radical challenge to systems thinking?* New York, NY: Routledge.

Straka, G. A. (2009). Informal and implicit learning: concepts, communalities and differences. *European Journal of Vocational Training. 48*(3), 133–145.

Tillart, H. V., Berg, S. V., & Warmerdam, J. (1998). *Work and learning in micro-enterprises in the printing industry.* European Centre for the Development of Vocational Training (CEDEFOP), Thessaloniki.

Watkins, K. E., Marsick, V. J., & de Álava, M. F. (2014). Evaluating Informal Learning in the Workplace. In *Promoting, Assessing, Recognizing and Certifying Lifelong Learning* (pp. 59–77). Springer Netherlands.

White, C. (2010). A socio-cultural approach to learning in the practice setting. *Nurse Education Today.* 30, 794–797.

Wofford, M. G., Ellinger, A. D., & Watkins, K. E. (2013). Learning on the fly: Exploring the informal learning process of aviation instructors. *Journal of Workplace Learning.* 25(2), 79–97.

Yamnill, S., & McLean, G. N. (2001). Theories supporting transfer of training. *Human Resource Development Quarterly, 12*(2), 195–208.

Zimmerman, B., Linberg, C., & Plesk, P. (2001). *Edgeware: Insights from complexity science for health care leaders.* Irving, TX: VHA.

PART I

SUPPORTING NEEDS OF ADULT LEARNERS:

Advancing Adult Learning in the Health Professions

CHAPTER 15

STAGED SELF-DIRECTED LEARNING MODEL

Leaving the Nest— From Novice to Professional

Julie Hall
Roane State Community College

Continuing education is a critical component in health care because professionals work in a complex discipline that is constantly evolving. Social, technological, and medical changes present many trials and challenges to professionals in health care. A report published by the Institute of Medicine (IOM) in 2010 concluded that the professional health care workforce is not prepared to guarantee delivery of the highest quality patient care and safety. Researchers found that health professionals tend to focus on meeting regulatory requirements rather than diversifying their skills or filling personal knowledge gaps (IOM, 2010). It is simply not possible for formal education programs to completely prepare graduates for the complex challenges and experiences encountered in the professional arena. Health professionals must be self-directed learners in order to obtain or advance

Building Sustainable Futures for Adult Learners, pages 325–339
Copyright © 2015 by Information Age Publishing

the knowledge and skills required to succeed; "faculty can no longer hope to convey all clinical information to students in the classroom. At best, faculty can assist students in learning broad concepts and then prepare them to keep up with the changing details" (Bonnel & Smith, 2010, pp. 15–16). Health professionals must embrace continuing education as a lifelong process and develop skills to remain motivated and independent in order to evolve with changing society and technology. Therefore, it is critical that programs provide a framework of education that allows graduates to succeed in the health care workplace through self-directed learning and continuing education.

Many educators who teach in professional health programs find themselves in a complex situation. They must ensure that students are obtaining the skills/information necessary to meet credentialing requirements as well as prepare them to grow professionally after graduation. Students are repeatedly exposed to the premise that teachers are to be viewed as experts who are there to provide knowledge. These recipients of a traditional educational process can acquire patterns of learning and motivation that are extrinsic or in response to simply fulfilling a course objective (Bolhuis, 2003). Within the scope of a health professional program, certain required and/or complex skills and knowledge must be mastered before students can safely start interacting with patients. Therefore, patterns of traditional teaching techniques are too often utilized. However, many professional experiences out in the field are complex and not predictable or straight forward; therefore, graduates must be able to function, think, and learn independently.

A possible solution to bridging this gap is to incorporate self-directed learning into the curriculum over a period of time, so that students are able to move from being dependent on traditional teaching methods to being more self-directed upon graduation (as well as meet all required competencies). One possible way to increase self-direction in learners is to utilize Grow's (1991a) Staged Self-Directed Learning Model (SSDL) with students during health professional preparation programs. The focus of this chapter is to describe the benefits, concerns, and teaching implications of incorporating SSDL into educational programs such as: dental hygiene, nursing, occupational therapy, physical therapy, radiologic technology, or respiratory therapy.

SELF-DIRECTED LEARNING

In the past, it was possible to learn a profession through an apprenticeship. However, that system has been replaced with an entirely new constantly evolving system of education. Candy (1995) identified the importance of continuing education:

It is almost truism to say that the rate of growth in knowledge in most technical areas, including medicine, is so great that no one can hope to learn in a few years at university all that they will need to know in a lifetime of practice.... Accordingly, practitioners' own individual and self-directed learning efforts must be the cornerstone of any program of continuing medical education... (p. 81)

Additionally, it is not practical for students to continually enroll in formal courses of study in order to keep up with new developments (Lwasi, 1987). Self-directed learning has been acknowledged as one method for professionals that rely heavily on students or adults being responsible for their own learning.

Self-directed learning examples can be traced as far back as Socrates in Rome (Merriam & Brockett, 2007). Since its identification, there have been multiple definitions presented by adult education theorists. The concept is based upon the work of adult education theorist, Malcolm Knowles. In the realm of formal education, the main theme is that students will have greater control over their learning. O'Shea (2003) found in a literature review that self-directed learning can provide "increased student confidence, autonomy, motivation, and the development of skills for lifelong learning" (p. 69). Self-directed learning can be thought of as a way in which successful lifelong learning can be facilitated among adults in professional fields of study. These types of individuals are in a constant learning mode; "people with this disposition are always striving for improvement themselves. They seize problems, situations, tensions, conflicts, and circumstances as valuable opportunities to learn" (Costa & Kallick, 2004, p. 15).

Graduates must be self-directed learners to obtain and develop the knowledge and skills required to succeed and progress (O'Shea, 2003; Patterson, Crooks, & Lunyk-Child, 2002; Westphal, 2008). Eventually, each student will be working as a professional in the workplace and must be adequately prepared to independently participate in continuing education. Self-directed learning is a practical method for professionals to constantly function effectively and deliver high quality healthcare.

Self-Directed Learning in Formal Education Programs

One of the major assumptions in andragogy presented by Knowles (1980) is that adults have a "reservoir of experience" and generally have a need to be self-directing. Many adult educators concur with Malcolm Knowles' writings and understanding of the advantages of using self-directed learning. As Candy (1991) recognized:

The world we live in demands self-starting, self-directing citizens capable of independent action. The world is changing so fast we cannot hope to teach each person what he/she will need to know in twenty years. Our only hope to meet the demands of the future is the production of intelligent and independent people. (p. 47)

However, many health and nursing curriculums continue to focus on content rather than the process of learning by utilizing traditional teacher-centered instruction (Kocaman, 2009). Many students in health care professional programs initially tend to desire direct or concrete teaching-centered approaches with highly organized activities and clearly stated requirements or expectations (Burnard & Morrison, 1992; Hewitt-Taylor, 2001; Levett-Jones, 2005; Turunen, Taskinen, Voutilainen, Tossavainen, & Sinkkonen, 1997). This is most likely attributed to the fact that health care delivery and these types of programs carry high levels of responsibility for both students and faculty.

Faculty Concerns

There is a lot of support for self-directed learning as a method of facilitating adults in formal educational programs (Lunyk-Child, Crooks, Ellis, Ofosu, O'Mara, & Rideout, 2001). However, health care programs have been historically dominated by traditional didactic teaching methods (O'Shea, 2003). Some faculty in formal education settings still have reservations about participating or facilitating self-directed learning. Due to the fact that most healthcare programs have restrictions imposed by professional or institutional requirements, it may be hard for faculty members to feel comfortable about integrating new teaching methods into their courses (Levett-Jones, 2005). However, more faculty members are increasingly becoming aware of the fact that self-directed learning will better prepare their graduates to become lifelong learners and better health care professionals. Some areas, such as the professional field of nursing, have increasingly published literature related to self-directed learning. O'Shea (2003) completed a literature review aimed at exploring the concept of self-directed learning and its function in nurse education.

According to a qualitative study completed by Lunyk-Child and colleagues (2001), some of the items that may hinder implementation of self-directed learning into courses include fear of failure, consistency, the need for increased faculty development, and a standard definition. The results of that study indicate that faculty members differ about the exact definition of self-directed learning and may not have the resources or time to participate in associated professional development. Additionally, faculty members struggle with being consistent in the classroom or across a division (i.e., when multiple sections of a particular class are being offered). This can contribute to insecurity; "I'm not going to measure up or do something wrong" (Lunyk-Child & et al., 2001, p.119). Standards and goals for health professional programs are usually set by accreditation agencies (e.g., licensure pass rates) and may create an atmosphere where faculty feel that they do not have the time or liberty to incorporate self-directed learning into their courses or across a program.

Student Concerns

Students in professional health care programs may also express concerns about incorporating self-directed learning into their studies. Many students are not familiar with self-directed learning terminology or what it exactly means (Lunyk-Child & et al., 2001). Individuals experience a majority of traditional teaching methods while maneuvering through educational systems; "From the first grade on, most students are trained to do what they are told. They are motivated from the outside, managed from the outside, and evaluated from the outside . . . " (Grow, 1991b, p. 58). Therefore, students are accustomed to viewing the teacher as an expert who provides their knowledge. Unfortunately, this dependent learning style based on early school experience can contribute to student struggles and resentment when trying to introduce self-directed learning into the classroom (Timmins, 2008). A study conducted by McCauley and McClelland (2004) indicated that previous learning experiences (in secondary level education) may be responsible for establishing dependency among students. The ones who are attempting to develop self-directed skills can feel lost if they are not given adequate guidance. A student participant in the Lunyk-Child and colleagues study (2001) stated:

> Coming into the first year, they want you to be self-directed, but this was such a foreign body of knowledge and way of learning that you couldn't be self-directed cause you didn't know where to start, that was the hardest part. (pp. 119–120)

Students have also stated that they dislike inconsistencies between professors or classes in a program associated with self-directed learning implementation. These differences can be perceived as confusing to members of the class who do not grasp or completely understand self-directed learning concepts. Students also seem to struggle with concerns that they may not be learning what they need to. Health professional programs can be considered "high-stakes" because if a particular student does not meet a specific standard or number of competencies, then she will be dismissed. Many healthcare programs have very strict readmission policies and may not allow readmission. Therefore, many students worry about guaranteeing that they are learning exactly what is needed to pass the course and move forward in the program; "Am I learning what I need to learn?" (Lunyk-Child & et al., 2001, p. 120).

STAGED SELF-DIRECTED LEARNING MODEL

The Staged Self-Directed Learning Model (SSDL) proposed by Grow (1991a) defines stages and activities that educational programs can integrate into their classes to prepare students with the necessary skills to become effective life-long learners. Each stage is designed to gradually introduce the student to self-directed learning and serves to ensure that core content and required information are delivered. This also helps the student adapt naturally to different learning options as they progress through a program and items are incrementally added or changed. Some students who are unacquainted with self-directed learning may become frustrated if they are suddenly immersed in an independent new concept or assignment that is quite different from more traditional ones (Staverdes, 2011). Instructors have reported that if they immediately introduce a self-directed learning approach into a class of unfamiliar students that there was immediate "apprehension or concern about having to do 'everything alone'" (Thompson & Wulff, 2004, p. 39). The overall goal is to facilitate the student's change from being a dependent teacher-oriented learner to being self-directed all in one continuum. Initially, all learners may not be ready to take responsibility for their own learning. If the stages are integrated appropriately throughout the curriculum of a health professional program, it is possible to address required educational objectives as well as develop independent learning skills.

The SSDL model could be used as a way to help educational programs produce graduates who have the ability for self-direction while working in a health care profession. It attempts to reconcile the fact that students initially desire to be led by the teacher when starting a new profession as well as satisfy the educator's critical need to pass on specific information. There are four stages (Figure 15.1) within the model and each one offer methods that can be utilized to achieve required goals and move towards the ability to become self-directed.

Stage 1: Dependent Learner or Low Level of Self-Direction

Overall, adult learners have a "deep psychological need to be generally self-directing" (Knowles, 1980, p. 43). It is important to point out that even

Stage	Student	Teacher	Examples
Stage 1	Dependent	Authority, Coach	Coaching with immediate feedback. Drill. Informational lecture. Overcoming deficiences and resistance.
Stage 2	Interested	Motivator, guide	Inspiring lecture plus guided discussion. Goal-setting and learning strategies.
Stage 3	Involved	Faciltator	Discussion facilitated by teacher who participates as equal. Seminar. Group projects.
Stage 4	Self-directed	Consultant, delegator	Internship, dissertation, individual work or self-directed study group.

Figure 15.1 Staged self-directed learning model. *Grow, Adult Education Quarterly, 41*(3), 129. Copyright 1991 by American Association for Adult and Continuing Education. Reprinted by permission of SAGE Publications.

though a student may start a health professional program with low self-direction because the material is new, that does not render the individual a dependent learner as a whole. As Grow (1991a) points out; "all learners of whatever stage may become temporary dependent in the face of new topics" (p. 129).

Most likely, students will begin a health professional program and prefer detailed instructions in their courses. Due to the nature of the information covered in the first semester, faculty members will also find the first stage of the SSDL model conducive to their teaching needs. Stage 1 provides information in a clearly organized manner and very explicit details about course or clinic expectations are provided. Teachers in these beginning courses would be providing subject matter information through lectures and straight-forward techniques (Grow, 1991b). Faculty members should provide frequent feedback to the students about their progress with recommendations for improvement.

Stage 2: Interested Learner or Moderate Self-Direction

Stage 2 may begin to be incorporated into health professional courses towards the beginning of the program. It is likely that stage 1 and stage 2 may overlap each other at times depending on the subject matter. Stage 2 teaching includes teacher-led discussion after a lecture, structured projects with predictable outcomes, or demonstration of a specific skill followed by guided student practice (Grow, 1991b). This stage of teaching is probably visible in laboratory sections where students may be learning a particular skill. There is an increased 'two-way' interaction between instructor and the students. The instructor should take the time to explain and justify each assignment and persuade students of its value (Grow, 1991a).

Stage 3: Involved Student or Intermediate Self-Direction

Stage 3 includes students who are ready to explore topics on their own, but still need an instructor to help guide or provide a sense of direction. This stage really begins to transition students to greater levels of self-direction and independence. The instructor may allow "student group projects approved and facilitated (but not directed) by the instructor, and group projects progressing from structured assignments with criteria checklists, to open-ended, student-developed group projects performed without close supervision" (Grow, 1991a, p. 134).

Stage 4: Directed Students or High Level of Self-Direction

Stage 4 is the ultimate goal of the SSDL model and optimally where health professional students will be upon graduation. Students in this phase are able to take responsibility for their own learning and are capable of utilizing their own resources for the gathering of educational information (Grow, 1991a). At this point, instructors progress into a role of consultant and are a source of enablement. They motivate students to remember that their health professional field is constantly changing and the key to success and providing safe patient care is linked to lifelong learning and continuing education; "the ability to learn on one's own has become a prerequisite for living in a dynamic world of rapid change" (Levett-Jones, 2005, p. 364).

Some examples of stage 4 activities would be honor projects or independent study as well as student-run organizations (publications). The students approach the instructor only when questions arise that requires increased guidance or input. Grow (1991a) states that:

> The role relationship between teacher and student is collegial and distinctly not intense; instead the relationship is high between student and world, students and task, and perhaps among students. The teacher actively monitors progress to ensure success, but steps in only to assist students in acquiring the skills to be self-directing and self-monitoring. The teacher weans the student of being taught. (p. 135)

Due to the limitations of formal education, stage 4 self-direction may not be fully recognized until after graduation. The ultimate goal is for students who enter health professional programs as dependent learners in stage 1 or 2 of the SSDL model to develop over the course of the program and graduate as stage 4.

Applying the Model to Health Professional Programs

The major advantage of the SSDL model is that the four stages lend themselves to being very beneficial within the curriculums of health professional programs. Educators within these degree programs usually retain the same students for at least two years at a time and have a great opportunity to assist graduates to be improved self-directed learners. For maximum benefit, faculty members should coordinate their efforts in order to facilitate graduates who are clinically and didactically proficient.

Stage 1 is beneficial in health professional programs because the first semester would be most likely focused on preparing students to start clinical fieldwork that would require hands-on patient care, specific skills, and clearly delineated expectations (e.g., attendance requirements or utilizing patient identifiers before proceeding with any type of care). During stage 2, the instructor may demonstrate how to position for a chest x-ray and then have the student simulate the same positioning for competency assessment (prior to any clinical patient contact). A stage 3 example for health care would be to review and dialogue about clinical case studies. The instructor and students will both be involved in the analyzing and interchange of related information; "the instructor concentrates on facilitation and communication and supports students in using the skills they have" (Grow, 1991a, p. 133). Stage 4 may become apparent by the formation of student-centered study groups where they convene and work collaboratively based on incentive or personal motivation to pass licensing exams in a respective field. To summarize, the SSDL model could be easily distributed across the curriculum (Figure 15.2).

For example, the SSDL model could be successfully applied across the curriculum of a radiologic technology program. Students in the beginning of the first semester of study would be considered in stage 1 and faculty would be focusing on teaching basic patient care skills (learning names of specific anatomy on a radiographic image). Students would also learn about x-ray positioning through lecture and image analysis classes. Stage 2 techniques would possibly overlap because students would also work in smaller laboratory groups where the instructor demonstrates positioning and guides students to simulate the radiographic exams. Stage 3 techniques would be eventually integrated later in the year via an instructor or student sharing case studies where the class must identify a particular pathology or evaluate errors seen on radiographic images. The instructor may work with

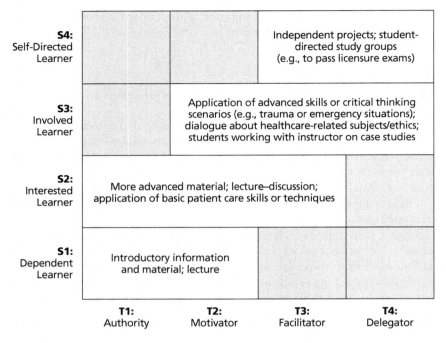

Figure 15.2 Application of the staged self-direction model to a health professional program. Adapted from Grow (1991a).

the class as an equal in some situations depending on the complexity and uniqueness of each presented case study (especially if a student shares it with the class and the instructor is learning as well). Students may also use stage 3 techniques during the second year of study in trauma labs where they collaboratively work to ascertain how to obtain diagnostic images on patients with advanced level injuries that would not fit basic textbook descriptions. Stage 4 would hopefully be reached just prior to graduation where students would decide to form their own study groups and work together or perhaps independently in order to study for their licensing exam.

TEACHING IMPLICATIONS OF THE SSDL MODEL

The advantage of using the SSDL model is that a matrix can be presented to the student that allows them to locate themselves in terms of readiness and comfort of being self-directed. This matrix allows an educator to match the learner's stage with appropriate instructional strategies (Merriam, 2001). Additionally, the model allows for the teacher to have different possible roles depending on the learners' willingness and ability to be self-directed (Caffarella, 1993).

Many instructors may not realize that they teach the exact same way to all of their students regardless of their position in the program (novice versus a more senior student). Grow (1991b) described that phenomenon after a conference:

> A professor told me he had been surprised to realize that he taught all his students—from freshman to graduate students—in exactly the same way. He was ready to consider changing his approach—now that the option had been brought to his attention. (pp. 60–61)

However, it is important that instructors work in combination with students to find the appropriate amount or balance of self-directed learning methods in each class. Educators need to appropriately identify what subject content is critical to the success of their students in the clinical setting as well as help develop their level of self-direction. They also need to recognize becoming self-directed is not an overnight occurrence and that frustration may occur. A possible challenge that some instructors may encounter in the implementation of SSDL teaching methods is resistant tendencies to relinquish direct control over the learning experiences in some situations (Hewitt-Taylor, 2001; Lunyk-Child & et. al., 2001).

Another task for educators will be to find the space within their content filled curriculums. The challenge is to find a way to incorporate both guidance and choice into the course. It is difficult to achieve full self-directed learning in a formal health education setting. However, with the SSDL model, introductory and lower-level courses could be more teacher-centered, using such methods as lecture, guided labs, and teacher-led discussion. As the students progress through the curriculum, the upper-division courses can incorporate teaching methods that prepare students for greater degrees of self-direction; "will increasingly employ such methods as student decision-making, collaborative learning, and independent projects, and faculty will shift from coaches to facilitators as students become more capable of directing their own work" (Grow, 1991b, p. 62). There will also be the challenge of balancing the SSDL model and specific grading requirements as needed for programs to maintain quality and high standards. The distinction between grades and learning is a concern for students (Douglass & Morris, 2014). Faculty members will also have an important job of integrating and managing grades into their courses and this should not be ignored; "Grades are the elephant in the classroom" (Walvoord & Anderson, 2010, p.1). Established learning goals for each class and program will aid educators in balancing these requirements. Ultimately, it is important that instructors encourage and facilitate students to be equipped for

336 ■ J. HALL

opportunities and challenges beyond their formal education (Dynan, Cate, & Rhee, 2008).

Criticisms of the SSDL Model

Grow recognizes that there could be a problem resulting from a mismatch between teaching styles and learning styles in the SSDL model matrix. The worst problems could arise when there are two extremes on the matrix paired with each other. Some examples of a severe mismatch could be seen between a stage 4 self-directed student and a stage 1 authoritarian teacher. On the opposite end of the spectrum, when a dependent learner (stage 1) is paired with a stage 4 teacher then the student will simply not be able to handle the assignments and expectations (Grow, 1991a). There are also milder mismatches that can occur which can stifle learning opportunities in the classroom.

Tennant (1992) published some criticisms of the SSDL model that have valid points. For example, the student moves through different levels of self-direction while progressing throughout the SSDL model. At what exact point should the student be deemed ready to move to the next level? Additionally, who should judge that the student is ready to progress? The argument of whether the student versus the instructor should be the one to initiate that change is brought into question. Tennant (1992) questions whether or not that responsibility should be given to the instructor or does the student need to be accountable for this advancement. Grow (1994) is not convinced that an instructor is able to ascertain the level of a student's self-directedness on his or her own experience or intuition:

> A recent experience has challenged my initial conviction that teachers can easily arrive at a correct diagnosis on their own. In a class consisting mainly of college seniors, I turned students loose on several projects intended to provide them an opportunity to extend and consolidate. . . . This freedom worked for two-thirds of the class. But before I detected the problem, a group of students mismatched to this non-directive approach worked up considerable discontent and suddenly began attacking me for not teaching them. (p. 112)

The SSDL model is applicable and valuable for facilitating students toward being independent or highly self-directed learners by graduation. However, it should be used with the practical realization that it will not work for everyone all the time. There are many advantages of utilizing the model, and as a whole it should help many students move towards a higher level of self-direction. Grow (1994) recognized that "there is no one way to teach or learn well. Different styles work for different learners in different situations" (p. 113). Even though the model will have general success in health professional programs, educators need to recognize that every student may not obtain stage 4 self-direction. However, the SSDL model does provide general workable phases or labels for each shift within the course of the curriculum (Grow, 1994).

SUGGESTIONS FOR FUTURE RESEARCH

Some future questions for research would be to ascertain the benefits of utilizing a self-direction readiness instrument such as the Oddi Continuing Learning Inventory (OCLI), Self-Directed Learning Readiness Scale (SDLRS), or the Personal Responsibility Orientation to Self-Direction in Learning Scale (PRO-SDLS) in conjunction with the SSDL model. Also, how could one approach teaching in a health professional course or program if it had students with radically different levels of self-directed readiness? Would the results still be beneficial to the students and ensure program standards and requirements are met? Additionally, how can educators influence graduates to remain self-directed in their continuing education activities over a long-span of time; "lifelong learning presents some difficulties in self-motivation, resistance to change, time and life constraints" (Westphal, 2008, p. 28).

CONCLUSION

Within health professional programs, the goal is to increase knowledge and competency of beginning practitioners to ensure that the highest level of patient care is always delivered. The other goal is facilitate graduates with developed skills that will continue to serve them well beyond the requirements of a particular college course or program. It may be hard for instructors who have relied on traditional teaching methods to embrace new ways of learning without the proper amount of continuing education. It would be beneficial for program faculty to collaborate and incorporate the SSDL model throughout the two-year period in the appropriate places. This would involve gaining support from all faculty members within a program; "the SSDL model might be used as a planning tool for coordinating faculty efforts so that the students do, in fact progress toward greater self-direction as they move to upper-level college courses" (Grow, 1991a, p. 144). An appropriate amount of professional development and involvement in the implementation by all instructors would be critical in order for everyone to feel invested and possess a strong understanding of what benefits the program and its students could earn through the endeavor.

Ultimately, all programs that are producing health professionals need to periodically re-evaluate teaching practices to ascertain if they staying up-to-date with the needs of the profession and community. Unfortunately, the IOM has found in its most recent report that there is a deficiency in the amount of quality continuing education that is being completed. Health professional educators should examine their own teaching styles and programs in order to reconcile the critical need to pass on specific information as well as facilitate graduates who are able to successfully engage in lifelong learning. By meeting this goal, the health care profession will be composed of professionals who are interested in diversifying their skills or creating a natural curiosity to keep up with new technology rather than being solely externally motivated to complete continuing education activities.

REFERENCES

Bolhuis, S. (2003). Towards process-oriented teaching for self-directed lifelong learning: A multidimensional perspective. *Learning and Instruction, 13*, 327–347.

Bonnel, W., & Smith, K. V. (2010). *Teaching technologies in nursing and the health professions.* New York, NY: Springer Publishing, LLC.

Burnard, P., & Morrison, P. (1992). Students' and lecturers' preferred teaching strategies. *International Journal of Nursing Studies, 29*, 345–353.

Caffarella, R. S. (1993). Self-directed learning. *New Directions for Adult and Continuing Education, 57*, 25–35.

Candy, P. (1991). *Self-direction for lifelong learning.* San Franciso, CA: Jossey-Bass.

Candy, P. (1995). Physician teach thyself: The place of self-directed learning in continuing medical education. *The Journal of Continuing Education in the Health Profession, 15*, 80–90.

Costa, A., & Kallick, L. (2004). *Assessment strategies for self-directed learning* Thousand Oaks, CA: Corwin Press.

Douglass, C., & Morris, S. R. (2014). Student perspectives on self-directed learning. *Journal of the Scholarship of Teaching and Learning, 14*(1), 13–25.

Dynan, L., Cate, T., & Rhee, K. (2008). The impact of learning structure on students' readiness for self-directed learning. *Journal of Education for Business, 84*(2), 96–100.

Grow, G. (1991a). Teaching learners to be self-directed. *Adult Education Quarterly, 41*, 125–149.

Grow, G. (1991b). Higher-order skills for professional practice and self-direction. *Journalism Educator, 45*(4), 56–65.

Grow, G. (1994). In defense of Staged Self-Directed Learning Model. *Adult Education Quarterly. 44*(2), 109–114.

Hewitt-Taylor, J (2001). Self-directed learning: Views of teachers and students. *Issues and innovations in nursing education, 36*(4), 496–504.

Institute of Medicine (2010). *Redesigning continuing education in the health professions.* Washington, DC: The National Academies Press.

Knowles, M. S. (1980). *The modern practice of adult education: From pedagogy to andragogy,* (2nd ed.). New York, NY: Cambridge.

Kocaman, G. (2009). A longitudinal analysis of the self-directed learning readiness level of nursing students enrolled in a problem- based curriculum. *Journal of Nursing Education, 48*(5), 286–290.

Levett-Jones, T. L. (2005). Self-directed learning: Implications and limitations for undergraduate nursing education. *Nurse Education Today, 25*(5), 363–368.

Lunyk-Child, O., Crooks, D., Ellis. P., Ofosu, C., O'Mara, L., & Rideout, E. (2001). Self-directed learning: Faculty and student perceptions. *Journal of Nursing Education, 40*(3), 116–123.

Lwasi, C. (1987, January). Role of the teacher in self-directed learning. *Nurse Education Today, 7,* 222–227.

McCauley, V., & McClelland, G. (2004). Further studies in self-directed learning in physics at the University of Limerick, Ireland. *International Journal of Self-Directed Learning, 1*(2), 26–37.

Merriam, S. B. (2001). Andragogy and self-directed learning: Pillars of adult learning theory. *New Directions for Adult and Continuing Education, 89,* 3–13.

Merriam, S., & Brockett, R. (2007). *The profession and practice of adult education: An Introduction.* San Francisco, CA: Jossey-Bass.

O'Shea, E. (2003). Self-directed learning in nurse education: A review of the literature. *Journal of Advanced Nursing, 43*(1), 62–70.

Patterson, C., Crooks, D., & Lunyk-Child, O. (2002). A new perspective of competencies for self-directed learning. *Journal of Nursing Education, 41*(1), 25–31.

Staverdes, T. (2011). *Effective online teaching, training manual: Foundations and strategies for student success.* San Francisco, CA: Jossey-Bass.

Tennant, M. (1992). The staged-self directed learning model. *Adult Education Quarterly, 42*(3), 164–166.

Timmins, F. (2008). Take time to facilitate self-directed learning. *Nurse Education in Practice, 8,* 302–305.

Thompson, T., & Wulff, S. (2004). Implementing self-directed learning strategies (GSDL) in intermediate and advanced level chemistry courses. *International Journal of Self-Directed Learning, 1*(2); 38–52.

Turunen, H., Taskinen, H., Voutilainen, U., Tossavainen, K., & Sinkkonen, S. (1997). Nursing and social work students' initial orientation towards their studies. *Nurse Education Today, 17,* 67–71.

Walvoord, B. E., & Anderson, V. A. (2010). *Effective grading: A tool for learning and assessment in college* (2nd ed.). San Francisco, CA: Jossey-Bass.

Westphal, C. (2008, April). Learning never stops: Keys to lifelong learning. *Access, 1,* 26–29.

CHAPTER 16

BLENDING FOR SUSTAINABILITY

Aligning the Needs of Adult Learners and the Needs of Health Sciences Education

Paige L. McDonald, Howard O. Straker,
and Laurie B. Lyons
*The George Washington University
School of Medicine and Health Sciences*

Creating sustainable futures for adult learners requires that higher education provide access to knowledge and skills learners require in a competitive economic environment. Barriers to adult participation in higher education such as accessibility, affordability, accountability, program structure and duration, and a lack of student support (Advisory Committee on Student Financial Assistance, 2012; Deggs, 2011) threaten the ability of adults to remain sustain a competitive edge in the workforce. Correspondingly, institutions of higher learning are receiving increasing pressure to "provide affordable, sustainable approaches" (Beckem & Watkins, 2012, p. 61) that

Building Sustainable Futures for Adult Learners, pages 341–360
Copyright © 2015 by Information Age Publishing
All rights of reproduction in any form reserved.

impart the skills their students need to survive in an ever changing, knowledge-based economy (Berrett, 2011; Newman, Couturier & Scurry, 2004).

Healthcare professionals are currently in high demand, and the Association of American Medical Colleges (2006) and other agencies have called for expanding the number of health professionals to be trained. Unfortunately, health professions education, particularly medical education, relies heavily on traditional delivery models with little flexibility in schedules, limiting access to adult learners (Prober & Heath, 2012). Health professions education begins with a classroom phase that provides introductory and background facts for expertise knowledge. It also introduces the profession's problem solving process, but in a simplified way. Next, students participate in an apprenticeship/internship/practicum where they learn from professionals on the job as they solve more complex problems. But, there is also recognition of the need to expand curricula and incorporate more interactive processes, such as problem-based and case based learning, which promote critical thinking and application of concepts (Liaison Committee on Medical Education, 2013), earlier in program curricula. This recognition challenges instructors to employ active learning strategies that allow content application in real-world settings, while also negotiating increasing class sizes.

Blended learning models offer promise in negotiating the competing demands in health professions education. Yet, questions remain as to how to redesign traditional model of face-to-face delivery into a blended model that meets the education needs of future healthcare professionals. Further, while adoption of blended learning may promote the flexibility required for adult learners to gain access to health professions education, little is known at this time about how alternative delivery models will be accepted within disciplines heavily reliant on traditional models of delivery.

This chapter reviews the redesign of *Health, Justice, and Society* (HSJ) from a traditional face-to-face model of delivery to a blended model. HSJ is a first semester course in the physician assistant (PA) program at the George Washington University (GWU). Adopting a blended delivery model promised to increase flexibility and negotiate the tension of increasing class size while adopting an instructional design that supports higher levels of learning and, ideally, encourages future reflective practice. Course redesign required an interdisciplinary approach that combined expertise in PA curricula, blended learning design, and adult learning theory. This chapter first reviews relevant literature, which includes learning models selected to guide our course redesign. Next, the chapter describes lessons learned after facilitating the newly designed course and our plans for future modifications. Finally, the chapter ends with a discussion of recommendations for other institutions considering adoption of blended learning in traditional programs.

RELEVANT LITERATURE AND PEDAGOGICAL APPROACH

Blended Learning

Blended learning, which comprises both face-to-face and online instruction (Bonk & Graham, 2006), has gained recent support in higher education because it offers the flexibility of online learning environments while permitting the face-to-face interaction promoted by the traditional model of delivery (Allen, Seaman, & Garrett, 2007; Graham, Woodfield, & Harrison, 2013; Norberg, Dzuiban, & Moskal, 2011). Research confirms that blended courses can provide meaningful learning experiences for adult learners because they allow learners to share their experiences in a variety of interaction mediums, minimize feelings of isolation and alienation some students experience in online courses, and offer exposure to a variety of learning resources (Dzakiria, Wahab, Sobri, Rahman, & Dato, 2012; Lotrecchiano, McDonald, Lyons, Long & Farber, 2013; McDonald, 2012). Moreover, adult learners value course designs that present options, allow personalization and self-directedness, present variety, and support a learning community (Ausburn, 2004; McDonald, 2012). McDonald (2012) also found that adult learners value the increased learning they feel they gain in blended courses as compared to other delivery models.

Adoption of blended models in traditional health sciences curricula, such as a PA programs, could prove critical to the sustainability and efficacy of those programs while securing greater access to education adult learners require to gain access to high demand professions. The established benefits of blended learning align with the demands of PA education: increased student participation in course activities (Geçer & Dag, 2012), student perceptions of improved analytical skills (Chen & Jones, 2007) and increased sense of community and connectedness (Carter-Brown, 2009; Comey, 2009; Lotrecchiano et al., 2013), increased ability to apply course concepts in the field (Chen & Jones, 2007), and increased reflection upon action and future reflective practice (Cooner, 2010). Some PA education programs have used online technology for one or two courses within a traditional face-to-face context (Brock, Ballweg, Wick, & Byorth, 2005; Day, Smith, & Muma, 2006; Day & Hale, 2005), most in conjunction with their traditional programs, such as University of Wisconsin and Wingate University. Yet, PA literature does not specifically address blended learning. However, organizers of a recent conference noticed that a handful of PA programs are beginning to use blended learning format in some classes (Physician Assistant Education Association, 2013 conference brochure).

Studies looking at blending learning are beginning to appear in the health sciences literature. Advanced practice nursing was one of the first health professions to use online learning with several online nurse practitioner programs; thus, it is no surprise that the nursing profession is using and studying blended learning (Hsu, 2012; Stephens & Hennefer, 2013). Blended learning studies are also appearing in relation to physical therapy (Bello-Hass, Proctor, & Scudds, 2013), pharmacy (Ortega-Rivas, Saorín, de la Torre, & Elsheikha, 2013) and medical education (Duque et.al. 2013; Sánchez-Mendiola et al., 2013; Stewart, Inglis, Jardine, Koorts, & Davies, 2013). Additional research is required regarding how to design blended courses for health professions education to align with the needs of adult learners.

Course Description and Pedagogical Approach

HSJ is a two credit, first semester course designed to introduce new PA students to the social dynamics of health. Because this is one of the first classes for a new cohort of students and because it deals with psychologically sensitive issues, promoting a sense of community among the students is essential. Yet, incorporating the social interaction required to promote a learning community and the individual reflection required to encourage future reflective practice in cohorts comprised of over 60 students can prove challenging in a traditional model of delivery. Fostering a sense of community becomes even more difficult given that classes are held in a theatre style lecture hall. In addition, students within the cohort represent different backgrounds, age groups, and levels of experience within healthcare settings, creating challenges with regard to designing a learning experience aligned with student needs and experience levels.

Redesigning HSJ as a blended course offered promise in negotiating pedagogical challenges. It also promoted increased flexibility in content delivery and course scheduling, creating a design more aligned with the needs of working adult learners (Allen et al., 2007; Dzakiria et al., 2012; Graham et al., 2013; McDonald, 2012; Norberg et al., 2011; Soares, 2009). Adding an online component allows didactic materials, such as readings and lectures, to be placed online, enabling increased autonomy in where and when students review course materials. It also allows for more distributed time for reflection and reduces the need for faculty to devote valuable face-to-face time to review concepts. Face-to-face class sessions can be reserved for the application of knowledge and further discussion of concepts among peers and faculty, which are critical to achieving higher levels of learning (Illeris, 2003).

While there are many definitions of blended learning, the designers had specific pedagogical goals for course redesign, so we adopted a definition aligned with those goals. Picciano (2009) defines blended learning as the integration of online and traditional face-to-face class activities "in a planned, pedagogically valuable manner" wherein a portion of face-to-face time is replaced by online activity (p. 10). In our redesign, we focused less on replacing face-to-face class sessions with online sessions and more on how we could purposively structure a relationship between online and face-to-face activities to support pedagogical objectives. As a happy consequence, we were able to reduce the amount of required face-to-face time.

Blending for Future Reflective Practice

The complexity of today's healthcare environment necessitates that future practitioners not only learn facts, procedures, and problem-solving but that they also learn to apply that knowledge in situations often more complicated than they experience in school. As a result, health sciences education has begun promoting to focus on developing reflective practitioners (Dannefer, 2013; Kinsella, 2009; Maree & Van Rensburg, 2013). One of our course goals was to structure the course to promote future reflective practice among our PA students. Correspondingly, we borrowed from Schön (1983, 1987), one of the more popular models in health sciences education.

Schön's (1983; 1987) theory of reflective practice borrows heavily from experiential learning theory, which conceptualizes learning as a process resulting from the interaction of an individual with his or her environment (Dewey, 1916, 1938). Reflection allows an individual to progress beyond mere memorization of facts and procedures, to critical assessment of current problems in comparison to previous experiences to determine appropriate future action (Dewey, 1916, 1938; Kolb, 1984). Schön describes the dialogic relationship between reflection and action as essential to reflective practice. Developing the ability to reflect-in-action and reflect-on-action enables practitioners to know how to respond skillfully to complex situations (Schön). When applied in educational situations, promoting reflection-in-action may involve providing learning experiences in which students can compare a new or surprising situation to previous knowledge to complete a task or solve a problem. Enabling reflection-on-action would require providing opportunities for students to think about how the learning experiences altered their knowledge or understanding of a concept and what they would do differently in future practice based upon their new knowledge (Schön).

Bliuc, Goodyear, and Ellis (2010) and McDonald (2012) found a relationship between perceptions of the integration of online and face-to-face class sessions in a blended course and perceptions of level of learning. So, structuring the relationship between online and face-to-face class sessions became a priority in course redesign, and we used Schön's (1983, 1987) as our guide. We designed our course to include online discussions, quizzes, or collaborative assignments prior to face-to-face class, which we hoped would promote meta-cognitive awareness of their own biases, beliefs, and assumptions prior to applying concepts to "real-world" scenarios in face-to-face classes. The face-to-face sessions were reserved for application of these concepts in simulated "real-world" scenarios, which were designed to promote reflection-in-action by posing new and perhaps more challenging questions and problems than previously considered, encouraging students to think differently about decisions or conclusions drawn in online postings. Debriefs following these scenarios allowed students to verbalize new ways they had come to consider course material or new challenges raised by the activities.

To facilitate reflection-on-action, we required that students complete an online journal entry at the end of each week. Journal prompts were carefully crafted to encourage students to reflect upon their interactions with course content during the week to capture how their thought processes may have changed and to promote meta-cognitive awareness of individual learning. Prompts also asked how students thought the knowledge they gained would influence their future practice, which is important given that the students would not begin clinical rotations until their second year in the program. Ideally, because the journals reside online, the students can keep them and perhaps use them once they are placed in clinical settings. At the least, we are hoping that the course structure will encourage students to adopt a formal mode of reflection (such as journaling) as a part of their future clinical practice.

Blending for Increased Interaction

The potential divergence between healthcare problems future PAs solve while in school and problems they face in actual practice (Tate, 2003) requires learners who can apply knowledge from previous experiences to new, perhaps more complex situations. Correspondingly, PA education must prepare them to engage in higher levels of learning characterized by the ability to apply knowledge to new and differing situations (Illeris, 2003; Kolb, 1984). McDonald (2012) found that students in blended courses report higher levels of learning when they experience a relationship among course components allowing a process of reflection, application, interaction, and self-regulation. Interaction in both the online and face-to-face class sessions facilitated this process. Students who reflected upon a topic (by answering an online discussion question) and discussed the topic with peers prior to class sessions reported that they could take their discussions to a deeper, more meaningful level in the face-to-face sessions. The blended format allowed all students to apply the content in multiple environments and to interact in multiple environments, which was critical to their understanding of course concepts and future application of those concepts in real-world scenarios. Finally, seeing their own responses to online discussions and their peers' responses to their answers made them think more critically and, perhaps, change their opinions on issues and ideas (McDonald, 2012).

Experiential learning theories (Dewey, 1916, 1938; Kolb, 1984) indicate how reflection and application can generate new knowledge for use in future situations. However, they fall short of explaining how interaction with peers and with the instructor in the learning contexts influences learning and self-regulation. Interaction is perceived of as "the defining attribute for quality and value in online learning experience" (Wagner, 2006, p. 44). Social learning theories (Bandura, 1986; Illeris, 2003) posit that feedback from the social environment facilitates knowledge generation because it enables determination of whether actions match desired intentions (Bandura, 1986; Illeris, 2003). Repeated interactions in learning environments enable anticipation of consequences of future actions, permitting the personal agency necessary for individuals to exercise control over learning (Bandura, 1986; 2001). Consequently, we designed our course to promote interaction and application of concepts in both the online and face-to-face learning environments to encourage a learning process involving reflection, interaction, application, and self-regulation.

Blending for Communities of Inquiry

PAs do not work in isolation. So, it is vital that their programs of study facilitate an understanding of how to work with others to solve complex problems and to negotiate constructively in the solution-building process. HSJ addresses controversial topics, which require students to think critically about their own assumptions and beliefs while negotiating and challenging the beliefs and assumptions of their peers. Recent trends in toward collaborative learning in online environments are based on the social constructivist assumption that "an individual person constructs his or her knowledge through the process of negotiating meaning with others . . . cognitive development is highly dependent on social interaction and collaboration with more capable and knowledgeable others" (So & Bush, 2007, p. 3) and stem from the need to shift focus from the delivery of content to the development of higher learning skills (So & Bush). The Community of Inquiry model (Garrison, Anderson, & Archer, 2003; Garrison & Kanuka, 2004) is based on social constructivist principles for online learning. Based on this model, instructors aim to build the sense of community required to create a safe environment in which students can negotiate the meaning of controversial issues related to future practice. Building communities of inquiry requires social, cognitive, and teaching presence whether in an online or face-to-face class setting (Garrison & Kanuka; Garrison et al.)

Building community in a course comprised of 67 students can prove challenging. So, for the online discussions preceding face-to-face class sessions, we divided students into smaller groups of six or seven students. Students remained in these groups for the duration of the course, which allowed them to build the social presence and familiarization necessary to feel comfortable sharing experiences related to controversial topics and to debate those topics without fear of reprisal. To negotiate the challenge of reading individual discussion posts of 67 students, we asked the groups to post summaries of their discussions in a whole-course discussion board. We used the summaries to guide our planning of face-to-face class sessions. Consequently, face-to-face sessions were somewhat emergent. In Week 4, in response to student feedback, we adopted a practice by which we allowed students to determine the content of face-to-face discussions to allow them more input into topics they wanted to discuss in more detail. Based on their online discussions in small groups, they could post a "Hot Topic" for discussion at the beginning of the next face-to-face sessions.

For discussions in the face-to-face class sessions, we reassigned groups to promote a sense of community among the larger group and to allow students to take their group discussions to a deeper level of understanding by encouraging them to apply the meanings they negotiated in their online groups to new scenarios, furthering opportunities to increase their own levels of learning and their consideration of how course concepts might related to future practice. Transitioning between their online groups with consistent membership and face-to-face groups with changing membership also exposed students to a wider variety of peer experiences, increasing their opportunity to consider the variety of ways concepts related to practice. Instructors ensured faculty presence by reading group discussions and summaries, commenting on them in the online forum and in the face-to-face class sessions, and monitoring discussions in the classroom.

Evaluation

We were very interested evaluating this course, since this was the first time using a blended learning format within the PA program. So, we used multiple sources of evaluation at different times throughout the semester to assess student satisfaction and the quality of work in course assignments. Table 16.1 captures the evaluation modes and results. We had five to ten minute check-ins at the start of each face-to-face session, which provided continuous feedback. At the semester mid and endpoints we administered surveys of various lengths to gage student satisfaction with the format and its structural elements as well as whether the online and face-to-face learning activities supported learning. Open comments were included with every survey, so we could obtain qualitative date. We also held a final face-to-face

TABLE 16.1 Evaluation of HSJ Course Redesign

Assessed Area	Evaluation Method	Time	Results
Student concerns	Oral discussion	Beginning of each face to face session	Students requested more structure
Student satisfaction with blended format	Online open ended survey	Mid-course	50% liked the blended format
Student perceptions of level of challenge and workload	Online University end-of-course evaluations	End of course	• One third felt challenged • One third felt unchallenged
Student perceptions of supports for learning • Online elements aligned with f2f • Online assignments prepared for f2f • F2F reinforced online activities	Online course specific blended learning survey	End of course	Mixed reviews on support for learning: • 40% agree 40% disagree • 38% agree 44% disagree • 32% agree 31% disagree
Student satisfaction with course elements: • VoiceThread assignment • Online lectures • Online journals • Online videos • Wiki assignment • F2F discussions	In-class audience response system poll	Final course session	• Approximately 50% satisfaction with VoiceThread, online lectures and journals • 60% unsatisfied with Wiki • 100% satisfied with f2f discussions
Faculty assessment of student learning	Faculty assignment review	Throughout course	Majority of students demonstrated synthesis of materials, reflection on personal assumptions

evaluation session using an audience response system survey to assess the student's satisfaction and experience with various course media. We then reviewed responses to each question during the class, which provided us with additional understanding of students' responses. To assess course effectiveness, we continuously assessed students' work throughout the semester, looking for evidence that they were meeting course objectives.

LESSONS LEARNED

With our course redesign, we achieved success in increasing interaction, guiding students toward deeper reflection, creating communities of inquiry, and pushing the students into levels of higher learning. However, we struggled with modulating the amount of interaction, the uniqueness of this course within the program, the amount of structure, student perceptions, and the use of technology. Herein are our lessons learned.

Increasing and Promoting Interaction

The new course structure greatly improved the level and quality of course interactions. Previous iterations of this course in a classroom setting did not foster interaction among students and between students and the instructor. Only a small number of voices were heard from the 60 plus students. Most did not actively speak, and several had expressed discomfort with spontaneous public speaking. In the redesigned course, students interacted in small groups both online and face-to-face. They enjoyed the interaction, which was one of the highest rated areas in the end of course evaluations. Many students commented that the online and small group discussions provided them an opportunity to have a voice in class, particularly those not comfortable speaking in class. Some commented that the online interactions forced them to compose their thoughts before posting, and they were then able to see their own thoughts as they interacted with their classmates. Many valued reading responses of peers in online discussions. These results correspond with previous findings on the value of online interaction to the blended course structure (McDonald, 2012).

However, while our blended course structure increased interaction among students and between students and faculty, students did not readily see the distinction between the levels of online and in face-to-face class discussions. Consequently, some did not consider the online discussion a valuable part of their learning experiences, even though faculty noted how the level of familiarity gained in online discussions improved the quality and depth of the in-person discussions. Additionally, students indicated a desire for more immediate feedback from faculty on individual discussion board postings, rather than faculty comments on group summaries. Student responses correspond to assertions from blended learning literature that the amount and type of faculty involvement in online discussions influences the level of student engagement (Lee & Dashew, 2011). While Lee and Dashew recommend that faculty respond to at least the initial postings of students and, perhaps, send private emails on quality of postings, they do not offer advice on how to manage the workload in high enrollment courses. Alternating weekly discussions with other types of assignments may be the best option for faculty responsible for large numbers of students. Ocak (2011) found that faculty reluctance to facilitating blended courses relates to the additional time it requires as compared to face-to-face courses, particularly in managing the online portion of the course. Ocak's recommendations include setting very clear guidelines on the type of faculty interaction and feedback students can anticipate. Still, additional research is required provide guidance on how to ensure adequate faculty participation online discussion in courses with high enrollments.

Reflection

The pattern of pre-classroom online discussions, face-to-face discussions, and post activity journaling produced a pattern of reflective practice (Schön's 1983, 1987). Reflection-in-action and reflection-on-action were evidenced through the student's online writings, during the face-to-face class sessions, and in journal entries. The face-to-face interactions were lively and built on the pre-classroom discussions. We observed the students reflection-in-action as they discussed answers to new questions combined with the new perspectives from their classmates or the activities in class (like role playing). The journals at the week's end demonstrated various depths of reflection stemming from the week's activities. Many students noted how their underlying assumptions were challenged or reinforced. This did not occur for everyone each week, but most had this type of reflection at some point in the course, confirming previous findings that blended courses can promote reflection in large cohorts (Cooner, 2010).

Collaboration and Building Communities of Inquiry

Another goal of our course design was to create communities of inquiry among these students new to the physician assistant program. The purpose for forming communities of inquiry was to socialize the students into learning collectively to promote critical thinking and negotiate meaning (Garrison & Vaughan, 2008). Our experience confirms previous findings that blended courses can promote the increased connectedness and sense of community (Carter-Brown, 2009; Comey, 2009; Lotrecchiano et al., 2013) required to allow meaning negotiation. Throughout the semester the students consistently worked on assignments and had online discussions with an assigned peer group. We sought to facilitate a safe environment in both the online and face-to-face environments, so the community of students could tackle controversial issues. These safety zones allowed them to critically think about personal assumptions that may affect care of their patients in future practice. Evidence of their learning through the communities of inquiry was found in the online and face-to-face discussions, VoiceThread comments on ethics cases, and in the evaluations.

Promoting Higher Levels of Learning and Application

Our course redesign achieved higher levels of learning, as demonstrated by the synthesis and application of course concepts in multiple scenarios (Illeris, 2003; Kolb, 1984). One example of application is the students' creation of a wiki about the epidemiology of locale populations. After learning some basic epidemiologic concepts, each team created a profile of an assigned community. The students took the newly acquired knowledge of epidemiology concepts and applied them to a specified community. Another example involves the learning that occurred in discussing ethics cases. Through readings and intense discussions followed by narrated team presentations, the students applied a synthesis of personal experiences, ethical principles, and a framework to ethical clinical dilemmas they could face in future practice. In face-to-face discussions the teams resolved their ethical dilemmas, reinforcing that the course structure facilitated opportunities for the students to demonstrate higher levels of learning.

However, we were challenged in another way while trying to promote higher levels of learning and learned the true meaning of reflection in action. Because this was the students' first semester and they were not yet in clinical settings, our reflection-in-action often involved further discussion (Schön, 1983, 1987). So, when they reflected later in their journals it was not upon actual actions taken. While we saw value in this reflect on action step, students perceived these additional discussions as redundant. Future course designs must include more activities that allow students to take action on the materials they have read or viewed in online lectures, so they can experience the actual application of knowledge in different situations required for higher levels of learning (Illeris, 2003; Kolb, 1984).

The impact of the physical environment provided a lesson for restructuring courses to encourage application of knowledge. In several weeks, we were successful in designing scenarios in which students could practice or act upon knowledge gained through readings and online lectures. However, the lecture hall setting of our face-to-face class inhibited these activities. The physical setting prohibited the more intimate interactions required for role-play or simulation of patient/provider interactions. As much consideration should be given to the physical course environment as is often given to the design of the virtual environment for online courses. Unfortunately, this is extremely difficult to do in a packed urban campus.

Encouraging a New Paradigm of Learning

An unanticipated challenge to our course structure was students' resistance to a new paradigm of learning. A sizeable portion of the class suggested that they did not learn during this course; one third of the students responded that they did not learn much or feel challenged by the course. Yet, faculty review of the assignments quizzes, wiki, discussions (online and face-to-face), and reflective journals demonstrate that the majority of the students achieved a level of intellectual and emotional growth. Students particularly admitted to this within their reflective journals.

Dzuiban, Hartman, and Moskal (2004) note that blended learning requires students to relearn how to learn because methods they have used in previous modalities do not work in blended courses. Our students indicated a resistance to adopting new methods of learning delivery; in fact, they continually expressed a preference for formal lectures delivered in person and requested the "right answers" to controversial assignments, such as ethics cases. They seemed more comfortable with the paradigm of learning as transmission of information from an expert instructor to a student through lecture. This discomfort with active learning strategies offers a new avenue for future research. White, Pinnegar, and Esplin (2010) argue that students such as these often resist active learning formats because they have a content-based approach to learning, anticipating learning to come as contextual facts. Davidson (2011) notes that students do not always recognize the merit of active instructional methods when they are introduced. However, Davidson also found that over a three-year period there was a significant decrease in student ratings of lectures and a parallel increase in their ratings of team-based and online learning. This change mirrored the instructor's expertise and comfort with the new design.

Our course was not designed to be one where students engaged in rote memorization of factual knowledge. Rather, it was designed to encourage reflection on how healthcare disparities and unconscious bias might influence patient/provider interactions in future practice. Unfortunately, student perception of the course cannot accurately reflect learning (Thorn, 2003; White et al., 2003). However, better scaffolding might allow students to learn how to learn in blended courses before encountering more challenging content. Still, our experience raises questions about how to address student dependency upon transmission models of learning delivery in blended courses.

In addition to better scaffolding within courses, a larger lesson learned relates to the placement of courses using new blended methods within the degree program as a whole. Ours was the only course in our program using a blended format. Moreover, ours was one of the first courses students took, making adjustment to a new structure even more difficult. We believe the marked difference in our course structure from other courses in the program invited student criticism and inhibited adaptation to a new model of learning delivery. We are currently encouraging other courses in our program to adopt more of an online presence to increase familiarity with using online strategies in support of learning, particularly courses offered during the same semester students are taking our course. Additionally, future cohorts will be made aware that they will be participating in blended courses prior to enrollment. Blended courses need to be considered in the context of the program, not just individually.

Creating a Structure

Providing the amount of structure learners required in a blended course was challenging. We thought we had anticipated all of the structural needs of the students, and perhaps created too much structure. But as it turned out, we underestimated the students' needs for structure. In the first few weeks of the course, they repeatedly requested additional guidelines. Feedback also emphasized the importance of establishing a rhythm to activities early in the course. For example, if we had an online discussion prior to the face-to-face session in the first week, we should continue that pattern for several weeks before changing it, to allow them to adapt to a new pattern of activities before changing the sequencing in later weeks. Another challenge related to our course week starting on a different day than other courses in their program of study. Students found it difficult to adapt to our course week because all of their other courses began on Monday and ended on Friday. This may help explain their initial resistance to the blended structure. However, we were assigned a face-to-face class day of Tuesday each week, and to allow students to reflect and discuss topics online prior to the face-to-face session, we needed to adjust the course week accordingly. In the future we will request a face-to-face class day later in the week to allow the course week to start on Monday.

Determining Content and Activities

When designing the learning materials and activities for the course, we carefully considered the amount of time it would take students to complete all weekly activities. We purposely removed readings, assignments, and activities or redesigned activities and interactions to avoid the class and a half syndrome in which online requirements are simply added to an existing face-to-face course without being integrated (Kaleta, Skibba, & Joosten, 2007). Despite this, many of the students commented that the course took up too much of their time or required more work than other courses. It is not usual for there to be perceptions of greater workload and more difficulty with time management in blended courses than in traditional format courses (Banerjee, 2011; Napier, Dekhane, & Smith, 2011). However, it is difficult to gage the average time the students spent on assignments and media as the range was large. When asked how many hours a week they were spending, responses were between four and six hours a week, which is appropriate for a two-credit course, depending on prior knowledge of course material and learning style. In another example, students reported they spent between one and six hours a week preparing VoiceThread presentations alone. Upon reflection, we have realized that this format may initially feel as if it takes more time than the traditional face-to-face format because students are adjusting to a new model of delivery while learning course content (Dzuiban et al., 2004). Also, research indicates the need to assess student skill in time management prior to engagement in blended courses (McDonald, 2012; Tabor, 2007), so we may need to prepare our students to manage their time in a blended courses differently than in their other courses. Also, future versions of the course will reconsider workload, perhaps lightening the workload at the beginning of the semester until students have adjusted to the course structure.

Selecting Technologies

It is challenging to determine how much and what types of technologies to adopt in a blended course. We decided to use online lectures and discussion boards as the primary technologies. However, we also included small group wiki and VoiceThread assignments. Student feedback indicated that we were a bit overzealous in our use of technologies. They would have preferred to use one or two tools consistently rather than alternating between them. Alternating between technologies may have proven even more challenging because students were adjusting to the first semester of a new program and ours was the only blended course. Picciano (2009) recommends selecting technologies to align with pedagogical goals, which we did. However, McDonald (2012) also found that students gain greater mastery over the use of technology after experiencing successive blended courses. So, in the future we will limit the use of new technologies early in the program to allow students to adjust to them. Subsequent courses can adopt more sophisticated and varied technologies once students have adjusted to the new model of learning.

CONCLUSION AND RECOMMENDATIONS

Through our redesign of PA 6210 we learned that adoption of a new learning model is achievable in a discipline reliant upon a traditional model of learning delivery. Redesign of this course was the first step in encouraging adoption of blended learning across our PA program, opening the door for increased adult learner participation in education leading to a career in this high demand field with an ever expanding curriculum. Yet, course redesign is not to be taken lightly. Even though we had the support of instructional designers and technological experts and based our redesign on pedagogically sound practices, after delivering our newly designed course we recognized the need for several improvements. We caution those considering adoption of new learning models that the first redesign may not be perfect. Utilizing several evaluation methods throughout the first delivery will allow continual refinement to achieve a design meeting both pedagogical goals and student needs.

Still, our redesign of *HSJ* suggests that a blended learning model can support development of skills and knowledge student physician assistants require in future practice, including reflective practice, application of knowledge in a variety of contexts, and the ability to work in teams to negotiate complex problems. The blended model also provides the flexibility that adult learners required when engaging in higher education. Yet, adoption of blended learning in traditional programs is challenged by both the learner's expectation of learning as a transmission process from instructor to student and by the need to scaffold courses to allow students to adopt technology skills for learning in order to focus more on the process of learning and less on learning the technologies. Our pilot also suggests that testing a new model in a program in which all other courses are delivered in a traditional format invites resistance and criticism from students. In order to promote acceptance of flexible learning models promoting the active learning that support adult participation in high demand fields, blended learning should be considered holistically within the context of the degree program.

REFERENCES

Advisory Committee on Student Financial Assistance (ACFSA) (2012). *Pathways to success: Integrating learning with life and work to increase national college completion.* Report to the U. S. Congress and Secretary of Education. Retrieved from www.ed.gov

Allen, I. E., Seaman, J., & Garrett, R. (2007). Blending in: The extent and promise of blended education in the United States. The Sloan Consortium. Retrieved from www.sloanconsortium.org/publications/survey/pdf/Blending_In.pdf

Association of American Medical Colleges. (2012). *AAMC Statement on the Physician Workforce 2006.* Retrieved from https://www.aamc.org/download/304026/data/2012aamcworkforcepolicyrecommendations.pdf

Ausburn, L. J. (2004). Course design elements most valued by adult learners in blended online education: An American perspective. *Education*

Media International, 41(4). Retrieved from http://www.tandfonline.com/doi/abs/10.1080/0952398042000314820

Bandura, A. (2001). Social cognitive theory: An agentic perspective. *Annual Review Psychology, F–52*, 1–26.

Bandura, A. (1986). *Social foundations of thought and action: A social cognitive theory.* Englewood Cliffs, NJ: Prentice-Hall.

Banerjee, G. (2011). Blended environments: Learning effectiveness and student satisfaction at a small college in transition. *Journal of Asynchronous Learning Networks, 15*(1), 8–19. Retrieved from http://search.ebscohost.com/login.aspx?direct=true&db=eric&AN=EJ918215&site=ehost-live; http://sloanconsortium.org/jaln/v15n1/blended-environments-learning-effectiveness-and-student-satisfaction-small-college-transi

Beckem, J. M., & Watkins, M. (2012). Bringing life to learning: Immersive experiential learning simulations for online and blended courses. *Journal of Asynchronous Learning Networks, 16*(5), 61–70.

Bello-Haas, V., Proctor, P., & Scudds, R. (2013). Comparison of knowledge and knowledge application confidence in physical therapist students completing a traditional versus blended learning professional issues course. *Journal of Physical Therapy Education, 27*(1), 10–19.

Berrett, D. (2011, September 25). Which core matters more? Differences in definitions of quality lead to new debates over the importance of teaching practical skills versus specific knowledge. *The Chronicle of Higher Education.* Retrieved from http://chronicle.com.proxygw.wrlc.org/article/In-Improving-Higher-Education/129314

Bliuc, A. M., Goodyear, P., & Ellis, R. (2010). Blended learning in higher education: How students perceive integration of face-to-face and online learning experiences in a foreign policy course. In *Higher Education Research and Development Society of Australasia (HERDSA) Conference, 2010.* Melbourne, 6–9 July 2010.

Bonk, C., & Graham, C. (2006). *Handbook of blended learning: Global perspectives and local designs.* San Francisco, CA: Pfeiffer Publishing.

Brock, D., Ballweg, R., Wick, K. H., & Byorth, K. (2005). On-line collaborative exercises: The implications of anonymous participation. *Journal of Physician Assistant Education, 16*(1), 13–17.

Carter-Brown, C. B. (2009). *Building communities: The effects of offering face-to-face meetings to students studying at a distance.* (Doctoral Dissertation). Retrieved from Proquest.

Chen, C., & Jones, T. (2007). Blended learning vs. traditional classroom settings: Assessing effectiveness and student perceptions in an MBA accounting course. *The Journal of Educators Online, 4*(1), 1–15. Retrieved from http://eric.ed.gov

Comey, W. (2009). *Blended learning and the classroom environment: A comparative analysis of students' perception of the classroom environment across community college courses taught in traditional face-to-face, online and blended methods* (Ed.D. The George Washington University). ProQuest Dissertations and Theses. Retrieved from http://search.proquest.com.proxygw.wrlc.org/pqdtft/docview/288045934/F5BED03F694041F4PQ/1?accountid=11243

Cooner, T. S. (2010). Creating opportunities for students in large cohorts to reflect in and on practice: Lessons learnt from a formative evaluation of students' experiences of a technology- enhanced blended learning design. *British Journal of Educational Technology, 41*(2), 271–286. doi: 10.1111/j.1467-8535.2009.00933.x

Dannefer, E. F. (2013). Beyond assessment of learning toward assessment for learning: Educating tomorrow's physicians. *Medical Teacher, 35,* 560–563. doi: 10.3109/0142159x

Davidson, L. K. (2011). A 3-year experience implementing blended TBL: Active instructional methods can shift student attitudes to learning. *Medical Teacher, 33*(9), 750–753. doi:10.3109/0142159X.2011.558948

Day, D. B., & Hale, L. S. (2005). Promoting critical thinking in online physician assistant courses. *Journal of Physician Assistant Education, 16*(2), 96–102.

Day, D. B., Smith, B., & Muma, R. D. (2006). The effectiveness of online courses in physician assistant education. *Journal of Physician Assistant Education, 17*(3), 33–36.

Deggs, D. (2011). Contextualizing the perceived barriers of adult learners in an accelerated undergraduate degree program. *Qualitative Report, 16*(6), 1540–1553.

Dewey, J. (1938). *Experience and education.* New York, NY: Kappa Delta Pi.

Dewey, J. (1916). *Democracy and education: An introduction to philosophy of education.* New York, NY: Macmillan.

Duque, G., Demontiero, O., Whereat, S., Gunawardene, P., Leung, O., Webster, P., & Sharma, A. (2013). Evaluation of a blended learning model in geriatric medicine: A successful learning experience for medical students. *Australasian Journal on Ageing, 32*(2), 103–109. doi:10.1111/j.1741-6612.2012.00620.x

Dzakiria, H., Mohd, S., Rahman, A., & Dato, H. (2012). Blended learning (BL) as pedagogical alternative to teach business communication course: Case study of UUM executive diploma program. *The Turkish Online Journal of Distance Education TOJDE, 13*(3), 297–315. Retrieved from http://files.eric.ed.gov/fulltext/EJ997824.pdfgoogl

Dziuban, C. D., Hartman, J. L., & Moskal, P. D. (2004). Blended learning. *EDUCAUSE Center for Applied Research Bulletin, 7,* 112.

Garrison, D. R., Anderson, T., & Archer, W. (2003). A theory of critical inquiry in online distance education. In M. G. Moore & W. Anderson (Eds.), *Handbook of Distance Education.* Mahwah, NJ: Erlbaum.

Garrison, D. R., & Kanuka, H. (2004). Blended learning: Uncovering its transformative potential in higher education. *The Internet and Higher Education, 7,* 95–105.

Garrison, D., & Vaughan, N. (2008). *Blended learning in higher education.* San Francisco, CA: John Wiley & Sons.

Geçer, A., & Dag, F. (2012). A blended learning experience. *Educational Sciences: Theory and Practice 12*(1), 438–442. Retrieved from http://akademikpersonel. kocaeli.edu.tr/akolburan/sci/akolburan18.10.2012_01.58.04sci.pdf

Graham, C. R., Woodfield, W., & Harrison, B. J. (2013). A framework for institutional adoption and implementation of blended learning in higher education. *Internet and Higher Education, 18,* 4–14, doi: 10.1016/j.iheduc.2012.09.003

Hsu, L. L. (2012). Qualitative assessment of a blended learning intervention in an undergraduate nursing course. *Journal of Nursing Research, 20*(4), 291–298. doi:10.1097/jnr.0b013e31827363bc

Illeris, K. (2003). Toward a contemporary and comprehensive theory of learning. *International Journal of Lifelong Education, 22*(4), 396–406.

Kaleta, R., Skibba, K., & Joosten, T. (2007). Discovering, designing, and delivering hybrid courses. In A. G. Picciano & C. D. Dziuban (Eds), *Blended learning: Research perspectives.* Needham, MA: Sloan-C.

Kinsella, E. A. (2009). Professional knowledge and the epistemology of reflective practice. *Nursing Philosophy, 11,* 3–14.

Kolb, D. A. (1984). *Experiential learning: Experience as a source of learning and development.* Englewood Cliffs, NJ: Prentice Hall.

Liaison Committee on Medical Education (LCME) (2013). *Functions and Structure of Medical Education: Standards for Accreditation of Medical Education Programs Leading to the M.D. Degree.* Retrieved from http://www.lcme.org/publications/functions2013june.pdf.

Lee, R., & Dashew, B. (2011). Designed learning interactions in blended course delivery. *Journal of Asynchronous Learning Networks, 15*(1), 72–80.

Lotrecchiano, G. R., McDonald, P. L., Lyons L., Long T., & Farber M. (2013). Blended learning: Strengths, challenges, and lessons learned in an interprofessional training program. *Maternal and Child Health Journal, 17,* 1725–1734. doi: 10.1007s/10995-012-1175-8

Maree, C., & Van Rensburg, G. H. (2013, September). Reflective learning in higher education: Application to clinical nursing. *African Journal for Physical, Health Education, Recreation and Dance,* (Supplement 1), 44–45.

McDonald, P. L. (2012). *Adult learners and blended learning: A phenomenographic study of variation in adult learners' experiences of blended learning in higher education.* (Doctoral dissertation, Ed.D. The George Washington University). ProQuest Dissertations and Theses. Retrieved from http://search.proquest.com/docview/992950856?accountid=11243.

Napier, N. P., Dekhane, S., & Smith, S. (2011). Transitioning to blended learning: Understanding student and faculty perceptions. *Journal of Asynchronous Learning Networks, 15*(1), 20–32. Retrieved from http://search.ebscohost.com/login.aspx?direct=true&db=eric&AN=EJ918216&site=ehost-live; http://sloanconsortium.org/jaln/v15n1/transitioning-blended-learning-understanding-student-and-faculty-perceptions

Newman, F., Couturier, L., & Scurry, J. (2004, October 15). Higher education isn't meeting the public's needs. *The Chronicle Review.* Retrieved from http://chronicle.com.proxygw.wrlc.org/article/Higher-Education-Isnt-Meeting/35297

Norberg, A., Dzuiban, C. D., & Moskal, P. D. (2011). A time-based blended learning model. *On the Horizon 19*(3), 207–216. Retrieved from http://search.proquest.com/docview/888254241

Ocak, M. A. (2011). Why are faculty members not teaching blended courses? Insights from faculty members. *Computers and Education, 56,* 689–699. Retrieved from www.elseviewr.com/locate/compedu

Ortega-Rivas, A., Saorín, J. L., de la Torre, J., & Elsheikha. H. (2013). Touch-pad mobile devices for blended learning in immunology practicals. *Medical Education, 47*(5), 518–519.

Physician Assistant Education Association (2013). 2013 PAEA Annual Educational Forum Proceedings/Educational Sessions. Retrieved http://forum.paeaonline.org/proceedings-ed-sessions/

Picciano, A. G. (2009). Blending with a purpose: The multi-modal model. *Journal of Asynchronous Learning Networks, 13*(1), 1–9.

Prober, C. G., & Heath, C. (2012). Lecture halls without lectures. *The New England Journal of Medicine, 366*(18), 1657–1659.

Sánchez-Mendiola, M., Martínez-Franco, A., Rosales-Vega, A., Villamar-Chulin, J., Gatica-Lara, F., García-Durán, R., & Martínez-González, A. (2013). Development and implementation of a biomedical informatics course for medical students: Challenges of a large-scale blended-learning program. *Journal of the American Medical Informatics Association, 20*(2), 381–387. doi:10.1136/amiajnl-2011-000796

So, H. J., & Brush, T. A. (2007). Student perceptions of collaborative learning, social presence and satisfaction in a blended learning environment: Relationships and critical factors. *Computers and Education.* doi: 10.1016/j.compedu.2007.05.009

Schön, D. A. (1987). *Educating the reflective practitioner.* San Francisco, CA: Jossey-Bass.

Schön, D. A. (1983). *The reflective practitioner: How professionals think in action.* New York, NY: Basic Books.

Soares, L. (2009, June). *Working learners: Educating our entire workforce for success in the 21st century.* Washington, DC: Center for American Progress.

Stephens, M., & Hennefer, D. (2013). Internationalising the nursing curriculum using a community of inquiry framework and blended learning. *Nurse Education in Practice, 13*(3), 170–175. doi:10.1016/j.nepr.2012.08.010

Stewart, A., Inglis, G., Jardine, L., Koorts, P., & Davies, M. W. (2013). A randomised controlled trial of blended learning to improve the newborn examination skills of medical students. *Archives of Disease in Childhood — Fetal & Neonatal Edition, 98*(2), F141–4. doi:10.1136/archdischild-2011-301252

Tabor, S. (2007). Narrowing the distance: Implementing a hybrid learning model for information security education. *The Quarterly Review of Distance Education, 8*(1), 47–57.

Tate, S. (2003). Educating for reflective practice. *The Journal of Alternative and Complementary Medicine, 9,* 773–777.

Thorn, P. M. (2003). *Bridging the gap between what is praised and what is practiced: Supporting the work of change as anatomy and physiology instructors introduce active learning into their undergraduate classroom.* (Ph.D., The University of Texas at Austin). ProQuest Dissertations and Theses. (305294245). Retrieved from http://search.proquest.com.proxygw.wrlc.org/docview/305294245?accountid=11243.

Wagner, E. (2006). On designing interaction experiences for the next generation of blended learning. In C. Bonk & C. Graham (Eds.). *The handbook of blended learning.* San Francisco, CA: Pfeiffer Publishing.

White, J., Pinnegar, S., & Esplin, P. (2010). When learning and change collide: Examining student claims to have "learned nothing". *Journal of General Education, 59*(2), 124–140. Retrieved from http://search.ebscohost.com/login.aspx?direct=true&db=eric&AN=EJ907008&site=ehost-live; http://dx.doi.org/10.1353/jge.2010.0007

CHAPTER 17

TRAINING MEDICAL FACULTY TO USE ADULT LEARNING PRINCIPLES AND MENTORING IN CLINICAL TEACHING

Kathy Peno
University of Rhode Island

Elaine M. Silva Mangiante
Salve Regina University

Rita A. Kenahan
Teacher's College, Colombia University

The cognitive apprenticeship model introduced to surgical training in the 1900s by William Halsted at Johns Hopkins continues to provide the framework for training surgeons (Kotsis & Chung, 2012). In surgical education, this model translates into academic surgeons serving their patients as well as trainees who include surgical residents receiving supervision before licensure and medical fellows seeking advanced specialty training. In their role as faculty, these surgeons may lack specific, deliberate training in

Building Sustainable Futures for Adult Learners, pages 361–383
Copyright © 2015 by Information Age Publishing

teaching skills to be effective teachers of trainees (Pernar, Ashley, Smink, Zinner, & Peyre, 2012). Recent changes have been implemented in medical schools in the way medical residents are assessed, with a move from time-based toward a competency-based model (Batalden, Leach, Swing, Dreyfus, & Dreyfus, 2002). A key principle of competency-based education, according to the Accreditation Council for Graduate Medical Education (ACGME), is a developmental view of professional knowledge and skill acquisition (Sullivan, Simpson, Cooney, & Beresin, 2013). To determine residents' development of proficiency in practice, specialty-specific milestones have been incorporated into their assessment process. As a result, it is vital that surgical faculty possess effective teaching and mentoring skills to assist residents' attainment of these milestones.

STATEMENT OF THE PROBLEM

While academic physicians assume a significant teaching and mentoring role, they have little formal training in education or a background in teaching and mentoring (Knapper, 1995; Pernar et al., 2012; Strowd & Reynolds, 2013). To be truly effective teachers, especially in light of the new ACGME milestones, surgical faculty need to possess skills in observation, assessment, feedback, instructional methods, mentorship, and small group teaching (Clark, Houston, Kolodner, Branch, Levine, & Kern, 2004). While surgical faculty may be experts in their particular domains of practice, they are called upon to teach a variety of adult learners including residents and fellows; yet, they are often left to rely on their former teachers as models for the development of their own pedagogical practice. The "see one, do one, teach one" concept that is the hallmark of the Halstedian cognitive apprenticeship model may be insufficient without the addition of the knowledge and use of adult learning principles and mentoring strategies (Kotsis & Chung, 2013). Therefore, this study sought to understand the effect of professional development in adult learning principles and mentoring on the teaching and mentoring practice of surgical faculty.

LITERATURE REVIEW

Surgical Faculty Development

Despite the lack of teaching instruction that surgical faculty have received, especially in adult learning theory and mentoring, research suggests that it is something they want and need (Kenahan, 2014; Peyre, Frankl, Thorndike, & Breen, 2011). While surgical faculty development programs are emerging around the country, a major lack of access to such instruction remains. In order to address this gap in pedagogical or, in terms of adult learners, andragogical knowledge and skills (Knowles, 1980), a professional development (PD) session was developed by the first author that included adult learning principles, adult learning styles, and mentoring training. This PD was requested by a medical device company to train surgical faculty how to improve their teaching of surgical residents and fellows in laboratory sessions.

Adult Learning Principles and Learning Style Preferences

According to Knowles (1980), adult learners are internally motivated and self-directed, bring valuable life experience and knowledge to their learning, are goal and problem-oriented, desire relevance, are practical in their pursuit of knowledge, and want to be treated with respect in the learning environment. These principles are especially useful for surgical faculty to understand and integrate into their interactions with trainees who come to the learning situation as highly educated and experienced individuals. Additionally important to adult learning is the notion of *teaching as learning* based on the work of Vygotsky (1986). Vygotsky termed the interaction of language and thought as the process of internalization, whereby language is transformed into inner speech and verbal thinking. Therefore, when a learner engages in teaching others what they have learned, this process can help them make sense of the concepts or skills being taught (John-Steiner & Mann, 1996). Use of this strategy is often called "teach back," whereby the trainee, after processing a new concept, must teach it back to the instructor in his own words (Kotsis & Chung, 2012).

In addition, the PD focused on developing and utilizing strategies for meeting the various sensory learning style preferences adults present – auditory, visual, tactile, and kinesthetic. Research suggests that adults learn best when their preferred sensory learning styles are met (Dunn, 1984). The PD provided an introduction to all of these principles and included instructors' roles, strategies for use, and a discussion about which strategies the faculty could integrate into their practice immediately.

Mentoring

Mentoring has an important place in the development of medical practitioners (Clark et al., 2004). Strowd and Reynolds (2013) offer a characterization of the role of the mentor as, "a voluntary and active participant in the personal and professional development of the mentee, offering knowledge, experience, guidance, support, and opportunity for advancement" (p. 244). While barriers to successful mentoring relationships exist, including time constraints and lack of resources, the most notable is the lack of adequate mentor training (Strowd & Reynolds, 2013). When assessing the prevalence and perceived importance of mentoring education in teaching hospitals in the U.S., researchers found that mentoring was rated fourth out of five on an importance scale, but only 38% of the programs reported teaching mentoring as part of their faculty development curriculum (Clark et al., 2004).

To meet the need for mentoring training, the PD included an introduction to the Purposeful Ongoing Mentoring Model (POMM) developed by the researchers (Peno & Silva Mangiante, 2012). This model provides a framework of mentoring for skill development, an obvious benefit in surgical training. The POMM contains three sections: *The Novice to Expert Model of Skill Acquisition* (Dreyfus & Dreyfus, 1980, 1986), *Goals* (for mentee development), and *Mentor Actions* (to assist mentee movement to a higher level of skill).

Novice to Expert Model of Skill Acquisition

Dreyfus and Dreyfus (1980, 1986) developed their model of professional skill development, the novice to expert model of skill acquisition (hereinafter referred to as "the skill model"), that illustrates growth over the course of a person's career in a particular domain. The skill model highlights a learner's movement across five levels of skill development: novice, advanced beginner, competent, proficient, and expert. As novices, new surgeons operate in a rules-based environment and lack the ability to understand the different contexts or situations they may encounter. As they move to advanced beginner, they begin to see exceptions to rules in some cases, but still struggle when handling challenging situations. As surgeons become competent in their practice, they begin to recognize which situations need attention and which can be ignored. They are able to see that general principles have application to a wide range of situations but can still spend a great deal of time deliberating over problems at this level. Proficient practice is recognized by the replacement of rules with situational intuition and the use of general principles tempered by experience; however, those who are proficient may still deliberate when making important decisions. At the expert level, practice is guided mainly by intuition and experience resulting from thousands of hours of reflective performance.

Goals for Skill Development and Mentor Actions

For this discussion, two sections of the POMM (goals and mentor actions) will be considered together. The goals portion of the POMM provides the mentor/mentee dyad with a focus for their interactions with attainment of the next level of skill in mind. Characteristics displayed at the succeeding skill level are utilized to set goals for the learning outcomes.

Mentor actions are grounded in the work of Vygotsky (1978), and in particular, employ the Zone of Proximal Development (ZPD) to describe how a mentor can scaffold the mentee's learning. Vygotsky defines the ZPD as "the distance between the actual development level as determined by independent problem solving and the level of potential development as determined through problem solving under adult guidance or in collaboration with a more capable peer" (p. 86). Therefore, the ZPD represents the difference between the learner's current level of development and the level that can be attained through effective collaboration with a more capable person. This collaboration consists of scaffolding on the part of the more capable person, a combination of challenge with support. The more capable peer provides a model for a higher level of practice through demonstration and/or explanation (challenge) while supporting (coaching and feedback) the learner's attempts to make sense of and emulate what is being taught. During the mentor/mentee collaboration, it may be the mentor, at first, who initiates the teaching and learning activities. Mentees may not be aware yet of what they do not know (Daley, 1999) or contexts they may face. As mentees gain experience, however, they may be more likely to initiate the collaborative learning process with questions and concerns about situations that arise. It is important to note that it is not sufficient for the more capable person or mentor to simply possess a higher level of knowledge or skill; he or she must exhibit the capability to scaffold effectively for maximum mentee learning to occur.

In a laboratory setting, the surgical faculty member, as mentor, would model the procedure being taught while verbalizing directions and providing examples or cases that relate to the procedure. The mentor would then provide the mentee with an opportunity to practice the procedure while offering specific feedback about the mentee's performance. Optimally, the trainee would teach-back the procedure to the surgical faculty member while practicing it. Once the surgical faculty as mentor was satisfied that the mentee's attempts at the procedure were correct, the mentor would fade the feedback and allow the mentee time to practice and hone the skill, thus advancing the mentee's skill level in the ZPD.

The Role of Reflection

The instruction and feedback process during scaffolding merits further explication. In his work, Schön (1983, 1987) explores the role of reflection in the learning process. According to Schön (1987), the mentor demonstrates with verbal instruction; the mentee observes, listens, and then imitates; and the mentor supplies critique on the mentee's practice. During instruction and demonstration, verbalizing the procedure on the part of the surgical faculty can "provide clues to the essential features" of the demonstration (Schön, 1987, p. 112). Allowing for the mentee's reflection during and/or after his practice can illuminate even subtle differences that need alteration. Then, the surgical faculty as mentor can take measures to help their trainees improve their practice. Faculty can encourage reflection on some particular aspect of practice, model alternate strategies, and provide feedback on the trainees' conception of a new approach. To do so, the surgical faculty could ask, "What happened when you tried that procedure?", "How well do you think that worked?", "Why do you think that happened?", "Explain, . . .", "An alternative approach might be . . .", "How effective do you think that strategy will be when working with x issue?", "How might you apply that strategy differently?", or "What result can you expect?" Together the surgical faculty and the trainee would discuss how the use of an alternate strategy might play out in the laboratory while performing a particular surgical procedure and, as a result, the trainee would be better prepared to perform that procedure in the future.

The researchers sought to understand the effect that PD comprised of adult learning principles, adult learning styles, and the POMM would have on the teaching and mentoring practice of surgical faculty participating in a weekend spine surgery course sponsored by a medical device company. The surgical faculty, as part of their agreement with the medical device company, provided instruction in the cadaver lab to the trainees. They were invited to a) attend the PD session, b) identify areas for improvement of their teaching, and c) integrate these strategies into their teaching of current spine surgery techniques with trainees during the course. To understand the effectiveness of the PD on the surgical faculty's teaching and the trainees' learning during the course, the following research questions were developed.

RESEARCH QUESTIONS

1. What was the nature of the surgical faculty teaching in the laboratory after the PD?
2. How do surgical faculty describe their use of adult learning principles, adult learning styles, and the POMM in their teaching in the laboratory with their trainees?
3. How do the trainees describe their experience as learners within the laboratory setting?

4. What recommendations do surgical faculty provide for the design of the PD and to sustain their implementation of strategies learned from the PD?

RESEARCH DESIGN AND METHODOLOGY

The research questions were investigated using qualitative design employing naturalistic inquiry (Erlandson, Harris, Skipper, & Allen, 1993). Naturalistic methodology was appropriate for this research given that the phenomenon under study involved examination of surgical faculty members' teaching practices and the trainees' learning in an authentic training setting.

Setting

The data were collected during a course sponsored by a medical device company where surgical faculty provided laboratory instruction in spine surgery techniques to trainees. As part of the course, surgical faculty voluntarily attended a PD session on effective teaching strategies. The PD, data collection activities, and the surgical training occurred over the course of three days at a clinical training site in Massachusetts.

Participants

The day prior to the spine surgery training, thirteen surgical faculty participated in a two-hour PD session. All attendees in the PD training were invited to volunteer for the study involving a twenty-minute interview and observation of their teaching in the laboratory. Of the twelve surgical faculty who agreed to participate in the study, nine were able to fit interviews into their schedule during the course, and eleven were observed teaching. The surgeons' pseudonyms are listed in Table 17.1 with their number of years experience as a surgeon and prior teaching experience and training in teaching. In addition, trainees taught by faculty participants were invited to participate in the study through focus group interviews rather than individual interviews due to their tightly scheduled course requirements. Four pre-fellows and one fellow participated in the interviews and were observed during a laboratory session under the tutelage of an assigned surgical faculty member.

Professional Development Session

The first author of this study facilitated the PD session presenting adult learning principles, adult learning styles, and the POMM in relation to the

TABLE 17.1 Experience Level and Prior Teaching of Surgical Faculty Interviewed and Observed

Pseudonym of Surgical Faculty	Years of Experience as a Spine Surgeon	Prior Education and Teaching Experience
Dr. Andrews	5	Some teaching in medical school (1st year medical trainees)
Dr. Davis	3	Academic assignment—3 years
Dr. Elwood	6	Academic assignment—6 years
Dr. Ferry	CV not provided	Unknown
Dr. Johnson	2	Academic assignment—2 years
Dr. Rasoud	<1	Taught for one year in medical school
Dr. Reed	13	Academic assignment—13 years
Dr. Samuelson	4	Clinical instructor in medical school—also received an MA in Education
Dr. Sewell	5	Academic assignment—5 years

surgical training context (Peno & Silva Mangiante, 2012). First, she introduced six adult learning principles (Knowles, 1980) via PowerPoint. Then, she provided participants with a worksheet outlining a faculty member's role in the use of adult learning principles with recommended instructional strategies. To assist the faculty members envision the strategies in practice, the facilitator showed viewed video clips of spine surgeons from a previous training session implementing the learning strategies with their trainees in a cadaver laboratory. Finally, the surgical faculty members who had consented to participate in the study were asked to select and commit to incorporating one or more strategies into their teaching during the laboratory sessions over the next two days. They listed their planned instructional activities on the worksheets, which were then collected and used as part of the data analysis. Copies were made and provided to the faculty for discussion during their interviews and were given to them to take as a reference for future teaching.

Additionally, the facilitator introduced the participants to the POMM (Peno & Silva Mangiante, 2012) and the five levels of the Dreyfus and Dreyfus Skill Model (1980, 1986) to help them understand skill development and strategies to use with their trainees in the laboratory. In small groups, the surgical faculty members identified characteristics and skill levels of their trainees, bearing in mind the skills they would teach them the following day. Once the surgical faculty placed their learners at a skill level, the facilitator introduced the goals component of the POMM, adapted from Ribeiro (2012). This component operationalizes movement from one level of the skill model to the next by considering the characteristics and abilities of individuals at the next level of skill and providing goals to attain these capabilities. With an understanding of the skill model levels and the goals to guide movement from one level to the next, the PD focused on the mentor actions component of the POMM. To assist faculty with implementation during the lab, the facilitator provided participants with a worksheet that outlined the skill levels along with goals for skill development and concomitant mentor actions. Each faculty member who agreed to participate in the study identified aspects of the POMM they would use in their teaching in the laboratory over the next two days. The facilitator collected these forms for data analysis as well.

Data Collection

As is typical with qualitative naturalistic inquiry, data were collected via observation, semi-structured interviews of both faculty and trainees, and document examination in an attempt to triangulate the data (Erlandson et al., 1993; Merriam, 1998). To minimize bias in the collection process, the first two authors engaged in observation of the laboratory training sessions as onlookers, not participants; thus, allowing them to separate the data collected from interviews from those observed in situ (Patton, 2002). The researchers, aware that the surgical faculty might behave differently when being observed for a scholarly study, took this factor into consideration in their analysis.

Observation
The observation data provided snapshots of time during the laboratory teaching. The surgical faculty members worked in pairs to teach two or three trainees in a laboratory at a table with a cadaver. There were a total of seven laboratory tables occupied by surgical faculty and their trainees. At five tables, one faculty member provided instruction. At two tables, a junior faculty member was paired with a senior faculty member whereby both provided instruction. The researchers observed surgical faculty as they taught trainees various spine surgery techniques and kept field notes on the teaching techniques observed during each three and a half hour lab session over a two-day period. The researchers spent equal time at each table observing teaching and learning interactions.

Semi-Structured Interviews
To eliminate conflict of interest, one researcher unaffiliated with the PD interviewed nine surgical faculty during the weekend between teaching sessions at a time convenient for each of them. Interviews were semi-structured and lasted approximately twenty minutes. Two of the nine surgical faculty members participated in a joint interview to accommodate their schedule.

Focus Group Interviews for Trainees

The researcher who provided the PD to the surgical faculty interviewed the trainees during focus group sessions held on the last day of the course at the completion of their training sessions. The focus group lasted approximately twenty minutes. Four of the five participants in the focus group had recently completed their surgical residency and were beginning their fellowship in a month's time. One of the participants had already completed one year as a surgical fellow and was returning for a second year with a different surgeon.

Document Examination

Each surgical faculty member provided the researchers with a curriculum vitae that indicated the extent of each member's teaching experience. In some cases, the documents showed evidence of training in teaching methods or awards for teaching. This information informed interview questions regarding each faculty member's knowledge of and experience with teaching methods. In addition, the researchers examined the worksheets the surgical faculty used to denote their intended actions for instruction and mentoring improvement.

Data Analysis

The analysis process involved a sequence of deductive and inductive examination of the data. First, the researchers read and reread observation field notes, document notes, and transcriptions of interviews using codes generated from the characteristics of adult learning principles (ALP) and the POMM to identify patterns in the data (Patton, 2002).

- Faculty provide modeling (POMM)
- Faculty provide feedback (POMM)
- Faculty have trainees reflect (POMM)
- Faculty draw on trainees experiences (ALP)
- Faculty ask questions (ALP and POMM))
- Faculty explain relevancy–the "why" of a procedure (ALP)
- Faculty provide hands-on experiences & real life examples (ALP)
- Faculty show respect for trainees (ALP)
- Faculty encourage trainees to teach each other (ALP)

Subsequently, three themes emerged inductively from a re-examination of the data corpus and the patterns among the categories using constant comparison (Erickson, 1986; Strauss & Corbin, 1990). Through this analysis, the researchers sought to identify themes to capture the similarities and differences between participants' teaching practices (Merriam, 1998). To increase the trustworthiness of the findings, a peer debriefer with expertise in adult education reviewed the data and analyses in order to clarify themes, provide alternative interpretations, and further refine the analysis (Erlandson et al., 1993).

RESULTS

Based upon examination of a) the worksheets that captured the participants' intended use of the strategies they learned in the PD, b) interviews with the participants of their reported use of strategies, c) interviews with trainees about their learning experience, and d) observations of surgical faculty teaching in the cadaver laboratory, a picture emerged of strengths and gaps in the faculty members' knowledge of teaching practices and adult learning strategies. The results from this study are reported in four sections to answer each of the research questions: a) nature of the surgical faculty teaching in the laboratory, b) surgical faculty members' description of their use of the PD in the course, c) description from trainees as learners in the lab setting, and d) recommendations from surgical faculty on the design of the PD session and how to sustain their implementation of the strategies learned.

Nature of the Surgical Faculty Teaching in the Laboratory

Based on analysis of the data from faculty reports and observations of the surgical faculty's use of the adult learning principles and mentoring techniques in their laboratory instruction, the following themes emerged, depicting the nature of their teaching after the PD:

1. The surgical faculty most readily implemented strategies based on practices that they could deliver through direct instruction that did not require trainees' responses.
2. Some surgical faculty implemented strategies that required engaging trainees in responses or thinking about trainees' performance.
3. The strategies least implemented by surgical faculty required more active processing of the learning with the trainees and more response expected of them.

Table 17.2 depicts the strategies that the surgical faculty wrote they intended to try in their teaching, those they reported actually trying, and those

TABLE 17.2   Faculty Intended Use, Reported Use and Observed Use of Strategies Learned in the PD

	Dr. Andrews	Dr. Davis	Dr. Elwood	Dr. Ferry	Dr. Rasoud	Dr. Johnson	Dr. Reed	Dr. Samuelson	Dr. Sewell
Model Skill	I R O	I O	O	I R O	R O	R O	O	R O	I O
Provide Feedback	O	O		I R O	R O	I	R O	I R O	
Time for Reflection	I	I R	I R		I R O				
Draw on trainees' experience	I R O	R	R	I R O	I R O	I	R O	R O	O
Ask questions	I O	R O			I R O	R	R O	R O	I R
Explain relevance	O	R O	O	O	R O	R O	O	O	I O
Hands on-and examples	R O	R O	O	R O	I R O	I R O	R O	R O	R O
Show respect for trainees	R O	R O	R O	I R O	R O	R O	O	R O	O
Encourage trainees to teach back	I	R O	I R	I R	R O		R O	R	

Note: I = Intended; R = Reported; O = Observed; Dr. Reed did not attend this professional development session and therefore did not complete the worksheet with his intended use of strategies. However, he attended the same PD three months prior.

the researchers observed. Since there were more laboratory tables than researchers, the two researchers were not always observing at each table throughout the entire course. The researchers are confident, however, that by spending a total of seven hours observing, they were able to capture the essence of the strategies employed by faculty.

Theme 1: Surgical Faculty Readily Implemented Direct Instruction, Not Requiring Trainee Response

Observation data indicated that every surgical faculty member provided role modeling, gave trainees an opportunity for hands-on experience and provided real-life examples, explained the relevancy or the "why" of a procedure, and showed respect for trainees. Each of these teaching strategies is an approach that involves faculty delivery without a need for trainee response. Though not all surgical faculty members reported using these strategies in the interview, each of these teaching approaches was clearly visible in their practice. The three approaches of providing modeling, offering hands-on experiences with application to real-life examples, and explaining reasons for a procedure were consistent with the way that these surgeons were taught their craft through the Halstedian approach of "see one, do one, teach one." Dr. Davis explained that "I was doing a lot of those things, but I was doing them intrinsically without having thought about it." Dr. Rasoud appreciated the focus on relevancy as an important aspect of instruction: "Just reinforcing why it's important to hold instruments correctly and use them safely and reminding them gently without any negative confrontation, I think, was very helpful."

It was noteworthy that the strategy of showing respect for trainees generated interest and discussion. Several surgical faculty members mentioned that their own experiences as residents or fellows learning from faculty had been abusive and belittling. Some surgical faculty reported they were determined not to repeat this commonly used, negative approach to instruction. Dr. Rasoud explained that he was pleased to learn strategies that were more positive and effective than the style used by his own teachers. He spoke of situations where his teachers would yell at trainees and call them disparaging names if they did something wrong. He was uncomfortable with these behaviors and he connected particularly with the strategies that dealt with respect and drawing on a trainees' previous experience. Other surgical faculty members were interested to learn that trainees are more receptive to learning when they are respected. It is noteworthy that respect was observed in each faculty-trainee interaction and reported by seven of the surgical faculty as an approach that they consciously implemented in the laboratory sessions, yet only one surgical faculty member chose this strategy as a goal for instruction.

Theme 2: Some Surgical Faculty Implemented Strategies That Required Engaging Trainees in Responses or Thinking About Trainees' Performance

The data indicated that some surgical faculty were observed or reported providing feedback, asking questions, drawing on trainees' experiences, and encouraging trainees to teach back to increase understanding. Common features of these strategies are that the surgical faculty members must think beyond their own delivery of information to focus on the trainee's performance and engage each trainee in providing responses. For example, Dr. Andrews noted that during the laboratory sessions he focused on acknowledging trainees' background:

> How do you do this at home? What techniques do you bring here with that? I'm trying to really formally say however you've done it before is probably very good. This is how I am slightly different as opposed to this is the way I do it. (Andrews, personal communication, July 27, 2013)

Some doctors focused on improving their questions to elicit trainee responses. Dr. Rasoud noted: "I wanted to make sure I did a better job of asking open-ended questions and if they had a response to open-ended questions using tactile feedback with the actual cadaver." Dr. Samuelson indicated the value of "checking in" with trainees particularly when "one of the trainees was getting it a lot more quickly than the other one." Dr. Samuelson also noted being able to identify a trainee's misconceptions or confusion by "the questions that he asked." Thus, the responses or questions by the trainees became indicators for the surgical faculty of how to proceed next with instruction.

Providing feedback was an area of intended focus for only three faculty members during the laboratory sessions, yet six faculty members were observed offering feedback to trainees. Dr. Samuelson explained:

> I was just trying to make a conscious effort of watching them and giving them feedback on technical things as they did them like how to hold the drill or how to gently retract tissue. As surgeons, we always tend to provide feedback but we always come out as negative because it comes in moments of stress once something goes wrong and so they have the negative stuff. So I always try to give some positive feedback. (Samuelson, personal communication, July 27, 2013)

Thus, he recognized the value of giving positive feedback to trainees early in the learning.

The strategy "encourage trainees to teach back" was emphasized by some surgical faculty members in the interviews. Dr. Reed noted that when residents "teach someone else, then you know whether they're at different levels or at the same level. And then you can relate different experiences with them or talk at a different level based on their answers." Dr. Elwood explained that as a "direct result" of the PD, he "asked them to teach me the techniques that we just learned and have them re-explain with their new knowledge about the anatomy and how they were going to do it." However, though six surgical faculty members reported using this approach in the laboratory, only three surgical faculty members were observed implementing it. Thus, the strategy of teaching back was included also for the following theme.

Theme 3: The Strategies Implemented Least Often by Faculty Were Those That Required More Active Processing and Responsiveness by the Trainee

These strategies included providing time for reflection and encouraging trainees to teach back what they had learned. While four faculty members indicated that they planned to incorporate time for reflection, three reported they did and only one was observed doing so. As for encouraging their trainees to teach back what they had learned, three of the faculty planned to incorporate that strategy, six reported that they did, but the researchers only observed three faculty actually using the strategy in their teaching. A common feature of both these strategies is that more ownership of the learning is given to the trainee and more response is expected of the trainee. Reflection requires that the surgical faculty actively process the learning with the trainee and this discourse can be time consuming. Based on observations, only Dr. Rasoud provided "time for reflection" in combination with "encouraging trainees to teach back" by expecting trainees to first explain a technique, then work on the cadaver, and finally explain and reflect on what happened after they completed a procedure.

It appears that the faculty may be more comfortable utilizing strategies that are more faculty-directed (modeling, providing feedback, asking for prior knowledge and questioning, allowing for hands-on activity) and less comfortable utilizing those strategies that tend to be more trainee-centered and require faculty facilitation (allowing time for reflection on practice and having the trainee teach back what they are learning).

Surgical Faculty Members' Description of their Use of the PD in the Course

As for the effectiveness of the PD on their teaching practice, the faculty delineated different areas they found helpful in their practice. They particularly appreciated the use of video examples derived from previously trained surgical faculty. As Dr. Davis explained, "I think having the videos and stopping the videos was very helpful because it really solidifies what your message is and it demonstrates in a very concrete manner what you're trying to accomplish." Dr. Johnson noted, "What I liked specifically was the case examples, the videos in terms of the reinforcement... applying a real-time scenario." These visual tools portrayed a variety of effective teaching techniques in a cadaver laboratory as models for the faculty.

For surgical faculty who were experienced teachers, many strategies were implicit to their practice, and only after discussion, did the strategies become more explicit to them. In reference to the adult learning principles, Dr. Davis felt, "It definitely made it more conscious just because I've never broken down adult learning as a procedure... I actively thought about what I was saying and what I was doing and that's different instead of just—when you do something as often, it just becomes a matter of fact to you." Dr. Ferry reiterated the notion that this PD was important for even seasoned faculty, "Maybe I was doing this in some way but it was not very organized so I think now, I was able to do a little more organizing." One faculty member, Dr. Samuelson, had four years of teaching experience and a master's degree in education and reported, "I think probably the most useful was just going through the list of things to consider. Just in terms for me of reviewing because you never really take inventory of yourself." It appeared that making their practice explicit as a result of the PD helped faculty be more conscious of the quality of their instruction.

The less experienced faculty felt the PD was important as a model of what they should be doing with their trainees. Dr. Rasoud, who had recently completed his fellowship and who had limited teaching experience, voiced that he appreciated learning teaching strategies that were different from the ineffective and inappropriate ways he had been taught. His use of every strategy is discussed later in the results section.

As for the mentoring portion of the PD based on the POMM, Dr. Davis explained:

> I think this sheet, your Purposeful Ongoing Mentoring and Coaching Model, the POMM, I think this is the most helpful for me because.... I think if you know your audience, then you can gauge how you want to interact with them, what their goals are, what your goals are, and what strategies are most effective to do that. (Davis, personal communication, July 27, 2013)

Having an idea of the proficiency level of the trainees at his table made his work more focused on each trainee's particular needs. Dr. Andrews also expressed this notion when he said,

> I had a better sense of what my objective was as opposed to feeling it out and guessing where I was trying to take people. I had some bins to put people in and say if this person is in this bin, my objective is to get them this piece of knowledge to move to the next step of the way. (Andrews, personal communication, July 27, 2013)

Thus, some faculty members felt that the POMM provided a framework from which to identify a trainee's knowledge base and then make appropriate instructional decisions. It appears that having a framework to use when gauging a trainee's knowledge and skill level as well as strategies to implement in order to guide trainees from where they are to where they need to be was a valuable part of this PD. However, while the faculty found it valuable and helpful, based upon their observed use of these strategies or lack thereof, the evidence indicates that they need more instruction using reflection as a mentoring tool for skill development.

Description from Trainees as Learners in the Lab

In addition to the faculty, the trainees were interviewed regarding their experience in the laboratory with surgical faculty. Due to the intensity of the course and a lack of time to meet with them individually, four trainees were interviewed as a group, and one was interviewed alone. The essence of their discussion was that they felt they had been provided a safe environment to practice what they were being taught and, in many cases, to explore or push beyond to see what could go wrong. They agreed that many of the faculty gave them a safe space to make mistakes and to learn from these mistakes, something they could not do in a real operation. Although they never used the word *respect*, they reported that they felt they were being treated as colleagues. They also felt that *their* learning was the primary focus of the faculty at all times. One trainee said it appeared that the faculty were highly motivated and excited to teach and that, in turn, provided him with a sense of excitement and motivation about his learning. They all agreed that the small faculty-to-trainee ratio at each table gave them opportunities to have one-on-one instruction and ask questions they might not have had the opportunity to ask in a larger teaching setting. The trainees also mentioned that the faculty frequently used models, cases, x-ray, stories, and examples that were very helpful.

Of particular note was the surgical faculty dyad of Dr. Rasoud and Dr. Reed. Dr. Reed is a seasoned faculty member with 13 years of teaching experience and Dr. Rasoud recently completed his fellowship and lacked teaching experience. There were three or four trainees at this table at any given time throughout the laboratory portion of the course. The researchers observed two levels of teaching and mentoring occurring at this table: faculty with trainees and seasoned faculty with junior faculty. During informal conversation with Dr. Rasoud, he reported that he would defer to Dr. Reed during instruction and then would mimic some of Dr. Reed's strategies. Fortunately, Dr. Reed was adept at using many of the strategies taught in the PD. Together, this dyad utilized every strategy taught in the PD and did so in an almost rhythmic manner. One of the trainees at this table was interviewed and reported that he felt he had been given the opportunity to try the skills being taught in a "safe environment" and was encouraged to push his skill further without fear of making a mistake. He reported that this was a valuable experience and an opportunity that a surgeon in training rarely receives. He felt this time to learn from seeing what a mistake would look like was of major importance because, as he said, "you can't do this stuff in the operating room."

In summary, although many surgical faculty were experienced teachers, they felt the PD helped them think about their instruction in a more organized, deliberate manner, attending to the quality of their instruction. The less experienced faculty appreciated having models other than their own teachers to help shape their teaching practice going forward. The faculty appeared to be most comfortable using teaching and mentoring strategies that were faculty-directed and demonstrated less comfort with those that required faculty facilitation for trainee responses.

Recommendations by Surgical Faculty

After the faculty engaged in professional development during the spine surgery training course and had applied their training in the laboratory, the surgical faculty were queried as to possible suggestions for improving future PD sessions. They made several recommendations they felt would enhance their learning and retention of skills in future sessions. They also recommended future topics to include in the PD.

Ways to Sustain the Professional Development

The surgical faculty reported that the insights they had acquired during the professional development could be sustained through explicit reminders and follow-up sessions. Several faculty members recommended that the course organizers send a "friendly" e-mail notification to the participating faculty every three months reminding them about the adult learning principles, adult learning styles, and the POMM (Peno & Silva Mangiante, 2012). Dr. Andrews noted, "These skills are the kinds of skills that need to be refreshed every once in a while." Dr. Ferry, Dr. Reed, and Dr. Sewell independently suggested that the learning principles be included as an electronic attachment sent to surgical faculty as a refresher prior to their teaching similar courses.

Another recommendation for an approach to refresh skills learned during the professional development was to offer a series of trainings. Dr. Davis suggested that the content areas of adult learning could be divided into different trainings providing more intensive, yet short courses, that repeat-faculty could attend each year or every couple of years. This approach would allow faculty to acquire more in-depth knowledge on particular aspects of adult learning, while also reinforcing their prior training.

Faculty Suggestions For Future Professional Development

The recommendations for future professional development in adult learning techniques included more hands-on experiences, additional videos showing the application of the principles to the surgical context, individual and group feedback, and training for how to deal with challenging trainees. One surgical faculty member, Dr. Elwood, provided a suggestion that the professional development should involve a hands-on experience in which the participants had to teach someone a skill (i.e., build a challenging structure out of Legos) in order to "do" and practice how to successfully teach. He felt the faculty could experience practical techniques in teaching through a workshop model in which they taught each other something that they did not already know how to do. Through a hands-on activity, surgical faculty could experience "different ways that might successfully engage me, that get me interested and teach me how to do something."

Each of the faculty members expressed that they appreciated the use of video clips of surgical faculty working in the laboratory to have a visual image of the adult learning principles in action. Several faculty suggested that more video clips in varied situations be provided.

Additionally, during the PD, the surgical faculty received copies of published articles about the stages of development from novice to expert in the medical community and how it is being used in medical education. Several faculty members mentioned that they appreciated reading evidence from white papers of how adult learning principles and the novice to expert stages are implemented in training. Dr. Davis recommended that research literature continue to be included as resources in their training materials. In line with this recommendation, Dr. Elwood suggested that brief reports of data regarding effective teaching techniques be presented. He explained, "We're data driven surgeons...we're more focused on the practical aspects of how do I teach this effectively." He noted that it was "incredibly useful to know just talking to somebody, they retain nothing...but put their hands on something and then all of a sudden, their retention goes up exponentially." Dr. Elwood regarded this succinct presentation of empirical findings as an efficient way for the surgical faculty to become aware of research-based practices.

A common theme among the surgical faculty was their interest in receiving feedback about their teaching in the laboratory with the trainees. The faculty members expressed the desire for both individual and group feedback. They welcomed objective observations not only from the adult educators, but also from the trainees themselves. Dr. Reed suggested this feedback could be provided face-to-face or via e-mailed communication. Dr. Elwood suggested that the PD providers compile a list of "ten strategies that worked very well for this group" based on the observations. In addition, surgical faculty could receive a list of suggestions for "when you're having a tough time engaging somebody; this is how you engage them." The faculty felt that they would benefit from a report of the strategies that the surgical faculty implemented well during the course as well as those strategies that could benefit from additional attention.

Finally, Dr. Samuelson, a surgical faculty member who had extensive experience teaching trainees, recommended that the professional development could be strengthened by devoting a portion of the training to how faculty members could deal with difficult trainees'... who are just very arrogant and just won't listen or ones who just don't get it." This faculty member expressed that "those are the ones that I struggle with because I get frustrated. If they won't listen to me, how do you get them to understand?" Dr. Samuelson felt this was a "challenge for all of us" and recommended that the faculty would appreciate considering alternatives in these difficult situations.

CONCLUSION

Given the demand for surgical faculty to possess the knowledge and skill to effectively perform their role as teachers and mentors to the trainees they serve (Kenahan, 2014; Pernar, Ashley, Smink, Zinner, & Peyre, 2012; Peyre, Frankl, Thorndike, & Breen, 2011), the results of this study can provide important insight into the types of PD and ongoing support they need. In this study, the surgical faculty were most comfortable implementing strategies that did not require trainee responses and that were characterized by direct instruction on their part, which most closely aligned with the Halstedian approach they are taught to use (Kotsis & Chung, 2012). They were less comfortable utilizing those strategies that required them to engage trainees in the teaching process or that required them to think about trainee performance while they were teaching. They were least comfortable with strategies that required more active processing of the learning with the trainee and with more response expected on the trainees' part. Based upon these findings, along with faculty recommendations, we suggest strategies for enhancing future professional development of surgical faculty. Table 17.3 depicts the strategies that were taught in the PD that faculty were most, less, and least comfortable utilizing in their teaching based upon observation, self-report, and recommendations for future PD offerings.

Based upon these findings, future PD activities with surgical faculty should provide focused instruction and experiential activities on providing feedback to trainees during the teaching process, asking open-ended questions during instruction that broadens trainee learning, utilizing information about trainees' prior experience(s) that serves as a starting point for instruction during the lab teaching session, and giving trainees the opportunity to demonstrate and provide verbal accounts of their learning by "teaching back" in the lab. It is vital to a learners' skill development to have the opportunity to reflect on their practice with their teacher as mentor facilitating the process (Carraccio, Benson, Nixon, & Derstine, 2008). Future PD activities should explore the importance of reflection in the learning process and the process of implementing effective reflection strategies during teaching.

Due to time constraints, the PD under study was limited to two hours and included three major components: adult learning principles, adult learning styles, and the POMM mentoring model. Based upon the recommendations of the faculty, future PD should include shorter, more intensive sessions, focused on a single concept such as, "effective strategies to provide trainee feedback in the lab," or "encouraging trainee reflection during surgery in a cadaver lab." These short, intensive sessions should include hands-on activities and the continued use of video examples of actual surgical faculty demonstrating the strategies while teaching in a cadaver

TABLE 17.3 Faculty's Comfort Level Utilizing Strategies from PD and Recommendations for Future PD

Strategies from PD	Recommendations for Future PD
Most Comfortable	
• Provide modeling • Provide hands-on experiences and real-life examples • Explain relevancy—the "why" of a procedure • Show respect for trainees	• Provide hands-on activities • Use video examples of surgeons teaching in the lab
Less Comfortable	
• Provide feedback • Ask questions • Draw on trainees' experiences • Encourage trainees to teach back	• Provide focused instruction and experiential activities on providing feedback to trainees, asking open-ended questions, utilizing information about trainee's prior experiences, and encouraging trainees to "teach back." • Shorter, more intensive sessions on a single concept. • Model and facilitate "teach back" process • Use video examples of surgeons teaching in the lab
Least Comfortable	
• Provide time for reflection • Encourage trainees to teach back	• Focus on importance of reflection to learning and implementation of reflection strategies • Model and facilitate "teach back" process • Use video examples of surgeons teaching in the lab

lab. The video approach was successful and should be enhanced in future PD. To continue to model the process for surgical faculty, the PD providers should scaffold the surgeon's development of these skills by providing pointed, individual feedback during the session with general feedback on their performance post-session.

In addition to the suggestions for future PD found in Table 17.3, some faculty expressed an appreciation for the journal article they were provided as part of the PD and suggested that, because they use data to inform their performance, receiving relevant literature enhanced the learning experience for them. This practice should be continued. Finally, future PD should include sessions on issues that are tangential to surgical teaching practice such as dealing with difficult trainees. Incorporating a needs analysis into the PD would provide a means for insuring that session topics are meeting the ongoing needs of faculty.

REFERENCES

Batalden, P., Leach, D., Swing, S., Dreyfus, H., & Dreyfus, S. (2002). General competencies and accreditation in graduate medical education. *Health Affairs, 21*(5), 103–111.

Carraccio, C. L., Benson, B. J., Nixon, J. L., & Derstine, P. L. (2008). From the educational bench to the clinical bedside: Translating the Dreyfus developmental model to the learning of clinical skills. Academic Medicine, 83(8), 761–767.

Clark, J. M., Houston, T. K., Kolodner, K., Branch, W. T., Levine, R. B., & Kern, D. E. (2004). Teaching the teachers: National survey of faculty development in departments of medicine of U.S. teaching hospitals. *Journal of General Internal Medicine, 19,* 205–214.

Daley, B. J. (1999). Novice to expert: An exploration of how professionals learn. *Adult Education Quarterly, 49*(4), 133–147.

Dreyfus, H. L., & Dreyfus, S. E. (1986). *Mind over machine: The power of human intuition and expertise in the era of the computer.* New York, NY: Free Press.

Dreyfus, S. E., & Dreyfus, H. L. (1980). *A five-stage model of the mental activities involved in directed skill acquisition* (ORC 80-2). Berkeley, CA: University of California, Berkeley, Operations Research Center.

Dunn, R. (1984). Learning styles: State of the science. *Theory into Practice. 23*(1), 10–19.

Erickson, F. (1986). Qualitative methods in research on teaching. In M.C. Wittrock (Ed.), *Handbook of research on teaching* (3rd ed., pp. 119–161). New York, NY: Macmillan.

Erlandson, D. A., Harris, E. L., Skipper, B. L., & Allen, S. D. (1993). *Doing naturalistic inquiry: A guide to methods.* London, England: Sage.

John-Steiner, V., & Mahn, H. (1996). Approaches to learning and development: A Vygotskian framework. *Educational Psychologist, 31*(3/4), 191–206.

Kenahan, R. (2014). *An exploratory case study of the professional teaching and learning practices of surgeons providing instruction in the medical devices and diagnostics industry: Implications for faculty development and endorsement by the professional field.* (Unpublished doctoral dissertation). Teacher's College, Columbia University, New York, NY.

Knapper, C. (1995). Understanding student learning: Implications for instructional practice. In W. Wright (Ed.), *Teaching improvement practices.* Bolton, MA: Anker.

Knowles, M. S. (1980). *The modern practice of adult education: From pedagogy to andragogy.* Englewood Cliffs, NJ: Prentice Hall/Cambridge.

Kotsis, S. V., & Chung, K. C. (2013). Application of the "see one, do one, teach one" concept in surgical training. *Plastic and Reconstructive Surgery Journal, 131*(5), 1194–1201.

Merriam, S. B. (1998). *Qualitative research and case study applications in education.* San Francisco, CA: Jossey-Bass.

Patton, M. Q. (2002). *Qualitative research & evaluation methods* (3rd ed.). Thousand Oaks, CA: Sage Publications.

Peno, K., & Silva Mangiante, E. (2012). The journey from novice to expert: Toward a purposeful on-going mentoring model. In C. J. Boden & K. P. King (Eds.), *Conversations about adult learning in a complex world* (pp. 211–221). Charlotte, NC: Information Age Publishing.

Pernar, L. M., Ashley, S. W., Smink, D. S., Zinner, M. J., & Peyre, S. E. (2012). Master surgeons' operative teaching philosophies: A qualitative analysis of parallels to learning theory. *Journal of Surgical Education, 69*(4), 493–498.

Peyre, S. E., Frankl, S. E., Thorndike, M., & Breen, E. M. (2011). Observation of clinical teaching: Interest in a faculty development program for surgeons. *Journal of Surgical Education, 68*(5), 372–376.

Ribeiro, R. (2012). Remarks on explicit knowledge and expertise acquisition. *Phenomenology and Cognitive Science.* doi: 10.1007/s11097-012-9268-9

Schön, D. J. (1983). *The reflective practitioner.* New York, NY: Basic Books.

Schön, D. J. (1987). *Educating the reflective practitioner: Toward a new design for teaching and learning in the professions.* San Francisco: Jossey-Bass.

Strauss, A., & Corbin, J. (1990). *Basics of qualitative research: Grounded theory procedures and techniques.* Newbury Park, CA: Sage.

Strowd, R., & Reynolds, P. (2013). The lost resident: Why resident physicians still need mentoring. *Neurology, 80*(23), 244–246.

Sullivan, G., Simpson, D., Cooney, T., & Beresin, E. (2013). A milestone in the milestones movement: The *JGME* Milestones Supplement. *Journal of Graduate Medical Education, 5,* 1–4.

Vygotsky, L. S. (1978). *Mind in society: The development of higher psychological processes.* Edited by M. Cole et al., Cambridge, MA: Harvard University Press.

Vygotsky, L. S. (1986). *Thought and language.* Cambridge, MA: MIT Press.

CHAPTER 18

WHEN ADULT LEARNING PRACTITIONERS ENCOUNTER EDUCATION IN THE HEALTH PROFESSIONS

Challenges to Theory and Practice

Teresa J. Carter and Laura P. Gogia
Virginia Commonwealth University

Adult education has a long tradition of learning-centered teaching that has contributed to theory development and forms the basis of practice in the field. Even before Knowles (1970) asserted his well-established assumptions about adults as learners, Lindeman (1926/1989), Dewey (1938/1963), Houle (1961) and others described humanistic underpinnings that have since shaped the values and philosophical orientation of many adult educators. As a field of practice, adult educators value the learner's life experience as the basis for constructing knowledge and encourage self-directedness within a learning climate that is both respectful and supportive. Engagement in critical reflection and critical self-reflection on experience, central

Building Sustainable Futures for Adult Learners, pages 385–401
Copyright © 2015 by Information Age Publishing

concepts in Mezirow's (1991) transformative learning theory, have been widely adopted as hallmarks of a constructivist orientation to learning that now dominates much adult learning practice, as well as theory.

Yet, when adult learning practices are carried into health professions education, adult educators often struggle to reconcile their language, values, viewpoints, and perspectives with those that have dominated these scientific disciplines for more than a century, even amid the current call for dramatic reform in the education of health professionals (Benner, Sutphen, Leonard, & Day, 2009; Cooke, Irby, & O'Brien, 2010; DePaola, 2008; Dezee, Artino, Elnick, Hemmer, & Durning, 2012; Ludmerer, 2012). Dezee and colleagues (2012) estimate that since 2005, 75% of medical schools in the United States have or are currently undergoing curriculum reform. Similar trends can be found in other disciplines within the health professions, such as dentistry and nursing (Benner et al., 2009; DePaola, 2008). Why do these professional fields of study all proclaim a dramatic need to revise their educational processes? The answers lie within current practices and their recognized shortcomings.

Clinical education is characterized by an emphasis on patient safety and zero tolerance for error as much as it seeks to train professionals who are critical thinkers, expert problem solvers, skillful communicators, and high-stakes decision-makers (Benner et al., 2009; Cooke et al., 2010; DePaola, 2008). The environment is one in which more must be learned during the years of professional training than ever before as medical knowledge expands dramatically with every passing year (Cooke et al., 2010; Ironside, 2004; Ludmerer, 2012). The result of this expanding knowledge base has led to what some scholars call the "additive" curriculum in which new content is continuously added without any deletion of what has been taught before (Giddens & Brady, 2007; Ironside, 2004).

As more must be learned within the defined period of study, students and trainees, terms used to describe beginning and advanced learners in professional education, are under enormous pressure to meet standards set by accrediting bodies and national licensure examinations that certify competence to practice. They learn under the tutelage of expert basic science faculty and skilled clinicians who were never trained in adult learning methods, but who continue to teach as they were taught (Dezee et al., 2012). The lecture-intensive curriculum has dominated early years of study in these professional fields for more than 100 years (Cooke, Irby, Sullivan, & Ludmerer, 2006). However, within the last 10 to 15 years, graduate education in the health professions has been organized around achievement of core competencies such as patient care, medical knowledge, interpersonal and communication skills, practice-based learning and improvement, professionalism, and systems-based practice. Even so, the mantra, "see one, do one, teach one" continues to be the mainstay of teaching in the clinical setting, and trainees both learn and pass on skills and knowledge largely through role modeling (Passi et al., 2013). Passi and colleagues argue that much of this role modeling contributes to a "hidden" curriculum in the health professions in which trainees model less than desirable practices and behaviors that contradict what they learn in the formal curriculum.

Within the last two decades, many of the concepts and theories that originate within adult education have found their way into the literature of the healthcare disciplines where they influence current competency requirements and undergird calls for curricular reforms (Benner et al., 2009; Cooke et al., 2010; DePaola, 2008; Ludmerer, 2012; Taylor & Hamdy, 2013). However, as health professions educators are encouraged to adopt many of the concepts and theories inherent in adult education, the humanistic underpinnings and philosophical orientations associated with them are re-cast against a backdrop of scientific, deductive reasoning, cause-and-effect thinking, and a strict preference for documented and measurable outcomes. As adult educators, we have discovered our challenges of practice are related to this philosophical and conceptual chasm. Familiar words often hold different meanings for our counterparts in the health professions, and practices borne within one discipline translate differently when used in another context with its different worldviews, traditions, and origins of thought.

As authors, we bring twin perspectives that spring from different educational pathways: one of us has an educational background in adult learning and now works in medical education to enhance professional instruction and faculty development, and the other is a medical doctor, trained in traditional methods of didactic instruction, now completing her PhD in Education. Our goal is to highlight the challenges presented in the education of today's health professionals through an examination of the literature and our own experiences in attempting to influence educators within these disciplines.

THE CONTEXT FOR EDUCATING THE HEALTHCARE PROFESSIONAL

In addition to being costly, undertaking advanced education in the health professions is a time and labor intensive effort which can take from seven to 12 years in some subspecialties (Accreditation Council for Graduate Medical Education, 2014; Liaison Committee on Medical Education, 2013b; Youngclaus & Fresne, 2013). The time invested in learning, however, is only one aspect of complexity in the education of healthcare professionals. During their training, learners in advanced stages of their education (residency training for physicians) are also employed by the healthcare system as providers of care, albeit under clinical supervision. This less expensive form of patient care is now built into the healthcare system; most university hospitals would not be solvent without the reduced labor costs of trainees during the years of their residency and fellowship training (Ludmerer, 2012). Health professions scholars have lamented this role conflict between learner and healthcare provider as detrimental to the educational mission but have scant alternatives to pose to the existing system in an era of reduced state and federal funding for health professions education (Ludmerer, 2012).

Certainly, for healthcare professionals, lifelong learning is a requirement, not an option. The ideal learner emerging from this extensive training period is a professional who is skilled in self-directed learning, aware of how to monitor his or her own learning by developing metacognitive abilities, cognizant of personal limitations and how to address them, interpersonally skilled and adept in communicating with a diverse population of patients and care providers, oriented toward providing care in a team setting, professional in every aspect of personal and work life, and adept in understanding and navigating a complex healthcare system. The current educational system for health professionals admittedly falls far short of achieving this ideal (Benner et al., 2009; Cooke et al., 2010; DePaola, 2008).

DISCONNECTS IN WORDS, THEORY, AND PRACTICE

One of the major challenges we see for adult educators who attempt to work in health professions education concerns the use of language familiar to adult learning theory and practice, but interpreted or applied differently in the healthcare context. Among these disconnects in language are some key theoretical concepts that undergird contemporary adult learning theory: meanings associated with self-directed learning (SDL), transformative learning, critical thinking, and reflective practice. After illustrating some of the differences we have observed in practices as well as in use of theory, we propose opportunities to bridge the divide in ways that can help to advance the aim of these noble professions during an era in which major changes are underway.

Conflating the Terminology of Self-Directed Learning

Self-directed learning has its theoretical roots in the works of Houle (1961), Tough (1967, 1971), and Knowles (1975) who first described it as a "process in which individuals take the initiative, with or without the help of others, in diagnosing their learning needs, formulating learning goals, identifying human and material resources for learning, choosing and implementing appropriate learning strategies, and evaluating learning outcomes" (p. 18). Recently, however, the Liaison Committee on Medical Education (LCME), the accrediting body for all United States medical schools, contributed to the confusion by redefining active learning as the ability for students to assess their learning needs, individually or in groups; identify, analyze, and synthesize information relevant to their learning needs; assess the credibility of information resources; and share information with their peers and supervisors (Liaison Committee on Medical Education, 2013a). While medical educators have been encouraged to adopt active learning methods to *engage* learners so they are not passive recipients but active constructors of knowledge, this new definition adds a further element of confusion by conflating active learning with self-directed learning.

Upon this redefined notion of active learning, which is an accreditation standard, medical schools across the country are re-considering what needs to happens in the classroom since they are being held accountable for producing self-directed learners under the guise of active learning. This has led many to perceive SDL as an educational intervention or a classroom technique, as opposed to a shift in philosophical orientation that encourages learners to develop skills in assessing their own learning needs and setting goals (Li, Paterniti, Co, & West, 2010; Stuart, Sectish, & Huffman, 2005; Van Schaik, Plant, & O'Sullivan, 2013).

A common theme that emerges in the health professions literature is of educators who are unprepared to encourage SDL, claiming they have no training or background to assume the role of facilitator (Van Schaik et al., 2013). In a systematic review of the effectiveness of SDL in health professions education, Murad and colleagues examined 59 studies involving more than 8,000 learners (Murad, Coto-Yglesias, Varkey, Prokop, & Murad, 2010). They discovered that only 8% of the published curricula organized around SDL as an educational premise provided a definition of SDL, and less than one in five published studies satisfied all the key components of SDL as identified by Knowles (1984). Instructional interventions labeled as SDL included problem-based learning, class discussions, one-minute paper writing techniques, affective response exercises, and educational interventions that consisted of a computerized module or self-study guide. Only seven studies of the 59 examined described the function of the teacher as facilitator, and only five involved learners who were involved in assessment of learning outcomes.

Similarly, when Nothnagle and her colleagues (2011) investigated the learning culture, including medical residents' perspectives of SDL in the Brown University Family Residency Program, they found numerous paradoxes and contradictions in residents' self-reports. While these advanced learners claimed to value the concept of SDL, they also said that they engaged in very limited goal setting or reflection, and they were not confident that they had the skills to manage their own learning, preferring a teacher-centered approach. The residents recognized that patient care situations were potent opportunities for engaging in SDL, but they also viewed patient care and learning as competing time priorities (Nothnagle, Anandarajah, Goldman, & Reis, 2011).

Van Schaik and colleagues (2013) examined the faculty mentor's perspective on the use of portfolios among medical students to reflect on progress, diagnose learning needs, and create learning plans to address gaps in knowledge or skills. These medical educators found wide variety in the faculty mentors' beliefs and approaches to SDL, definitions of SDL, and perceptions of students' SDL skills. They discovered that portfolio mentors did not uniformly accept the notion that self-directed learning skills could be taught, believing, instead, that self-directedness was an inherent quality present in some students. The discrepancies between the aims of the portfolio as a learning strategy and faculty use of it were large enough to justify recommendations for the school that included explicit faculty development with instruction in SDL skills as well as the need for institutional culture change.

In a qualitative analysis of responses to a national survey of pediatric residents, residents (advanced physician trainees) had difficulty with personal reflection, goal generation, and in creating and implementing a personal development plan. They also cited competing time demands and environmental role strain as issues that prevented SDL (Li et al., 2010). The time-constrained context for educating health professionals appears to affect not only what is learned but how it is learned. Hays' (2009) investigation of self-directed learning of clinical skills in the United Kingdom also found evidence that trainees were unprepared to assume responsibility for their own learning, a finding that mirrors conclusions reported frequently among researchers in U.S. medical settings (Murad et al., 2010; Nothnagle et al., 2011). Hays (2009) suggested that SDL may be more of an aspirational goal for medical schools rather than a reflection of current reality by viewing it as an expression of the breadth of training provided:

> What is known about self-directed learning in basic medical education? Most medical school mission statements include a claim that graduates will be adult learners who will become self-directed learners. These statements are rarely challenged, but, instead, are accepted, perhaps erroneously, as indicators of an aspiration, the achievement of which is difficult to measure.... [S]elf-directedness in medical school may be linked more to gaining breadth of experience than to achieving mastery of the core curriculum. (p. 505)

Such confusion about the nature of what it means to be self-directed as a learner, the ability or interest of learners in assuming responsibility for their learning, and the reported lack of facilitation skills claimed by faculty do not bode well for development of professionals who will engage in learning throughout the lifespan.

While current calls for reform in health professions education uniformly assert the importance of SDL, the literature is replete with studies that report student and trainee's assertions of preference for external guidance on what and how to learn (Murad et al., 2010; Nothnagle et al., 2011; Van Schaik et al., 2013). For some educators in the health professions, the ability to be self-directed appears to be a personal trait or learner characteristic, and lack of knowledge that self-directedness can be learned and fostered through educational practices seems widespread. Very few appear to be aware of Grow's (1991) conception of self-directedness as a continuum in which the educator's responsibility is to match the developmental level of the learner and, thus, scaffold the learner into greater independence.

Reflecting for What Purpose?

Self-direction is not the only area within adult learning in which we found theoretical concepts poorly understood or misapplied in the context of health professions education. Other areas of difference are evident in the meanings and practices associated with reflective practice, critical reflection and self-reflection, and transformative learning (Wear, Zarconi, Garden, & Jones, 2012; Wittich, Reed, McDonald, Varkey, & Beckman, 2010). J. A. Moon (2005) describes the source of this dilemma as emanating from the nature of reflection as a multi-disciplinary area of study with little integration across disciplines.

Certainly, not all of the educational literature in the health professions reflects different interpretations of critical reflection, since we found scholarship consistent with adult learning theory and practice. For example, P. J. Moon (2008) used transformative learning as the lens to examine "death talks," the conversations between physicians and their terminally-ill patients. He claimed these were potent opportunities for physicians to become aware of their own existential views as a prerequisite for a more authentic self when interacting with patients.

However, we found sufficient misunderstandings to warrant concern that transformative learning and the ideas around critical reflection and critical self-reflection, as well as the body of literature on reflective practice, has been interpreted with a preference for measurable outcomes or with an orientation toward error correction and single loop learning (Argyris & Schön, 1992). Such views are inconsistent with the premises of transformative learning as described by Mezirow (1991), reflective practice as described by J. A. Moon (2005), and double-loop learning as described by Argyris and Schön (1992).

In our review of the literature in the health professions, we found transformative learning described as an outcome of hospital quality improvement efforts (Wittich et al., 2010) or as an intervention strategy for improving the attitudes of nurses on the job (Thomas, 2012). For example, Thomas (2012) developed a three-part educational program to reframe staff perceptions of the role of charge nurse. Upon completion of the educational intervention, a majority of the program attendees reported valuing the time for the educational sessions which gave them an opportunity to examine their thoughts and feelings about their roles as charge nurses, and 75% said that they learned new words to describe and explain their experiences. In terms of transformative learning theory (Mezirow, 1991), this outcome, worthy as it may have been for the nurses concerned, would not rise to the level of a perspective transformation.

In another study, researchers reported on the results of a 10-hour bioethics course designed to prepare future physicians for discussing advance directives with patients (Mueller et al., 2010). In a post-course survey, students reported feeling more empathetic and knowledgeable, which the authors viewed as evidence of transformative learning. While we cannot know the depth of experience for individual students with any degree of certainty, the manner in which this intervention was described leads us to believe that knowledge gains were more likely to be in the realm of instrumental learning, and not at all what Mezirow (1991) intended as evidence of life-changing transformation. In other studies, transformative learning was used as a learning intervention strategy to foster disorienting dilemmas in an attempt to address disruptive physician behavior (Samenow, Worley, Neufeld, Fishel, & Swiggart, 2013) or to create disorienting encounters in simulation exercise debriefs (Parker & Myrick, 2010). Examples such as these are indicative of a more cursory understanding of the process of transformation and express lack of understanding of the relative rarity and depth of a transformative learning experience. They also call into question the ethical dimensions that may be associated with intentional attempts to produce disorienting dilemmas as part of the educational process in working with adult learners (Ettling, 2006).

Our conclusion is that many educators in the health professions have been exposed to the terminology of transformative learning, with its intuitive appeal as a valued educational outcome, but without sufficient depth to fully appreciate the differences between instrumental, communicative, and emancipatory learning (Mezirow, 1991). Cranton and King (2003) claim that professional development for educators needs to incorporate learning activities that foster content, process, and premise reflection to encourage critical self-reflection on habits of mind about teaching. We believe that too few educators in the health professions have had opportunity to engage in intensive learning experiences that would enable them to do this, given the preponderance of faculty development initiatives offered as short seminars or workshops.

A similar approach to the practices inherent in reflective practice as an educational strategy also surfaced in our literature review in which we observed attempts to measure the outcomes of reflection. In one thoughtful critique of reflective practice, Wear and colleagues (2012) describe the widespread adoption of reflection and reflective writing throughout the medical curriculum by questioning the extent to which reflection can be captured in measurable outcomes:

> Similar to other teaching and learning trends, such as professionalism or competencies, which medical educators have widely accepted over the past several decades, "reflection" and "reflective writing" have become familiar terms and practices.... We argue that the use of "reflection" in medical education requires more thoughtfulness and precision, especially because, as educators, we ask students to do so much of it, and we ourselves sprinkle it so liberally across academic discourse.... [E]ducators often use the term carelessly and casually, embedding it throughout local curricula and within national organizations, boards, and accrediting agencies—even as something to be quantitatively assessed ... How can the authenticity of learners' experiences be encouraged and sustained in an environment of formulaic approaches and growing demands for documented outcomes and demonstrated competencies? (p. 603)

Within the context of curricular reform, reflective learning activities are likely to remain a valued and important aspect of professional training; the challenge will be how to advance a more complete understanding of the theoretical basis for these important areas of practice in ways that are true to the meanings associated with adult learning theory.

Thinking Critically about Critical Thinking

Brookfield (2012) describes critical thinking as having four basic components: identifying the assumptions that frame our thinking and determine actions; confirming the basis of these assumptions and whether or not they are accurate and valid; being able to look at ideas and decisions from a variety of perspectives; and taking informed actions on the basis of testing assumptions and ideas (p. 1). These aspects of critical thinking are very much in line with what occurs when an individual questions the underlying assumptions, values, and beliefs that may result in transformative learning according to Mezirow's (1991) theory. In the health professions, critical thinking is a much discussed and written about topic, and the basis for workshops and faculty training.

In 2011, Krupat and colleagues undertook a study to determine the extent to which clinician-educators agreed on definitions of critical thinking and whether the clinical practice examples they provided were consistent with their definitions. The 97 participants in the study from five medical schools were asked to define critical thinking, describe a clinical scenario in which they viewed critical thinking as important, and to provide two examples, one of a clinician who was thinking critically and another of one who was not. Using qualitative methods that examined patterns and themes, their results indicated that most clinicians described critical thinking as a process or ability, with a few describing it as a personal disposition. Those who viewed critical thinking as a process, however, described it as a compilation of complex pieces of information from a patient's illness, including history, examination findings, laboratory, and radiologic results. In none of the examples described was there any mention of examining assumptions or testing ideas from a variety of perspectives. Instead, critical thinking was largely viewed as a process of complex data integration and interpretation, a form of sophisticated problem-solving.

These authors described well the need for clinicians to teach students to embrace complexity and be open to uncertainty by asking challenging questions, probing assumptions, and seeking justification for knowledge claims (Krupat et al., 2011). However, their findings indicated a "significant disconnect" in how clinicians conceptualized critical thinking through their definitions and in the manner in which it was described in the clinical setting. They concluded "if we are to foster critical thinking among medical students, we must reconcile the way it is defined with the manner in which clinician-educators describe critical thinking—and its absence—in action" (p. 625). Since so much testing in the health professions aims to assess critical thinking capacity, largely through multiple choice questions, the disjuncture between espoused beliefs and actual descriptions of what critical thinking looks like in practice poses an even larger issue in the assessment procedures for students and trainees during their education.

Learning from Role Models: What the Hidden Curriculum Teaches

Historically, health professionals have learned through an apprenticeship process, particularly in medical education, in which vocational identity and professionalism are developed through careful observation and imitation of role models (Sternszus, S. Cruess, R. Cruess, Young, & Steinaert, 2012). In this form of acculturation, newcomers gain skills and knowledge and come to embrace the attitudes and ideals of the profession through socialization into a community of practice (Lave & Wenger, 1991). Role models who promote humanistic views of empathy, respect, and compassion cannot be underestimated for the valued lessons they teach (Chuang et al., 2010; Passi et al., 2013).

Unfortunately, learners in the health professions are often exposed to less-than-ideal role models who model cynical, disrespectful, and other unhealthy workplace behaviors (Leape et al., 2012). Since the 1990s, this dark side of informal learning experiences in the clinical setting, often labeled the hidden curriculum, has been attributed to a culture of unforgiving perfectionism, individualistic competition, and a hierarchy of power relationships that exist in the healthcare environment (Haidet & Stein, 2006; Leape et al., 2012). The culture of disrespect that feeds and is fed by the hidden curriculum surfaces in many ways, but one of the most obvious is in humiliating and demeaning treatment of nurses, residents, and students by physicians (Leape et al., 2012). This problem is well-recognized as unacceptable by institutions involved in medical training, but ridding the culture of instances of student and trainee abuse has proven difficult, so much so that each year, the graduation survey conducted of all fourth year medical students by the LCME asks specifically about whether students have experienced abusive behaviors during their training (Association of American Medical Colleges, 2013).

For most adult educators, instances in which students and trainees might be publically embarrassed or ridiculed seem unthinkable given the humanistic underpinnings embraced by the field. However, adult educators are not training learners in the high stakes environment of a hospital setting, in operating rooms, or emergency rooms in which errors of practice can endanger the life of a patient within seconds. Medical education training clearly does not condone these practices as acceptable teaching techniques, but they may be more understandable given this different culture and the high costs to patient safety for mistakes. However, occasions of student-reported instances of humiliating remarks or public embarrassment in the clinical setting continue to cast a shadow within the culture of medical education (Haizlip et al., 2012). We see a need for andragogical principles to be more widely understood and encouraged by clinician-educators within this environment so that in addition to creating a safe learning climate, the setting embraces what Rogers (1969) so eloquently claimed as the foundation of learner-centered teaching: qualities of acceptance, prizing, and trust.

Moving Forward

The challenges we present in this chapter represent a few of the disconnections we have experienced as we attempt to reconcile our understanding of adult learning with the views of educators in the health professions. The differences we see in how theory is being used to guide practice are not uniformly dispersed among those who teach, but we have observed sufficient discrepancies in how adult learning theory is conceptualized in the literature and used in practice to give us reasons to reflect on both how and why this occurs. We do see many opportunities, however, for adult educators to promote greater depth and appreciation for what adult learning theory and practice can offer the health professions. A number of hopeful endeavors are on the horizon that hold promise to contribute to the reform of educational practices, reform that has been embraced by leadership and institutions of all disciplines around the country (Benner et al., 2009; Cooke et al., 2010; DePaola, 2008).

OPPORTUNITIES TO BRIDGE THE DIVIDE

Since history, culture, and prior experience always filter how new concepts are understood and used, we recognize that our ability to influence education in the health professions depends upon how well we can relate to the unique contexts for teaching and learning that exist within these complex worlds of practice. Our hope is to develop the relationships and experiences that will enable us to work side-by-side with our educational colleagues to meet the challenges they face in educating the next generation of doctors, nurses, dentists, pharmacists, and allied health professionals.

The culture that exists within these institutions of higher learning is well-entrenched and highly resistant to change (Hafferty, 1998). Curriculum reform is only one aspect of what will be needed to improve health professions education. Fifteen years ago, Hafferty described the problem within medical education when he said, "Indeed, a great deal of what is taught—and most of what is learned—in medical school takes place not within formal course offerings but within medicine's 'hidden curriculum'" (p. 403). Changing the educational culture within the health professions, particularly within medicine, will undoubtedly require effective leadership at many levels. Leadership in teaching and learning will be necessary, but not sufficient, since many of the issues that form the basis of calls for reform are embedded within policies, reward systems, accreditation practices, and faculty selection and promotion procedures of our institutions (Cooke et al., 2010).

Within the educational mission, however, there are some promising new initiatives that seek to provide opportunities for teaching faculty to hone their facilitation skills, develop more in-depth understanding of adult learning theory and practice, and contribute to scholarship in ways that can influence the health professions disciplines. In the past ten years, a number of master's degree programs designed especially to introduce adult learning concepts to health professions educators have emerged in institutions across the country, as have graduate certificate programs designed specifically for time-constrained clinician-educators (Tekian & Artino, 2013). Some of these are offered in online formats; others are in hybrid delivery or face-to-face learning environments. Several are programs developed within Schools or Colleges of Education in partnership with health professions education units to enhance faculty development.

Other innovations are emerging in the realm of inter-professional education for faculty in which educators in various disciplines within the health professions are taught together as they develop new skills, knowledge, and attitudes for teaching and learning. These programs hold great promise for bridging differences among educators in various professions who must also work together in teams within the healthcare setting. By creating inter-professional learning settings with doctors, nurses, and a variety of health professionals from different disciplines, the sense of community that builds in the classroom may well support the development of better interpersonal relationships among care providers. In doing so, our educational efforts may also be able to combat some of the persistent effects of status and rank that contribute to the hidden curriculum.

Educational practice for students and trainees in the health professions is undergoing radical change within the formal curriculum as reforms take place in institutions of higher education in the U.S. (Benner et al., 2009; Cooke et al., 2010; DePaola, 2008). In spite of some misconceptions that we have observed in the use of adult learning theory for practice, those who teach in the health professions are gaining experience with active methods for learner engagement that are replacing the mainstay of didactic lecture. These early efforts in using new methodologies are often practiced with incomplete understanding of adult learning theory, but we do see progress in a direction that adult educators would recognize as promising. What remains to be seen is whether the historical and cultural components of the educational environment can evolve to include ideas from adult learning theory and practice that will contribute to the development of a sustainable future for the large number of professionals who will be needed to care for society's health needs in the future. Within this health professions context, more adult educators will be needed to share best practices and contribute leadership to educational reform efforts now underway. The doors are open for those who want to take part in the challenges of change, with opportunities to make a difference in ways that matter.

REFERENCES

Accreditation Council for Graduate Medical Education. (2014). *Program and institutional accreditation.* Retrieved from http://www.acgme.org/acgmeweb/tabid/83/ProgramandInstitutionalAccreditation.aspx

Argyris, C., & Schön, D. A. (1992). *Theory in practice: Increasing professional effectiveness.* San Francisco, CA: Jossey-Bass.

Association of American Medical Colleges. (2013). *2013 Graduation Questionnaire.* Retrieved from https://www.aamc.org/download/352546/data/2013gqsurvey.pdf

Benner, P., Sutphen, M., Leonard, V., & Day, L. (2009). *Educating nurses: A call for radical transformation.* San Francisco, CA: Jossey-Bass.

Brookfield, S. D. (2012). *Teaching for critical thinking.* San Francisco, CA: Jossey-Bass.

Chuang, A. W., Nuthalapaty, F. S., Casey, P. M., Kaczmarczyk, J. M., Cullimore, A. J., Dalrymple, J. L., & Peskin, E. G. (2010). To the point: Reviews in medical education—taking control of the hidden curriculum. *American Journal of Obstetrics and Gynecology, 203*(4), 316.e1-6. doi: 10.1016/j.ajog.2010.04.035

Cooke, M., Irby, D. M., & O'Brien, B. C. (2010). *Educating physicians: A call for reform of medical school and residency.* San Francisco, CA: Jossey-Bass.

Cooke, M., Irby, D. M., Sullivan, W., & Ludmerer, K. M. (2006). American medical education 100 years after the Flexner Report. *The New England Journal of Medicine, 355,* 1339–1344.

Cranton, P., & King, K. P. (2003). Transformative learning as a professional development goal. *New Directions for Adult and Continuing Education, 2003,* 31–38. doi: 10.1002/ace.97

DePaola, D. P. (2008). The revitalization of U.S. dental education. *Journal of Dental Education, 72*(Supplement), 28–42.

Dewey, J. (1963). *Experience and education.* New York, NY: Collier Books. (Originally published 1938)

Dezee, K. J., Artino, A. R., Elnicki, D. M., Hemmer, P. A., & Durning, S. J. (2012). Medical education in the United States of America. *Medical Teacher, 34,* 521–525.

Ettling, D. (2006). Ethical demands of transformative learning. [Special edition]. *New Directions for Adult and Continuing Education, 2006,* 59–67. doi: 10.1002/ace.208

Giddens, J. F., & Brady, D. P. (2007). Rescuing nursing education from content saturation: The case for a concept-based curriculum. *Journal of Nursing Education, 46*(2), 65–69.

Grow, G. O. (1991). Teaching learners to be self-directed. *Adult Education Quarterly, 41*(3), 125–143. doi: 10.1177/0001848191041003001

Hafferty, F. (1998). Beyond curriculum reform: Confronting medicine's hidden curriculum. *Academic Medicine, 73*(4), 403–407.

Haidet, P., & Stein, H. (2006). The role of the student-teacher relationship in the formation of physicians: The hidden curriculum as process. *Journal of General Internal Medicine, 21,* S16–20. doi: 10.1111/j.1525-1497.2006.00304.x

Haizlip, J., May, N., Schorling, J., Williams, A., & Plews-Ogan, M. (2012). The negativity bias, medical education, and the culture of academic medicine: Why culture change is hard. *Academic Medicine, 87*(9), 1205–1209. doi: 10.1097/ACM.0b013e3182628f03

Hays, R. (2009). Self-directed learning of clinical skills. *Medical Education, 43*, 505–506. doi:10.1111/j.1365-2923.2009.03378.x

Houle, C. O. (1961). *The inquiring mind.* Madison, WI: The University of Wisconsin Press.

Ironside, P. M. (2004). "Covering content" and teaching thinking: Deconstructing the additive curriculum. *Journal of Nursing Education, 43*(1), 5–12.

Knowles, M. S. (1970). *The modern practice of adult education: Andragogy versus pedagogy.* New York, NY: Association Press.

Knowles, M. S. (1975). *Self-directed learning.* New York, NY: Association Press.

Knowles, M. S. (1984). *The adult learner: A neglected species* (3rd ed.). Houston, TX: Gulf.

Krupat, E., Sprague, J. M., Wolpaw, D., Haidet, P., Hatem, D., & O'Brien, B. (2011). Thinking critically about critical thinking: Ability, disposition, or both? *Medical Education, 45*, 625–635.

Lave, J., & Wenger, E. (1991). *Situated learning: Legitimate peripheral participation.* Cambridge, UK: Cambridge University Press.

Leape, L., Shore, M., Dienstag, J., Mayer, R., Edgman-Levitan, S., Meyer, G., & Healy, G. (2012). Perspective: A culture of respect, Part 1: The nature and causes of disrespectful behavior by physicians. *Academic Medicine, 87*, 845–852. doi: 10.1097/ACM.0b013e31828338d

Li, S. T., Paterniti, D. A., Co, J. P., & West, D. C. (2010). Successful self-directed lifelong learning in medicine: A conceptual model derived from qualitative analysis of a national survey of pediatric residents. *Academic Medicine, 85*(7), 1229–1236. doi:10.1097/ACM.0b013e3181e1931c

Liaison Committee on Medical Education, (2013a). *ED-5A, Active learning.* Retrieved from http://www.lcme.org/connections/connections_2013–2014/ED-5-A_2013-2014.htm

Liaison Committee on Medical Education (2013b). *Functions and structure of a medical school.* Retrieved from http://www.lcme.org/publications/functions2013june.pdf

Lindeman, E. (1926/1989). *The meaning of adult education.* Research Center for Continuing Professional and Higher Education. Oklahoma City, OK: Oklahoma. (Original work published 1926)

Ludmerer, K. M. (2012). The history of calls for reform in graduate medical education and why we are still waiting for the right kind of change. *Academic Medicine, 87*(1), 34–40.

Mezirow, J. (1991). *Transformative dimensions of adult learning.* San Francisco, CA: Jossey-Bass.

Moon, J. A. (2005). *Reflection in learning and professional development.* New York, NY: RoutledgeFalmer.

Moon, P. J. (2008). Death-talks: Transformative learning for physicians. *American Journal of Hospice & Palliative Medicine, 25*(4), 271–277. doi: 10.1177/1049909108318567

Mueller, P. S., Litin, S. C., Hook, C. C., Creagan, E. T., Cha, S. S., & Beckman, T. J. (2010). A novel advance directives course provides a transformative learning experience for medical students. *Teaching and Learning in Medicine, 22*(2), 137–141.

Murad, M. H., Coto-Yglesias, F., Varkey, P., Prokop, L., & Murad, A. (2010). The effectiveness of self-directed learning in health professions education: A systematic review. *Medical Education, 44*, 1057–1068.

Nothnagle, M., Anandarajah, G., Goldman, R., & Reis, S. (2011). Struggling to b self-directed: Residents' paradoxical beliefs about learning. *Academic Medicine, 86*, 1539–1544.

Parker, B., & Myrick, F. (2010). Transformative learning as a context for human patient simulation. *Journal of Nursing Education, 49*(6), 326–332. doi: 10.3928/-1484834-20100224-02

Passi, V., Johnson, S., Peile, E., Wright, S., Hafferty, F., & Johnson, N. (2013). Doctor role modeling in medical education: BEME Guide No. 27. *Medical Teacher, 35*, e1422–e1436.

Rogers, C. R. (1969). *Freedom to Learn.* Columbus, OH: Charles E. Merrill.

Samenow, C. P., Worley, L. L., Neufeld, R., Fishel, T., & Swiggart, W. H. (2013). Transformative learning in a professional development course aimed at addressing disruptive physician behavior: A composite case study. *Academic Medicine, 88*(1), 117–123. doi: 10.1097/ACM.0b13e31827b4cc9

Sternszus, R., Cruess, S., Cruess, R., Young, M., & Steinaert, Y. (2012). Residents as role models: Impact on undergraduate trainees. *Academic Medicine, 87*, 1282–1287. doi: 10.1097/ACM.0b013e3182624c53

Stuart, E., Sectish, T. C., & Huffman, L. C. (2005). Are residents ready for self-directed learning? A pilot program of individualized learning plans in continuity clinic. *Ambulatory Pediatrics, 5*(5), 298–301.

Taylor, D. C., & Hamdy, H. (2013). Adult learning theories: Implications for learning and teaching in medical education: AMEE Guide No. 83. *Medical Teacher, 35*(11), e1561–e1572.

Tekian, A., & Artino, A. R. (2013). AM last page: Master's degree in health professions education programs. *Academic Medicine, 88*(9), 1399.

Thomas, P. L. (2012). Charge nurses as front-line leaders: Development through transformative learning. *Journal of Continuing Education in Nursing, 43*(2), 67–74.

Tough, A. (1967). *Learning without a teacher* (Educational Research Series, No. 3). Toronto, CA: Ontario Institute for Studies in Education.

Tough, A. (1971). *The adult's learning projects: A fresh approach to theory and practice in adult learning.* Toronto, Canada: Ontario Institute for Studies in Education.

Van Schaik, S., Plant, J., & O'Sullivan, P. (2013). Promoting self-directed learning through portfolios in undergraduate medical education: The mentor's perspective. *Medical Teacher, 35*, 139–144.

Wear, D., Zarconi, J., Garden, R., & Jones, T. (2012). Reflection in/and writing pedagogy and practice in medical education. *Academic Medicine, 87*(5), 603–609. doi: 10.1097/ACM.0b013e31824d22e9

Wittich, C. M., Reed, D. A., McDonald, F. S., Varkey, P., & Beckman, T. J. (2010). Transformative learning: A framework using critical reflection to link the improvement competencies in graduate medical education. *Academic Medicine, 85*(11), 1790–1793. doi: 10:1097/ACM.06013e3181f54eed

Youngclaus, J., & Fresne, J. A. (2013). *Physician education debt and the cost to attend medical school: 2012 update.* Washington, DC: Association of American Medical Colleges.

PART II

SUPPORTING ADULT LEARNING IN ORGANIZATIONS, INSTITUTIONS, AND COMMUNITIES:

Leading Change toward a Sustainable Future for Adult Learning

CHAPTER 19

COLLABORATIVE LEADERSHIP FOR SUSTAINED PARTNERSHIPS

Margaret H. Rice
University of Houston–Victoria

Leadership of adult education in the twenty-first century, particularly in planning educational programs, means working in partnership with many groups. Caffarella and Daffron (2013), professors and authors in the field of adult education, pointed out that building and sustaining partnerships help create a solid base of support for adult learning programs. These partnerships, whether formal or informal, often include stakeholders who have varying social, economic, cultural, and political interests. However, they also noted that not all partnerships fulfill their purpose. The author remembers early in her experience with educational partnerships a valued mentor saying, "Collaborations are messy and they take a lot of work." As Cervero and Wilson (2006) emphasized, program planning takes place "in complex, messy settings in which people gather at planning tables to make decisions about the educational objectives and the social and political objectives of educational programs" (p. 6). Because of the "messy" nature of negotiating the various political, social, cultural, and economic interests

Building Sustainable Futures for Adult Learners, pages 405–419
Copyright © 2015 by Information Age Publishing
All rights of reproduction in any form reserved.

that are represented when people engage in educational planning, leadership becomes crucial. Many are calling for a more collaborative form of leadership to address the challenges planners face today, both in education as well as other fields.

Rubin (2009), founder and senior consultant at the Institute for Collaborative Leadership, asserted that "the first decade of the twenty-first century has been littered with political divisiveness, partisanship and an international image of aggressiveness. Our options are either isolation or bridge-building; polarized encampments or collaboration" (p. xv). O'Hara-Devereaux (2004), founder and CEO of Global Foresight, wrote that contemporary leadership challenges require a new leadership paradigm, one in which "leadership is neither a solo act nor a celebrity role." The successful leader must incorporate self-leadership "with others across generations and cultures, times and places" (p. 14). Collaborative Leadership meets these requirements, and fits well within the contemporary theories of adult education, particularly the transformative learning theorists (Boyd, 1991; Daloz, 1986; Mezirow, 2009), with their emphasis on discourse or dialogue, openness to others' perspectives, critical reflection, concern for others' feelings, withholding judgment, awareness of context, holistic orientation, and authentic practice. It also contains concepts significant to the learning organization theorists (Marsick & Watkins, 2005; Senge, 1990), who emphasize inquiry, dialogue, team learning, collaboration, and collective vision (Merriam, Caffarella & Baumgartner, 2007; Mezirow, Taylor, & Associates, 2009).

With the aforementioned considerations, a collaborative leadership approach for program planners and strategists in the field of adult education can greatly increase the success of partnership endeavors. The purpose of this chapter is threefold: first, to further the rationale for increasing the use of collaborative leadership in the current adult education environment; second, to increase understanding of this leadership style through a look at some definitions related to it; and, last, to help program planning leaders with developing the characteristics and skills needed for this leadership style through examination of a model designed by the author and author's spouse, and used successfully for many years in leadership training.

RATIONALE FOR COLLABORATIVE LEADERSHIP

Collaborative Leadership provides a leadership paradigm that has the capacity to bring together a diverse group of stakeholders to solve the complex challenges that adult education, as well as many other organizations, face today. As Jones, Lefoe, Harvey, and Ryland (2012) stated in their article on distributed leadership, models that emphasize "collective collaboration rather than individual power and control" are needed for twenty-first century leadership (p. 67). Rubin (2009) made a similar statement, saying the kinds of changes that are being demanded of institutions in general, and education in particular, are changes that:

> no one public leader, organization or sector can make on its own; changes that call on leaders to reach beyond their own borders to build sustained and broad-based support; changes that can best emerge from strong and coherent systems that build clarity, trust, aligned visions, passionate commitment, and shared resources through collaboration. (p. xv)

Humphreys, (2013) vice-president for policy and public engagement at the Association of American Colleges and Universities, also discussed the complexity of educational institutions, pointing out that the environment is often difficult to comprehend and navigate, even for insiders, much less for external constituents. She asserted,

> If we are to meet increasing demands for a more highly educated populace while also maintaining quality and navigating changes in technology, funding patterns, accountability frameworks, and the diversity of our student bodies, we urgently need more effective and widespread collaborative leadership. (Humphreys, 2013, para. 4)

Although a collaborative leadership approach is not the answer for every leadership situation, it offers advantages in those ever increasing situations involving multifaceted viewpoints and many stakeholders who have much at stake.

DEFINITIONS RELATED TO COLLABORATIVE LEADERSHIP

Rubin (2009) defined a collaboration as a "purposeful relationship in which all parties strategically choose to cooperate in order to achieve shared or overlapping objectives" (p. 2). Many groups such as social groups, committees, task forces, churches, and teams could fit this definition because the two main concepts are "purpose" and "relationship." Its purpose justifies its convening, and it is a "collective, and interactive endeavor" (p. 3). Participants choose to engage with one another. Engaging and contributing to the process is a key aspect of collaboration. Adult education leaders live and breathe in this broad range of entities. As Cervero and Wilson (2006) pointed out in their influential work on negotiating the social and political interests that are integral to successful planning, roles and settings for planners of adult education include "leaders and continuing educators in community colleges and higher education, human resource and organizational development specialists in business and government, labor and union educators, social movement activists, instructional developers for distance education, adult literacy educators, community educators and organizers, and educators in professional associations" (p .ix). Collaboration is implicit in the role of adult educator.

Stoner (2013), writing for the Seapoint Center for Collaborative Leadership, added an important point that collaboration is "working together to create something new in support of a shared vision" (para. 5). This "something new" results from each participant's willingness to contribute his or her perspective, while keeping an open mind to others' viewpoints. This synthesis of existing viewpoints to develop a new perspective is supported by transformational learning theory. Mezirow, Professor of Adult Education at Columbia University, who launched this theory in 1978 (Illeris, 2009) spoke of "perspective transformation," which occurs as learners (or collaborators) examine their assumptions and beliefs. Through the four components of experience, critical reflection, discourse (or dialogue), and action, a new understanding is formed (Merriam, Caffarella, & Baumgartner, 2007), one that is neither mine nor yours, but "ours."

People often use "teamwork" and "collaboration" interchangeably. Stoner (2013), along with Campbell (2011), Director of the Ashridge Strategic Management Center in England, expressed concern that collaboration is often confused with teamwork. Stoner pointed out that although teamwork might be collaborative, it is just as often hierarchical, as in sports, the military, and many business and educational settings. Collaboration is "based on respect, trust, and the wise use of power." Leaders must be willing to let go of control. Campbell, contrasting teamwork and collaboration continued:

> Now, so long as the team has someone with the authority to resolve disputes, ensure coordinated action and remove disruptive or incompetent members, teams work well.
>
> . . . Collaborators face a different challenge. They will have some shared goals, but they often also have competing goals. Also, the shared goal is usually only a small part of their responsibilities. Unlike a team, collaborators cannot rely on a leader to resolve differences. (p. 1)

Teamwork may foster innovation, but it is not integral to its processes. Coordination and cooperation are the mainstays of teamwork, while reflection and dialogue that leads to innovation is a distinctive component of collaboration.

What, then, defines and distinguishes collaborative leadership from other types of leading? According to Rubin (1998), "Collaborative Leadership is the skillful and mission-oriented facilitation of relevant interinstitutional relationships" (p. xvii). Rubin further stated,

It is the juncture of organizing and management. Whereas teachers, community, and labor organizers are trained to patiently build their movements through one-on-one conversations with each individual they want to recruit, collaborative leaders do this and more by building structures to support and sustain these productive relationships over time. (2009, p. 3)

Others emphasized the relational aspect of collaborations. Witte and McCormack (2014), in writing about building collaborative partnerships, describe collaboration as being a "mutually beneficial and explicit relationship between two or more individuals or organizations to achieve specific goals. It requires more long-term, committed efforts than cooperation or coordination" (p. 252). This distinguishing characteristic of collaborative leadership—building lasting relationships—is what makes this style of leadership significant for sustaining partnerships.

The challenge for collaborative leaders is to develop the needed abilities to build and manage these ongoing, voluntary, and purposeful relationships. This type of leadership requires a commitment to personal growth as well as skills development in communication and group processes. It requires the ability to reflect on one's own actions and make changes to improve one's leadership in light of the actions and viewpoints of the group one is leading. It requires the skills and tools to negotiate the various political agendas, ethical constructs, and social persuasions that participants bring to the planning process. It requires dedication to the task and confidence in the participants' ability to create a shared vision and stay with a process that enables attainment of their vision. And, it requires the leader/facilitator to have the self-confidence and know-how to guide the group to their destination. *Building Blocks of Collaborative Leadership*, the model shown in Figure 19.1, can serve as a guide to those who want to increase their effectiveness as collaborative leaders through development of the personal characteristics, relationship skills, and leadership processes needed to be an effective.

BUILDING BLOCKS OF COLLABORATIVE LEADERSHIP: A CONCEPTUAL FRAMEWORK

Model Overview

This model or conceptual framework is designed for leaders committed to developing a collaborative style. It is adapted from a model, designed by the author and the author's spouse (Rice & Rice, 1997), who used it in leadership training seminars for many years to help leaders and organizations develop effective relationships for working together. The model identifies basic components and competencies required for collaborative leadership.

COLLABORATIVE LEADERSHIP

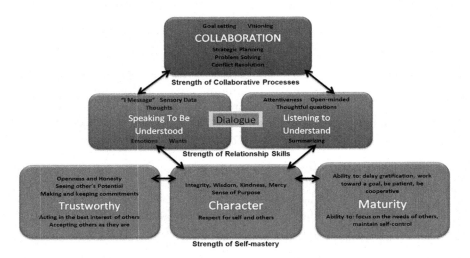

Figure 19.1 Building blocks of collaborative leadership. © 2013 Margaret & Gene Rice, adapted from *Building Blocks of Effective Relationships*, 1997.

The model has six components or "building blocks" which are important characteristics for the collaborative leader. These traits should also be, or become over time, descriptive of the participants and group as well. These components reflect the characteristics that Rubin (1998) noted are needed for a collaborative leader to build and sustain the relationships to accomplish the task: "respect, humility, trustworthiness, interpersonal and organization skills, credibility, and focused self-discipline" (p. 1).

The three levels of the conceptual framework—self-mastery, relationships, and processes—illustrate an orderly progression to the development of sustainable collaborative partnerships. This is true to the extent that it is difficult to work in each successive level without having some degree of proficiency in the prior level. Additionally, if one attempts to use the relationship and collaborative process skills, without the solid foundation provided by the foundational level, that leader will be seen as manipulative, consequently losing the very trust that is needed for long-term relationships. Rubin (2009) addressed this subject, suggesting "As collaborative leaders, we have to be trustworthy, otherwise our collaborative partners will not be comfortable sacrificing a little bit of control over their decision making and public image to join our collaboration" (p. 62). The initial level of the framework is foundational for all that follows. However, at the same time the leader/group grows in one area, growth is enhanced in all areas, as indicated by the arrows connecting the various components. These arrows represent the connectedness of the components and the reality that leaders can grow continuously in all the areas of collaborative leadership. The six main components of the model are identified in the larger print, with some examples of the component provided in smaller black print. These examples are not intended to be exhaustive, but to give fodder for thought and awareness.

Level One: The Strength of Self-Mastery

The first three components—trustworthiness, character, and maturity—are located on the first tier because they are foundational to building long term relationships. A case could be made for combining all three under one heading (character or trustworthiness); however, they are separated for the purpose of exploring them more fully and creating awareness and opportunity for reflection around these traits.

These foundational components are considered self-mastery attributes because unlike skills that are developed through practice, the foundation-level traits result from commitments individuals make about the way in which they will relate to others. Senge (1990), a strong influence in development of learning organization theory, spoke of "personal mastery," describing it as the "discipline of continually clarifying and deepening our personal vision, of focusing our energies, of developing patience, and of seeing reality objectively" (p. 7). Senge's description aligns well with the qualities listed in the level-one blocks.

To be seen as a person of character—one on whom others would rely in interpersonal interactions—and one who is able to facilitate collaboration requires maturity and trustworthiness. The more one can develop these traits, the better he or she will become at collaborative leadership. Qualities of maturity include the abilities to delay gratification, work toward achieving long-term goals, exhibit patience with others' perspectives, and focus on the needs of others.

Trustworthiness includes being open and honest, which sets the tone for others to express themselves with honesty. Witte and McCormack (2014) noted that collaborative partnerships are built on the basis of trust. They emphasized "mutual respect, trust, and a shared desire to pursue a common goal" as foundations of collaboration (p. 251). One of the most important traits in this category for a collaborative leader is accepting others as they are, while at the same time seeing their potential and valuing what they bring to the table. When people know they can count on their leader to act in their best interest, as well as keep commitments, they will trust that leader. This correlates with the concept of developing "authentic practice" in transformative learning theory. Mezirow et al. (2009) noted, "Developing authentic practice is significant for fostering trusting relationships between learners and teacher which often provides the safe environment for learners to engage in critical reflection, ultimately allowing transformative learning to take place"(p. 4). Authentic practice is essential for a collaborative leader/facilitator in creating the environment of trust necessary for success.

Rubin (2009) pointed out that people who choose to relate to us as a leader must be "confident in the consistent morality of our behavior and the predictable pattern of our ethics" (p. 62). As leaders of collaborations, "we are compelled to come to grips with our central defining principles: that is, those values and elements of our character that are central to our identity and self-image" (Rubin, 2009, p. 62). The more one exercises maturity and trustworthiness, the more that leader will be seen as a person of character who acts with integrity and naturally projects a sense of purpose. The leader has established the credibility needed for collaborative work to progress.

Building Self-Mastery Skills

In using this model as a development tool for collaborative leadership, the following will be helpful exercises for the foundational areas.

1. Review the traits listed in the three level-one blocks and think of others you might want to add to them. (Remember, these are examples.)
2. Reflect on those areas that are strengths in your life, as well as those in which you need growth.
3. Select one or two traits that you want to improve, and make a commitment to positive change in these areas.
4. Identify a situation, time or place in which you can demonstrate your commitment and imagine yourself following through in that situation. Think of the words you will use and the behaviors you will express. It may be helpful to think of someone who you admire in the area you have chosen to strengthen, and follow their example.

Level Two: The Strength of Relationships

The strength of self-mastery sets the stage for skills development in communication, the level at which relationships are enriched and expanded. As Rubin (2009) described, leaders' reach "beyond their own borders to build sustained and broad-based support; changes that can best emerge from strong and coherent systems that build clarity, trust, aligned visions" (p. xv). The best leaders realize both the importance of and the challenges to successful communication. Rubin, in emphasizing the importance of interpersonal communication suggested that leaders contribute to this by:

- modeling honest and productive communication skills,
- asking more questions than we answer,
- attentively ensuring that all partners participate in key discussions,
- noting and addressing nonparticipation, and
- never permitting decisions to be made by tacit endorsement but, rather, by making sure that each partner is engaged in the decision with at least an active vote or affirmation of support. (pp. 70–71)

Communication that best furthers the goals of collaboration is often referred to as dialogue (Daloz, 1986) or discourse (Mezirow & Associates, 2000), and is integral to collaborative efforts. Discourse, according to Mezirow, is a process through which we "transform our taken-for-granted frames of reference... to make them more inclusive, discriminating, open, emotionally capable of change, and reflective so we may generate beliefs and opinions that will prove more true and justified to guide actions" (pp. 7–8). The skillful facilitator continually sharpens the skills that engender dialogue and helps the group to develop their dialogical skills. In the spirit of true dialogue, speakers want to speak in a way that conveys meaning, and listeners want to listen attentively to understand the speaker's meaning. The aim for the leader of collaborative groups is to enable this dynamic exchange change to occur. As group members present their viewpoints, while others listen with an open mind, what Mezirow identifies as "perspective transformation," takes place. Rather than "your way" or "my way, a "new way" begins to emerge.

Skilled collaborative leaders continually work to enhance their own dialogue skills and model them for the group, as well as providing guidance before and during collaborative discourse. From a practical standpoint, these leaders generally present some "ground rules" for group interaction and encourage input from the group for additions or deletions to these rules, until the group agrees on the guidelines by which they will relate. These generally include items such as listening without interrupting, encouraging everyone in the group to express their opinion, respecting others' viewpoints, and so on. Such guidelines set the tone for respectful interaction, and the leader can remind the group, if needed, during the course of their work together.

Building Communication Skills

Communication involves the sending of a message and the receiving of a message as it was intended by the sender. This is where collaborations often get messy. While it is not within the purview of this chapter to discuss the many ways that messages can be misunderstood and misinterpreted, most leaders have experienced the challenges of creating an environment in which communication strengthens relationships within the group. Some good general communication tips for the collaborative leader to remember and encourage in the "speaking to be understood" category include the following.

1. Use an I-message, which shows ownership of one's observations, thoughts, feelings and wants. This is particularly important if the discussion has become a little tense.
2. Provide sensory (observation) data to provide documentation for those listening.
3. Present thoughts (interpretations, conclusions, beliefs) to help listeners understand your perspective.
4. Share emotions to help others empathize.
5. Express wants to help others understand your intent and to persuade or motivate.

An easy acronym to remember these speaking skills is STEW: Sensory data (observations), Thoughts (beliefs, interpretations, opinions, viewpoints, assumptions), Emotions (feelings, such as fear, relief, joy, sadness), and Wants (desires, objectives, dreams). For example, consider the following hypothetical statement made by a university safety task force member.

> When I look at our facilities, I am very concerned about the safety and security of our students, especially at night when they leave classes. I think we're very fortunate that we haven't had an incident so far, and I want us to take some measures to ensure that we don't. I get really nervous when I see that there are no security lights or cameras around our buildings. Additionally, our buildings remain open to anyone during our hours of operation. I have heard students express concern about walking out to their cars at night. I would like to see us install security cameras and lighting. I believe it would make students feel better also—plus, it would make a statement about the priority we place on student safety.

Notice in the above example the speaker uses an "I-Message" reflecting ownership of their viewpoint. Sensory data is provided (When I look... no security cameras or lighting;... I have heard...); thoughts are presented (I think we're very fortunate... I believe it would make students feel better... it would make a statement); emotions are shared (I am very concerned... I get really nervous); and, wants are expressed (I want us to take some measures... I would like to see us put up a fence).

Learning to really listen for understanding is critical to the success of collaborative endeavors. In today's environment, listening can be made more difficult if participants are distracted by using electronic devices to send text messages, check e-mail, check Facebook, or any of the variety of other diversions these handy devices offer. Leaders often include a statement related to this in the ground rules to which the group agrees. Listening skills are the most important skills to develop when trying to understand another's perspective, and they can be continually improved. Following are some ideas that help increase understanding.

1. Attentiveness—focusing on the speaker, noticing non-verbal expression as well as the words that are being spoken.
2. Encouraging the speaker by responsive body language.
3. Keeping an open mind, that is, listening with a non-judgmental attitude.
4. Asking open-ended questions to get additional information, especially when you don't fully understand the speaker's viewpoint. (Open-ended questions require a thoughtful response, rather than just a "yes" or "no.")
5. Summarizing in your own words what you understood as a listener, and asking the speaker to correct any misunderstanding.

Just as with the self-mastery (level one) attributes, collaborative leaders can increase their effectiveness by reviewing and paying attention to their dialogical skills. As the leader/facilitator models communication that enhances relationships and enables better collaboration, group members will tend to follow suit. Questions for reflection and commitment to improvement in the second-tier components include:

1. Am I communicating in a way that builds relationships?
2. Do my speaking skills reflect taking responsibility for self? Do I consistently leave out an important aspect of my experience, such as emotions or wants?
3. Am I listening with an open mind?
4. Am I open to changing my viewpoint?
5. Am I listening for the meaning behind others' words?
6. Am I asking open-ended questions?

Level Three: Strength of Collaborative Processes

As the foundational elements, along with the elements for effective dialogue (the first two levels) are working together, then a group is able to do the work on the complex issues for which they were brought together. The top tier of the pyramid is collaboration. It is placed at the top because it is the ultimate aim of the process, and also because the components of the first two tiers must be present to some extent before a group will be able to work collaboratively.

The top tier is where the real work takes place. It includes such elements as visioning, goal-setting, problem-solving, conflict resolution, and strategic planning, the last of which incorporates multiple processes brought together in a plan that is then implemented. The successful collaborative leader oversees the preparation needed for this level of work and selects quality tools designed to produce the results needed for the collaboration to move forward.

A glimpse into a very small "process among processes" of a collaborative group might go as follows, with the leader/facilitator providing a structure that ensures that each person is heard on the issues of importance. The facilitator divides a group of 30 "representative stakeholders" into six teams of five members each. Each team would be directed to select roles for each member, such as team leader, recorder, materials coordinator, time-keeper, and clean-up manager. The team leader's job is to keep the team on task to complete their assignments in the allotted time. The recorder's responsibility is to write down team member input, the reporter for each team reports to the large group what their team has agreed upon, and so on.

This scenario could unfold as follows. The teams are assigned the task of brainstorming ways of creating the safest environment for students. Each team member writes three ideas on a 3×5 card; when this activity is completed, each team member shares their ideas, and the recorder writes each unduplicated idea on a large sheet of paper. The group then has the chance to dialogue about the ideas they have identified, to give their viewpoints, and ask questions of their team members. Next, the group votes on their three best ideas using a method determined by the facilitator. This often is done by giving each team member five "stick-on" dots to distribute among the ideas. Each reporter then presents their team's three top ideas to the large group along with a summary of the dialogue that took place. Each unduplicated idea is posted on a flipchart or by other means visible to all. Team members are then asked to go back into discussion and, as a group, determine the most important ideas. Again this can be done by giving each team some "stick-on dots" and asking them to place the dots accordingly. Often a facilitator will tell a group, "You have nine dots to distribute in any way you choose. If you want to place five dots on one idea you can, but decide as a group how you want to place them. Team leaders, you are responsible for ensuring that each team member has the opportunity to express his or her opinion."

This example is illustrative of the ways in which a leader/facilitator involves the entire group, ensuring that every person provides input, and the group has opportunity to discuss and reflect on the ideas presented. It encourages shared decision-making based on the best thinking of the group at a particular time. There are many methods and tools for accomplishing this, and each leader must determine what facilitates the best outcomes with a particular group. This requires the leader to be attuned to the group dynamics, as well as keeping the group on task and moving toward their stated goals. In the collaborative framework, a plan is always a work in progress. Implementation begins, but progress is assessed along the way, and adjustments are made as needed to achieve the aims the group has decided upon. For this reason, collaborations must be sustained to be successful. A skilled leader/facilitator safeguards this sustainability.

Building Collaborative Leadership Skills

Becoming skilled at collaborative leadership requires a commitment to growth. It requires critical reflection upon one's own beliefs and assumptions about people, places, and things. It requires being open to others' viewpoints, while ensuring that the group moves forward toward their goals. And, it requires confidence that the group has the ability to make wise choices and move forward. One could say it requires continual transformation. Although each aspiring collaborative leader must find their best way forward, the following are some suggestions for growth in this third-tier area. (1) Select a skilled collaborative leader/facilitator to mentor you. This could be a formal mentoring relationship, or learning from a skilled leader of a group in which you are involved; (2) Familiarize yourself with the skills needed to lead collaborative processes by reading experts in the field, such as Rubin; or, publications by organizations dedicated to collaborative leadership, such as Partnership for Excellence, One World, Inc., or Seapoint Center for Collaborative Leadership; (3) Begin incorporating collaborative leadership principles and tools in every meeting you lead or attend; and (4) Let colleagues know that you are available to facilitate strategic planning using a collaborative style. The more you lead using this paradigm, the more comfortable you will become with it.

CONCLUSION

Collaborative Leadership offers a much needed paradigm to solve problems creatively in adult education, as well as in other fields. It incorporates multiple stakeholders and viewpoints, innovative solutions to complex problems, and shared vision and goals. Reflecting back on Rubin's statement, "You are a Collaborative Leader once you have accepted responsibility for building—or helping to ensure the success of—a heterogeneous team to accomplish a shared purpose" (Rubin, 2009, p.2), reminds one that collaborative leadership implies responsibility and commitment.

ACKNOWLEDGEMENTS

I would like to acknowledge Judy Phillips, CEO of Partnership for Excellence, who is the best collaborative leader I've ever worked with. Six years ago, I was asked to serve on the Victoria Independent School District (VISD)

"District Leadership Team" in Victoria, Texas where I live and work. At that time, VISD was divided by many problems and conflicts. A new superintendent arrived and asked Phillips to assist the district in strategic planning. A diverse group of individuals was asked to serve on the leadership team, representing every internal and external stakeholder group. Phillips' collaborative style of leadership and her expertise in using the skills associated with this paradigm have enabled VISD to create a shared vision and goals, and make outstanding, measurable progress toward achievement of these goals. Phillips has been an inspiration, role model, and an informal mentor in helping me improve my collaborative leadership skills; and, most significantly, confirmed the importance of collaborative leadership in maintaining partnerships. I thank Phillips and the VISD administration for the privilege of being part of this leadership team that has made a positive difference in our community.

REFERENCES

Boyd, R. D. (1991). *Personal transformations in small groups: A Jungian perspective.* New York, NY: Rutledge.

Caffarella, R. S., & Daffron, S. R. (2013). *Planning programs for adult learners: A practical guide.* San Francisco, CA. Jossey-Bass Publishers.

Campbell, A. (2011). *Collaboration is misunderstood and overused.* Retrieved from http: blogs.hbr.org/2011/09/collaboration-is-misunderstood/

Cervero, R. M., & Wilson, A. L. (2006). *Working the planning table: Negotiating democratically for adult, continuing and workplace education.* San Francisco, CA: Jossey-Bass Publishers.

Daloz, L. A. (1986). *Effective teaching and mentoring: Realizing the transformational power of adult learning experiences.* San Francisco, CA: Jossey-Bass Publishers.

Humphreys, D. (2013) Deploying collaborative leadership to reinvent higher education for the twenty-first century. *Peer Review, 15*(1). Retrieved from http:// www.aacu.org/peerreview/pr-wi13/Humphreys.cfm

Illeris, K. (2009). Introduction to "An overview on transformative learning." In K. Illeris (Ed.), *Contemporary theories of learning: Learning theorists . . . in their own words* (p. 91). New York, NY: Routledge/Taylor and Francis Group.

Jones, S., Lefoe, G., Harvey, M., & Ryland, K. (2012). Distributed leadership: A collaborative framework for academics, executives and professionals in higher education. *Journal of Higher Education Policy and Management, 34*(1), (67–78).

Marsick, V. J., & Watkins, K. E. (2005). Learning organization. In L. M. English (Ed.), *International encyclopedia of adult education* (pp. 355–360). New York, NY: Palgrave Macmillan.

Merriam, S. B., Caffarella, R. S., & Baumgartner, L. M. (2007). *Learning in adulthood: A comprehensive guide* (3rd ed.). San Francisco, CA: Jossey-Bass.

Mezirow, J., & Associates. (2000). *Learning as transformation: Critical perspectives on a theory in progress.* San Francisco, CA: Jossey-Bass.

Mezirow, J. (2009). An overview on transformative learning. In K. Illeris (Ed.), *Contemporary theories of learning: Learning theorists . . . in their own words* (pp. 91–105). New York, NY: Routledge/Taylor and Francis Group.

Mezirow, J., Taylor, E. W., & Associates. (2009). *Transformative learning in practice: Insights from community, workplace, and higher education.* San Francisco, CA: Jossey-Bass.

O'Hara-Devereaux, M. (2004). *Navigating the badlands: Thriving in the decade of radical transformation.* San Francisco, CA: Jossey-Bass.

Rice M., & Rice, D. (1997). *Building blocks of effective relationships.* Unpublished manuscript.

Rubin, H. (1998). *Collaboration skills for educators and nonprofit leaders.* Chicago, IL: Lyceum Books, Inc.

Rubin, H. (2009). *Collaborative leadership: Developing effective partnerships for communities and schools.* Thousand Oaks, CA: Corwin Press.

Senge, P. M. (1990). *The fifth discipline: The art and practice of the learning organization.* New York, NY: Currency Doubleday.

Stoner, J. L. (2013). *Let's stop confusing cooperation and teamwork with collaboration.* Retrieved from http://seapointcenter.com/cooperation-teamwork-and-collaboration/

Witte, M. M., & McCormack, T. J. (2014). Building collaborative partnerships through personal relationships. In C.J. Boden-McGill & Kathleen P. King (Eds.), *Developing and sustaining adult learners* (pp. 249–265). Charlotte, NC: Information Age Publishing.

CHAPTER 20

SHAPING LEADERSHIP CULTURE

The Role of Adult Education in Developing and Sustaining the Next Generation of Women Leaders

Carmela R. Nanton
Palm Beach Atlantic University

Leadership and learning are indispensable to each other.
—J. F. Kennedy (1963, p. 869)

Women bring considerable talent, experience, and educational background to leadership in industry today. Despite that fact, we do not see them represented in the top leadership positions. Organizations ordinarily aggressively vie with each other to recruit and promote these candidates. However, whether we are talking about countries, Fortune 500 companies, governments, healthcare, or other service industries, there is clear evidence of a real and persistent disconnect between the obvious qualifications (educational preparation, workforce presence, and managerial experience) and the presence of women as top leaders (McKinsey & Company, 2012).

Building Sustainable Futures for Adult Learners, pages 421–445
421

Women's leadership is sometimes problematic as an embodied form of leadership that presents potential risk. Senge (2006) points out that women leaders are "...people who do not come from the traditional centers of power but from the cultural, economic and demographic periphery..." (p. 367); thus, they can immediately engender mistrust and unfavorable judgments by observers who may be unconsciously predisposed to disqualify top candidates from being recruited, promoted, or selected for leadership positions. Sinclair (2005) points out "Leadership is a bodily practice, a physical performance in addition to a triumph of mental or motivational mastery" (p. 388). As leaders, women increase the level of complexity across all dimensions of leadership. They continue to present a challenge to organizational search committees as the ongoing underrepresentation of women in chief or executive (C-level) level positions suggest. Because organizations and nations still continue to struggle with accepting women as leaders, there remains critical learning to be done in this area. In the quote that began this chapter, Kennedy (1963) points out that "learning and leadership are indispensable to each other" (p. 869). Therefore, this chapter's primary purpose is to undertake a cross-disciplinary examination of social role theory (Eagly & Johnson, 1990; Moss, 2008), gender and leadership theory (Eagly, 1987; Eagly & Carli, 2007; Hoyt, 2013), and adult education theory (Elias & Merriam, 2004). The proposed strategies to address the identified barriers to women as leaders will be discussed within the framework of the radical adult education philosophy (Elias & Merriam, 2004; Freire, 1970; Merriam, Caffarella, & Baumgartner, 2007), highlighting the role adult education can or needs to play in shaping contemporary leadership culture and the development of the next generation of women leaders. The chapter will conclude with proposed strategies for the learning (Wenger, 2000) and practice strategies for creating a more inclusive leadership environment and culture for women.

THE SIGNIFICANCE OF WOMEN'S LEADERSHIP

There is currently some resistance to women as leaders. This resistance to women's leadership can be attributed to conflicting values, roles, and power dynamics consciously or unconsciously perpetuated by ingrained stereotypical reactions. Research has shown that a plausible reason for these reactions is that people are trapped in bodily performances by wider relations of power and discourse (Sinclair, 2005). They are played out in gender regimes (appropriately masculine and feminine performances), class-based assumptions (shop floor versus managerial masculine performances), and around socially and culturally constructed taboos (Sinclair, 2005, p. 388). Thus, when women take on leadership positions, they are in effect operating outside of their socially prescribed roles in ways that can result in "disruption, and contestation, resistance and experimentation" with traditionally held normative roles and expectations. A brief look at social role theory can provide further insight and understanding of this phenomenon.

SOCIAL ROLE THEORY

One plausible reason for the slow change in the organizational culture is that western culture has gender-based roles and expectations that are largely contradictory to the idea of women as leaders (Eagly, 1987; Moss, 2008). Thus, when men and women alike have negative reactions to women as leaders, the cause runs deeper than what is immediately evident. Eagly (1987) has spent several decades analyzing and explaining the significant influence that social norms exert on social behavior. Her seminal work on social role theory brought four salient considerations to the forefront that present a foundation from which to view the challenges women in leadership face. First, she wrote, that men and women behave differently in social situations, taking on roles specified and expected by the society in which they are a part. Second, the primary emphases of women's roles are related to domestic, home-making or relational tasks; for men, the roles are public, work-related, or agentic. Third, the occupational roles that women are expected to fulfill are not only different from men's, but they are lower in positional power and status. Fourth and finally, those women who operate or seek to step outside of those roles are faced with pressure to conform that hinders their progress in the achievement of agentic roles and behaviors. These role expectations are socialized into the psyches of the society at large, are passed down from generation to generation, and influence the behavioral and decision making processes of individuals (Eagly 1987; Moss, 2008). In organizations these expectations can also influence the perceptions of who could (or should) lead: "not only are the decision makers influenced by the stereotypes that disadvantage women in the leadership role, but they may succumb to homosocial reproduction, a tendency for a group to reproduce itself in its own image" (Hoyt, 2013, p. 359).

Leadership and Social Role Theory

The nature of leadership practice also influences the very perception of the roles that are appropriate for certain individuals. For example, Moss (2008) indicates that individual roles can be considered flexible depending on context and responsibility: "work roles, such as leadership positions...might override... gender roles and reduce gender differences" (para. 5). On the other hand, Moss also indicates that "individuals might question the capacity of women in particular positions, such as leadership roles" (para.7), because of social role expectations. Holding a leadership position can require specific behaviors of the leader that supersede social role expectations.

So, Eagly and Johnson (1990) assert that "when social behavior is regulated by other, less diffuse social roles [a leader's] as it is in organizational settings, behavior should primarily reflect the influence of these other roles and therefore lose much of its gender stereotypic character" (p. 249). Thus, a position of authority can serve to mitigate the perceptions of gender stereotypes. Whereas under the usual circumstances, social role prescriptions can prevent women from being nominated for promotions, and women showing agentic traits can be seen as unappealing or cold; the currently-held concept of leadership can reduce these perceptions and behaviors (Eagly & Johnson, 1990; Heilman, Wallen, Fuchs, & Tamkins, 2004; Rudman, 1998).

Thus, it is the responsibility of incumbent leaders, throughout the processes of leadership development and succession planning, to be open to moving beyond the limitations of prevailing mental models and to initiate strategies to develop female high-potential followers for the future strategic benefit of the company as a whole. Frequently, according to Senge (2006) in the Fifth discipline, "the first or second generation of women in senior executive positions have to be 'more like men than the men,' in order to prove that they are 'real leaders' by the masculine criteria that are still dominant" (p. 368). The hindrances and obstacles that will be discussed are those that have been experienced by the first generation of women leaders, and they shed important light on what might be actually happening as society and organizations transition into a more inclusive leadership culture.

Naturally, given that women are visibly different from the masculine embodiment of leadership that has prevailed from early trait theories to today's prevailing leadership personas, this transition will not come without challenges and struggles. This difference further complicates matters by triggering even more dissonance: women as leaders are operating outside their gender-prescribes roles (Sinclair, 2005). Organizational culture must change in response to the increase of female workers and the inevitable rise of women to leadership positions (McKinsey & Company, 2012). As one studies the issue, the question arises: what exactly is it that needs to be changed? A look at the state of leadership and the barriers that currently exist will provide some specific areas of change that will be required.

CONTEMPORARY STATE OF WOMEN IN LEADERSHIP

According to the research literature, actual barriers against women as leaders are in place, and many experience role conflicts and tensions as they take on leadership roles (Evans & Breinig Chun, 2007; Shyns & Sanders, 2005; Sinclair, 2005). For the purposes of this discourse, it will be assumed that the educational and experiential qualifications have been met or exceeded. One could argue that women have increasingly had opportunity to assume leadership roles in an ever broadening range of disciplines, fields, and organizations. Generally, that is indeed true. However, the paucity of those who have had opportunity to make it, as well as the protracted pace of their advancement, is the intriguing and concerning phenomenon. There is ample historical evidence that women can and have successfully and effectively lead countries through times of turmoil, challenge, and transformation. Well-known leadership icons such as Golda Meir, Bhenazir Bhutto, Eva Peron, Margaret Thatcher, and Angela Merkel are powerfully clear examples of such leadership. These women have undeniably demonstrated their competency, skill, and effectiveness.

Women's Leadership Capability and Effectiveness

Highlighting the effectiveness of women's leadership is critical because the focus of the discussion goes beyond leader competencies to address areas that are usually subsumed within a competency paradigm. The discussion on social role theory addressed this in part; the specific barriers that follow this section will identify several non-competency related concerns that have significant impact on women's leadership opportunities. Even if women were to simply lean in to their ambitions, as Sandberg & Scovell's (2013) book encourages them to do, they would be doing so in the face of underrepresentation, prejudice, challenges to their authority, second guessing, insubordination, ongoing vulnerability, unnaturally high or conflicting expectations, and those who would force them in line with the status quo they are destined to change (Evans & Breinig Chun, 2007; Shyns & Sanders, 2005; Sinclair, 2005). Hoyt (2013) points out that the research supports "social costs and backlash experienced by women when they promote themselves or are competent in positions of authority" (p. 357). In the end, it really is about attitude and perception because, "being out of role in gender-relevant terms has its costs for leaders..." (Eagly & Johnson, 1990, p. 248). To add scope and context, a brief review of the literature on women's leadership effectiveness follows.

Women's Leadership Effectiveness

Ultimately, leaders are judged by their perceived effectiveness. Eagly and Johnson's (1990) meta-analysis points out that when we speak of leadership

426 • C. R. NANTON

effectiveness, we are reminded that it is "contingent on features of the group or organizational environment' (p. 249). Further, their analysis found that "women's leadership styles were more democratic than men's even in organization settings..." (p. 249). DuBrin's (2007) research with over 1800 male and female managers identified some differences between men and women's leadership skill tendencies: women were "rated higher on relationship-oriented leadership skills" while men were "...rated higher on task-oriented leadership skills" (p. 125). However, the findings indicated that on "overall [leadership] effectiveness, the sexes were perceived the same" (p. 125). Hoyt (2013) confirms that although women are less likely to negotiate or promote themselves for leadership positions, "...women are no less effective at leadership, committed to their jobs, or motivated for leadership roles than men." (p. 358). It is important to establish women's leadership effectiveness and ability at the outset because it sets up an important premise for examining the challenges, tensions, and inconsistencies that will be highlighted in the following discussion of barriers.

BARRIERS TO WOMEN'S LEADERSHIP

In Fortune 500 companies, the top of the leadership ladder is precarious, lean, and scarce for women (McKinsey & Company, 2012). Scholars agree that a range of obstacles exist: for the sake of clarity, only a few relevant to understanding the complexity of women's leadership will be highlighted here. Research suggests that informal organization barriers (Barbuto, Fritz, Matkin, & Marx, 2007; Evans & Breinig Chun, 2007; Lips & Keener, 2007; Shyns & Sanders 2005), lack of access to relevant social networks (Olsson & Walker, 2004; Nanton, 2009), and entrenched perceptions of women (Eagly & Johnson, 1990) can result in negative workplace ramifications. Yet women such as Carly Fiorina and Andrea Jung are powerful examples of strong proven leadership effectiveness across male and female dominated industries.

Nonetheless, the persistent reality is that women have not been able to attain leadership positions at the rate one would expect. As Olsson and Walker (2004) point out, "...while the number of women entering management positions continues to increase; women remain underrepresented at the senior executive level" (p. 244). This trend is so clearly evidenced across industries and business sectors alike, the inequities so pronounced, that the term "glass ceiling" has been used to describe the "... invisible, yet quite impenetrable, barrier that serves to prevent all but a disproportionately few women from reaching the highest ranks of the corporate hierarchy, regardless of their achievement and merits" (Lampe, 2001, p. 346). More recently, Eagly & Carli (2007) present the metaphor of a labyrinth to describe the challenges encountered all along the way of women's advancement to leadership positions.

Hillary Clinton's losing bid for the U.S. presidency in 2008 is an example with both adult education and leadership implications. It illuminated a classic and sobering reminder that this trend is still relevant today. Clinton's subsequent position as Secretary of State simultaneously acknowledged her prodigious leadership capability and competency even as it illuminated the significant barriers to women and leadership that yet remain. The glass ceiling remained intact between the tried and proven relationship-oriented position of Secretary of State, in which women have so far been allowed to lead and have proven themselves effective, and the ever elusive position of the Presidency that has yet to be won. Clinton's vivid words accurately depict what happened:

> Although we weren't able to shatter that highest, hardest glass ceiling this time, thanks to you, it's got about 18 million cracks in it,...And the light is shining through like never before, filling us all with the hope and the sure knowledge that the path will be a little easier next time. (Cilizza, 2008)

America's boardrooms and executive offices have had a similarly perplexing and persisting pattern of organizational leadership emerge. Furthermore, when women do arrive at the top, many find that they are not equitably compensated, and that the positional reward is anti-climactic in relation to the struggle to get to the senior executive level (Evans & Breinig Chun, 2007). The ubiquitous barriers in place that contribute to the underrepresentation of women in the executive or chief level positions of companies and nations are the biggest aspect of leadership of culture that needs to be reshaped to develop and sustain the next generation of women leaders. The work of re-shaping the leadership culture will result in "individual embodied practices [that can positively] interrupt systemic power" (Sinclair, 2005, p. 388).

Perception Barriers of Women's Leadership Effectiveness

Eagly and Johnson (1990), discussing perception barriers, point out that "women may tend to lose authority if they adopt distinctively feminine styles of leadership in extremely male dominated roles. Women who survive in such roles probably have to adopt the styles typical of male role occupants" (p. 248). Fletcher (2001) confirms that they disappear from the attention of co-workers and male-oriented colleagues because of leading as women. Though they may be well-qualified, they are not necessarily at the forefront when promotions are discussed. Their disappearance from the sight of co-workers and selecting officers is likely because they have neatly fit into the gender role stereotypes for supportive rather than leadership positions. This sets up a conflicted existence for aspirant women leaders as they also need to learn how to hurdle or circumvent existing barriers within leadership culture.

Conflicts and Consequence Barriers of Women's Leadership

Lips and Keener (2007) identified experiencing social disapproval, gender role strain, being judged less likeable if women promote their own competence, needing to continuously prove themselves, and balancing work and family as tension points not felt by male counterparts (p. 564). Evans and Breinig Chun (2007) point to informal organizational barriers which, "like behavioral forms of discrimination, may be invisible, difficult to pinpoint, covert, and cumulative in impact" (p. 57) in higher education. Barbuto, Fritz, Matkin, and Marks (2007) highlight the complexity created with the simultaneous expectations of women to behave like leaders on the one hand and to remain feminine on the other –even as they are punished for their femininity: "The more women violate the standards for their gender, the more they may be penalized by prejudiced reactions that would not be directed to their male counterparts" (p. 72). Because these roles are prescribed, stepping away from them or operating in a manner that is counter to the expectations can create a significant challenge for the woman as leader. In the face of these additional consequences, some women abandon their aspirations for leadership because it is perceived as unfeminine (Lips & Keener, 2007).

Barrier of Leadership as Unfeminine

Tension develops in women as they assume leadership roles, if "leadership is viewed as unfeminine" (Lips & Keener, 2007, p. 564) and the antithesis of the essence of whom they are. Lips and Keener point out that "people are more tolerant of dominant behavior in men than in women and that women receive more penalties for dominance than men do" (p. 564) and that the reward/cost ratio is not favorable to them. The cost can be perceived as being too high due to difficulty with subordinates who challenge the required dominant behavior of women as leaders. So, some high-potential candidates make the determination that no compensation is worthy of this stress. Thus, the perception of leadership as unfeminine becomes one of the covert organizational barriers causing women a loss of economic value (Lips & Keener, 2007).

Barrier of Abandoning Career Ambitions

The response to the cumulative effect of barriers can cause some well-qualified women to choose to walk away from their aspiration to be leaders (Fels, 2004). Collective wisdom, as a result, is that women are not ambitious, or that they are not interested in leadership roles. Contrary to this assumption, in an insightful study of women who had walked away from their dreams, Fels (2004) sought to examine whether women truly lacked ambition for leadership positions. Fels's findings suggested that women did not lack ambition, but that they lacked "an evaluating, encouraging audience" (2004, p. 3) which, according to Fels, must be present as such recognition is critical for fostering the development and mastery of skills. As these women are consistently presented with negative evaluations coupled with lack of encouragement, they become de-motivated in their quest for leadership positions and take themselves out of the running. The consequence is knowledge drain in organizations and job dissatisfaction.

A cumulative effect begins to emerge as even these few barriers are identified. According to Evans and Breinig Chun (2007) and Shyns and Sanders (2005), covert and invisible barriers can be the underlying cause for what can be occurring in organization search committees as well. Because such actions are covert or invisible, they ultimately result in many highly competent women, potential leaders, being prevented from advancement opportunities and compensation that are more readily available to men. These barriers are significant to the women who are hindered by them, for at least two reasons: first, candidates unaware of the barriers may attribute their negative experiences to other more tangible things, including their performance. Second, because these barriers are not easily identifiable, it becomes more difficult for women to remove these obstructions to their career advancement. There is salient economic value linked to informal workplace barriers as they can translate into women's salary inequities, lack of promotions, or even promotions without appropriate salary compensation and marginalization from critical networks (Evans & Breinig Chun 2007; Nanton, 2009; Shyns & Sanders 2005).

Social Networks Barriers

Women have also been blocked from access to beneficial social networks (Nanton, 2009). Career advancement is so often linked to social networks that a brief examination is warranted, even necessary. Olsson and Walker (2004) point out that "executive culture is constituted as a male domain," framed as "corporate masculinity" (p. 244). This can have a negative effect on women along two fronts. First is in relation to status and power by association. Women can be marginalized from status, power, politics, and informal social events, making them outsiders to critical networks that create career advancement benefits as they are not associated with these powerful networks. Second, they are positioned at a disadvantage when they compensate by creating their own less powerful networks with limits placed on their involvement in decision making, their social mobility, and career advancement (Nanton, 2009; Shyns & Sanders, 2005).

Conflicts of Role Expectations

Another conflict-ridden aspect of role expectations is related to women's work-life balance. Gender role expectations continue to persist even though many women bring home a bigger paycheck than their partner (Eagly & Johnson, 1990; Insch, McIntyre, & Napier, 2008; McKinsey & Company, 2012). These role expectations have influence on their lifestyle and career choices. Personal challenges, increased tension, stress, and conflict occur when women as leaders "are both primary breadwinners and primary caregivers" (McKinsey & Company, p. 6). They are pushed to integrate both roles: some choose to "hold themselves back from accelerated growth" (p. 7). While some organizations have sought to address this work situation, movement to make these organizational changes lags behind the growing needs of women as leaders as company response is often reactive rather than proactive (Sandberg & Scovell, 2013).

From a practical organizational perspective, women are traditionally placed in assistant, secretarial, support, and or relationship-oriented management positions which reduce the odds of their advancement to leadership roles (Hoyt, 2013; McKinsey & Company, 2012). Insch, McIntyre, and Napier (2008) point out that "...constantly being aware of being a woman in a man's world, having to prove themselves to others, and having to work harder and be better than their male counterparts" (p. 21) also serves to prevent women's advancement to senior management positions. This is exacerbated by the lack of women in senior management positions who can either hire in more women, serve as mentors, or at minimum serve as examples of those who have mastered the hurdles of their leadership interactions and developed a "professional style with which male managers were comfortable" (p. 21). Quite often these women collectively suffer in silence. They believe that they are the only ones with that problem. The guilt and shame of it all keeps them silent and isolated.

Brookfield (1987) astutely observes that "most personally problematic situations do have some social dimension to them" (p. 61): "Perceiving the connection between personal troubles and social forces leads to social as well as individual change" (p. 59). So it is vital to the leadership change process for women to not only see their problem as part of the socio-cultural context that both creates and supports it, but to move beyond this recognition to dialogue, talking about it publicly. In so doing, they can collaborate on questioning "prevailing, predominantly white male modes of knowledge, the generation of alternative perspectives and framework of interpretation, and the collective attempt to create new ways of thinking and living" (p. 60).

However, many women in the public sphere are not yet at this place. Thus, women are largely left with having to prove their capability to lead, without having the benefit of role models who have successfully learned to navigate the organizational environment and scale the hurdles presented to them. Proposed changes that will be required need to occur at several levels in the organization, and even across society, for it to be truly effective, meaning that learning and change also needs to occur. How can today's organizations effectively and strategically respond with formal and informal leadership development strategies that take into consideration the complexity of the leadership context for female high-potential candidates without jettisoning all of the problems at the feet of women? It is here that adult education in various forms can take on a significant role in shaping leadership culture.

THE ROLE OF ADULT EDUCATION IN SHAPING LEADERSHIP CULTURE

The women who take to leadership positions naturally are under much pressure and lead with skill under great difficulty in a workplace context that is not always friendly or accepting (Insch, McIntyre, & Napier 2008). The dynamic interactive relationship between leader and follower is premised on perceptive judgments made by both parties that result in either the success or the failure of the leadership experience of followers. This relational context of leadership also has salient implications for the participants.

It is also in this situated context that the leader-mentor can work to shape organizational culture to be more inclusive of the needs of women leaders as their needs are articulated and expressed: they are then functioning as transformational leaders (Northouse, 2013). It is this aspect of the leader-follower interchange which is influenced by the mental models shaped by the societal, cultural, and professional normative expectations that we will now explore. The discussion will begin with the role that adult education could play through the appropriate philosophical approach, recognition of the forms of learning that best apply to this leadership development context, and the adult education practices that most efficiently facilitate the needed organizational change in perspective and practice.

Adult Education Philosophy

The proposed approach for shaping leadership culture to be more in-clusive of women's leadership involves adult education and learning. From an adult education perspective, the philosophical approach as the entity that undergirds actions, decisions, and behavior is *Radical-Progressive*. The rationale for this blended approach speaks to the problematic complexity of women's leadership, and a fundamental need to change society. This complexity is culturally influenced with oppressive overtones as evidenced by social role theory and the organizational barriers previously discussed. The radical philosophical approach, as well as Freire's theory, according to Elias and Merriam (2004), "challenges the status quo" and "stands outside of the mainstream of adult education philosophy" (p. 147) because it is one where "radical changes to society" are proposed (p. 148). Elias and Merriam point out:

> Most educational philosophies accept given societal values and attempt to propound educational philosophies within those value structures. While pro-gressives... attempt to utilize education to reform society, it is only the radical critics that propose profound changes in society. (p. 147)

They further recognize that "individual liberation and societal liberation are closely tied together..." (p. 156).

This connects to Brookfield's assertion that individual crises are usually linked to societal crises also. The goal for education in Freire's (1970) radi-cal adult education theory is radical conscientization: "...where dialogue and social activity are essential to the learning process, and descriptive of human and social consciousness (Elias & Merriam, 2004, p. 156). The four levels of consciousness, according to Elias and Merriam (2004), begin with the lowest level *intransitive consciousness*, which involves a "culture of silence" and a preoccupation with the most basic needs, much as would be the case when a woman keeps silent at injustices because she is new and really needs the job, not yet relating her oppressive present to the historical context. So she blames herself, or attributes it to just her luck. The second level is *semi-intransivity*; here the "individuals have internalized negative values that the dominant culture ascribes to them (p. 156). These women will put them-selves down, believe that they really do not qualify, or concede that they are best when working for, supporting, or emotionally dependent on someone.

Third is the *naïve transitiveness* level, where the people, though still main-taining the culture of silence, "begin to experience their reality as prob-lem" (p. 156). At this point the woman begins to recognize the problem that exists and may even criticize and pressure when she experiences being passed over, for example, but because she still is in the culture of silence, when she is given a plausible reason, it will be accepted even though it is manipulative. This manipulation can be coercive through the use of harassment, hostile work environments, threat of future opportunity, or even overt communication that women do not make good leaders. The woman capitulates and reverts to frustrated silence until the next similar occurrence. It should be noted at this juncture that there may be women leaders in place who are in the first three stages, still bound by the code of silence for very different reasons. Some because they are first and have no one to talk to, others because they are now too busy watching their back and defending their selection to position in the first place, given that they are leading in unchanged and or unaccepting organization and socio-cultural environments.

The final stage is *critical consciousness*. This is when the individual has experienced conscientization "marked by depth in the interpretation of problems, self-confidence in discussions, receptiveness, and refusal to shirk responsibility" (p. 157). At this stage of dialogical critical consciousness, the women are able to recognize discrimination, make the related connections, and are self-confident enough to initiate a "radical denunciation of dehumanizing structures, accompanied by an announcement of a new reality to be created" (p. 157). They engage in "a rational critique of the ideology supporting these structures" moving to "praxis, the authentic union of action and reflection" (p. 157). Thus conscientization, according to Freire (1970) is an open social activity, dialogic in that it facilitates the breaking of the silence. It is because of the social nature of conscientization that the author proposes social learning for shaping leadership culture.

Application of the radical adult education philosophical approach to the issue places women's contemporary leadership as being in the conscientization process. Having more recently arrived at the critical consciousness stage, a large percentage of women are still in the second and third level stages of semi-intransitivity and naïve transitiveness. Initial analysis would confirm a problem with the needed emancipation of women as leaders, and the requisite shift in leadership and organizational culture. Thus the articulation of the new reality has not yet been finalized: consensus on the announcement yet remains in the dialogical stages. Thus, adding to part of the dialogue and discourse on what the new reality could look like is an underlying goal of this chapter. The radical adult education philosophy presents "both a theory and a method for cultural and political change" (p. 163) in a situated context that is social and oppressive.

The adult learning that is required involves the raising of awareness: what Freire terms as conscientization. It will also require a re-education of society, organizations, and men with new words, idioms, and practices. The new knowledge is applied and results in the emancipation and empowerment of the formerly oppressed group because "knowing is inseparable from deciding to do something in reference to the knowledge" (p. 166). The goal is a social movement that results in increased equity in that community of practice.

The *progressive* approach (Elias & Merriam, 2004), premised on "education as socialization and ... enculturation" (p. 61), is significant to women's leadership challenges in that it is learner focused: "centering upon individuals and their needs" (p. 65), "... adjusted to the learners, to the problems they need solved, to the situation confronting them" (p. 66), and based in the "personal experiences" (p. 68) of the learner. Thus this philosophical approach can, for example, facilitate the breaking of the silence, recognizing and learning new ways to address some of the workplace barriers that are encountered. The salience of this approach, according to Elias and Merriam, is that it is extensive and "not restricted to schooling, but includes all those incidental and intentional activities that society uses to pass on values, attitudes, knowledge and skills" (2004, p. 61). It is also inclusive of the "work of many institutions of society: family, workplace, school, churches, and the entire community" (p. 61): all the essential arenas of society where the perspectives and cultural expectations described in social role theory can be mitigated, re-learned, and re-shaped. All these aspects must be addressed in the strategies so that the inferior roles to which women have been socialized to can be changed to leadership roles if they so desire. Two forms of learning in particular are appropriate here in a holistic approach to women's leadership development.

Social Learning and Women's Leadership Development

Social Learning is an integrative view of the adult learning that occurs from observing other's behaviors in social settings. In the leadership development context in particular, "knowledge transfer of tacit knowledge occurs through socialization with others" (Merriam, Caffarella, & Baumgartner, 2007, p. 179). Merriam, Caffarella, & Baumgartner contend that "by observing others, people acquire knowledge, rules, skills, strategies, beliefs, and attitudes" (p. 288). Leadership development therefore involves a form of learning that is clearly described in social cognitive learning theory (Bandura, 2001), which occurs in a situated context which prepares aspirant high-potentials for their anticipated leadership opportunity.

The presence of a leader-model to guide the developing protégé fits clearly into this adult learning theory. The learner has a model they observe; they internalize their observations, reinforce that learning with feedback, and reproduce the learned behavior in the appropriate situation and time. Two of the essential points of social learning theory are that learning can be vicarious and can occur without immediate evidential demonstration of such learning. The other is that social learning is context based (Bandura, 2001). Vicarious learning (observed but not personally experienced) can be knowledge high potential or aspiring candidates acquire from the observed experiences of their predecessors, which can result in recognition of barriers, role conflicts, or abandoned career aspirations.

Situated Learning Theory and Women's Leadership Development

Because social learning is context based, another important form of adult learning occurs as described by situated learning theory. In this instance, Lave (1988) points out that situated learning needs to occur in a specific context where the learned behavior is required and appropriate. Lave holds that the learner is part of a community of practice (the organization) where the beliefs and behaviors to be appropriated are defined. Starting out at the periphery of the community of practice learning, engagement and development cause them to become deeper parts of the community, increasing their expertise.

In the leadership development context, the candidate starts out at the periphery as the new recruit. Over time, as they demonstrate their potential and competency to the group and are selected for leadership development and mentoring, they become deeply invested in the community. One of the key points that Lave raises early on is that situated learning is primarily incidental. In the leadership development social learning experience, however, situated learning is not only deliberate, but the knowledge the mentor-expert transmits to the candidate is occurring in the context of the workplace they will potentially be called to lead (Lave & Wenger, 1991). The knowledge is best acquired through social interaction and collaboration within the community of practice and between the mentor and protégé.

Social Capital Networks for Learning and Career Advancement

In the organization, women engaged in leadership development initiatives are developing, or are already connected to, networks that are institutionalized and durable enough for them to engage in and learn specific norms and behaviors that translate into beneficial relationships and recognition for them. The networks provide access to resources "through affiliations, contacts, and services allowing them to gain knowledge and information essential for achieving their goals" (Nanton, 2009, p. 14). They also become communities of practice where collaboration can occur and the place where upcoming projects or anticipated organizational changes, behavioral criteria or advancement opportunities, and other benefits provide increased bargaining (and decision making) power to the women in well-connected networks.

Leadership development and learning experience "within a collaborative context of social networks enhances, rather than diminishes, the learner's self-determination and ability to self-manage..." two critical characteristics leaders are going to need (Nanton, 2009, p. 16). The mentor-model also becomes a lynchpin of their protégé's networks, contributing to the development, need for connectedness and sense of belonging (Nanton, 2011). Therefore, as part of the social learning environment, it becomes important for women to have membership in, and belong to, social networks where they can develop and add to their behavioral repertoire the behaviors acceptable to male managers, where they can demonstrate their competency in collegial settings so their abilities do not pose a major threat, and where the perceived differences that can hinder their future opportunities can be reduced. A brief conceptual look at the leadership context and community of practice in which the social and situated learning are taking place follows.

CONTEXT AND COMMUNITY OF PRACTICE

From an adult education perspective, both social learning and situated learning are context based. Leadership development occurs in both a relational and organizational context and is situated in a relational and cultural context. Social role theory (Moss, 2008) prescribes basic gender roles for both the relational and cultural context. It is understandable then that any push toward a changing of those prescribed roles, even in a workplace context, would be met with strong resistance on several fronts. While the organizational context is often mutually agreed on by employees under a common goal and vision, the gender role assumptions or expectations are not so easily categorized or submerged to the emergent organizational needs of women leaders.

It is in this dynamic social learning space, conceptualized in Figure 20.1, that trust or mistrust, synergy or conflict, is sensed and acted on by the leader and follower. And it is this dynamic space on which we will focus attention for transforming leadership culture. In this invisible yet permeable interactive space, the author proposes that connection and commitment are developed, leadership of the other is validated, and both leader and follower walk away perceiving that they have developed (mostly sub-consciously and cognitively), decision making skills, self-regulation, and self-efficacy (Bandura, 2001; Nanton, 2011). Figure 20.1 provides a view of the social

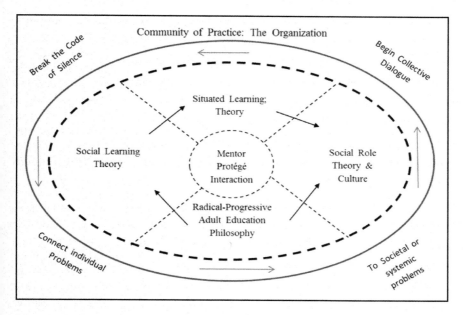

Figure 20.1 Context and community of learning and practice.

learning situated context and theoretical framework and how the organizational context, societal and cultural contexts can potentially interact.

The protégé is learning in within a situated leadership development context and developing skills to be practiced in a similar future situated context. It is in this space that leader identity is shaped through the modeling of the leader-mentor. This powerful interchange, in part, determines whether the protégé will accept the leader's identity, and by extension their leadership practice. The observation of consequences to the leaders' behaviors and decision making, coupled with reinforcement, determines whether the protégé will internalize and adopt that behavior. Here is also where collaborative dialogue can occur, that new strategies can be developed to address identified problems, and that the culture of the organization can be re-shaped to be more inclusive of women leaders. Some of these proposed strategies and implications will be described next.

ADULT EDUCATION IMPLICATIONS FOR WOMEN'S LEADERSHIP DEVELOPMENT

Top priorities for twenty-first century organizations are to develop and sustain viability, competitiveness, agility, product quality, and service excellence. Diversity and women's leadership have been linked to increases in all these areas. DuBrin (2007) challenges top management to increase awareness and sensitivity to "the need for more diversity in choosing successors" (p. 475). High-potential candidates, particularly women in leadership in collaboration with top management, can help usher in a new generation of women leaders who have the freedom and capacity to lead as women in their most natural ways (Insch, McIntyre, & Napier, 2008; Senge, 2006). These candidates will no longer be overlooked, nor will they "disappear" once the leadership development process experience is over because their leadership style preferences and behaviors will have been legitimated throughout the company.

How can this happen when the current climate is still resistant and oppressive? As women leaders in organizations seek to shape a path to a new organizational leadership culture, they will also need to develop a bridging or transitional leadership style which includes (1) agility for adjustment to the dynamic situational context that presents itself; (2) fluidity of selection and movement between a durable accepted (or newly acquired) repertoire of behaviors; and (3) creating a new form of leadership that bridges both new social role requirements and organizational expectations while demonstrating competencies and skills to lead effectively and authentically as they remain true to their gender.

The goal is to ensure that this new leadership culture and climate will not include untoward personal cost or sacrifice and that barriers to equity or opportunity will be eliminated. Given that it is clearly apparent that both organizations and society need assistance in achieving these transformative goals of inclusion and change, the following learning and practice strategies are proposed for shaping contemporary leadership culture to one that is more inclusive of women as leaders.

STRATEGIES FOR INITIATING CHANGE IN PERCEPTION AND PRACTICE

The proposed strategies have been connected together as puzzle pieces that must fit together to provide a holistic picture for effecting and sustaining simultaneous, lasting change in contemporary societal (and organizational) perception and practice. The four identified parts to this puzzle are organizational and individual initiatives embodied in the roles of adult education, top leadership and men sponsors, women executives, and the aspiring high potential candidate (Figure 20.2).

Because the challenges in women's leadership are undergirded by the social role prescriptions of society, the strategies for overcoming them must employ an approach that seeks to change the societal and workplace

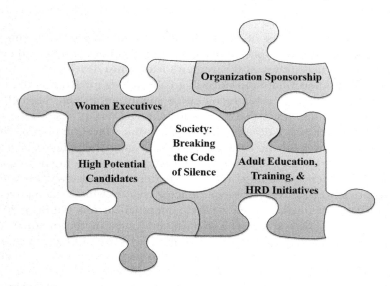

Figure 20.2 Critical roles for changing perception and practice.

perceptions that fosters those challenges and provide new knowledge and solutions for resolving individual problems and experiences within both contexts. Next, two overarching actions need to occur to make room for the pieces to effectively come together: first, breaking the code of silence and reaching the level of critical consciousness that causes stakeholders to engage in open dialogue with each other and the organization. Second, that there is movement beyond just dialogue to action that is responsive to the changes that are needed. The radical adult education approach described by Elias and Merriam (2004) can be employed to bring awareness and change leadership culture through critical consciousness of the players; the progressive adult education approach focuses on solving the problem of changing society's perceptions and expectations specific to the individual needs.

The recent Shriver report (2014) presented thought provoking information with salient relevance for this chapter's focus. It reported "trends re-shaping the American landscape" and included a comprehensive examination of American attitudes about the role of women in today's world" (p 7). The expectation, according to Podesta (2014) is to "spur a national conversation about what women's emerging economic power means for our way of life" (p.7). It is this type of conversation that can break the code of silence for women in general about the transformation that has already begun to unfold and the need for responsive action to what is now known in society and in organizations.

Adult Education Strategies

We begin with the role of adult education in focusing on removing the presenting barriers and work toward developing, implementing, and evaluating best practice strategies for women's leadership development. Knowing what works and what does not will go a long way toward holding each party accountable and challenging those organizations that lag behind, while still rewarding those that have made changes.

The human resource development arm of adult education plays a significant role as a powerful and strategic driver for change by using social learning methods for on-the-job training, observation, coaching, mentoring, and growth assignments. Building on prior experience, knowledge, and skills, a more transactional and explicit experience is created, which, when linked to appropriate incentives, can reduce the perceptual barriers (DuBrin, 2007). Introducing diversity initiatives can raise awareness of the organization's formal and informal practices that systematically keep women out of leadership positions. At the basic level, training in the human resource recruitment, selection, and compensation must be strategic to ensure that there are enough qualified women in the pipeline so that they are available for the leadership development and placement in promotion openings (Petroni & Colacino, 2008). It is critical that salary inequities are addressed and monitored to counteract demotivation; and that practical and attitudinal perspectives be addressed that would remove the challenges of the labyrinth and the barriers of the glass ceiling. Increased focus on recruiting more women to leadership development programs and mentoring can be purposive, leading to more women leaders at the executive level with selections based on equity and qualifications and not based on gender (Hoyt, 2013).

Mentoring relationships, whether cross-gender, formal, or informal, create the ideal context for the processes of social and situated learning, and both are relational, collaborative, and context based learning. They also serve to create vital social networks that facilitate career advancement. Training throughout the company, including for executives, that addresses sensitivity to and awareness of the prevailing mental models and practical ways to reframe them is critical.

Top Leader's Sponsorship

Lasting change in organizations happens from the top down (Kotter, 1996). So, the second critical piece of this puzzle is leaders' sponsorship behaviors bolstered by an in-depth understanding and awareness of the prevailing perceptions. This would be exceptionally helpful to the candidate's ability to navigate the complexity of her leadership development process in the organization; it would help remove the barriers that currently exist while serving as a catalyst for social re-structuring of company culture to where women's leadership development can flourish. Leader-sponsors and male colleagues need to actively contribute to the needed change. After all, they still hold the positions women aspire to and can lead by implementing positive reinforcement and putting related workplace incentives in place that will exponentially increase the likelihood of desired behaviors. Executive sponsorship is a powerful driver for organizational and leadership culture change. Executive coaching can become an invaluable method to influence individual and group attitudes and behaviors, positively initiating and sustaining changes in approach for the next generation of women leaders.

It also would be essential to hold executives accountable for following through on the succession plan, moving beyond merely completing the social learning cycle to actually placing qualified candidates as the openings come up (Petroni & Colacino, 2008). It will take innovation and commitment to ensure that fairness is practiced throughout the organization. Organizations can link corporate reward systems and/or executive bonuses to succession initiatives in order to communicate the seriousness of the required changes. Women's skills and competencies would be more prone to recognition when attention is paid to objective and equitable evaluations of their work (Fels, 2004), and they would be encouraged to move into leadership positions.

Women Executives

The third puzzle piece is finding powerful advocates and mentors for the aspiring leader candidates. As executives, they have successfully made it through the glass ceiling and have learned how to navigate or circumvent the barriers and gender role challenges. As mentors, they can foster consciousness and facilitate the development of effective skills and career trajectories in aspiring women. They can consciously work on not being characterized as 'queen bees,' erecting new barriers in the way of strong and promising candidates: and in so doing, they can affect the situated learning that needs to occur and re-shape the leadership culture into one that is more inclusive. It is a challenging responsibility as they are often still working out their own situation. However, they are in a prime position to recognize and mitigate some of the challenges they have faced for others that follow.

Through social learning, they can facilitate, evaluate, and provide active follow-up and feedback in the areas where the aspirant's social learning processes are not strong. They can also assist with breaking the code of silence by sharing their stories and experiences, contextualizing it in both the organization and society. This normalizes the aspirant's experiences by connecting their individual problems to broader societal problems. Through strategic social networking, other women leaders, the organization, and even community groups need to partner together to reduce the wage and hiring gap for women workers and push the agenda for women's leadership progress and organizational cultural change across all sectors.

Female executives can serve as advocates to motivated selection panels as well as for better work-life balance in practice while also being models of fair distribution of promotion rewards and diversity in the succession talent pool. They can also help reduce some of the challenges by purposively mentoring and developing potential candidates in the behaviors accepted by the organization and understanding leadership complexities, and they can coach candidates on choosing the right social networks so that they are linked to key relationships and related opportunities for advancement to leadership positions (Nanton, 2011; Insch, McIntyre & Napier, 2008).

The High-Potential Candidate

This last piece of the puzzle is one of the most critical ones. Candidates are urged to take strategic ownership of their careers to stop the still prevalent self-perpetuating cycles. This will require either personal leadership or the ability to be sufficiently self-aware to self-lead, self-adjust (self-regulate), self-encourage, and shift to make the best out of every presenting situation (Bandura, 2001; Ramsey & Schaetti, 2011). With their new knowledge, women must shift from supportive roles to being assertive in managing their career advancement by the choices they make to take leading roles.

Candidates must be proactive in connecting to critical formal and informal social networks and leveraging or re-negotiating their current network memberships for career advancement (Nanton, 2011, 2012). These networks also need to include supportive learning and dialogical communities where awareness is created and self-confidence is developed as the women learn to interpret and address their experiences in light of the social context in which they work (Brookfield, 1987; Elias & Merriam, 2004; Wenger, 2000). Potential women leaders must be proactive in their organizations about addressing their needs as leaders and candidates for leadership positions. It is in these communities that the silence is broken and courage to re-shape leadership and societal culture is born. Furthermore, candidates need to take responsibility for being well-informed, being insistent in salary negotiations, and persisting in self-promotion.

CONCLUSION

In conclusion, leadership effectiveness has never really been the issue facing women in leadership. There is too much evidence in business, industry, and across the world to the contrary. The perception of leadership capability, driven by prescribed social roles, is at the crux of the problem, which in turn causes conscious and unconscious barriers to be erected between women's aspirations for leadership and their actual opportunities to lead.

Two main things need to occur if women are to fully realize the possibilities for change in leadership culture: the code of silence must be broken, and women's individual leadership problems need to be consciously connected to the broader societal problem. Only then can there be any hope for the subsequent waves of the women's movement to reach their crest, with women fully equal in terms of wages, inclusion, and access to leadership positions. Only then can the leadership and societal culture be changed to one where women can thrive as we all benefit from what they have to offer.

Transitioning to this model leadership context is still in progress; so in the meantime, contemporary women leaders will need to be integrated and agile in the workplace, with fluidity of movement between the best behavioral characteristics of both men and women. This new form of leadership bridges social role expectations and organizational expectations. It also demonstrates competency and effective leadership while remaining true to gender and it will become the future norm.

The needed changes are great and will take concerted effort on all fronts. Women's collaborative, purposive action can change the socio-cultural environment through their vote in the larger social context, for example. Similarly, women can effect significant leadership culture change within their organizations with persistent, confident, collective, and purposive action. However, the foundational pieces need to be put in place with urgency (Kotter, 1996). It is the urgency that propels action: organizations that pro-actively remove the burden of proof for women through conscientization will become more viable and effective in twenty-first century.

Adult education is a primary and essential factor. The other factors are organizational leader sponsorship, women executives, and of course the aspirant candidates. Addressing the issue on all fronts moves beyond the rhetoric and research to action that signals what could well be the cresting next wave of the women's movement, not just for equality of entry into the workplace, but for access to the leadership positions women have worked for and earned. It will secure a fundamental shift in organizational perceptions of women's leadership capability, the legitimization of their leadership, and ultimately the re-shaping of organizational culture. In so doing, the next generation of women leaders will be strengthened and sustained, and the culture of leadership will have been fundamentally changed to include them well into the future.

REFERENCES

Bandura, A. (2001). Social cognitive theory: An agentic perspective. *Annual Review of Psychology. 52*, 1–26.

Barbuto, J. E., Fritz, S. M., Matkin, G. S., & Marx, D. B. (2007, January). Effects of gender education, and age upon leaders' use of influence tactics and full range leadership behaviors. *Sex Roles, 56,* 71–83.

Brookfield, S. (1987). *Developing critical thinkers: Challenging adults to explore alternative ways of thinking and acting.* San Francisco, CA: JosseyBass.

Cilizza, C (2008). Hillary Clinton, 18 million cracks, and the power of making history. *The Fix.* Retrieved from: http://www.washingtonpost.com/blogs/the-fix/wp/2013/06/13/hillary-clinton-18-million-cracks-and-the-power-of-making-history/?wprss=rss_politics&clsrd

DuBrin, A. J. (2007). *Leadership: Research findings, practice, and skills.* Mason, OH: South Western.

Eagly, A. H. (1987). *Sex differences in social behavior: A social-role interpretation.* Hillsdale, NJ: Lawrence Erlbaum Associates.

Eagly, A. H., & Carli, L. L. (2007). *Through the labyrinth: The truth about how women become leaders.* Boston. MA: Harvard Business School Press.

Eagly, A. H., & Johnson, B. T. (1990). Gender and leadership style: A meta-analysis. *Psychological Bulletin, 108,* 233–256.

Elias, J., & Merriam, S. (2004). *Philosophical foundations of adult education.* (3rd ed.). Malabar, FL: Krieger Publishing Company.

Evans, A., & Breinig Chun, E. (2007). Are the walls really down? Behavioral and organizational barriers to faculty and staff diversity. *ASHE Higher Education Report, 33,* 1.

Fels, A. (2004). "Do women lack ambition?" *Harvard Business Review, 9424,* 2–11.

Fletcher, J. (2001). *Disappearing acts: Gender, power, and relational practice at work.* Boston, MA: MIT Press.

Freire, P. (1970). *Pedagogy of the oppressed.* New York, NY: Seabury Press.

Heilman, M. E., Wallen, A. S., Fuchs, D., & Tamkins, M. M. (2004). Penalties for success: Reactions to women who succeed at male gender-typed tasks. *Journal of Applied Psychology, 89,* 416–427.

Hoyt, C. (2013). Women and leadership. In P. G. Northouse, (2013). *Leadership, theory and practice.* (5th ed., pp. 349–382). Los Angeles, CA: Sage.

Insch, G. S., McIntyre, N., & Napier, N. K. (2008). The expatriate glass ceiling: The second layer of glass. *Journal of Business Ethics, 83,* 19–28. DOI:10-1007.

Kennedy, J. F. (1963). Memorial addresses in the Congress of the United States and tributes in eulogy of John Fitzgerald Kennedy a late President of the United States. Washington, DC: U.S. Government Printing Office.

Kotter, J. P. (1996). *Leading change.* Boston, MA: Harvard Business School Press.

Lampe, A. C. (2001). Book reviews. *Gender, Work and Organization 8*(3), 346–351.

Lave, J. (1988). *Cognition in practice: Mind, mathematics, and culture in everyday life.* Cambridge, UK: Cambridge University Press.

Lave, J., & Wenger, E. (1991). *Situated learning: Legitimate peripheral participation.* Cambridge, UK: Cambridge University Press.

Lips, H., & Keener, E. (2007). Effects of gender and dominance on leadership emergence: Incentives make a difference. *Sex Roles, 8* (56). 563 –571. DOI:10.1007/s11199-007-9210

McKinsey & Company. (2012). Women matter: Making the breakthrough. Retrieved from http://www.mckinsey.com

Moss, S. (2008). Social role theory. Retrieved from http://www.psych-it.com.au/Psychlopedia/article.asp?id=77

Nanton, C. R. (2009). Ties that bind: Cultural referent groups and coping strategies of adult women as learners. In C. R. Nanton & M. V. Alfred (Eds.), *Social capital and women's support systems: Networking, learning and surviving* (pp. 13–22). NDACE I122. San Francisco: Jossey-Bass.

Nanton, C. R. (2011). Creating leadership legacy: Social learning and leadership development. *International Journal of Learning, 7*(12), 181–193.

Nanton, C. R. (2012). Learning to lead: Leveraging social learning, social capital, and social media in leadership development. In C. J. Boden-McGill & K. P. King (Eds.), *21st Century adult learning in our complex world.* Charlotte, NC: Information Age Publishing.

Northouse, P. G. (2013). *Leadership, theory and practice.* (6th ed.). Los Angeles, CA: Sage.

Olsson, S., & Walker, R. (2004). The wo-men and the boys: Patterns of identification and differentiation in senior women executives' representations of career identity. *Women in Management Review, 19*(5/6), 244–251.

Petroni, A., & Colacino, P. (2008). Motivation strategies for knowledge workers: Evidences and challenges. *Journal of Technology Management and Innovation, 3*(3), 21–32.

Podesta, J. (2014). Preface. In H. Boushey, & A. O'Leary, (2014). *The Shriver Report: A woman's nation changes everything. A Study by Maria Shriver and the Center for American Progress.* Washington, DC.

Ramsey, S., & Schaetti, B. (2011). Leading through the 'I' of the storm. Flying Kite Publications. pp. 1–12. Retrieved from www.PLSeminars.com

Rudman, L. A. (1998). Self-promotion as a risk factor for women: The costs and benefits of counter stereotypical impression management. *Journal of Personality and Social Psychology, 74*, 629–645.

Sandberg, S., & Scovell, N. (2013). *Lean in: Women, work and the will to lead.* New York, NY: Alfred Knopf, Borzoi Books.

Schyns, B., & Sanders, K. (2005). Exploring gender differences in leaders' occupational self-efficacy. *Women in Management Review, 20*(7/8), 513–523.

Senge, P. M. (2006). *The fifth discipline: The art and practice of the learning organization.* Currency Edition. New York, NY: Doubleday.

Sinclair, A. (2005). Body possibilities in leadership. *Sage Publications.* London, England: Thousand Oaks. DOI: 10.1177/174271500505723

Wenger, E. (2000). Communities of practice and social learning systems. *Organization, 7*, 225–246. Sage Publications. DOI: 10.1177/135050840072002.

CHAPTER 21

ADVANCING INNOVATION IN HIGHER EDUCATION

Anna K. Hultquist
Capella University

The United States is committed to developing an educated populous positioned to drive economic growth in the global marketplace (Obama, 2012). This national strategy joins agendas from across the globe preparing workers to compete for market share in the international arena. The call to expand access to effective lifelong learning opportunities designed to support, "...competitive economies, and to boost individuals' ability and capacity to work and adapt to the changing demands of today's dynamic labour markets" (G20, 2011, pp. 2–3) is now critical to success in our global knowledge-based economy. According to the Partnership for 21st Century Skills report, "economic, technological, informational, demographic, and political forces have transformed the way people work and live. These changes—and the rate of change—will continue to accelerate. Schools, like businesses, communities, and families, must adapt to changing conditions to thrive" (Partnership for 21st Century Skills, 2003, p. 6).

In this fast-paced, technologically advanced global environment, adults are being asked to adapt to dynamic changes stimulated by globalization, economic fluctuations, corporate changes, and the continued evolution of

Building Sustainable Futures for Adult Learners, pages 447–464
Copyright © 2015 by Information Age Publishing
All rights of reproduction in any form reserved.

social organizations and cultural norms (Heifetz & Laurie, 2012). These evolving demands heighten the need for effective lifelong learning on a national and global scale. To meet the needs of adults in this highly complex and changing environment, educational institutions serving the adult population are working diligently to develop educational solutions.

In response to increasing job-skill requirements, adults are entering institutions of higher education in record numbers. Between the years 2000 and 2010, the percentage of undergraduate students aged 25 and older rose nearly 30%, from 6.1 million out of a total undergraduate student population of 15.3 million to 8.9 million out of 21.0 million students enrolled in undergraduate programs. The National Center for Education Statistics forecasts the adult student population to increase at the moderate rate of 14% increase in students aged 25 and older from 2011 to 2021 (National Educational Statistics, 2012).

Institutions of higher education are also faced with a growing expectation for non-degree offerings designed to enhance job skills as well as stimulate the minds of the aging baby-boomer population seeking continued learning opportunities (Kasworm, 2012). As a result, traditional and non-traditional public and private institutions alike are working to develop new ways to service the evolving needs of the adult population while, at the same time, grappling with the global forces facing higher education today.

The growing educational needs of the adult population are among a collection of forces impacting higher education today. Globalization, the emerging knowledge-based culture, and rapid advances in technology are stimulating change throughout the industry (Altbach, Reisberg, & Rumbley, 2010). New regulatory requirements, student performance goals, gainful employment benchmarks, and enhanced curricular standards add to the challenges facing colleges and universities worldwide causing them to reevaluate how to effectively educate the populous (Fathi & Wilson, 2009). These pressures, exacerbated by budgetary constraints generated from thinning public funds, are challenging institutions already struggling to find ways to demonstrate increased program relevance, affordability, and accessibility.

In addition to shifting student demographics, the demand for career-relevant knowledge across the lifespan and emerging educational modalities are adding to the forces impacting higher education worldwide (Culkin & Mallick, 2011; Khan, Ahmed, & Nawaz, 2011; Omerzel, Biloslavo, & Trnavčevič, 2011). As these forces converge on institutions of higher education, colleges and universities are realizing the need for innovative and effective strategies that will transform the industry (Tikhomirova, Tikhomirova, Maksimova, & Telnov, 2011). The ability of the industry to respond effectively to these complex needs, however, is still under review. In the meantime, the American people are waiting to see how colleges and universities across the land adapt to the transformative forces facing the industry

(Mogilyanskaya, 2012). According to Christensen and Eyring (2011), failure to transform in response to these forces will cause institutions of higher education to decline.

HIGHER EDUCATION RESPONSES TO GLOBAL FORCES FOR CHANGE

There are a group of colleges and universities embracing the challenges of our changing global landscape as they design innovative solutions in the higher education space. The programs and platforms being developed represent a wide range of responses. Some delivery models that meet the unique needs of the adult student population won legitimacy over time and are, therefore, expanding to a wider audience. Other models are relatively new and will require further investigation before they are adopted by the field.

MODELS EMERGING IN THE HIGHER EDUCATION INDUSTRY

Universities seeking to keep pace with changes sweeping the globe are rushing to develop new ways to educate a changing populace buffeted by emerging global demands. The first wave of transformation in higher education took the form of fully online universities. This technology-driven format offered greater accessibility to credible academic programs taught by faculty active in their respective fields, an option that proved attractive to students across the age spectrum. Many traditional colleges and universities seeking to catch the wave of this disruptive innovation in the industry have launched online courses and fully online programs to augment their regular offerings. To manage the demand for online courses, other traditional universities created distinct units to house their virtual program offerings. Southern New Hampshire University's College of Online and Continuing Education serves as one example of a traditional university that established a separate academic entity dedicated to advancing beyond the institution's current models of teaching and learning. Penn State's World Campus was also created to provide technology-enhanced distance learning programs linked to the larger institution's brand reputation (Shearer, 2004). The development of a separate business unit within an established university setting allows the new department to benefit from the larger institution's reputation and financial resources. In addition, by establishing a distinct unit to house innovative developments, the university is able to benefit from increased revenue generated by the adaptive unit making this model an attractive one (Kamenetz, 2012; Parry, 2013).

Another adaptation developed to meet the forces impacting higher education today takes the form of university spin-outs. Developed in China, this model takes the form of a university-created company that benefits directly from knowledge generated from academic research. Spin-outs in the United States were made possible by the 1980 passage of the Bayh-Dole Act that allowed universities to patent inventions coming out of federally-funded research efforts (Meyers, 2009). The development of university spin-outs in the United States over the past three decades have contributed to innovations in industries that range from national defense to medical diagnosis and treatment (Chandra, 2009). Clearly, this extension of the university into the business community demonstrates one of the values of employing entrepreneurial strategies to guide innovation in higher education.

The massive open online course, or MOOC, is another innovation developed in response to pressures facing educational institutions today (Baggaley, 2013). According to Rollins (2014), a 1998 venture by New York University opened the door to MOOCs in America. Columbia University followed in 2000 with its own efforts in this arena. While the longevity of these initial attempts spanned just three years, they laid the foundation for the many successful ventures that followed. In 2004 the Kahn academy, an online educational center, created its first MOOC-like offering. Four years later, a free online course entitled, *Connectivism and Connect Knowledge*, was developed in Canada by Downes and Siemens. Then in 2011, Stanford University launched its own free online course in artificial intelligence that attracted over 160,000 students from all over the globe. Stanford's highly successful entrance into the MOOC arena energized this growing movement that provides free and accessible education to anyone who registers (Flynn, 2013). In the two years following Stanford's open-access online course, MOOCs have proliferated. Established academic institutions such as Harvard, Princeton, and MIT are collaborating across institutional lines and national borders to create a range of free online learning opportunities. While the success of MOOCs continues to grow, this educational model is generating both supporters and critics. Some believe MOOCs are the "most easily implemented form of education ever invented" (Baggaley, 2013, p. 368). Others, however, find the challenges underlying the creation and management of MOOCs fraught with difficulty. Therefore, the ability of MOOCs to enjoy a sustainable future in the higher education industry is still unknown (Rollins, 2014). One thing is clear, however; MOOCs are making an impact that is shaping the future of higher education across the globe.

Another evolution in the industry that is pressing higher education institutions into new territory is competency-based learning. Emerging as a legitimate model in the higher education industry, this model was designed to prepare career-ready graduates by building academic programs on externally validated career-relevant competencies needed in the global workforce.

The roots of this model go back as far as the early 1970s when Regent University established Excelsior College in order to provide academic offerings to the adult student population. Excelsior's programs focused on the development of competencies through clearly articulated student learning outcomes and the application of prior learning to program achievement. Western Governor's entrance in this arena in 1997 expanded the use of competency-based education leading to academic degrees (Laitinen, 2013). To accommodate this educational model, in 2006 the federal government added direct assessment of student learning to the traditional credit hour to qualify for financial aid dollars. Several years later, Southern New Hampshire University received approval to offer academic programs built on a student's mastery of program-specific competencies leading directly to degree conferral. Other schools, such as Capella University, link student mastery of career-relevant competencies with credits earned in pursuit of an academic degree (Parry, 2013). Today, institutions across the country are examining the competency-based approach to education as a viable and perhaps improved means of gauging student learning. Needless to say, such innovative approaches are being studied closely to determine the strengths and opportunities inherent in these emerging models.

Future Innovation in Higher Education

Continued transformation of the higher education industry driven by institutional innovation is underway in countries across the globe. Researchers Wisseman and Verloop (2009) predicted the next evolution in higher education will involve greater collaboration with surrounding community and business organizations. These partnerships will allow universities to broaden their reach and widen their horizontal scope by applying knowledge created within the academy to conditions emerging in relevant industries. In return, valuable data generated in these external settings is channeled back to the academy to support continued learning. Developing viable alliances between higher education and external stakeholders will, however, depend on the academy's ability to lower its walls of the academy to allow the dynamic interplay between its research laboratories and its partners in such a way that the needs of all stakeholders are met. Fundamental shifts in the industry are required in order to achieve the level of transformation needed to restage higher education for the opportunities of tomorrow. Higher education's organizational capacity to respond to the dynamic global environment will determine the success of each institution's transformative efforts (Cinite, Duxbury, & Higgins, 2009).

ORGANIZATIONAL CHANGE WITHIN HIGHER EDUCATION

Tension between traditional higher education institutions and innovative program design and delivery is challenging academic leadership's ability to deliver high-quality educational offerings as these strategic initiatives come face-to-face with an organizational culture that, by its very nature, generates constraints. This strain is rooted in what some are calling a lack of alignment between the mission statements of many academic institutions and the pragmatic business strategies being developed to improve efficiencies and drive innovation (Drew, 2010). The potential difference between the purpose of colleges and universities to educate the populous and the large-scale institutional changes originating in operational and fiscal efficiencies can create a unique challenge for institutional leadership. This stress is often exacerbated when the prescribed changes include a revision of traditional roles and the transformation of organizational structures that have guided the academy over the past century (Loomis & Rodriguez, 2009). In order to overcome the barriers that emerge from the interface of these two distinct systems, the industry needs to determine how it can best respond to the forces assailing higher education today, assess their capability to respond to the educational evolution taking place, design innovative strategies to meet evolving student expectations, and execute changes undergirding the innovative revolution now underway.

The Role of Strategic Planning in Higher Education

A process developed to guide the United States military and adopted by the business community is now being applied to institutions in higher education in an effort to meet a range of goals with varying degrees of success (Sullivan & Richardson, 2011). The strategic planning process is a straightforward method of evaluating and planning that guides leaders to strengthen the viability of their respective institution. In order to craft effective strategies, organizations start by articulating their ideal state. It is important that the vision statement emerging from this step expresses the place this particular institution would like to hold in their industry, the level of operational effectiveness the organization is seeking to achieve, the resources it has developed to fund current and future states, and other elements that contribute to the institution's ideal future. Once complete, the vision statement informs the organization's statement of purpose or mission. The mission statement itself is built on the institution's vision by articulating the university's identity in the industry and the most important functions it offers in the service of reaching its goals (Özdem, 2011).

The mission statement plays a central role in the organization, serving as the backbone for the organization's culture and shaping how the institution will go about meeting its goals. Key cultural characteristics that enable the institution to fulfill its mission naturally arise from the vision and mission statements, taking the form of values and policies that promote and protect institutional norms. As institutions of higher education move through these turbulent waters of change, it is important that they align their vision, mission, values, and policies to ensure they have a solid foundation on which to build their future.

The fundamental role of the institution's vision and mission statements in the strategic planning process make their accuracy critical. As institutions of higher education face a swiftly evolving environment demanding innovative approaches for educating the populace, it is important that the vision statement undergoes regular review to ensure it remains current. Once these cornerstones are in place, leaders are ready to move into the core of the strategic planning process. However, since this model of organizational review and goal setting emerged from the highly regulated military segment of the government, and subsequently adopted by the business community, institutions of higher education are finding this rather linear approach to planning foreign to their own culture. In particular, colleges and universities reported that the mission statement is fundamentally disparate with the business practices being employed to improve efficiencies and drive innovation (Drew, 2010). The perceived incongruence between the university's mission and prescribed corporate protocol can, therefore, create challenges for academic institutions seeking to implement large-scale institutional changes. This is particularly true when those changes include the revision of traditional roles and the transformation of the organizational structures that have guided the industry over the past century (Loomis & Rodriguez, 2009). As colleges and universities today face a time of rapid and substantial change, the application of proven business strategies can actually prove beneficial in helping them adapt and succeed in this highly competitive industry. The first step in bridging the divide between the academy and the business world, however, requires leadership to take a close look at the dynamic nature of their own institution's mission statements to ensure it captures their evolving purpose within a changing environment. To ensure the statement remains relevant, a regular cycle of review is highly advised. Of equal importance, however, is the care leaders need to take in approaching the review process due to the deeply held beliefs about the purpose of higher education contained within the mission statement itself. It is often useful, therefore, to include multiple layers of the organization in the review and revision process to ensure voices from key stakeholders are heard. By involving key parties across the university in the review or revision itself, the institution positions itself to craft a mission statement that is internally meaningful and externally relevant. In addition, input from both academic units and operational areas can expand the focus of the institution in today's marketplace while more fully representing the whole organization. Furthermore, creating a mission statement that inspires, clarifies, and motivates internal and external stakeholders, the university sets the stage for academic and business leaders alike to reach across the divide and work together in service of the institution and its students.

With the vision and mission statements in place, and the values and policies clearly aligned, the strategic planning process begins in earnest. A detailed review of data sets revealing the overall fiscal and operational health of the organization is the next step that lets leadership know how well the institution is doing in fulfilling its mission and achieving its goals. Placing the organization's performance within the external market is another important step at this stage of the planning process. This outward focus lets the institution better understand its position relative to competitors.

A review of these initial data sets helps leadership gauge institutional performance within the industry, articulate how best to differentiate itself within the marketplace, set specific performance goals to meet emerging challenges, and determine ways to adapt to the demands of a rapidly changing global economy. Moreover, a review of these key metrics enables leaders to identify high functioning areas, pinpoint opportunities in areas where challenges exist, and articulate steps to reduce risks related to poorly performing parts of the organization. Once this phase of the strategic planning process is complete, action items can be developed to guide the institution forward.

Routine strategic planning has the potential to provide a consistent and predictable process that examines current and future priorities, identifies opportunities that support growth, allocates resources in support of specific strategic goals, and prepares the organization to respond to trends in the internal and external environments. Colleges and universities that engage in strategic planning are found to increase their ability to direct resources, operational processes, and organizational functions in support of institutional goals (Fathi & Wilson, 2009). Therefore, as the higher education industry designs methods to meet the demands of students and businesses in the twenty-first century, the effective use of strategic planning can lead to industry-enhancing innovations that will guide higher education forward in the global marketplace of today (Chance & Williams, 2009).

As previously stated, the linear framework that characterizes the business approach to strategic planning often creates tension as colleges and universities attempt to apply this model to their own planning process. In order to meet the unique needs of educational institutions, specific elements of academic performance are added to the standard review of the organization's fiscal and operational status. Key performance metrics included in academic settings include instructional quality, program-specific, new, and total enrollment and graduation rates, individual course enroll-ment trends, program and course currency, and faculty and student publi-cations (Karpagam & Suganhi, 2012). In addition to leadership's review of these academic metrics, it is vital that academics join in the review of these data and help shape the goals emerging from this review. It is important to include representatives from both business and academic areas in the stra-tegic planning process in order to gain a more comprehensive perspective that can support future innovation.

With increased competition confronting every level of the higher edu-cation industry, strategic planning has the potential to influence the fu-ture success of institutions willing to follow this protocol. With the rapid pace of change in the global marketplace today, institutions are beginning to engage in strategic planning periodically throughout the year in order to respond to emerging challenges and opportunities more quickly. This growing trend allows institutions to integrate strategic planning into their organizational culture. Relevance of the planning process can be increased through alignments between the strategic goals and individual work re-sponsibilities. With individual performance evaluated through the current strategic initiatives, change efforts can be infused more readily throughout the academic and operational units (Sullivan & Richardson, 2011).

The services of an experienced consultant familiar with business acumen and academic protocol are a valuable resource for colleges and universities facing the changes of today. For institutions new to the strategic planning, gaining the expertise of a consultant familiar with the practice in the higher education setting can prove very beneficial. Institutions that are comfort-able with strategic planning, but are seeking to increase its positive impact, can also find an experienced consultant useful in helping them realized greater gains from this planning process.

Strategy Execution in Higher Education

The effective execution of goals emerging from the strategic planning process can prove challenging for many organizations (Decker et al., 2012). The scope of the changes identified, the culture of the organization, the characteristics of the individual units impacted by the change, and the ac-curate alignment of organizational resources with change efforts combine to impact the organization's ability to make progress toward specific stra-tegic goal achievement. Nearly 70% of organizational changes have failed to reach completion and produce the desired outcomes (Reeves, 2008). Clearly, organizations of all types face challenges in implementing change. Higher education institutions, however, have unique features that make successful change even more challenging. The dispersed management structure that characterizes many universities creates a complex, multidivisional structure that can impede the speed and success of large-scale change efforts. Moreover, individual units within institutions of higher education are often given significant levels of independence to create and deliver academic programs. The personnel within each unit, therefore, have the ability to directly influence the unit's respond to strategic change initiatives (Makins, Nagao, & Bennett, 2012). Ensuring genuine alignment between the institution's internal culture and the goals emerging from the strategic planning process, therefore, is essential in executing organizational change (Makins et al., 2012).

In addition to the institution's internal features, it is essential to examine the external environment during the strategic planning process. The need to maintain competitive advantage by offering an effective value proposition that meets student and employer expectations is vital in positioning an organization for optimal success (Pacheco-Ornelas, Cuevas-Rodriguez, & Rodriguez-Pacheco, 2012). Innovative delivery models stimulated by online segments of the industry, competency-based approaches, business partnerships, and evolving student needs are all stimulating change in institutions of higher education as they reevaluate their own relevance in the rapidly changing external environment (Falin, 2012).

The clear evaluation of an organization's alignment to internal and external factors will provide the academy with a more direct path to strategic goal achievement. Moreover, an assessment of the organization's overall readiness for change is critical to successful strategic planning process as it will highlight the organization's overall, and unit-specific, capacity to integrate changes effectively. The successful implementation of innovative solutions within the industry of higher education, therefore, requires a clear assessment of both external and internal factors that stimulate and drive change.

Capacity for Change

Organizational readiness to change is valued in corporations where innovation is vital to the competitive landscape. Executing pioneering initiatives successfully allows an organization functioning within a rapidly changing environment to shape its future while maintaining strategic advantage over rivals. Organizations that struggle to implement change effectively, however, often fall short of achieving their strategic goals, thereby weakening their competitive position in the market place and reducing their overall fiscal strength (Washington & Hacker, 2005). To reduce the likelihood of a poorly executed strategic plan, organizations today are looking for ways to utilize key competencies in support of their initiatives. In response, researchers studying organizational capacity for change are discovering key factors that contribute to the effective implementation of innovative strategic goals.

Capacity for change is a dynamic capability within an organization that supports its ability to adapt to evolving conditions and implement innovative solutions. The organizational capabilities undergirding these adaptive efforts are found to be multidimensional, creating a complex network of interdependent dynamics. According to Judge (2011), the eight key components to consider when assessing an organization's change capacity include the trustworthiness of leaders, level of innovation that already exists, efficacy of the organizational communication, commitment levels of mid-level management, degree of employee trust, extent of organizational accountability, level of system's thinking present, and the presence of strategically-placed change champions. As the rate of change-stimulating innovations impacting institutions across the globe accelerates, developing a culture ready and able to adapt is becoming essential. Finding a balance between current operations and change efforts, therefore, moves to center as leaders guide their organizations to fulfill current obligations while shaping the future of their industry (Meyer & Stensaker, 2006). To achieve this balance, it is the responsibility of leaders to be selective in the changes they institute and effective in managing the change process developed in response to emerging demands. To assist leaders in this complex task, researchers are working to identify key factors that will have the greatest impact on organizational change initiatives. For example, Decker et al. (2012) determined that poorly articulated goals, inadequate understanding of the change process, deficits in leader or employee competence, and an ineffective grasp of the organization's internal and external environment were key predictors of unsuccessful organizational change. In contrast, Judge, Naoumova, and Douglas (2009) found that the effective use of human capital and the skilled management of the organization's infrastructure at all levels supported overall capacity to change successfully.

Saran, Servier, and Kalliny (2009) added to the discussion by identifying six key areas of the organization that prove critical to successful plan execution. These organizational areas include: corporate culture, organizational structure, level of functional differentiation between units, function of leadership, employee job satisfaction, and overall job involvement and empowerment. Identifying the organizational capabilities in each element reveals areas needing particular attention during the change effort. Moreover, a clear assessment of the organization's internal status enables the effective deployment of corporate resources needed for successful execution.

Clearly, change capacity across organizations is comprised of multiple inter-related forces, with implementation and outcome impacting a range of stakeholders. According to the investor, an organization that produces results quickly by acting with a sense of urgency is highly prized (Kotter,

2008). To the consumer, the recipient of the changes, improved quality at an affordable price is expected. To the employee implementing the change effort, the organization's change readiness is found to be dependent on the level of change commitment from senior management, the competence of those driving the change, the level of change in specific job tasks, and the change support received from one's immediate supervisor (Cinite, Duxbury, & Higgins, 2009). Furthermore, the organization's ability to communicate effectively during the change is seen as a critical factor that influences the level of success achieved in any change. A clear understanding of each stakeholder's perspective will provide leaders with valuable insights on where to focus time and energy in order to produce an organizational culture ready for change.

Capacity for Change in Higher Education

Institutions of higher education face some unique challenges that can influence the success of change efforts. As described earlier, cultural features, governance structures, and faculty roles are among the factors that contribute to a highly complex organization. Another important fact relevant to many colleges and universities today is their status as public institutions. Organizations within the public sector generally have highly bureaucratic internal environments embedded within a highly complex structure. Therefore, leaders seeking to implement change successfully within public higher education institutions will likely have additional factors to consider such as institutional governance, faculty centrality, and disbursed power bases. Clearly, advancing innovation in higher education is proving to be a complex undertaking as changes inherent in innovative efforts interface with the established mores of the academy. Still, colleges and universities across the globe are rising to the occasion with varying levels of success. The remainder of the chapter will look at the importance of leaders in driving innovation that will shape the future of the industry.

The Role of Leadership in Driving Innovation

Leaders play a vital role in guiding their organization to implement changes in service of adaptive innovation. From crafting the institutional vision statement to evaluating changes undergirding innovative initiatives, leaders influence the process and can help shape the future success of their organization. For leaders in academic institutions, however, the effective use of this influence is shaped by the unique characteristics inherent in these educationally focused systems.

Institutions of higher education today have grown out of deeply engrained traditions that endorse a dispersed governance structure driven by high levels of faculty and staff involvement. Moreover, multiple centers of decision making emanating from faculty-centered processes make the academic environment particularly complex. This model of organizational structure and process has served the academy well for decades. However, in the face of growing demands for change in higher education today, the traditional structure of the institutions within the industry is under pressure to change. It is at this juncture that the unique characteristics of the academy take on special importance. At this point in time, academic leaders are being called upon to stimulate large-scale innovation that will position their institution for success. In order to accomplish this task, leaders are developing strategies to meet the challenges impacting the industry today. Often these strategies require significant levels of change.

One of the most significant barriers to the execution of innovative initiatives and their accompanying changes is the decentralized power base functioning within many colleges and universities today. These dispersed power centers often function independently and maintain only a loose connection to other centers and to the institution at large. This organizational structure makes the job of implementing changes that much more challenging. Some academic leaders have found it useful to identify key stakeholders across the university to serve as advocates or promoters of the change initiatives within their own spheres of influence. This approach to change management enables senior leadership access to each of the dispersed areas impacted by the change, solicit feedback about the change efforts, and evaluate progress made during each phase of the change roll-out. When used effectively, promoters are able to support the successful implementation of innovation and change in settings where governance is dispersed and power is shared across units (Husig & Mann, 2010).

As academic leaders today guide the transformation of instructional units, processes, and delivery methods, they will need to employ leadership skills aligned with the job at hand. Much like the transformation they are leading, the skills found to be most effective in guiding innovation and change in higher education today are transformational in nature. By influencing faculty and staff, stimulating their intellect, and motivating them toward the change, leaders are able to facilitate the desired changes (Chipunza & Gwarinda, 2010).

While the skills of the transformational leader are proving effective in guiding institutional change in higher education, the specific tasks inherent in the change process can remain unclear as newly emerging innovations enter uncharted territory. In an effort to clarify the process followed by one academic institution in implementing large-scale change, Randall (2012) identified six fundamental steps employed to transform a two-year college into a four-year institution. These steps include: (a) Identifying the challenge (technical vs. adaptive); (b) Recognizing the difficulty of change; (c) Framing the issues and focusing attention; (d) Securing ownership; (e) Managing stakeholder conflict and stress; and (f) Creating a safe haven (pp. 8–13). Randall (2012) also noted that the successful execution of the tasks that led to the desired transformation was predicated on ongoing collaboration between leadership, faculty, and staff.

Leading others by facilitating and maintaining effective collaboration utilizes the expertise from members within and across teams to position organizations to compete effectively in the marketplace (Ansell & Gash, 2008; Judge, Naoumova, & Douglas, 2009). Moreover, collaborative governance within the public sector has been guiding administrative action to effectively create and sustain collective actions that support the effective use of resources while benefiting a wide range of stakeholders (Emerson, Nabatchi, & Balough, 2012). This collaboration can be designed so that the intellectual capital available within higher education today benefits the development and implementation of innovative change efforts. In addition, aligning organizational resources to respond to a rapidly changing global context supports a collaborative leadership approach that gathers input and knowledge from across the firm in support of effective change. Internal forces supporting collaborative styles of leadership noted by Penney (2011) include generational expectations of a growing workforce. Therefore, effective collaborative leadership will be important in supporting the institution's vitality and relevance as faculty and staff are given the opportunity to stimulate greater interdependence, and the external environment demands quick and effective changes to drive competitive advantage.

CONCLUSION

Higher education today is facing significant pressure to develop innovative solutions to meet the emergent needs of a changing world. The demands created by our increasingly connected global economy and fueled by rapid technological advances call for skilled workers and the continuous retooling of the existing workforce. Adults today are entering colleges and universities in record number in order to secure work in this transforming economy, and to stay relevant within its swiftly moving job market. In response, innovative approaches to teaching and learning are being developed across the globe that address the needs of lifelong learners in the 21st century. As the industry continues to evolve, individual institutions can play central roles in shaping the future of higher education. To increase the success of such efforts, many institutions within the academy are adopting strategic planning to gauge their performance, set goals that support continued success, and develop action plans to operationalize innovative strategies that meet the evolving needs of today's adults.

The importance of implementing change efforts is highlighted today as universities respond to a quickly changing landscape. New forms of delivery are emerging each year as the industry addresses the needs of a growing adult student population seeking relevant and accessible credit-bearing and non-credit-bearing programs. Each innovative solution represents a change in the way higher education programs are built and delivered. Such change efforts can be challenging. In order to increase the likelihood for success, researchers have identified a number of factors that contribute to an organizations readiness for change. By incorporating an assessment of an institution's unique capacity to change into the strategic planning process itself, academic leaders will incorporate knowledge of organizational strengths and opportunities in the change management plan undergirding each initiative. This added insight gives the university an increased chance of success while executing each of its strategic initiatives.

Meeting the needs of the adult student population in today's evolving global economy is a challenge being addressed by colleges and universities across the country. Advancing innovation in higher education, however, is a monumental task. The unique characteristics of higher education institutions worldwide are built on centuries of tradition that have proven useful over many years. Moreover, the dispersed governance structure and shared power-base across areas within the university present particular challenges to leaders seeking to guide their institutions into a successful future. Leaders who learn to work within the culture of their institution to guide it through a process of transformation are proving that innovation is not only possible, but attainable. Clearly, institutions of higher education are well suited to meet the challenges ahead as they embrace their own knowledge and expertise and partner with those outside the academy to create an innovative approach to education that meets the emergent needs of our world today.

REFERENCES

Altbach, P. G., Reisberg, L., & Rumbley, L. E. (2010). Tracking a global academic revolution. *Change, 42*(2), 30–39.

Ansell, C., & Gash, A. (2008). Collaborative governance in theory and practice. *Journal of Public Administration Research & Theory, 18*(4), 543–571.

Baggaley, J. (2013). MOOC rampant. *Distance Education, 34*(3), 368–378.

Chance, S., & Williams, B. T. (2009). Assessing university strategic plans: A tool for consideration. *Educational Planning, 18*(1), 38–54.

Chandra, A., & Fealey, T. (2009). Business incubation in the United States, China and Brazil: A comparison of role of government, incubator funding and financial services. *International Journal of Entrepreneurship, 13,* 67–86.

Chipunza, C., & Gwarinda, S. A. (2010). Transformational leadership in merging higher education institutions: A case study. *South African Journal of Human Resource Management, 8*(1), 1–10.

Christensen, C. M., & Eyring, H. J. (2011). *The innovative university.* San Francisco, CA: Jossey Bass.

Cinite, I., Duxbury, L. E., & Higgins, C. (2009). Measurement of perceived organizational readiness for change in the public sector. *British Journal of Management, 20*(2), 265–277. Doi:10.1111/j.1467-8551.2008.00582.x

Culkin, N., & Mallick, S. (2011). Producing work-ready graduates. *International Journal of Market Research, 53*(3), 347–368.

Decker, P., Durand, R., Mayfield, C. O., McCormack, C., Skinner, D., & Perdue, G. (2012). Predicting implementation failure in organizational change. *Journal of Organizational Culture, Communications and Conflict, 16*(2), 39–59.

Drew, G. (2010). Issues and challenges in higher education leadership: Engaging for change. *Australian Educational Researcher, 37*(3), 57–76.

Emerson, K., Nabatchi, T., & Balogh, S. (2012). An integrative framework for collaborative governance. *Journal of Public Administration Research & Theory, 22*(1), 1–29.

Falin, P. (2012, December). More cracks in the credit hour. *Inside Higher Ed.* Retrieved from http://www.insidehighered.com/news/2012/12/05/carnegie-foundation-considers-redesign-credit-hour#.UMIt_UPnFxw.email

Fathi, M., & Wilson, L. (2009). Strategic planning in colleges and universities. *Business Renaissance Quarterly, 4*(1), 91–103.

Flynn, J. T. (2013). MOOCS: Disruptive innovation and the future of higher education. *Christian Education Journal, 10*(1), 149–162.

G20 (2011). *Policy coherence position statement prepared for: The G20 high-level conference on strengthening the social dimension of globalization.* Paris. Retrieved from http://comunidadilgo.org/public/files/IOE-IAC_Policy_Coherence_Position_Statement_ to_the_G20_%28June_10_version%292.pdf

Heifetz, R., & Laurie, D. (2012). Mobilizing adaptive work: Beyond visionary leadership. In J. Conger, et al. (Eds.), *The leader's change handbook: An essential guide to setting direction and taking action* (pp. 55–86). San Francisco: Jossey-Bass.

Husig, S., & Mann, H. (2010). The role of promoters in effecting innovation in higher education institutions. *Innovation: Management, Policy & Practice, 12*(2), 180–191. doi:10.5172/impp.12.2.180

Judge, W. (2011). *Building organizational capacity for change.* New York, NY: Business Expert Press, LLC.

Judge, W. Q., Naoumova, I., & Douglas, T. (2009). Organizational capacity for change and firm performance in a transition economy. *International Journal of Human Resource Management, 20*(8), 1737–1752.

Kamenetz, A. (2012). Southern New Hampshire University: For relentlessly reinventing higher ed online and off. *Fast Company*, (163), 94–96.

Karpagam, P. L., & Suganthi, L. L. (2012). A strategy map of balanced scorecard in academic institutions for performance improvement. *IUP Journal of Business Strategy, 9*(3), 7–16.

Kasworm, C. E. (2012). US adult higher education: One context of lifelong learning. *International Journal of Continuing Education & Lifelong Learning, 5*(1), 1–19.

Khan, M., Ahmed, I., & Nawaz, M. (2011). Student's perspective of service quality in higher learning institutions: An evidence based approach. *International Journal of Business & Social Science, 2*(11), 159–164.

Kotter, J. P. (2008). *A Sense of Urgency*. Boston, MA: Harvard Business School Publishing.

Laitinen, A. (2013). Changing the way we account for college credit. *Issues in Science & Technology, 29*(2), 62–68.

Loomis, S., & Rodriguez, J. (2009). Institutional change and higher education. *Higher Education, 58*(4), 475–489.

Makins, Q., Nagao, D., & Bennett, N. (2012). Enterprise alignment and inertia risks during transformation. *Information Knowledge Systems Management, 11*(1/2), 151–168.

Meyers, A. (2009). Spin-outs: Creating businesses from university intellectual property. *Journal of Commercial Biotechnology, 15*(3), 281–282. doi:10.1057/jcb.2009.6

Meyer, C. B., & Stensaker, I. G. (2006). Developing capacity for change. *Journal of Change Management, 6*(2), 217–231.

Mogilyanskaya, A. (2012, November 30). Americans are proud of U.S. colleges but not of their direction. *The Chronicle of Higher Education.* Retrieved from http://chronicle.com/article/Americans-Are-Proud-of-US/135942/

National Center for Education Statistics. (2012) *Digest of education statistics: 2012.* Retrieved from http://nces.ed.gov/pubs2014/2014015.pdf

Omerzel, D. G., Biloslavo, R., & Trnavčevič, A. (2011). Knowledge management and organizational culture in higher education institutions. *Journal for East European Management Studies, 16*(2), 111–139.

Obama, B. (2012). *State of the union.* Speech presented in the U.S. Capitol, Washington DC.

Özdem, G. (2011). An analysis of the mission and vision statements on the strategic plans of higher education institutions. *Educational Sciences: Theory & Practice, 11*(4), 1887–1894.

Pacheco-Ornelas, M. C., Cuevas-Rodriguez, E., & Rodriguez-Pacheco, R. H. (2012). Organizational competences and competitiveness: The effect of business strategies. *Advances in Competitiveness Research, 20*(3/4), 16–31.

Parry, M. (2013). Helping colleges move beyond the credit hour. *Chronicle of Higher Education, 59*(34), B7–B8.

Partnership for the 21st Century (2003). *Learning for the 21stcentury.* Retrieved from http://www.p21.org/storage/documents/P21_Report.pdf

Penney, S. H. (2011). Voices of the future: Leadership for the 21st century. *Journal of Leadership Studies, 5*(3), 55–62.

Randall, L. M. (2012). Transforming a university: A study of process leadership. *Academy of Educational Leadership Journal, 16*(2), 1–20.

Reeves, D. B. (2008). Making strategic planning work. *Educational Leadership, 65*(4), 86–87.

Rollins, T. M. (2014). MOOCs: Been there, done that. *Chronicle of Higher Education, 60*(19), B4–B5.

Saran, A., Serviere, L., & Kalliny, M. (2009). Corporate culture, organizational dynamics and implementation of innovations: A conceptual framework. *Asian Journal of Marketing, 3*(1), 10–19.

Shearer, R. (2004). Penn State World Campus adds live e-learning to its online curriculum. *T H E Journal, 32*(3), 59–60.

Sullivan, T., & Richardson, E. (2011). Living the plan: Strategic planning with practice and assessment. *Journal of Continuing Higher Education, 59*(1), 2–9.

Tikhomirova, N., Tikhomirov, V., Maksimova, V., & Telnov, Y. (2011). The competence approach to the creation and updating of academic knowledge in the smart economy. *Proceedings of the International Conference on Intellectual Capital, Knowledge Management & Organizational Learning*, 563–570.

Washington, M., & Hacker, M. (2005). Why change fails: knowledge counts. *Leadership and Organizational Development Journal, 26*, 400–411.

Wisseman, J. G., & Verlopp, J. (2009). *Toward the third generation university: Managing the university in transition.* Cheltenham, United Kingdom: Edward Elgar Publishing, Ltd.

PART II

SUPPORTING ADULT LEARNING IN ORGANIZATIONS, INSTITUTIONS, AND COMMUNITIES:

Implementing Forward-Looking, Compentency-Based Measures of Adult Learning

CHAPTER 22

PRIOR LEARNING ASSESSMENT

Trends and Issues in U.S. Post-Secondary Education

Henry S. Merrill
DePaul University School for New Learning

Prior learning assessment (PLA), with its origins in the ferment of the Carnegie Commission on Non-traditional Education in the 1970s, is seeing a resurgence of interest 40 years later. PLA began during the innovative reforms of post-secondary education in the 1960s–70s. It was sustained as an important option in adult degree completion programs and services existing on the margins of post-secondary education through the end of the twentieth century. There is a renewed interest in PLA as an important strategy and set of processes for assessing learning in the context of important contemporary forces: competency-based degrees using direct assessment, career credentials and pathways, and the explosion of learning opportunities and open education resources available via Web 2.0. The focus of the chapter is on the reasons for this increased interest on the part of many

Building Sustainable Futures for Adult Learners, pages 467–490
Copyright © 2015 by Information Age Publishing

different stakeholders. In addition to post-secondary institutions, this interest comes from affiliated organizations, philanthropic institutions, federal and state government agencies, the military, and regional accrediting associations. The primary questions explored are: What are the driving forces behind the issues concerning PLA both as an innovation in the 1970s and today? What forces are driving the related trends in post-secondary education? What is the outlook for PLA in theses challenging times?

These two quotations, from Eduard Lindeman and Curtis Bonk, provide some perspective on how experiential learning, a fundamental concept of adult learning, has both remained the same and changed during the last 90 years, especially in relation to PLA.

> A fresh hope is astir. From many quarters comes the call to a new kind of education with its initial assumption affirming that education is life—not merely preparation for an unknown kind of future living. . . . The whole of life is learning, therefore education can have no endings. E. C. Lindeman. (*The meaning of Adult Education,* 1926, p. 3)

> Anyone can now learn anything from anyone at anytime. C. J. Bonk (*The World is Open: How web technology is revolutionizing education,* 2009, p. 7)

Lindeman's idea that education has no ending shows how things have remained the same: as adults we recognize learning from our experience throughout our lifetime. Bonk's description of the twenty-first century world of open-anyone-anything-anytime learning posits how access to the theory and practice of any subject matter has opened up learning opportunities for those with the technologies to access the content.

Origins of PLA in the 1970s

It has been 45 years since the publication of the Carnegie Commission on Nontraditional Education, funded by the Carnegie Corporation in 1971, reports calling for substantial reforms and innovation in post-secondary education. Stimulated by the turbulent spirit of the 1960s and converging demographics of traditional college students with returning adult learners, these reports and the Higher Education Act, passed in 1965 and reauthorized in 1974, stimulated a wave of interest in and increased funding for institutions and students. PLA was one of those innovative reforms. PLA was a result of the development of reliable assessment processes so adults may demonstrate and document college-level learning gained outside the traditional classroom walls (Klein-Collins, 2013; Maehl, 2004).

During the 1960s and 1970s, there was great interest in developing alternative approaches to deliver post-secondary education with more flexibility, especially with regard to the traditional requirements of time and place. Post-secondary education had expanded greatly to accommodate the wave of children born to the Boomer generation (Cross, 1976). However, as that demographic segment graduated there was a need to replace them with new audiences. The focus became the non-traditional student or adult learner (Cross, 1976). The 1973 Commission on Non-traditional Study provided much of this impetus. Their work sounds very familiar and almost current albeit 40 years later. One of their reports, Diversity by Design, explores ways for increasing opportunities and access for adults and creating alternative, external degrees within traditional post-secondary institutions. One brief section sketches a proposal for a National University using a direct assessment model that presages the model of Western Governors University. This is a summary list of their important recommendations:

1. Lifetime learning—basic, continuing, and recurrent—has a new appropriateness today and requires a new pattern of support.
2. Colleges and universities must shift emphasis from degree-granting to service to the learner, thus countering what has become a degree-granting obsession.
3. Faculty understandings and commitments must be reoriented and redirected, particularly through in-service development, so that knowledge and use of non-traditional forms and materials will increase.
4. An organized effort must be made to promote intelligent and widespread use of educational technology with special emphasis on programming for cable television, computers, videotape recorders, and possibilities of satellite broadcasting.
5. New agencies must be created to make possible easy access to information and develop better ways to disseminate it, to perform guidance and counseling services, and to be assessors and repositories of credit for student achievement.
6. New evaluative tools must be developed to match the non-traditional arrangements now evolving, so that accreditation and credentialing will have appropriate measures of quality.
7. Cooperation and collaboration must be encouraged among collegiate, community and alternative educational entities so that diverse educational programs and structures may come into being." (Gold, 1973, pp. xvii–xix)

The work of the Carnegie Commission provided the foundation for what became the non-traditional and external degree models, evening colleges, and general studies programs to meet the needs of adult learners later in the 1970s and 1980s. These innovations marked a shift from traditional institutional convenience models to focusing on the needs of adult learners (Maehl, 2004).

There are many examples of the innovative reforms generated during this period. At the federal level, there were amendments to the Higher Education Act of 1965 creating the Fund for Improvement of Post-secondary Education (FIPSE) to provide grants to institutions supporting innovative programs (Cross, 1976). One initiative from the American Council on Education (ACE) was assessing and recommending academic credit for training completed while in military service. Another was a three-year collaboration, begun in 1974, between the Educational Testing Service (ETS) and a group of 10 post-secondary education institutions called the Cooperative Assessment of Experiential Learning (CAEL) Project. The research focused on the current uses of experiential learning and identifying best practices to provide valid and reliable ways for assessing the outcomes to document college-level credit for prior learning. This collaboration resulted in an initial draft set of principles for PLA (Keaton, 1976). The name and work of CAEL was refocused as a non-profit organization. The name was changed to the Council for Adult and Experiential Learning with an enhanced mission to improve access for adults to attain meaningful learning, credentials, and work. Today CAEL consults with colleges and universities and trains faculty to assess prior learning for college credit. CAEL is recognized internationally for research and expertise on the portfolio assessment method of PLA. The Ten Standards for Assessing Learning developed by CAEL are used by colleges and universities and accrediting organizations across the country (Klein-Collins, 2013).

PLA and Experiential Learning

What exactly is PLA? How is experiential learning defined? There are, of course, books that focus on these questions. For our purposes, this section provides an overview for readers not thoroughly familiar with these concepts. CAEL, a prominent proponent for PLA, provides this definition:

> PLA is the process by which an individual's learning is assessed and evaluated for purposes of granting college credit, certification, or advanced standing toward further education or training. That learning may have been acquired through on-the-job experiences, corporate training, military training or experience, volunteer work or self-guided study. PLA methods include exams, individual portfolios, or the formal review of a course or training program to determine whether it is at the college level. Typically the first two methods assess the learning outcomes or what the individual knows and can do; the last method assesses inputs, what materials and learning activities a course or training program presents. (Klein-Collins and Wertheim, 2013, p. 2)

Fenwick (2003) describes as one "basic conceptualization of experiential learning: an independent learner, cognitively reflecting on concrete experience to construct new understandings, perhaps with the assistance of an educator, towards some social goal of progress or improvement" (2003, p. 12). Fenwick provides a useful summary of the categories of activities usually included under the term experiential learning in adult education: (1) Internships, apprenticeships, or service learning as examples of field-based learning; (2) credit for prior learning programs in post-secondary education; (3) Active learning exercises used in classroom-based, non-collegiate instruction; (4) outdoor (a. k. a. wilderness) programs in post-secondary education or corporate training programs focused on leadership development, creative problem solving, self-awareness, and group processes and communication; (5) informal learning developed through reflection on everyday activities for meaning-making (a. k. a. practical intelligence); and (6) learning developed through social action, either as an active community citizen or when engaged in resisting a dominant force as part of a collective action (2003, pp. 4–5). The recognition of the value of experiential learning that may be assessed by subject matter experts as equivalent to college-level learning is the fundamental innovation of PLA.

The concept of reflecting on experience to learn or make meaning from concrete activities is at the core of PLA. It is a common misunderstanding that the PLA process recognizes all life experience as college-level learning. It is true that some institutions may award credit or advanced standing based on the review of an applicant's resume without any careful assessment of learning with a PLA process documenting whether college-level learning actually occurred. The PLA process in use at post-secondary institutions with credible PLA programs requires the learner to reflect on and provide documentation for college-level learning derived from specific experiences, such as those described by Fenwick. These PLA programs and processes are based on the principles established by the Ten Standards for Assessing Learning and rigorous review by faculty and other appropriate subject matter experts (Fiddler, Marienau, & Whitaker, 2006).

PLA Methods In Post-Secondary Education Programs

There are four generally accepted approaches to PLA that, when conducted well, ensure academic quality. These approaches include nationally standardized exams, challenge exams developed by faculty (usually for use only at their post-secondary institutions), credit recommendations from other educational organizations, and individualized portfolio assessment processes. Examples of national standardized exams in specified disciplines include Advanced Placement (AP) exams as used in high schools, the College Level Examination Program (CLEP) tests, Excelsior College exams (formerly Regents College Exams), and DANTES Subject Standardized

Tests (DSST). At the institutional level, college faculty may develop challenge exams for select courses at their campus. These exams may be used to determine credit and advanced standing in a subject. An exam may also be used to assess competency and credit for college-level learning from local workplace programs or other experiential learning not included in the national compilations created by two national non-profit organizations, National College Credit Recommendations Service (NCCRS—formerly known as National PONSI), and the American Council on Education (ACE) (Klein-Collins, 2010).

Since the 1970s, NCCRS and ACE have developed processes to evaluate non-college programs and make recommendations for academic credit. These affiliate organizations provide evaluations of corporate professional development and military training programs. The compilations of college credit recommendations of courses or examinations available from non-academic organizations (outside of the traditional college classroom setting) provide important resources to link workplace learning with post-secondary education for adults seeking college degrees. The current proliferation of academic courses and other learning experiences, such as Massive Open Online Courses (MOOCs) and digital badges now offered by post-secondary institutions and other providers, add more complexity to these options. These recent developments will be discussed below.

The fourth example of ways to approach prior learning is portfolio assessment by local faculty or other appropriate subject matter expert. A portfolio is a student's documentation of college-level learning achieved through non-collegiate experiences. Post-secondary institutions adopt one of several different options when developing local policy to govern this individualized approach. One institutional policy option is to allow students to develop learning outcomes that are equivalent only to existing courses at that institution. This is often described as a course matching system. Another option is to allow the student to identify equivalent courses taught at other institutions for use in developing learning outcomes to be assessed in their portfolio. A third option is to document block credit for learning outcomes that are assessed by faculty as college level learning but have no exact course equivalency at their institution. An example of the block credit approach could be awarding a certain amount of credit that does not match existing courses by directly assessing a demonstrated competency, such as a performance skill or demonstration of content mastery, on the basis of performance and demonstrated knowledge of specific skills and subject matter (Fiddler, Marienau, & Whitaker, 2006).

One important product of CAEL's work has been to define and publish their Ten Standards for Assessing Learning. Table 22.1 presents a summary of the Ten Standards for institutions to guide the development of PLA policy and program administration. The first five Standards focus on the

TABLE 22.1   CAEL's Ten Standards for Assessing Learning

Standard 1	Credit or its equivalent should be awarded only for learning, and not for experience.
Standard 2	Assessment should be based on standards and criteria for the level of acceptable learning that are both agreed upon and made public.
Standard 3	Assessment should be treated as an integral part of learning, not separate from it, and should be based on an understanding of learning processes.
Standard 4	The determination of credit awards and competence levels must be made by appropriate subject matter and academic or credentialing experts.
Standard 5	Credit or other credentialing should be appropriate to the context in which it is awarded and accepted.
Standard 6	If awards are for credit, transcript entries should clearly describe what learning is being recognized and should be monitored to avoid giving credit twice for the same learning.
Standard 7	Policies, procedures, and criteria applied to assessment, including provision for appeal, should be fully disclosed and prominently available to all parties involved in the assessment process.
Standard 8	Fees charged for assessment should be based on the services performed in the process and not determined by the amount of credit awarded.
Standard 9	All personnel involved in the assessment of learning should pursue and receive adequate training and continuing professional development for the functions they perform.
Standard 10	Assessment programs should be regularly monitored, reviewed, evaluated, and revised as needed to reflect changes in the needs being served, the purposes being met, and the state of the assessment arts.

Source: Fiddler, Marienau, & Whitaker, 2006, pp. 14–24.

process of assessing learning. The last five Standards focus on program administration and quality control of the PLA process.

These Ten Standards provide specific goals as the foundation for local institutional policies and processes governing PLA. Ensuring accurate and credible learning assessment, whether the learner participated in formal, non-formal or informal learning, is the ultimate goal for PLA practitioners (Fiddler, Marienau, & Whitaker, 2006).

Initiatives with PLA and Access To Post-Secondary Degrees

Increased interest at national and state levels in developing goals for and ways to increase the number of people completing associate and bachelor degrees is one force driving this renewed interest in PLA (Sherman, Klein-Collins, & Palmer, 2012). The degree completion goal of doubling college graduates by 2020 is one example of this renewed interest. President Obama stressed the importance of education to America's future prosperity in a speech at Macomb Community College in Michigan, on July 14, 2009. Reminding the audience of Goal 2020 calling for the U.S. to have the highest proportion of college graduates in the world, he announced the American

Graduation Initiative "to help an additional five million Americans earn degrees and certificates in the next decade" (Obama, 2009, July 14).

There is a resurgence of interest in the concepts, policies, and best practices that provide the foundation for PLA (Klein-Collins & Wertheim, 2013). Postsecondary education institutions, foundations, and non-profit organizations have identified many initiatives to reach these goals for building a sustainable future for adult learners. Examples of the initiatives include hybrid distance learning courses, accelerated degree programs, and competency-based programs using PLA strategies and methods while adhering to high academic standards in program delivery (Sherman, Klein-Collins, & Palmer, 2012).

Examples of Stakeholder Initiatives

There are many examples of recent initiatives for institutions and individual learners to provide individualized assessments, particularly for portfolio-based assessments. One of these initiatives is the Learning Counts™ service started by CAEL in January 2011. Learning Counts is a national online service providing advisors to help learners prepare documentation for portfolios. CAEL-trained faculty subject matter experts then assess the portfolios. CAEL provides transcripts of these credit recommendations for consideration by post-secondary institutions selected by the student. If accepted, the credits are added to the student's academic record as transfer credit. This initiative was developed with support from eight foundations (Council for Adult and Experiential Learning, 2014).

The American Council on Education (ACE) has developed the Credits to Credentials™ program to improve the pathways towards completing a degree or other credential. This initiative is described as "a large-scale strategy to develop and implement clearly-mapped education and career pathways for adults that have successfully completed workforce and military training and occupations with ACE credit recommendations" (ACE Credits to Credentials, 2014). This is done in collaboration with post-secondary education institutions and ACE corporate and institutional clients, such as employers, professional associations, unions and government agencies. ACE seeks to provide guaranteed transfer credit, shorten time to credential completion, and decrease education costs for both learners and employers with these education and career pathways (ACE Credits to Credentials, 2014).

Another ACE initiative is Maps to Credentials, a three-year project is funded by FIPSE. This program designs and pilots credential road maps for student veterans; it applies ACE credit recommendations for military occupations and training and incorporates other PLA methods to accelerate veterans' postsecondary attainment. One example of this kind of map is a Credential and Military Crosswalk created by Ivy Tech Community College, one of the institutions that participated in the pilot. It is available at: www. ivytech.edu/pla/ (ACE Maps to credentials, 2014).

ACT published a white paper in 2011, *Breaking new ground, Building a national workforce skills credentialing System*. The intent of this report, similar to many other reports published in the last 20 years, is to support an orderly and transparent system of meaningful workplace credentials in addition to post-secondary credentials. These reports typically focus on the essential skills needed for success in the workplace, the human relations, writing, math, and critical thinking skills as well as industry-specific skills that employers want to be able to validate via this kind of credential system.

> The value of assessing current workforce skills and translating that performance into meaningful and industry-recognized workplace credentials should not be underestimated. For employers, utilizing a national skills credential is a way for them to fill critical positions, build the talent pipeline, and compete globally. For workers, having a national work ready credential improves their labor market experience, demonstrates essential skills aligned to the requirements of the workplace, and provides a national, across-industry, portable credential. Today, approximately 40 states are at various stages of implementing a general work/career ready certificate. These certificates provide a standard way to measure worker knowledge and skills, all within a standardized, easy-to-understand common language, and are compatible with traditional credentials." (ACT, 2011, p. 9)

The Lumina Foundation is an interesting example of a philanthropic institution developing initiatives to increase access to post-secondary education and degree completion. Lumina articulated this graduation initiative: "Goal 2025: To increase the proportion of Americans with high-quality college degrees or other credentials to 60% by 2025" (Lumina Foundation, 2013). Lumina developed two strategic initiatives to achieve Goal 2025. Taking advantage of the proliferation of competency-based models and open courseware to create new pathways to degrees is the first strategy. The second is expanding the availability of prior learning assessment (PLA) and other approaches to accelerate progress toward degrees (Lumina Foundation, 2013, p. 7).

Lumina's Degree Qualifications Profile (DQP) framework is another example of an initiative related to its strategic imperative of developing a twenty-first century educational system. The DQP is a tool developed with the intent to "help transform U.S. higher education. A Degree Profile—or qualifications framework—illustrates clearly what students should be expected to know and be able to do once they earn their degrees—at any level" (Lumina, DQP, p. 3). Lumina projects that use of the Degree Profile over time would impact post-secondary education in several ways, including the development of a common vocabulary for sharing good practice, a clearer explanation for understanding the outcomes of higher education, and improved accountability descriptors (Lumina, 2011).

The intent of the DQP is to define competencies in ways that emphasize both the cumulative integration of learning from many sources and the application of learning in a variety of settings with the ability to offer benchmarks for improving the quality of learning. The DQP is presented graphically as a web with the associate's degree at its center, surrounded by the bachelor's degree, with the outer region being graduate study, specifically the master's degree. The graphic image has five 'anchor lines' moving from a central point outward, forming a pentagram-shaped web. These anchor lines represent the basic areas of learning that should comprise a degree. The first anchor line is Broad, Integrative Knowledge and the second anchor line is Specialized Knowledge. The third, Intellectual Skills, includes analytic inquiry, fluency in oral and written communication, and fluency in quantitative applications. Civic Learning is the fourth anchor line and includes preparing students for responsible citizenship and engaging diverse perspectives. Fifth is Applied Learning including opportunity to demonstrate analytic inquiry, active learning, real-world problem solving, and innovation (Lumina, 2011). The DQP provides a model that might be used to stimulate innovate degrees within the framework of a traditional post-secondary institution using traditional degrees, much like the external degree model in the 1970s and 1980s. Or the DQP might provide an institution the model to radically redefine the entire academic program.

Post-secondary Institution Initiatives and Competency-Based Education

The reforms proposed by the Commission for Non-traditional Education in the 1970s to improve access to college for adults and lifelong learning opportunities for continuous professional development had marginal impact on the traditional delivery of post-secondary education. There were, however, some notable initiatives started in the 1970s at a few institutions that provide a basis of theory and practice applicable to developing models for the twenty-first century. Vermont is one state that built a PLA process on the foundation provided by the Commission reports. The Vermont State Colleges (VSC) system created a centralized Office of External Programs administered by the Community College of Vermont (CCV) in 1975. This office conducts all the PLA for the VSC system, including exams and portfolio assessment. A semester-long, three-credit course is available to assist students in creating a portfolio to document college-level learning based on non-collegiate experiences. A standing faculty committee is responsible for assessing all the portfolios submitted and making recommendations for college credit. CAEL reported that more than 7000 students have successfully earned college-level credit through this program, and the credits are recognized throughout the VSC system and at some independent institutions (Sherman, Klein-Collins, & Palmer, 2012).

In addition to CCV, several other innovative post-secondary institutions founded in the 1970s provided alternative paths to degree completion using some combination of PLA, generous credit transfer policies, credit by exam, and independent study strategies for adult learners. These institutions include Charter Oak State College and Thomas Edison State College. DePaul University's School for New Learning is an example from the private, non-profit university sector. The State University of New York (SUNY) System created two innovative institutions: Empire State College and Regents College. Empire State College was founded to provide access statewide with nontraditional teaching and learning strategies using faculty mentors guiding learners through designing and completing individualized degree programs in 12 broad areas of study. Regents College developed a credit-by-exam program that provided expanded options beyond CLEP and DSST exams for adults to document their learning for college credit. Regents College was part of the SUNY System from 1971 until 1998 when it became a private, non-profit institution. In 2001 the name was changed to Excelsior College. Excelsior continues this direct assessment program as UExcel Exams, making them available globally in a computer-based format. The exams are recommended for college under the ACE CREDIT service (Laitinen, 2012).

Confusing Terminology: Competency-Based Education and Outcomes-Based Education

It is beyond the scope of this chapter to fully explore the complex interaction of teaching and learning theories, political contexts, and social issues embedded in sorting through the differences in outcomes-based education (OBE) versus competency-based education (CBE). However, these terms are used, often interchangeably, in contemporary discussions of education reform and in reference to PLA. This section outlines some of the basic terms and arguments to clarify understanding of these types of education. There is a fundamental change in the underlying premise of the teaching-learning exchange incorporated in both OBE and CBE: a shift from instructor-defined learning objectives or goals to defining outcomes identifying what students will learn (Spady, 1994). Peter Ewell defined learning outcomes in terms of "the particular levels of knowledge, skills, and abilities that a student has attained at the end of (or as a result of) his or her engagement in a particular set of collegiate experiences" (Klein-Collins, 2012, p. 9).

Outcomes-based education (OBE) and competency-based education (CBE) also have their roots in the Commission for Non-traditional Education inspired reforms in the 1970s and 80s; however, the focus at that time was primarily on K–12 and vocational-technical education and some areas of clinical and professional education. Spady (1994) provides three premises of OBE, outlining a holistic approach that may resonate with some adult educators: "(1) All students can learn and succeed, but not on the same day and in the same way; (2) Successful learning promotes even more successful learning; (3) Schools control the conditions that directly affect successful school learning" (1994, p. 20). According to Spady (1994), the purposes of OBE are, one, ensuring that all students demonstrate the knowledge, competence, and qualities needed to be successful after completing their education and, two, designing and operating schools so all students achieve the intended outcomes. Spady defines outcomes as "Learning results that are clearly demonstrated at or after the end of an instructional experience. Outcomes can take many forms (from simple to complex) depending on the content, competencies, performance contexts, and consequences embodied in their definition" (1994, p. 198). It is important to note that competencies are included within this definition of outcomes.

CBE has often been characterized as having a narrow focus on strategies and methods seen as only appropriate for vocational-technical education. Despite some initiatives in the 1970s at the post-secondary level, CBE was not regarded as useful or appropriate for college programs with a liberal arts focus on goals including the development of critical thinking and making meaning. However, CBE purposes were actually broader than vocational technical education as described by Spady (1978):

> competencies ultimately require role performance, not just the acquisition of skills or knowledge of appropriate methods. They are, in other words, reflections of both what one is and what one can do. Competency-oriented programs should, therefore develop assessment tools that focus on the more qualitative aspects of performance as well as the more concrete demonstrations of cognitive and manual skill tapped by conventional measurement devices. (1978, p. 17)

There is renewed interest in CBE as an important way to conceptualize twenty-first century education reform. The shift in focus since the 1980s from academic inputs to outcomes assessment strategies for planning and measuring improvement in institutional quality is an important influence in this renewed interest in OBE and CBE. A major force behind moving from defining learning outcomes to even more specific competencies needed for professional performance has been continued criticism of graduates who do not demonstrate the required skills needed. Ewell discusses outcomes defined as competencies that describe "not only what is to be learned but also the specific levels of performance that students are expected to master" (as cited in Klein-Collins, 2012, p. 9). Ewell goes on to specify: "While learning outcomes typically include specific skills and knowledge, competencies are at a higher categorical level...a competency requires students to process that learning in a way that enables them to apply it in a variety of situations" (op. cit., p. 9). Thus it seems that a primary argument in making the case for CBE is that competencies are more objectively measurable than learning objectives or outcomes because of the specificity and applicability of the CBE course and curriculum.

Alternatives for Documenting Learning

Another force for educational reform happening simultaneously is the search for more effective ways to document learning beyond the traditional time-based formula of the academic credit hour. The New America Foundation report, "*Cracking the Credit Hour*" (2012), is another example of philanthropic support for educational reform funded by the Bill & Melinda Gates Foundation and the Lumina Foundation. This report reviews the history of the credit hour from a unit of measure of faculty workload developed to determine faculty eligibility for pensions to the standard Carnegie unit formula for number of minutes of classroom time per credit hour and the formula for high school and college graduation requirements. Although this focus on time spent in a class per credit hour formula was not what the Carnegie Foundation intended, and tried to shift away from in later publications, it became the accepted standard unit for secondary and post-secondary education administration as a convenient metric. Over time the credit hour was applied to student enrollment to determine full-time status, award financial aid, guide recording courses on transcripts, scheduling, and state and federal enrollment-based funding in addition to faculty workload (Laitinen, 2012).

The primary focus of *Cracking the Credit Hour* is to further the argument that seat time is not a useful measure for or guarantee of student learning. The emergence of online learning, hybrid delivery and post-secondary institutions using a variety of accelerated course formats are examples of other challenges to the validity and usefulness of the credit hour. The process of institutional self-regulation to determine the content and credit hour value of a course, reviewed by regional accrediting agencies, has been the standard for decades. However, the credit hour has been used as the metric determining federal, state, and institutional financial aid so it is enmeshed in many complex financial formulae. In 2009, the U.S. Department of Education's inspector general decided additional regulation was needed because accrediting agencies were not providing adequate oversight and approving programs with courses that awarded too many credit hours for the length of the course. One example cited was a for-profit institution that awarded nine hours of credit for a 10-week course. The U.S. Department of Education, in a set of regulations to combat financial aid fraud and abuse issued in 2010, did provide a definition that referred to learning outcomes but also included the traditional in-class and out-of-class formula as a measure. A 15-page letter of clarification issued in 2011 tried to clarify the definition and not discourage innovative practices. From the perspective of most institutions, the letter was of little help, so in the face of uncertainty the credit hour formula remains the standard measure (Laitinen, 2012).

There have been some recent adaptations of innovative strategies that build on the work of pioneering institutions using assessment methods developed in the 1970s at Charter Oak University, DePaul University's School for New Learning, Thomas Edison State College, Alverno College, Empire State College, and Regents College. These innovations focus on defining the learning outcomes for a course and documenting how those outcomes are achieved. Once the focus shifts to learning outcomes, or competencies as they are also described, there are more ways to document the individual's learning no matter where it was attained. This leads to the renewed focus on CBE and the variety of direct assessment strategies available to document competencies, such as PLA, simulations, performance, exams, portfolios, etc. (Klein-Collins, 2013).

Analysis of examples of CBE degree programs emerging in the last 20 years helps identify some common characteristics. Western Governors University (WGU) started as a collaboration of the member states of the Western Governors Association (WGA). The idea for a virtual CBE university to increase access to post-secondary education in the western states was formulated and discussed by WGA during 1996 and 1997. WGU began operations in September 1998. By July of 2012, celebrating the first 15 years, WGU reported 16,000 graduates and more than 33,000 students enrolled. There are about 1,100 full-time faculty and 200 part-time faculty (Western Governors University, Timeline, 2014).

The primary components of the WGU program provide an example of one model for institutions that have created CBE programs in recent years. The primary focus is on a personalized learning experience that allows the student to identify the competencies she wants to incorporate in an individualized degree plan within a broad framework of general education and discipline areas of study. The associate's, bachelor's and master's degree programs available through WGU are in the professional areas of education, business, information technology, and health professions.

Each student is assigned a faculty mentor as primary contact to provide guidance through the process of developing the degree plan relevant to career needs and goals, suggesting learning resources, and providing feedback on assessments of competencies. The student and mentor develop a personalized degree plan consistent with the student's academic background, career experience, readiness for independent learning, and the amount of time the student has to commit to studying. The mentor recommends learning resources (including textbooks, simulations, online learning communities, web-based tutorials from partner vendors, and online courses) and determines when the student is ready to complete required assessments. Students demonstrate mastery of specific competencies by completing assessments such as a traditional exam, a research or other authentic project, essay, or other practical demonstration of a required competency. Students with competencies (skills and knowledge) in a field of study from prior academic and work experience draw upon all these experiences while completing assessments to document learning. WGU focuses on developing competence, rather than using seat time as a metric, so the length of the degree program is determined by passing the required assessments (Western Governors University, Student Experience, 2014).

There are several other non-profit institutions offering CBE in course-based degrees or using direct assessment methods as a way to improve access, provide more flexibility and personalization, and reduce the cost of earning a 2-year or 4-year degree. The University of Maryland University College, Northern Arizona University, University of Wisconsin System, DePaul University School for New Learning, and the College for America at Southern New Hampshire University are examples of such institutions incorporating CBE. Capella University, one the largest for-profit institutions, is also offering a degree based on the CBE model (Klein-Collins, 2012).

State Postsecondary Education Initiatives

There has been a strong focus on improving American schools and colleges to meet the needs of the workplace by many individuals and organizations during the last 25 years. One of the first reports describing the skills and attitudes necessary for success in the twenty-first century was the Secretary's Commission on Achieving Necessary Skills (SCANS) report, "*What Work Requires of Schools*," from the U.S. Department of Labor. The SCANS report focused primarily on what high schools needed to improve to meet the need of employers for better prepared workers (U.S. Dept. of Labor, 1991). The National Governor's Association, U.S. Chamber of Commerce, and many other organizations have issued additional reports calling for secondary and post-secondary educational reform during the last 25 years. One common theme of these reports has been calls, such as President Obama's American Graduation Initiative, for more citizens to pursue postsecondary education or to complete credentials on a career pathway that leads to developing skills needed for employment in the turbulent, global economy of the twenty-first century as well as additional qualifications such as associate's and bachelor's degrees.

Another result of these calls for reform, especially for improved career ladder credentials and access to lifelong learning for adults, has been initiatives at the level of state post-secondary education governance bodies or university systems. Many states have shown a renewed interest in approaches to PLA and/or adult degree completion program initiatives. CAEL's 2012 report, *State Policy Approaches to Support Prior Learning Assessment,* provides a summary of legislative and state higher education governance policies that specifically encourage PLA and/or improved access for adults. In some states there was also focus on specific sectors like workforce development system linkages and the needs of military veterans. The 23 states CAEL identified where there has been significant activity in these areas are: Alabama, Alaska, Colorado, Florida, Hawaii, Idaho, Indiana, Kentucky, Louisiana, Maryland, Minnesota, North Dakota, Ohio, Oklahoma, Oregon, South Carolina, Tennessee, Texas, Virginia, Utah, Washington, Wisconsin and West Virginia (Sherman, Klein-Collins, & Palmer, 2012).

One example of a state legislative initiative is seen in the state of Washington. This legislation required the state post-secondary education boards that provide oversight for state-supported post-secondary education, community and technical colleges, private independent post-secondary education and private career schools, to work together on the following specific goals:

[I]ncrease the number of students who receive PLA credits; increase the number and type of PLA credits that count toward a major or earn a degree, certificate or credential, while ensuring quality; develop transparent PLA policies and practices in awarding academic credit for prior learning; create PLA tools to develop faculty and staff and share exemplary policies and practices; develop articulation agreements; and develop outcome measures to track progress on goals. (Sherman, Klein-Collins & Palmer, 2012, p. 9)

The response to this legislation by the oversight organizations was to form a taskforce of their representatives and include representatives from other stakeholders. Participants representing stakeholders were from the state department of labor, workforce development agencies, labor unions, military, legislative staff, college administrators, and faculty. One of the products of this taskforce has been a PLA policy and procedures manual for statewide use by all post-secondary institutions (Sherman, Klein-Collins, and Palmer, 2012).

Accrediting Agencies and Direct Assessment Competency-Based Programs

All the higher education regional accrediting agencies have approved PLA in some form at the institutions they review for decades. In the last few years, the accrediting agencies have encouraged post-secondary institutions to innovate with CBE programs using direct assessment strategies to document competencies. The Higher Learning Commission (HLC) created a Substantive Change Screening Form and Application for institutions interested in developing innovative degrees utilizing direct assessment strategies (Higher Learning Commission, 2014). The HLC has approved some institutions to initiate direct assessment competency-based programs in disciplines ranging from nursing to liberal arts. These programs were approved after conducting a pilot project to better understand the CBE program model and enable the HLC to develop a protocol for program reviews. After receiving HLC approval, the next step is for these institutions to participate in Title IV federal financial aid programs. This approval process has not been completed as of early 2014 (Higher Learning Commission, 2014).

The U.S. Department of Education defines a direct assessment program as an instructional program that, in lieu of credit hours or clock hours as a measure of student learning, utilizes assessment strategies such as an examination or paper, or recognizes the direct assessment of student learning by subject matter experts such as a PLA portfolio or assessing performance or other competency measure (Higher Learning Commission, 2014). Direct assessment of student learning means measuring what a student knows and can do to demonstrate competency in the theories and practices of the selected subject matter for a degree. Methods of assessment will vary depending on the learning outcome(s) to be measured and whether the goal is assessing student learning or program quality effectiveness. A sample list of methods or instruments for gathering evidence to show whether students have achieved the expected learning outcomes (or competencies) related to program or course goals may include: course-embedded assessment (homework assignment, essays, locally developed exams), grading with criteria or rubrics, internal/external juried review of performances and exhibitions, comprehensive exams, National Major Field Tests, GRE subject exams, certification or licensure exams, senior thesis, capstone or major project, portfolio evaluation, case studies, simulations, internship or clinical evaluation, and external examiners/peer review (Klein-Collins, 2013).

Open Educational Resources (OER), MOOCs and Badges

The proliferation of opportunities available for learners to gain and document new knowledge and skills through distance learning technologies has been recognized for two decades as a disruptive force in education (Bonk, 2009). These opportunities, examples of Bonk's world of open-anyone-anything-anytime learning, fall in the broad category of open educational resources (OER). According to Wiley (2007), the term OER was first used at a UNESCO meeting in spring 2002. The participants, including representatives from universities and six international and non-governmental organizations, declared "their wish to develop together a universal educational resource available for the whole of humanity, to be referred to henceforth as Open Educational Resources." (Wiley, 2007, p. 3). The participants in this UNESCO meeting provided a more detailed definition of OER:

> Open Educational Resources are defined as "technology-enabled, open provision of educational resources for consultation, use and adaptation by a community of users for non-commercial purposes." They are typically made freely available over the Web or the Internet. Their principal use is by teachers and educational institutions to support course development, but they can also be used directly by students. Open Educational Resources include learning objects such as lecture material, references and readings, simulations, experiments and demonstrations, as well as syllabi, curricula and teachers' guides. (UNESCO, 2002)

OER is a term many in post-secondary education first noticed when used to describe the free access to course materials made available by MIT's Open-CourseWare project, and other initiatives at Rice, Yale, and other institutions soon after UNESCO's definition. OER is one example of a global open initiative that is reacting to the dominance of information communication technology (ICT) by large international corporations and national government intrusions that dampen innovation. Some other examples of the open movement are the alternative Creative Commons copyright, Wikipedia, open source software applications (for word processing, spreadsheets, etc.), open source coding for course management systems, and open access to academic and research publishing. An Internet search using the term "open movement" provides links to many groups and organizations challenging public policy and commercial interests internationally with respect to freedom of creativity, innovation, expression, and privacy issues.

The Open Educational Resources Foundation (OERF) was created as a non-profit organization at Otago Polytechnic in New Zealand in April 2009. The OERF focuses on open education, described in the first three of 14 points in its policy statement, by providing leadership, securing funding for institutions and communities of learners to support innovative OER projects, and creating a collaborative International Centre for Open Education (Wikieducator, 2014). The OERF is also responsible for the Wikieducator, described as an evolving community for collaboration on projects to develop open content to be made available as OER on Wikieducator (Wikieducator, 2014). The Wikieducator is a source of useful information and resources, although it should be noted that some of the content has not been updated in more than five years. There are several other online sources for OER, and some examples include the Open Learning Network, Open-CourseWare Consortium, Connexions, OER Commons, OpenContent

Alliance (part of the Internet Archive), OpenLearn (The Open University), GLOBE (Global Learning Objects Brokered Exchange), Khan Academy, Apple's iTunes U, TED-Ed, and YouTube. These resources range from projects involving one university (OpenLearn) to projects involving many international collaborators. Funding for these initiatives has come from many universities, philanthropic organizations, and corporations.

The rapid rise of Massive Open Online Courses (MOOCs) is another type of open learning opportunity providing access to knowledge for individual learners, whether participation is for academic credit or personal and professional development. During the first few years of their existence, MOOCs have been primarily examples of the one-to-many distribution of information model. Often the sage is still on the stage. Learner interaction has often been left to individual initiatives or voluntary dialog groups. One can raise the question if MOOCs are really a new phenomenon—or simply using the increased bandwidth and development of ICT as a new delivery platform. There are many examples of programs that provided access to knowledge on a broad scale during the last 40 years, such as Sunrise Semester on broadcast TV, Carl Sagan's "COSMOS: A Space Time Odyssey" seen on PBS and distributed worldwide, and the broad range of Discovery and History channel programs. The development of YouTube and TED-Ed are also large-scale examples of open access for creating new or adapting existing content.

There have been many initiatives exploring ways to use MOOCs effectively. One has been to explore a MOOC for delivery of developmental writing and math courses. Another milestone in the development of MOOCs in 2013 was demonstrated by ACE when it provided credit recommendations for five MOOC-based courses delivered by Coursera, a corporation providing a technology platform for educational institutions and other organizational partners to offer free online courses. Here we see again that philanthropic support, in this case from the Bill & Melinda Gates Foundation, has been important in funding some initiatives to transform post-secondary education and open access to learning (Klein-Collins & Wertheim, 2013). It is too early to know where the MOOC phenomena will lead, but it clearly provides a very interesting opportunity for the individual learner to access knowledge, whether delivered by a university or a corporate learning program, that may be incorporated into a request for PLA.

Another example of a new approach to documenting learning accomplishments is the development of open, digital badges. The Mozilla Foundation is one of the leaders in developing these badges with the Open Badges Initiative (OBI) to demonstrate how digital badges allow learners to obtain recognition for and document skills learned anywhere (Mozilla Foundation and Peer2Peer University, 2012, August 27). The MacArthur Foundation is a funding partner and the Humanities, Arts, Science, and

Technology Alliance and Collaboratory (HASTAC) is also developing the use of this digital badge initiative. Open Badges are described as a twenty-first century credentialing approach connecting businesses and their talents needs with individuals with badges documenting those talents, so both thrive:

> More learning is rewarded and more employers get the precision, diversity and breadth in talent they seek. By 2016, we envision an Open Badge ecosystem that at least a million workers and a million students can access—the emergence of an assessment approach designed for our times. (Mozilla, MacArthur Foundation, and Humanities, Arts, Science, and Technology Alliance and Collaboratory, 2014)

Open Badges use digital technology to create badges that recognize and document learning accomplishments capturing skill descriptions and translate them with specific detail. Since badges are digital and information based, they allow learners to represent, verify and communicate interests, skills, and achievements for employment, education, or lifelong learning. They are based on an open standard developed by Mozilla that enables learners to combine multiple badges from different issuers to tell the individual's complete story of achievements (Alliance for Excellent Education and Mozilla, 2013).

This ecosystem of open badges is composed of organizations that issue badges (issuers), learners that earn badges (earners), and entities or audiences (consumers) that need to be able to verify or document the skills and achievements of the earners (Alliance for Excellent Education and Mozilla, 2013). This opportunity to develop the model for digital badges as a useful credential is open to a wide variety of groups to promote literacy in the areas of health, finance, citizen engagement, and digital communication in addition to reading, numeracy, and writing skills. A report from the American Institutes of Research (AIR) in 2013 focuses on using digital badges for adult learners. The authors suggest that badges have promise as a more effective way to certify the skills achieved by adult learners in basic education programs where learners gain functional skills; however, there are few types of formal recognitions such as a diploma or verifiable certificate. By the end of 2013, the Open Badges Initiative (OBI) had issued 235,100 badges by a total of 1,915 issuers. This growth is a 470% increase in badges issued and 425% increase in the number of issuers since the end of 2012 (Mozilla Open Badges Blog, 2013). In the near future, badges may be very useful in a variety of employment settings to verify a specific level of skill achievement (Finkelstein, Knight, & Manning, 2013).

Kahn Academy is another example of an organization using badges to reward learners for developing skills using the Academy's own content library. It has developed a set of six badge types to recognize effort invested by an individual and to motivate learners to continue to make progress. The badge types have a specific set of badges for learners to earn, ranging from as few as three badges to more than 40 related to that type for learners to pursue (Khan Academy, 2014).

Badges are another example of a seemingly new phenomenon. Or is a Badge simply another way to designate something similar to the CEU (continuing education unit) and certificates for completing a specific set of professional development requirements? Once again, it is difficult to project the impact of this new ecosystem for documenting an individual's lifelong learning. It will take persistence and commitment on the part of these organizations providing leadership in collaboration with many other partners to develop an effective model demonstrating how digital delivery and recording enhance career development opportunities and improve career pathways for adult learners.

What is the impact of these open initiatives on individual learners and PLA? The primary point is that learning and access to knowledge have increased exponentially with the growth of the Internet. Distance learning has been a disruptive force in post-secondary education, part of the turbulent environment besetting post-secondary education for the last 40 years. Learning opportunities for the individual, and her personalized learning agenda, have never been as plentiful and exciting. Bonk reminds us, however, that despite myriad formal and informal learning opportunities, we are still early in the development of technologically enhanced learning: "Technology innovations in the coming decades will bring unfathomable opportunities. For this reason, it is crucial to remind ourselves continually that human learning is the primary goal.... Without some lingering imprint on the human brain, what is the purpose?" (Bonk, 2009, p. 361).

PLA and Future Possibilities

PLA arose from a wave of innovation in the 1970s and still finds its place in the turbulence, calls for reform, and initiatives besetting post-secondary education early in the twenty-first century. There are diverse stakeholders promoting innovation that value PLA as a way to assist adults to complete degrees, thus helping reach increased degree completion goals. These degree completion initiatives may be within the context of degree formats in traditional institutions, in CBE degree formats using direct assessment, or the DQP framework proposed by the Lumina Foundation. PLA and its practitioners will have an important role in navigating through these degree formats and help learners interested in attaining affordable degrees or certifications that support their career pathways on their schedule.

There is a strong demand for educational reform from many different stakeholders to provide citizens with degrees or career credentials that develop documented competencies that meet the needs of employers. Postsecondary institutions are responding to these forces by experimenting with new models of degree programs not based on credits determined by clock hours and traditional or narrowly focused disciplines. These new CBE models using individualized (often multidisciplinary) degree plans and direct assessment strategies will provide alternatives for traditional age and returning adults to personalize their programs for career advancement or preparing for transitions and change as necessary for their chosen career pathway.

The development of OER, including MOOCs and Open Badges to deliver and document learning, are still in the early stages of development. The many ways for the individual to learn, and her choices from many types of content, represented by OER, provide exciting opportunities for learners in the twenty-first century. These increased opportunities will provide challenges for assessing learning as well. One thing is certain, the basket of "Here's what I've learned!" brought by an individual in the future to a PLA assessor at a post-secondary institution will have many more interesting types of artifacts to examine than ever before.

REFERENCES

ACE Credits to credentials. (2014). Washington, DC: Author. Retrieved from http://www.acenet.edu/news-room/Pages/Credits-to-Credentials.aspx

ACE Maps to credentials. (2014). Washington, D. C.: Author. Retrieved from http://www.acenet.edu/news-room/Pages/Maps-to-credentials.aspxACT.

ACT Breaking new ground: Building a national workforce skills credentialing system. (2011). Iowa City, IA. Author. Retrieved from http://www.act.org/research/policymakers/reports/breakingnewground.html)

Alliance for Excellent Education and Mozilla. (2013). Expanding education and workforce opportunities through digital badges. Washington, DC. Author. Retrieved from http://www.2mbetterfutures.org/wp-content/uploads/2013/11/Expanding-Workforce-and-Education-Opportunities-through-digital-badges.pdf.

Bonk, C. J. (2009). *The World is open: How web technology is revolutionizing education.* San Francisco, CA: Jossey-Bass Publishers.

Council for Adult and Experiential Learning. (2014). Learning counts: How it works. Chicago, IL: Author. Retrieved from http://www.learningcounts.org/how-it-works/

Cross, K. P. (1976). *An introduction to non-traditional education in the United States.* Paper prepared for the US-USSR Seminar on Higher Education, October, 1976. Retrieved from https://diva.sfsu.edu/bundles/210857/79907/download

Fenwick, T. J. (2003). *Learning through experience: Troubling orthodoxies and intersecting questions.* Malabar, FL. Krieger Publishing Company.

Fiddler, M, Marienau, C., & Whitaker, U. (Eds). (2006). *Assessing learning: Standards, principles, & procedures (2nd Ed.)*. Chicago, IL: Council for Adult and Experiential Learning

Finkelstein, J., Knight, E., & Manning, S. (2013). The potential and value of using digital badges for adult learners. Washington, DC: American Institutes for Research. Retrieved from lincs.ed.gov/publications/pdf/AIR_Digital_Badge_Report_508

Gold, S. B. (1973). *Diversity by design*. San Francisco, CA: Jossey-Bass Publishers.

Higher Learning Commission. (2014). Background information on direct assessment competency-based programs. Chicago, IL: Author. Retrieved from http://www.ncahlc.org/Information-for-Institutions/direct-assessment-competency-based-programs.html

Keaton, M., & Associates. (1976). *Experiential learning: Rationale, characteristics and assessment*. San Francisco, CA: Jossey-Bass Publishers.

Khan Academy. (2014). Badge types. Mountain View, CA: Author. Retrieved from https://www.khanacademy.org/badges

Klein-Collins, R. (2012). Competency-based degree programs in the U.S.: Postsecondary credentials for measurable student learning and performance. Chicago, IL: Council for Adult and Experiential Learning.

Klein-Collins, R. (2010). PLA Fueling the race to postsecondary education: A 48-institution study of prior learning assessment and adult student outcomes. Chicago, IL: Council for Adult and Experiential Learning. Retrieved from http://www.cael.org/pdfs/PLA_Fueling-the-Race

Klein-Collins, R. (2013). Sharpening our focus on learning: The rise of competency-based approaches to degree completion. Champaign, IL: National Institute for Learning Outcomes Assessment. Retrieved from http://learningoutcomesassessment.org/occasionalpapertwenty.html

Klein-Collins, R., & Wertheim, J. (2013). The growing importance of prior learning assessment in the degree completion toolkit. In R. G. White & F. R. DiSilvestro (Eds.), *New directions for adult and continuing education, No. 140, Winter 2013*, (pp. 51–60). San Francisco, CA: Jossey-Bass Publishers. doi: 10.1002/ACE.20073

Lindeman, E. C. (1926). *The meaning of adult education*. New York, NY: New Republic.

Lumina Foundation. (2013). Lumina Foundation Strategic Plan 2013–2016. Indianapolis, IN: Lumina Foundation. Retrieved from http://www.luminafoundation.org/goal_2025.html

Lumina Foundation. (2011). The degree qualifications profile: Defining degrees: A new direction for American higher education to be tested and developed in partnership with faculty, students, leaders and stakeholders. Indianapolis, IN: Lumina Foundation for Education, Inc. Retrieved from http://www.luminafoundation.org/publications/The_Degree_Qualifications_Profile.pdf

Laitinen, A. (2012). *Cracking the credit hour*. New York, NY: New America Foundation and Education Sector.

Maehl, W. L. (2004). Adult degrees and the learning society. *New Directions for Adult and Continuing Education, 2004*(103), 5–16.

Mozilla Foundation and Peer 2 Peer University. (2012, August 27). Open badges for lifelong learning: Exploring an open badge ecosystem to support skill development and lifelong learning for real results such as jobs advancement. Working document in collaboration with the MacArthur Foundation. Retrieved from https://wiki.mozilla.org/File:OpenBadges-Working-Paper_012312.pdf.

Mozilla Open Badges Blog. (2013). *2013: The year in review.* Mountain View, CA: Author. Retrieved from http://openbadges.tumblr.com/post/71643223520/2013-the-year-in-review

Mozilla, MacArthur Foundation, & Humanities, Arts, Science, and Technology Alliance and Collaboratory (2014). *Open badges: 2 million better futures.* Mountain View, CA: Author. Retrieved from http://www.2mbetterfutures.org/.

Obama, B. (2009, July 14). President's remarks in Warren, MI. Retrieved from http://www.whitehouse.gov/the_press_office/Excerpts-of-the-Presidents-remarks-in-Warren-Michigan-and-fact-sheet-on-the-American-Graduation-Initiative/

Sherman, A., Klein-Collins, R., & Palmer, I. (2012). State Policy Approaches to Support Prior Learning Assessment. College Productivity Resource Guide. Chicago, IL: Council for Adult and Experiential Learning and HCM Strategists. Retrieved from http://www.cael.org/pdfs/College-Productivity-Resource-Guide2012

Spady, W. G. (1994). *Outcomes-based education: Critical issues and answers.* Arlington, VA: American Association of School Administrators.

Spady, W. G. (1978). The concept and implications of competency-based education. *Educational Leadership, October 1978.*

UNESCO. (2002). UNESCO Promotes New Initiative for Free Educational Resources on the Internet. Retrieved from http://www.unesco.org/education/news_en/080702_free_edu_ress.shtml

U.S. Department of Labor. (1991). What Work Requires of Schools; A SCANS report for America 2000. Washington, DC: U.S. Government Printing Office.

Western Governors University. (2014). WGU Timeline. Salt Lake City, UT: Author. Retrieved from http://www.wgu.edu/about_WGU/timeline

Western Governors University. (2014). Student Experience. Salt Lake City, UT: Author. Retrieved from http://www.wgu.edu/student-experience/life

Wikieducator. (2014). Open education resource foundation: About. Otego Polytechnic University, Aukland, NZ: Author. Retrieved from http://wikieducator.org/OERF:About

Wiley, D. (2007). On the sustainability of open educational resource initiatives in higher education. Paris, FR: Organisation for Economic Development. Retrieved from http://www.oecd.org/edu/ceri/38645447.pdf

CHAPTER 23

WHAT'S IN YOUR CREDIT HOUR?

Quantifying Intended Learning Outcomes in Education

Frederick Carl Prasuhn
Western Governors University

Scott R. Frasard
Ebay, Inc.

An intricate element of United States education is the credit hour. The credit hour is a unit of measure that is associated with course completion, administrative decisions, financial aid, and other education components. The commonly practiced credit hour definition is learning associated with one instructional hour plus two additional student study hours. Over the last century this commonly accepted meaning became a foundational element of United States education. Further, application and use of credit hours were based on subjective decisions made by those developing curriculum. In 2010, however, the United States Department of Education placed

Building Sustainable Futures for Adult Learners, pages 491–506
Copyright © 2015 by Information Age Publishing
All rights of reproduction in any form reserved.

into federal rule that a credit hour is equivalent to the learning occurring in one instructional hour and two student study hours. In essence, the Department of Education formalized the practiced credit hour meaning without changing its definition and use within U.S education system. None of the credit hour information quantified how much learning actually occurs within one instructional hour plus two student study hours. Additionally, there were no guidelines on how to determine credit hour values. Thus, the federal rule only served to formalize a definition for a credit hour and continues practice as-is (U.S. Department of Education, 2013).

This study sought to answer the question found in the U.S. Department of Education's formalized credit hour definition: "How much learning occurs within one instructional hour plus two student study hours?" We began with a systematic review of Department of Education, regional accrediting agencies, and higher education regulations and documents. The research did not reveal any guidelines or defining characteristics of the learning associated with a credit hour. We found that credit hour values were assigned by curriculum developers, which include faculty and instructional designers. By exploring the curriculum developers' intended learning outcomes as indicated by the learning objectives, an important element of credit hour assignment may be found.

Literature Review

The lack of information discussing learning and credit hour use further supported the need for this study. Review of literature did provide foundational understanding of a credit hour and how the unit was used within United States education. We did not find objective guidelines for credit hour production.

Credit Hour History

The current United States educational structures were built from efforts that began in the late 1800s. Societal and governmental changes fostered the need to develop educational standards. Maeroff (1994) discussed how early twentieth century society required more education and began placing greater value on higher education. During the late 1800s and into the early 1900s, the formation of what became known as the K–12 system developed. The Carnegie Foundation developed a system in an effort to equalize college entrance standards. The instrument was the Carnegie Unit, or now known as the credit hour. Maeroff (1994) and Shaw (1993) discussed how The Carnegie Foundation for the Advancement of Teaching with the support of the National Education Association implemented 14 standard units for college entrance requirements. Each unit required a minimum of 130 instructional hours over the course of an academic year. Lewis (2000) and United States Network for Education Information (2008) explained how the credit hour value changed little in the 100+ years of use. One credit hour now equals 45 "learning" hours per semester, or 90 hours per academic year. The 45 hours per credit hour equates to the minimum of one hour of classroom instruction and two student preparation or study hours per week over the course of a term. We found in the literature that the "1+2 hours" is standard practice.

Credit Hour Production

It appeared in literature that credit hour values were determined at a local level by course developers such as faculty, instructional designers, and the like. Prasuhn (2011b) discussed that credit hour values were subjectively decided and varied from one institution to another. The regional accrediting commissions permitted institutions to determine how values were decided as long as the school could associate its decisions with traditionally practiced higher education standards (Middle States Commission on Higher Education, 2009; New England Association of Schools and Colleges Commission on Institutions of Higher Education, 2005; North Central Association of Colleges and Schools—The Higher Learning Commission, 2003; Northwest Commission on Colleges and Universities, 2003; Southern Association of Colleges and Schools Commission on Colleges, 2009; Western Association of Schools and Colleges Accrediting Commission for Senior Colleges and Universities, 2010). The Department of Education (Office of Postsecondary Education, 2001; Program Integrity Issues: Final Rule, 2010) relied on accrediting commissions and higher education systems to oversee curricular matters to ensure quality educational decisions and offerings. Thus, arbitrary processes from curriculum design to system level reviews assessed if credits, courses, and programs were academically appropriate and met expected higher education praxis. Educators used professional judgment during accreditation reviews assessing institutional course offerings. We did not find any concrete and quantifiable measures to associate learning with credit hour values other than learning objectives.

Credit Hour Values

Credit hour values essentially remained the same as when first introduced during the late 1800s (Integrated Postsecondary Education Data System, 2011; Maeroff, 1994; Shaw, 1993; Program integrity Issues: Final Rule, 2010; Watkins & Schlosser, 2000). A credit hour, in general, has been associated with one hour of classroom instruction plus two student study hours per credit, per week, per semester. Varied values existed in the amount of student study time and amount of course work. Researchers found that learning was associated with time spent learning: one instructional hour

TABLE 23.1   Credit Hour Learning Time by Regional Accreditation Commissions Time Expected per One Credit Hour

Organization	Instructional Hours/Week	Student Study Hours/Week	Total Learning Hours/Week
Original Carnegie Unit	5	0	5
Middle States Commission on Higher Education	1	2	3
Commission on Institutions of Higher Education	Combination to equate to 3 hrs		
Northwest Commission on Colleges and Universities	Combination to equate to 3 hrs		
Commission on Colleges	"Sound and acceptable practices for determining the amount and level of credit awarded for courses, regardless of format or mode of delivery." Principle 3.4.6, p. 26.		
Accrediting Commission for Senior Colleges and Universities	Combination to equate to 40–45 hrs/semester. (3 hrs/wk)		
Western Association of Senior Credit Hour Values	Combination to equate to 40–45 hrs/semester. (3 hrs/wk)		

Note: This table is adapted from Prasuhn, F. C. (2011a). *Virtual seat time: Translating asynchronous online education "class time" into credit hours.* (Ph.D. Dissertation), The University of Georgia, Athens, GA.

plus two student study hour. The exact amount of time varied based on type of learning, place of learning, intended learning outcomes, and operational definitions. However, all definitions closely aligned to 1 + 2 hours as the foundation of courses.

As shown in Table 23.1, application of the credit hour fluctuated. As a generalization, governing bodies associated the credit hour with the expectation that one instructional hour plus two student study hours per credit hour per week. Additionally, the number of expected learning time lessened from 5 hours per week to 3 hours per week. We consistently found the allotted 3 hours of learning time expected. However, we did not find any guidelines quantifying learning with credit hour values. Found throughout the data was that professional educator judgments projected learning associated with credit hours.

Adult Learning

Enrollments of adult nontraditionally aged learners are increasing in higher education. Educational institutions, according to Poley (2008), should consider seriously on how best to meet adult learners' educational needs. This sentiment is further discussed by Bishop and White (2007) and Jones, Voorhees, and Paulson (2002). Higher education institutions should begin offering courses and programs outside the confines of traditional education. Today's adult learners are in a global market that require learning on demand, flexibility, and recognition of skills already attained (Hrastinski, 2008; Poley, 2008; DiMartino & Castaneda, 2007). Howell, William, and Lindsay (2003) reported that nontraditional aged learner enrollments, 25 years of age and older, were increasing each year. Allen, Seaman, and Garrett (2007) also reported like results. Hussar and Bailey (2008) indicated that enrollments of adult learners aged 25 years of age and older were increasing at a greater rate than those under the age of 25 years old. More recently, Hussar and Bailey (2011) updated their report by indicating the trend would continue to the year 2020. Adult learners may now be considered educational consumers. They are looking for flexibility of scheduling, convenience, and coordination with career and life. Adults were also looking for recognition of work experience and skills toward courses (Amarsaikhan, Lkhagvasuren, Oyun, & Batchuluun, 2007; Fox, 2007; Lee & Nguyen, 2007; Reisetter, LaPointe, & Korcuska, 2007).

With the many technology advancements and societal changes, educational needs and instructional modalities are no longer limited to traditional classrooms and parameters (Web-Based Education Commission, 2000). Traditional classroom based learning and tracking learning with credit hours is no longer feasible due to the many changes in education (Maeroff, 2003; Maeroff, 1994). The education of today offers accelerated programs, varied class times, instruction outside of the classroom setting, and the like. How education is tracked is a system that is outdated and requires changing (Scott, 2009a, 2009b, 2009c; Shaw, 1993; Maeroff, 1994). Adams and Morgan (2007), DiMartino and Castaneda (2007), and Watkins and Schlosser (2002) argue that today's educational structures, standards, measures, and systems should be changed. More specifically, the credit hour system no longer is applicable in its present form. Life and work experiences and knowledge, competencies, and skills gained outside of the classroom should receive recognition in a fair and equitable manner.

The Department of Education recognized the need for change in credit hour production (Scott, 2009c). The Office Inspector General released memorandums to three of the regional accrediting agencies questioning credit hour practices. Accreditors agreed and urged the Department of Education to establish standards. Inconsistencies and lack of policies and procedures leave earned credit hours vulnerable for misuse (Lew, 2003). Articulation of credit hours between institutions was an example of how credit hour judgments often hurt students. Simply, not all credit hours are viewed nor evaluated the same across higher education (Patton, 1945; Miller, 2007). Buchen and LeCornu (2005) added to the argument by indicating that learners are the ones who ultimately suffer due to inconsistencies in the credit hour system. More recently, the Department of Education (2010) placed into federal regulation the credit hour definition. This policy was put into place to improve integrity within higher education and to standardize credit hour production. In doing so, "a credit hour is an amount of work represented in intended learning outcomes . . . [that approximates] one hour of classroom or direct faculty instruction and a minimum of two hours of out of class student work" (Program Integrity Issues, 2010). The policy, however, does not provide guidelines for establishing number or type of learning outcomes nor quantifying learning represented within the three learning hours. In essence, the Department of Education perpetuated credit hour meaning and praxis without any defining parameters.

METHODS

To address the issue of how much learning is associated with one instructional hour plus two student study hours, we needed to learn about curriculum designers' intended student learning outcomes. This descriptive study used data from a large two-year technical college located in the southeastern United States, which provides continuing education, technical, and undergraduate transfer credit courses. This institution was purposefully selected based on the following criteria: (1) familiarity of the institution by both researchers; (2) wide variety of programs and course subjects taught; and (3) publically available syllabi on the institution's web site. Permission to use the publicly available course syllabi was obtained by the school's Executive Vice President. Given the institution's characteristics, data obtained could realistically be generalized to other two-year technical colleges within that system.

Data Collection

We considered what institutional records would provide consistent data collection relative to courses, course work, and intended learning. All of these data are found in course syllabi. Common higher education praxis is to assign credit hour values based on course academic rigor, level, amount of work, and type of work required, which are found in the course syllabus. Thus, the syllabus represents curriculum designers' intended learning design and outcomes. The syllabus also provides various course details. All publicly available syllabi were included in this study, 575 in total. This set of syllabi were randomly divided into two sets for evaluation; one set per researcher. We scanned the documents to evaluate and clarify what information may be useful in determining intended learning outcomes. We generated a list of 24 potential variables by comparing syllabi structure and information against literature. The possible variables were reduced to a final list of 14 variables based on whether or not each was included on the syllabi (see Table 23.2). Not all syllabi provided the same structure or the same information consistently.

The 15 variables selected were those most commonly found on the syllabi. These data points include: (1) number of credit hours; (2) number of class hours; (3) number of lab hours; (4) course type; (5) course instructional format; (6) if attendance effected grade; (7) if class participation effected grade; (8) if extra credit was offered; (9) required resources listed; (10) required assignments listed; (11) required assessments listed; (12) grading categories listed; (13) number of cognitive domain objectives; (14) number of psychomotor domain objectives; and (15) number of affective domain objectives. We defined each variable to ensure similar data collection.

Using a random sampling of 30 of the available syllabi, we independently collected data. After this analysis trial, we discussed: (1) presence/absence of each variable in the syllabi; (2) challenges in identifying each variable in the syllabi; and (3) continued relevance of each variable for the present study. At this time, we determined that only 7 of the 15 variables were present on all syllabi. These variables included the basic course information: (1) *course ID*; (2) *number of credit hours*; (3) *number of class hours*; and (4) *number of lab hours*, which allowed for analysis within each group membership level. Additionally, three variables were always present but in varying amounts and without a definitive pattern or rationale for their individual presence or absence (*cognitive objectives, psychomotor objectives*, and *affective objectives*). Considering all data characteristics, the decision made focused our analysis on the seven consistently found variables. Finally, we conducted collaboration sessions to ensure we were coding the syllabi in a similar manner. Since we are both adult educators and instructional designers, we had no problem with coding learning objective types and found that we coded each type the same each time.

Given the institution's standard syllabus formatting, the presence or absence of each variable, and the potential of each variable to be a legitimate component of a credit hour, we decided to include only *number of credit hours, number of class hours, number of lab hours*, and the *number of cognitive objectives, number of psychomotor objectives*, and *number of affective objectives* in the final analyses. While all 15 variables were collected from all syllabi, only these six variables were considered as potentially useful in examining the learning associated with one credit hour. This decision coordinates with the information found in literature discussing how course developers created courses and made decisions about assigned number of credit hours, learning outcomes and objectives, and other course matters. Since the project was to study intended learning associated with a credit hour (see prior discussion about the Department of Education's *Program Integrity Issues:*

Final Ruling), the six variable closely examined were most directly related to credit hours and intended learning.

RESULTS

To determine instructional commonalities, descriptive statistics were calculated for each of the six variables. Given the exploratory nature of this study, descriptive statistics provided insights into whether learning objectives could feasibly be used as a credit hour component. Specifically, for each level of credit hour, the total number of objectives, means, and standard deviations were calculated for each of the three learning domains and overall. Additionally, correlation coefficients were calculated for credit hours, clock hours, and number of objectives to describe any relationships among these variables along with $r2$ values to indicate shared variance between the variables.

For the 575 syllabi evaluated for this study, there were a total of 20,657 learning objectives, with a mean of 12.1 (SD = 23.3) per syllabus, which provides some indication of intended learning amounts per course. Separated by learning domain, cognitive and psychomotor objectives were most and similarly prevalent with means (and standard deviations) of 18.7 (SD = 26.2) and 16.6 (SD = 27.5), respectively. While these learning objectives types were well represented in the syllabi, the affective learning domain was noticeably fewer or absent with a mean of 0.9 (SD = 2.7) per syllabus. Total credit hours per syllabus ranged from 1 to 12. Table 23.2 provides the total number of learning objectives, the overall mean and standard deviation, as well as the number, mean, and standard deviation for each learning objective domain by credit hour to illustrate differences. The variable *required resources*, was present 92% of the time, depending on actual need for the course while the variable *grading categories* was present only 29% of the time. The remaining five variables were present between 0% and 3% of the time (attendance, 1%; participation, 1%; extra credit, 0%; required assignments, 3%; and required assessments, 3%).

To explore how the three learning objective types related to the number of credit hours, class hours, and lab hours, correlation coefficients and r^2 statistics were calculated (see Table 23.3). The correlation analysis revealed that the total number of objectives were positively correlated with the total credit hours assigned for the course ($r = .211$, $r^2 = .045$, $p < .001$). Additionally, all three learning objective types were positively correlated with the total number of objectives: cognitive $r = .669$, $r^2 = .448$, $p < .001$, psychomotor $r = .702$, $r^2 = .493$, $p < .001$, and affective, $r = .110$, $r^2 = .012$, $p < .05$. These relationships suggest that learning objectives may indeed prove useful as explanatory variables when determining credit hours.

TABLE 23.2 Summary Descriptive Statistics by Credit Hour

Cr Hrs	Total			Cognitive			Psychomotor			Affective		
	n	M	SD	n	M	SD	n	M	SD	n	M	SD
1	379	4.4	6.1	74	4.6	2.6	291	10.0	6.2	14	0.5	1.2
2	3050	13.9	27.9	1674	22.9	28.6	1324	18.1	35.4	52	0.7	2.2
3	9028	11.1	22.3	5278	19.5	24.0	3534	13.0	27.0	216	0.8	2.2
4	3741	10.3	15.9	1674	13.8	17.9	1956	16.2	17.1	111	0.9	3.1
5	1260	13.5	19.1	1260	13.5	19.1	638	10.3	13.6	57	1.8	4.7
6	1881	20.2	29.6	1881	20.2	29.6	1023	16.5	28.7	41	1.3	2.6
7	3673	24.9	61.1	673	24.9	61.1	280	15.6	39.9	18	2.0	2.4
8	415	34.6	78.8	365	91.3	127.1	38	9.5	11.0	12	3.0	2.9
9	172	57.3	99.3	0	—	—	172	172.0	0.0	0	—	—
10	—	—	—	—	—	—	—	—	—	—	—	—
11	14	4.7	3.8	3	3.0	0.0	9	9.0	0.0	2	2.0	0.0
12	44	7.3	11.3	2	1.0	1.4	42	21.0	8.5	0	0.0	0.0
Total	**20657**	**12.1**	**23.3**	**12884**	**18.7**	**26.2**	**9310**	**16.6**	**27.5**	**523**	**0.9**	**2.7**

Note: There were no classes worth 10 credit hours.

TABLE 23.3 Correlations Among Credit Hours, Clock Hours, and Number of Objectives

	Credit Hr	Class Hrs	Lab Hrs	Cognitive	Psychomotor	Affective	Total Objs
Credit Hrs	1.000						
Class Hrs	0.161**	1.000					
Lab Hrs	0.654**	−0.448**	1.000				
Cognitive	0.083*	0.280**	−0.183**	1.000			
Psychomotor	0.195**	−0.174**	0.269**	−0.055	1.000		
Affective	0.107	0.013	0.073	0.054	−0.002	1.000	
Total Objs	0.211**	0.070	0.076	0.669**	0.702**	0.110*	1.000

* Significant at $p < 0.05$
** Significant at $p < 0.001$

While both cognitive and psychomotor objectives were positively correlated with credit hours ($r = .083$, $r^2 = .007$, $p < .05$ and $r = .195$, $r^2 = .038$, $p < .001$, respectively), affective objectives were not statistically related. These results suggest that more value is placed on knowledge and performance relative to how many credit hours a course is worth, while attitude has less, if any value. Further, cognitive objectives were positively related to the number of class hours ($r = .280$, $r^2 = .078$, $p < .001$) while psychomotor objectives were negatively related to the number of class hours ($r = -.174$, $r^2 = .030$, $p < .001$) while both cognitive and psychomotor objectives are positively correlated to the number of lab hours ($r = .183$, $r^2 = .033$, $p < .001$ and $r = .269$, $r^2 = .072$, $p < .001$, respectively). These results, combined with the correlation of lab hours to credit hours ($r = .654$, $r^2 = .427$, $p < .001$), suggest that achieving performance objectives has a higher value than achieving knowledge objectives relative to the total number of credit hours assigned to a course.

DISCUSSION

As presented previously, this study sought an answer to "How much learning occurs within one instructional hour plus two student study hours?" The question raised is in response to the Department of Education formal credit hour definition found in the *Program Integrity Issues: Final Rule* (2010). The Department defined the credit hour but did not provide guidance or parameters for institutions to consistently determine credit hour values to curricular intended learning. Therefore, this study examined quantifiable data related to credit hour values in a higher education institution. Systematic data collection and data analysis occurred. The following discussion is offered based on study findings.

The institution chosen for this study is representative of other two-year institutions within the region. Dynamics of this type of school place focus on preparing learners with practical workplace skills. While considered important, we did not use this characteristic within the analysis given the homogeneity of technical college missions; however, we speculate that institutional mission and purpose affect courses' design and course objectives. We found a relationship among the number of lab hours and psychomotor objectives, which supports this assumption. Additionally, emphasis on skills attainment was clear given the supported psychomotor objectives and lab hours. Since skill attainment is critical, psychomotor objectives naturally should be considered for all learning. Further research of other two-year institutions and of other higher education institutional types is needed to test this proposed correlation.

The concept and use of a master syllabus system is not a new idea within higher education. This system often is associated with courses with many related sections. Also, there may be multiple instructors teaching classes. In an effort to provide uniformity, the master course syllabus serves as the foundation of each course. Faculty are permitted to create supplemental course syllabi to provide additional course details and structure. This uniformity provides more consistent course alignment across the institution and with other colleges. We found, however, that the master syllabi examined did not provide as much detail as expected. Assignment information and how learners were assessed was not found. Overall, course details were not sufficient to determine anything beyond intended learning outcomes.

As the number of learning objectives increased, so did the assigned credit hours. (See Figures 23.1–23.4.) We discovered great changes, however, in the ratio of objectives to credit hours beginning with 7 credit hours courses and ending with 11 credit hour courses, though why this occurred is unknown.

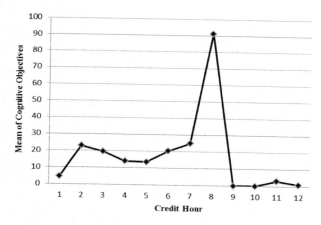

Figure 23.1   Mean cognitive objectives by credit hour.

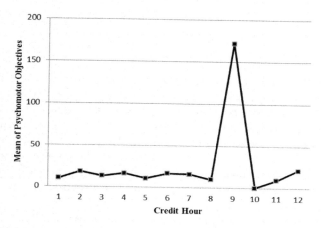

Figure 23.2   Mean psychomotor objectives by credit hour.

Figure 23.3 Mean affective objectives by credit hour.

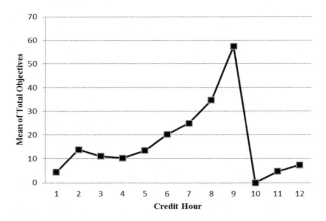

Figure 23.4 Mean total objectives by credit hour.

Perhaps the greatest findings were the information presented in the course learning objectives. There was a lack of consistent objective format between courses. Many objectives were written so vaguely that the reader had to interpret their meaning. Others objectives were written using terminology that could not be easily assessed to determine if learners achieved the objective. When assessing actual learning outcomes as compared to intended learning outcomes, vaguely written learning objectives create challenges for faculty, especially when objectives are written as compound or complex objectives.

We found through this study factors that may correlate credit hours and course objectives. Future research should include four-year institutions in addition to two-year schools as well as comparisons among public, for-profit, and not-for-profit higher education bodies. Student learning outcomes and degree level should also be included. Having a more holistic understanding may provide a more concrete and objective foundation to build course credit hour values, which could be consistently applied among higher education institutions.

Limitations

While this study collected data in a methodical approach, limitations existed. First, the institution chosen and the syllabi collected represent one specific college and do not apply generally to higher education. Second, the college chosen was a two-year institution focusing on career and workplace skill development. The focus of the school taints the dynamics of information collected resulting in high counts of psychomotor objectives. These factors did not represent the various types of higher education institutions within the United States. For example, we speculated that studying four-year institutions would produce results other than observed with this study. Baccalaureate schools are expected to produce more balanced results encompassing the learning domains, which is contrary to work skill focus by two-year institutions. Third, the "master syllabus" format used by the institution studied did not allow for full disclosure of course information. The premise of the master syllabus system was designed to more fully align courses between instructors while allowing each faculty member to adjust for class nuances and specific teacher expectations.

REFERENCES

Adams, J., & Morgan, G. (2007). "Second generation" e-learning: Characteristics and design principles for supporting management soft-skills development. *International Journal on E-Learning, 6*(2), 157–185.

Allen, I. E., Seaman, J., & Garrett, R. (2007). *Blending in: The extent and promise of blended education in the United States.* Retrieved from https://www.sloanconsortium.org/publications/survey/pdf/Blending_In.pdf

Amarsaikhan, D., Lkhagvasuren, T., Oyun, S., & Batchuluun, B. (2007). Online medical diagnosis and training in rural Mongolia. *Distance Education, 28*(2), 195–211.

Bishop, M. J., & White, S. A. (2007). The clipper project: Discovering what online courses offer residential universities. *EDUCASE Quarterly, 30*(1), 14–20.

Buchen, I. H., & Le Cornu, D. J. (2005). International academic equivalence: A primer *DETC Occasional Paper* (Vol. 22, pp. 1–30). Washington, DC: Distance Education Training Council.

DiMartino, J., & Castaneda, A. (2007). Assessing applied skills: The Carnegie Unit, awarding course credit for seat time, is working against efforts to teach and test 21st century workforce skills. *Educational Leadership, April*, 38–42.

Fox, B. (2007). Teaching through technology: Changing practices in two universities. *International Journal on E-Learning, 6*(2), 187–203.

Howell, S. L., Williams, P. B., & Lindsay, N. K. (2003). Thirty-two trends affecting distance education: An informed foundation for strategic planning. *Online Journal of Distance Learning Administration, 6*(3), 1–19. Retreived from http://www.westga.edu/~distance/ojdla/fall63/howell63.html

Hrastinski, S. (2008). Asynchronous and synchronous e-learning: A study of asynchronous and synchronous e-learning methods discovered that each supports different purposes. *EDUCASE Quarterly, 31*(4), 51–55.

Hussar, W. J., & Bailey, T. M. (2008). *Projection of educational statistics to 2017.* Washington, DC: National Center for Education Statistics.

Hussar, W. J., & Bailey, T. M. (2011). *Projections of education statistics to 2020.* (NCES 2011–026). Washington, DC: U.S. Government Printing Office. Retrieved from http://nces.ed.gov/pubs2011/2011026.pdf

Integrated Postsecondary Education Data System. (2011). Glossary: C section. Retrieved June 18, 2011, from http://nces.ed.gov/ipeds/glossary/?charindex = C

Jones, E. A., Voorhees, R. A., & Paulson, K. (2002). *Defining and assessing learning: Exploring competency-based initiatives* (United States Department of Education Ed.). Washington, DC: National Center for Education Statistics.

Lee, Y., & Nguyen, H. (2007). Get your degree from an educational ATM: An empirical study in online education. *International Journal on E-Learning, 6*(1), 31–40.

Lew, H. (2003). *Memorandum: Final audit report.* (ED-OIG/A09-COOI4). Washington, DC: Department of Education. Retrieved from www2.ed.gov/about/offices/list/oig/auditreports/a09c0014.pdf.

Lewis, L. (2000). *University of Phoenix's management of student financial assistance programs.* (ED-OIG/A09-70022). Sacramento, CA: U.S. Department of Education. Retrieved from http://www2.ed.gov/about/offices/list/oig/auditreports/a0970022.pdf

Maeroff, G. I. (1994). The assault on the carnegie unit. *NCA Quarterly, 68*(3), 408–411.

Maeroff, G. I. (2003). *A classroom of one: How online learning is changing our schools and colleges.* New York, NY: Palgrave Macmillan.

Middle States Commission on Higher Education. (2009). *Guidelines: Degree and credits.* Philadelphia, PA: Middle States Commission on Higher Education. Retrieved from http://www.msche.org/documents/Degree-and-Credit-Guidelines-062209-FINAL%5B1%5DDec09.pdf

Miller, H. N. (2007). Legislation can end bias against career colleges. *Chronicle of Higher Education, 53*(48), B8.

New England Association of Schools and Colleges Commission on Institutions of Higher Education. (2005). *Statement on credits and degrees.* Beford, MA: New England Association of Schools and Colleges Commission on Institutions of Higher Education. Retrieved from http://cihe.neasc.edu/downloads/POLICIES/Pp110_StatementonCreditsandDegrees.pdf

North Central Association of Colleges and Schools—The Higher Learning Commission. (2003). *Handbook of accreditation* (3rd ed.). Chicago, IL: North Central Association of Colleges and Schools—The Higher Learning Commission.

Northwest Commission on Colleges and Universities. (2003). *Accreditation handbook* (2003 ed.). Redmond, WA: Northwest Commission on Colleges and Universities.

Office of Postsecondary Education. (2001). *Student financial assistance and nontraditional educational programs (including the "12-hour rule"): A report to Congress.* Washington, DC: U.S. Department of Education. Retrieved from www2.ed.gov/policy/highered/guid/12hourrulereport.doc

Patton, L. T. (1945). The abuse of the credit-hour system. *The Journal of Higher Education, 16*(5), 258–260.

Poley, J. (2008). Asynchronous learning networks: Policy implications for minority serving institutions and for leaders addressing needs of minority learners. *Journal for Asynchronous Learning Networks, 12*(2), 73–82.

Prasuhn, F. C. (2011a). *Virtual seat time: Translating asynchronous online education "class time" into credit hours.* (Ph.D. Dissertation), The University of Georgia, Athens, GA.

Prasuhn, F. C. (2011b, March 26, 2011). *What is a credit hour?* Paper presented at the Adult Education and HROD Research Symposium, Athens, GA.

Reisetter, M., LaPointe, L., & Korcuska, J. (2007). The impact of altered realities: Implications of online delivery for learners' interactions, expectations, and learning skills. *International Journal on E-Learning, 6*(1), 55–80.

Scott, W. A. (2009a). *Alert memorandum.* (ED-OIG/L13J0006). Washington, DC: Department of Education. Retrieved from http://www.ed.gov/about/offices/list/oig/auditreports/AlertMemorandums/l13j0006.pdf

Scott, W. A. (2009b). *Review of the Middle States Commission on Higher Education's standards for program length.* (ED-OIG/I13J0005). Washington, DC: Depart of Education. Retrieved from www.ed.gov/about/offices/list/oig/aireports/i13j0005.pdf

Scott, W. A. (2009c). *U.S. Department of Education's inspector general credit hour 2009.* Washington, DC: Office of Inspector General. Retrieved from http://www2.ed.gov/about/offices/list/oig/aireports/i13j0004.pdf

Shaw, R. (1993). A backward glance: To a time before there was accreditation. *North Central Association Quarterly, 68*(2), 323–335.

Southern Association of Colleges and Schools Commission on Colleges. (2009). *Principles of accreditation: Foundations for quality enhancement* (S. A. o. C. a. S. C. o. Colleges Ed. 4th ed.). Decatur, GA: Southern Association of Colleges and Schools Commission on Colleges.

Program Integrity Issues: Final Rule, 75 Fed. Reg. 66,890 (2010), U.S. Department of Education, § 34 C.F.R. §600.2, §602.24, §603.24, and §668.8 pp. 66832–66975 (2010).

U.S. Department of Educaton. (2013). Program integrity questions and answers—credit hour. Retrieved from http://www2.ed.gov/policy/highered/reg/hearulemaking/2009/credit.html

U.S. Network for Education Information. (2008). *Structure of the U.S. education system: Credit systems.* Washington, DC: U.S. Department of Education. Retrieved from http://www2.ed.gov/about/offices/list/ous/international/usnei/us/credits.doc

Watkins, R., & Schlosser, C. (2000). The impact of technology on educational equivalency: capabilities based educational equivalency units. *Educational Technology, 40*(6), 49–54.

Watkins, R., & Schlosser, C. (2002). Moving past time as the criteria: The application of capabilities-based educational equivalency units in education. *Online Journal of Distance Learning Administration, 5*(3). Retreived from http://www.westga.edu/~distance/ojdla/fall53/watkins53.html

Web-Based Education Commission. (2000). *The power of the Internet for learning: Moving from promise to practice.* Washington, DC: U. S. Department of Education.

Western Association of Schools and Colleges Accrediting Commission for Senior Colleges and Universities. (2010). *Policies manual.* Alameda, CA: Western Association of Schools and Colleges Accrediting Commission for Senior Colleges and Universities. Retrieved from http://www.wascsenior.org/findit/files/forms/Policy_Manual_current.pdf

PART II

SUPPORTING ADULT LEARNING IN ORGANIZATIONS, INSTITUTIONS, AND COMMUNITIES:

Supporting Professional Development for Adult Educators

CHAPTER 24

A HYPOTHETICAL MODEL TO HELP FACULTY MEMBERS IN THE USE OF LEARNING CONTRACTS WITH THE STUDENTS

Monica Fedeli, Ettore Felisatti, and Mario Giampaolo
University of Padua

It is important to begin this chapter by describing the context of the Italian university system because this description may help the reader understand its internal heterogeneity and complexity. In 1999, the Ministry of Education, University, and Research (MIUR), with Ministerial Decree n. 509, established the criteria and objectives within which each single university has the ability to design their degree programs to match the specific needs of the territory. The programs are built using "crediti formativi universitari" (university credits that quantify the required hours of study to complete each course of the degree program according to the European credit system; one credit corresponds to 7 hours of lessons and 25 hours of independent study). "The introduction of 'crediti formativi universitari' is one of the first innovations,

Building Sustainable Futures for Adult Learners, pages 509–528
Copyright © 2015 by Information Age Publishing

which is evidence of the tendency to place the student and his/her learning ahead of the faculty member and methods of teaching" (Luzzato & Stella, 2010, p. 16). The Ministerial Decree also introduced the "classi di corsi di studio" (general guidelines to create degree programs) with the aim of giving degree programs a unique value at the national level. Each "classe di corso di studio" sets minimum objectives and training activities with which universities must comply to reach the same legal value. To design degree courses, faculty members will choose between basic, typical, related, or supplementary courses from different "settori scientifico disciplinari" (groups of subjects). Ministerial Decree n. 509, in concert with the "Processo di Bologna" (the political process through which European countries are trying to unify the higher education systems), transformed most degree programs of 4 or 5 years into two cycles. The first cycle is called the "Laurea" (bachelor degree program) and has a duration of three years; the second cycle is called the "Laurea Magistrale" (master's degree program), to be attended for a period of two years (Luzzato & Stella, 2010).

The "Comitato Nazionale di Valutazione del Sistema Universitario" (CNVSU) (National Committee for the Evaluation of the University System) report published in January 2011 describes the performance of the Italian university system in the academic year 2009–2010. There are 95 universities in total across the country; most of them state and very few private, and the committee estimated that in 2009, they collected 13.2 million Euros in tuition fees. The university system, in the academic year to which the report refers, had 5,493 degree programs, including bachelor's and master's degrees, and more than 159,000 courses. The system, the CNSVU, employed approximately 114,000 people, including professors and administrative staff, at the end of 2010 (Commissione Nazionale di Valutazione del Sistema Universitario [CNVSU], 2011).

In 2013, two important documents drafted a clear picture of the condition of the university system in Italy. The first was published by the Italian organization "Consiglio nazionale Universitario" (CUN) (the National University Council is the same organization, namely the "Commissione Nazionale di Valutazione del Sistema Universitario" in the previous paragraph above, under a new name) and was titled: "Declaration of the National University Council on the Emergencies of the Higher Education System." The second important document was the annual publication of the Organization for the Economic Co-operation and Development (OECD) on the conditions of education all over the world. "The OECD Directorate for Education and Skills devotes a major effort to the development and analysis of the quantitative, internationally comparable indicators that it publishes annually in Education at a Glance" (Organization for the Economic Co-operation and Development [OECD], 2013, p. 1). It is necessary to highlight the data that clarify some important problems that have inspired the work that is described in this chapter. The first data to take into account were reported by the "Consiglio Universitario Nazionale" and are related to the decrease in the number of bachelor's and master's degree programs since the 2007–2008 academic year. This decrease and the consequent growth in the number of attending students create a situation in which it is not possible "to develop a didactic centered on the student's learning" (CUN, 2013, p. 12). The second important type of data was reported in the OECD Education at a Glance and is about the relationship between the number of faculty members and the number of students. In Italy, there are an average of 19 students per faculty member compared to an average of 15.6 for the OECD countries and an average for European countries of 15.9 (OECD, 2013, p. 375). These data are evidence of a situation in which the high number of students per course does not allow faculty members to provide student-centered learning, limiting the opportunity for participation in individual activities and laboratories, with a consequent loss of the skills needed by the learner.

The introduction of learning contracts (LC) in our university system can be a way to contrast the lack of a student-centered didactic because this instrument helps students become more self-directed and permits their involvement in activities with peers and experts that will improve their knowledge, understanding, skills, attitudes, values, and interest in relation to a subject. The aim of this chapter is to describe to faculty members the themes and findings we discovered after having used the learning contract in two different academic courses. We hypothesized a model for the use of LC in the Italian university academic classes, giving faculty members the opportunity to begin their practice with the LC. The research questions that led our work and helped us to explore how LCs can fit into the Italian university context are:

1. How is it possible to introduce LCs into the Italian university system?
2. Which aspects can be observed in the implementation of LCs in an online platform?

LITERATURE REVIEW

The theories of self-directed learning and andragogy and their differing approaches and perspectives compose our literature framework. Specifically, the linear model of self-directed learning (Knowles, 1975; Tough, 1979) adopted by the authors in their practice helps "learners move through a series of steps to reach their learning goals in a self-directed manner" (Merriam & Caffarella, 1999, p. 293). Knowles (1975) describes the linear model by offering different steps in which learning occurs:

1. Climate setting
2. Diagnosing learning needs
3. Formulating learning goals
4. Identifying human and material resources
5. Choosing and implementing learning strategies
6. Evaluating outcomes

Moreover, Salmons's (2000) theory of teaching and learning online offers an interesting model for supporting students through online discussion forums.

One of the resources Knowles (1986) provides to learners to complete steps autonomously and independently is LCs. The LC approach to education is consistent with a theoretical model of learning and education developed during the 1960s and 1970s: "It was labeled andragogy, the art and science of helping adults to learn" (Knowles, 1986, p. 41). The assumptions of this theoretical model are:

1. The need to know why to learn something
2. The need to be self-directed
3. The need to take experience into account
4. The need to wait for the learners' readiness to learn
5. The need to organize learning of tasks and real-life problems
6. The need to be driven by an intrinsic motivation

Knowles (1986) argues that the LC "is an alternative way to structure the learning experience: It replaces the content plan with a process plan" (p. 39), which includes how the content will be acquired by students. The theoretical and philosophical foundations of LCs are to be found in the theory and practice of independent study, which originates from John Dewey's philosophy. The basic premise that characterizes the theory and practice of independent study is that the major goal of education is to transform dependent learners into independent students. During the 1960s, studies and research on self-directed learning enriched the theoretical foundations of LCs. These studies emphasized the concept of life-long learning and identified the main objective of education as the development of self-directed learning skills (Knowles, 1986). "The LCs are agreements negotiated between students and staff regarding the type and the amount of study to be undertaken and the type and amount of assessment or credit resulting from this study" (Stephenson & Laycock, 1993, p. 17). An LC is a formal written agreement that details what is to be learned, the resources and strategies to assist students, the products they can use to give evidence of the learning and the completion date (Anderson, Boud, & Sampson, 1994). "LCs are formal agreements written by students" (Berger, Caffarella & O'Donnel, 2004, p. 290), and in writing this contract, they have to describe the topics they will learn, the resources they will use, and the results or evidence of the learning process they will produce. An important component of the LC is a new type of relationship that is created between the student and the faculty member. The student is not a passive container of knowledge but becomes an active creator of his or her own learning process. Conversely, the teaching tradition in Italian universities is characterized by passive learning, and students are not encouraged to have a direct experience of learning. This tradition and the needs of the institution forced faculty members to bear the responsibility of deciding what is important to study, how, where, and when to study, and how to evaluate the student. The use of the LC during the students' learning process allows them to become responsible and to negotiate the learning path with the instructor. The role of the faculty member becomes that of an expert and a resource that facilitates learning. Their role "shifts from that of a didactic transmitter of content and controller of learners to that of a facilitator of self-directed learning and content resources" (Knowles, 1986, p. 43). The relationships between student and faculty member and between student and institution are not the only ones affected by the practice of the LCs. "This instrument provides the means by which the student, the institution, and employers can negotiate, approve, and assess the outcomes of study whilst both institution and employer act as a resource for learning" (Stephenson & Laycock, 1993, p. 24). In this way, universities can help students enter the labor market by developing the real skills needed. Berger et al. (2004) describe the responsibilities and tasks of a faculty member who, thanks to the LC, facilitates learning with students. These are (a) helping students to develop their contracts; (b) suggesting resources to study; (c) meeting students when they need help; (d) evaluating the evidence of students; (e) giving feedback on the students' learning; and (f) creating a supportive environment.

Online discussion forums, through which students receive support during the LC activities we will describe, have influenced this work. Discussion forums are implemented in the institutional online environment provided by the university in which this work takes place to offer blended courses to students. "Online discussions are an important component of both blended and online courses" (Armstrong, 2010, p. 217). Discussions in an online environment can be synchronous when students have conversations in real time or asynchronous when students post at different times. It is important to understand the characteristics of asynchronous online discussions because they are the equivalent of face-to-face discussions in the traditional classroom (Andresen, 2009). One of the most popular conceptual frameworks in the process of developing interaction among participants in online discussion is Salmon's Model of Teaching and Learning Online (2000). In the first step of the model, called access and motivation, and in the second, named online socialization, participants become familiar with the technology and start to make connections with other participants; they start to develop technical skills and to send and receive messages. In the third stage, called information exchange, participants develop skills in searching for information and in personalizing the environment while continuing the exchange of information process. In the fourth and fifth stages of the model, respectively called knowledge construction and development, participants construct personal knowledge and understanding and are ready to develop new content (Salmon, 2000). Armstrong (2010) explains the challenges students and instructors have when working with online discussions. The lack of verbal cues in the communication process, especially if participants have never met each other, is the major challenge in online communication. Eye contact, intonation, tone, and use of humor, for example, are verbal cues that are highly important in face-to-face communication and are missing in an online forum discussion. Furthermore, the lack of visual cues makes it more difficult to understand student participation and presence in online discussions. Another problem is the difficulty associated with hardware in general, such as crashes and unexpected server problems, and the skills needed regarding navigation. Last but not least, in online discussion spaces and online environments in general, students and instructors can experience a feeling of lack of privacy because in discussion environments, every thought shared is recorded and archived. Andresen (2009) identifies the relationship between the instructor and the learner as a success factor of an online asynchronous discussion. The loss of visual cues forces the instructor to find new ways to express feelings and communicate ideas, necessitating the faculty member to become more cognitively involved in the learning materials, pay more attention to details of the course, and be more precise and formal in setting assignment expectations. In order to stimulate good discussion, the faculty members have to consider the personality of the learners, the time they need to prepare their participation in the discussion, and the time they need to develop online relationships. Another important issue is the level of intervention that depends on what the faculty member wishes to accomplish with her/his learners (Mazzolini & Maddison, 2003, as cited in Andresen, 2009). There are many positions in literature considering whether an instructor has to be present in an online discussion or not, but it is always better to support learner-learner interactions that really engage participants and allow the sharing of ideas that truly improve the learning process.

METHOD

As previously stated, the explorative questions which oriented our work in adapting the Knowles's LC model for the Italian university context and in evaluating this instrument are (a) how is it possible to introduce LCs in the Italian university system? and (b) which aspects of LCs experience can be supported through an online platform? We considered relevant the premise that we conducted the evaluation of our practice with two different groups of students using the multi method approach: quali-quantitative (Trinchero, 2002). In the non-normed surveys used to collect students' perceptions on the LC practice, we used open questions to give students the opportunity to express their personal opinions on their learning process. We also used closed questions to confirm some aspects of particular interest for the faculty members such as reflection and planning of learning. Another source we used to collect data, with the aim of understanding the interests and involvement of the students in the proposed activities, was the content analysis of students' posts in the online discussion forums. In the following paragraphs, we will focus on participants, procedures, data collection, and analysis of the method we used with our students.

Participants

We proposed LCs, for the first time, to a group of students in the 2011–2012 academic year. The second group was involved in the last academic year, 2012–2013. The number of students who decided to use the LC in the first group was 37, with an average age of 35. Of the participants, 57% were practicing schoolteachers, while the remaining 43% were working in educational social services. These students were enrolled in the "Risorse Umane, Valutazione e Gestione dei Servizi Educativi" (Human Resources, Evaluation, and Educational Services Management) course, which is part of a blended master's degree program in "Programmazione e Gestione dei Servizi Educativi, Scolastici e Formativi" (Design and Management of Educational Services).

The second group involved in the learning contract experience was comprised of 17 students, with an average age of 36.5 and of which 18% were schoolteachers, 18% were teachers of adults, 27% were social workers, and the remaining 37% were working in a variety of different settings. These students were attending the second year of a blended master's degree program in "Educazione Continua" (Continuing Education) and were enrolled in the course of "Comportamento Organizzativo" (Organizational Behavior).

Procedure

The procedure of our practice consisted of three main phases. In the first phase, the LCs were presented to the students; the faculty member used one hour during the lesson to explain why it is important to use LCs and how to create their own contracts following Knowles's (1986) guidelines. In this presentation, the faculty explains and provides visual and textual resources to allow students to understand the LC's aims, the theoretical framework, and how to use the instrument. Faculty members prepared a video to help students who were absent during the face-to-face presentation and saved all the resources provided during the lesson on the online environment. The video was not shown to the second group.

In the creation phase, the students began by articulating their learning objectives. For each objective, students indicated resources (material and human) and strategies (techniques and tools) that would allow them to achieve their identified objectives. In addition, students indicated the evidence they would produce to validate a successful achievement. In this phase, students also assessed the time needed to achieve each objective. The faculty member supported students by answering questions using LCMS forum discussion. The LCMS provided additional support, allowing group work and private messages. At the end of this phase, each student showed evidence of their learning process and product and presented it in front of their colleagues. In this phase, an assessment process also took place. A self-assessment, a peer evaluation, and an evaluation from the instructor were adopted. The results of the evaluation were indicated on a 30-point scale, where 18 was the minimum grade to pass the evaluation. Items reported in the evaluation template included the following areas: (a) Level of preparation (knowledge of the topics); (b) Conceptual clarity; (c) Use of an appropriate lexicon; (d) Richness of theoretical references; (e) Critical thinking; (f) Commitment; (g) Group participation and contribution; (h) Working method; and (j) Product realized (output).

The final stage of our practice involved the narration of the learning experience. This is the part of the procedure that allows the realization of a qualitative and quantitative analysis to understand student perception and how it is possible to improve the LC practice. The analysis of the learning experience through the student's narration allowed the faculty member to reflect on the evolution of a personal practice and the adaptation of the LC to a person's own specific teaching situation. In this case, we used a questionnaire with open and closed questions.

Data Collection and Analysis

Data collection included the survey, which was proposed to students in the last phase of our procedure. In the survey, we used open-ended questions in order to collect the opinions of the students more quickly and closed questions to obtain the confirmation of the characteristics of the LC that were of particular interest for faculty members, such as reflection in learning. For the second group of participants, data collection also included a qualitative analysis of the discussion forum because, during our second year of practice, we used forum discussions more than during the first year. This method of collecting data is aligned with our two research questions. For the first question, the use of open-ended questions to collect data seemed to be the best way to explore the possibility of adapting the LC in our context and took into account student perceptions. The qualitative analysis of the forum discussion helped faculty members to better understand which characteristics of LC are supported through this technology.

In the survey, the two open-ended questions asked students to (a) indicate their opinions with respect to the presentation phase of the LC; and (b) indicate their opinions with respect to the creation phase of a LC. Using a categorization process (Creswell, 2008), faculty and a collaborator read the data, marked it, and divided it into two categories: positive and negative judgments. Later, answers were more specifically categorized using constant-comparative methods (Glaser & Straus, 1967). For example, the student's answer "Completing the Learning Contract, I became more practical in the technique and I understood the value of monitoring my learning" has been categorized by the two coders as "capacity of the LC to enable strategies of self-monitoring." In the third open-ended question, one student answered "...an unnecessary repetition...a big waste of time...and all that time I could study!" This answer has been categorized as a negative judgment and more precisely as "LC evokes negative feelings." The closed-ended questions asked about some characteristics of the instrument that were important for the faculty (questions related to the LC's ability to identify learning objectives, to develop reflection, and a sense of control on learning). To answer the closed-ended questions, students used a four-point ordinal scale where 1 = *never* and 4 = *always*. We used a scale with 4 levels to divide *undecided* into favorable and contrary responses (Lalla, 2001).

The qualitative analysis of the discussions in the forum was performed using Dedoose, a user-friendly Web-based software developed for qualitative and mixed-method analysis. The coders in this case started with a definition of the principles by which the analysis of the discussion forum would have been realized. They identified the unit of analysis in a syntactic unit such as the single sentence (Fahy et al., 2000; Hillman, 1999) with the ability to use multiple codes for the single unit. The two coders independently conducted a general reading of the text and agreed on the codes that would be used for the coding phase. Eleven codes emerged from the first reading of the texts; they were: (a) reflection on the learning process; (b) reflection on the effectiveness of the instrument; (c) negative feelings on the learning process; (d) awareness of the learning process; (e) awareness of the effectiveness of the LC; (f) difficulty in using the LC; (g) transfer of the LC in other contexts; (h) research for other resources; (i) production of artifacts, (j) collaboration with the faculty member, (k) and collaboration with pairs.

The encoding phase took place in two successive stages. In the first, a coder or "trainer" identified the sentences that were considered important and coded using one or more codes up to a maximum of four. Then, the second encoder or "trainee" performed the coding analysis independently on the sentences identified by the trainer. The software completed a reliability analysis between the codes assigned by the two coders. The value of the Pooled Cohen's Kappa coefficient, which shows the overall result for the reliability of tests that include more than one code (de Vries, Elliott, Kanouse, & Teleki, 2008), was 0.48, which does not reflect good agreement between the coders. The syntactic units were examined again and the differences in the understanding of the codes initially established by the coders were clarified (Haney, Russell, Gulek, & Fierro, 1998). The second reliability test that was run produced a good Cohen Pool Kappa coefficient of 0.68 (Fleiss, 1971; Landis & Koch, 1977).

FINDINGS

In this section, we report the findings we have seen when using LCs in an institutional context similar to that in an Italian academic class. Some of the findings are in line with the limitations and benefits that the literature acknowledges in learning processes conducted using LCs (Knowles, 1986). Others allow one to think of LCs as an instrument that can be used in personalized learning plans (Waldeck, 2006) for their characteristics of flexibility, reflexivity, and of allowing participation and the sharing of knowledge. We will present the main important themes we discovered after two years of practice using LCs that helped us in the design of a model of practice, analyzed later in the discussion paragraph.

Findings in the Analysis of Survey

From the open-ended question, "What are your impressions about the presentation phase of the Learning Contract? Please indicate strengths and weaknesses," the researchers highlighted interesting negative opinions by the students of the first group. These opinions included "misunderstanding of the task" (more explanation requested or the tool's unclear purpose). The second group of students expressed opinions in response to the same question, referring to the initial difficulties in understanding how and why to use LC. Some significant responses were: "At the beginning, I was floored because what to do was not clear. I focused more on the difficulties to be overcome, deadlines to be met, etc., rather than on the meaning of the LC." The perception of lack of clarity is the first problem a faculty member must take into account; his duty is to explain clearly what the real value of an LC is. Again, "The first impression was not very positive.... I did not understand the effectiveness and it seemed to me a constraint with respect to the learning method of each person." To evoke negative feelings and constraints is contrary to the objectives that a learning experience through LCs aims to reach. Generally, it is possible to find in the sentences expressed by the students of the two different groups, words that denote characteristics of difficulty, misunderstanding, and uselessness of the instrument.

For the open-ended question, "What are your impressions about the process of creating a Learning Contract? Please indicate strengths and weaknesses," positive opinions for the students of the first group included the ability to activate "reflexive" and "organizational" strategies, the opportunity "for clarifications of what has been learned" and "to become aware of what has been learned," the possibility of "control of what has been learned," and "focusing on what has been learned." Negative judgments included LCs "evoke negative feelings," "produce over commitment," "are too complex," and "an unnecessary practice." For the second group of students, most of the opinions focus on the difficulties encountered and on the feelings experienced by the students. Moreover, eleven out of the eighteen answers speak explicitly of reflection and collaboration with peers and with the faculty as facilitator as key elements of their learning process. More significant responses include: "My impressions were positive, particularly in the negotiation phase, where [it] is possible to express thoughts and reflections. Through the advice of the teacher and colleagues the work can be refined or be subjected to significant changes, always in the perspective of improvement." "The discussions in the classroom and in-group have been the key to calibrate our goals. I reassessed the objective in the light of advice from colleagues and teachers." These examples give the idea of LCs as a flexible structure that allow students, with the help of reflection both alone and in a group, to change the objectives of learning, resources and evidence, tailoring these to the development of their own knowledge and skills.

In the survey we formulated three closed-ended questions to comprehend the characteristics of LCs that interested the faculty. These characteristics are the reflection on the learning process, the sense of control on the knowledge and skills acquired, and the ability to identify learning objectives (see Table 24.1).

Findings in the Analysis of Forum Discussions

From the analysis of the discussion forums conducted on the students of the second group, we defined three major themes. These three themes are: (a) using LCs to develop student-centered learning; (b) using LCs to

TABLE 24.1 Percentage of Students' Answers to the Closed Ended Questions

Closed-ended questions		Always	Often	Rarely	Never
Do you think that the Learning Contract is an appropriate tool to develop a better reflection on your learning processes within the subjects studied?	Group 1	31%	49%	17%	3%
	Group 2	76%	24%	0	0
Do you think that the Learning Contract is an appropriate tool to develop a sense of control over the topics studied?	Group 1	23%	51%	20%	6%
	Group 2	59%	41%	0	0
Do you believe that the LC is an appropriate tool to develop a process to identify your learning objectives?"	Group 1	17%	57%	23%	3%
	Group 2	53%	47%	0	0

develop students' reflections; and (c) using LCs to develop student participation. Through the forum discussion, we tried to understand how technology and forum discussion in particular can help a faculty member to fully develop the potentiality of LC.

Using LCs to Develop Student-Centered Learning

The first theme individuated through the textual analysis is the possibility that the LC has of transforming the learning into a more student-centered experience (see Figure 24.1). Students report their engagement to find other resources to develop and create their evidence. By doing so, students start motivated, autonomous, and self-directed research (Bray & McClaskey, 2013) that allows them to became participants in the learning process. In this active research, the strategies we employ to make use of the learning resources have a great importance. One student pointed out, "...I have also found other resources on internet like this one http://www.studiculturali...." Resources are books, academic articles, updated information on a website, multimedia resources, but also experts who facilitate the learning of techniques and tools (Knowles, 1986). Another student pointed out, "I found a John Rachal article on future prospects of Knowles's andragogical model...I have also the possibilities to find an Adult Education expert at the University of Trieste."

Students of the second group of participants are also starting to use LCs in other contexts, especially those who work as teachers. This transfer of knowledge allows us to understand not only how it is easy to adapt an LC from learning to working situations (Stephenson & Laycock, 1993) but also how

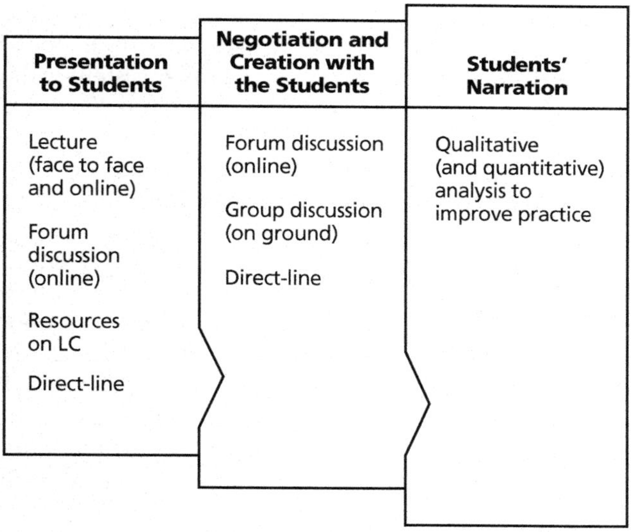

Presentation to Students	Negotiation and Creation with the Students	Students' Narration
Lecture (face to face and online)	Forum discussion (online)	Qualitative (and quantitative) analysis to improve practice
Forum discussion (online)	Group discussion (on ground)	
Resources on LC	Direct-line	
Direct-line		

Figure 24.1 The hypothetical model to help faculty members in the use of learning contract with the students.

LCs can be used to generate a process of learning that is adaptable to different aspects of our life. One student said, "Now, in my work, during the preparation of each didactic module, I ask myself which are my objectives, which resources I can use, which criteria to validate the evidence I will use?..." The LCs ease in this transfer and the possibilities to use it in other contexts means flexibility. The LC is a "flexible concept" and "is virtually impossible to organize it in a defined classification system" (Knowles, 1986, p. 38).

Using LCs to Develop Students' Reflections

The following statements show different aspects of the reflection on the students' learning process that emerged from the analyzed text. "I realized that this methodology helps me to focalize the starting point and the result that I want to achieve through a continuous learning process." "Creating my Learning Contract, I had the opportunity to review what I'm learning in practice and reflect on what I'm learning." Reflective learning is generated by the analysis of a personal or group experience, whether intentional or accidental, occurring in any of the contexts of everyday life. Reflective learning creates and clarifies some situations, changing the conceptual perspective of the person and the relative frame of reference. People learn from their experience, reflect on it in a process that provides a continuous transition between reflection and action, and reflect on the action itself with the aim of improving. The reflection takes place if what one is learning is challenging, meaningful, (Moon, 2004, p. 87) consistent with what is being experienced, and engaging for the person (Moon, 2004, p. 89).

Using LCs to Develop Student Participation

Comparisons with peers and with the faculty are key elements of students' learning processes. In the questionnaire that was provided at the end of the course, the majority of students' perceptions speak explicitly about the relationship with other students and the faculty (see Figure 24.2). Some of the more significant opinions in this regard include: "I lived in initial confusion and uncertainty solved with the help of the instructor and the sharing with others students"; "The creation phase has been challenging. I waited for my colleagues to share their Learning Contracts and for their feedback"; and "The discussions in the classroom and in groups were key elements to calibrate our goals." Moreover, there are many posts that report a good level of collaboration with the instructor. One student wrote, "The faculty clarified our doubts, specifying to focus our attention not only on the delivery date but on the active participation and on the learning process we are producing." From the text analysis, it is possible to determine that for students, it is important to share not only the final evidence they realized but also the evidence in progress to receive suggestions. A student shared, "I read the works of my colleagues, they do not have particular criticisms, and they are functional to the objectives...."; while another added, "I read the map you posted, a suggestion I can give to you is to verify the correct use of terminology." Comparison and collaboration with peers and instructors in all the stages of learning

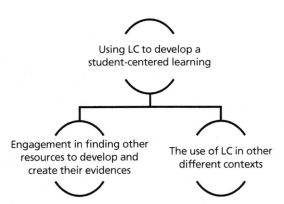

Figure 24.2 Subthemes of the theme "Using LC to develop a student-centered learning."

is a fundamental component for each kind of learning, especially in the LC practice, which enhances the importance of the students' experiences and the use of other learners as resources.

DISCUSSION

The aim of our work is to hypothesize a possible model to facilitate the use of LC in the Italian university setting, and specifically, our practice is realized within the context of a single course. The model is the result of the qualitative and quantitative analysis (Fedeli, Giampaolo, & Coryell, 2013) mentioned above and realized during two years of practice in using learning contracts with Italian students in the institutional university context. The real purpose of this model is to use students' opinions, expressed at the end of their learning experience, to tell other Italian faculty who want to propose LCs to their student which characteristics need to be taken into account for them to be used effectively (see Figure 24.3). The model hypothesizes three phases: the "presentation to the students" of the instrument; the "negotiation and creation with the students" of the learning contents; and the "students' narrations" of the experience, through which the learners express their opinions, feelings, and judgments on the instrument in relation to the learning process in general. These three phases cannot be distinguished, but overlap. In the first two phases, the cognitive component of understanding is important. Understanding what the sections of the LC mean is important, but above all, understanding that a LC goes beyond the superficial appearance of a table divided into columns to become criteria by which it is possible to conduct, actively and autonomously, one's own learning process. Between the phases of "negotiation and creation" and "narration," reflection is the metacognitive component. It is both

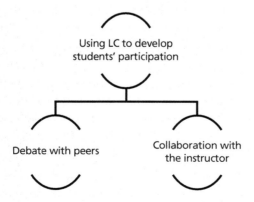

Figure 24.3 Subthemes of the theme "Using LC to develop students' participation."

intrapersonal and interpersonal. The production of the evidence involves an intrapersonal reflection on the dynamics of the group discussion and negotiation with the facilitator, which allows for an interpersonal reflection. The metacognitive component of reflection is of fundamental value for the success of the LC experience as reported in our findings.

During the presentation of the instrument, one or more lessons must be used to explain how to create the learning contract. Starting from some important topic in the subject or from a list of learning outcomes, the faculty explains how to describe a learning objective in terms of "statements of what will be learned" (Berger et al., 2004, p. 311) "in terms of content acquisition, behavior and the direction of growth" (Knowles, 1986, p. 29). It is important that those who use the contract are able to formulate their own learning objectives, but it is also very important to explain the concepts of resources and strategies to prevent misunderstandings between "what to learn and what to do to learn" (Knowles, 1986). In this first phase, it is important to clearly establish the criteria for the evaluation and self-evaluation of the evidence. By specifying criteria, students are able to produce consistent evidence. This process can be one of the most problematic steps in the design of LCs in the classroom. In an academic context, the students must perform a written or an oral test to demonstrate their acquired knowledge. This practice of evaluation is not consistent with the practice of assessment that characterizes andragogical learning experience (Rachal, 2002), self-directed learning, and the LC practice. It is also important to give appropriate weight to the explanation of why it is important to indicate the delivery date for the activities. This will allow more in-depth organization and awareness of time management. During the presentation phase, resources should be provided to the students to understand what an LC is, how to create it, and the purpose of this instrument. Finally, it could be important to provide students with a direct line such as Skype or a discussion forum dedicated to a specific topic; this way the faculty member will receive requests for clarification.

The second phase, called "negotiation and creation with the student," is central to the model. In this phase, as we analyze the surveys and the discussion forum, the process of reflection on the contents of the LC and on the activities relating to the production of evidence begins. After defining the learning objectives and resources formulated by the students, the faculty member gives initial feedback on these and suggests changes or integrations if necessary. The facilitator should also discuss various aspects for the fulfillment of the evidence with the students. In this phase, the model proposes the division of students into groups to discuss the issues and contents of the LC. Our model does not recommend specific criteria to divide students into groups, but it is possible to aggregate students on the basis of similar learning objectives. At the end of this phase, a subsequent negotiation with the faculty is necessary to define the LC. This does not mean that the learning contract cannot be changed. Our model proposes a limit to this negotiation. This limit is established with the single purpose of facilitating the development of independence and autonomy in the learners.

The use of a Learning Content Management System, as said in Fedeli et al. (2013), is an important part of the work. Our university adopted the Moodle platform system to manage online activities. Since 2012, we have been integrating the forum discussion into the LC experience conducted with the students. The discussion forum can be used by the students not only as an instrument to communicate in an asynchronous way with colleagues and faculty members, but also as a repository of information, resources, thoughts, emotions, and suggestions to solve different problems. It is important to organize the forum discussion to avoid confusion and disorientation due to the quantity of interventions and discussions that can frustrate the students. For this reason, it is important to divide the discussion forum into themes and sub-themes. It is possible to start with the creation of three sections for each of the different phases of the LC experience: Sections for the presentation phase, the creation and the negotiation phase, and finally for the narration phase. In each of the three sections, different discussions can take place. In the first section, spaces can be opened to discuss the meaning of the LC, the different components of the instrument, and another space to provide and discuss examples. In the negotiation and creation section, it is necessary to open a space to facilitate discussion about each component of the LC, including learning objectives, resources, evidence, and evaluation. In the third section, it is possible to open a general discussion about the feelings generated by the experience, about the way in which students have collaborated with others, and a specific discussion related to the problems identified.

CONCLUSION

These findings offer us the opportunity to reflect on our efforts to introduce LCs in an Italian university setting, help us to develop our proposed model of practice, and allow us to implement changes in our future courses of study. We are also interested in identifying the best online instrument to help faculty support students' efforts in adopting LCs. After two master's degree courses, which were conducted by negotiating students' learning plans through contracts in our university, we found by analyzing students' opinions and discussions on the online forum that four components are very important in the use of learning contracts with students.

First, during the initial introduction of the students to the learning contract, it is important that faculty members ensure the understanding of what the sections of the LC mean and their importance to the learning process, but above all, students need to understand that a LC goes beyond the superficial appearance of a table divided into columns. Second, during the learning process, the metacognitive component of reflection is of fundamental value for the success of the LC experience. Third, as stated in our most recent paper, Fedeli et al. (2013), one of our directions of growth in the use of LCs was that of analyzing group dynamics in class and online. With the second group of students, we organized different occasions to work in groups with their learning contracts in class during the course, and this was very much appreciated by the students as a supportive method to encourage their own learning. In these small groups of 3–4 people, the students were able to share their doubts and their fears and to be supportive of their colleagues. Fourth, we gave students the opportunity to know the evaluation criteria from the beginning. Criteria of evaluation are an important part of the learning contract and, in our opinion, guide the students by orienting them towards the production of evidence. For example, if a criterion in the evaluation model is to engage people with the evidence, students know that their evidence must in some way engage other students. The list of criteria is a means to evaluate students' evidence and products (as part of their final exam), learner self-directedness and the learning process in a more effective way.

A future direction is to introduce learning contracts from the beginning of the master's degree program and not restrict their use to only one course. Accordingly, we are also aware that in order to progress further, we need to train and sensitize colleagues and find integration strategies among the different teachings. In the 2011/2012 academic year, we started implementing contracts in one course; currently, in the academic year 2013/2014, we have proposed the use of learning contracts to students in five master's degree courses, engaging three faculty members in the realization of the learning process with contracts. In the future, we hope to sensitize even more Italian faculty members and students to the culture of self-directed learning. We understand the importance of doing so as reflective practitioners and researchers who are mindful of the complexities of bridging research and theory from other countries to instruction and evaluation in our own context in Italy.

REFERENCES

Anderson, G., Boud, D., & Sampson, J. (1994). Expectations of quality in the use of learning contracts. *Capability: The International Journal of Capability in Higher Education, 1*(1), 22–31.

Andresen, M. A. (2009). Asynchronous discussion forums: Success factors, outcomes, assessments, and limitations. *Educational Technology and Society, 12*(1), 249–257.

Armstrong, K. (2010). High wire act: The perils, pitfalls and possibilities of online discussions. *Word Academy of Science Engineering and Technology, 46,* 217–222. Retrieved from http://www.waset.org/journals/waset/v46.php

Berger, N. O., Caffarella, R. S., & O'Donnell J. M. (2004). Learning contracts. In M. W. Galbraith (Ed.), *Adult learning methods: A guide for effective instruction* (3rd ed., pp. 289–320). Malabar, FL: Krieger.

Bray, B., & McClaskey, K. (2013). A step-by-step guide to personalized learning. *Learning & Leading with Technology, 40*(7), 12–19.

Consiglio Universitario Nazionale. (2013). *Le emergenze del sistema.* [Report on the system emergencies] Retrieved from http://www.cun.it/media/118417/dichiarazione_cun_su_emergenze_sistema.pdf

Comitato Nazionale per la Valutazione del Sistema Universitario. (2011). *Undicesimo rapporto sullo stato del sistema universitario* [Eleventh report on the state of the university system]. Retrieved from http://www.cnvsu.it/_library/downloadfile.asp?id=11778

Creswell, J. W. (2008). *Educational research: Planning, conducting, and evaluating quantitative and qualitative research.* Columbus, OH: Pearson Merrill Prentice Hall.

de Vries, H., Elliott, M. N., Kanouse, D. E, & Teleki, S. (2008) Using pooled kappa to measure inter-rater agreement across many items. *Field Methods 20*(3), 272–282.

Fahy, P. J., Crawford, G., Ally, M., Cookson, P., Keller, V., & Prosser, F. (2000). The development and testing of a tool for analysis of computer mediated conferencing transcripts. *Alberta Journal of Educational Research, 46*(1), 85–88.

Fleiss, J. L. (1971) Measuring nominal scale agreement among many raters. *Psychologica Bulletin. 76*(5), 378–382.

Fedeli, M., Giampaolo, M., & Coryell, J. (2013). The use of learning contracts in the Italian University System. *Adult Learning, 24*(3), 104–111.

Glaser, B., & Strauss, A. (1967). *The discovery of grounded theory: Strategies for qualitative research.* Chicago, IL: Aldine

Haney, W., Russell, M., Gulek, C., & Fierros, E. (1998 January-February). Drawing on education: Using student drawings to promote middle school improvement. *Schools in the Middle, 7*(3), 38– 43.

Hillman, D. (1999). A new method for analyzing patterns of interaction. *The American Journal of Distance Education, 13*(2), 37–47.

Knowles, M. S. (1975). *Self-directed learning: A guide for learners and teachers.* New York, NY: Association Press.

Knowles, M. S. (1986). *Using learning contracts.* San Francisco, CA: Jossey-Bass Publishing.

Lalla, M. (2001). La scala di Likert per la valutazione della didattica [The Likert scale for the assessment in teaching]. *Rivista Italiana di Economia Demografia e Statistica, 1* (LV), 149–175.

Landis, J. R., & Koch G.G. (1977). The measurement of observer agreement for categorical data. *Biometrics. 33*(1), 159–74.

Luzzato, G., & Stella, A. (2010). L'intreccio tra riforma didattica e Processo di Bologna. In C. Finocchietti, D. Giacobazzi, & P. G. Palla (Eds.), *Lo spazio europeo dell'istruzione superiore* [The European space for higher education] (pp.13–28). Retrieved from http://www.cimea.it/files/fileusers/UQ25Luzzatto.pdf

Merriam, S. B., & Caffarella, R. S. (1999). Learning in Adulthood. A Comprehensive Guide. San Francisco: Jossey-Bass.

Moon, J. A. (2004). *A handbook of reflective and experiential learning: Theory and practice.* London, England: Routledge Falmer.

Organization for the Economic Co-operation and Development. (2013). *Education at a glance 2013: OECD indicators.* OECD Publishing. Retrieved from http://dx.doi.org/10.1787/eag-2013-en

Rachal, J. R. (2002). Andragogy's detectives: A critique of the present and a proposal for the future. *Adult Education Quarterly: A Journal of Research and Theory, 22*(3), 210–227.

Salmon, G. (2000). *E-moderating: The key to teaching and learning online.* London, England: Kogan Page.

Stephenson, J., & Laycock, M., (1993). Learning contract: Scope and rationale. In J. Stephenson (Ed.), *Using learning contracts in higher education* (pp. 17–28). London, England: Kogan Page.

Tough, A. (1979). *The adult's learning projects: A fresh approach to theory and practice in adult learning.* Toronto: Ontario Institute for Studies in Education.

Trinchero, R. (2002). Manuale di Ricerca Educativa [Handbook of Educational Research] Milano: Franco Angeli.

Waldeck, J. H. (2006). What does "Personalized Education" mean for faculty, and how should it serve our students? *Communication Education, 55*(3), 345–352.

CHAPTER 25

PERSONAL AND PROFESSIONAL EXPERIENCES TO DEVELOP LEARNING IN TEACHERS' PROFESSIONAL QUALIFICATION

Ettore Felisatti, Cristina Mazzucco, Monica Fedeli, and Mario Giampaolo
University of Padua

Teaching in a formal context develops interaction dynamics that link teachers with teachers. In a formal learning situation, teachers bring their own social, cultural, cognitive, and relational dimensions, which are often difficult to define in a precise manner, making the interaction complex and unique. The cognitive, personal, and professional objectives that teachers pursue require a central investment in the teacher. Teaching becomes effective only if it changes the learner. This result is only possible all with a qualified teacher who prepares the ideal context for the development of learning.

The process organization of the learning environment and the strategies for dialogue, support, and facilitation as they relate to the teacher's characteristics influence the quality of the teacher. In accordance with the European

Building Sustainable Futures for Adult Learners, pages 529–539

Commission, teachers must possess specific qualifications, must be lifelong learners, and must be aware that they are operating within a professional and social community (COM, 2007). The quality of teaching reflects the acquisition of a competence system that covers many aspects: (a) quality of performance (Margiotta, 1999); (b) professional practices (Paquay, Altet, Charlier, & Perrenoud, 2012; Perrenoud, 2002); and (c) the integration of knowledge and know-how (Danielson, 2007; Toch & Rothman, 2008).

The development of competences requires the acquisition of knowledge related to planning, management, didactics, methodology, and relationships and also requires personal reflection. Reflection in this context means "the process by which is possible to critically evaluate the content, the process, or the premises of our efforts to interpret and give meaning to an experience" (Mezirow, 2003, p. 106). Reflection intervenes in the construction of meanings related to the profession, bringing into play representations, value judgments, beliefs, and feelings (Montalbetti, 2005) that are rooted in actual experience but also in relation to the past, giving answers to the questions arising from our transformative act. For this reason, reflection requires a space in training both in reference to learning linked to action (Schön, 1993) and in relation to the experiences that develop our expectations and our prospects for significant change (Mezirow, 2003; Quaglino, 2004).

The Educational Reference Context

The course Didactics and Cooperative Learning in the online Master's Degree Program in Education Science, Childhood, and Preadolescence at University of Padua is the context of our research. The master's degree program lasts for 180 "Crediti Formativi Universitari" (CFU); these are a quantification of the hours of study required to complete a degree program according to the European Credit System. One credit consists of seven hours of lessons and 25 hours of independent study. The Master's Degree Program aims to enhance teacher's professional practice, realizing personalized learning paths and giving teachers the possibility to transform previous educational qualifications and professional activities into hours of study. The program finishes with a final exam in which teachers present a written dissertation about the skills acquired during their courses and their reflections on professional practice. The Master's Degree Program is completely developed online through an open source online platform, but with a final test conducted on site. The platform offers teachers access to educational resources and to a series of interactive and collaborative learning activities, realized individually and in groups and guided by teachers and tutors.

The course Didactics and Cooperative Learning (which has a value of 9 CFU) offers teachers the fundamental theories of teaching, operational models to interpret the teaching practice, and methods to facilitate cooperative learning in the classroom. The course promotes the development of theoretical knowledge, teaching skills, and interpersonal skills to qualify for the teacher profession. By the end of the course, the teachers have acquired skills in analyzing the educational system and the teaching profession, skills in planning educational activities, and skills in facilitating cooperative learning. The course ends with a final evaluation of the outcomes achieved by the teachers during the online activities and with a final written exam conducted on site.

Knowing the personal and professional experiences of our participants could help us to understand how to design better learning paths for developing teaching skills. In the attempt to achieve this research objective, we formulated a general research question: how can analyzing the teachers' reflections help us to improve the design of our training course to develop teaching skills? Specifically the questions that we use to guide the analysis of teachers' experiences are as follows: What types of teachers did we have in the course? What were these teachers' aspirations? How was their previous training? Why did they decide to become teachers? What were the most significant experiences they had in their work?

METHOD

An online course titled Teaching and Learning Cooperative in the online master degree program Education Science, Childhood, and Preadolescence is the context of our research. During the academic years 2010/2011, 2011/2012, and 2012/2013, we involved 251 teachers in activities through a discussion forum. We have collected their discussions, read them, and analyzed them to identify some significant indications regarding the research questions above with the aim of understanding the personal and professional experiences upon which the teachers' teaching practices are based. This analysis can be useful to outline the possible directions for the design and implementation of training projects for teaching professional development.

Participants

The 251 teachers involved in the research were mostly females (F = 236; M = 15). The average age of the entire group was 42 years old, with a modal value between 40 and 49 years old. More than 90% of the teachers (228 of 251) had a primary school teaching certificate, which was required in Italy until 2001 to teach in primary schools and kindergarten; 31% had a bachelor's degree, and 89% already worked as a teacher. Sixty-two percent were working in a primary school, 26% in a kindergarten, 3% in a high school, and the remaining 9% were at nursery schools.

Procedure

The topics proposed in the course were structured in three lesson plans: (a) lesson plan 1—cooperative methodologies for teaching and learning, in which we developed the issues of learning, using a social perspective, the models of cooperative learning and, in particular, the learning together method (Johnson & Johnson, 1994); (b) lesson plan 2—instructional planning, in which we analyzed the planning dimension in school, curriculum design, and models of instructional planning; (c) lesson plan 3—didactics and teacher professionalism, which deepened the teacher's didactic action and outlined a quality professional profile. Each lesson plan had the following structure: (a) three video-recorded lectures, with a presentation of contents; (b) a video introduction to motivate and lead the teachers to an initial reflection about the themes that would be developed online; (c) online activities developed in groups, with the support of an expert tutor; (d) a discussion forum to clarify, analyze and interpret the topics; and (e) an individual assessment with an online test.

This research is focused on the online experience conducted in lesson plan number 3, where we analyzed through a specific process the professional profile of a quality teacher. The educational lesson plan proceeds by adopting two fundamental paths. These paths include reflection on the social, cultural, cognitive, and relational dimensions of teaching and the comprehension of a useful framework to understand the complexity of the teaching profession.

The proposed activity was anticipated by the introductory video, including some short film clips about different learning situations and different models of professionalism. With the video, we intended to stimulate the personal concern of the teachers by soliciting projective and emotional dimensions with regard to the occupation. During the free discussion forums, we invited the teachers to consider their choice to be teachers and the situations related to that choice; they had the opportunity to express and share in pairs some personal impressions, highlighting internal representations with strong communicative significance: telling is an educational experience for both the teller and for those who take part in it.

We invited the teachers to reflect on different aspects of their professional profile such as values, beliefs, relationships, and performance, which often tacitly come into play in the teaching practice (Striano, 2001). We considered three aspects of reflection on the teaching profession (Wittorski, 1998):

1. The social biographical aspect related to life experiences, personal motivations, personal skills and competences, life events, attitudes, family circumstances, etc.
2. The educational aspect, which includes all the educational opportunities encouraging the development of basic skills for the profession.
3. The professional experience aspect, in which learners develop specific skills in relation to the contexts and practices shared by the professional community through internships, induction procedures, professional imprinting, experiments, research projects, and qualified experience.

Data Analysis

The analysis of the content posted by the teachers in the discussion forum allowed the extrapolation of the most significant parts, the identification of recurring themes as well as the identification of the expressive and communicative forms most commonly used (Fahy et al., 2000; Hillman, 1999). More specifically, the analysis of the content posted by the teachers in the discussion forum took place with the support of ATLAS.ti. 5.0, which is a Computer Assisted Qualitative Data Analysis Software (CAQDAS). In particular, we created a hermeneutic unit (which provides the data structure for research in ATLAS.ti). This hermeneutic unit is a type of container concept into which we put everything that is relevant to the research: that is, the data to analyze, the quotations, the codes, the conceptual linkages (families, networks), the memos (which are similar to a code, but usually contain longer passages of text), etc. We appointed all of the forum discussions to our hermeneutic unit by creating primary documents (PD). We then selected single sections of the documents (words, sentences, paragraphs . . .) that we considered relevant to the aims of our research: the quotations. We assigned to each quotation a specific code. Then, we created three families (a family is a way to form and organize clusters of codes) to analyze the three research topics:

1. The social biographical aspects.
2. The educational aspects.
3. The professional aspects.

Finally, we created some network views that allowed us to conceptualize the structure by connecting sets of similar elements together in a visual diagram, allowing us to find relationships between codes, quotations, and families.

FINDINGS

In the majority of the data analyzed, a highly emotional tone emerges describing the teachers' motivation for their career choice. Generally, this motivation stems from childhood, and it is often linked to a pleasant memory (sometimes a bit nostalgic) of their teachers (especially primary school teachers). Some stories are very engaging and personal, full of interesting biographical details and evoking an idea, maybe slightly romantic, of the teacher figure. Discursive and conversational language is mostly used, but generally the stories are also scientifically correct from an educational and teaching viewpoint. Teachers often used terms such as design, curriculum, methodologies, teaching techniques, learning strategies, coordination, taxonomies, research, and teamwork. The strong need for lifelong learning reveals an attitude toward the search and development of their professional skills; in this way, teachers make a continuous effort to improve the quality of their performance. In the teachers' reflections, we found a contrast between theory and practice, exemplified in the persistence, on some occasions, of a view in which the practice is not connected to the theory. However, the most important findings are related to the aspects of reflection mentioned above.

Social Biographical Aspects

With regard to the social biographical aspects, 90% of the teachers, those possessing a primary school teaching certificate, claimed an innate desire to be a teacher that is, for them, their lifelong ambition. This passion was acquired in childhood during primary school. It appears that the most popular game for these teachers when they were children was simulating lessons with dolls, chalk, chalkboards, and more or less improvised grade books. For example, one of the most significant posts states, "When I was a child attending the primary school, I passionately loved school and, in particular, my teacher. I liked so much to correct my brothers' exercises books, and I liked to help my friends in difficulty. I liked to play the teacher with my little dollies. My parents gave me a little blackboard and some colored chalk. I spent a lot of time writing and erasing, getting angry with and pampering my dollies/pupils..." Seven percent of the teachers noted an initial indecision between the wish to become a teacher and that to become a nurse. For example, one teacher states, "To tell the truth, when I enrolled at the institute for the primary school teaching certificate, I hadn't a clear idea about what I wanted to do. At the beginning, I believed I would become a nurse, but later, during the training hours at an elementary school,

I felt in love with teaching; furthermore, I have always had an innate love for children, which probably was given to me from my mother."

Approximately 10% acknowledged that they became teachers by chance, considering this profession to be a way to obtain a safe career and a means to achieve economic independence from their family; moreover, these teachers declared that they made this choice following their parents' recommendations (usually the father). Referring to this finding, we can read in our data, "I started this job by chance, led by the desire to be economically independent in a short time. My father insisted that I did this work, then over time it has become my passion . . . "

However, all of the teachers claim to be satisfied with their job, and they recognize (even beyond their initial expectations) that they acquired, in time, a great passion for teaching. These teachers say, in fact, throughout most parts of the discussion forum, that they take great satisfaction from this profession (70%), especially from the relational point of view. In particular, the relationships with the children are considered to be motivating, but in many cases, the relationships with colleagues are also very important and meaningful. The cognitive aspect linked to the need to experience lifelong learning also appears to be very gratifying: these teachers recognize, in particular, the possibility of always being in training and in close contact with the topic of continuing education. Analyzing again the biographical field, in many contributions, being a teacher is more of a mission than a profession (70%): it appears to be a vocation. In general, we discover the profile of a person wishing to take care of others, interested in educational themes, and satisfied by working in contact with children. Further, there is an expressed desire to take care of the weak, the helpless, and the disabled (30%). In this regard, one participant said, "Among the various possibilities of study, I felt more inclined towards something that would allow me to cultivate relationships; I felt attracted toward the world of children. The experience from the internship confirmed this. I think also that a genetic predisposition led me to be interested in others, to get close to my friends in difficulty, and a desire to share and help them, had an influence in my choice."

Many of these teachers, more than 30%, are active in the social and cultural fields. Many of them, approximately 35%, have volunteered in the parish or were part of scout groups when they were younger. More than 10% claim to be politically engaged in their municipality of residence. For example, one teacher stated,

> When I was fourteen, I became a cultural educator in the town parish, and so with other cultural educators, we planned some educational activities, finding the right tools. I liked so much staying with pupils and going with them through new experiences and new knowledge. Several times, I went with them to summer camps as an educator.

The Educational Aspects

With reference to the educational component, these teachers took many courses to update their skills. In fact, they consider lifelong learning to be very important. These teachers declare a constant passion for learning. Just over 20% claim to have already attended other undergraduate courses for long or short periods (usually in the Faculty of Psychology or Pedagogy) early in their teaching careers, but they abandoned their university studies to focus on family (marriage and the birth of children). For them, enrollment in this online degree course represents a form of revenge. For example, one teacher stated,

> I graduated 25 years ago, and then I enrolled in the faculty of psychology. At the same time, I started working in a private kindergarten school shortly after I won a competition in public school. I got married, I had two children... Family commitments, school commitments were too demanding and so I had to abandon the study... Now enrolling in this course is for me a way to take revenge and to make up for lost time.

However, many of these teachers have attended various training courses. Most of the courses they took were media and technology courses (8%), courses for teaching methods to use with pupils presenting specific learning difficulties (8%), official qualifications for educators courses (8%), instructional strategy courses for specific disabilities (5%), literacy courses for pupils not speaking Italian (5%), applied psychology courses (5%), and music and psychomotor courses (5%). Finally, activities carried out in groups with colleagues are considered to be particularly beneficial for professional development. Among these activities, for example, the teachers mentioned the opportunity to participate in research projects with universities, with the National Institute for Learning Outcomes Assessment (10%), with the board of the supervisors, or with the different Regional Institutes of Research. These experiences, in many cases, have allowed these teachers the possibility of testing new designs, innovative teaching methods, new strategies for learning, and new systems and evaluation criteria.

Professional Aspects

With regard to professional aspects, many of the teachers (60%) started as substitute teachers and, in time, they became tenured teachers. Many of them worked, for long or short periods, as a teacher's aide (20%), finding in this role a great passion and much satisfaction (sometimes unexpectedly). Thirty percent recognize the importance of experience in the field and sharing the practice and group reflection. These teachers admit that they learned much from the comparison with their older colleagues. The opinion that knowledge is the cornerstone, perhaps dominant, in teaching practice is shared. In other words, these teachers recognize the great importance of educational training, participating in various events and taking theoretical courses, but they believe that practice is the key to developing teacher competence. Seventy percent recognize teaching skills as being particularly important, and 45% highlight the relevance of competences related to design, communication skills (35%), and relational skills (40%). Furthermore, it appears to be essential that a good teacher be flexible and able to manage the risks and emergencies related to ongoing social and demographic changes, particularly migratory flows (20%).

CONCLUSIONS

The analyzed forum discussions reveal several aspects that characterize the professional profiles of the teachers involved. In effect, (a) they appear to be highly motivated teachers who are emotionally involved in their work, which is considered to be important in terms of interpersonal relationships and interpersonal and social improvement; (b) they intend the teaching profession to be a process of care that works for the welfare of the teacher and in defense of the weakest in the school community and in the wider social community; (c) they are willing to strengthen their professional dimension, accepting the lifelong learning logic as a progressive and integrated process in addition to initial and in-service training; and (d) they welcome the experiential dimension as an effective device for professional growth, enhancing direct contact with teachers, peers, and senior tutors.

The analysis of the teachers' contributions also raised three interesting questions that, in our opinion, are particularly crucial for training and university curricula quality. The first question concerns the relationship between theory and practice, a topic that is generally not adequately detailed in the academic context; this question introduces the problem of the type of professionalism that must be possessed by a university professor called to train teachers. We rather hope that theory and practice will be seen as two elements that interact in a circular manner, where theory is combined with practice as a reflection on it and practice combines with theory when teachers meet and try to make explicit (also in writing) their tacit knowledge (Polanyi, 1966). The second question concerns the enhancement of research training, a competence that today is more indispensable than ever for teachers, who operate in uncertainty, and that is much appreciated by our group of teachers (Sagor, 2004). The third question regards the social dimension of learning (Bruner, 1982; Vygotsky, 1934/1986), an approach that, unfortunately, in the Italian university has been difficult to establish in an appropriate manner.

Ultimately, our position, within the limits of our research, is that the analyzed forum discussions invite us to focus on the importance of an education that places a person at the center of learning the subject. The emotional involvement expressed by the teachers reflected in diachronic form in their biographical, training, and professional experience, has placed in the foreground the need to reflect more deeply on the relationship between the educational and transformative character of training. Together with disciplinary and instrumental learning processes, it is necessary to develop meaningful learning connecting knowledge and know-how in practice (Wenger, 1998) to the personal method for being a professional and a subject in change. In other words, it is necessary for training to allow the transformative dimension of the self (Mezirow, 2003) by the subject inserted in professional learning paths. In this direction, it appears to be useful to create a learning space in which the trainee can develop a greater awareness of his or her personal path, offering a reflection that helps to make explicit the implicit links and meanings that are always present in training choices (Schön, 1987). Uncovering the interconnections between the technical-instrumental acquisitions of the profession and internal motivations, desire for knowledge and personal fulfillment helps to relocate training in terms of new values.

REFERENCES

Bruner J. (1982). *Verso una teoria dell'istruzione* [Toward a Theory of Instruction]. Roma: Armando.

COM. (2007). Communication from the Commission to the Council and the European Parliament *Improving the quality of teacher education* SEC (2007) 931 and SEC (2007) Brussels

Danielson, C. (2007). *Enhancing professional practice: A framework for teaching* (2nd ed.). Alexandria, VA: Association for Supervision and Curriculum Development.

Fahy, P. J., Crawford, G., Ally, M., Cookson, P., Keller, V., & Prosser, F. (2000). The development and testing of a tool for analysis of computer mediated conferencing transcripts. *Alberta Journal of Educational Research, 46*(1), 85–88.

Hillman, D. (1999). A new method for analyzing patterns of interaction. *The American Journal of Distance Education, 13*(2), 37–47.

Johnson, D. W., & Johnson, R. T. (1994). *Learning together and alone: Cooperative, competitive and individual learning.* Needham Heights, MA: Allyn and Bacon.

Margiotta, U. (1999). *L'insegnante di qualità* [The quality teacher]. Roma: Armando.

Mezirow, J. (2003). *Apprendimento e trasformazione.* [Transformative dimension of adult learning]. Translated by R. Merlini. Milano: Raffaello Cortina.

Montalbetti, K. (2005). *La pratica riflessiva come ricerca educativa dell'insegnante* [The reflexive practice as educational research for the teacher]. Milano: Vita e Pensiero.

Paquay, L., Altet M., Charlier, E., & Perrenoud, P. (2012). *Former des enseignants professionnels. Quelles stratégies? Quelles compétences?* [Training teachers. Which strategies? Which competencies?] (12th ed.). Bruxelles: De Boeck.

Perrenoud, P. (2002). *Dieci nuove competenze per insegnare* [Ten new competencies to teach]. Roma: Anicia.

Polanyi, M. (1966). *The tacit dimension*, New York, NY: Anchor Books.

Quaglino, G. P. (2004). *Autoformazione. Autonomia e responsabilità per la formazione di sé nell'età adulta* [Self-directed learning. Autonomy and accountability in adult training]. Milano: Raffaello Cortina.

Sagor, R. (2004). *The action research guidebook: A four-step process for educators and school teams.* Corwin Press: Thousand Oaks, CA.

Schön, D. A. (1987). *Educating the reflective practitioner.* San Francisco: Jossey Bass.

Schön, D. A. (1993). *Il professionista riflessivo.* [The reflexive professional]. Bari: Dedalo.

Striano, M. (2001). *La "razionalità riflessiva" nell'agire educativo* [The "reflexive rationality" in the educational action]. Napoli: Liguori.

Toch, T., & Rothman, R. (2008). *Rush to judgment: Teacher evaluation in public education.* Washington, DC: DC Education Sector.

Wenger E. (1998). *Communities of practice: learning, meaning and identity.* New York, NY: Cambridge University Press.

Vygotsky, L. S. (1934/1986). *Thought and language.* Cambridge, MA: MIT Press (original work published in 1934).

Wittorski, R. (1998). De la fabrication des competences [Building competencies]. *Education Permanente, 135*(2), 57–69.

CHAPTER 26

INTEGRATING TECHNOLOGY INTO PEDAGOGICAL CONTENT KNOWLEDGE IN K–12 AND UNIVERSITY PROFESSIONAL DEVELOPMENT

Kathleen B. Fabrikant
Armstrong Atlantic State University

Cindy S. York
Northern Illinois University

Megan E. Morris
Armstrong Atlantic State University

BACKGROUND

Learners in the current millennium are wired to think digitally and expect instant access to knowledge. The need for educators to integrate new teaching tools is driven by the ever-increasing speed of technological advances

Building Sustainable Futures for Adult Learners, pages 541–558
Copyright © 2015 by Information Age Publishing
All rights of reproduction in any form reserved.

and as a way to engage the newest generation of learners with the ability to gain critical pedagogical content mediated by constant change. Research has shown this is true on a global basis (Doherty, 2010; Florian, 2012; Northcote, Reynaud, & Beamish, 2012; Whitchurch, Skinner, & Lauwerys, 2009).

If professional development is to remain sustainable and able to effectively support developing generations of educators, the authors of this chapter believe one of the most deciding factors is the integration of technology into pedagogical content knowledge supported by professional development efforts. Little (2006) asserted the term "pedagogical content knowledge," currently used by many, was first used by Dewey as he linked educational objectives with experiential activities outside the classroom. "Broadly defined, pedagogical content knowledge is the practical knowledge that enables teachers to transform the content and epistemology of a subject discipline for purposes of teaching" (Little, 2006, p. 7).

There can be many incentives for the development of high quality teacher training. The dizzying speed of available technological teaching tools for classroom use is one of the most obvious. How can educators be taught fast enough, and how can educators teach K–12 students in a world where those learners seem to be born with an innate digital knowledge? A second incentive is driven by the adoption of Common Core State Standards by many states, which requires a new level of pedagogical content knowledge (PCK). PCK has since been expanded to Technological Pedagogical and Content Knowledge (TPACK) (Thompson & Mishra, 2008). "T" signifies Technology. The addition of the "A" was meant to demonstrate that technology, pedagogy, *and* content were equal building blocks for educators to utilize as they used technology to improve their instruction and learning (Thompson & Mishra, 2008).

Van Driel and Berry (2012) renewed the spotlight on the "... importance of forms of professional development for teachers that are built on collaboration, collegial interactions, and the fostering of relationships" (p. 26). They discussed collaboration among educators within their professional environments as an essential part of the creation of high-level professional development. However, Van Driel and Berry warned of the dangers of mandated training sessions that can often have the opposite effect, resulting in a greater lack of communication and collaboration among educators.

OVERVIEW OF THIS CHAPTER

This chapter discusses how faculty development was used to enhance the quality of content knowledge pedagogy using technological tools. This starts with a discussion about an exploratory research study on the professional development of K–12 teachers in a newly implemented iPad program.

University professional development will then be discussed in terms of best practices. Finally, this chapter concludes with a comparison of professional development in the two different settings and implications for professional development of teachers and faculty.

Philosophy Driving Professional Development

Studies on professional training have described the tenets of andragogy (Knowles, 1988), which forms the foundation for the teaching of adults (Thompson & Mishra, 2008, Van Driel & Berry, 2012). The principles of andragogy are an integral part of faculty development, which is, in essence, adult education. Brookfield's (2006) core assumptions of skillful teaching included the premise "skillful teaching is whatever helps students learn," "skillful teachers adopt a critically reflective stance towards their practice," and finally, "the most important knowledge skillful teachers need to do good work is a constant awareness of how students are experiencing their learning and perceiving teachers' actions" (pp. 18, 24, 28). These principles are implicit in adult education.

A logical progression of knowledge is that educators first develop their own knowledge, and then implement that knowledge in their classrooms, which can lead to specific learner outcomes. Literature has shown "PCK development is a complex process that is highly specific to the content, situation, and person" (Van Driel & Berry, 2012, p. 27). Therefore, PCK should be aligned with educators' existing practice and they should be given the opportunity to structure this knowledge in their own classroom communities.

Technology Competencies

Thompson and Mishra (2008) described the tendency to only teach the use of technology in professional development without including the vitally important areas of pedagogy and content knowledge as one reason why the field of education is behind in the effective inclusion of technology as a teaching tool. "Merely introducing technology to the educational process is not enough. The question of *what* teachers need to know in order to appropriately incorporate technology into their teaching has received a great deal of attention recently" (Mishra & Koehler, 2006, p. 1018). Mishra and Koehler (2006) demonstrated the framework of connections "between and among content, pedagogy, and technology," which should be taken together "rather than treating these as separate bodies of knowledge, this model additionally emphasizes the complex interplay of these three bodies of knowledge" (p. 1025).

Harris and Hofer (2009) suggested educators first design a lesson and instructional strategies, then infuse technology into the delivery of those strategies, rather than plan lessons around the use of technology. Mishra and Koehler (2006) agreed with that assessment of the use of technology when they asserted simply because an educator is skilled in the use of technology, it does not follow that the technology will be successfully incorporated into their classroom. Emphasis should be on the *what*, not the *how* (Mishra & Koehler, 2006, p. 1033). According to Mishra and Koehler (2006), "standard checklists of technology skills are very efficient means of listing what teachers need to know, but offer little suggestion on how teachers are to achieve these skills" (pp. 1032–1033). "Merely knowing how to use technology is not the same as knowing how to teach with it" (Mishra & Koehler, 2006, p. 1033).

Merriam and Bierema (2014) discussed how quickly the use of technology has changed the practice of adult education. Although more and more adults are connected through online social media, that does not translate to the effective use of technology and may lead to superficial learning instead of the kind of learning that promotes deep thought and critical thinking. "Technology is changing and challenging the role of adult educators" (Merriam & Bierema, 2014, p. 211).

Professional Learning Communities

Professional development appears to have shifted away from a "training" concept to one of creating a professional learning community (Vescio, Ross, & Adams, 2008). This places K–12 teachers and higher education faculty into positions of collaborators and planners of professional development, instead of simply the receivers of new updates. As both givers and receivers of instruction through technology, educators at all levels may need to become facilitators, bringing together a diverse and physically separated community of learners. A professional community of learners is most successful when learners are part of their own ongoing professional development, when the topics are relevant and immediately useful, when development is connected to learners' own content pedagogy, when content is organized and to the point, and resources are shared (Barnett, 2004, pp. 12–13).

THE STUDY

The first two authors of this chapter conducted a three-year study (2010–2013) that chronicled how a small, independent school (St. Andrews) in the southeast (one of the first in the United States to implement one-to-one iPads) infused the use of technology into teaching practice professional development. The school labeled the project, iDiscover21c, (the school's name of Internet/technologically-based learning, appropriate for the twenty-first century), which was their adaptation of TPACK. In other words, the teachers at the school were learning how to infuse technology into instruction for twenty-first century teaching and learning. The administrators and teachers of the K–12 knew the school was lagging in the area of technology in terms of both equipment and expertise prior to the one-to-one iPad integration.

History Behind the iPad Project

At the end of the 2009–2010 school year, the administration at St. Andrews made the decision to purchase iPads for each student and teacher and Mac laptops for each teacher. This created an immediate, and rather steep, learning curve for the teachers and administration as iPads were first released in April 2010 and school would start again in August 2010. The teachers were given the laptops and iPads to take home for the summer to get acquainted with them. Apple trainers conducted several iPad training sessions for teachers over the summer and fall semester. Training was also provided to parents and they were encouraged to use the iPads when their children brought them home.

METHODS

A qualitative, exploratory study was designed to examine how the administrators, teachers, and students perceived the implementation of iPads into instruction school-wide. However, this chapter will only discuss the administrator and teacher perceptions of the iPad integration and subsequent professional development. Institutional Review Board approval was sought and granted from Armstrong Atlantic State University and permission from St. Andrews was also granted to do the study.

Participants and Setting

St. Andrews on the Marsh school is located on Wilmington Island, Georgia. There were approximately 480 students, five administrators, and 28 teachers. Eight administrators participated in the study over the three years. Of the original five, three left before the end of year two. Their replacements participated (for a total of eight). A total of 36 teachers also participated in the study, 28 in year one. In year two, eight new teachers participated when others left the school.

Data Collection

Data collection consisted of surveys, interviews, and focus groups over the three years. Surveys will be described via participant type in the next sections. Instruments were neither validated nor used prior to this study, as the questions were specific to the school and its unique situation. As previously mentioned, this was an exploratory study. In addition, the researchers performed classroom observations and professional development observations. Interviews, focus groups, and professional development observations were all audio and/or video-recorded. Transcripts were done for all interviews and focus groups. All transcripts utilized pseudonyms, as administrator and teacher quotes are all confidential.

Administrators

Surveys were provided via a secure online survey tool, Qualtrics. Surveys (consisting of 46 questions, both open-ended and Likert-type) for administrators consisted of topics such as: rating how comfortable they and their teachers were with the iPad, technical competency with the iPad both prior to and after the implementation, as well as advice they would provide to other administrators wanting to implement a similar program. Demographic information (14 questions), level of buy-in by stakeholders, impact, technical support, parental support, and level of commitment were also addressed on the survey. During the first year, all five administrators completed the survey. The three new administrators did not complete the online survey because they came to the school two years after the iPad implementation and did not feel qualified to answer questions which focused on the beginning of the process.

Interviews were also conducted with administrator participants. Interviews were semi-structured with open-ended questions. The interview protocol started with 28 questions, but some of the questions were answered by participant responses and were not asked. Interviews lasted about 90 minutes each. Interview questions consisted of topics such as how technology was infused into the school's culture, types of technology support services that were available for teachers using the iPad, types of training that was required for anyone receiving an iPad, curricular issues, technology support issues, and so on.

Eight administrators overall were interviewed across the three years. Of the original five, three left before the end of year two. Their replacements were interviewed during year two using the same questions to determine if their perceptions were different based on the length of time they had spent as part of the iPad implementation.

Teachers

Teacher surveys consisted of 17 demographic questions and 61 other questions, both open-ended and Likert-type. Topics included general technology professional development, iPad specific professional development, frequency of technology use in their classrooms for computers and iPads, as well as specific iPad applications and ways they used them. Perceptions of the iPads and their uses in the classroom were also queried using a Likert-type scale. All 28 teachers were surveyed, however 14 started the survey and only 9 completed the survey. This could be due to the long length of the survey.

Teachers were interviewed via focus groups of two and three. Questions for focus groups were semi-structured and open-ended and consisted of 12 questions. Topics consisted of the use of iPads in the classroom and professional development. Eight teachers took part in the focus groups. Focus groups were all conducted by one researcher. Focus groups took between 60 and 120 minutes each.

Four teachers were also observed in their classrooms during the use of iPads in instruction by one researcher. One classroom had two teachers team teaching. Classroom observations were as long as the class periods.

Study Timeline

Year one of iPad implementation:

- Fall—5 administrators completed surveys
- Spring—5 administrators interviewed
- Spring—3 hour end-of-year technology professional development showcase presented by 24 teachers

Year two of iPad implementation:

- Fall—8 teachers participated in focus groups
- Spring—3 new administrators interviewed

Year three of iPad implementation:

- Spring—classroom observations (Grades K, 1, and 4)
- Spring—3 hour showcase for grades K–5, which showed student research of various topics using iPads as interactive tools

Data Analysis

Qualitative data analysis procedures were followed. Data was examined for common themes related to professional development and technology integration. Triangulation took place via interviews, focus groups, surveys, and observations of both classrooms and professional development sessions over the three years.

FINDINGS AND DISCUSSION

The following sections will discuss findings as they pertain to professional development for each of the three years of the project.

Professional Development Year One

The first professional development meetings focused solely on Internet use, ethics, and the principles of its use by students, teachers, staff, and administration. The subsequent meetings were focused on the use of iPads as a tool for classroom instruction. Each regularly scheduled faculty meeting included a segment of *iPad show and tell* (later called *tech talks* and/or *tech share*), during which teachers demonstrated an instructional use of the iPad in their content area, a new iPad application (App) they had discovered, or in some cases, something they and/or their students had designed and customized for use in their classes.

At the end of the first year, a three-hour teacher-driven professional development seminar was conducted. Teams of teachers comprised of two from each level of the school (lower, middle, and high school) showcased an iPad App used by them in their classrooms. This meant that each team had appropriately customized that App to the level of their learners. Teachers further showed how they tailored the use of each App to meet the needs of each specific age group. This seminar was the culmination of the first year experiences with the iPads. Teachers and administrators worked to create this seminar to showcase how far they had come in just one year of iPad use. This final showcase of teacher professional development was meant to summarize the *tech talks* held during weekly faculty meetings throughout the year and illustrate the value of *teachers teaching other teachers*.

At the end of year one with iPads and Mac laptops in place, the administration wrote a letter targeted toward parents. In it they discussed the progress of the iDiscover21c throughout the school. Becoming a twenty-first century school would mean a shift from teacher-centered to learner-centered classes, which is a fundamental component of the twenty-first century learning model. "Instead of a clear road map, we have chosen to discover as we go. While this has served us well in this first year, now is the time to create a more definite plan. Essential to creating a plan is a clearer understanding of our goals" (Fabrikant & York, 2011).

The following outcomes were identified as some of the lessons learned from the first year of iPad implementation in the school. These outcomes reflect the principles of collaboration and of andragogy, both among teachers, and in their classrooms, which had become increasingly learner-driven.

- Most of the participants agreed that they had gained a better understanding of twenty-first century teaching and learning.
- Teams modeled this style of teaching, which gave colleagues models for their own teaching.
- The cross-divisional teams strengthened their respect and understand of all parts of the school.
- All teams appeared to enjoy learning together throughout the process.
- Teams discovered new ways to use the iPads and Apps (Fabrikant & York, 2011).

Professional Development Year Two

During year two, teachers were applying what they learned in year one. By the second year of the iPad implementation, the school had developed a wiki forum, which was used to store their own discoveries and those showcased in the weekly *tech talk* section of their faculty meetings. This proved to be a valuable and lasting resource to which all teachers contributed and from which all could benefit. Teachers at the school now voiced very specific ideas of how they wanted staff development to be implemented. Their perceptions had changed from one of dreading the time and commitment to learn, to one of a desire to explore new teaching strategies using iPads.

Teachers appeared less concerned about the new technology and how to use it, which emerged during the focus group interviews. Teachers now understood how to incorporate it into their school day and felt they were making progress integrating it into their curriculum. Teachers also indicated a strong desire to modify the use of the iPads based on the experiences of their learning new technology to understanding its implications and future uses in their classrooms.

Table 26.1 contains direct quotes from the teachers that were recorded during the teacher focus groups in fall of year two. Only questions that specifically pertained to teacher professional development were included in this table.

TABLE 26.1 Quotes from Teacher Focus Groups about Professional Development

1. What types of professional development occurred for the use of iPads?
   - "For the professional development with these (iPads), this past summer we had . . . three, four days of professional development. So about 15 hours with that and we have had intermediate pieces with that. Aside from the first three days of training, which was great, but was really focused on learning the iWord software."
   - "We fall on our faces and we would get right back up and try again. Do it less poorly than the last time and try to make it work. The training that has come on the iPads is . . . it has come from other faculty members as faculty have found something to use and found a way to do it. They've stood up at a faculty meeting and said, "Hey, look what I found." So, it's really become internal."
   - "There was a lot of professional development last year for lower school, middle school and high school. Lower school would like to see more professional development specific to their needs."
   - "At this point, we need someone who is better trained to help us incorporate iPads use into the curriculum."
   - "The in-house training from faculty is the best, most useful. The outside sessions were not well done. Apple does some training, but not specific enough to meet our needs."

2. How is this integrated into regular faculty meetings?
   - "Yes, Tech Share at the beginning of meetings."
   - "Tech share at the faculty meetings- faculty shared what they have discovered, or in some cases, what learners have discovered. We need time to explore and/or implement these discoveries."

3. Do you think that professional development opportunities are useful and practical in helping educators use iPads and integrate them into the classroom?
   - "Yes, I would like to see more, at least monthly, driven by our faculty."
   - "Yes, but we would like to see the professional development geared more to our lower school needs."
   - "The high school faculty would like to see a laptop and iPad assigned to each learner. Middle school is happy with the iPads alone, as is the lower school. There has been quite a bit of planning for the future and we will go forward with technology."

4. Other comments
   - "The iPads have not changed the curriculum or pedagogy. iPads are a tool to supplement what they are doing in the classroom."
   - "The future looks like traditional texts will be replaced" (Fabrikant & York, 2011).

Professional Development Year Three

By the end of year three, the teachers felt the iPad had reinvented the way they learn and teach. Both teachers and staff felt that using the iPad made student learning more creative and engaging and improved students' critical thinking as well as students' collaborative and communication skills. Teachers noted that the students could now take information, synthesize it and make it into a technology piece (Fabrikant & York, 2013).

At the end of year three, the teachers were ready to move on to more specifically designed types of faculty professional development. They were interested in sessions geared toward specific grade levels and skills. The use of iPads as an instructional tool was well established throughout the classrooms and comments from discussions with the teachers being observed pointed toward the development of more specific ways to use iPads in each grade level, especially the K–4 levels. At the end of three years, a teacher-driven model of professional development was the norm at the school.

UNIVERSITY FACULTY PROFESSIONAL DEVELOPMENT

As a professional development trainer at the university level for faculty who teach pre-service teachers, the third author conducted informal surveys at the end of each professional development training session. The perceptions in the following sections were derived from those surveys and her personal experiences training College of Education faculty at the university level.

One main problem often observed with most faculty development offered at higher education institutions is that it does not appear to be faculty-driven, but instead comes from an administrative level and focuses on what professors should know and be able to do in order to adequately prepare pre-service teacher candidates. Research has elucidated the fact that there are a number of unanswered questions about utilizing information technologies effectively (Bingimlas, 2009; Elsaadani, 2013; Gu, Zhu, & Guo, 2013; Levin & Wadmany, 2008; Schrum, Skeele, & Grant, 2003; Surry & Land, 2000; Tabata & Johnsrud, 2008). Rice and Miller (2001) concluded that with technology advancements, faculty "need to make an effort to understand new technologies and realize the benefit when their institutions invest in information technology" (p. 334). As "faculty will be the individuals most affected by the use of instructional technologies and are the best judges of what they require to effectively use instructional technologies in their courses" (p. 334–335). Thus, faculty are a critical core resource as "studies on teacher attitudes revealed that teacher confidence affects the use of technology more than variables such as access to equipment, administrative support, and time" (Levin & Wadmany, 2008, p. 237; Tabata & Johnsrud, 2008).

When designing technology integration professional development for faculty who teach pre-service teachers, the third author of this chapter started with the single most defining element of learning, which was to ask *what value does this training provide the learner* (Harris, 1997). The value is added through what the learner takes into their environment to maximize not only their potential but also the potential of the environment in which they operate.

It was the goal of the third author's professional development design to promote change and learner transformation, consistent with the theory of life-long learning. Knowles' (1988) principles of andragogy explained that a person's readiness to learn information that would have an impact on their lives has a great deal to do with how well new information is learned. If what is learned is useful and relevant, the adult learner is more likely to be motivated to learn and apply that information. In this particular instance, the focused efforts were on technology integration in the learning environments of the higher education faculty at a small, state university in Savannah, GA. As literature has discussed, adults learn best when training incorporates *learn by doing* strategies, and engaging in authentic learning with direct relevance to their teaching (Doherty, 2010). Faculty must feel a connection to the professional development, find value in the learning, and be able to readily apply it in their normal setting.

The higher education faculty members who participated in the professional development training were involved in the education of pre-service teacher candidates. Thus, their ability to model and support technology integration in various learning environments and content areas had an exponential impact on generations of future educators. To elaborate, "today's students are no longer the people our educational system was designed to teach" (Prensky, 2001, p. 1). "Today's teachers have to learn to communicate in the language and style of their students" (Prensky, 2001, p. 4).

At the university, a professional development setting was created in which learning would engage faculty in progressively more demanding levels, meeting them where they were, challenging them to go beyond their comfort zone, sparking their curiosity into how technology integration would be to their maximum benefit. They were asked to keep in mind throughout all professional development sessions the fundamental question from the work of Judi Harris: "Is it worth it?" (Harris, 1997, p. 14). The professional development training sessions were built to offer more specific training using available resources that encouraged faculty to adapt their pedagogy to fit both their personal preferences and their learners' needs.

To ensure success of the professional development efforts, and to evaluate professional development offerings, feedback was solicited from faculty via an online survey form with questions tailored to the type of instruction received (e.g., device or software specific) of both the college's on-site training and the University System of Georgia's live online webinars. Feedback gathered helped form a new needs assessment evaluation, professional development offerings, and technology purchase recommendations during the following semester. These professional development offerings were proactive, addressing gaps in knowledge regarding available resources. All resources utilized in the professional development sessions were compiled into a web page for those unable to attend, those wanting references to something learned, or for those faculty who wanted their students to work with the resources with the emphasis being on best practices and classroom modeling.

University/K–12 Professional Development Comparison

Van Driel and Berry (2012) discussed that the complex nature of PCK for educators' professional knowledge is highly topic, person, and situation specific—essentially ruled by strong personal beliefs regarding what educators view as good teaching. Therefore, grounding professional development training in specific professional contexts is influenced by institutional factors (culture, available time, resources, and leadership support). Additionally, Van Driel and Berry's (2012) research noted that designing professional development using PCK is a complex process, intended for educators to reflect, individually and collectively, on their experiences. It is important to note that educators must be able to adapt newly learned ideas into their practice and make meaningful connections to old ideas as a necessary way to enhance effectiveness when teaching.

Best practices for professional development have been noted in the literature (Barnett, 2004; Brookfield, 2006; Harris & Hofer, 2009; Van Driel & Berry, 2012). Best practices included hands-on training, training required by educators to meet a perceived need in the workplace, speakers who are interesting, who are speaking on a topic of interest to the educators, a prior understanding by educators of the need for the training, presentations by peer educators, training that has an immediate and apparent use, and top-down required sessions. Table 26.2 represents the alignment of reflections from both the K–12 and university settings previously discussed against the list of best practices synthesized from several sources (Barnett, 2004; Brookfield, 2006; Harris & Hofer, 2009; Van Driel & Berry, 2012).

Each best practice listed in column one of Table 26.2 was compared at both settings to see if the opinions of the K–12 teachers aligned with the opinions of the university faculty. It was determined that hands-on training and relevance was important in both settings. If the training was immediately useful, it was viewed as more valuable. Training that was required to meet a need in the workplace was viewed as important if the teachers and faculty had some input into the sessions. Speakers who were interesting as well as presentations by peer educators were perceived as trainings that were targeted toward specific needs in both settings. A prior understanding of the need for training served as a means of motivation for both settings because the teachers and faculty had input into their own needs. Training with an immediate use was seen as helpful because there would be no gap between the training and its application. Top-down required sessions were

TABLE 26.2 Examples of Best Practices by Setting

Best Practice	K–12 Teachers	Higher Education Faculty
Hands-on training: Sessions where educators can actually produce or complete a project that is useful to them.	This was true at many of the K–12 professional development sessions, where teachers were able to use their iPads during the short "Tech Talk" part of their regular weekly faculty meetings to download and use the newly introduced App.	Faculty were provided with learning challenges (e.g., scavenger hunt) where they had to utilize the skills learned during the training in order to solve a problem or answer a question posed. This not only created an environment for immediate application but also positive reinforcement in the confidence of the skills learned.
Training required by educators to meet a perceived need in the workplace.	In the K–12 school, the lower school (grades K–5) teachers were very interested in professional development geared to their students' developing literacy needs. The weekly faculty meetings were also an excellent venue for teachers to communicate their needs and for other teachers to share their own discoveries.	Faculty were informally surveyed at the beginning of each semester using a targeted needs assessment with an emphasis on technology and following each training session to gather data from which to make adjustments to the focus of the training.
Speakers who are interesting, who are speaking on a topic of interest to the educators.	In this regard, the K–12 teachers were most engaged when their colleagues were presenting a new idea. While many did appreciate the Apple training, they also found it very general and designed to learn software, but not how to apply it to their instructional strategies.	Faculty were encouraged to participate in professional development with invited speakers who offered training on educational devices utilized in the contemporary classroom (SmartBoards, iPads, presentation software).
A prior understanding by educators of the need for the training (for example: training through a voluntary basis on how to create online courses that are 508 compliant, rigorous, and interactive for students).	The K–12 teachers were well aware of the need for the professional development sessions used to help them learn how to interact with the iPads and Mac laptops. With a very short implementation timeline of 40 days to fully integrate a new platform with both iPads and Mac laptops, teachers were anxious to attend as much professional development as possible. They recognized that this was only the beginning.	Faculty expressed interest in training, not only as a means for maintenance but also for expanding their skill set to include more contemporary tools. Therefore, faculty were seeking training on a voluntary basis.

(continued)

TABLE 26.2   Examples of Best Practices by Setting (continued)

Best Practice	K–12 Teachers	Higher Education Faculty
Presentations by peer educators.	As stated previously, the K–12 teachers used presentations by their colleagues to fill gaps between the technical use of iPads and how to implement the iPad as an instructional tool. As teachers shared Apps and their integration into classroom pedagogy, the weekly faculty meetings became an important part of their learning community.	Presentations were conducted by people at both the college and university level (presentations of various initiatives at college faculty meetings, a faculty showcase hosted by the University Office of Online and Blended Learning where faculty developed courses and components that contribute to overall success).
Training that has an immediate and apparent use.	The K–12 teachers' use of weekly meetings to share small amount of TPACK with each other proved to be the most useful vehicle for the timely delivery of immediately useful information.	The goal of the professional development sessions was to enable the faculty to integrate lessons learned into their daily teaching practice.
Top down required sessions.	While the K–12 teachers understood the usefulness of the sessions delivered by Apple, they voiced a much greater appreciation of those short professional development sessions given by their own colleagues. By the end of the first year, teachers were also comfortable in voicing exactly what kind of professional development they felt would most benefit them as they moved the use of iPads to a higher level.	Perceptions from professional development training sessions appeared to show that mandated, or top-down, sessions were not as successful as those training sessions initiated or requested by the faculty.

understood as perhaps necessary, but neither teachers nor faculty reported being motivated by them.

PROFESSIONAL DEVELOPMENT IMPLICATIONS

There are a number of implications for the professional development of educators as they infuse technology into pedagogical content knowledge. The implications of this chapter combine the principles of adult education and those of TPACK. Brookfield's (2006) core assumption that "skillful teaching is whatever helps students learn" (p. 17) contains within it principles of andragogy. Adults, including teachers and faculty, who have input into their own training, are motivated to absorb and synthesize that training more successfully, as shown in Table 26.2. Therefore, giving teachers and faculty choices about what professional development they would like is extremely important.

Teachers and faculty in both settings also viewed training that was relevant and immediately useful to be good. Therefore, making sure that professional development ideas and products can be immediately put into use in the classroom is very important. Having the professional development participants bring examples of their current lessons or curriculum with them to the professional development session and then apply the new material to actual classroom lessons, increases its meaning and allows for immediate implementation of the new ideas. Giving participants fictitious examples to use is not as good as having them use authentic examples from their current teaching. As a final thought, when the integration of technology in pedagogical content knowledge is taught through professional development, it is more likely to be better received by teachers and faculty if the professional development best practices are followed.

CONCLUSION

It is fairly certain that professional development needs will continue to exist, driven by the need for education to stay aligned with the speed of technological innovations. There is a necessity for institutions to support these needs and is vital to educator success. This also includes preparing and maintaining educators' skill sets to teach future generations of evolving learners. Most notably, educators and learners are increasingly diverse and these professional development sessions must be reflective of these new innovations and theoretical ideas about learning (Northcote et al., 2012).

The basic principles of andragogy can, and often are, easily incorporated into the educational needs of adults, teachers and faculty, to learn new technologies to enhance their teaching methods (Knowles, 1988). It is important for administrators and the planners of professional development to use the principles of andragogy as they plan new training sessions for teachers and faculty. To our twenty-first century students, what has become a more common way of learning (iPad) was not yet invented just five years ago. Our teachers and faculty must learn to teach students to prepare for careers that may not even exist yet, and this will be done more successfully if we teach adults the way adults learn best.

REFERENCES

Barnett, E. (2004). Characteristics and perceived effectiveness of staff development practices in selected high schools in South Dakota. *Education Research Quarterly, 28*(2), 3–18.

Bingimlas, K. A. (2009). Barriers to the successful integration of ICT in teaching and learning environments: A review of the literature. *Eurasia Journal of Mathematics, Science & Technology, 5*(3), 235–45.

Brookfield, S. D. (2006). *The skillful teacher: On technique, trust, and responsiveness in the classroom.* San Francisco, CA: Josey-Bass.

Doherty, I. (2010). A learning design for engaging academics with online professional development modules. *Journal of Learning Design, 4*(1), 1–14.

Elsaadani M. A. (2013). Exploring the relationship between teaching staff age and their attitude towards information and community technologies (ICT). *International Journal of Instruction, 6*(1), 215–226.

Fabrikant, K. B., & York, C. S. (2011). [The implementation of one-to-one iPads in a K–12 school]. Unpublished raw data.

Fabrikant, K. B., & York, C. S. (2012). [The implementation of one-to-one iPads in a K–12 school: Year two]. Unpublished raw data.

Fabrikant, K. B., & York, C. S. (2013). [The implementation of one-to-one iPads in a K–12 school: Year three]. Unpublished raw data.

Florian, L. (2012). Preparing teachers to work in inclusive classrooms: Key lessons for the professional development of teacher educators from Scotland's inclusive practice project. *Journal of Teacher Education, 63*, 275. doi: 10.1177/0022487112447112

Gu, X., Zhu, Y., & Guo, X. (2013). Meeting the "digital natives": Understanding the acceptance of technology in classrooms. *Educational Technology & Society, 16*(1), 392–402.

Harris, J. (1997). Wetware: Why use activity structures. *Learning and Leading with Technology, 25*(4), 13–17.

Harris, J., & Hofer, M. (2009). Grounded tech integration. *Learning and Leading with Technology, 37*(2), 22–25.

Knowles, M. (1988). *The modern practice of adult education: From pedagogy to andragogy.* Cambridge Adult Education, Prentice Hall, Englewood Cliffs, NJ.

Levin, T., & Wadmany, R. (2008). Teachers' views on factors affecting effective integration of information technology in the classroom: Developmental scenery. *Journal of Technology and Teacher Education, 16*(2), 233–263.

Little, J. W. (2006). *Professional community and professional development in the learning-centered school.* Arlington, VA: National Education Association, 1–26.

Merriam, S. B., & Bierema, L. L. (2014). *Adult learning: Linking theory and practice.* San Francisco, CA: Josey-Bass.

Mishra, P., & Koehler, M. J. (2006). Technological pedagogical content knowledge: A framework for integrating technology in teacher knowledge. *Teachers College Record, 108*(6), 1017–1054.

Northcote, M., Reynaud, D., & Beamish, P. (2012). Teaching the lecturers: Academic staff learning about online teaching. *US-China Education Review, 2*(4), 384–393.

Prensky, M. (2001). Digital natives, digital immigrants. *On the Horizon, 9*(5), 1–6. doi: 10.1108/10748120110424816

Rice, M. L., & Miller, M. T. (2001). Faculty involvement in planning for the use and integration of instructional and administrative technologies. *Journal of Research on Computing in Education, 33*(3), 328–336.

Schrum, L., Skeele, R., & Grant, M. (2003). One college of education's effort to infuse technology: A systematic approach to revisioning teaching and learning. *Journal of Research on Technology in Education, 35*(2), 256–255.

Surry, D. W., & Land, S. M. (2000). Strategies for motivating higher education faculty to use technology. *Innovations in Education and Training International, 37*(2), 145–153.

Tabata, L. N., & Johnsrud, L. K. (2008). The impact of faculty attitudes toward technology, distance education, and innovation. *Research in Higher Education, 49*, 625–646. doi:10.2307/25704589

Thompson, A. D., & Mishra, P. (2008). Breaking news: TPCK becomes TPACK! *Journal of Computing in Teacher Education, 24*(2), 38, 64.

Van Driel, J. H., & Berry, A. (2012). Teacher professional development focusing on pedagogical content knowledge. *Educational Researcher, 41*(26), 26–28. doi: 10.3102/0013189X11431010

Vescio, V., Ross, D., & Adams, A. (2008). A review of research on the impact of professional learning communities on teaching practice and student learning. *Teaching and Teacher Education, 24*, 80–91.

Whitchurch, C., Skinner, M., & Lauwerys, J. (2009). Recent developments in relation to professional staff in UK higher education. *Australian University Review, 5*(1), 56–60.

CHAPTER 27

DEVELOPING A REPERTOIRE OF PRACTICE

Online Instructor Dispositions and Personalities

Jeral R. Kirwan
Ashford University

Elizabeth Ann Roumell
North Dakota State University

INTRODUCTION

The traditional face-to-face delivery of postsecondary education content has been changing dramatically due to Information and Communications Technologies (ICTs) for the past 20 years, and educational institutions in adult, continuing, and higher education around the globe have been scrambling to adapt. "Harnessing innovative technology in higher education" (King & Griggs, 2006) has been a staple discussion within our field for at least two decades, and has much in common with the scholarship in online learning. The emergence of Internet and Web-based learning has significantly impacted how professional learning and development programs have been designed,

Building Sustainable Futures for Adult Learners, pages 559–581

delivered, and assessed (Hardy, 2006). In fact, some herald a paradigm shift in the field of adult and continuing education, or at least a "paradigm creep" as described by Donavant (2009). Even as online and blended programs have become more common, the quality of online education, in comparison with more conventional face-to-face forms of education, remains an area of contention (Blustain, 2006; Meyer, 2002). If a distinct and effective environment of online learning is to emerge, the roles, characteristics, and dispositions of instructors in the virtual learning environment need to be explored in more depth. As more adult educators accept the responsibility of delivering courses utilizing various constellations of ICTs, it is imperative new frameworks are developed and tested to provide them with useful feedback about their online teaching potential and repertoire of practice.

The use of self-assessment tools may be helpful to improve virtual instruction by supplying educators with feedback about the characteristics, skills, and dispositions that have been identified as essential for creating and delivering quality virtual and blended instruction. The main benefit of this type of feedback is that instructors can use the framework for self-assessment to improve their ability to identify and develop an effective presence and practice (Nicol & Macfarlane-Dick, 2006) in the online learning environment. A framework addressing online instructor dispositions provides a useful tool for research and practice in the area of online instruction, where educators can be empowered as autonomous and self-directed professionals (Merriam, 2002; Mezirow, 1985) who actively and consistently engage in reflective practice (Brookfield, 1995; Ferraro, 2000), work toward improving learning strategies (Cercone, 2008; Heimlich & Norland, 1994), improve decision-making processes (Ferry & Ross-Gordon, 1998), and develop educator dispositions and practices applicable to learning in virtual environments (Anderson, 2004).

In this chapter, we introduce and explain a framework for virtual instructor dispositions and characteristics based on foundational online learning and adult and continuing education literature. Our aim for this chapter is to offer an expanded understanding of virtual instructor "personas" including identified characteristics, beliefs, and behaviors of online educators. An extension of this goal is to provide insight into the online educators' role(s), but also to provide a starting point for self-assessment where they can continue identifying strengths and preferences and developing their online teaching style toward a more reflective practice (Cox, 2005; Marienau, 1999).

FACILITATING ONLINE LEARNING

In a virtual learning environment, a substantial portion of course content is delivered via the Internet, and the majority of communication and interaction between all participants is facilitated with ICTs (Curran, 2008;

King & Griggs, 2006). Online learning offers learners temporal and geographic flexibility and convenience which expands accessibility, choice, and provides them with greater control over their own learning (Bastiaens & Martens, 2000; Belanger & Jordan, 2000; King & Griggs, 2006; Lau, 2000). Andragogical assumptions have long been debated, but the main characteristics of online adult learning, in many ways, parallel these principles (Blondy, 2007; Frey & Alman, 2003). While online and blended learning are now quite common in postsecondary education, these virtual modalities of instruction delivery continue to be heavily critiqued for the social distance experienced by learners and the hindered communication between instructor and learners (Erichsen & Bolliger, 2011; Gibson, 2006; Lau, 2000; Mason, 2007; Russel, 2005). It is also still often argued that learners must have access to dependable technology (Clarke, 2002), and that some learners may lack the technology skills or self-directed learning skills (Berge, 2001; Mason, 2007) necessary to learn successfully in virtual environments.

COMPONENTS OF DISPOSITIONS

In identifying the dispositions of educators, three components are typically addressed, including characteristics of individual personality, the values and beliefs that serve as a justification for action, and regular patterns of an individual's behavior. Together, these three areas can help identify the tendencies of an educator within various learning environments.

In order to understand people's behavior, it is necessary to understand their general perceptions of the world. From a perceptual viewpoint, behaviors are considered symptoms of underlying values, beliefs, and perceptions of the world. Therefore, understanding one's general world perceptions is the key to understanding one's actions. Thus, it is understood that the notions of dispositions and personalities are not seen as causes of behavior. An educator does not praise students because she has a disposition to be supportive or an agreeable personality, but rather, an educator who is observed to make use of praise across contexts and on frequent occasions may be described as having a supportive disposition or an agreeable personality. In this sense, the concepts of dispositions and personalities are descriptive characteristics and may have a predictive element. For example, someone who demonstrates supportive behavior over time is more likely to be supportive the next time as well. Descriptors of effective educator personalities, beliefs, and behaviors, then, can be used as indicators for successful online instructional practice. For the purpose of developing *dispositions* for the virtual learning environment, we take three components of dispositions into consideration, namely personality traits, beliefs pertaining to educational practice, and frequency and types of behavior.

Educator Dispositions

Research on teacher dispositions is found primarily in the K–12 realm, where "dispositions indicate a teacher's tendency to act effectively on the behalf of the learning and well-being of his or her students" (Carroll, 2012, p. 38). Katz (1993) defined a teacher's disposition as an attributed characteristic of a teacher, one that summarizes the trend of a teacher's actions in specific contexts. Ennis (1987) defined dispositions as a tendency to do something given certain conditions. The notion of dispositions represents not just a summary of behaviors, but also an individual's beliefs, values, and other personality traits. In adult education, Cranton (2004) crafts a relevant model for educators with five dimensions of "authenticity in teaching," namely self-awareness, awareness of others, relationships with learners, awareness of context, and critical reflective practice.

One may think of the term dispositions as the process of developing an educator identity and a set of instructional practices (Blythe and associates, 1998). It is the professional development process in which educators engage in the intellectual, cultural, ethical, and social actions and practices necessary to become effective educators, which can lead educators to become more authentic, individuated, and critically reflective practitioners (Cranton & King, 2003). In adult and continuing education, we are not unfamiliar with these components of developing educator dispositions, as "teaching style" (Heimlich & Norland, 1994), refining one's artistry or craft (Ferraro, 2000), and transformative learning theory as a practitioner model (Dirkx, 1998) in adult and continuing education have been discussed in depth. Schussler, Stooksberry, and Bercaw (2005) see the combination of these as the development of an educator disposition that is increasingly able to perform with flexibility and intentionality within a particular context. As Katz (1995) states, "dispositions comprise habits of mind rather than mindless habits" (p. 90).

Dispositions connect values and other kinds of inner commitments with actions. They function as a process that connects valuing with strategies, or an established instructor practice, directed with intentionality toward deliberate outcomes (Centra, 1993). Dispositions for ambitious teaching become a reliable pattern and character of a particular educator's practice with the development of a professional identity that grows out of acting strategically, achieving desired outcomes, and recognizing oneself as a person capable of doing so (Carroll, 2012). Gutiérrez (2003) suggests that it is the contexts of engagement and experience that influence practitioners' proclivities, meaning the context of experience in interaction and activities needs to be the focus, thus calling our attention to the contextual differences of a virtual learning environment. Ritchhart (2001) also suggests that dispositions are situation specific, meaning the shift in the medium of instruction to virtual learning environments necessitates that new instructional dynamics, demands in communication, and social competencies are expected of virtual educators (Comeaux & McKenna-Byington, 2003).

Personality Types

Personality research is useful in identifying more stable characteristics that people bring to a given environment. For example, personality may affect an instructor's willingness to embrace technology in the learning environment (Chambers, Hardy, Smith, & Sienty, 2003). Personality may also be related to a person's willingness to adapt to the diffusion of innovations (Gilbert, 1995), or their inclination to become online educators (Fuller, Norby, Pearce & Strand, 2000). For the purpose of developing an online dispositions framework, we adopted the Five Factor Model personality inventory (also known as the "Big 5" or "OCEAN") as a basis for exploring personality traits. The Five Factor Model represents an "organizing scheme" for understanding teaching dispositions—personality trait relations. With regard to the latter point, the Five Factor Model of personality traits of Openness, Conscientiousness, Extraversion, Agreeableness, and Emotional Stability (the inverse of the trait of Neuroticism) is a widely used, parsimonious model of normal personality that has been utilized across many settings (De Raad, 2000; Digman, 1997), with supporting studies across many personal characteristics and demographics (Costa & McCrae, 1994), including learning dispositions like self-direction (Kirwan, Lounsbury, & Gibson, 2010).

A fair amount of empirical research has been conducted on the relationships between personality and student satisfaction and performance in online learning, but fewer empirical studies exist that explore the relationships between personality and various measurements regarding online educators (Bolliger & Erichsen, 2013). Research on student perceptions and experience may contribute to our understanding of the relationship between an educator's personality type and their instructional environment.

Researchers suggest that individual personality differences are important in how students perceive their distance learning experiences, making it plausible that personality also plays an important role in understanding distance educators' practice. Moehl (2011) recently explored the relationship between personality type (MBTI) and instructional perspectives of higher education faculty. Moehl's (2011) findings suggest that not only are there significant relationships between personality types and instructional perspectives and practices, but that similar instruments can be useful for the development of faculty in providing tools that aid educators in reflective practice and help them "achieve a more holistic approach to selecting and designing teaching strategies that accentuate their personal strengths, introduce variety in lesson planning, and incorporate activities that maximize student learning and understanding" (p. 5).

ONLINE INSTRUCTOR PRESENCE

It is necessary to know what dimensions of online educational practice are important in developing quality online learning. "To develop quality online teachers, we need to understand what makes online educators not only effective but also exemplary and to consider changes face-to-face teachers need to make in order to succeed in the online milieu" (Edwards, Perry, & Janzen, 2011, p. 102). The roles for online educators identified in the literature include pedagogue, facilitator, instructional designer, social organizer, manager, and ICT troubleshooter (Baran, Correia, & Thompson, 2011). A number of similar online teacher roles can be discerned from online distance and continuing education research including professional, pedagogical, social, evaluator, administrator, technologist, advisor/counselor, and researcher (Anderson, Rourke, Garrison, & Archer, 2001; Bawane & Spector, 2009; Berge, 2009; Coppola, Hiltz, & Rotter, 2002; Gousch, Alvarez, & Espasa, 2010; Goodyear, Salmon, Spector, Steeples, & Tickner, 2001; Salmon, 2004; Smith, 2005; Williams, 2003). One of the most influential ideas in both online as well as adult education literature is that of establishing learning communities (Shapiro & Lavine, 1999; Wang, Sierra, & Folger, 2003), which comprises of similar roles and educator responsibilities. Bawane and Spector (2009) assert that virtual educators are required to possess a diverse set of competencies and the ability to apply them in shifting contexts.

Effective Instruction for Adult Learners in Virtual Higher Education

Appel (2006) purports that online learning involves features of teaching, learning, and communication that are fundamentally different than in conventional learning environments. Similar to Knowles' (1970) principles on the differences that adult learners bring to their environment, it is suggested here that virtually mediated learning also differs from our traditional conceptions of adult learning based on our face-to-face learning experiences (Huang, 2002; Mason, 2007). Regarding the expanded use of ICTs as a primary medium for education, Bonk, Kirkley, Hara, and Dennen (2001) note, "these events are changing the fabric of higher education. One important piece of the fabric is the instructor. What is the role of the online instructor?" (p. 2). As adult and continuing educators who increasingly work in these shifting environments, we must also ask ourselves what dispositions and professional identities shall we cultivate as adult and continuing educators? While online learning offers flexibility and many rewards for both learners and instructors, Rose (2012) emphasizes that "it takes a special set of skills and attitudes to excel at it" (p. 28). But what entails quality virtual instruction?

Bangert (2006) suggests we look back to Chickering and Gameson's (1991) classic theoretical model for effective postsecondary instruction. Chickering and Gameson argue that student success is related to instruction that encourages student-faculty contact, cooperation among students, active learning, prompt feedback, time on task, high expectations, and respect for diverse ways of learning.

Feldman (2007) revisited the idea of utilizing student ratings to identify dimensions of exemplary postsecondary teaching and found the following (in descending order as correlated with student achievement):

- Teacher's preparation
- Clarity and understandableness
- Perceived outcome or impact of instruction
- Teacher's stimulation of interest in the course and subject matter
- Teacher's encouragement of questions and openness to opinions of others
- Teacher's availability and helpfulness
- Teacher's elocutionary skills
- Clarity of course objectives and requirements
- Teacher's knowledge of the subject
- Teacher's sensitivity to, and concern with, class level and progress
- Teacher's enthusiasm (for subject and for teaching)
- Teacher's fairness, impartiality of evaluation of students, quality of examinations
- Intellectual challenge and encouragement of independent thought
- Teacher's concern and respect for students, friendliness of the teacher
- Nature, quality, and frequency of feedback from the teacher to students

While these components seem broadly relevant to postsecondary instruction, Relan and Gilliani (1997) claim that virtual and blended learning are distinct and dependent on different conditions than conventional instruction. McCombs and Vakili (2005) identify four factors that contribute to effective online instruction: (1) student–instructor interaction; (2) student-centered learning environment; (3) time-on-task; and (4) quality of interactive learning activities. King and Biro (2006) offer six principles in planning online and virtual programming, including "being formative, cyclical, visionary, scalable, sustainable, and supportive of lifelong learning" (p. 177).

Chua and Lam (2007) emphasize pedagogical interaction, personalization, pluralism of learning methods, and monitoring and feedback. Kyong-Jee and Bonk's (2006) work concludes that teaching strategies, course design, and online teaching skills are all important for the quality of online education. And echoing these, Pelz (2004) found that educators who become exemplary online teachers tend to create carefully designed online courses that promote cognitive, social, and teacher presence, not dissimilar to Cranton's (2004) notion of authenticity in teaching. Thus, yoking online and adult education literature, we have adopted these three components of virtual instruction—cognitive, instructor, and social *presence*—to serve as the primary categories for organizing the key instructor qualities for virtual instructor dispositions.

Instructor Presence

While the term disposition is not common in the field of online learning, the concept of online *presence* is, which parallels the idea that particular competencies, attitudes, and habits of practice contribute to higher quality leaning experiences. Rourke, Anderson, Garrison, and Archer (2001) defined *presence* as a person's ability to project themselves socially and affectively into a learning environment. The notion of social presence is related to the concept of teacher *immediacy*, described as an educator's communication behaviors that reduce social and psychological distance between teachers and learners (Andersen, 1979; Mehrabian, 1971). This idea was extended in relation to technology mediated communication, and social presence was then understood to be the "felt presence" of the other person in technology-mediated communication, and the resulting "felt presence" of their interpersonal interactions. Anderson et al. (2001) define teaching presence as "the design, facilitation, and direct instruction of cognitive and social processes for the purpose of realizing personally meaningful and educationally worthwhile learning outcomes" (p. 5). Three main threads can be identified regarding the roles and effective habits of practice in the online environment: *cognitive presence, pedagogical presence*, and *social presence* are the critical dimensions that contribute to effective virtual learning environments.

Presence as Virtual Dispositions

Teaching presence refers to "designing and managing learning sequences, providing subject matter expertise, and facilitating active learning"

(Rourke et al., 2001, para. 2). Coppola et al. (2002) reiterate the importance of the cognitive, managerial, and affective roles of a virtual educator, focusing on their unique roles. We adopted the commonly referenced Community of Inquiry model (COI) (Archer, Garrison, Anderson, & Rourke, 2001) as a framework of three overlapping circles that represent content expertise (cognitive), instructor presence (pedagogical), and social presence, which together form the virtual educational experience.

While the purpose of the COI model originally pertained to developing community in online learning environments, the three dimensions of presence are particularly useful in helping identify the kinds of interactive behaviors and educator dispositions that have been described as contributing to quality virtual learning experiences. Notably, when looking back at the instructional characteristics suggested for exemplary conventional postsecondary teaching, adult education components for teaching authenticity, as well as the factors identified by several studies for effective online learning, these three categories (See Figure 27.1) provide a useful framework in conceptualizing what might be considered to be a desirable online teaching disposition.

In order to clarify what we understand to be part of a virtual instructor's disposition, we define *cognitive presence* as 'ideas,' or the interactive behaviors that contribute to active learning, provide content matter, offer explanation/clarification, and build ideas, and understanding. We define *instructor presence* as the interactive behaviors that enhance instructional design, organization, management, effective communication and feedback, and facilitation of active learning. *Social presence* is defined as the interactive behaviors that reduce perceived social distance between the instructor and learners, and between learners, and enhance social cohesion in the learning environment. And while an educator's inclination to work with technology is an important contextual factor, many studies and instruments already exist to assess online educator's levels of comfort and competencies in working with ICTs.

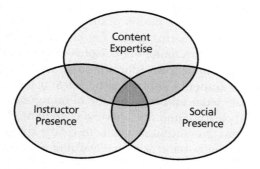

Figure 27.1   COI model as an online educator disposition framework.

The scope of this conceptual framework, then, is focused on examining these three primary domains of presence required of virtual educators.

It is through social interaction within the learning environment (Vygotsky, 1978) that an individual's personality, beliefs, and common behaviors are expressed within the context of online instruction, meaning greater attention must be paid to the specific development of interactive behaviors within a virtual learning community. Identifying and examining interactive behaviors as indicators of each form of presence in the online learning environment may help researchers and practitioners improve strategies in facilitating deeper and more meaningful adult learning experiences.

Altogether, the conceptual framework for virtual instructor dispositions includes the three areas that make up a disposition—personality, beliefs about instruction, and behavioral patterns—which are taken into consideration within the three areas of virtual presence—subject expertise and knowledge (cognitive), instructor (pedagogical), and social interaction. The three tables below provide an overview for each of the three domains that make up the virtual dispositions framework we are presenting. In each table are some descriptive actions for each of the components of the respective form of online presence. We also included some basic example questions that could be used to start developing a self-assessment that educators could use to reflect on their personal practice. Following the tables for each of the forms of presence, we provide an example application of the framework and how it could potentially be used to guide professional development for virtual educators.

Cognitive Presence

Literature and scholarship in online instruction strongly emphasize course management (the pedagogical dimensions) as well as social presence, with a common oversight of subject area expertise and the cognitive dimension, which is often treated as a given. However, several of the items developed in Feldman's (2007) research on the qualities exhibited by exemplary teachers pertain to the notion of subject area expertise, indicating the domain of cognitive presence should not be overlooked.

Within this domain, we examine the personal characteristics and interactive behaviors that contribute to an educator's ability to clearly communicate and demonstrate the content within the given learning context. Here, an educator's content knowledge and expertise are of importance, as well as their ability to select and clearly communicate subject content. Within the virtual learning environment, an educator's ability to clearly communicate in written form is incredibly important, as virtual learning tends to be heavily text-driven. Young (2006) states, "effective communication is one of the most important elements of a successful online course . . . Effective instructors model good communication skills and, following their example, students learn to do the same" (p. 73). Clear communication and elaboration of content is essential. Table 27.1 outlines aspects of personality, beliefs about instruction, and behavioral patterns that comprise the domain of cognitive presence.

TABLE 27.1 Cognitive Presence: Content Expertise and Intellect

	Descriptions	Example Questions
Personality Traits	Openness to Experience/Intellect	– Do you enjoy collecting new information for your class? – Do you get excited to learn something new?
Cognitive Roles	• Selecting appropriate content • Demonstrating expertise and depth of knowledge • Modeling scholarly habits and communication • Communicating comfortably and confidently in writing • Reinforcing concepts, ideas, content • Offering cognitive reciprocity • Anchoring learning strategies in experience • Developing/performing summative and formative assessment	– Do you set high standards for your students? – Do you know how to get things done?
Patterns of Instructor Behavior	• Writing clearly and using accurate language conventions • Regularly offering explanations/ elaborations, clarification, and disambiguating content • Providing accurate information & adequate scholarly references and resources • Founding comments/ arguments/ positions in evidence/literature/ experience • Paraphrasing literature and others to help learners construct personal meaning • Providing additional material, examples, and evidence related to content • Relating content to real world experience • Synthesizing and summarizing information for learners • Building on and extending ideas in discussion	– Do you enjoy reading new literature in your field? – Do you like to think of new ways to present ideas?

Instructor Presence

The roles of online educators are often described as pedagogical, facilitator, instructional designer, social, managerial, and technical. Instructional design is particularly important in virtual education, which is concerned with planning, organizing, and structuring the elements of a virtual learning environment (Anderson et al., 2001). Teaching competencies (Goodyear et al., 2001), communication competencies (Williams, 2003), and course management competencies (Berge, 2009; Coppola et al., 2002; Guasch et al., 2010) all weigh in as essential skillsets for virtual instruction.

Research has found that teaching presence is a significant predictor of students' perceptions of learning, satisfaction, and sense of community (Baran, Correia, & Thompson, 2011). In a study that examined more than 1,200 student evaluations of online courses along with surveys of the instructors, Spangle, Hodne, and Schierling (2002) found that a pedagogy including well developed written communication skills, the careful design of learning activities that promote discussion, as well as prompt feedback were important contributing factors to a successful virtual learning experience. The roles of virtual educators—instructional design and content organization, facilitating discourse and learner interaction, and direct instruction including clarification, disambiguation, and instructor feedback—are all crucial in developing the interactions that are critical for online learning. In addition to cognitive presence, a virtual educator must develop and effectively project their instructor presence into the online learning environment. Table 27.2 illustrates elements of personality, beliefs about instruction, and behavioral patterns that comprise the domain of instructor presence.

Social Presence

A fair amount of literature exists covering the importance of social presence in online learning. "The social role is one of most emphasized roles and it refers to teachers' functions related to building and improving student-teacher relationships in a virtual learning environment" (Baran, Correia, & Thompson, 2011, p. 429). Leners and Sitzman (2006) emphasize the affective qualities required within the domain of social presence. In this domain, we examine an educator's social tendencies, interpersonal competencies, emotional intelligence, their ability to personalize and establish a "safe" learning environment, and their ability to relate to the learners (see Table 27.3). Knowles, Holton, and Swanson (2012) emphasize the notion of understanding how the adult learner comes to the learning environment with individual competencies, preferences, and experiences, and how an instructor must be able to recognize and support these differences. This

TABLE 27.2 Instructor Presence: Facilitation and Responsiveness

	Descriptions	Example Questions
Personality Traits	Conscientiousness Work Drive	– Are you a detail oriented person? – Do you finish things despite obstacles in the way?
Instructor Roles	• Providing leadership • Designing learning environment • Providing for course structure • Organizing content and information • Scaffolding learning content • Managing course and learning activities • Facilitating active learning • Sustaining interaction and timely communication • Providing quality feedback • Instigating, supporting, and sustaining critical thinking • Offering review and providing recursive learning strategies • Offering appealing, engaging, and rewarding opportunities for individual and group interactions	– Do you closely follow your course plan? – Are you well-prepared for class?
Patterns of Instructor Behavior	• Providing prompt and detailed feedback • Continuing and responding to threads • Promptly responding to questions • Answering emails and questions in a timely fashion • Responding to learner posts • Providing rejoinders and prompts to further discussion • Posing new questions for discussion • Challenging positions and drawing out explanations • Giving directions and providing suggestions • Requesting clarification and further elaboration from students • Providing for student-student interaction	– Do you complete tasks successfully? – Do you excel as an instructor?

can be particularly important when working with adult learners in an online environment, where typical face-to-face interaction is not present. Wlod-kowski (2008) also describes the core characteristics of expertise, empathy, enthusiasm, clarity, and cultural responsiveness required for creating a safe

TABLE 27.3 Social Presence: Immediacy and Interpersonal Cohesion

	Descriptions	Example Questions
Personality Traits	Agreeableness Extraversion	– Do you believe your students have good intentions? – Are you comfortable communicating with students?
Social Roles	• Projecting oneself socially • Projecting oneself affectively • Inviting participation and conversation • Building trust • Constructively resolving conflicts • Maintaining contact and communication • Expressing appreciation • Encouraging learners and participation • Affirming individual and group identities • Building and sustaining relationships • Attending to learners' current needs • Sharing feelings and mood, as well as respecting those of others • Reducing felt social distance	– Do you get along well with people you have just met? – Do you understand why people do what they do?
Patterns of Instructor Behavior	• Offering self-disclosure and sharing personal experiences • Communicating care, concern, and interest in individuals • Respecting the wide variety of experience, learning, and ways of knowing • Welcoming many forms of participation • Using inclusive pronouns and language • Offering complements and encouragement to learners • Acknowledging each individual participant • Offering affirmation to individuals • Communicating in a cordial and professional manner • Welcoming diverse ideas, cultures, identities and styles of learning	– Do you know what to do to help students feel welcome? – Do you like to think of new ways to present ideas?

and motivating learning environment that supports critical consciousness. We believe our proposed model not only adequately takes these described characteristics and behaviors of an effective adult educator into account, but also provides a framework that can support and guide personal awareness and professional development for adult educators.

The model of virtual educator dispositions we are presenting here provides for a more systematic means of connecting individual traits, personal values, and other kinds of inner commitments with patterned actions within the virtual learning environment. We did not list behavior-anchored indices for each of the domains of presence, but observations of behavioral, communication, and social interaction patterns can also provide insight into an educator's strengths and weaknesses. Identifying online educator dispositions helps us connect personal characteristics and valuing with educators' habits of mind and practice, as well as instructional strategies.

In self-identifying predispositions and tendencies, online educators can claim and maintain ownership and agency in their professional development pursuits, exercising personal intentionality toward improved practice. Aspiring online educators can leverage the dispositions model to develop more effective patterns and interactive behaviors in their practice and to recognize one's potentials and limitations. Such self-assessment contributes to more purposeful and reflective educator practices in the online environment and to the growth of their professional identity.

AN EXAMPLE APPLICATION

As we have been developing this framework, we found ourselves asking the question, as online educators, how could we gather information about our own personalities and preferences to improve our practice. How could such a tool for self-assessment and reflective practice be used to improve our skills as online educators? We believe understanding our preferences and areas of strength in the virtual classroom are very helpful in identifying areas for individual professional development, as well as continuous course and program improvement. In Figure 27.2, we provide a snapshot of what part of an online dispositions feedback report might look like.

In identifying one's personal inclinations, predispositions toward certain behaviors, as well as strengths and weaknesses in the classroom, and receiving some recommendations for professional development and improvement, virtual instructors in adult, continuing, and higher education may be able to purposefully select and reflect on areas for improvement and seek out appropriate professional development training.

PREFERENCE FOR STABILITY	◆				PREFERENCE FOR CHANGE
You value familiarity, predictability, and precedent and find comfort in stability, routine, and tradition. New tasks and new learning may be uninteresting or demanding for you.					You value new learning, change, and innovation and find motivation in novelty, variety, and possibilities for improvement. New tasks and new learning are stimulating and attractive to you.

Your scores indicate a strong preference for stability in the classroom. You are comfortable with your methods of instruction, routine, and format of your courses. You are more interested in continuing to utilize successful teaching strategies, rather than finding new technologies and methods.

Strengths

- You value stability and will help sustain continuity in your courses.

- With your interest in predictability, you like to establish a set routine in the classroom and try to make sure that there are no sudden changes or surprises.

- You are inclined to become proficient with certain content and to develop your specialized expertise. You would rather be a master of one trade than a jack-of-all-trades.

Weaknesses

- You tend to be uncomfortable with too much change and innovation in the classroom; you are likely to have difficulty adjusting to abrupt shifts in direction, modifications in procedures, and changes in priorities in your instructor role.

- Your preference for stability may put you at risk becoming too specialized in your skills, knowledge, and content, which can limit your adaptation of new materials and methods of instruction.

- You may be seen by some people you work with as being stuck in a rut and set in your ways. It may be difficult for you to hear new ideas and embrace innovation initiatives in the classroom.

Areas for Development

- Consider whether you are growing professionally and developing any new skills or abilities. When was the last time you signed up for a seminar, course, training program, or workshop to learn something new?

- When you have to be involved in change in the classroom, try to familiarize yourself with as many of the new elements as soon as possible. You may want to ask peers how they are coping with change.

Figure 27.2 Personality report example (derived from Lounsbury, Gibson, & Sundstrom, 2000).

In the example in Figure 27.2, we look briefly at the personality dimension of Openness to New Ideas, which has been identified as a predictor to other traits such as learner self-directedness (Kirwan et al., 2010; Oliveira & Simões, 2006), and Intellect (Nusbaum & Silvia, 2011) in adult students. Within this dimension, educators vary in their preferences for stability and continuity or their preferences for novelty and change. Having an inclination in one direction or another may have a strong impact on how the educator performs within a virtual learning environment. This predisposition could lead a person to create very structured courses with routine and predictability built in, or to create a course that integrates a wide variety of new ideas, techniques, technologies, and so forth. Literature on effective online learning suggests that both stability and innovation are important to virtual learning, but the extreme in either direction could also lead to barriers and obstacles that may be worth examining. Figure 27.2 illustrates what this feedback could look like for an instructor for one personality trait. Sample survey items could be developed for this personality dimension where educators would respond using a Lickert-like scale to items such as:

- I enjoy integrating new technologies into my classes.
- I am excited when learning something new.
- I like to develop new courses.
- I enjoy reading new literature in my field.

In identifying our tendencies as individuals, we may also be more capable of identifying areas that we can address as online educators. For example, if I love to throw new ideas, technology, and approaches into my online course, but I do not provide for an element of structure or predictability, I may be confusing the learners. On the contrary, if my courses are too rigid and do not provide for novelty and innovation, I may unintentionally be stifling the learning potential for diverse ideas, means, and individuals. Knowing more about our tendencies as educators can help us build more intentionality into our everyday instructional practice and developing more sustainable learning environments for a broader audience.

SUMMARY

At a time when virtually mediated instruction has become a staple within adult, continuing, and higher education, it has become an educational imperative that we take a closer look at the traits, characteristics, and habits of practice that help build efficacious adult learning environments. A key, and often overlooked, element of this is the dispositions that educators bring to virtually mediated education. If a distinct and effective practice for virtually mediated education is to emerge, the roles, characteristics and dispositions of educators in the virtual learning environment need to be explored in more depth. Therefore, the development of new self-assessment tools may provide educators with formative feedback they can use to improve their performance as educators and to establish an effective repertoire of practice.

A model for virtual educator dispositions provides a useful framework for research and practice in the area of online and virtual instruction by establishing defined categories of interactive instructional behaviors and exemplar dispositions that can be examined in more depth. Such a framework also provides a foundation for developing tools to help educators become empowered as autonomous and self-directed professionals who actively and consistently engage in reflective practice and work toward effective instructional strategies that are congruent with virtually mediated learning environments.

Such a framework may also contribute to improving decision-making processes related to virtual instruction, promoting action research, creating quality measures, assisting course and professional development, designing instructor training, and fostering communities of learning. All of these avenues potentially contribute to the sustainability of adult, continuing and higher education—we need new models for educators that fit our current learning ecologies.

REFERENCES

Andersen, J. (1979). Teacher immediacy as a predictor of teaching effectiveness. In D. Nimmo (Ed.), *Communication yearbook 3* (pp. 543–559). New Brunswick, NJ: Transaction Books.

Anderson, T. (2004). Towards a theory of online learning. In T. Anderson & F. Elloumi (Eds.), *Theory and practice of online learning*. Athabasca, AB Canada: Athabasca University.

Anderson, T., Rourke, L., Garrison, D., & Archer, W. (2001). Assessing teaching presence in a computer conferencing context. *Journal of Asynchronous Learning Networks, 5*(2), 1–17. Retrieved from http://sloanconsortium.org/publications/jaln_main

Appel, J. (2006, September 29). New standards aid in virtual instruction. *eSchool News Online*. Retrieved from http://www.flvs.net/areas/aboutus/NewsArchives/Documents/Headlines/2006/ESN.Oct%2006.pdf

Archer, W., Garrison, D., Anderson, T., & Rourke, L. (2001). A framework for analyzing critical thinking in computer conferences. Paper presented at EURO-CSCL 2001, Maastricht. Retrieved from http://www.communitiesofinquiry.com

Bangert, A. (2006). The development of an instrument for assessing online teaching effectiveness. *Journal of Educational Computing Research, 35*(3) 227–244.

Baran, E., Correia, A., & Thompson, A. (2011). Transforming online teaching practice: Critical analysis of the literature on the roles and competencies of online teachers. *Distance Education, 32*(3), 421–439.

Bastiaens, T. J., & Martens, R. L. (2000). Conditions for web-based learning with real events. In B. Abbey (Ed.), *Instructional and cognitive impacts of Web-based education* (pp. 1–31). Hershey, PA: Idea Group Publishing.

Bawane, J., & Spector, J. (2009). Prioritization of online instructor roles: Implications for competency-based teacher education programs. *Distance Education, 30*(3), 383–397. doi: 10.1080/01587910903236536

Belanger, F., & Jordan, D. H. (2000). *Evaluation and implementation of distance learning: Technologies, tools and techniques*. Hershey, PA: Idea Publishing Group.

Berge, Z. L. (Ed.). (2001). *Sustaining distance training: Integrating learning technologies into the fabric of the enterprise*. San Francisco, CA: Jossey-Bass.

Berge, Z. (2009). Changing instructor's roles in virtual worlds. *Quarterly Review of Distance Education, 9*(4), 407–415. Retrieved from http://www.infoagepub.com/quarterly-reviewof-distance-education.html

Blondy, L. C. (2007). Evaluation and application of andragogical assumptions to the adult online learning environment. *Journal of Interactive, Online Learning, 6*(2), 116–130.

Blustain, H. (2006). Policy affecting distance education, program development, and delivery. In K. P. King & J. K. Griggs (Eds.), *Harnessing innovative technology in higher education* (pp. 29–46). Madison, WI: Atwood Publishing.

Blythe, T., & Associates. (1998). *The teaching for understanding guide.* San Francisco, CA: Jossey-Bass.

Bolliger, D. U., & Erichsen, E. A. (2013). Student satisfaction with blended and online courses based on personality type. *Canadian Journal of Learning and Technology, 39*(1). Retrieved from http://cjlt.csj.ualberta.ca/index.php/cjlt

Bonk, C. J., Kirkley, J., Hara, N., & Dennen, V. (2001). Finding the instructor in post-secondary online learning: Pedagogical, social, managerial and technological locations. In J. Stephenson (Ed.), *Teaching and learning online: Pedagogies for new technologies* (pp. 76–97). London, England: Kogan Page.

Brookfield, S. (1995). *Becoming a critically reflective teacher.* San Francisco, CA: Jossey-Bass.

Carroll, D. (2012). Examining the development of dispositions for ambitious teaching: One teacher candidate's journey. *The New Educator, 8*(1), 38–64.

Cercone, K. (2008). Characteristics of adult learners with implications for online learning design. *AACE Journal, 16*(2), 137–159.

Centra, J. A. (1993). *Reflective faculty evaluation: Enhancing teaching and determining faculty effectiveness.* The Jossey-Bass Higher and Adult Education Series. San Francisco, CA: Jossey-Bass.

Chambers, S., Hardy, J., Smith, J., & Sienty, S. (2003). Personality indicators and emergency permit teachers' willingness to embrace technology. *Journal of Instructional Psychology, 30*(3), 184–188.

Chickering, A. W., & Gameson, Z. F. (1991). Seven principles for good practice in undergraduate education. *New Directions for Teaching and Learning, 47*, 63.

Chua, A., & Lam, W. (2007). Quality assurance in online education: The universitas 21 global approach. *British Journal of Educational Technology, 38*(1), 133–152. doi:10.1111/j.1467–8535.2006.00652.x

Clarke, A. (2002). *Online learning and social exclusion.* Leicester, United Kingdom: National Institute of Adult Continuing Education.

Comeaux, P., & McKenna-Byington, E. (2003). Computer mediated communication in online and conventional classrooms: Some implications for instructional design and professional development programmes. *Innovations in Education and Teaching International, 40*(4), 348–355.

Coppola, N., Hiltz, S., & Rotter, N. (2002). Becoming a virtual professor: Pedagogical roles and asynchronous learning networks. *Journal of Management Information Systems, 18*(4), 169–189. Retrieved from http://www.jmis-web.org/top-page/index.html

Costa, P., & McCrae, R. (1994). Stability and change in personality from adolescence through adulthood. In C. F. Halverson, G. A. Kohnstamm, & R. P. Martin (Eds.), *The developing structure of temperament and personality from infancy to adulthood* (pp. 139–155). Hillsdale, NJ: Erlbaum.

Cranton, P. (2004). Perspectives on authenticity in teaching. *Adult Education Quarterly, 55*(1), 5–22.

Cranton, P., & King, K. P. (2003). Transformative learning as a professional development goal. *New Perspectives on Designing and Implementing Professional Development for Teachers of Adults, 98,* 31–38.

Cox, E. (2005). Adult learners learning from experience: Using a reflective practice model to support work-based learning. *Reflective Practice: International and Interdisciplinary, 6*(4), 459–472.

Curran, C. (2008). Online learning and the university. In W. J. Bramble & S. Panda (Eds.), *Economics of distance and online learning: Theory, practice, and research* (pp. 26–51). New York, NY: Routledge.

De Raad, B. (2000). *The big five personality factors (the psycholexical approach to personality).* Seattle, WA: Hogrefe & Huber.

Digman, J. (1997). Higher-order factors of the big five. *Journal of Personality and Social Psychology, 73,* 1246–1256.

Dirkx, J. M. (1998). Transformative learning theory in the practice of adult education: An overview. *PAACE Journal of Lifelong Learning, 7,* 1–14.

Donavant, B. W. (2009). The new, modern practice of adult education: Online instruction in a continuing professional education setting. *Adult Education Quarterly, 59*(3), 227–245.

Edwards, M., Perry, B., & Janzen, K. (May 2011). The making of an exemplary online educator. *Distance Education, 32*(1), 101–118.

Ennis, R. (1987). A taxonomy of critical thinking dispositions and abilities. In J. Baron, & R. Sternberg (Eds.), *Teaching thinking skills: Theory and practice* (pp. 9–26). New York, NY: W. H. Freeman and Company.

Erichsen, E. A., & Bolliger, D. U. (2011). Towards understanding isolation of international students in traditional and online learning environments. *Educational Technology Research and Development, 59,* 309–326. doi: 10.1177/2158244011403804

Feldman, K. A. (2007). Identifying exemplary teachers and teaching: Evidence from student ratings. In R. P. Perry & J. C. Smart (Eds.), *The scholarship of teaching and learning in higher education: An evidence-based perspective* (pp. 93–143). New York, NY: Springer.

Ferraro, J. M. (2000). *Reflective practice and professional development.* Washington, DC: ERIC Clearinghouse on Teaching and Teacher Education. Retrieved from http://www.ericfacility.net/ericdigests/ed449120.html

Ferry, N. M., & Ross-Gordon, J. (1998). An inquiry into Schön's epistemology of practice: Exploring links between experience and reflective practice. *Adult Education Quarterly, 48*(2), 98–112.

Frey, B. A., & Alman, S.W. (2003). Applying adult learning theory to the online classroom. *New Horizons in Adult Education and Human Resource Development, 17,* 4–12.

Fuller, D., Norby, R. F., Pearce, K., & Strand, S. (2000). Internet teaching by style: Profiling the on-line professor. *Educational technology & Society, 3*(2), 1–23.

Gausch, T., Alvarez, I., & Espasa, A. (2010). University teacher competencies in a virtual teaching/learning environment: Analysis of a teacher training experience. *Teaching and Teacher Education, 26*(2), 199–206. doi: 10.1016/j. tate.2009.02.018

Gibson, C. C. (2006). Increasing equity: Seeking mainstream advantages for all. In K. P. King & J. K. Griggs (Eds.), *Harnessing innovative technology in higher education* (pp. 133–150). Madison, WI: Atwood Publishing.

Gilbert, S. (1995, March). An "online" experience. *Change Proquest*, 28–46.

Goodyear, P., Salmon, G., Spector, J., Steeples, C., & Tickner, S. (2001). Competences for online teaching: A special report. *Educational Technology Research and Development, 49*(1), 65–72. doi: 10.1007/BF02504508

Gutiérrez, K. D. (2003). Cultural ways of learning: Individual traits or repertoires of practice. *Educational Researcher, 32*(5), 19–25.

Hardy, D. W. (2006). No time to spare: Technology assisted professional development. In K. P. King & J. K. Griggs (Eds.), *Harnessing innovative technology in higher education* (pp. 151–168). Madison, WI: Atwood Publishing.

Heimlich, J. E., & Norland, E. (1994). *Developing teaching style in adult education.* The Jossey-Bass Higher Education Series. San Francisco, CA: Jossey-Bass.

Huang, H. (2002). Toward constructivism for adult learners in online learning environments. *British Journal of Educational Technology, 33*(1), 27–37.

Katz, L. G. (1993). Dispositions: Definitions and implications for early childhood practices. *Perspectives from ERIC/ECCE: a monograph series* (Urbana, IL, ERIC Clearinghouse on ECCE).

Katz, L. G. (1995). *Talks with teachers of young children: A collection.* Norwood, NJ: Ablex.

King, K. P., & Biro, S. C. (2006). Conclusion. In K. P. King & J. K. Griggs (Eds.), *Harnessing innovative technology in higher education* (pp. 169–182). Madison, WI: Atwood Publishing.

King, K. P., & Griggs, J. K. (2006). *Harnessing innovative technology in higher education.* Madison, WI: Attwood Press.

Kirwan, J. R., Lounsbury, J., & Gibson, L. (2010). Self-directed learning and personality: The big five and narrow personality traits in relation to learner self-direction. *International Journal of Self-Directed Learning, 7*(2), 21–34.

Knowles, M. (1970). *The modern practice of adult education: From pedagogy to andragogy.* Englewood Cliffs, NJ: Cambridge.

Knowles, M. S., Holton, E. F., & Swanson, R. A. (2012). *The adult learner.* Routledge.

Kyong-Jee, K., & Bonk, C. J. (2006, November 22–30). The future of online teaching and learning in higher education: The survey says …. *Educause Quarterly, 28*(4), 23–30. Retrieved from http://www.educause.edu/eq

Leners, D. W., & Sitzman, K. (2006). Graduate student perceptions: Feeling the passion of caring online. *Nursing Education Perspectives, 27*(6), 315–319.

Lau, L. (Ed.). (2000). *Distance learning technologies: Issues, trends, and opportunities.* Hershey, PA: Idea Group Publishing.

Lounsbury, J., Gibson, L., & Sundstrom, E. (2000). *eCollege sample report.* Resources Associates: Knoxville, TN.

Marienau, C. (1999). Self-assessment at work: Outcomes of adult learners' reflections on practice. *Adult Education Quarterly, 49*(3), 135–146.

Mason, R. (2007). Learning technologies for adult continuing education. *Studies in Continuing Education, 28*(2), 121–133.

McCombs, B. L., & Vakili, D. (2005). A learner-centered framework for e-learning. *Teachers College Record, 107*(8), 1582–1600.

Mehrabian, A. (1971). *Silent messages.* Belmont, CA: Wadsworth Publishing Company.

Merriam, S. B. (2002). Andragogy and self-directed learning: Pillars of adult learning theory. *New Directions for Adult and Continuing Education. Special Issue: The New Update on Adult Learning Theory, 89*, 3–14.

Meyer, K. A. (2002). Quality in distance education: Focus on on-line learning. ASHE-ERIC Higher Education Report. *Jossey-Bass Higher and Adult Education Series, 29*(4). San Francisco, CA: Jossey-Bass.

Mezirow, J. (1985). Concept and action. *Adult Education Quarterly, 35*(3), 142–151.

Moehl, P. J. (2011). *Exploring the relationship between Myers-Briggs type and instructional perspectives among college faculty across academic disciplines.* Proceedings of the Midwest Research-to-Practice Conference (MWR2P) in Adult, Continuing, Community and Extension Education, Lindenwood University, St. Charles, MO.

Nicol, D. J., & Macfarlane-Dick, D. (2006). Formative assessment and self-regulated learning: A model and seven principles for good feedback practice. *Studies in Higher Education, 31*(2), 199–218.

Nusbaum, E. C., & Silvia, P. J. (2011). Are openness and intellect distinct aspects of openness to experience? A test of the O/I model. *Personality and Individual Differences, 51*(5), 571–574.

Oliveira, A. L., & Simões, A. (2006). Impact of socio-demographic and psychological variables on the self-directedness of higher education students. *International Journal of Self-Directed Learning, 3*(1), 1–12. Retrieved from http://www.sdlglobal.com

Pelz, B. (2004). Three principles of effective online pedagogy. *Journal of the Asynchronous Learning Network, 8*(3), 33–46. Retrieved from http://sloanconsortium.org/publications/ jaln_main

Relan, A., & Gillani, B. B. (1997) Web-based instruction and the traditional classroom: similarities and differences. In B. H. Khan (Ed.), *Web-based Instruction* (pp. 41–46). Englewood Cliffs, NJ: Educational Technology Publications.

Ritchhart, R. (2001). From IQ to IC: A dispositional view of intelligence. *Roeper Review, 23*(3), 143–50.

Rose, R. (2012, June/July). What it takes to teach online. *Distance Learning*, 28–30.

Rourke, L., Anderson, T., Garrison, D. R., & Archer, W. (2001). Assessing social presence in asynchronous text-based computer conferencing. *Journal of Distance Education, 14*(2), 50–71.

Russel, G. (2005). The distancing question in online education. *Innovate.* Retrieved from http://www.innovateonline.info/index.php?view=article&id=13

Salmon, G. (2004). *E-moderating: The key to teaching and learning online.* London, England: Routledge Falmer

Schussler, D., Stooksberry, L., & Bercaw, L. (2005, April). *Conceptualizing dispositions: Intellectual, cultural, and moral domains of teaching.* Paper presented at the American Educational Research Association Annual Conference, Montreal, Canada.

Shapiro, N., & Levine, J. (1999). *Creating learning communities: A practical guide to winning support, organizing for change, and implementing programs.* San Francisco: Jossey-Bass Publishers.

Smith, T. (2005). Fifty-one competencies for online instruction. *The Journal of Educators Online, 2*(2), 1–18. Retrieved from http://www.thejeo.com

Spangle, M., Hodne, G., & Schierling, D. (2002). Approaching value-centered education through the eyes of an electronic generation: Strategies for distance learning. *Paper presented at the Annual Meeting of the National Communication Association,* New Orleans, LA. ERIC, ED 474581.

Vygotsky, L. S. (1978). *Mind in society: The development of higher mental processes.* Cambridge, MA: Harvard University Press.

Wang, M., Sierra, C., & Folger, T. (2003). Building a dynamic online learning community among adult learners. *Educational Media International, 40*(1–2), 49–62.

Williams, P. (2003). Roles and competencies for distance education programs in higher education institutions. *American Journal of Distance Education, 17*(1), 45–57. doi: 10.1207/ S15389286AJDE1701_4

Wlodkowski, R. J. (2008). *Enhancing adult motivation; A comprehensive guide for teaching all adults.* San Francisco, CA: John Wiley & Sons.

Young, S. (2006). Student views of effective online teaching in higher education. *American Journal of Distance Education, 2*(2), 65–77.

PART II

SUPPORTING ADULT LEARNING IN ORGANIZATIONS, INSTITUTIONS, AND COMMUNITIES:

Exploring Local and Global Partnerships to Sustain Adult Learning

CHAPTER 28

CREATING STRONG PARTNERSHIPS THROUGH COMMUNITY COALITIONS

Clint E. Cummings and Karen Franck
University of Tennessee Extension

This chapter focuses on characteristics of effective coalitions as identified by coalition members with the goal of providing recommendations for community leaders who are interested in developing and sustaining their own community groups. The study described herein was conducted specifically to identify effective practices to assist county Family and Consumer Sciences (FCS) Extension agents with Cooperative Extension who are implementing a nutrition education program for low-income audiences. Cooperative Extension was established by the Smith-Lever Act of 1914 and is regarded as the largest adult education institution in America (Griffith, 1991). Cooperative Extension has a history of building partnerships to improve individuals, families, and communities and is often the lead organization on community coalitions for a variety of issues. An important aspect of the program described in this chapter is that counties participating in this nutrition education federal grant are required to have active coalition involvement. Important aspects of developing and maintaining an active and

Building Sustainable Futures for Adult Learners, pages 585–597
Copyright © 2015 by Information Age Publishing

effective coalition from the viewpoint of coalition members are identified. These factors are translated into recommendations and guidelines that can be used by any agency or organization that is interested in forming an effective community coalition.

The connection to adult learning focuses on three different groups: Extension educators, community partners and volunteers, and adult program participants. FCS Extension agents are professional educators who have at least a bachelor's degree when hired, and concepts related to effective coalitions are being shared for their professional growth and development. This occurs at regional staff development trainings and one-on-one meetings. As their practice is informed, influenced, and improved by what they learn, Extension agents are better equipped to provide leadership for coalitions consisting of community partners and volunteers. It then serves to inform their practice as a group as coalitions plan and implement nutrition education activities for the target audience. Program participants are the ultimate beneficiaries when coalitions are active and effective. By understanding the characteristics of effective coalitions, Extension agents and coalitions are better able to carry out the mission of the program so that participants are more likely to make positive lifestyle changes.

A coalition is an alliance of people and organizations that come together to work jointly toward a specific goal that they would not be able to reach alone (Butterfoss, 2007). Coalitions are commonly used by groups and organizations to address issues or problems in the community such as environmental or public health concerns (Kegler, Steckler, McLeroy, & Malek, 1998; Lodl & Stevens, 1999; Roussos & Fawcett, 2000; Tavernier & Hartley, 1995; Wells, Ford, McClure, Holt, & Ward, 2007; Zakocs & Guckenburg, 2007). Reviews of the literature show numerous approaches to defining characteristics and strategies of effective coalitions (Butterfoss, Goodman, & Wandersman, 1993; Foster-Fishman, Berkowitz, Lounsbury, Jacobson, & Allen, 2001; Zakocs & Edwards, 2006). While coalitions are a popular means to address specific community needs and achieve positive outcomes, their effectiveness can be difficult to define and measure (Kegler et al., 1998; Roussos & Fawcett, 2000; Wells et al., 2007). In their review, Zakocs and Edwards (2006) found a great deal of variety across studies about how factors of coalition building and functioning were defined and how effectiveness was measured. Part of the complication with measuring coalition effectiveness is that assessment can occur at different levels, including how the coalition itself functions and operates, the effectiveness of actual programs and interventions carried out by the coalition, and change in the community based on coalition efforts (Butterfoss & Francisco, 2004). Success at one level does not necessarily translate to success at another level. As Kegler et al. pointed out, "it is possible that coalition members can be satisfied and actively involved but not accomplishing much that will lead to improved... outcomes" (1998, p. 350).

Due to the complexity of factors involved in designing, implementing, sustaining, and evaluating coalition efforts, there is no single best approach that will work for all groups. There are practices, however, which have shown to be promising and could be encouraged and replicated across a variety of coalitions. Through their literature review, Zakocs and Edwards (2006) identified six coalition building factors that appear to enhance coalition effectiveness: formal governance procedures, strong leadership, active participation from members, diverse memberships, collaboration among member agencies, and group cohesion. In addition, Foster-Fishman et al. (2001) suggested that collaborative capacity can be developed through "enhancing community member competencies, building new relationships, strengthening intracoalition operations, and promoting the design and implementation of effective community-based programs" (p. 257). Kegler et al. (1998) suggested that good communication, a sense of belonging, a task orientation at meetings, and the identification and nurturing of capable leaders were factors related to coalition effectiveness. Other studies included skill building for coordinators and ongoing training (Butterfoss, 2004; Kegler, Norton, & Aronson, 2007).

As part of Extension programming in Tennessee, county FCS Extension agents who receive funding to conduct nutrition education for low-income audiences are required to create and maintain effective coalitions. Activities are planned and conducted by local coalitions made up of partners from a variety of organizations, as well as community volunteers. Coalition members contribute to the program in several ways. They assist with the local needs assessment to help prioritize efforts and identify other opportunities to reach eligible participants. They also give general guidance to nutrition education activities. An important function of coalition members is to provide access to eligible audiences through their agency, organization, or community group. They utilize curricula and materials to reach eligible audiences and, ultimately, help plan and implement nutrition education activities in the county. The reach and effectiveness of the program is largely attributable to coalition efforts. Despite the advantages of having a coalition, these groups can sometimes be challenging to establish and maintain. It can be difficult to attract and engage members and to sustain the coalition over time. Furthermore, like any group, coalitions go through transitional periods in which experienced members leave and new members join, forcing the group to restructure. In summary, the focus of this study was to help inform best practices related to working with community coalitions.

METHOD

For this project qualitative and quantitative methods were used to collect data from coalition members to provide information about how coalitions were functioning from their unique perspective. Prior to collecting any data, all procedures were approved by the Institutional Review Board at the University of Tennessee. Using active adult coalition members, focus groups were conducted first and then an online survey was completed.

Focus Groups

Two focus groups were conducted with a total of 18 members from two active coalitions. The two counties were selected to participate based on the first author's assessment that the coalitions were working effectively. The author defined effective coalitions as meeting all of the following criteria: regular meetings were being held (at least bimonthly), coalition projects were being planned and implemented on a regular basis with participation from several members, and a sufficient number of volunteer hours were documented. For the program described here, each county is given a target number of volunteer hours that they need to document to show program impact.

To be included, focus group participants had to meet all of the following criteria: 18 years of age or older, active coalition member, English speaker. To recruit participants, the FCS Extension agent provided the authors with a list of coalition members. The FCS Extension agent e-mailed invitations to their coalition members explaining the purpose of the project to identify the characteristics of an effective coalition. Potential participants were given a scheduled meeting date, time, and place and were asked to contact the FCS Extension agent if they would be available and interested in participating in the study. The FCS Extension agent forwarded contact information for coalition members who agreed to participate in the focus groups to the first author. The first author e-mailed a follow-up letter to everyone who agreed to participate. This letter explained that the focus groups would be audiotaped, all information would be confidential, and that their feedback would help "strengthen ... coalitions across the state and will result in a stronger program."

The two focus groups were held in their respective county Extension offices during afternoon hours. The county FCS Extension agent did not attend the meeting so members could speak freely. Each group lasted between 1 to 1.5 hours and a light snack was provided. Each participant received a small gift for participating that was valued under $4.00. All participants read and signed an informed consent at the start of the group.

The first author facilitated both groups. Participants were asked to respond to an initial opening question: "Tell us about some successful projects you have planned as a group in the last few years. What do you think made those projects successful?" Participants were prompted to describe the planning process for this project including how the group worked together as a team and how the group was organized (e.g., was one person in charge, how did group members decide what and when to do things.)

After this opening discussion, participants were asked a series of questions and prompts that were developed by the authors based on themes identified by a previous survey with FCS county Extension agents regarding coalitions. Questions centered on three main areas: how the coalition operates, the purpose of the group, and the perceived value. Regarding how the coalition operates, prompts focused on how the coalition functions including how often meetings were held and who lead the groups. For coalition purpose, prompts included defining the purpose of the overall program and the purpose of the coalition. Prompts related to value included reasons for participating in the coalition and how individuals and agencies benefit from coalition participation. Participants were also asked to talk about any experiences that they had with groups and other coalitions that did not function well. They were asked to describe characteristics of those groups and the group leadership. They were also asked to describe barriers that they faced that inhibited their ability to work on coalitions.

Most of the focus group participants were women and the majority were white (12 White females, 4 African American females, 1 African American male, 1 White male). The groups were audiotaped, and the second author took notes during the focus groups. The audiotapes were transcribed. The second author analyzed the transcripts by coding data related to major trends and themes. The focus presented here was on common or similar ideas expressed across groups and participants related to having strong coalitions (Krueger, 1994).

Online Surveys

As a follow-up to the focus group findings, an anonymous online survey was conducted with a sample of coalition members from across the state. County FCS Extension agents are required to enter active coalition members in an online database each year. Selected members who had a valid e-mail address were included in the sample. To ensure feedback from counties across the state, potential participants were selected based on regional location. In this state, Extension offices are split into three regions. Because of the nature of this grant, counties in these regions have varying degrees of funding and coalition involvement. Efforts were made to recruit coalition members from each of the regions to ensure representation from areas with high coalition involvement to lower coalition involvement. Ten counties from each region were selected for participation for a total of 30 counties. For each county, two to five coalition members were identified to receive the online survey for a total of 104 potential participants. All potential participants were e-mailed an invitation to participate in the survey with information about the project and informing them that their feedback would be anonymous. Participants received a link to the survey. The survey was constructed using Survey Monkey. Participants provided informed consent when they completed the survey. Out of the original 104 potential participants, 11 e-mail addresses were not valid reducing the sample size to 93. Thirty-seven complete surveys were received out of 93 for a response rate of 39.8%.

Participants completed 10 questions related to the organization, purpose, and value of the coalition. These questions were based on a 10 point Likert scale with 1 being the lowest to 10 being the highest rating. In addition, four open-ended questions were asked to collect members' comments about their perception of the coalition. SPSS 20.0 was used to calculate descriptive statistics including central tendency and measures of dispersion (Fink, 2003).

RESULTS

Focus Groups

Five major ideas emerged as important themes for having and maintaining a strong and effective community coalition based on coalition members' statements: unity, connection, action, equality, and organization. These five themes are described in detail below. When using actual quotes from participants pseudonyms were used to protect confidentiality.

Unity
Members described the importance of being interested and concerned about addressing the same social issue—in this case, helping low-income individuals and families. Sue stated: "I think our common goal is that we are all working for the same population . . . We all have that common need and passion for what we do" (personal communication, April 12, 2011). Julie stated that, in order for coalitions to be successful and to work together well, "you have to bring people to the table with the same common goals and purpose" (personal communication, April 12, 2011). Several members also talked about the importance of community to group members sharing comments like "we are truly concerned about what happens in the community," "our community is important to us," and "we are very involved in community affairs" (personal communication, April 12, 2011).

Connection

A related characteristic to sharing a common goal was the ability of group members to use meetings and activities to form connections with people from other agencies; this included being able to support each other as well as network with others in the community. As Elaine put it, "If we were out there swimming upstream by ourselves, I think we would have all drowned by now... It is comforting that we have this whole group of people who are working together for this common goal" (personal communication, April 12, 2011). Joe said, "We're all together helping people and it's nice to know we're not in this by ourselves" (personal communication, April 12, 2011). Several members described the group as a support system.

Action

Several members commented on the importance of the group actively working together to address community needs. As Helen explained, "if it was just sitting here talking about what we could do and who could help who and not doing anything that would really help then you would have lost me at the first meeting." Sue described the coalition as "a group of doers" (personal communication, April 12, 2011). Elaine stated, "if [we] see a need, [we] don't just sit around and talk about it, [we] get it done. I feel if we can't save the world, then we can try to work with that family" (personal communication, April 12, 2011). Members were able to see the value in what they do and in their contributions. They also expressed feelings that their time is well invested in projects and meetings because they were actively involved in getting things done.

Equality

Members also identified the importance of being valued as equals. Coalitions bring together a diverse group of people ranging from actual program participants to case managers to agency directors. Several members talked about how everyone was treated the same in the group and distinctions were not made based on status or job title. Julie stated, "we don't have big egos" (personal communication, April 12, 2011). Helen commented about feeling "respected as a member of the coalition" where "your opinion really does count" (personal communication, April 12, 2011).

In addition, members spoke about the importance of being appreciated and valued by the county FCS Extension agent. Rita explained, "she really makes you feel like she values what you're saying and what you do when you're doing a project" (personal communication, April 12, 2011). Several members mentioned the importance of being thanked by the agent for their service to the group.

Organization

Although group members talked about their appreciation for coalition meetings being less formal than other meetings they attended, they also recognized the importance of organization. In particular, they described the importance of the county FCS Extension agent's role in keeping the group connected and on-task through regular meetings as well as e-mail communication between meetings. They described the importance of regularly scheduled meetings with the possibility of some flexibility as needed. The county FCS Extension agents were important in this process and members recognized the agent as the key to the group's ability to function successfully.

Online Survey

Most respondents were positive about their involvement with the coalition and reported high levels of understanding about the purpose of the coalition, their role, and the county FCS Extension agent's role. Most also indicated that meetings are a good use of their time and that the coalition does a good job reaching those in need. Out of the 37 total survey respondents, 14 rated at least one question at or below the midpoint of the scale (5 or less out of a possible 10), indicating that they were less satisfied with how their county coalition was functioning. Respondents rated themselves the lowest for being involved in planning coalition activities (see Table 28.1).

The survey also included open-ended questions about the role of coalition members, the role of the Extension agent, and what could be done to improve their county coalition. Positive responses to the open-ended

TABLE 28.1   Mean Scores of Coalition Members' Responses to Online Survey

Survey Question	Mean Score	Standard Deviation
I understand the purpose of the program.	8.89	1.75
The role of the Extension agent is clear.	8.78	2.13
The purpose of the coalition is clearly defined.	8.58	2.23
Coalition meetings are well-led.	8.44	2.51
The coalition does a good job reaching those in need.	8.42	2.77
My role as a coalition member is clear.	8.42	2.42
Coalition meetings are a good use of my time.	8.23	2.58
I am satisfied with the way the coalition functions.	8.17	2.87
I help carry out [program] activities.	7.81	2.99
I help plan [program] activities.	6.92	3.32

questions reflected some of the major themes identified in the focus groups including statements about how coalitions provide an opportunity for strong partnerships, collaborations, and networking. Comments also included the importance of coalitions for providing opportunities to learn about other activities in the community.

Other responses to the open-ended questions diverged from focus group comments in that they described what was not working as well. Several respondents reported not being involved in the coalition or not feeling that their opinion and input was valued. For example, John stated, "I was asked to make recommendations on topics for this fiscal year. I did and never heard anything else."

Several members felt that more meetings would be helpful and that recruiting more members and increasing the scope of the membership would be important steps to strengthen their coalition. Ann stated, "we need to get more people involved around the county." Heidi called for "more active members." Finally, Robert reported that there needed to be more involvement because "it is usually the same small group doing all the work."

DISCUSSION

The findings discussed here align with factors that have been identified as important for a successful coalition, including a common mission, commitment to the cause, effective leadership, specific goals and objectives, action plans, and an effective use of resources that maximizes services while minimizing duplication of efforts (Lodl & Stevens, 2002; Radhakrishna & Snider, 1995). A formalized structure with written agreements, agendas, and minutes has been seen in more active coalitions (Jackson & Clark, 1996). Since coalitions by definition involve people working together effectively, interpersonal skills are important as well (Conone & Smith, 1997).

Commitment to a common cause was evident in participant comments. Leadership by the FCS Extension agent was valued, as was the ability to collaborate and maximize resources. Though not specifically asked about, developing agendas and writing minutes were regular practices that helped formalize and organize the meetings. To the extent that these things were happening, members viewed the coalitions positively. When these things were not happening, members reported less satisfaction.

By their very nature, coalitions are centered around a common purpose (Lodl & Stevens, 1999). The purpose of the coalitions described here is to provide nutrition education to eligible low-income audiences. Members most often come from agencies and organizations that also provide programming to this audience so their participation is mutually beneficial. What became clear in the focus groups, however, was that members participated not only because it helped them carry out their job responsibilities but because they were personally invested in helping others. They believed in the mission of the work they were performing and found a great deal of personal satisfaction from being part of the coalition. These members have a passion for the cause and are actively involved in the betterment of their communities through helping people take control of their own lives. These traits are common to community-based adult learning programs (Merriam, Caffarella, & Baumgartner, 2007).

While active involvement was identified as an important factor for members participating in the focus groups, survey respondents were less likely to report that they were planning and carrying out coalition activities. In fact, they disagreed with these two statements more than any other. This suggests a discrepancy between what is found to be an important characteristic of an effective coalition and many respondents' experience in practice.

Another important factor of an effective coalition identified in the focus groups was a sense of value and equality. Members have different roles at their agencies, and some are volunteers from the community. Some of the community volunteers were program participants receiving nutrition education for low-income populations. There is the potential for a power differential amongst members from the group as some are in positions that may be perceived to be of higher status than others. This was not found in the focus group interviews. Members recognized the sense of equality they felt as part of the group and felt they were valued by the Extension agent.

The value of connection should not be underestimated. In both the focus groups and surveys, members identified the value of networking as an important benefit for participating in the coalition. When asked what they gained from participating in the coalition, survey respondents indicated partnerships, collaboration, and networking more than any other factor.

PRACTICAL IMPLICATIONS

For groups who are interested in forming and maintaining an effective coalition, several recommendations are key. *First, coalitions should be focused on a common cause in keeping with its purposes and goals.* Coalitions should have a clearly identified issue and need to determine their purpose and how they will address this issue. For example, the coalitions discussed here actively worked together to identify community projects that they could implement related to nutrition education. Other types of coalitions might be centered around advocacy efforts or media campaigns and would need members with skills related to those types of efforts in order to be successful. For any type of coalition, it is likely that members would come from a number of different organizations and have a variety of job responsibilities so their frame of reference could be broader than the issues that the coalition is designed to address. Leaders may need to focus the group on what can and cannot be conducted through a particular program or funding stream. As an important next step, members should cultivate their individual and collective commitment to the common cause that they are addressing as a group.

Second, all coalition members should be viewed equally—as active participants with an important role in the process, and it is important for both leaders and coalition members to have this orientation. Leaders who understand this will address and engage members in such a way as to invite their involvement in planning and conducting activities. Leaders should be aware of perceived power differences and demonstrate that ideas from all members are valuable. All members should be appreciated and recognized for their contribution. Members who understand their role to be actively engaged are more likely to have the mindset that they should be involved in planning and implementing activities. Meetings in which everyone plays an active role are more likely to result in purposeful activity than those in which the leader simply reports what activities have been conducted by the lead agency since the last meeting.

Third, meetings need to be managed to encourage participation and engagement. Coalitions are designed to come together regularly to address a problem. To facilitate the process and keep members informed and involved, meetings should be held on a regular basis. Frequency of meetings depends on a variety of factors and a balance needs to be achieved so that members' time is put to good use. At a minimum, coalitions should plan to meet at least four times per year. Fewer meetings than this, limits the potential for ongoing momentum and the group serves in more of an advisory capacity. For active coalitions expected to result in impact, monthly or bimonthly meetings are recommended. Also, communication about and between meetings is key. Meetings should be well-planned and organized, but there should also be enough flexibility to accommodate a dynamic group.

Finally, ample opportunity for networking should be provided before, during, and after the meetings. Coalition members have a number of different responsibilities that may go beyond the scope of the coalition. By facilitating networking time before and after the meeting, leaders are able to focus on the mission of the coalition as discussed above while providing an opportunity for members to connect and discuss other topics. Meeting time and location should be chosen to facilitate networking, and these factors will vary depending on the needs and constraints of the local coalition.

As an implication for adult educators, the principles described in this chapter can be used in staff development activities to equip practitioners with the knowledge and skills necessary to be successful in their coalition development efforts. Messages should be routine and consistent, and general concepts shared in large group settings on a regular basis help to provide background information. To be most effective, individualized guidance should be offered through one on one discussions and site visits to help practitioners think about how to apply the concepts in the context of the local coalition. The information can also be used to train coalition members, either by the coalition leader or through more formalized group training.

CONCLUSION

Coalitions provide an opportunity to address community problems in a systematic way by bringing together the people and organizations with the knowledge and skills to address them. Problems do not exist in isolation, and it is rare that one organization can address and mitigate an ongoing problem on its own. Despite the common use of coalitions, their effectiveness should not be taken for granted. Attention must be given to practices that make success more likely. Some of these practices have been highlighted throughout the chapter, and the characteristics of successful coalitions that were described and discussed are largely in line with what others have found. The information presented in this chapter can be used to help local coalition leaders and members maximize their effectiveness.

REFERENCES

Butterfoss, F. D. (2004). The coalition technical assistance and training framework: Helping community coalitions help themselves. *Health Promotion Practice, 5*(2), 118–126. doi: 10.1177/1524839903257262

Butterfoss, F. D. (2007). *Coalitions and partnerships in community health.* San Francisco, CA: Jossey-Bass.

Butterfoss, F. D., & Francisco, V. T. (2004). Evaluating community partnerships and coalitions with practitioners in mind. *Health Promotion Practice, 5*(2), 108–114. doi: 10.1177/1524839903260844

Butterfoss, F. D., Goodman, R. M., & Wandersman, A. (1993). Community coalitions for prevention and health promotion. *Health Education Research, 8*(3), 315–330.

Conone, R. M., & Smith, P. L. (1997). Coalition intelligence. *Journal of Extension* [Online], *35*(3) Article 3TOT2. Retrieved from http://www.joe.org/joe/1997june/tt2.php

Fink, A. (2003). *How to manage, analyze, and interpret survey data.* Thousand Oaks, CA: Sage.

Foster-Fishman, P. G., Berkowitz, S. L., Lounsbury, D. W., Jacobson, S., & Allen, N. A. (2001). Building collaborative capacity in community coalitions: A review and integrative framework. *American Journal of Community Psychology, 29*(2), 241–261.

Griffith, W. S. (1991). The impact of intellectual leadership. In J. M. Peters & P. Jarvis (Eds.), *Adult education: Evolution and achievements in a developing field of study* (pp. 97–120). San Francisco, CA: Jossey–Bass.

Jackson, D. G., & Clark, R. W. (1996). Predictors of effectiveness of collaborative relationships of the USDA Youth at Risk Coalitions. *Journal of Extension* [Online], *34*(6) Article 6RIB3. Retrieved from http://www.joe.org/joe/1996december/rb3.php

Kegler, M. C, Norton, B. L., & Aronson, R. (2007). Skill improvement among coalition members in the California healthy cities and communities program. *Health Education Research, 22*(3), 450–457. doi: 10. 1093/her/cyl 109

Kegler, M. C., Steckler, A., McLeroy, K., & Malek, S. H. (1998). Factors that contribute to effective community health promotion coalitions: A study of 10 project ASSIST coalitions in North Carolina. *Health Education & Behavior, 25*(3), 338–353. doi: 10.1177/109019819802500308

Krueger, R. A. (1994). *Focus groups: A practical guide for applied research.* Thousand Oaks, CA: Sage.

Lodl, K. A., & Stevens, G. L. (1999). Community coalitions: Identifying changes in coalition members as a result of training. *Journal of Extension* [Online], *37*(2) Article 2RIB2. Retrieved from http://www.joe.org/joe/1999april/rb2.php

Lodl, K. A., & Stevens, G. L. (2002). Coalition sustainability: Long-term successes and lessons learned. *Journal of Extension* [Online], *40*(1) Article 1FEA2. Retrieved from http://www.joe.org/joe/2002february/a2.php

Merriam, S. B., Caffarella, R. S., & Baumgartner, L. M. (2007). *Learning in adulthood* (3rd ed.). San Francisco, CA: Jossey-Bass.

Radhakrishna, R. B., & Snider, A. B. (1995). Community coalition for tobacco-free youth: Results of a needs assessment. *Journal of Extension* [Online], *33*(2) Article 2RIB2. Retrieved from http://www.joe.org/joe/1995april/rb2.php

Roussos, S. T., & Fawcett, S. B. (2000). A review of collaborative partnerships as a strategy for improving community health. *Annual Review of Public Health, 21*, 369–402.

Tavernier, E. M., & Hartley, M. P. (1995). A model for coalition building in urbanized areas. *Journal of Extension* [Online], *33*(5) Article 5FEA2. Retrieved from http://www.joe.org/joe/1995october/a2.php

Wells, R., Ford, E. W., McClure, J. A., Holt, M. L., & Ward, A. (2007). Community-based coalition's capacity for sustainable action: The role of relationships. *Health Education & Behavior, 34*(1), 124–139. doi: 10.1177/1090198105277851

Zakocs, R. C., & Edwards, E. M. (2006). What explains community coalition effectiveness? A review of the literature. *American Journal of Preventive Medicine, 30*(4), 351–361. doi:10.1016/j.amepre.2005.12.004

Zakocs, R. C., & Guckenburg, S. (2007). What coalition factors foster community capacity? Lessons learned from the fighting back initiative. *Health Education & Behavior, 34*(2), 354–375. doi: 10.1177/1090198106288492

CHAPTER 29

THE DEVELOPMENT OF APPALACHIAN ADULT LEARNERS UNDER GLOBALIZATION

A Transformative Perspective

Fujuan Tan, Lee Nabb, and Robert Sammons
Morehead State University

INTRODUCTION

Appalachian culture has historically been one of seclusion and homogeneity (Anglin, 2004; Bauer & Growick, 2003; Massey, 2007). These characteristics have influenced the development of this culture as well as how it is perceived from inside and out (Ellis, 2013; Keefe, 2000). Notwithstanding a history of isolated development, Appalachia, like most, if not all, other cultures in the world, is now arguably, unavoidably exposed to influences of diversity and globalization. The third author being an Appalachian and a collective seven-year exposure of the first two authors to this culture, has prompted a probe into the impacts of these influences, as well as their

Building Sustainable Futures for Adult Learners, pages 599–617
Copyright © 2015 by Information Age Publishing
All rights of reproduction in any form reserved.

transformative affects, from an inside perspective. With data gathered from interviews with Appalachian graduate students, the following chapter provides a unique, inside perspective concerning the effects of diversity and globalization on Appalachian culture and concomitant transformation of its members.

APPALACHIAN CULTURE

Appalachian culture is unique. A combination of mountainous terrain and consequential self-sufficient communities kept the culture isolated and relatively homogenous for centuries (Anglin, 2004; Bauer & Growick, 2003; Massey, 2007; Matvey, 2005). As a term, Appalachia (or Appalachian) is difficult to define. Geographically, its borders have been redrawn numerous times since the seventeenth century. Currently, the Appalachian Regional Commission (ARC), a federal, state, and local governmental economic development agency, defines Appalachia as a 205,000 square mile region following the spine of the Appalachian Mountains. According to the ARC, Appalachia encompasses 420 counties in all of West Virginia, and parts of Alabama, Georgia, Kentucky, Maryland, North Carolina, South Carolina, Tennessee, Virginia, Ohio, Pennsylvania, New York, and Mississippi (inclusion of land in these latter two states is controversial). This patch of land extends over 1000 miles and contains over 25 million people, 42% of whom live in areas classified as rural compared to 20% of the U.S. population at large (The Appalachian Region, n.d.). According to Commission statistics from 2007 to 2011, 16.1% of the population lived in poverty during this time period, with 108 of the 420 counties averaging high poverty rates—1.5 times higher than the national poverty level (Appalachia's Economy, n.d.)—and 93 counties classified as "distressed," the worst designation in a four-category economic classification index (Appalachian Region, n.d.; County Economic Status and Distressed Areas in Appalachia, n.d.). This condition is an improvement from past decades. In 1965, Appalachian counties in distress numbered 223, with 295 averaging high poverty (The Appalachian Region, n.d.; Appalachia's Economy, n.d.). Mining, forestry, agriculture, chemical industries, and heavy industry have historically driven Appalachian economy, with manufacturing and service industries as recent additions, mostly in urban portions of the region (Hurst, 2006). According to the Appalachian Regional Commission, although the Appalachian region has made progress, it still lags behind the rest of the nation in economic vitality:

> Central Appalachia in particular still battles economic distress, with concentrated areas of high poverty, unemployment, poor health, and severe educa-

tional disparities. And recent economic data show that the Region has fared far worse in the current recession than the rest of the nation. (Appalachia's Economy, n.d., para. 2)

The most economically distressed area lies in the heart of Appalachia, mostly in Eastern Kentucky (County Economic Status in Appalachia, FY 2014, n.d.), where data for this study were gathered.

Demographically, Appalachia is 83.9% White, 9.1% Black, 4% Hispanic, and 1.5% Other, compared to the United States, which is 64.2% White, 12.2% Black, 16.1% Hispanic and 7.6% Other. The Appalachian region of Kentucky is even more homogenous than Appalachia as a whole breaking down as 95.5%, 1.8%, 1.2%, and 1.5%, respectively (Pollard & Jacobsen, 2013). As with any other people, the history that leads to the ethnic makeup of Appalachia is complex, but Scotch-Irish, German, and English settlers migrating to the region throughout the eighteenth century has given the region its predominantly White makeup (Fischer, 1989; Newhall, 2006; Rouse, 1992).

Geography, economics, and demographics aside, Appalachia as a culture is more nebulous and difficult to generalize. As Clark and Hayward (2013) state,

> Appalachia is both a real place to those who live there, and a sometimes-mythic land to outsiders. For inhabitants, what it means to live in Appalachia and how they identify themselves varies from person to person, just as what it means to be an American is a matter of individual experience. (pp. 1–2)

Notwithstanding, homogenous and secluded, Appalachian culture is often also characterized as self-sufficient and more collective in nature than those in the rest of the United States. Appalachians take pride in being independent and close knit with strong family values (Drake, 2001; Fischer, 1989; Hofstede, 2001; Tang & Russ, 2007). With these traits come a strong sense of commitment to extended family and a strong trust in, and willingness to help or receive help from, community members (Bauer & Growick, 2003).

These common characteristics may derive from a common stake in historical economic drivers such as agriculture, logging, and the coal industry. Although agriculture has been a continuing economic medium in Appalachia, the nature of the terrain has kept farm size small. Most farms are run by nuclear families (LaLone, 2008). Moreover, the land is not conducive to popular cash crops like cotton. Tobacco has long been a popular crop in Appalachia, but an increasingly difficult economic environment for family farms has decreased the number of such entities over several decades, and tobacco has become a controversial crop, adding to the challenges faced by the Appalachian farmers (Algeo, 1997). Similar to agriculture, logging was limited in Appalachia early on because of the difficult terrain. Later, logging would boom and then wane as advances in technology and increases in demand were followed by the development and implementation of environmental and sustainable resource policies (Paulson, 2006). The Appalachian coal industry was most prevalent in the late nineteenth and early twentieth century. Appalachia produced approximately 80% of the nation's coal by 1930 (Jackson, 2005). However, coal demand decreased in the following decades due to competition from cleaner burning fuels, regulations concerning high-sulfur coal, and attention to controversial, mountain top removal, mining practices (Abramson, 2006; Bingman, 2004; Smith, 2004). Challenges in the nature of these main industries have fostered a reliance on community, while governmental and corporate conflicts, mishaps, and misdealings have advanced a healthy distrust of outsiders (Drake, 2001).

The mix of geographical elements, and ethnic makeup has led to a certain uniqueness in the religion (McCauley, 1995), music (Olson. 2006), literature (Miller, Hatfield & Norman, 2005), and folklore (Richmond & Walkup, 2011; Rivers, 2012) of the Appalachian region, but of more pertinence for this chapter is education. As DeYoung and Herzog (2006) assert, "the scope of education in Appalachia is a broad as the region itself" (p. 1517). Notwithstanding, some common generalities are widely known and now accepted. Ethics and religious beliefs have been major forces in the development of education in the greater United States as well as Appalachia (DeYoung & Herzog, 2006; Teets, 2006). Two other major factors affecting education in Appalachia in particular were the notions of "place and community"—workable land and cooperative relationships with people (DeYoung & Herzog, 2006, p. 1518). Initial schools in Appalachia were attached to, or affiliated with, churches, with the teaching of morality in mind.

Throughout the nineteenth century, as government and other organized initiatives for education ensued, the latter two imperatives affected the type and quality of educational opportunities for children and adults. Elementary schools were small and local; attendance was relatively low and school terms relatively short as place and community took precedence over academics (McNeil, 1995; Teets, 2006). Organized education for adults and students of high school age concerned agriculture and associated topics. For instance, food preservation and nutrition were mainly taught to women (Lee. 2006).

The Appalachian population increased through the twentieth century, and larger scale agricultural operations began replacing the family farm. As a result, governments began consolidating schools, eliminating local one- and two-room schoolhouses in favor of larger schools in central locations to improve curricula and schools and use resources more efficiently. Consolidation conflicted with Appalachian values and exacerbated dissension with government in general. Adult education, remaining practical, shifted from agriculture to vocational education (Teets, 2006) such as ornamental horticulture, forestry, and natural resources (Lee, 2006). Appalachia obtained national attention in the 1960s for its impoverished conditions, including its below par educational systems, which prompted Appalachian leaders to become increasingly involved in education reform. As a result, although significant progress was made in improving education at all levels, Appalachian values have exacerbated advances in educational attainment (DeYoung & Herzog, 2006; Lee, 2006; Teets, 2006), creating apprehension among those, especially women, contemplating leaving their communities, even temporarily, to pursue advanced degrees (Miewald, 2006). In short, for Appalachia, rural, agrarian and religious values, distrust of government, and difficulty with government funding have kept the Appalachian population lagging behind the national norm regarding educational attainment. Although progress has been made in recent decades, the culture has difficulty seeing the practical value of education, and social pressure for more traditional uses of time and resources remains (DeYoung & Herzog, 2006; Shaw, DeYoung & Rademacher, 2004).

Perhaps the most popular and ready identifier of an Appalachian, at least one from the South is the dialect of English they speak. As Montgomery and Johnson (2007) explain,

> Appalachian English is a broad term for the social and geographic varieties found in a large mountain and valley region encompassing all or parts of eight southern states: West Virginia, eastern Kentucky and Tennessee, western Virginia, and North Carolina, northern Georgia and Alabama, and northwestern South Carolina. Historically and structurally it is closely related to Ozark English, and it shares many features with the English of the Lower South. (p. 42)

Isolation has caused the Appalachian dialect to develop slightly different variances to what is widely held as standard English in all respects. In contrast to modern standard English, Appalachian English has preserved "an unequaled record of usages common in colonial American English that have disappeared elsewhere" (Montgomery & Johnson, 2007, p. 43). However, like other dialects around the world, Appalachian English has developed characteristics all its own, making it a clear signal to Appalachians and non-Appalachians alike, to what culture its user belongs. Linguists and other social scientists understand that, regardless of the dialect or language, the users are simply effective communicators, using the tools they have mastered to function in society. In this respect, no language, dialect, or user is superior or inferior to another (Boonlong, 2007; Parker & Riley, 2010). Yet language does not operate in a vacuum. It is inextricably infused in aspects of life; it is social, economic, and political (Goshgarian, 2012; Parker & Riley, 2010). Although the dialect signifies a strong cultural identity and cohesion among its users, development of these aspects in relation to larger society through the years has caused the Appalachian dialect to be associated with unflattering misconceptions and stereotypes (Fedukov-ich, 2009; Hayward, 2013). The dialect has often been associated with lazy "hillbilly" pronunciations, low economic status, and unsophisticated, rural living. As such, its users have commonly fallen victim to various forms of discrimination from others (Ellis, 2013).

As one might gather from the discussion above, Appalachian culture is not always bound to geographic, economic, or political borders. People need not live in the region, be poor, or hold active affiliations to be considered Appalachian. Those raised, or who have family—extended or nuclear—within the culture, and who still hold those values, typically identify as Appalachians.

DEFINITIONS

To ensure a comfortable level of understanding, before moving to a discussion of research, the use of some terminology in this chapter should be clarified. *Diversity* and *globalization* have deservedly become popular terms in very recent decades. Increasing populations and advancing technology are causing the world to seem a smaller place and evoking interactions between different peoples like never before. Because the use—perhaps overuse—of these words in the various contemporary media forms can potentially cause confusion, a brief discussion of their definition and use here is warranted. In contrast, *transformation* has a specific meaning in the discipline of adult learning, as it will be used here, and thus requires brief discussion to ensure common understanding.

Diversity and Globalization

Diversity is perhaps a shortened version of cultural diversity. At least this chapter intends it so. Perusing the Internet, one can find myriad definitions for cultural diversity, or diversity hence forward, from myriad sources. Still other sources assume a common definition is understood, which may or may not be the case. No such assumption is made here. For purposes of this chapter, diversity simply means the existence of different cultures, ethnicities, or peoples. This treatment uses this simple, broad meaning and places no emphasis on the quality of such difference; neither does it imply what people do in the face of such difference, as related specifics are presented or discussed outright.

Likewise, this chapter uses globalization in its broadest sense. Thus, for immediate purposes, globalization means "worldwide integration and development" (Globalization, 2013). Arguably substantially influenced by economics (Globalization: A framework for IMF involvement, 2002), it is a human, social phenomenon that includes interplays, exchanges, interchanges and growing interdependence of all kinds, and occurs at various levels, local to inter and multinational. Perhaps noteworthy is the tension some see between the alleged movement toward a large monoculture and the healthy existence and celebration of various separate unique cultures.

Transformation

Transformation is used here in the sense coined by Jack Mezirow in the 1970s. It concerns transformative learning, which generally involves an experience not easily assimilated into the mental matrix (known as a dilemma in transformative theory), critical reflection on the experience and its effects, and the formulation of a new perspective, often called development (Mezirow, 1978, 1990, 1991). In short, "transformative theory is about change—dramatic, fundamental change in the way we see ourselves and the world in which we live" (Merriam & Caffarella, 1999, p. 319). Implicit within this definition description is an element of personal growth.

METHODOLOGY

The first two researchers have been collectively teaching in adult and higher education graduate programs at a regional university in eastern Kentucky for seven years—one researcher for five years, one for two. Having lived in Appalachia all his life, the third author is a bonafide member of the culture. Conversations between the three eventually lead to exposure and confirmation the mutual opinion that, among Appalachians, who comprise the majority of our student body, some kind of transformation must be occurring as a result of increasing diversity and impacts of globalization coming to the region. However, reviews of literature offered little information on this subject. Although a substantial literature base exists that describes the region and various aspects of Appalachian culture from an objective vantage, a sparsity exists in the exploration of how adult Appalachians see themselves, let alone how they might perceive the abovementioned transformation, assuming it is occurring. This sparsity and assumption spawned this research project. The researchers conducted the study with the following questions in mind: How do Appalachian adults view their culture and language? Have they been affected or transformed by diversity and globalization?

From the researchers' vantage, the desire to understand perspectives and experience combined with the aforementioned lack of available information called for a qualitative methodology (Bernard, 2000; Bogdan & Biklen,

2003). Furthermore, the focus of the targeted information, and the desire of "getting comparable across subject" (Bogdan & Biklen, 2003, p. 96), made the use of in-depth, or semi-structured interviews preferable (Bernard, 2000; Bogdan & Biklen, 2003; Lindlof & Taylor, 2002). The researchers wanted to get directly at the desired data without leading the interviewees, or inducing them to "tell us their experience in terms that they think we want to hear" (Lindlof & Taylor, 2002, p. 195). Given the access, and assuming such participants would have sufficient understanding and awareness of the transformation to be investigated, the targeted pool of potential interviewees was the adult and higher education student body at the researchers' university, a substantial portion of who were Appalachian. This pool of interviewees had the added benefit of the already-established rapport conducive to such interviews (Bernard, 2000; Bogdan & Biklen, 2003; Lindlof & Taylor, 2002) with the first two authors, who would conduct the interviews.

Under these conditions and criteria, the researchers developed the following six interview questions: (1) Why do you consider yourself Appalachian? (2) How do you view Appalachian culture and language and their relation to culture and language in the rest of the world? (3) Has your view (for Question 2) changed gradually or recently? If so, what has influenced this change? (4) How do you perceive cultural diversity in your area and its influence on your life? (5) Describe globalization in relation to you and your culture? (6) Do you have any other comments? These questions were reviewed by three peers and one former Appalachian graduate student, and modified accordingly, to ensure clarity and objectivity.

In the fall of 2013, the researchers used six online adult and higher education graduate courses—adult and higher education programs are online at this institution—to invite enrolled students who consider themselves Appalachian to participate in the study via separate interviews. 11 students—three males and eight females, with an average age of 44 years—volunteered and participated. Because of the same logistical issues that cause students in these programs to opt for online programs and courses, participants were given the option of answering interview questions face-to-face or by email. Four participants chose face-to-face interviews while seven chose to respond by email. Consent forms indicating the voluntary and confidential nature of participation were signed by face-to-face interviewees in person; email interviewees received the forms in Word documents, and returned electronic copies of the signed documents.

In the interest of gathering thoughtful, introspective, and thus, more detailed and valuable, responses, face-to-face participants were given the interview questions at least one week in advance of the interview, and email participants received the interview questions through their university accounts as attached word processing files and asked to respond within those files and send them back as attachments within two weeks to submit responses. Of course, face-to-face interviewees were given prompts and asked follow-up questions for clarification, and further probing (Bernard, 2000; Bogdan & Biklen, 2003) in a "minimal encouragement" fashion (Evans, Hearn, Uhlemann & Ivey, 2004, p. 44). Email interviewees were re-sent new word processing documents asking new questions, or to elaborate on, or explain particular previous responses, which were also included as quotations in the new document. Face-to-face interviews were recorded and transcribed, and email files containing responses were downloaded onto researcher computers for later coding and analysis. Emails were then deleted. Each of the two researchers coded and analyzed data gathered by the other, and then both researchers reviewed results.

For determining the scope and applicability of the research, that the 11 participants were graduate students solicited from, and with significant ties to, the Appalachian region in or around eastern Kentucky is worth reiterating. Perhaps also worth reiterating is that seven of the interviews were conducted via email instead of face-to-face. Although the researchers noticed no difference in the quality of that data gathered between the two types— email responses were shorter, but more concise—whether electronic interviews offer the same richness as face-to-face interviews is a question that is yet to be decisively answered (Fontana & Frey, 2005). Readers can weigh the benefits and liabilities of these and other previously discussed factors in deciding the particular value and relevance of the results.

RESULTS

With respect to the first question of why participants consider themselves Appalachian, all responded that they had been raised in the region. Most still live close to where they lived as children. Although two had since relocated to areas outside their original Appalachian communities (arguably they live in proximity to, if not still within, the region), they asserted a strong Appalachian identity, still having family in the area and adhering to the values they were taught. Emotional attachment was evident. Fondness for the environment, and the kindness, loyalty, and honesty of the people were commonly expressed notions in responses.

Culture and Language

Participants, described by pseudonyms, consistently answered the second question—how do you view Appalachian culture and language and their relation to culture and language in the rest of the world?—by way of contrast, taking care to describe Appalachian culture in detail, but perhaps assuming the culture(s) outside to be mostly understood. As one participant, Charles, asserted, "we are different to others, but so are others different to us" (personal communication, October 11, 2013). All responders were quick to point out what they considered the qualities of their culture, several likening people to a "big family" (Adam, personal communication, November 7, 2013; Ann, personal communication, October 8, 2013; Deloris, personal communication, October 9, 2013; Evelyn, personal communication, October 24, 2013) where loyalty, trust, mutual aid, and selflessness are uniquely strong. As another participant, Ann, explained, Appalachians are "friendly," and "genuinely seem to care for others" (personal communication, October 8, 2013). All expressed or directly mentioned a pride and satisfaction, even happiness, in being Appalachian. Most mentioned the characterization of a strong work ethic, or, as Feona described, a "mountain ethic...alive for generations" (personal communication, October 29, 2013). Gretta recounted her father as a coal miner going to work "even when he was sick" (personal communication, October 15, 2013). A minority of the respondents (two) expressed an importance of religion, crediting it as a factor in tying people closer together, associating their locale with the "bible belt" (Gretta, personal communication, October 15, 2013; Feona, personal communication, October 29, 2013).

Not all comments about culture were complementary. Three of the respondents pointed out some faults. Betty mentioned "superstition," and "closed-mindedness," as liabilities, creating barriers between Appalachians and non-Appalachians (personal communication, September 24, 2013). Brian and Deloris discussed the challenges of poverty. The condition, which was evident to them, leads to a "hopelessness" (Deloris, personal communication, October 9, 2013) that manifests in social ills like obesity and substance abuse (Brian, personal communication, November 12, 2013; Deloris, personal communication, October 9, 2013).

Notwithstanding, all were quick to defend the culture against the popular misconceptions and "bad publicity" (Adam, personal communication, November 7, 2013) they perceive it receiving. Evelyn, recounted situations in her work, where outside media people deliberately targeted, or requested, leads and exposure to situations and people representing stereotypically bad characteristics. Such media representatives were "put off" or "upset" when directed to people she saw as more representative of the current cultural situation (personal communication, October 24, 2013). Participants made clear that they did not perceive their culture to be inferior to others in any way; evident in responses was a desire for more respect.

Regarding language, only one, Feona, responded by characterizing the Appalachian dialect as "a little lazy" (personal communication, October 29, 2013). Recognizing the difference from "standard" English, the rest of the participants expressed healthy pride in the distinction, connecting the dialect with cultural roots and heritage. For them, their dialect preserves usages and accents of an older form of English. While other respondents alluded to this point, Brian was particularly adamant to point out that the dialect was equally unique, but not inferior to, other dialects, including "standard English." Moreover, use of the Appalachian dialect in no way indicates a lack of intelligence. In making his point, he recounted an experience in which he was advised by an instructor not to take a specific college course (not an English course), as his preferred dialect indicated an improbability of successful completion (personal communication, November 12, 2013). Adam identified the tension between standardizing the English and preserving uniqueness of the Appalachian dialect. Seeing each as a separate language, his solution was in becoming bilingual. "It's best to learn two Englishes," he said (personal communication, November 7, 2013).

Differences between the Appalachian and standard dialects are complex and extensive. As an example, Appalachian dialect uses "jine" or "join" to mean "join" in standard English; "holler" is used for hollow," "knowed" means "knew" and the prefix "a" is routinely attached to verbs (Montgomery & Johnson, 2007). So, the standard English sentence "I knew they were joining him in the hollow," would be stated something like "I knowed they was ajionin him in the holler" in the Appalachian dialect. For an Appalachian, knowing both ways to say it may be advantageous.

Question three, "has your view (for Question 2) changed gradually or recently?" elicited little initial and direct response. The reaction to this question came out indirectly in responses to subsequent questions, presumably as participants reflected upon it over more time. Responses to this question are therefore treated later in discussions of transformation. At this point, the discussion moves directly to perceptions of diversity.

Diversity

Responses to question four, "how do you perceive cultural diversity in your area and its influence on your life?" were uniform. All recognized the homogeneity of their part of the region, seeing only modest increases in diversity. Seeming to know a bit of the history of the region, Charles explained that his area was even more diverse in the mid-twentieth century as a "local boom" occurred, attracting workers from outside the region, presumably in the coal and logging industries. He also noted that people are now leaving the area to pursue employment opportunities elsewhere (personal communication, October 11, 2013). Betty perceived a relationship between the close-knit ties of the community and the lack of diversity, each aspect supporting the other, thereby hindering diversity growth (personal communication, September 24, 2013). Gretta attributed the continued lack of diversity in part to religion, stating, "Some cultures have a difficult time fitting in here because our area is part of the bible belt..." (personal communication, October 15, 2013).

Globalization

With respect to describing globalization in their area(s) (question 5 of the interview), all participants recognized its affects. According to Hallie, the effects are subtle. "It is almost like a whisper spoken into the wind. You can't see it or touch it, but once you think about what you encounter and do in your daily lives, it's not hard to realize some form of globalization is apparent" (personal communication, October 17, 2013).

Others expressed the necessity and benefit of globalization. As Ann explained, "globalization is becoming a must. For years we have remained in our comfort zone. We only knew coal mining and farming. As the economy changes, and industry evolves, we're going to have to reach out and bring new industries to our area" (personal communication, October 8, 2013). Betty elaborated these ideas. "We must think outside our inherited way of life. And bring about change if we're going to survive. I think we have the intelligence and integrity to grow in different directions without losing our cultural roots" (personal communication, September 24, 2013).

All comments concerning perceptions of globalization were not benign or positive. In her response to this topic, Evelyn recalled the construction of a prison in her area. She suggested that, although bringing some employment opportunities and "a new road" to the community, this development had mostly ill effects, compromising Appalachian values and disrupting local lives (personal communication, October 24, 2013). Evelyn and Cindy commented on the increased availability of "welfare" assistance and what they perceive as its resulting abuse. While Evelyn simply expressed a concern of how this more recent occurrence is affecting the region (personal communication, October 24, 2013), Cindy was more adamant: "I DO NOT like the disability mentality that has infested Appalachia in the last 15–20 years. This is different than the culture I am familiar with, which is an independent, as opposed to a dependent, way of living" (personal communication, October 7, 2013).

Transformation

To the researchers, transformation of the participants was evident. Several participants recounted the discomfort of transforming thought in their formative years as influences from outside the culture imposed new ideas upon them. Responses to globalization presented an overall perspective that the phenomenon is indeed occurring, and that it is forcing Appalachians to reevaluate their culture and its relationship to others. Apparent from the responses was that the main impetus behind transformative experience was education—formal and informal.

Culture

As one might imagine, transformation of cultural perspective can be complex, as the story of Adam demonstrates. As he explained, the proudness he now holds for his culture was not always present. "The media—T.V. and newspapers—described Appalachian people as stupid and backwards and everything . . . when you hear a lot of these publications, you can't avoid questioning about yourself and what you belong to . . ." (personal communication, November 7, 2013), not until later college experience did this perspective change.

> As I was exposed to diversity, several people at school who were from outside Appalachia thought my culture was pretty cool. . . . This made me think what was cool about it. After I thought about it for a period of time, I concluded that, yes, my culture is very cool. It has been a treasure to me. I should have cherished it from the beginning. (Adam, personal communication, November 7, 2013)

From this example, and the preceding discussion, one might see the progression of more than one level of transformation. To begin with a perspective of cultural normalcy, change to a perspective of cultural inferiority due to outside influence, and then graduate to a perspective of cultural comfort and pride, seems typical, at least for those Appalachians participating in higher education.

Language

The overall tenor of the responses provided a similar picture to the above description of culture regarding language. Several participants recalled the frustration of early education when they were initially, and then continuously, informed that the language they had learned from birth was "incorrect" (Adam, personal communication, November 7, 2013; Deloris, personal communication, October 9, 2013; Gretta, personal communication, October 15, 2013). Some still express feelings of animosity toward elementary teachers. This conflict and confusion contributed to a lack of motivation for learning. Positive transformation occurred later as higher education and travels provided healthy exposure to other ideas. They learned to see their dialect as unique rather than wrong, and then to appreciate the "beauty" of it. Feona expressed appreciation that the dialect was "a heritage handed down from generation to generation" (personal communication, October 29, 2013).

Betty stated, "I learned to see my language as unique rather than wrong" (personal communication, September 24, 2013).

Education

Underscored in this study is the importance of education in the positive transformation of Appalachians in particular, and any people in general. The discomfort and unpleasant experience of primary education these participants expressed could have been avoided. Today's Appalachian youth are hopefully enjoying the benefits of improved educational practices. However, perhaps a more important consideration here is the cultural attitude of Appalachians toward education. Participants attest it was not highly valued. As Brian explained,

> To my parents, feeding the cattle is by far more important than my school. As you can imagine, our whole family relies on the cattle to feed us and maintain a life. If I missed the school bus because I had to finish feeding the cattle, it was not a big deal. (personal communication, November 12, 2013)

In the context of familial support, Charles stated "it was rather traumatizing when I had to leave home and the whole family to go to school" (personal communication, October 11, 2013). Betty admitted, "the sense of duty to take care of family could easily make me give up the [educational] opportunity" (personal communication, September 24, 2013).

Remember that these participants are graduate students—people who have defied the pressure of traditional Appalachian values in order to pursue the education that has, according to their own accounts, afforded them the transformative experience leading to a healthy perception of their culture. Their portrayal is at once concerning and uplifting. Knowing that educational success is not at par with the national level raises the question of how current youth view other aspects of their culture, and, if necessary, how constructive transformative perspectives might occur for more people in this culture. Conversely, participants of this study highly value education, have observed an increase in this perspective in others within their culture, and are actively promoting such value in their families and in their communities, which is of considerable influence considering they all are, or plan to be, working in educational settings.

DISCUSSION

Appalachia has been identified as a region with distinct geographical features containing a people with distinct, if varied, cultural features. At least some of these features were instrumental in how the people developed in this area, which is unique compared to other inhabitants in the U.S. The literature is replete with accounts of the consequences and challenges such features have caused throughout the region's history. The literature also leaves unanswered the question of where Appalachia is heading in the face of two major forces affecting most, if not all of the rest of the world—globalization and diversity. This is a question the authors of this chapter have sought to illuminate.

As attested by the data, being Appalachian depends more on a state of mind than physical borders. It is an identity based on community values and culture. Participants in this study have come to appreciate their heritage and espouse the Appalachian way of life, acknowledging both its positive and negative effects. Participants noted Appalachians are caring people with a strong work ethic, challenged by closed-mindedness and possibly superstition, which may impede efforts to globalize and diversity the region, and may contribute to social ills like poverty and substance abuse that continue to affect the area. Likewise, participants expressed a healthy appreciation for the Appalachian dialect of English, while realizing the deleterious effects the unique but minority tongue has caused in the past, fostering and perpetuating mainstream ethnocentric perceptions of ineptness. Still, all participants recognized the effects of globalization, gradual in coming as they may be. Most seem willing to embrace globalization seeing the benefits it can provide; the caveat to manage it carefully to avoid consequences conflicting with Appalachian values, or wellbeing was both directly and indirectly expressed.

Transformation of the participants of the study was evident. Revelations and realizations concerning the perceptions and effects of culture and language—first adverse, and then empowering—were popular themes. Also salient was the essential role of education in the transformative experience. Recognizing the conflict between their traditional cultural values and the development of education systems within the region, participants recalled their personal challenges in pursuing education, and the benefits of the transformation that occurred as a result. Such transformation altered perspectives on Appalachian culture and its relationship to the world outside in ways beneficial to the individuals. Now what seems important to the participants is encouraging others in their communities to value and continue education, which should ultimately improve its quality and benefits. The idea is that ever more Appalachians will transform, using the strengths of the culture to embrace and manage the inevitable social changes like diversity and globalization to maximize benefits and minimize liabilities. The transformation resulting from education escalates from an individual to a collective, or community experience and the benefits and power it bestows expand exponentially.

Once more, for purposes of applicability of the results of this study, readers should note that participants were Appalachian graduate students in adult and higher education, and that data was collected via email as well as face-to-face interviews. The data may therefore not be representative of the Appalachian population as a whole, diverse as it is in itself. Also, the researchers must acknowledge the argument that data gathered electronically may not be of the same quality as that gathered face-to-face as researchers were not present to take advantage of visual and inflective communication cues and input.

Notwithstanding, some lessons to adult educators interested in facilitating transformative, or at least positive, education are obvious. Culturally sensitive design and instruction are key. Educators should understand the values of the communities from which the students come in developing and implementing educational experiences. Moreover, education should be itself culturally value-free, instead helping students critically examine their own cultures, their relationships to other influential cultures, and their effects on educational and life experiences.

CONCLUSION

The research presented here began as a curiosity about the state and effects of diversity and globalization on the Appalachian culture. Results of interviews with 11 adult and higher education students identifying as Appalachian express aspects of the effects of the increasing exposure to globalization on a culture gradually losing its relatively strong isolation. Even remaining substantially value-neutral in their interpretation, the researchers see highlighted in the articulated responses the perceived benefits and liabilities of such change, as well as the tension created in finding a balance between progressive change and the preservation of a unique and valued culture. More evident than anticipated to the researchers is the central and crucial role of education, primary and continued, in cultural perspective transformation. Educators and people in general should heed the very important message in this research. Culture should never be devalued, but respected and celebrated. Only then can people maximize potential at individual and societal levels.

REFERENCES

Abramson, R. (2006). Bituminous coal industry. In R. Abramson & J. Haskell (Eds.), *Encyclopedia of Appalachia* (pp. 457–460). Knoxville: University of Tennessee Press.

Algeo, K. (1997). The rise of tobacco as a Southern Appalachian staple: Madison County, North Carolina. *Southeastern Geographer, 37*(1), 46–60.

Anglin, M. K. (2004). Erasures of the past: Culture, power, and heterogeneity in Appalachia. *Journal of Appalachian Studies, 10*(1/2), 73–84.

Appalachia's economy. Appalachian Regional Commission. Retrieved from http://www.arc.gov/appalachian_region/AppalachiasEconomy.asp

Appalachian region. (n.d.). Appalachian Regional Commission. Retrieved from http://www.arc.gov/appalachian_region/TheAppalachianRegion.asp

Bauer, W., & Growick, B. (2003). Rehabilitation counseling in Appalachian America. *Journal of Rehabilitation, 69*(3), 18–24.

Bernard, H. (2000). *Social research methods: Qualitative and quantitative approaches.* Thousand Oaks, CA: Sage Publications, Inc.

Bingman, B. (2004). To save the land and people: A history of opposition to surface coal mining in Appalachia. *Journal of Appalachian Studies, 10*(1/2), 227–228.

Bogdan, R., & Bilken, S. (2003). *Qualitative research for education: An introduction to theories and methods* (4th ed.). Boston, MA: Pearson Education Group, Inc.

Boonlong, F. (2007). The language rights of the Malay minority in Thailand. *Asia-Pacific Journal on Human Rights & The Law, 8*(1), 47–63. doi:10.1163/157181507782200259

Clark, A., & Hayward, N. (2013). Introduction. In A. Clark & N. Hayward (Eds.), *Talking Appalachian* (pp. 1–21). Lexington: The University Press of Kentucky.

County economic status in Appalachia, FY 2014. Appalachian Regional Commission. Retrieved from http://www.arc.gov/research/MapsofAppalachia.asp?F_CATEGORY_ID=1

DeYoung, A., & Herzog, M. (2006). Introduction to education. In R. Abramson & J. Haskell (Eds.), *Encyclopedia of Appalachia* (pp. 1517–1521). Knoxville: University of Tennessee Press.

Drake, R. (2001). *A history of Appalachia.* Lexington, KY: University Press of Kentucky.

Ellis, M. (2013). The treatment of dialect in Appalachian literature. In A. Clark & N. Hayward (Eds.), *Talking Appalachian* (pp. 163–181). Lexington: The University Press of Kentucky.

Evans, D., Hearn, M. Uhlemann, M., & Ivey, A. (2004). *Essential interviewing: A programmed approach to effective communication* (6th ed.). Belmont, CA: Thomson.

Fedukovich, C. (2009). Strange imports: Working-class Appalachian women in the composition classroom. *Journal of Appalachian Studies, 15*(1/2), 140–154.

Fischer, D. (1989). *Albion's way: Four British folkways in America.* New York, NY: Oxford University Press.

Fontana, A., & Frey, J. (2005). The interview: From neutral stance to political involvement. In N. Denzin & Y. Lincoln (Eds.), *The Sage handbook of qualitative research* (3rd. ed.). Thousand Oaks, CA: Sage.

Globalization: A framework for IMF involvement. (2002). International Monetary Fund. Retrieved from http://www.imf.org/external/np/exr/ib/2002/031502.htm

Globalization. (2013). Dictionary.com. Retrieved from http://dictionary.reference.com/browse/globalization?s=t

Goshgarian, G. (2012). *Exploring language* (13th Ed.). New York, NY: Longman.

Hayward, N. (2013). Think locally: Language as community practice. In A. Clark & N. Hayward (Eds.), *Talking Appalachian* (pp. 70–80). Lexington: The University Press of Kentucky.

Hofstede, G. H. (2001). *Culture's consequences: International differences in work related values.* Thousand Oaks, CA: Sage.

Hurst, J. (2006). Introduction to business, technology and industry section. In R. Abramson & J. Haskell (Eds.), *Encyclopedia of Appalachia* (pp. 441–447). Knoxville: University of Tennessee Press.

Jackson, K. (2005). Coal and culture: Opera houses in Appalachia. *Journal of American Culture, 28*(4), 440. doi:10.1111/j.1542-734X.2005.00248.x

Keefe, S. (2000). *Mountain identity and the global society in a rural Appalachian county.* Paper presented at the National Conference on Ethnicity and Gender in Appalachia (Huntington, WV, March 2000).

LaLone, M. B. (2008). Running the family farm: Accommodation and adaptation in an Appalachian region. *Journal of Appalachian Studies, 14*(1/2), 62–98.

Lindlof, T., & Taylor, B. (2002). *Qualitative communication research methods* (2nd. Ed). Thousand Oaks: Sage Publications.

Lee, J. (2006). Agricultural education. In R. Abramson & J. Haskell (Eds.), *Encyclopedia of Appalachia* (pp. 404–405). Knoxville: University of Tennessee Press.

Massey, C. (2007). Appalachian stereotypes: Cultural history, gender, and sexual rhetoric. *Journal of Appalachian Studies, 13*(1/2), 124–136.

Matvey, J. J. (2005). *Regionalism and globalization: Essays on Appalachia, globalization, and global computerization.* New York, NY: IUniverse.

McCauley, D. (1995). *Appalachian mountain religion: A history.* Champaign: University of Illinois Press.

McNeil, W. (1995). *Appalachian images in folk and popular culture* (2nd ed.). Knoxville, TN: University of Tennessee Press.

Merriam, S. B., & Caffarella, R. S. (1999). *Learning in adulthood: A comprehensive guide.* San Francisco: Jossey-Bass.

Mezirow, J. (1978). *Education for perspective transformation: Women's re-entry programs in community college.* New York, NY: Teachers College.

Mezirow, J. (1990). How critical reflection triggers transformative learning. In J. Mezirow & Associates (Eds.), *Fostering critical reflection in adulthood: A guide to transformative land emancipator learning* (pp. 1–20). San Francisco: Jossey-Bass.

Mezirow, J. (1991). *Transformative dimensions of adult learning.* San Francisco: Jossey-Bass.

Miewald, C. (2006). Women's Roles. In R. Abramson & J. Haskell (Eds.), *Encyclopedia of Appalachia* (pp. 195–196). Knoxville: University of Tennessee Press.

Miller, D., Hatfield, S., & Norman, G. (2005). *An American vein: Critical readings in Appalachian literature.* Athens: Ohio University Press.

Montgomery, M., & Johnson, E. (2007). *The new encyclopedia of southern culture: 5.* Chapel Hill, NC: Univ. of North Carolina Press.

Newhall, D. (2006). English. In R. Abramson & J. Haskell (Eds.), *Encyclopedia of Appalachia* (pp. 253–255). Knoxville: University of Tennessee Press.

Olson, T. (2006). Music—introduction. In R. Abramson & J. Haskell (Eds.), *Encyclopedia of Appalachia* (pp. 1109–1120). Knoxville: University of Tennessee Press.

Parker, F & Riley, K. (2010). *Linguistics for non-linguists: A primer with exercises* (5th Ed.), Boston, MA: Pearson.

Paulson, L. (2006). Lumber industry. In R. Abramson & J. Haskell (Eds.), *Encyclopedia of Appalachia* (pp. 501–504). Knoxville: University of Tennessee Press.

Pollard, K., & Jacobsen, L. (2013). The Appalachian region: A data overview from the 2007–2011 American community survey. Appalachian Regional Commission. Retrieved from http://www.arc.gov/research/researchreportdetails.asp?REPORT_ID=103

Richmond, N., & Walkup, M. M. (2011). *Appalachian folklore: Omens, signs and superstitions.* S.l: s.n.

Rivers, M. (2012). *Appalachia mountain folklore.* Atglenn, PA: Schiffer Publishing Ltd.

Rouse, P. (1992). *The great wagon road: From Philadelphia to the South.* Richmond, VA: Dietz Press.

Shaw, T., DeYoung, A., & Rademacher, E. (2004). Educational attainment in Appalachia: Growing with the nation, but challenges remain. *Journal of Appalachian Studies. 10*(3), 307–329.

Smith, D. A. (2004). To save the land and people: A history of opposition to surface coal mining in Appalachia (Book). *American Historical Review, 109*(1), 216.

Tang, M., & Russ, K. (2007). Understanding and facilitating career development of people of Appalachian culture: An Integrated Approach. *Career Development Quarterly, 56*(1), 34–46.

Teets, S. (2006). Education in Appalachia. In G. Edwards, J. Asbury & R. Cox (Eds.). *A handbook to Appalachia: An introduction to the region.* Knoxville, TN: University of Tennessee Press.

CHAPTER 30

GLOBALIZATION OF CURRICULA THROUGH PARTNERSHIPS

Building Competitive Global Learner Capacity

Amy Rell and Roxanne Gonzales
Granite State College

Within the context of a global market, internationalization and globalization are key initiatives at many post-secondary institutions. The objective of graduating engaged, informed, skilled citizens infused with a global perspective and global understanding is a mutual goal among colleges and universities. Equally common are learners seeking programming that accommodate learners' desires and the necessity to market themselves post-graduation as competitive in a global marketplace. Colleges and universities have a shared responsibility to build programming that enhances learners' abilities to succeed post-graduation, including programs aimed at internationalizing and globalizing. Accordingly, the preeminent organization for

Building Sustainable Futures for Adult Learners, pages 619–631
Copyright © 2015 by Information Age Publishing
All rights of reproduction in any form reserved.

international education, NAFSA (The Association of International Educators), notes that "there is a growing sense that internationalization is an institutional imperative, not just a desirable possibility" (Hudzik, 2011, p. 7).

Before discussing how campuses can achieve this lofty aim, it is critical to define internationalization. Referring again to NAFSA, "Comprehensive Internationalization" is

> A commitment, confirmed through action, to infuse international and comparative perspectives throughout the teaching, research, and service missions of higher education. It shapes institutional ethos and values and touches the entire higher education enterprise. It is essential that it be embraced by institutional leadership, governance, faculty, learners, and all academic service and support units. (Hudzik, 2011, p. 6)

Just how do post-secondary institutions progress toward this end? With such an all-encompassing definition, the ramifications for implementation are complex.

An additional caveat emerges when internationalization and globalization is expected at institutions serving post-traditional learners, defined as "individuals already in the workforce who lack a postsecondary credential yet are determined to pursue further knowledge and skills while balancing work, life, and education responsibilities" (Soares, 2013, para 1). Regis University, a Jesuit-Catholic institution situated in the Rocky Mountain Region of Denver, Colorado, has succeeded in launching and sustaining multiple global programs designed with the hallmark of comprehensive internationalization for post-traditional learners and has done so in a systematic manner through key strategic partnerships. This chapter will briefly describe the history, demographics, mission, and vision of Regis University followed by a detailed analysis of four innovative partnership-based international degree models that address the needs of underrepresented adult learners and prepare them to be competitive in a global marketplace. As a result, readers will have a greater understanding of how to develop internationally based partnership programs using innovative, accelerated models. Each program is offered in an accelerated format that serves adults working with populations of Latin America, Ireland, the Middle East, and Africa. The impact of these programs cannot be overstated in today's world economy and marketplace. With the expansion of the Internet and e-commerce, global competence and agility is essential to stand-out and succeed in the modern corporate world.

JESUIT EDUCATION AND INTERNATIONALIZATION

There are 28 Jesuit institutions of higher education in the United States, and many more in the world represented on five continents. At its core,

Jesuit education, the Society of Jesus, and Ignatius philosophy embrace and encourage globalization and internationalization as part of their mission. From the inception of the Society of Jesus in the mid-sixteenth century, Jesuits have traveled the world conveying a message of the importance of education and, specifically, education from a global perspective. In the modern spirit of this 500 year tradition, The Society of Jesus declared in 1995 in the Decree Four of the Society's Thirty-Fourth General Congregation that

> It is part of our Jesuit tradition to be involved in the transformation of every human culture, as human beings begin to reshape their patterns of social relations, their cultural inheritance, their intellectual projects, their critical perspectives on religion, truth, and morality, their whole scientific and technological understanding of themselves and the world in which we live. We commit ourselves to accompany people, in different contexts, as they and their culture make difficult transitions. (Association of Jesuit Colleges and Universities [AJCU], n.d., p. 8)

This sentiment was echoed by Father Pierre Teilhard De Chardin, S.J.: "The age of nations is past. The task before us now, if we would not perish, is to build the earth" (as cited in DiLeonardo, 2007, p. 2). The history of globalization with the Jesuit tradition is lengthy as is the importance placed in Jesuit philosophy of education via globalization.

In essence, internationalization is a constant study within the Jesuit community of post-secondary institutions. Several publications elucidate the current projects undertaken at Jesuit institutions that respond to the need to globalize. One such survey, disseminated in 2006 by the American Society of Jesuit Universities (AJCU), provides data and examples from the twenty-eight Jesuit institutions in the United States regarding internationalization of curriculum, study abroad, institutes and centers, faculty exchange, and institutional partnerships. From this study and others like it, it is evident that Jesuit institutions place high value on internationalization efforts, that many institutions within the Jesuit network are operating from a global perspective, and that much work is yet to be done to increase these efforts. When specifically assessing how the Jesuit network has created partnerships that allow for globalization, it becomes clear that partnership programs have "led to some ground breaking programs, networks and relationships that promote global awareness and cultural appreciation" (Association of Jesuit Colleges and Universities [AJCU], 2006, p. 12). The partnership programs Regis University has successfully developed contribute to this end.

REGIS UNIVERSITY

Regis University inaugurated in 1877 in Las Vegas, New Mexico with the goal of serving the Spanish speaking population of New Mexico. The University moved to Morrison, Colorado in 1884 and the current campus in Denver, Colorado in 1887. In Regis' 150-year legacy, it has grown to an enrollment of nearly 15,000 learners within three unique colleges. Regis College, with an enrollment of approximately 2,000 learners, is a traditional liberal-arts college offering an array of undergraduate and graduate degrees. Reukert-Hartman College for Health Professions, enrolling 3,000 learners, offers undergraduate, graduate, and professional doctoral degrees in the health fields. Finally, the College for Professional Studies (CPS) enrolls approximately 10,000 learners.

Separated into four schools offering undergraduate and graduate programs, CPS is home to the School of Education, School of Management, School of Computer and Information Sciences, and the School of Humanities and Social Sciences, all of which serve post-traditional learners in an accelerated format. Learners come to CPS already having college credit and work experience, in an effort to complete their degrees. Classes are offered on-ground and online in five and eight week formats. On-ground classes meet once per week for four hours. Facilitators are primarily affiliates (adjuncts) who continue to work outside of academia in their respective professional fields.

CPS is intentional in its application of andragogy, a construct that approaches learning from its operational structure, academic programming, and service to learners. The model provides for flexibility in how learners experience their education. This changes the role of the faculty as well as the learner; faculty become facilitators and learners become responsible for their learning (Knowles, 1990). The concept of andragogy has transformed over time to focus more on the learner experience, knowledge the learner brings to the learning environment, as well as what occurs in the learning environment. CPS has embraced the model to the fullest (Knowles, Holton, & Swanson, 2011). The CPS curriculum is a praxis; theory and practice blended with the implication that learners bring knowledge into the learning environment and apply new learning in their daily lives. Social justice is a basic tenant of adult education as is Jesuit education; Regis's CPS melds the two concepts, andragogy and social justice, in the approach to programming and rationale for international partnerships.

The CPS model also borrows from other models associated with adult learning such as accelerated learning formats based on the Council for Accelerated Programs best practices (CAP, 2014), and the Council for Adult and Experiential Learning's (CAEL) best practices for prior learning assessment. It retains currency in the field through professional organizations focused on adult learning such as the University Professional and Continuing Education Association (UPCEA) and the Association for Continuing Higher Education (ACHE). In essence, the CPS model identifies the gap of what learners need to know in specific content areas, defines, through programming, how that learning will occur, and aligns the learning as to its importance to the learner's life situation (Knowles et.al, 2011).

The three-tiered college approach allows CPS to focus on a model of serving adult learners while still embracing the Jesuit mission and values that all three colleges share, of learners becoming leaders in the service of others. Embedded in the Regis mission and vision, in addition to teaching, is a commitment to cultivating understanding and awareness that we are citizens of a global world who must be prepared to do work beyond our backyard. The College for Professional Studies has benefited from the ideological and fiscal support necessary to develop partnership programs that meet the goal of creating internationalized programs and subsequently, globally-minded graduates.

MBA IN EMERGING MARKETS: PARTNERSHIP WITH INSTITUTO TECNOLÓGICO DE ESTUDIOS SUPERIORES DE OCCIDENTE (ITESO)

ITESO and Regis partnered in 2010 creating the first online bilingual MBA in Emerging Markets. Located in Guadalajara, Mexico, ITESO offers undergraduate and graduate degrees ranging from engineering, business, and humanities to vocational programming. The Emerging Markets MBA degree partnership between ITESO and Regis University is "designed for entrepreneurs, business people and executives from Latin America and the US Latino business communities who are looking for business opportunities and managerial careers in the global economy." (*Global MBA*, n.d.). Courses emphasize an international, multi-cultural, global economic focus. As a similarly positioned Jesuit institution, ITESO shares a similar mission and vision with Regis.

The MBA in Emerging Markets is an online program consisting of 12 courses (36 credit hours) in an accelerated eight-week format. In order to be admitted, learners must demonstrate a high-level mastery of English and Spanish, among other content area requirements such as the Graduate Management Admissions Test (GMAT). Once admitted, learners complete six courses taught in English by Regis faculty and six courses taught in Spanish by ITESO faculty. All coursework is designed and developed jointly by both institutions' faculty and vetted through each school's curriculum approval process. An additional component of the program includes an optional summer intensive taken on-ground one year at Regis University and the subsequent year at ITESO. Graduating learners earn a joint degree with a seal from both institutions. While still in its initial years, enrollments have been small but steady. The inaugural year enrolled 14 learners (11 from Mexico, 2 from the United States, 1 from other), the 2011 academic year enrolled 36 learners (26 from Mexico, 9 from the United States, 1 from other), and the 2012 academic year enrolled 28 learners (20 from Mexico and 8 from the United States). With little to no galvanized marketing efforts on the part of Regis or ITESO, the small enrollments to date are seen as a victory by both institutions. Learners tend to be post-traditional (Soares, 2013, para. 1). Many are mid- to high-level business executives seeking to augment their credentials while simultaneously enhancing their language skills. As noted above, the demographic data indicates that the majority of learners come from the United States and Mexico.

Dual Language Degrees: Partnership with Ana G. Mendez University System (SUAGM)

In 2011, Regis partnered with the Ana G. Mendez University System (SUAGM) in Puerto Rico to offer eight undergraduate and four graduate degrees in a variety of disciplines, including a dual language modality, with the aim to graduate bilingual professionals capable of functioning within their disciplines at a professional level in both English and Spanish. As such, Regis provided the curricula, accreditation, faculty, and accelerated degree completion model previously described while the for-profit entity aligned with SUAGM, Agmus Ventures Incorporated (AVI), provided the dual language model that consists of alternating instruction on a weekly basis between English and Spanish (*Agmus Ventures*, n.d.) and the daily operational management of the campus. The admission requirements include demonstration of proficiency in English and Spanish. Learners, however, are not turned away should their language proficiency require improvement. Embedded within the degrees are remedial and immersive language courses in both English and Spanish designed to bolster language ability. Graduating learners earn a degree with a seal from Regis University.

During the five and eight week accelerated on-ground courses, identical in outcomes to the CPS monolingual courses, learners gain content area expertise along with English and Spanish language skill development. This is accomplished through alternating the language of instruction on a weekly basis. One week, all assignments, class-work, homework, and readings are conducted in English followed by Spanish the subsequent week. While Dual Language is widely accepted as a bilingual learning model of excellence in the primary and secondary level settings (Thomas & Collier, 2012), its use at the post-secondary level is vanguard with no scholarly academic literature describing its effectiveness.

The Dual Language degree partnership between SUAGM and Regis University originally conceived the target audience as bilingual professionals, both English and Spanish dominant, seeking to complete their degrees in a bilingual setting. The model instead serves a largely Spanish dominant population (93%) of first-generation degree seekers, often with little to no college credit. The majority of learners come from a Mexican background, parallel to the Denver Hispanic community at large. Unlike the Emerging Markets Global MBA offered with ITESO that draws primarily mid and high-level bilingual business executives, the Dual Language degrees draw a wide range of learners from first-generation post-secondary degree seekers with little to no college experience to highly successful Spanish dominant professionals seeking a U.S. credential.

As a result of the many first-generation degree seekers and English language learners, students require an extensive network of in-person, high-touch, intrusive support services in a bilingual format whereby students are proactively contacted on a continuous basis to insure satisfactory course progression and engage in detailed advising. Furthermore, although courses are offered face-to-face, unlike the majority of CPS online offerings, an electronic lab with tools specifically designed to enhance language proficiency in English and Spanish complements each course. The extension campus where Dual Language courses are taught functions as a community center where learners, families, and the community frequently gather for different cultural and civic functions and events. After two years, enrollments peaked at approximately 150 learners. Because of the slow enrollment growth despite marketing efforts, the partnership between SUAGM and Regis for the Dual Language degrees ended in late 2013. Regis now assumes the daily operation and management of the extension campus and degrees.

MS IN SOFTWARE ENGINEERING AND DATABASE TECHNOLOGIES AND IRISH STUDIES CERTIFICATE: PARTNERSHIP WITH NATIONAL UNIVERSITY OF IRELAND (NUI), GALWAY

Similar to the ITESO partnership is an online Master's degree in Software Engineering and Database Technologies between Regis and the National University of Ireland (NUI). As with the ITESO program, Regis faculty and Galway faculty each teach half of the courses. This degree is intended to "prepare students to take their place in this in-demand industry with training in the areas of computer architecture and operating systems, software engineering, Oracle® database administration, and enterprise portal design and development" (*Prepare for success*, n.d.). Upon completion, graduates receive a diploma from their respective institutions; however, the graduates also receive a certificate signed by both institutions' presidents. These learners tend to be older adults seeking the flexibility of an online degree. Because distance education is a rather new course delivery model in Ireland, this program offers Irish learners the flexibility they seek while providing all learners an international experience.

Another partnership is the Irish Studies Certificate, a joint effort between Regis and the National University of Ireland (NUI) at Galway. Aligned with the online-accelerated model described in the previous sections, the Irish Studies Certificate consists of multiple accelerated, online courses that provide an introduction to Irish life and culture through the disciplines of archaeology, history, literature in English and in Irish (presented in translation), political science, sociology, and traditional Irish music and dance. The Irish Studies courses are developed, written, and taught by staff and adjunct faculty at the Centre for Irish Studies at NUI Galway. According to the President of the NUI Galway

> This joint venture allows The National University of Ireland to offer its expertise in the field of Irish Studies to a wider audience and builds on the success Galway has experienced in the past with our internationally recognized Summer School, as well as a broad range of undergraduate programs and the highly successful Master's in Irish Studies Program. Our partnership with Regis will alert learners from around the globe to the strength of Irish Studies as an academic discipline at NUI, Galway, where it is a designated Area of Excellence. (*Undergraduate Irish*, n.d.)

Designed as an articulation agreement between the two institutions, all learners admitted to the College for Professional Studies at Regis have access to this program. Successful completion of four courses yields a Certificate of Completion in Irish Studies from Regis University. Successful completion of five courses yields a Diploma in Irish Studies from NUI, Galway. In addition, learners have the option to take courses at NUI Galway in lieu of in an online environment. Over 750 students have participated in the Irish Studies Certificate, which began in 2001. Enrollments jumped from five in the inaugural year to 98 in the second year. Enrollments peaked in 2003–2004 academic year at 113 and again at 112 in the 2006–2007 academic year. Since 2007, there has been a slight decline each year with the 2012–2013 academic year enrolling 49 learners.

DIPLOMA OF LIBERAL STUDIES PARTNERSHIP WITH JESUIT COMMONS: HIGHER EDUCATION AT THE MARGINS

The final partnership we describe highlights an international effort that could not be realized without creative incorporation of a partner. The Diploma of Liberal Studies and Community Service Learning is offered as a global partnership between the network of Jesuit institutions known as Jesuit Commons: Higher Education at the Margins (JC:HEM). Initiated in 2009, the partnership targets un-served and under-served populations of refugees living in camps located in Dzaleka, Malawi and Kakuma, Kenya, with ambitions to expand programming to Afghanistan, Syria, and Jordan. The partnership offers higher education to those at the margins of society who would not customarily have access to post-secondary education. The goal is the transformation in the lives of refugees and their communities through education that encourages learners to apply learning to their local communities.

Faculty from 36 Jesuit universities and other similarly situated institutions develop and deliver online courses towards a Degree in Liberal Studies, with the degree granted by Regis. Admission requirements for the 45-credit degree, offered in an accelerated eight week, online format, include evidence of being a refugee, evidence of engagement in refugee camp life, evidence of English proficiency via a written essay and an oral interview that confirms "commitment to be of service to others and an educated person" (*The Diploma in liberal studies*, n.d.). The admission interviews occur in the refugee camps conducted by the staff Jesuit Commons. Currently, there are 145 learners enrolled in Kakuma and 148 in Dzaleka. In September of 2013, the first cohort of 52 learners graduated. Executive administrators from various contributing institutions attended a graduation largely designed by the learners.

DISCUSSION

The partnerships described represent mission-driven initiatives that allow for globalization and internationalization of curricula and learners that could not otherwise be accomplished. The opportunity to serve under-represented learners, to expose learners to global issues, and to prepare learners for competing in the global market are lofty rationale that justify the dedication and commitment necessary to make the partnerships and programs viable. Through Regis' extensive history with design, development, and execution of global partnerships, opportunity has presented itself for learners, the institution, and the community alongside with challenges and many lessons learned. Possibly of the greatest significance is support from the highest levels of leadership within the institution. For partnership programs to succeed in globalizing curricula within an institution, the executive leadership must understand and support such programming. Because global partnership programs require extensive time investment to launch, said partnerships necessitate fiscal support as well as a keen understanding of how to align programming with the strategic initiatives with the university. Regis discovered pockets of global initiatives and partnership programs throughout the three colleges. As a result, a Presidential-appointed strategic planning solution group on internationalization has stated its primary recommendation that of rewriting the mission and vision of the University to include a global perspective (Adkins et al., 2013). The committee recognizes that for internationalization to be successful, it must be embedded in strategic orientation of the University and seen as critical from the highest levels of leadership.

Executive commitment to partnerships with a global scope allows for the minimization of other challenges, such as streamlining services across institutional silos and upholding policy exceptions and challenges related to growth, sustainability, and scalability. Upon creation and execution of global partnerships, many institutions of higher learning discover the need to work across departmental divisions and create exceptions to policies previously viewed as standard operating procedures. For instance, in the Dual Language degree model, because many learners and faculty arrive with Latin American transcripts, Regis quickly learned the need to analyze the common practice and requirement of prospective students and faculty providing an official, sealed transcripts in terms of timing and accreditation ramifications. Latin America operates distinctly as to obtaining transcripts. For example, an individual often must appear at the institution in person to request a copy of their transcript. In some cases, institutions have closed and there is no way of recovering a transcript. Most commonly, requesting and receiving a transcript from a Latin American institution can take several months to process. These can be a barrier to access if relationships and policies between the program, the Registrar's office, and the Admissions office are not discussed and developed.

Growth, sustainability, and scalability merit discussion as well. As evidenced by the partnerships detailed in this chapter, enrollments have not grown substantially. As a result, one of the four, the Dual Language model, exposed the challenge of a for-profit and non-profit partnership that subsequently terminated. All require significant human resources during planning and execution including the support of executive leadership and dialogue between institutional departments in preparation and development of creative procedures and processes that allow the potential for sustainability and scalability.

The partnerships explored in this chapter were developed to meet specific goals and target audiences within a global context; however, there are common lessons beyond the executive commitment that Regis experienced that are worth discussing. While these areas seem obvious, each of the partnerships in this chapter required a different approach in each of these areas.

- *Curricular attention to the audience and content*: The Jesuit Commons partnership is an excellent example of a dynamic curricular process. When the program began, it started with courses from Jesuit universities, using existing westernized curriculum. As the program matured, students began to express an interest in content that spoke to their culture, knowledge, and skill needs in the camps. Over time, the curriculum team has expanded to include faculty from across Africa, Europe, and the United States. The model of program development today is one of inclusiveness and flexibility to meet the specific needs of the targeted populations.

- *Faculty training*: Although ITESO is well known for its technology programs, the University had not moved into full online degrees. During the co-development of the partnership, faculty required training in the use of a learning management system as well how to develop courses for online environments. NUI was a similar experience. A benefit to both institutions is the ability to expand their own online programming to meet their own student populations.

- *Student interaction*: A common challenge and critique in online learning is how to engage students in online classrooms to ensure the experience is of high quality. While the curriculum includes activities online, there are ways to increase the student interaction in a face to face manner. Each of these partnerships approached the challenge differently. As mentioned, ITESO had an optional yearly onsite intensive in Mexico or Denver, CO. There were on average ten students from that participated annually. Jesuit Commons retains tutors in the camps who assist the students daily. NUI students have an annual reception with Regis faculty and leadership in Galway after graduation.

- *Administrative coordination*: There is administrative complexity when partnering with institutions within international institutions; database incompatibilities, credit transfers, term lengths, credentialing, laws, and language barriers. Add to this short list cultural distinctions, what might seem on the surface a straight and fairly quick process, but can expand into a much longer and complicated process. Institutions with international partnerships learn quickly to negotiate those elements that are the most critical to move forward with the partnership. The Dual Language partnership is an excellent example; policies such as official transcripts had to be reviewed early on in the partnership to determine what was best for the student while ensuring academic integrity.

Ultimately, the lessons learned enabled the partnerships to function: the process itself became a globalization experience for all students, faculty, staff, and administration on both sides of the partnership.

CONCLUSION

Partnership programs with an international framework have a potentially significant impact on the institution, learners, the community, and society at large. Regis University has demonstrated a commitment to the internationalization of curricula through partnerships that has allowed for an incredibly diverse and unique body of programming with countless benefits. It is remarkable that Regis has been able to succeed in developing and executing the four partnerships described, all of which focus on the post-traditional learner rather than the prototypical international or study-abroad learner. Through an accelerated, online model embedded with deep support services and taking advantage of a partnership model, Regis has succeeded in contributing to the post-traditional learner's ability to compete and succeed in a global market.

REFERENCES

Adkins, K., Cook, M., DeSisto, L., Gorrell, C., Johnson, P., Lee, J., & Yeap, S. B. (2013). *International students solution group report.* Retrieved from http://www.regis.edu/About-Regis-University/Strategic%20Planning/Progress.aspx

Agmus Ventures (n.d.) Retrieved from http://agmusventures.com/index_ing.html

Association for Continuing Higher Education (n.d.). Retrieved from http://acheinc.org/

Association of Jesuit Colleges and Universities (n.d.). In *A History rooted in mission: Jesuit higher education in the United States.* Retrieved from http://www.ajcunet.edu/Assets/Publications/File/A%20History%20Rooted%20in%20Mission.pdf

Association of Jesuit Colleges and Universities (2006). In *Internationalization of U.S. Jesuit colleges and universities: A preliminary analysis.* Retrieved from http://www.ajcunet.edu/International?Page=063ED464-F4D4-4210-A485-49D1AF3B12D5

Council for Accelerated Programs. (2014). *CAP model for good practice in accelerated programs in higher education.* Retrieved from http://www.capnetwork.org/modules.php?op=modload&name=UpDownload&file=index&req=viewdownload&cid=59

DiLeonardo, M. C. (2007). *Education for a globalized world: A profile of the internationalization of U.S. Jesuit campuses.* Retrieved from http://www.ajcunet.edu/Assets/Publications/File/EFGW20071.pdf

Global MBA in emerging markets (n.d.). Retrieved from http://www.mba-regis.iteso.mx/

Hudzik, K. H. (2011). *Comprehensive internationalization: From concept to action.* Retrieved from http://www.nafsa.org/uploadedFiles/NAFSA_Home/Resource_Library_Assets/Publications_Library/2011_Comprehen_Internationalization.pdf

Knowles, M. (1990). *The adult learner: A neglected species.* Houston, TX: Gulf Publishing.

Knowles, M., Holton, E., & Swanson, R. (2011). *The adult learner: The definitive classic in adult education and human resource development.* New York, NY: Elsevier.

Prepare for success with a Masters in software engineering and database technologies (n.d.). Retrieved from http://cps.regis.edu/lp/computer_degree/database_program.php

Regis University offers training and hope to refugees (n.d.) Retrieved from http://www.regis.edu/Signature-Story-Directory/Education-at-the-Margins.aspx

Soares, L. (2013). *Post-traditional learners and the transformation of postsecondary education: A manifesto for college leaders.* Retrieved from http://www.acenet.edu/news-room/Documents/Post-Traditional-Learners.pdf

The diploma in liberal studies (n.d.). Retrieved from http://www.jc-hem.org/

Thomas, W. P., & Collier, V. P. (2012). *Dual language education for a transformed world.* Albuquerque, NM: Fuente Press.

Undergraduate Irish Studies (n.d.). Retrieved from http://www.regis.edu/CPS/Academics/Degrees-and-Programs/Undergraduate-Programs/Irish-Studies

University Professional and Continuing Education Association (n.d.). Retrieved from: http://upcea.edu/

CONCLUSION

Jennifer K. Holtz
University of Arkansas at Little Rock

Carrie J. Boden-McGill and Stephen B. Springer
Texas State University

The 30 chapters in *Building Sustainable Futures for Adult Learners* represent leading edge praxis in adult education and learning by both well-known colleagues and emergent scholars who presented their work at the 2013 joint conference of the Adult Higher Education Alliance (AHEA) and the American Association of Adult and Continuing Education (AAACE). In addressing, as AHEA President Gabriele Strohschen put it, diverse "similarities of needs and commonalities of corresponding solutions" (Preface), the authors of these chapters make recommendations that serve the field well. As is often true with intricate thought and probing research, readers are left with questions to ponder, some of which might be quite unexpected. This concluding chapter looks at a few questions that broadly incorporate conclusions drawn from reading the preceding chapters.

IS IT TIME TO UPDATE HOULE'S CATEGORIES?

There is no question that the primary focus of this book, as represented by its chapters, is on what Houle (1993) would describe as goal-directed

Building Sustainable Futures for Adult Learners, pages 633–638
Copyright © 2015 by Information Age Publishing
All rights of reproduction in any form reserved.

learners, yet there is a wide variety of goal direction, with an equally wide variety of techniques and expectations that work and do not work in achieving the identified goal. It is clear that a single conceptualization of *goal-directed* no longer seems appropriate. Perhaps it is time for adult educators to pay attention to defining groups within "goal directed" to better optimize available methods. Having a more detailed understanding of goal-directed learners can make adult education both stronger as a field and more focused.

For example, those who are degree-seeking do not necessarily expect or desire the degree of flexibility in learning plans that a social learner may desire. As documented in Chapter 3, Collins, Coddington, and Williams' examination of formal goal setting as a means to enhancing persistence toward graduation, such goal setting does not necessarily work. Other aspects of life sometimes are more of a priority than goals that are internal to a student's academic plan. Similarly, doctoral level female students have learning, organizational, and personal needs, as discussed by Wu (Chapter 5), that result in competing high-stakes goals. At the same time, readers have seen that learners in the medical field have goals that are nonnegotiable. The rigidity of medical education means that goal direction for a medical learner is far different than the goal directed learning needs of Voelkel's displaced workers (Chapter 1), who sought fulfilling work that was not uniformly achieved through degree completion.

Some might argue that the variety of learning methods available for use with goal directed learners can be selected judiciously considering the type of goal direction at hand. This may be true. What is certain is that additional research is needed as to how the types of goal direction differ, so that adult educators can best select and engage these methods to meet learner needs.

IS THE TRADITIONAL EDUCATIONAL CLASSROOM STRUCTURE WORTHY OF A SECOND LOOK?

No, this is not a call for a return to the instructor-centered bastion of formality, rather an attempt to acknowledge a truism: To move ahead, one needs to know what to leave behind (Tasler, 2013). Goal-directed learners seek the vast majority of their learning through traditional learning environments— college and universities. Job seeking individuals need skills now, not later (especially at a time of economic instability, as the world faces now), and degree-seekers are typically on a schedule that rewards rapid completion. This is certainly true for those in medicine, where applicants compete for positions. The argument that learners prefer the traditional, structured environment only because that is what they know is legitimate, but taking time to become acclimated to an unfamiliar learning environment or structure is not necessarily something of interest to current adult learners. The question becomes, then, which methods work best when time is a factor?

In this volume, there is undoubtedly a call for more active learning. Bergman, Rose, and Shuck (Chapter 2) associate active learning with increased learner persistence while Lockhart and Jackson (Chapter 9) report high faculty and student satisfaction with "flipped" Technology Enabled Active Learning (TEAL) classrooms as well as significantly higher grades for students enrolled in TEAL classrooms verses their counterparts enrolled in classes that met in a traditional lecture halls. Similarly, Kuo (Chapter 8) advocates for incorporating more active learning techniques in online learning environments using Web 2.0 applications. In the arena of medical education, McDonald, Straker, and Lyons (Chapter 16) call for "active learning strategies that allow content application in real-world settings, while also negotiating increasing class sizes." In addition to more active learning strategies, Peno, Mangiante, and Kenahan (Chapter 17) and Carter and Gogia (Chapter 18) call for active, affective elements of adult education such as teaching through mentoring, scaffolded self-direction, critical reflection, and critical self-reflection. While these authors shed light on the benefits of active approaches, further research is needed into what methods work best and, equally important, which do not work, regardless of their theoretical appeal, in formal learning environments where learners focus on timely development of a knowledge base and skill set.

WHAT ELECTRONIC DELIVERY SYSTEMS ARE BEST-SUITED FOR VARIOUS AUDIENCES OF ADULT LEARNERS?

As Ross-Gordon (2011) pointed out, so called nontraditional students are now the "new traditional" in colleges and universities across the country, comprising more than 50% of part-time and 33% of full-time enrollment in higher education in the United States (Aud, Wilkinson-Flicker, Kristapovich, Rathbun, Wang, & Zhang, 2013). As adult students juggle the multiple roles of employee, parent, child, spouse, bread-winner, homemaker, and student, universities have adapted by offering blended and online courses, which have become a preferred delivery system for many adult learners (Allen & Seaman, 2013; Parsad & Lewis, 2008). Between 2002 and 2011, the percentage of students taking classes online has increased from 9.6% to 33.5% (Allen & Seaman, 2014). Which online delivery models and systems best fit the needs of diverse groups of adult learners?

Many authors in this volume shared effective strategies for delivering online classes and programs to assorted groups of learners. Some of these strategies consist of "converting" effective face-to-face strategies to an online format while others focused on using distinctly digital tools. For example, in Chapter 24, Fedeli, Felisatti, and Giampaolo took a tested and much-used tool, the learning contract, and utilized it in an online format for graduate students while Felisatti, Mazzucco, Fedeli and Giampaolo (Chapter 25) did the same with cooperative learning methods for students preparing to be teachers. Conversely, Springer, Lopez, Eichler, Lasker-Scott, and Boden-McGill (Chapter 13) used a web-based tool, blogging, to promote interdisciplinary graduate students' inquiry, reflection, and sharing learning with one another. In her chapter on innovation, Hultquist (Chapter 21) both praises universities for embracing online programs, spin-offs, and MOOCs while also encouraging universities to adopt new innovations as they become available in order to better serve students by keeping up and adapting to rapidly changing conditions.

Other authors promoted blended or hybrid approaches to best meet the needs of adult learners, especially in disciplines that are arguably best served by hands-on instruction. Peterson and McGuire (Chapter 10) see hybrid teaching and learning as an ideal way to capitalize on technological advances, ease financial constraints for students and institutions, and address quality concerns of faculty and students regarding electronic delivery. Likewise, in a health sciences program, McDonald, Straker, and Lyons (Chapter 16) chose a hybrid approach in order to implement more problem-based and case based learning to promote students' critical thinking and application of concepts.

The trends are undeniable, as evidenced in part by the number of chapters in this volume addressing distance learning. Recent studies have predicted a significant drop in students enrolled in face-to-face courses and simultaneous increase in the number enrolled in blended and hybrid courses (Moskal, Dziuban, & Hartman, 2012). The flexibility offered by distance education classes and programs may make a college education possible for many Americans who are balancing family and work obligations along with school (Kolowich, 2010). The question for our field is how we can explore which delivery systems best fit various groups of adult learners, without compromising the critical and, typically, time-sensitive learning needs of the groups being studied.

HOW DOES AN ADULT LEARNER-FRIENDLY UNIVERSITY OPERATE?

In this and other volumes in the series, an underlying theme is the question: How can colleges and universities adapt in order to better serve the needs of adult learners? A corollary that should be addressed in tandem is this: How does an adult learner-friendly university operate? As administrators know well, every system is multidimensional; any change to one component affects every other. While several suggestions are posed in this volume in answer to changes needed, what is missing is the operational component.

In Chapter 2, Bergman, Rose, and Shuck point out that demographic changes are forcing colleges and universities to consider more adult-friendly practices in order to adapt and to reach this underserved population. These changes may include reaching parents, an approach lauded by Lovell and Barnes (Chapter 4), or other underrepresented groups, such as non-native English speakers or foreign students in the developing world, as described by Rell and Gonzales (Chapter 30). In each case, the call is for additional services at flexible times.

Other authors suggest the reorganization of university structures and systems. Prashun and Frasard (Chapter 23) question the credit hour unit of measure and research the amount of learning that occurs per credit hour, with recommendations for additional research to promote greater standardization. Merrill (Chapter 22), conversely, promotes greater reliance on competency-based-education with incorporation of Prior Learning Assessment (PLA), both of which are currently based on credit hours when used in degree programs. Hultquist (Chapter 21) suggests that as institutions scramble to adapt to meet the needs of adult learners, an evaluation of key organizational dynamics that support an institution's *capacity to change* is needed to assess resources and challenges that will impact the change efforts.

CONCLUSION

There are opposing positions to each of the questions raised here, as there always will be in a field as broad as adult education. Opposing ideas and positions are to be respected, of course. This diversity informs and shapes our field and practice and our "similarities of needs and commonalities of corresponding solutions." In the increasingly technology-oriented and fast-paced workplace, adults must adapt to constant changes prompted by globalization, economic variations, and evolving corporate and organizational cultures (Heifetz & Laurie, 2012). To address the rapid change, a goal of institutions is to create what Weimer (2013) calls a learner-centered environment where the product is not learning, which could be static in time, but rather learners, who can learn throughout the lifespan. The work of building a sustainable future for adult learners is underway, evidenced by the professionals in our field in this volume and beyond who respond to learners' needs, revise the curriculum, expand delivery options and methods, include "real world" experiences in the learning environment, explore PLA and competency-based models, and create local and global partnerships.

REFERENCES

Allen, I. E., & Seaman, J. (2014). *Grade change: Tracking online education in the United States.* Retrieved from http://sloanconsortium.org/publications/survey/grade-change-2013

Allen, E., & Seaman, J. (2013). *Changing course: Ten years of tracking online education in the United States.* Retrieved from http://www.onlinelearningsurvey.com/reports/changingcourse.pdf

Aud, S., Wilkinson-Flicker, S., Kristapovich, P., Rathbun, A., Wang, X., & Zhang, J. (2013). *The condition of education 2013* (NCES 2013-037). U.S. Department of Education, National Center for Education Statistics. Washington, DC. Retrieved from http://nces.ed.gov/pubsearch.

Heifetz, R., & Laurie, D. (2012). Mobilizing adaptive work: Beyond visionary leadership. In J. Conger, et al. (Eds.), *The leader's change handbook: An essential guide to setting direction and taking action* (pp. 55–86). San Francisco, CA: Jossey-Bass.

Houle, C. O. (1961/1993). The inquiring mind (3rd ed.). Norman, OK: Oklahoma Research Center for Continuing Professional and Higher Education. (Original edition published in 1961).

Kolowich, S. (2010). Buying local, online. *Inside Higher Ed.* Retrieved September 6, 2011. Retrieved from http://www. insidehighered.com/news/2010/07/ 23/ online

Moskal, P., Dziuban, C., & Hartman, J. (2012). Blended learning: A dangerous idea? *Internet and Higher Education, 18,* 15–23.

Parsad, B., & Lewis, L. (2008). *Distance education at degree-granting postsecondary institutions: 2006–07.* Retrieved from http://nces.ed.gov/pubs2009/2009044.pdf

Ross-Gordon, J. (2011). Research on adult learners: Supporting the needs of a student population that is no longer nontraditional. *Peer Review, (13)*1. Retrieved from http://www.aacu.org/peerreview/pr-wi11/prwi11_rossgordon.cfm

Tasler, N. (2013, August 7). To move ahead you have to know what to leave behind. Harvard Business Review Blog. Retrieved from http://blogs.hbr.org/2013/08/to-move-ahead-you-have-to-know-what-to-leave-behind/

Weimer, M. (2013). *Learner-centered teaching: Five key changes to practice.* San Francisco, CA: John Wiley & Sons.

ABOUT THE CONTRIBUTORS

Dustin Barnes, A.S., is a non-traditional student attending the University of Montana with a Davidson's Honor Scholarship Fall 2014. He attended Helena College of the University of Montana (2012–2014) earning an Associate Degree in Science with a concentration in Mental Health Direct Care. His accomplishments include: Participant in 2012 Student Psychology Research Day at Helena College 12/17/2012; Participant in First Annual Student Statewide Research Day for Two-Year Colleges at Highlands College of Montana Tech 04/19/2013; Participant in Second Annual Student Statewide Research Day for Montana's Two-year Colleges 04/04/2014; worked on Independent Study–Research with Elyse Lovell, Ed.D. and worked on study-research with Nathan Munn, M.D. Interviewed on "Home Ground with Brian Kahn" Public Broadcast Service (PBS) about the Mental Health Direct Care Program and research opportunities at Helena College 2014; Recipient of the 2014 University of Montana Circle of Success Scholarship.

Matt J. Bergman, Ph.D., is Assistant Professor of Organizational Leadership and Learning at the University of Louisville. He was awarded the Innovation in Educational Attainment Prize from the Gheen's Foundation of 2013 for his advancement of national adult degree attainment. He was also the recipient of the AAACE Malcolm Knowles Award for Adult Education Program of the Year. His research is focused on adult degree programs and adult student persistence.

Carrie J. Boden-McGill, Ph.D. is Associate Professor and Chair of the Department of Occupational, Workforce, and Leadership Studies at Texas State

Building Sustainable Futures for Adult Learners, pages 639–661
Copyright © 2015 by Information Age Publishing
639

University. Dr. Boden-McGill's research is primarily focused in the areas of teaching and learning strategies, mentoring, transformative learning, and personal epistemological beliefs. She has presented papers in over 25 states and foreign countries and published articles in journals such as *Adult Learning Quarterly, The International Journal of Learning*, and *National Teacher Education Journal*. Her latest books are *Pathways to Transformation: Learning in Relationship*, co-edited with Dr. Sola Kippers, and *Conversations about Adult Learning in Our Complex World* and *Developing and Sustaining Adult Learners*, co-edited with Dr. Kathleen P. King. Dr. Boden-McGill serves as a Director on the AHEA Board and co-chairs the research and theory SIG of the Commission of Professors of Adult Education.

Lisabeth Eames Capozzi, M.S., is a doctoral candidate at Penn State University, Harrisburg, and Adjunct Professor in the Human Resources Master's Program at Villanova University. She has over 25 years of management experience in Organizational Development and has trained and taught adults throughout her adult life. Her research interests include arts-based learning, career issues facing returning military veterans, leveraging employee engagement, complexity science, and storytelling within organizations.

Teresa J. (Terry) Carter, Ed.D., is Associate Professor of Teaching and Learning and Associate Dean for Professional Instruction and Faculty Development in the School of Medicine at Virginia Commonwealth University in Richmond, Virginia. She holds a Master's degree in Education and Human Development (1991) and the Doctor of Education degree in Human and Organizational Learning (2001) from The George Washington University. She directed the Adult Learning graduate program in the School of Education for eight years before assuming her current position in the School of Medicine in 2012, where she currently directs a graduate certificate program for medical educators. Dr. Carter's research interests include transformative learning among professionals, the scholarship of teaching and learning, and organization development. She has been published in *Performance Improvement Quarterly, The Journal of Business Communication, Advances in Developing Human Resources, Learning Communities Journal*, and the *International Journal of Teaching and Learning in Higher Education.*

Nora Lisa Cavazos, B.A., earned a Bachelor of Arts from Texas State University and is pursuing a Masters of Arts in International Studies from Texas State University. Her focus and interests include foreign policy, Mexico-U.S. relations, and Mexican immigration. She currently works as a Graduate Research Assistant for the Department of Occupational, Workforce, and Leadership Studies, where she served as an Associate Editor for *Building Sustainable Futures for Adult Learners* and *Developing and Sustaining Adult Learners*. After graduation, Nora plans to work in the political and foreign policy arena where she hopes to bring change in the Mexican-American community.

Jill Coddington, Ph.D., is a faculty member of Computer Science at Regis University. She earned her doctorate from The Union Institute in Mathematics, and has master's degrees in Software Engineering and Business Administration. She teaches undergraduate and graduate classes in computer science. She is also actively involved in curriculum development both at Regis University and other universities and colleges. She has developed a number of full-degree programs for video game programming as she worked in this industry for more than a decade. She has taught for over 15 years and has more than 20 years of computer programming and related management experience. Her most recent publication is The Relationship of Goal Setting to Persistence. She has presented at various conferences including AAACE (American Association of Adult and Continuing Education) and HICE (Hawaii International Conference on Education). Her research interests include online learning techniques and effectiveness and retention.

Robert D. "Bob" Collins, Ed.D., Bob is Professor in the Master of Arts degree program at Regis University. His work at Regis is focused on his interest and expertise in adult learning theory and practice, higher education leadership, program development, and organizational change. Bob brings a diverse set of experiences from higher education and public school education as well as the small business world to his work at Regis. He was formerly a faculty member at Western State College, teaching in the educational leadership program and was Associate Vice President and Dean of the Graduate School. While in public education, he was Superintendent of Schools in two Colorado school districts, was Assistant Superintendent in Colorado Springs, and was an elementary school principal and classroom teacher in Colorado and Kansas. Bob's current research is focused on goal setting theory. He presented at the Hawaii International Conference on Education in 2012–2014.

Joellen E. Coryell, Ph.D., is Associate Professor of adult, professional, and community education and Program Coordinator of the M.A. in Adult Education at Texas State University. She earned her Ph.D. in Educational Human Resource Development with a specialization in Adult Education at Texas A&M University, M.Ed. in Curriculum and Instruction from Texas State University, and a B.A. in International Economics from the University of Illinois. Her research focuses on (1) international cross-cultural adult and higher education; and (2) the investment in the professional development of adult educators and leaders, and she has conducted research/ taught in Italy, Malawi, and New Zealand. She has also published articles in journals such as *Adult Education Quarterly, Adult Learning Quarterly, Journal* on *Excellence in College Teaching, Journal of Further and Higher Education,* and the *Journal of Studies in International Education.* Dr. Coryell has been recognized for her work with awards such as the Early Career Award from the Commission of Professors of Adult Education and Top 25 Texas Education Professors from Online Schools Texas. She has served the profession of adult education as Chair of the Adult Education Research Conference Steering Committee and as Co-Chair of the Instructional Improvement SIG for the Commission of Professors of Adult Education.

Thomas D. Cox, Ed.D., earned his doctorate in higher and adult education at the University of Memphis in 2004. He is an assistant professor of higher education and policy studies at the University of Central Florida (UCF). Prior to UCF, he was the founding director of the adult and higher education master's degree at the University of Houston-Victoria. His research interests include research on adult learners' experience within institutions of higher education, first-year experience best practices, and the use of technology and online teaching. He has previously published an edited book with Dr. Kathleen King of the University of Southern Florida entitled *The Professor's Guide to Taming Technology.* He recently published an edited book entitled *Case Studies for the New Professor* (2014).

Clint E. Cummings, M.S., is an Extension Specialist with the University of Tennessee Extension in the Department of Family and Consumer Sciences. He holds an M.S. from the University of Tennessee in Educational Psychology: Adult Education and a B.S. from the same institution in Human Ecology: Family Studies. He coordinates statewide training efforts with professional and paraprofessional field staff conducting nutrition education with low-income audiences. He also oversees partnership and coalition development efforts by providing ongoing training and technical assistance to Extension agents leading coalitions. He has led successful coalition efforts at the county level in both rural and urban settings. Mr. Cummings serves as Chair of the Cooperative Extension Special Interest Group (SIG) for the American Association for Adult and Continuing Education (AAACE).

Diane L. Dick, Ph.D., is Academic Appeals Specialist for Capella University. She holds a Ph.D. in Organization and Management with an emphasis in adult education from Capella University, a Master of Arts in English Literature with emphases in Irish Modernists and Dramatic Literature from the University of Minnesota, and a B.A. in Literature from The College of St. Scholastica. Dr. Dick's research emphases include cognition and literary aesthetics, adult-focused dissertation mentoring, and general education curriculum revision. Dr. Dick has presented papers on medieval literature, Irish literature, prior learning assessment, and adult-focused general education at international, national, and regional conferences, and is a published poet, composer, and playwright, with more than 12 plays and 1 opera produced.

A. Steven Dietz, Ph.D., graduated from the University of Texas at Austin in May 2005 in Adult and Organizational Learning, focusing on executive problem recognition and decision-making. He has been on faculty with Texas State University since 2004 in the Department of Criminal Justice (Fall 2004–Summer 2008) and is currently an Assistant Professor in the Department of Occupational, Workforce and Leadership Studies. Dr. Dietz is an experienced organization dynamics consultant working with both private and public organizations over the past 20 years. He has extensive experience with police departments and military organizations and was the Director of the Texas Institute for Public Problem Solving (TIPPS) from 1997–1999. Steven is also a veteran of the U. S. Navy where he served for 11 years and currently serves in the Texas Army National Guard. Dr. Dietz has numerous publications and professional and academic presentations that focus on the systemic issues faced by organizations and how those issues are resolved.

Matthew A. Eichler, Ph.D., is an Assistant Professor of Occupational, Workforce, and Leadership Studies at Texas State University. In this role, he teaches, serves as the faculty coordinator of graduate programs, and serves as the chair of the university's Distance and Extended Education Steering Committee. He holds a Ph.D. in Education with an Emphasis in Work, Community, and Family Education; a M.Ed. in Work, Community, and Family Education; and a B.S. in Agricultural Education all from the University of Minnesota. Dr. Eichler researches LGBTQIA (lesbian, gay, bisexual, transgender, queer, intersex and ally) learners and identity, distance learning, interdisciplinary problem solving, and cross-cultural collaboration. He has presented widely throughout the United States, Canada, and the Philippines. He serves as an associate editor for two journals and regularly referees book chapters and manuscripts. He has keynoted several international research conferences and has been recognized for his outstanding teaching, mentorship, and service at the university.

Kathleen B. Fabrikant, Ed.D., is an Assistant Professor of Education in the Department of Adolescent & Adult Education at Armstrong Atlantic State University in Savannah, GA. She earned her doctorate from Georgia Southern University with an emphasis on literacy and has a Master's degree in special education. She was formerly the Executive Directory of Royce Learning Center in Savannah, whose unique Adult Education program continues to serve the greater Savannah area. She teaches graduate classes in the Adult Education & Community Leadership at Armstrong Atlantic State University and works with the students on several community outreach efforts.

Monica Fedeli, Ph.D., is Assistant Professor and Aggregate Professor at the University of Padua in the Department of Philosophy, Sociology, Pedagogy, and Applied Psychology. She is member of the professor committee for the Doctoral School in Educational Sciences at University of Padova. She is member of the American Association for Adult and Continuing Education (AAACE) and a member of the Italian Society for Research in Didactic (SIRD). Dr. Fedeli's research is primarily focused in the University Business Dialogue, Personalized Didactics and Human Development in Organizations. Since 2008 she participated in several national and international research projects: ex 60% projects on apprenticeship and employability, junior research fellowships for skills mapping, and European Social Found (ESF) projects on non-formal skills validation. She is coordinator of the Project of National Research Interest (PRIN) for the University of Padua.

Ettore Felisatti, Ph.D., Full Professor at the University of Padua in the Department of Philosophy, Sociology, Pedagogy, and Applied Psychology. He is the director of the Interdepartmental Study Centre for Social Services (CISSPE) and peer reviewer for the National Agency for the Evaluation of University and Research (ANVUR). He is a member of the AAACE American Association for Adult and Continuing Education, of the Italian Societies for Research in Didactic (SIRD), and of the Italian Society for Research in Media Education (SIREM). Dr. Felisatti's research is primarily focused in school and university teaching, educational and training planning and assessment, and in initial and continuous teacher training. He participates in various research groups, in particular those investigating university teaching assessment, the promotion of teachers' competencies, teaching and learning in higher education. He has also studied issues related to training, promoting research, training and assessment activities using a blended learning approach.

Bonnie Flynn, Ed.D., is an Associate Professor at National Louis University (NLU). She teaches courses in healthcare and general management at the undergraduate and graduate level. She holds an Ed.D. in adult and continuing education from NLU, a Master in Public Health from Benedictine University, and master's degrees in both adult education and written communication from NLU. Dr. Flynn's research primarily focuses on transformative and accelerated learning. She has designed and taught courses in blended and online formats and is a certified Quality Matters™ peer reviewer. In service to the profession, she is an active member of the Illinois Public Health Association (IPHA) and the American Association of Adult and Continuing Education (AAACE); she served as past secretary of the Adult Higher Education Alliance (AHEA). Prior to her teaching career, she worked at the Joint Commission, a health care accreditor, for 15 years where she held a variety of positions.

Karen Franck, Ph.D., is an Extension Specialist for the University of Tennessee Extension Family and Consumer Sciences (FCS). She is the program evaluator for two federally funded nutrition education interventions including the Expanded Food and Nutrition Education Program (EFNEP) and the Supplemental Nutrition Assistance Program Education (SNAP-Ed) program. Dr. Franck has conducted program evaluations for a variety of diverse programs including drug and alcohol rehabilitation programs for women with children, domestic violence programs, and programs for at-risk youth including runaways and youth in foster care. She has served as Co-Principal Investigator on several grants evaluating the effectiveness of nutrition education interventions on children and adults as well as health and safety project and a national needs assessment for 4-H Healthy Living programs.

Scott R. Frasard, Ph.D., is the Global Manager of Training Measurement & Evaluation at eBay, Inc. He holds a Ph.D. in Adult Education and a M.Ed. in Adult Education with an emphasis in Human Resources and Organizational Development from The University of Georgia. He has presented papers at several national and international conferences such as *The Academy of Human Resource Development, Adult Education Research Conference,* and *The International Conference on Knowledge, Culture, and Change in Organizations.* He serves on the editorial board for *The Journal of Leadership and Organizational Effectiveness* and reviews manuscript submissions for journals and conferences such as *The Academy of Management* and *The American Evaluation Association.* Dr. Frasard is an adult educator of 20 years, a scholar-practitioner, and consultant. His research explores alternative teacher effectiveness evaluation methods in multicultural and multinational contexts and teacher characteristic influences on learning outcomes.

Iris J. Fulton, B. A., earned a Bachelor of Arts from Texas State University and is pursuing a Masters in Adult Education from Texas State University. Her focus is on mass communications, and continuing and community adult education. She currently works as a Graduate Research Assistant for the Department of Occupational, Workforce, and Leadership studies, where she served as an Assistant Editor for Building Sustainable Futures for Adult Learners.

Mario Giampaolo, M.S., in Experimental Psychology and Neuroscience at University of Padua. He is Doctoral Candidate in the School of Educational Sciences at University of Padua. In 2013, he was a visiting student at Lindenwood University, St. Charles Missouri, in the Doctoral School of Instructional Leadership with Emphasis in Andragogy. He is a member of the AAACE American Association for Adult and Continuing Education. Dr. Giampaolo's research is primarily focused in self-directed learning, personalized learning, and technology enhancing learning. Since 2012, he served as assistant project manager at the Interdepartmental Study Centre for Social Services (CISSPE).

Laura P. Gogia, M.D., practiced as an obstetrician/gynecologist in rural Virginia before returning to Virginia Commonwealth University to earn a Ph.D. with an emphasis in Adult Education and Research. She holds a M.D. from Virginia Commonwealth University and a B.S. from the College of William and Mary. Dr. Gogia's research is primarily focused on adult education in professional school contexts.

Roxanne Gonzales, Ph.D., is Academic Dean of the College for Professional Studies at Regis University. She has over 35 years of experience with classroom, online, blended, and independent study models. Dr. Gonzales is past President for the Association for Continuing Higher Education (ACHE) and has a long history of service to the community including membership on the Kansas City Hispanic Economic Development Corporation, the New Hampshire Governor's Advisory Commission on Latino Affairs, the Board of Trustees of Wentworth Military Academy and Junior College, and the City of Denver Hispanic Chamber of Commerce. Dr. Gonzales earned her Master's degree from Creighton University and her doctorate in higher education administration from the University of Massachusetts, Boston.

Portia M. Gottschall, B.A.A.S., is a nontraditional, adult, and first-generation college student. She graduated Summa Cum Laude with a Bachelor of Applied Arts and Science from Texas State University and is currently pursuing a Masters of Arts in Interdisciplinary Studies (MAIS) though the Department of Occupational, Workforce, and Leadership Studies (OWLS) at Texas State University. In addition to the MAIS degree, Portia is pursuing Texas State Certificates in Mediation, Professional Ethics, and Corporate Communication and Training. Portia is a Graduate Research Assistant for the OWLS department, where she served as Assistant Editor for Building Sustainable Futures for Adult Learners. She is the recipient of the Texas State Graduate Merit Fellowship and the College of Applied Arts Dean's Fellow Graduate Research Assistantship. Her research interests include social justice actions, women and gender studies, municipal nondiscrimination policies, and LGBTQIA advocacy and leadership.

Julie Hall, M.P.H., R.T. (R)(CT)(ARRT), is an Assistant Professor and Program Director in the Radiologic Technology Program at Roane State Community College. She is completing her doctorate from the University of Tennessee in Educational Psychology and Research with a concentration in Adult Learning. She has a Master of Public Health and Bachelor of Science Degree in Biochemistry, Molecular, and Cellular Biology from the University of Tennessee. She also has an Associate of Applied Science degree in Radiologic Technology from Roane State Community College. Her research interests include self-directed learning, transformative learning, and positive psychology. Prior to higher education, she worked in the healthcare field as a radiologic technologist and computed tomography technologist for approximately 15 years (including extensive radiography experience at a level-1 trauma center).

Michael D. Harner, Ed.D., is Director of Financial Affairs at the University of Illinois College of Medicine-Rockford. He holds an Ed.D. from Northern Illinois University department of Adult and Higher Education, M.A. in International Relations from Boston University-Brussels, Belgium, M.B.A. from Rockford College (University), and B.B.A from University of Iowa in accounting. He is a Certified Public Accountant. The foundation of this chapter was his dissertation.

Brian S. Hentz, M.B.A., M.A., is Associate Director of the Business Communications Center for the University of Connecticut's School of Business, as well as a Ph.D. candidate in Adult Learning (Neag School of Education, UConn). Mr. Hentz regularly teaches M.B.A. courses in professional writing and managerial communications, and his research interests include transitional learning, adaptive change, and sustainability, especially with respect to older adults. To support his cross-disciplinary research, Mr. Hentz has also completed graduate work in gerontology (University of Georgia's Institiute of Gerontology) and faculty development work in sustainable development (University of Queensland, Australia). For his dissertation, Mr. Hentz is exploring how older, professional men cope with involuntary job loss and learn through the uncertainties and complexities that underpin these unanticipated life transitions. A regular presenter at professional conferences, Mr. Hentz has also published in *Adult Learning* and *Business Communication Quarterly.*

Jennifer K. Holtz, Ph.D. is Assistant Professor of Adult Education and Program Coordinator of the Masters' degree in Adult Education at the University of Arkansas at Little Rock. Dr. Holtz's research focuses on the intersection of medical education, online education, and adult education, with emphasis on optimizing experiential learning online. Her publications include *Best Practices for Online Paleontology Instruction* (Journal of Paleontology Special Issue: Teaching Paleontology in the 21st Century), *Incorporating 3D Virtual Laboratory Specimens to Enhance Online Science: Examples from Paleontology and Biology* (The Professor's Guide to Taming Technology Leveraging Digital Media, Web 2.0. Kathleen P. King and Thomas D. Cox Eds.) and *Online Science Learning: Best Practices and Technologies,* each with Dr. Kevin Downing. She has designed multiple online courses in the fields of human biology, adult education, and research methods.

Anna K. Hultquist, Ph.D., serves as the Dean for the Department of Counseling, Social Work, and Human Behavior in the Harold Abel School of Social and Behavioral Sciences at Capella University. Dr. Hultquist has over 20 years of experience as an educator, academic administrator, and licensed therapist. She has earned a COAMFTE accredited Master of Science from the University of Rhode Island, pursuing graduate work in Guidance and School Counseling, and a Ph.D. in Adult Education from the University of Connecticut. In support of excellence in higher education, Dr. Hultquist's professional responsibilities include performance analytics, regional and specialized accreditation, accessibility, and career-relevant academic programming for adult students. Dr. Hultquist's contributions to the profession include appointment to the Oregon State Board for Professional Counselors and Therapists and numerous conference presentations and professional articles. Dr. Hultquist holds the distinction as a Certified Family Life Educator from the National Council on Family Relations, Clinical Member and Approved Supervisor from the American Association for Marriage and Family Therapy, and professional member of the American Counseling Association, Association for Conflict Resolution, and International Association of Coaches.

Yvonne Hunter-Johnson, Ph.D., is an Assistant Professor within the School of Education at The College of The Bahamas. She holds a Ph.D. in Curriculum and Instruction with emphasis in Adult Education, Training, and Development and Evaluation from the University of South Florida, M.B.A. and a Bachelor's in Professional Management from Nova Southeastern University. Dr. Hunter-Johnson's research is primarily focused in the area of teacher education, adult education, and workplace learning and development. She has presented papers in over 15 states and countries and has published articles in journals such as *Adult Learning, International Journal of Human Resource Development, The Qualitative Report, International Journal of Special Education,* and *International Journal of Bahamian Studies.* Dr. Hunter-Johnson has designed and taught courses both nationally and internationally in traditional, hybrid, and online formats. In regard to service, Dr. Hunter-Johnson mentors graduate and undergraduate students with research initiatives.

Lindsey R. Jackson, B.A., is studying Adult and Higher Education at Montana State University in Bozeman, Montana. After completion of her Master's degree program, she plans to enroll in a doctoral program. She earned her Bachelor's degree in Sociology from Montana State University at Bozeman. She has experience teaching and training and a Master's Certificate in Instructional Design. Her research interests include active learning classrooms and teaching strategies, online learning, technology in the classroom, educational law and policy, and diversity education.

Carrie Johnson, Ed.D., has worked with adult college students for over 20 years. She currently directs the B.A. in General Studies, an adult degree program, at Eastern Illinois University. She has presented several workshops for the Adult Higher Education Alliance and the American Association of Adult and Continuing Education at their annual conferences. She has spoken internationally on her research which focuses on adult accelerated courses, adjunct faculty development, teaching adults, and supporting underprepared adult learners in higher education. She has also published several journal articles and book chapters in those areas.

Melisa Kakas, M.A., in International Studies, is a former Graduate Research Assistant in the Department of Occupational, Workforce, and Leadership Studies at Texas State University and Associate Editor of *Building Sustainable Futures for Adult Learners.* Her interests include international business, economic development, sociology, and education.

Rita A. Kenahan, Ed.D., recently completed her Doctor of Education studies in Adult Learning and Leadership at Teachers College, Columbia University, New York, NY. She is a Group Manager of Professional Education at DePuy Synthes, a Johnson & Johnson company in the Medical Devices & Diagnostics (MD&D) industry. She holds a M.Ed. in Instructional Design from the University of Massachusetts, Boston, and B.S. in Nursing from Rhode Island College. Dr. Kenahan's research is focused on the areas of teaching and learning practices of surgeons who provide instruction to their peers on behalf of the MD&D industry with recommendations for faculty development. Her areas of research interest are (1) faculty preparedness and development; and (2) competency development and career planning for Professional Education associates in the MD&D and pharmaceutical industries. She has presented her work in the U.S. at the International Self Directed Learning Symposium, the American Association for Adult and Continuing Education, and the Women's Summit at Bryant University. Dr. Kenahan provides faculty development workshops for surgeons from various medical institutions to enhance their teaching skills and effectiveness.

Jeral R. Kirwan, Ph.D., is an Assistant Professor and Faculty Research Fellow in the College of Health, Human Services, and Science at Ashford University. He holds a Ph.D. in Educational Psychology and Research—Adult Learning; an M.S. in Educational Psychology—Adult Education; a Graduate Certificate in Applied Statistics and Research in Education; and a Bachelor of Arts in Psychology and Anthropology from the University of Tennessee, Knoxville. His varied professional experience includes working as a research consultant, psychometrician, child and family counselor/case manager, psychological technician, and teacher at the university level. Currently he teaches Statistics for the Behavioral Sciences, Research Methods, Theories of Personality, and provides research design assistance to both faculty and students. His research agenda includes adult learner personalities and development, learning in online modalities, and self-direction in learning.

Yu-Chun Kuo, Ph.D., is Assistant Professor of Instructional Design and Development in the School of Lifelong Learning at Jackson State University. She received her doctorate from the Department of Instructional Technology and Learning Sciences at Utah State University. She was a course designer and instructional technologist at other institutions. Dr. Kuo has designed and taught undergraduate courses in research, instructional design, and human resource development, and she has offered technology workshops and training sessions to non-traditional students in continuing education. Dr. Kuo's research focuses on the areas of instructional design, technology integration into teaching and learning, online learning, adult learning, and professional development. She was the recipient of the 2013 Alex Charters Research Grant from the Association for Continuing Higher Education (ACHE). Dr. Kuo has presented her research in international conferences and published articles in the academic peer-reviewed journals in instructional technology and adult education.

Tennille J. Lasker-Scott, M.Ed., received a master's degree in Adult Education at the University of Arkansas at Little Rock and is currently attending The University of Georgia's Adult Education, Leadership, and Organizational Development Doctoral program, where her research includes educating the disenfranchised, the participation of minority groups in adult educational opportunities, and issues of race, class, and gender in education and workforce development. Ms. Lasker-Scott is a recipient of The Irene and Curtis Ulmer Scholarship for Adult Education and fellowships from the Southern Regional Education Board the Predoctoral Fellowship Program at Texas State University-San Marcos.

Marilyn Lockhart, Ed.D., has worked with adults in various educational settings for over 25 years. She is currently the Director of the Center for Faculty Excellence and an Associate Professor in the Adult and Higher Education Graduate Program at Montana State University in Bozeman, Montana. She is a past president of the Adult Higher Education Alliance. Her area of research is adult learning and college teaching and has over 30 published works and numerous presentations on these topics. Recent publications include Developing a Holistic Faculty Development Program, The Importance of Authenticity in the Classroom, and Collaboration for College Student Improvement. Her previous work has been in the area of administration at the University of Virginia and in various capacities in adult education. She earned her doctorate in higher education administration from the University of Virginia.

Omar S. López, Ph.D., is an Assistant Professor in the Department of Occupational, Workforce, and Leadership Studies in the College of Applied Arts at Texas State University–Round Rock Campus. He is a transdisciplinary researcher who draws from the fields of engineering, strategic management, and economics, but also from learning theory and sociology to solve some of the thorniest problems confronting society's most vulnerable populations. His current research interests include evaluating the efficacy of STEM workforce development through career and technical education programs for at-risk populations in secondary and post-secondary education. Dr. López earned a B.A. in Biophysics from Trinity University, an M.B.A. from the University of California at Irvine, and an M.S.B.A. in Strategic Planning from the University of Southern California. He earned his Ph.D. in strategy and educational policy from the Public School Executive Leadership Program in the College of Education, The University of Texas at Austin.

Elyse D'nn Lovell, Ed.D., is a General Education Instructor at Highlands College of Montana Tech. Her interests include teaching and mentoring community college students in research projects and curricula related to psychology, sociology, and gerontology. Peer reviewed publications (2013–2014): I Have to Take This Psychology Stuff with Research Too—Really?! *International Journal of Adult Vocational Education and Technology*; Female College Students Who are Parents: Motivation Clarified by the Ages of Their Children, *Community College Journal of Research and Practice;* The Phenomenon of Facebook Journaling in the Classroom, *About Campus,* and Predictors for Intrinsic Motivation: Students' Ages and Project Based Learning, *Developing and Sustaining Adult Learners.* Her memberships include American Psychological Association (APA), Society for the Teaching of Psychology (STP), and Adult Higher Education Alliance (AHEA). For additional information elysednnlovell@gmail.com

Laurie B. Lyons, M.A., is the Director of Instructional Technology and Design for the Health Sciences Programs at the George Washington University, which encompasses both on-campus and distance health science programs. She previously worked with an interdisciplinary group of faculty to convert a federally funded two-semester face-to-face training program to a blended format. Laurie has a Master's degree in Educational Technology Leadership from the George Washington University and is certified as an online facilitator for the Quality Matters Applying the Rubric Online Workshop.

Paige L. McDonald, M.A., Ed.D., is the Director of Health Sciences Core Curriculum and Visiting Assistant Professor of Clinical Research and Learning at The George Washington University. Paige's doctoral research focused on adult learners in blended environments in higher education. She is currently working to promote blended learning and develop blended courses in Health Science disciplines. Paige's research interests include blended learning, adult learning, reflective practice, and course design for higher levels of learning.

Daniel M. McGuire, B.A., currently serves as Team Lead of the Hybrid Teaching and Learning Team at Augsburg College. Dan has 30+ years of experience with innovative development and implementation of Information Communications Technology systems. His early business career included opening a successful telecom market in China, creating two new branches for a national telecom vendor, and participation in the start-up of two new companies in the emerging micro-computer industry. More recently, he has helped pioneer the use of Moodle as a blended learning instructional tool and a staff development process and tool in both K–12 and higher education. He holds a B.A. degree in Humanities from St. John's University, Collegeville, MN, is a recipient of the Archer B. Gilfillan Prize for poetry, and is an urban park program baseball coach.

Elaine M. Silva Mangiante, Ph.D. is an Assistant Professor in the Education Department at Salve Regina University where she works closely with pre-service teachers and their cooperating teacher mentors. She received an M.A. degree in Counseling and a Ph.D. in Education from the University of Rhode Island. Her research interests include teacher development from novice to expert, urban education, science learning for critical thinking, and effective teaching practices. She formerly served as a professional development specialist with The Education Alliance at Brown University for educational reform in high-poverty districts. As a science specialist and mathematics curriculum coordinator for a K–8 school, she mentored early career teachers, provided consulting services in science education to schools, and received the state-level Presidential Award for Excellence in Elementary Science Teaching. She has most recently completed a study of the planning practices of elementary teachers in urban schools identified as effective in teaching inquiry science.

Cristina Mazzucco, Ph.D., is Research Fellow at University of Padua in the Interdepartmental Study Centre for Social Services (CISSPE). She holds the Ph.D. from the Doctoral School of Educational Sciences at University of Padua. She is member of the AAACE American Association for Adult and Continuing Education and member of the Italian Society for Research in Didactic (SIRD). Dr. Mazucco's research is primarily focused in the community schools, in the socio-educational interventions for adults and elderly people, and in the training and skills assessment of young people. In 2010 she participated in the Project of National Research Interest (PRIN): Models, policies and evaluation of educational research through video and digital artifacts in the context of semantic web. In 2007 she participated in the

Project funded by the European Social Found (ESF) Model for Integrated Operational Recognition and Certification of Competencies (MOIRC).

Henry S. Merrill, Ed.D., is Emeritus Associate Professor in the M.S. in Adult Education, Indiana University School of Education. He currently serves as primary facilitator at DePaul University for the Prior Learning Assessment (PLA) Certification Workshops offered by the Council for Adult and Experiential Learning (CAEL). PLA is an important learning assessment option; he has guided students through in both undergraduate and graduate degrees in the Indiana University School of Continuing Studies. His teaching and research interests include adult development and learning, program planning, instructional design, and distance education systems. He began teaching online in 1998. He earned the Doctorate in Adult Education at Ball State University. Dr. Merrill also provided leadership in adult and continuing education at IUPUI and IU East. In Act I of his career, he was a faculty member in Drama at Earlham College for 11 years.

Megan E. Morris, M.Ed., is the LiveText Administrator for the College of Education at Armstrong Atlantic State University in Savannah, GA. She earned her Master of Education in Adult Education and Community Leadership from Armstrong with an emphasis in human resource management and a post-graduate certificate in educational technology. She held positions in higher education including a part-time professor for the Department of Adolescent and Adult Education teaching a pre-service teacher candidates technology application courses focusing on classroom application.

Lee Nabb, Ph.D., acquired a B.A. from Southern Illinois University with a major in Religious Studies and a minor in Classical Civilization. He went on to study religion for one more year in Temple University's doctoral program before returning to Illinois and acquiring a M.S. Ed. in Adult and Continuing Education from Northern Illinois University. From there he went to Law School at Syracuse University and worked as a consultant in environmental legal issues for three years. He then attended the University of Wyoming where he received his Ph.D. in Adult and Post-Secondary Education and worked as an Assistant Lecturer for a year. He is currently licensed to practice law in New York and Illinois, and is an Assistant Professor of Adult and Higher Education at Morehead State University.

Carmela Nanton, Ed.D., is Professor of Education and Chair of the Professional Education Program for MacArthur School of Leadership, Palm Beach Atlantic University. Education: Ed.D., Columbia University's Organization & Leadership AEGIS program, specialty in Adult Education; M.S. in Human Resource Development, and M.S. in Counseling Psychology; and is a Board Certified Executive Coach. Named one of Palm Beach County's

Top Black Educators in 2013, she teaches undergraduate courses in organization management and graduate courses in leadership. Dr. Nanton is Past Chair of the Women and Leadership Affinity Group of the International Leadership Association. She is a Co-Chair of the CPAE HRD SIG in the American Association of Adults and Continuing Education; member for Education & Youth Advisory Board, and the Building Board of Adjustment & Appeals for the City of Boynton Beach, FL. Research Interests include human resource and leadership development, women and leadership, multiculturalism, and educational decision making.

Joann S. Olson, Ph.D., is Assistant Professor and Program Coordinator in the Adult and Higher Education program at the University of Houston-Victoria. She holds a Ph.D. in adult education from Penn State University and a M.A. in religious education from Wheaton College. Her research explores the intersection of adult learning and higher education, specifically for first-generation college students and adult learners returning to and exiting from higher education. Her 20-year career as an adult educator has included corporate training and workplace learning, religious education, and extensive work with undergraduates and young adults. She has published and presented work in a variety of adult education, higher education, and career development venues. She was recently presented with UHV's "Student's Choice Award" for outstanding service to students and School of Education and Human Development's "Outstanding Teaching" award. Dr. Olson also co-chairs the faculty development SIG of the Commission of Professors of Adult Education.

Kathy Peno, Ph.D., is Professor of Adult Education at the University of Rhode Island where she prepares teachers of adults in the Military, in health fields including Nursing, Pharmacy, and Dentistry, and in corporate and higher education organizations. She holds a Master's and Ph.D. in Adult Learning and Human Resource Development from the University of Connecticut. Her scholarship focuses on professional learning and skill development from novice to expert. She has written, consulted, and presented extensively on workforce development, professional development, and mentoring as a vehicle for continuous performance improvement in organizations. She is a former board member of AAACE and currently serves as executive board member and treasurer of The Coalition of Lifelong Learning organizations (COLLO).

Lori A. Peterson, Ph.D., is Assistant Vice President of Academic Affairs and Dean of Graduate and Professional Studies at Augsburg College. Lori came to this role after serving as Director of Augsburg's adult learning initiatives and as a faculty member, teaching in Augsburg's M.B.A., Master of Arts in Leadership, and undergraduate business programs. She earned her doctorate in Organization Development, with a specialization in international human resource development, from the University of Minnesota; has a master's degree in human resource development with a specialization in adult education; and is a registered Organization Development Consultant. Outside of academe, Lori has 20 plus years of experience in U.S. and international organization management and leadership, organization structural analysis, development and implementation of growth initiatives, human resource management and development, quality, and customer service.

Frederick Carl Prasuhn, Ph.D., is an Instructional Designer at Western Governors University, a practical scholar, and a consultant. He holds a Ph.D. in Adult Education, M.Ed. in Instructional Technologies, and other degrees. His presentations include Adult Higher Education Alliance and American Association of Adult and Continuing Education conferences and various regional symposiums. He has published in the *American Journal of Distance Learning, Internet Learning*, and the *Adult Higher Education Alliance Book Series*. Dr. Prasuhn serves on various boards and committees including Adult Higher Education Alliance, Commission of Distance Learning and Technology, and Commission of Professors of Adult Education. His interests include higher education policies, online learning, competency-based education, and evaluating commonly accepted practices in nontraditional manners. His background includes non-profit, corporate, and higher education positions.

Anne Rapp, Ph.D., is an Associate Professor at Lewis University, where she is Director of the B.A. in Professional Studies and Coordinator of Prior Learning Assessment. She holds a Ph.D. in U.S. History from the University of California, Santa Barbara. Dr. Rapp's research fields include the study of social movements, focusing primarily on feminism and civil rights, as well as Occupy Wall Street. Her interest in social justice led her to become involved in the service learning movement, designing experiential projects for adult learners that potentially trigger perspective transformation and meet social needs in disadvantaged communities. This led to her interest in critical theory and adult education. Presently, she conducts research on the role of critical reflection and transformative learning in prior learning assessment. She has presented at more than 20 national conferences in a variety of disciplines and has published articles on critical theory and transnational feminist activism.

Amy Rell, Ph.D., is Associate Dean of Dual Language at Regis University. She holds a Ph.D. with an emphasis in Second Language Acquisition and Applied Linguistics from UCLA and a B.A. in Spanish Language and Literature from Tulane University. Dr. Rell's research is primarily focused in the areas of globalization and internationalization, applied linguistics, theoretical linguistics, Yiddish, Spanglish, Dual Language and serving Hispanic students. She has presented numerous papers at national and international conferences. Dr. Rell was inducted into Phi Beta Kappa and awarded a Fulbright Scholarship as well as a National Endowment for the Humanities Fellowship. In service to the profession, Dr. Rell is a board member for the Hispanic Chamber Education Foundation and a committee member for Jewish Family University and the Temple Emanuel Leadership, Education, Advocacy and Development Program.

Margaret H. Rice, Ph.D. is Visiting Assistant Professor in the School of Education and Human Development and Special Assistant to the Provost at the University of Houston-Victoria (UHV) in Victoria, TX. She earned her doctorate from Texas A&M University in the field of Educational Human Resource Development. She holds a Master's of Religious Education from Southwestern Seminary and a B.S. from Baylor University. She has worked as a practitioner of Adult and Higher Education fulfilling roles in student services, program development, and strategic planning, as well as serving for seven years as Chief of Staff to the university president. Her research interests include leadership development, especially women's leadership issues, and transformational learning. She was instrumental in the recent expansion of UHV from an upper division and graduate university to a four-year residential campus and assisted in the creation of the Adult and Higher Education program at UHV. She is active in Texas Women in Higher Education, having served as chair of this organization for two years. With her transition to the School of Education and Human development, she looks forward to more teaching, research, and writing.

Kevin J. Rose, Ed.D., is a scholar-practitioner in residence in the Organizational Leadership and Learning Program at the University of Louisville. He has worked in various training and development areas including executive education and small business development. He is active in organizations such as the American Society for Training and Development and the Society of Human Resource Management. Dr. Rose maintains active research in the areas of executive education, workplace diversity, and applied human resource development.

Elizabeth Anne Roumell, Ph.D., is an Assistant Professor in the Education Doctoral Programs at North Dakota State University. She earned a Ph.D. in Education in the cognates of Adult and Post-secondary Education from the University of Wyoming. Currently she teaches doctoral courses including the Philosophical Foundations of Education, Advanced Qualitative Research, Technologies for Teaching and Learning, Empowerment and Transformative Education, International and Comparative Education, and Coordinating Connected Learning Environments. Her research agenda includes adult learner identity development, distance and continuing education, international and comparative education, and issues in diversity and inclusion. She also serves as the co-PI and state evaluator for the Strategic Prevention Framework State Incentive Grant (SPF SIG) for the North Dakota Department of Human Services, a 5-year $1.2 contract aimed at building the State's capacity and infrastructure for alcohol prevention programming. She also serves on the North Dakota Governor's State Epidemiological Outcomes Workgroup (SEOW).

Leah Katherine Saal, Ph.D., is an Assistant Professor of Literacy in the School of Education at Loyola University Maryland. Saal earned her Ph.D. in Curriculum and Instruction with an emphasis in Literacy and a M.A. in Educational Leadership, Research, and Counseling with an emphasis in Applied Educational Research Methodology and Evaluation from Louisiana State University in 2013. Her research focuses on the intersectionality of literacy and social justice within adult and community literacies. Her scholarship is informed by over nine years of experience teaching literacy skills to adults and older adolescents in community and higher education settings. In 2012, she was awarded the Literacy Research Association (LRA)'s J. Michael Parker Award for developing the theory of the adult "burgeoning" reader. She is an active member of the American Educational Research Association, the Literacy Research Association, the International Literacy Association, and the American Association for Adult and Continuing Education.

Robert Sammons, has a B.A. in Sociology with a minor in Psychology from Morehead State University. After many years working in mental health, he shifted focus to work in the Appalachian Collection at Camden Carroll Library on the campus of Morehead State University. Rob is the Special Collections Specialist working to preserve, conserve, and make accessible the works of Appalachian authors.

Todd Sherron, Ph.D., earned his doctorate from the University of North Texas where he studied applied technology, training, and development and econometrics. He earned a Master of Science in Interdisciplinary Studies from Texas State University in San Marcos, and a Bachelor of Arts from The University of Texas at Austin where he majored in government. As a researcher and evaluator, Dr. Sherron has lead studies in industry and conducted both federal and state program evaluations. As a writer, Dr. Sherron has written in the area of mathematics achievement, leadership, professional development, data analysis, marketing research, measurement, and organizational knowledge. As an educator, Dr. Sherron serves as Lecturer and Prior Learning Coordinator at Texas State University.

M. Brad Shuck, Ed.D., is Assistant Professor of Organizational Leadership and Learning at the University of Louisville. He was the 2010–2011 Malcolm Knowles Dissertation of the Year Runner-Up and recipient of the 2011 Advances in Developing Human Resources Issue of the Year Award for the special issue on employee engagement. His research is focused on the use of employee engagement and positive psychology in HRD.

W. Franklin Spikes, Ed.D. is Professor of Educational Leadership and Director of the Doctoral Program in Adult Education at Kansas State University. He received his doctorate at Northern Illinois in Adult Education and is a recipient of the Outstanding Alumni Award from the Department of Leadership and Educational Policy Studies. He teaches graduate level courses in program planning, human resource development, policy issues, and research. He is a Past-President of the American Association of Adult and Continuing Education and is a former Fellow in Academic Administration of the American Council of Education. He has also served as President of the Faculty Senate at Kansas State University. He is the first non-attorney to be appointed to the Kansas Supreme Court's Commission on Continuing Legal Education. He recently was elected Vice Chairman of the Commission and presently leads its work in the area of educational research and evaluation. His research interests are related to program evaluation, human resource development, and continuing professional education with a focus upon continuing legal education.

Stephen B. Springer Ed.D., C.P.M., L.P.C. is an Associate Professor in the Department of Occupational, Workforce, and Leadership Studies at Texas State University. He holds an Ed.D. in Adult and Extension Education with support areas in Vocational Counseling and Educational Administration from Texas A&M University-College Station, a M.Ed. in Psychology and Guidance from Our Lady of the Lake University, and a B.A. in Political Science from St. Mary's University. He also holds four public education certifications and is a Licensed Professional Counselor and Certified Public Manager. He is a retired Colonel in the Texas State Guard having served as Deputy J-3 for Professional Military Education. He has held public office having served as a school board member and President. His instructional experience includes elementary through graduate studies. In addition to his administrative service with the military, he has been a Program Chair with Texas State University and also a Director in the public schools. Dr. Springer has published and presented in various areas related to distance learning, equity, career counseling, and inclusion of older adults. He currently is working on research related to college instructors assisting service members exhibiting signs of PTSD.

Howard O. Straker, PA-C, M.P.H., is a physician assistant and the Director of Community Medicine of the George Washington University Physician Assistant (PA) Program where he has been a member of the faculty for 12 years. His interest in blended learning grows from a need to address the pedagogical challenges he faces teaching a large group of clinically oriented students. Howard is a candidate for a doctoral degree in education and holds faculty appointments in both the School of Medicine and Health Sciences and the School of Public Health and Health Services. He has been a PA for 23 years and has interests in the intersection of public health and clinical medicine. He is also interested in developing meta-cognition in future clinicians.

Dr. Gabriele Strohschen, Ed.D., is Associate Professor and Faculty Mentor at DePaul University's School for New Learning (SNL), where she also served as Director for the Graduate Programs. She designed and implemented SNL's first transnational graduate program in Thailand, and co-developed several of the school's graduate program options. She was the inaugural director of National-Louis University's online graduate program in adult education from 1989 through 2003. Her international work focuses on action research and program development and evaluation in Kenya, Germany, Thailand, China, and Mexico, within and emancipatory/popular adult education praxis. She has consulted with UNESCO, conducting adult education program evaluations in Afghanistan. Dr. Strohschen was Visiting Professor and Dissertation Advisor at Assumption University and Burapha University (Thailand), and currently serves as Dissertation Advisor for Alagappa University, Andhra University (India), and Argosy University and National-Louis University (USA). Prior to working in academia, she was a community organizer in Chicago's Latino immigrants and Black neighborhoods, and continues this work as a volunteer now through *Community Connexxions,* a cooperative of educators, activists, and artists. Dr. Strohschen is President of the Adult and Higher Education Alliance and President of the Phi Beta Delta Honor Society – Delta Theta Chapter, DePaul University.

Fujuan Tan, Ph.D., is an assistant professor of Education in the College of Education at Morehead State University, KY. She holds a Ph.D. in Adult and Post-secondary Education from the University of Wyoming (UW) in Laramie, Wyoming. She has taught for several years in adult and higher education settings and courses. In addition, Fujuan has considerable experience in coordinating international exchange programs. Her research interests include transformative learning for adults, international and comparative adult and higher education, adult ESL education, and culturally responsive education. Her most recent publication is Advancing Transformative Theory: Multi-fold and Cyclical Transformation.

Jonathan Taylor, Ph.D., coordinates the adult and postsecondary educations programs at Troy University's Montgomery Campus. He earned his Ph.D. in educational psychology and research at the University of Tennessee. Prior to his academic work, Dr. Taylor spent over a decade in public and private law enforcement training. His research interests are in the areas of learning resistance, workforce and professional training practices, and conceptual change.

Margaret A. Voelkel, Ed.D., is Associate Professor of Computer Technology in the Center for Business and Professional Development in the College of Applied Science and Technology at University of Arkansas-Fort Smith. She earned her doctorate in Workforce Development Education from the University of Arkansas in Fayetteville. She has a master's degree in Adult Education from the University of Arkansas and a bachelor's in Performance Studies from Northwestern University. She teaches undergraduate courses in computer applications, personal effectiveness, project management, time management, and quality processes. Her research interests include displaced workers, encore careers, generativity, and narrative inquiry.

Dorothy Williams, Ph.D., has over 24 years of experience teaching undergraduate and graduate adult students and designing curriculum; she specializes in Communication and Leadership. She has held various management positions in industry and in higher education. Williams earned her Doctorate in Education from Walden University, her Master of Science in Mass Communication from San Jose State University, and her Bachelor of Science in Business from the University of Colorado. She serves as professor and director of Regis University in Colorado. She has served on a variety of non-profit boards and committees. She is a recipient of the Colorado Springs Business Journal's 2011 Women of Influence, received the Regis University 2005 Communication Faculty of the Year, and is Regional Chair for the Association for Continuing Higher Education (ACHE). Her recent publication is The Relationship of Goal Setting to Persistence. She has presented at various national conferences.

Aimee Tiu Wu, Ed.D., is a higher education professional and adult educator. She earned her doctorate from Teachers College Columbia University, with specialization in adult learning and leadership through the *AEGIS* program and a master's degree in TESOL from New York University. She currently serves as managing partner and co-founder of *LearnLong Institute for Education and Learning Research* (NFP), an independent educational think-tank informing individuals, organizations, and local and global communities about higher and continuing education. Her research interests include motherhood and academia, cross-cultural consciousness, collaborative and appreciative inquiry, women and meaning making, and leadership development of women.

Cindy S. York, Ph.D., is an Assistant Professor at Northern Illinois University in the department of Educational Technology, Research, and Assessment. Her research interests include the examination of practitioners in order to better prepare students in the areas of instructional design and the integration of technology into teacher education. Her past includes K–12 teaching and corporate experiences. These experiences are continually applied to her current teaching and research. She is a Past-President of the Division of Distance Learning for AECT.

CPSIA information can be obtained
at www.ICGtesting.com
Printed in the USA
LVOW01s1932220216

476198LV00001B/1/P

9 781623 968871